AF386232

PORTRAIT OF A MUSE

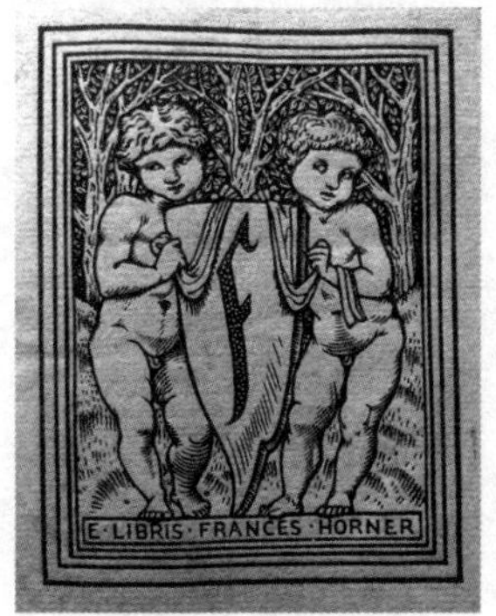

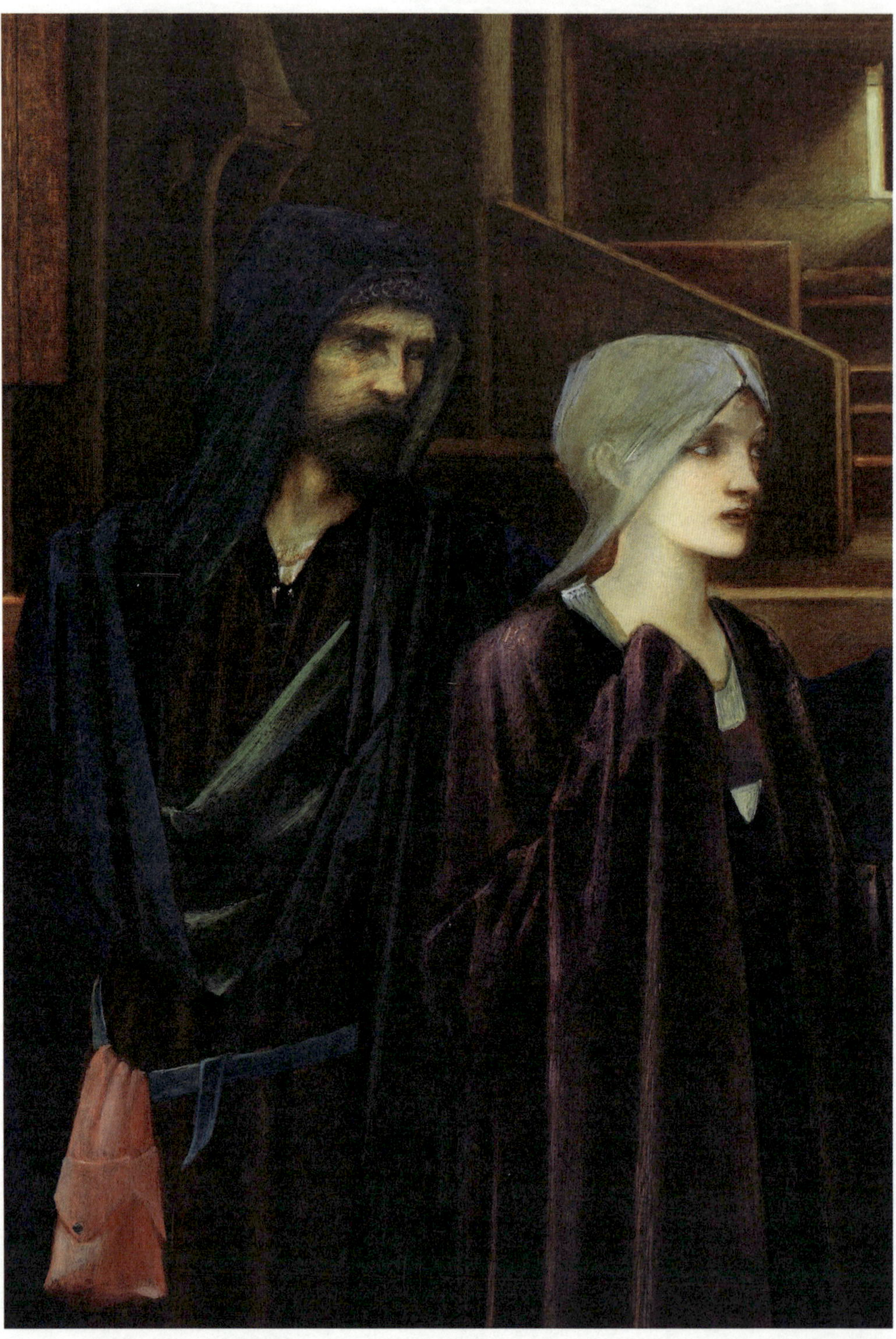

Portrait of a Muse

Frances Graham, Edward Burne-Jones
and the Pre-Raphaelite Dream

ANDREW GAILEY

WILMINGTON SQUARE BOOKS

an imprint of Bitter Lemon Press

WILMINGTON SQUARE BOOKS
an imprint of Bitter Lemon Press

First published in 2020 by
Wilmington Square Books
47 Wilmington Square
London WC1X 0ET

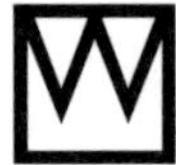

www.bitterlemonpress.com

ISBN 9781913394400
Edited, designed and typeset by Sally Salvesen

Printed in Wales by Gomer Press
2 4 6 8 9 7 5 3 1

HALF-TITLE PAGE: *Frances Horner's bookplate, designed by Edward Burne-Jones*
FRONTISPIECE: *Detail of The Wizard, by Edward Burne-Jones*

Contents

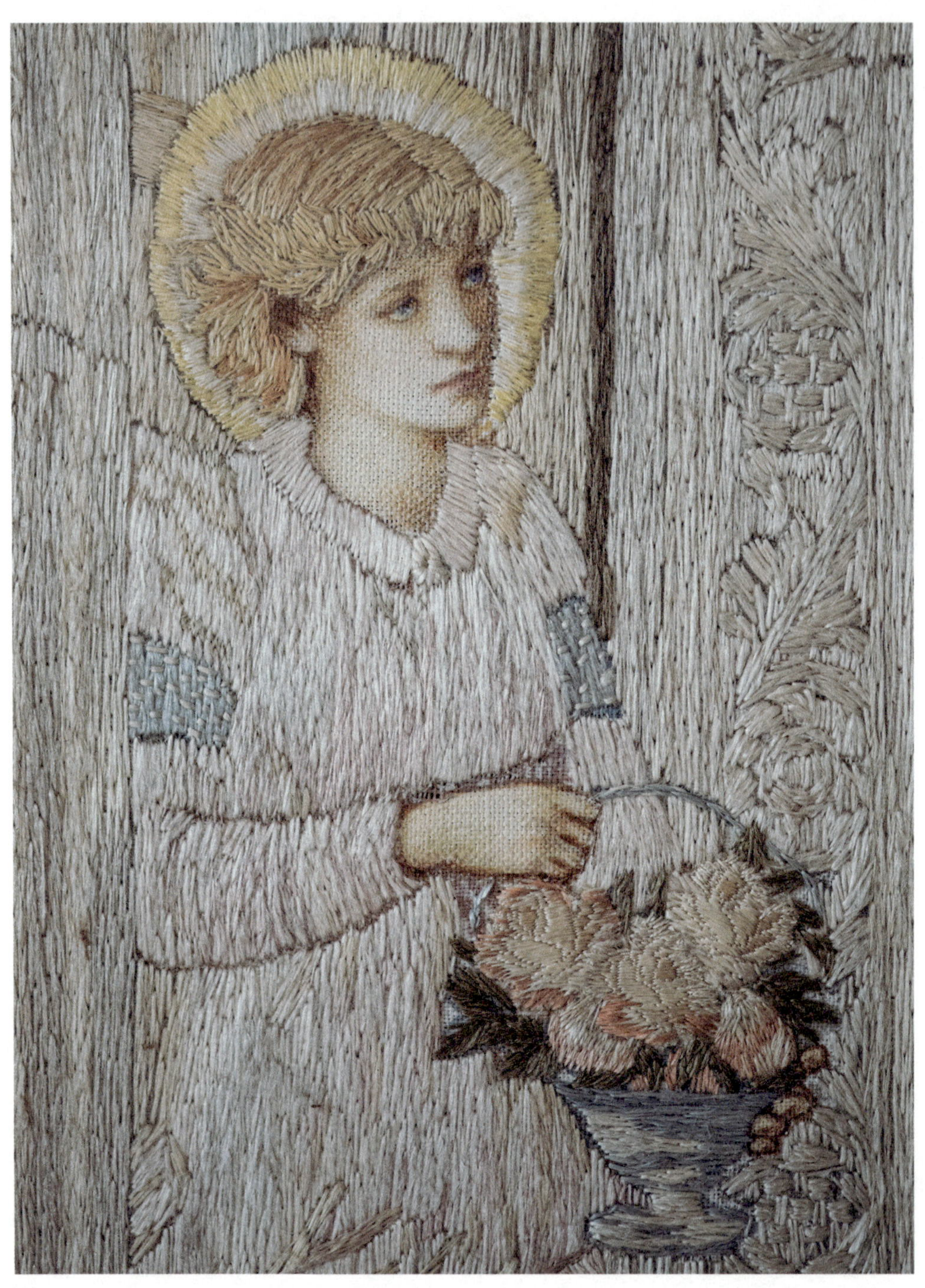

St Elizabeth of Hungary, detail of an embroidery designed by Burne-Jones and executed by Frances Horner

Preface

Once upon a time Non-fiction meant History. Go into a bookshop today and 'history' is to be found languishing amid self-help manuals and celebrities promoting their wares. For the most part it is made up of the lives of Great Men (many still living), War (the more gore the better) and Cookery. A book that can combine all three will have publishers and agents salivating. Less exotic are the hundreds of tomes written on Hitler or Churchilll. Do we really need another biography of Churchill? For all Great Men (and Great Women) are exceptions. Centre stage they stand, blinded by the lights that cut them off from the audience beyond. Studies in power, their lives often tell us little beyond themselves. Conversely, one can often learn much more about society and human nature in all its diversity from those men and women who under lit their age rather than commandeer the limelight.

One of those was Frances Graham, later Horner. I first came across her while researching another forgotten soul, James Hannay, an Irish clergyman who made a name for himself by alienating all sides in Victorian Ireland before escaping to England via Budapest. Under the *nom de plume* George A. Birmingham, this erstwhile provocateur would thereafter tickle the palate of the English middle classes with a series of very light novels and social comedy. Rather incongruously, after the Great War he had found himself in the parish of Mells, which lay lost in deepest Somerset and where seemingly time had stood still. In the adjacent Manor House, however, lived one who would never stand still. Frances Horner, now in her eighties, and Hannay would become fast friends, tearing round Europe in the 1930s (to the consternation of their children), beacons of a lost age as Hitler's armies mustered on the horizon.

Few remember Frances today, but in her day she led an extraordinary life despite the constraints of being a woman of ambition and imagination in a man's world. While her father (with Frances in tow) created one of the greatest private collections of Pre-Raphaelite and Old Master art ever seen, Frances became the muse and model of Edward Burne-Jones – then the most famous artist of his day. With the artist torn between lust and the discipline of purity, there followed a battle of wits that continued for twenty-five years over the role of a muse – a battle that would inspire some of his greatest paintings, but which Frances would ultimately win. In the aftermath of his death, she would bring such arts to the world of pre-war politics, becoming the 'High Priestess of the Souls' (who included Curzon and Balfour among their ranks), confidante of Liberal cabinet ministers and a future Prime Minister.

In a gilded age of excess, Frances lacked the fortune to compete. Yet her personality would draw to her table leading politicians, artists, writers and musicians; and exotica in the shape of Oscar Wilde and Einstein. Like her father, she too would become a patron of the arts, helping to launch the careers of Lutyens, Eric Gill and William Nicholson. At Mells, Burne-Jones's paintings and needlework designs hung alongside her father's Bellinis, a spectacular display that largely passed unremarked on by her young and their glamorous friends of the Coterie. The Great War would destroy this generation and with them the world Frances had known. Undaunted she opened Mells up to the new generations. Here Evelyn Waugh would come to write, and Siegfried Sassoon would explore his Catholicism, while under the loggia nervously entertaining his formidable hostess would be a young Cambridge student en route to the diplomatic service called Donald Maclean.

This was a life of tremendous dynamism and colour. Frances was not one of the great, but an acute observer of them and above all a connector of those who sought greatness. By contrast, hers is one of the forgotten lives. But dust these lives down and they are still vibrant, full of vigour, and with great stories to tell.

Andrew Gailey, February 2020

Acknowledgements

In the course of writing this book I have accrued many debts but few greater than that owed to the Earl and Countess of Oxford and Asquith. Not only has Clare fed and watered me on numerous occasions, but the family archive has been laid open to me. Moreover, Raymond has frequently gone searching for an elusive document – often at considerable peril to himself as he sought out boxes lurking on the highest shelves. Generously they have shared insights and family history, patiently correcting errors and responding enthusiastically to any unexpected finding. There can be few more delightful places to study than Mells and its beauty was matched by the warmth of the welcome and for that I am very grateful.

For their early encouragement that there was a book to be written about Frances Graham, I would like to thank my agent Eve White, Robert Gray, Richard Dorment, and Charlotte Gere. In particular, they alerted me to John Nicoll and Wilmington Square Books. I could not have asked for a more supportive publisher. Are there many authors who have been told to put in *more* illustrations rather than fewer? In an industry grown cautious, I am grateful to him for taking a risk. Thanks also to Sally Salvesen for her sensitivity and rigor in the prolonged process of producing a book out of the text. Amid the tedium of lockdown, her emails invariably raised the spirits as well as tightened many loose ends. Thank you also to Lady McFarland, Sarah Lynch, Emily Gailey and Kay Deane for reading the script in its various stages and their comments; and especially to William and Caroline Waldegrave for their friendship, encouragement and hospitality. I also benefitted from the generous advice of Caroline Dakers, Ralph Townsend and Oliver Garnett. As always, Roy Foster has been a great ally and mentor, ever ready to rally morale.

I am grateful to the following institutions and individuals for their permission to quote from collections under their care: The British Library; The Bodleian Library, Oxford; Ashmolean Museum;

The Fitzwilliam Museum, Cambridge; The National Library of Scotland; Hertfordshire Archives and Local Studies; The Earl of Wemyss & March; Churchill College Archives, Cambridge; The National Archives of Scotland; Library of Trinity College Dublin. By far the most important resource for a life of Frances Graham was the family archive at Mells and I am very grateful to the archivist, John D'Arcy, for all his help in my researches.

The illustrations for the book have drawn on collections with the National Portrait Gallery, Tate, the V&A, the Paul Mellon Centre for Studies in British Art, Christie's, Bridgeman, and other private collections. A significant majority of the illustrations come from private family albums. Thanks are owing to Charles Cator, Tamsin Evernden and Christopher Tennant for their help in tracking down the whereabouts of certain images. I am particularly grateful to Caroline True for her splendid photographs, especially those taken when feeling at death's door.

Finally, my greatest debt is to my family – Shauna, Emily and Rob – who have had to put up with Frances Graham for some years and done so with understanding and forbearance. I thank them for being unwavering in their love.

A. G.

Connections

ASQUITH, ARTHUR ('OC') (1883–1939) and HERBERT ('BEB') (1881–1947). Raymond Asquith's younger brothers who resisted funding Julian Asquith's education at Ampleforth. Beb married CYNTHIA CHARTERIS, Mary Elcho's daughter and once friend of Katharine.

ASQUITH, HERBERT HENRY ('HHA') (1852–1928). Liberal politician and Prime Minister. Long-standing friend and briefly lover of Frances. Married his second wife Margot Tennant in 1894.

ASQUITH, KATHARINE (née Horner) (1885–1976). Younger daughter of Jack and Frances Horner. Married Raymond Asquith in 1907; mother of HELEN, PERDITA (who married Billy Jolliffe, eldest son of neighbours Lord and Lady Hylton) and JULIAN ('Trim') heir to the Asquith earldom. Received into the Catholic Church and led the Catholic renaissance in Mells.

ASQUITH, RAYMOND (1878–1916). HHA's eldest son, he married Katharine Horner in 1907. Glittering academic career and much admired by Frances. Killed 1916.

ASQUITH, VIOLET (1887–1969). Raymond's sister, became a good friend of her brother's mother-in-law Frances. Married to Maurice Bonham Carter ('Bongie') who was HHA's Private Secretary in Downing Street.

BALFOUR, ARTHUR ('AJB') (1848–1930). Leading Conservative politician, Cabinet Minister from 1885 and Prime Minister 1902–1905. 'King Arthur' among the Souls. Never married. Frances's brother Rutherford dashed Balfour's languid pursuit of May Lyttelton. Thereafter had a lifelong relationship with Mary Elcho. Frances found it hard to engage with him.

BALFOUR, GERALD (1853–1945). Brother of Arthur, academic and briefly a politician, led astray by a flirtatious Laura Tennant. Married instead the energetic BETTY BALFOUR (née Lytton), sister of Lutyens's wife Emily.

BEECHAM, SIR THOMAS (1879–1961). International conductor and founder of the Royal Philharmonic Orchestra among others. Heir to a pharmaceutical fortune. Apparently, his father cleared Edward Horner's debts.

BELLOC, HILAIRE (1870–1953). Author of highly successful children's books and vigorous advocate of Catholicism's cause. Influential in Katharine's conversion. Fell out spectacularly with Frances ('hag Horner').

BURNE-JONES, EDWARD ('EBJ') (1833–1898). 'The Last Pre-Raphaelite' and leading painter of his day. Married to GEORGIANA MACDONALD and had two children: Margaret and Phil. Georgie stoically held their marriage together after EBJ's torrid affair with his model, MARIA ZAMBACO. William Graham was his leading patron and his daughter, Frances, became the artist's muse for the last twenty-five years of his life.

CAMPBELL, MRS PATRICK (1865–1940). Popular actress 'in the grand manner' with 'a gift for portraying passionate complex women'. Lived for a while with the Horners.

CECIL, VIOLET (née Maxse) (1872–1958). One of Frances's young acolytes, she married Lord Edward Cecil in 1894 but soon fell in love with Sir Alfred Milner, Britain's High Commissioner in South Africa during the Boer War. They eventually married in 1921 and she became Viscountess Milner. Both strong imperialists.

CHAMBERLAIN, JOSEPH (1836–1914). Birmingham industrialist and local politician who quickly rose to Cabinet rank. A determined imperialist, he did much to drag Britain into the Boer War. Uniquely he split two major parties in his career: Gladstone's Liberals over Home Rule in 1886 and Balfour's Tories over economic protection in 1903–5. Frances thought him a cad.

COCKERELL, SYDNEY (1867–1962). Bibliophile and Director of the Fitzwilliam Museum who advised Frances after the Mells Park fire.

COLEFAX, SIBYL, LADY (1874–1950). Hostess and interior decorator and later friend of Frances. Katharine found her insensitive especially over Katharine's discreet conversion to Catholicism.

COLVIN, SIDNEY (1845–1927). Art critic and Keeper of Prints and Drawings at the British Museum (1883–1912). He approved of William Graham's collection and even more so of his daughter.

COOPER, DUFF (1890–1954). Member of the Coterie, often gambled and drank to excess. Decorated soldier in last years of the war. As politician spoke out against Appeasement of dictators. Later Ambassador in Paris. Married Lady Diana Manners.

CURZON, GEORGE (1859–1925). A prominent member of the Souls, appointed Viceroy of India by Balfour. Frances admired his success but found him too egotistical and snobbish towards the 'Cosquiths'. Suffered from being too sure of himself.

CUST, HARRY (1861–1917). Editor of the Pall Mall Gazette and Conservative MP. A Soul. 'He was the Rupert Brooke of our day. Gold-haired, well-born, a poet. Irresistible', remembered Frances. Although she did resist him, many others did not. Still she chose not to judge him during the scandal of his marriage to Nina Welby-Gregory.

DESBOROUGH – see Grenfell

ELCHO, HUGO CHARTERIS, LORD (1857–1937). Inherited the Earldom of Wemyss in 1914. He married Mary Wyndham in 1883. It was not a love match and both sought solace in other relationships. MARY ELCHO was devoted to ARTHUR BALFOUR, although her daughter Mary was the result of a brief fling in the desert with Wilfrid Blunt. Another daughter, Cynthia, married Asquith's son Beb. Among their other children Hugo ('Ego') and Yvo were both killed in the First World War. Stanway in Gloucestershire was one of the favourite gathering places of the Souls.

FRENCH, SIR JOHN, later 1st Earl of Ypres (1852–1925). Commander-in-Chief of the British Expeditionary Force, 1914–16. In this role, he attempted to protect the sons of his friends. Edward Horner refused the opportunity.

GASKELL, MAY (HELEN MARY) (1853–1940). An occasional Soul whose affair with Burne-Jones forced Frances into 'triangular company'.

GLADSTONE, MARY (1847–1927). Daughter of the Prime Minister; Frances's partner in 'slumming' who in 1870s also introduced her into the musical world of Lytteltons and Balfours. Mary acted as her father's secretary until she married Revd Harry Drew in 1886.

GRANBY, VIOLET (née Lindsay) (1856–1937). Married Henry Manners in 1882, becoming Lady Granby in 1886 and Duchess of Rutland in 1906. Talented artist and a Soul, quite Bohemian, longstanding affair with Harry Cust – widely regarded as the father of her daughter DIANA MANNERS. Another daughter 'LETTY' married Ego Charteris.

GRAHAM, WILLIAM (1817–1885). Glasgow entrepreneur and port importer, Liberal MP, leading art collector of the day and patron of Rossetti and especially Burne-Jones. Married Jane Lowndes, talented pianist who trained under Mendelssohn, like her husband a firm Presbyterian. Parents of FRANCES GRAHAM who married Jack Horner of Mells. Her siblings included Alice (who married Quintin Hogg), Florence, Rutherford, Amy (who married Muir MacKenzie), Willie, Lily (who was a missionary) and Agnes ('AGGIE' who married Herbert Jeckyll and was created DBE in 1918 for her considerable public service. In later years she became a popular commentator on domestic management through a series of articles in The Times). RUTHERFORD and WILLIE both died young.

GRENFELL, ETTIE (née Fane)(1867–1952). Society hostess married in 1887 Willie Grenfell, MP and renowned sportsman, who was elevated to the peerage as Lord Desborough in 1905. They entertained in considerable splendour at Taplow and Panshanger. Two sons, Julian and Billy, were killed in the War.

GREY, SIR EDWARD (1862–1933). Foreign Secretary in pre-war Liberal cabinets. Prior to that made the Relugas Pact with Haldane and Asquith. Keen ornithologist. After his wife died became close to Pamela Wyndham.

HALDANE, R.B. (1856–1927). Scottish Lawyer and Liberal MP, held the offices of War Secretary and Lord Chancellor under Asquith. The victim of a press witch-hunt during the War. Jilted by his fiancée (Val Munro-Ferguson). Never married but was devoted to Frances. His centenarian mother disapproved of their close friendship; as did his sister ELIZABETH HALDANE (who was one of the first women to make a high-level career in public service).

HANNAY, REVD JAMES O. (1865–1950). Church of Ireland clergyman and writer of satirical novels. Appointed by Frances to revitalise the Anglican provision in the wake of Katharine's conversion. They became very good friends, often travelling abroad together and in so doing arousing the moral disapproval of his long suffering wife, Ada, and his children, especially his daughter Althea. A son, Seamus, was briefly a friend of Katharine's daughter, Helen, when they were at Oxford.

HIPPISLEY, SIR JOHN (1745/6–1825). Diplomat and fixer who recruited Papal support for the war against Napoleon; made his fortune with the East India Company before becoming an MP and prison reformer. Keen if idiosyncratic advocate for Catholic Emancipation for Ireland.

HOLLIS, CHRISTOPHER (1902–1977). Catholic convert and friend of Waugh and Knox and neighbour of Katharine in Mells. After an academic career and service in Intelligence during the Second World War, he was a Conservative MP. Prolific author.

HORNER, SIR JOHN ('JACK') FRANCIS FORTESCUE (1842–1927). Eldest son of Revd John Stuart Hippisley Horner and his wife Sophia, and heir to Mells Park and its estates. Among his siblings were four unmarried sisters of whom Gertrude was the most formidable. Just as challenging was his brother George who held the living and imposed a strict moral order on his flock. Neither approved of their brother 'Forte' marrying Frances in 1883. Frances called him 'Jack' and it stuck. Their children were CICELY (later Lambton), KATHARINE (later Asquith), EDWARD (d.1917) and MARK (d.1908). They let Mells Park and moved into the Manor House ('Mells Manor') in 1902.

IRVING, SIR HENRY (1838–1905). Leading Shakespearean actor of the day.

JEKYLL, HERBERT (1846–1932). Brother of Gertrude Jekyll, the garden designer, and husband of Aggie Horner. Private Secretary to two Lords Lieutenant in Ireland and later commissioner for the British section of the Paris Exhibition of 1900.

KNOX, FR RONNIE (1888–1957). Contemporary of Edward's at Eton and Oxford, converted to Catholicism and was ordained a priest, becoming a popular commentator and promoter of the Catholic faith. Among his writings was a translation of the Bible, which he completed at Mells to where he had moved after the Second World War.

LIDDELL, ADOLPHUS ('DOLL') (1846–1930). Contemporary at Oxford of Frances's brother Rutherford; a lawyer in the Lord Chancellor's office. An occasional Soul, he fell in love with Laura Tennant and then 'DD' Lyttelton – in both cases they married Alfred Lyttelton instead.

LISTER, CHARLES (1887–1915). Contemporary of Edward's at Eton and Oxford and a member of the Coterie, a passionate socialist, sent down from Oxford for one scrape too many, died at Gallipoli in 1915.

LUTYENS, SIR EDWIN (1869–1944). As a young architect he was taken up by Frances, building numerous country houses for her richer friends. Is most remembered for his design of the Cenotaph (1919). Among many other war memorials, he designed one for Mells and later collaborated with Frances in the design of Campion Hall, Oxford (1934). In 1897 he married Emily Lytton, daughter of the Viceroy of India and sister of Betty Balfour who had married Arthur Balfour's brother Gerald.

LYTTELTON, ALFRED (1857–1913). Brother of May Lyttelton and husband of first Laura Tennant and then 'DD' Lyttelton. Made his name as a first-class cricketer and later served in Arthur Balfour's cabinets.

Lyttelton, 'DD'. Edith (née Balfour) (1865–1943). A member of the Souls and very close confidante of Frances. After an affair with 'Doll' Liddell, she married Alfred Lyttelton in 1892. Keen supporter of Empire. Given the fate of most of the Coterie, remarkably her son Oliver survived the whole war on the Western Front unscathed.

Lyttelton, Edward (1855–1942). Brother of Alfred and Spencer Lyttelton, Anglican Priest and later Head Master of Eton. Unfairly sacked in 1916 for being thought to be pro-German.

Lyttelton, May (1850–1875). Adored by Arthur Balfour who was much shaken by her engagement to Frances's brother Rutherford Graham. As indeed were her parents.

Lyttelton, Spencer (1847–1913). Brother of Alfred and Edward and like them a talented cricketer. Served as Private Secretary in W. E. Gladstone's three governments. Early admirer of Frances.

Marsh, Eddie (1872–1953). Churchill's private secretary; man of letters and art collector; editor of Georgian Poetry. Publisher of the collected poems of Rupert Brooke.

McKenna, Reginald (1863–1943). Liberal politician who held a number of offices under Asquith including the Admiralty, the Home Office, and Chancellor of the Exchequer. Married Aggie's daughter Pamela. Restored Mells Park but not to Frances's design and later sold it too quickly for Frances to raise the funds to buy him out.

Manners, Con (née Constance Hamlyn-Fane) (d.1920), She married John, 3rd Baron Manners in 1885. They lived in Avon Tyrrell – a house built from the winnings of riding his horse Seaman to victory in the 1882 Grand National. Helped Frances recover from post-natal depression after the birth of Mark.

Manners, Diana (1892–1986). Daughter of the Duke and Duchess of Rutland (although Harry Cust was almost certainly her father), golden girl of the Coterie who married Duff Cooper, politician and later Ambassador to France. Confidante of Katharine's.

Milner, Violet (1872–1958). See Violet Cecil.

Moore, George Gordon (b. 1879). Sinister young American railroad millionaire with a remarkable hold over Sir John French, the Commander in Chief of the British Expeditionary Force. Moore shared a house with French and bankrolled his lifestyle, and later became his unofficial personal adviser at GHQ. Obsessed with Diana Manners, he was crucial in ensuring that her brother John escaped the battlefield. Moore returned to America under a cloud in 1916 and led a glamorous life until he lost all his fortune in the Wall Street crash.

Morris, William (1834–1896). Poet and designer whose influence on the decorative arts was profound. A leading light in the Arts and Crafts movement. A close friend of Burne-Jones from their Oxford days, they would collaborate on a range of projects, most especially in Burne Jones's stained-glass designs and in the works produced by the Kelmscott Press. Later they fell out over Morris's growing commitment to Socialism.

MUIR MACKENZIE, KENNETH (1845–1930). Oxford contemporary of Rutherford Horner. Married Frances's sister Amy (1874). Permanent Secretary in the Lord Chancellor's office; he was a powerful figure in the reform of the legal profession, often overcoming strong internal opposition. As Frances would note he was a hard man to shift from his own opinion. Worked well with Haldane when he was Lord Chancellor and indeed Haldane secured a peerage for Mackenzie in 1924. Later Mackenzie went on to serve in two Labour administrations and he was buried in Westminster Abbey in 1930.

PARRY, HUBERT (1848–1918). English composer whose repertoire included the anthem I Was Glad and Jerusalem, the famous setting of Blake's poem 'And did those feet in ancient time'. A major influence on the emerging English school of composers including Ralph Vaughan Williams, Gustav Holst, Herbert Howells and Arthur Bliss. A young Frances sent Burne-Jones away as a visit from Parry was imminent.

PEMBROKE, LORD (1850–1895). 13th Earl; Frances's neighbour in Wiltshire where Wilton offered glamour and culture. A leading Soul and a promoter with Frances of 'The New Morality'. Frances would join him on his yacht every autumn. The epitomy of gentlemanly manner and delicate sensitivity, by contrast with whom his wife, Gity, could seem tactless.

ROOKE, THOMAS. Burne-Jones's long suffering assistant, noted for his timidity. He adored Frances but rather unfortunately compared her to Marie Antoinette.

ROSEBERY, THE EARL OF (1847–1929). Liberal Statesman and Prime Minister 1894–95. An unreliable President of the Liberal League. Racehorse owner who won the Derby three times.

ROSSETTI, DANTE GABRIEL (1828–1882). Pre-Raphaelite artist. William Graham was one of his major collectors in the 1870s and remarkably tolerant of Rosetti's shameless tardiness. Following the death of his model, Lizzie Siddal, he had a long-standing affair with William Morris's wife Jane. Frances, having thought him wonderfully romantic at first, came to despise him.

RUSKIN, JOHN (1819–1900). The leading art critic of the Victorian era who did much to promote the Pre-Raphaelite painters. Much as Frances was flattered to be courted by such a national figure, she resisted his overtures.

RUSSELL, CONRAD (1878–1947). Aristocratic [nephew of the 9th Duke of Bedford], cultured and a little eccentric. Close friend of Raymond Asquith. After Raymond's death became devoted to Katharine who withstood his overtures but not his friendship. A sensitive mediator between Frances and Katharine.

SHAW STEWART, PATRICK (1888–1917). Contemporary of Edward's at Eton and Oxford. Member of the Coterie and the last of them to be killed on the Western Front.

STEAD, W. T. (1849–1912). Editor of *The Pall Mall Gazette* and campaigning journalist whose exposé of child prostitution ('the Maiden Tribute of Modern Babylon') saw him imprisoned. Died in the sinking of the Titanic.

STANLEY, VENETIA (1887–1948). Daughter of Lord Sheffield and close friend of Katharine. H. H. Asquith developed an obsession for her, despite his marriage and age, and in their frequent correspondence he would share with her confidential wartime information. In an effort to escape his close attention, she married his Private Secretary, Edwin Montagu in 1915. Asquith was devastated and the marriage was not a success.

TENNANT, SIR CHARLES ('THE BART') (1823–1906). Not a man hampered by scale, being both a hugely wealthy Scottish businessman and the father of sixteen children. Among his offspring, four were Souls. LUCY GRAHAM SMITH (1862–1942) who compensated for her unhappy marriage by flirting with Harry Cust; Charlotte ('CHARTY') (1858–1911) who married Lord Ribblesdale and who went on several jaunts with Frances; MARGOT (1864–1945) who provided much of the energy behind the Souls and married Henry Asquith, to Frances's regret; LAURA (1862–1886) who idolised Frances and who, after mesmerising many, married Alfred Lyttelton.

TERRY, ELLEN (1847–1928). Leading Shakespearean actress of the late Victorian period. Painted by and briefly married to G. F. Watts. Would lend Frances her box at the theatre.

TREE, IRIS (1897–1968) AND VIOLA (1884–1938). Thespian daughters of Beerbohm Tree, the actor and theatre manager. Iris was a member of the Coterie and it was she who defended them in court after the boating party scandal.

WAUGH, EVELYN (1903–1966). Novelist, Catholic convert and part of Katharine's circle at Mells. His most famous novel was Brideshead Revisited. Katharine strongly disapproved of it.

WEBB, BEATRICE (née Potter) (1858–1943). Broke her heart over Joseph Chamberlain before marrying Sidney Webb. Together they embarked on a life of social reform on Fabian principles. Frances threw dinner parties for Beatrice to meet influential politicians.

WHITE, DAISY (d. 1916) was the glamorous wife of the First Secretary at the American Legation in London and with her husband a fringe Soul.

WHITING, RICHARD (1461–1539). The last Abbot of Glastonbury, who was executed on the orders of Thomas Cromwell. Thomas Horner was a member of the jury that condemned him. Regarded as a Catholic martyr, Whiting was beatified by Pope Leo XIII on 13 May 1895.

WYNDHAM, GEORGE (1863–1913). Brother of Mary Elcho and Pamela Wyndham and leading Soul, he epitomised the late-Victorian ideal of masculinity, combining good looks and military dash with being a man of letters. Member of Balfour's cabinet, whose career was destroyed in 1905 by the Ulster Unionists.

ZAMBACO, MARIA (1843–1914). Burne-Jones's favourite model, with whom he had a tempestuous affair in the late 1860s which almost destroyed his marriage.

Prologue

Ancient Magic

You have gone into a magical land that I dream about
Edward Burne-Jones[1]

This was ancient land. A land of fable where King Arthur had first claimed Excalibur and where, wounded, he sought refuge among the enchantresses on the great Tor at Glastonbury. Rising five hundred feet out of the mists from the surrounding marshes, this outcrop was held a place of mystery, magical – its summit the gateway to Avalon. It would be ever thus. This had been sacred ground too in the Dark Ages and the site of religious ceremonies long lost in time. And in time also these would be absorbed by the all-consuming advance of Christianity. It was the Saxons who built the first church on the Tor; a timber framed structure that didn't survive the great earthquake of 1275 (so great it could be felt as far afield as London). Rebuilt in the next century in local sandstone, St Michael's church stood sentinel over Glastonbury Abbey below – a symbol of clerical authority in a land of pagan legend.

As such the Tor was perfect for his needs. For in November 1539 Thomas Cromwell, Vice-Gerent in Spirituals and Henry VIII's all-powerful lieutenant, wished to make a statement at the height of his Protestant campaign to dissolve the monasteries; one that would echo outside the county boundaries of Somerset to his enemies beyond. In his sights was Glastonbury Abbey – after Westminster the richest monastery in the land with huge estates stretching from Devon and west Somerset to Wiltshire and Oxford.

The old man who waited patiently on the outskirts of Glastonbury was frail and sickly. Enfeebled too after months incarcerated in the Tower of London subjected to 'investigations'. Stripped of all dignity, at the given signal he was spread-eagled and bound to a flimsy hurdle. Tethered to a horse, he was dragged through the streets past

1

sullen crowds and the now deserted Abbey. From there and with each jolt tearing into the old man's body, he endured a painful ascent of the Tor. Waiting for him at the top were a set of gallows, hastily assembled beside the church tower. After the briefest of absolutions and with little more ado, the executioner set about his grim work. The condemned man was hanged until barely alive, then drawn and quartered – the hideous fate of common traitors. So on 15 November 1539 died Richard Whiting, the last Abbot of Glastonbury, his dismembered body despatched to nearby Wells, Bath, Ilchester and Bridgewater; and his head stuck unceremoniously above the gateway of the Abbey, where once he had held great sway.[2]

*

Four years later in 1543, while visiting the Abbey's former lands at Mells on behalf of the King, John Leland reported that

> There is a praty maner place of stone harde at the west ende of the churche. This be likelihood was partely builded by Abbate Sewodde of Glasteinbyri. Sins it served the farmer of thys lordship. Now Mr Horner hath boute the lordship of the King.[3]

Mentioned in Domesday Book, the manor of Mells had been acquired by the Abbey in 1197. It was sufficiently valuable to be worth investing in and under Abbot Selwood not only was the farm house built but he commissioned the development of 'New Street' (one of the earliest examples of 'town planning'). For the Abbots of Glastonbury, Mells Manor was a favourite resting place. Indeed Whiting had spent his last night of freedom there. There is no record that he consulted with his local steward that day, but the next time Whiting saw Thomas Horner, the steward was in the jury at the show trial that condemned the abbot to death. Very soon this Thomas Horner was in the courts asserting his new rights and styling himself Thomas Horner of Mells.[4] Such could be the rewards of jury service.

Who was Thomas Horner? There were Horners with land holdings in Leigh on Mendip in the 1470s. As one of a number of Abbey stewards, Thomas would have combined the roles of farm manager and land agent, setting and collecting rents and resolving disputes. He would have known all the accounts, rentals, tithes, various manorial court rolls of the Abbey, but only for his area and Horner's remit at Mells was very local: the Mells area, including Leigh on Mendip,

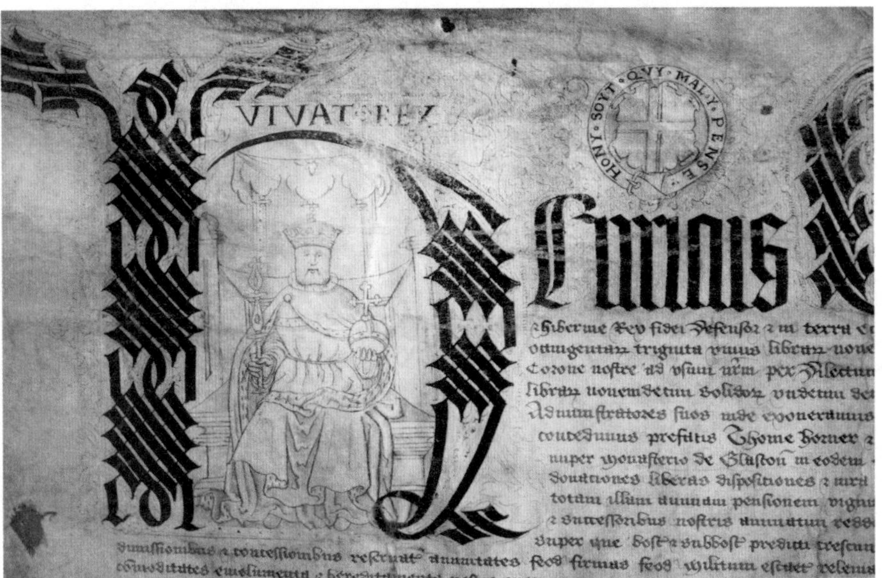

1.   *The Grant from Henry VIII to Thomas Horner providing for the acquisition of land at Mells and elsewhere, 10th July 1543 (detail)*

Nunney, Cloford, and possibly Doulting as well. All this was decidedly small scale compared to the aristocracy and gentry who had made up most of the jury. For him to serve on this jury he would have had to be known to be reliable to Cromwell's cause and ready to support a verdict against the Abbot. Possibly, he was a strong Protestant, but certainly he must have been already sympathetic to reform. It is inconceivable that the Crown would have sold the Abbey's land to someone they couldn't trust. That said, he was still made to pay a significant sum: £1831 2s. 3¾ d. (which equates to £1.4 million today) to acquire the manor (fig. 1). That and the fact that he moved into the farmhouse at Mells, where once the abbots stayed, suggest that he was a new man of means seeking to establish himself as a landed gentleman. His arrival in 1543 represented the coming of a new order as well as the demise of Catholic Mells. Gone was a Catholic outpost with ties to national and international affairs. In its place a Protestant regime, reinforced by the proximity of church and house, and peopled by a family that was energetic, pragmatic, provincial and socially ambitious. Little did Thomas Horner know that his gain would return to haunt his family in centuries to come.

*

By the summer of 1885, William Graham M.P. knew he was dying. The stomach cancer, which he had whimsically dismissed as the 'mischief within', had taken its toll and reduced to a shell a man once of vigour and imagination; who had made a fortune abroad and then spent it on assembling one of the greatest collections of contemporary art of his generation. For one so frugal in the accumulation of wealth, he could be wonderfully extravagant in the dispersal of it – especially in furthering the causes of the Pre-Raphaelite artists Dante Gabriel Rossetti and Edward Burne-Jones. The latter felt the impending loss particularly keenly and not simply for Graham's boundless generosity. He had become a mentor and father figure, welcoming Burne-Jones into his house, smoothing out what perplexed and agitated him, sharing his vision – someone through whose affection Burne-Jones had grown and flourished.

So it was too with Graham's daughter, Frances, whom Burne-Jones had known and loved since she was a child. She was not in the classic sense a Pre-Raphaelite 'stunner' – tempestuous, flame haired and barely repressed carnality. Instead, with her golden fair hair and girlish figure she embodied wide-eyed innocence and set off in him a conflict between moral sentiment and aching desire. For the rest of his life she would be his confidante and muse and he the greatest inspiration and love of her life. 'You haunt me everywhere', he once declared. 'I haven't a corner of my life or my thoughts where you are not'. He drew her obsessively, included her in some of his most famous paintings, and showered her with gifts. To him 'all the romance and beauty of my life means you'. But first and foremost, she was her father's favourite companion, his playmate as well as his partner in his great artistic adventure. Summoned now to his death bed ('I want you so much to come'),[5] she would keep vigil by his side until the end.

Dying he may have been but Graham was not yet dead. Wracked with pain, he was nevertheless determined to complete two last tasks. The first was to secure the financial future of Burne-Jones. Much to his family's astonishment he spent the last two months of his life negotiating from his bedside a series of commissions and revaluations that would provide the artist with the modern equivalent of £1,800,000. The second was no less important to him and concerned

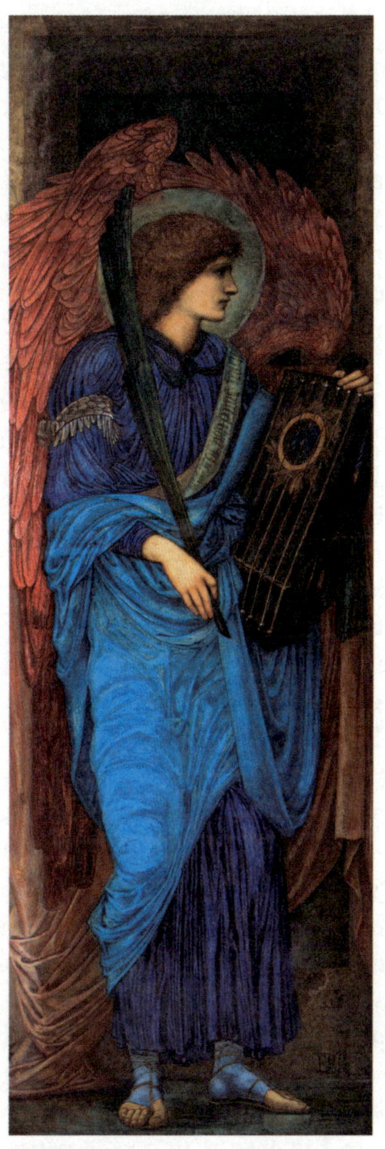

2.   *Edward Burne-Jones,*
'My Bright Robed Angel'

Frances. From his sick-bed he asked Burne-Jones if 'my bright robed Angel' was ready and to send it to his London home in Grosvenor Place 'while Frances is there, as it will be a pleasure to them both'. Two weeks later he was even more insistent. 'I don't want my Angel to be seen by anyone except Frances … So if you are sending it to Grosvenor Place, order it to be sent upstairs to Frances's boudoir and not shewn'.[6] This gift was private and personal – a last symbol of their shared passion for art and one, as so often in the past, that had to be shared privately. In truth, there was nothing discreet about this picture (fig. 2). Sumptuous in blue and towering over the onlooker, the Angel was an expression of glad confidence and enduring faith; ready to stand guard over Frances as once her father had done.

First it was to stand over him. Overriding her father's wishes, Frances brought the picture down and hung over her father's bed. Curiosity, she knew, would get the better of him. Burne-Jones also knew how to comfort his patron, sending daily moss roses from his garden and little paintings to whet his appetite for colour. 'When you write to me' Graham had asked, 'put three dabs of colours in the corners, [it is] just like having a grape when my mouth is dry'. And along with this came a last request: to bring 'the other drawing of Frances'.[7] For one last time they were a triumvirate again: father-daughter-protégé, patron-artist-model; an intimate world in which Frances became muse to them both. It was this that Burne-Jones sought to capture in an extraordinary letter written while stricken with grief at the passing of his friend. 'My heart has been full of love and blessing for you from years ago – when you were little…You were so like him to me from the first, like a womanly form of him – and that was why I so cared for you – and both lives were wonderfully interwoven in my imagination'.[8]

And so they were for her too. Her father and the artist, as one, had drawn her into their shared vision and a mission to create beauty in the face of industrial advance. With them she had been sucked into a vortex of emotions and experiences; a kaleidoscope of colour and imagination and opportunities ('treasures' she would call them) as few Victorian girls would know. Together there had been laughter amid the seriousness, excitement along with endeavour. Together also boundaries would be blurred and roles reversed as they sought to love her – each in his own way or seemingly so. Eventually their protective warmth proved claustrophobic and with a single decisive act she caught the old men by surprise and broke up the troika.

*

Frances would never be quite what Burne-Jones longed her to be. Behind the 'soft and gentle' manner was one determined to make her own way in the world. Still at least he could take solace that fate would take her to Somerset and the ancient land over which Glastonbury

Tor stood in lonely memory. 'All the way from Amesbury on to Glastonbury is romance land', he wrote to his young friend:

the most beautiful and sweet that ever was, I think – soaked in wonderful tales … and it is pretty for me that you have gone into a magical land that I dream about.[9]

Yet with Frances's arrival in Camelot, Mells would never be the same again. With her would come a different England, one that was metropolitan, artistic, radical and romantic. For, as many would discover, Miss Frances Graham was well used to getting her own way.

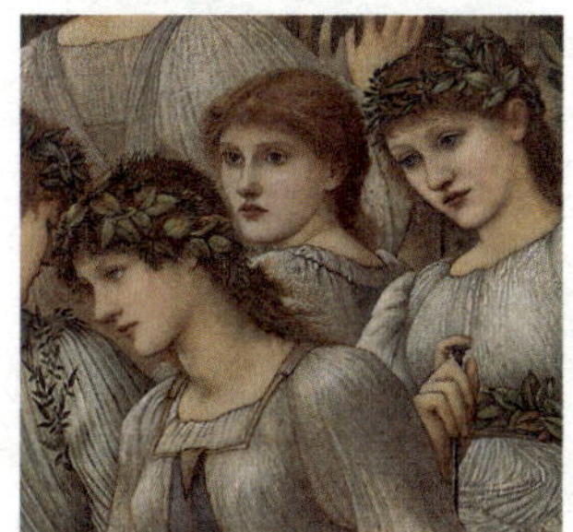

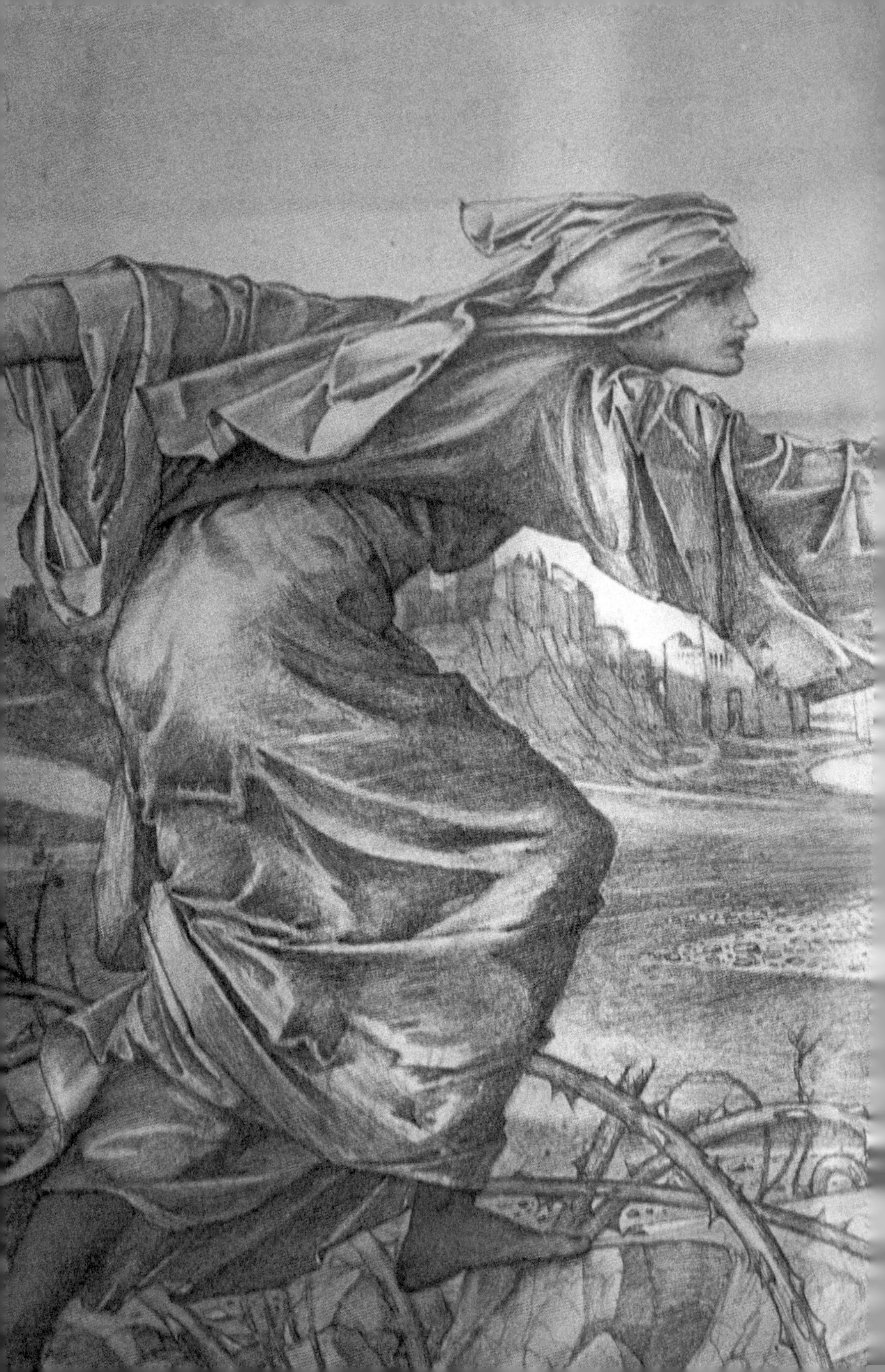

Part One

'The Blissfullest Years'
('1860'–1880)

F. has got such a beauty from Mr Burne-Jones – a big
picture of Cupid dragging a maiden through all the
meshes and mazes of Love

Mary Gladstone, 14 February 1875[1]

3.   *Love and the Pilgrim, by Edward Burne-Jones,*
detail of the cartoon Frances received on Valentine's Day 1875

~ 1 ~

THE MAKING OF A MUSE

I'm afraid Mamma won't approve of this, Panza

William Graham to Frances[2]

William Graham had looked extraordinary when first he settled in London in 1865. Tall and athletic he may have been, but it was the hair that caught the eye. Fair in colour and frenetic as if tightly sprung, it enveloped his head in a halo. From under it huge eyes stared out in child-like innocence on the world. 'He had a beautiful face' remembered one of Frances's friends, 'with an aureole of misty hair which made him look like a saint in a frock coat'. Eccentric, generous of heart, and walking around London with the 'spring gait of a Swiss guide', William Graham was different (fig. 4). All of which was hard to reconcile with the hard-nosed Glaswegian businessman making his fortune, employing thousands in his cotton mills and importing dry goods from India and port from Portugal. If the last maintains the family name to this day, he also had the confidence to risk investing in a small oil franchise in the 1860s that still retains the shell motif he once designed for them. Nor, for all that he was in 1865 the newly elected Liberal Member of Parliament for Glasgow, was he driven by political ideas or even preferment. Apart from the occasional intervention in defence of religion, he contributed little. But then that little mattered to him. A devout Presbyterian and Sabbatarian and later an enthusiastic follower of the American evangelists, Moody and Sankey,[3] Graham would lead his household in daily prayers. His was a belief that empowered rather than constricted, that was about having faith rather than seeking judgement. Hence 'his face was that of a saint', wrote Burne-Jones's wife, Georgiana, 'and at times like

10

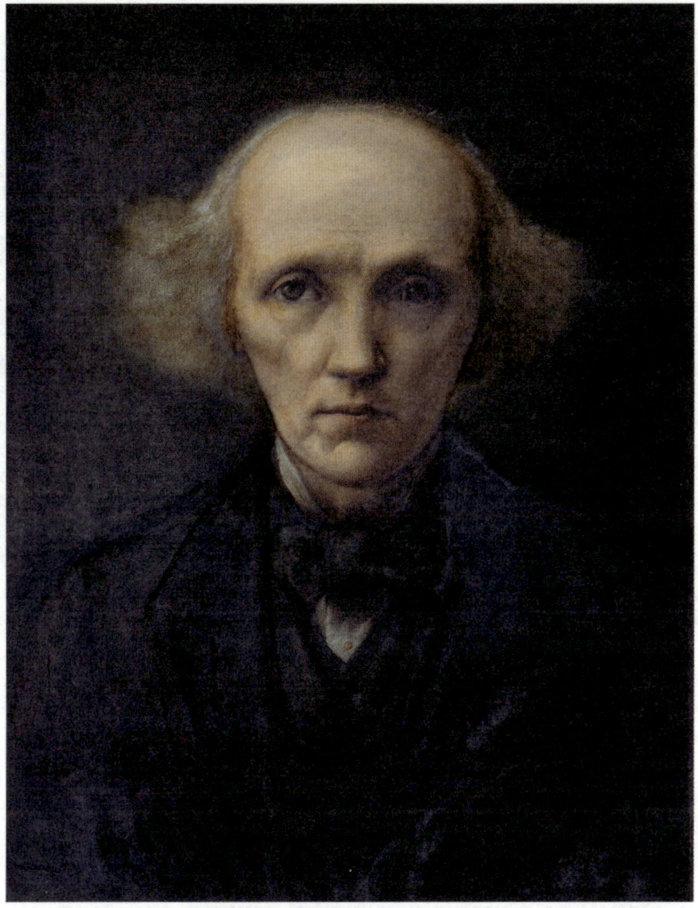

4.   *William Graham, by Edward Burne-Jones, c. 1880*

one transfigured'. The simplicity that comes with such conviction left him free to be curious.

Indeed this pillar of moral rectitude on arriving in London in 1865 was responsible for commissioning some of the most sensuous and erotically charged paintings of the Victorian era. At the outset of their friendship Burne-Jones hid the more explicit pictures from his new patron only to be surprised to find that these were the ones he liked best.[4] Nor did he let public notoriety deflect his taste. In 1870 Burne-Jones found himself embroiled in scandal over his painting *Phyllis and Demophoön*, which he had offered to the Old Water Colour Society's Summer exhibition. Amid the staid conventional work that

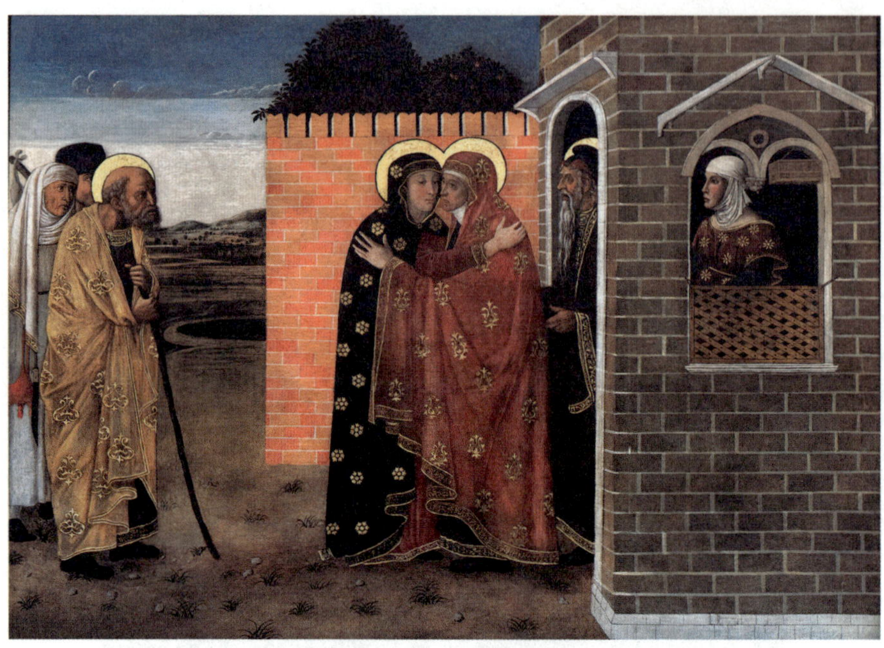

5.   *The Visitation, by Jacopo Bellini*

traditionally filled the exhibition, Burne-Jones's striking portrayal of desperate attraction was always going to stand out. If the display of male genitalia proved too much for the Society, others were outraged by the portrayal of a woman in lustful pursuit of a man. While the *cognoscenti* would also have spotted that both protagonists were given the face of Burne-Jones's mistress, Maria Zambaco, and reflected on a torrid affair that threatened to destroy his marriage. Asked to cover up the offending article, Burne-Jones refused and withdrew the painting, his reputation and confidence so damaged that he would not exhibit for another seven years.

None of this disturbed Graham. Having earlier in 1865 commissioned *Le Chant d'Amour* from Burne-Jones, he now ordered a companion piece *Laus Veneris* (1873–78) (fig. 15). Within a theme of Music and Love, it picks up on the legend of Tannhauser who lost his soul to his licentious desire for Venus, here portrayed as a fading libertine surrounded by her attendants and 'gnawed away with disappointment and desire.'[5] Graham was equally ready in 1872 to provide a haven in Scotland for a traumatised Rossetti when his affair with William

Morris's wife threatened to become public. In the Congregational Chapel where his family worshipped, almost all would have kept their distance from such company, but not William Graham.

A more cynical age might have condemned him as a voyeur and hypocrite. But the paintings he commissioned were never explicitly sexual. More importantly, William had a natural eye for what made a good picture. Burne-Jones pronounced him 'a genius for his perception and instinct for painting. He was infallible. He was never wrong'.[6] There was integrity to his taste, unaffected as it was by the opinions of others. In fact he was rather suspicious of connoisseurs. The appeal of a painting for him was less intellectual and more emotional. On one occasion he was so moved at first sight of one of Burne-Jones's pictures that he simply went up and kissed it.[7] Unencumbered by convention and fashion, he had the courage to trust his instincts when investing in contemporary art. Margot Asquith would later compare 'old Mr Graham who discovered and promoted Burne-Jones and Frederick Walker' with her billionaire father who was a much more competitive collector and corrupted his taste as result.[8] Nor was Graham narrowly focussed on commissioning new work, combining a much larger collection of Old Masters (then going very cheap) alongside his Pre-Raphaelites (fig 5). The two are not unconnected and he was frequently encouraging Burne-Jones 'to think in Italianate terms' especially praising Giorgionesque compositions. At its most basic, he liked his pictures 'Venetian in concept, rich in colour, romantic or elegiac in mood.'[9] Not for him the great moralistic narratives beloved of Victorians and he was ahead of his time in admiring the ambiguities of mood and subject in Burne-Jones's later works.

His was a collection built on the simple thrill of witnessing the creative process and a passion to pursue beauty in an often ugly world. True at times his veneration of some pictures as if they were icons almost verged on the idolatrous. Nevertheless those contemporaries who questioned his 'curious combination of … unaffected piety and a devotion to art that was almost pagan' failed to see that there was for Graham no contradiction. In creating beauty one was reaffirming the Divine.[10] Part of the appeal to him of Burne-Jones's talent was that it was untrained and thus God given. As he declared to Rossetti, art was 'chiefly precious as it shadows out to us and echoes in our hearts the music of that fair and sweet and stainless world unseen.'[11] Away from the world of business he could reclaim the innocence of one who has still 'the heart of a child and [who] is full of hope.' This prelapsarian fantasy of an innocent at large cannot of itself account for the deal maker and the election winner; and they in turn cannot explain his bewildering disregard for the opinions of others and the apparent depth of his *naïveté*. In truth he was more complex figure for whom the certainties of faith covered ambiguities of taste.

Graham bought art 'on a princely scale'. As Frances recalled, 'he bought pictures so large, that our house in Grosvenor Place was literally lined with them in every room from floor to ceiling, old and modern, sacred and profane; they stood in heaps on the floor and on the chairs and tables.'[12] He was the perfect patron. Calling in on a studio he would 'appear and disappear very swiftly' and was extraordinarily tolerant of artistic licence and delay. *Found*, which Graham commissioned from Rossetti in the late 1860s was only acquired after the artist's death in 1882. Another painting sent back for some minor repairs was returned with the subject's face repainted to take account of Rossetti's latest mistress. Most famous was the debacle of *Dante's Dream at the Time of the Death of Beatrice*. Commissioned in 1871 from Rossetti for the then huge sum of £1,500 guineas and with firm instructions that it should be six by six foot, it arrived eventually measuring ten by seven foot – too large for what space remained in his dining room.[13] For once Mrs Graham – no lover of art and resentful of the clutter – had her way and the picture was returned. It was not until 1881 that Rossetti produced a version that fitted.

Burne-Jones was much easier to work with (if no better a keeper of deadlines). To inspire him Graham would lend him works by Mantegna and Carpaccio from his collection. Best of all were notes asking Burne-Jones 'may I send you more £sd?' Because it was 'such a pleasure if one can, so that you may think only of making beautiful work.'[14] So devoted was he, that, for all his business acumen, he never kept any records of his financial commitments to his favoured artists. Such munificence came at a cost. Pre-Raphaelite commissions were rarely less than £1,000 and on average Graham was spending £4,000 a year (or £453,387 in modern values). Although wealthy, Graham was not super-rich like his fellow Scottish émigré in London, Charles Tennant (Margot Asquith's father), and in the fifteen years after 1866 when he bought his first significant picture,

Rossetti's *Morning Music*, he spent a third of his capital on art. In the process he created one of the greatest contemporary art collections of the nineteenth century.

In addition to Rossetti and Burne-Jones, Graham owned major works by Millais, Holman Hunt, Leighton, G.F. Watts, Legros, Fred Walker and Arthur Hughes. When Ruskin wrote his seminal article on 'The Three Colours of Pre-Raphaelitism', it would be based on three pictures he had found hanging in his bedroom at Graham's Scottish retreat. Just as significant (especially as so poorly regarded at the time) was his substantial collection of Old Masters, including Antonello's *Virgin and Child,* Dosso Dossi's *Circe and her lovers*, Pesellino's *Virgin and Child with St John*, and Piero di Cosimo's *The Finding of Vulcan*. Fittingly in the year before he died Gladstone recognised his achievement and made him a Trustee of the National Gallery.[15]

In 1886 he had been hardly dead a year before his collection was no more. His long-suffering wife, having been left everything in his will, finally took her revenge, putting it all up for sale at Christie's. To be fair, Graham had over-spent and possibly capital was needed for the annuities that provided for his many daughters. The house in Grosvenor Place was to be let go and they had nowhere to hang the pictures, many of which were already out on loan. That her children had to instruct Agnews to buy back some of the pictures suggests, however, that their mother had acted on her own initiative. But with the sale generating £69,168 (almost £69 million in today's terms), her offspring were quickly priced out. Thus for Frances, looking on helplessly as her father's creation was dispersed over four days, this sale marked the end of her early life and encapsulated the loss, in the most brutal of ways, of the influence that had been the making of her.[16]

*

Right from the start Frances Graham was never what she seemed (fig. 6). Even her date of birth was shrouded in ambiguity. In her memoirs the opening chapter on her early life is suggestively entitled (including inverted commas) '1860–1880'. Most historians plump for 1858, to which she would no doubt have acquiesced. But her gravestone didn't lie and Francie Graham was born in Glasgow in 28 March 1854.[17] A common vanity perhaps. So too was her desire in old age to reconstruct the past on her own terms.

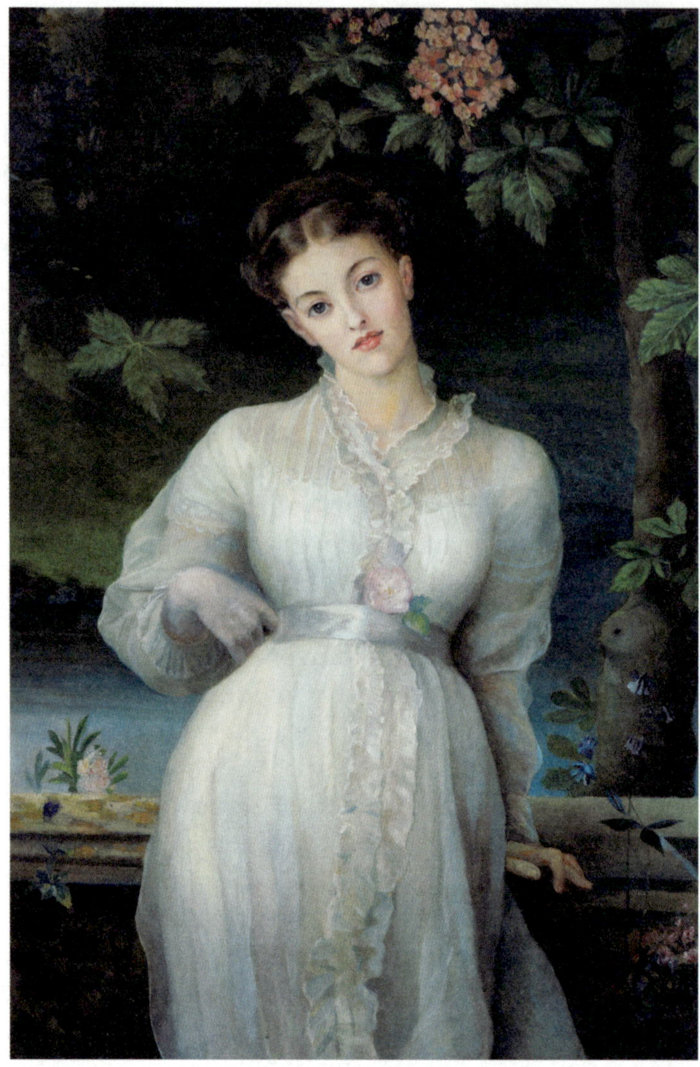

6.   *Frances Graham (Anon.)*

'Our family was rather divided', she claimed, so setting herself up as the eternal rebel railing against the bourgeois conventionality and religious sentimentality of the Graham household. With her father, they would be portrayed as lone voices against the prevailing philistinism. None in her eyes embodied the latter more than her mother. Frances never forgave her for seeming not to 'care' for her husband's pictures.

Yet Jane Graham (née Lowndes) was not insensitive to the arts. A talented pianist in her youth, she had once studied under Mendelssohn and Liszt and it was she who nurtured in Frances a lifelong interest in music.[18] She was certainly very religious but then so too was her husband. And it was his extemporary prayers and favourite hymns that Frances would remember fondly – not least as she struggled for him on the organ he had installed. Sundays would see two services and no visitors. But they would be enlivened, in Frances's memory, by her father's vivid recounting of the Scripture stories; of which 'his telling of the Good Shepherd and the wandering sheep would always make me cry.'

Two of Frances's sisters,[19] Alice and Florence remained strongly evangelical all their lives, while another, Lily, became a missionary in China. Yet Frances's declaration that she and her youngest sister Aggie 'were not religious' was belied by the Christian mission for handicapped children she established in the stable block of her family home.[20] Frances would never do anything to hurt her father. It would only be after his death and finding herself in more sophisticated society that her faith wavered. Nor was her upbringing restrictive: 'we younger children were allowed to do very much as we pleased, living in a home in which money was not much considered, and where discipline, such as it was, was very loving, and more concerned with the spirit than the mind or the body.' When she was very young they had moved to Langley Hall, outside Manchester, and she lived a comfortable childhood of nannies and baked cereal around the nursery fire, while in a paddock was 'a fat grey called Stella'. It was a privileged existence in which 'a good deal was done for our pleasure and well-being.'[21]

If the Grahams were deemed 'advanced' in their attitudes towards the upbringing of children, in one crucial regard they could not have been more conventional. In the matter of education, it was only Frances's two brothers who were sent to school. Her elder brother, Rutherford, 'a handsome, brilliant creature' was soon enjoying too much the freedoms of Oxford, while Willie, to whom she was closer, was at Eton. For the girls there was instead a stream of French and German governesses to provide a smattering of European culture. Frances picked up languages easily and was clearly very able. But any knowledge of literature, philosophy or the classics was largely self-taught. This left her lacking the cumulative framework that

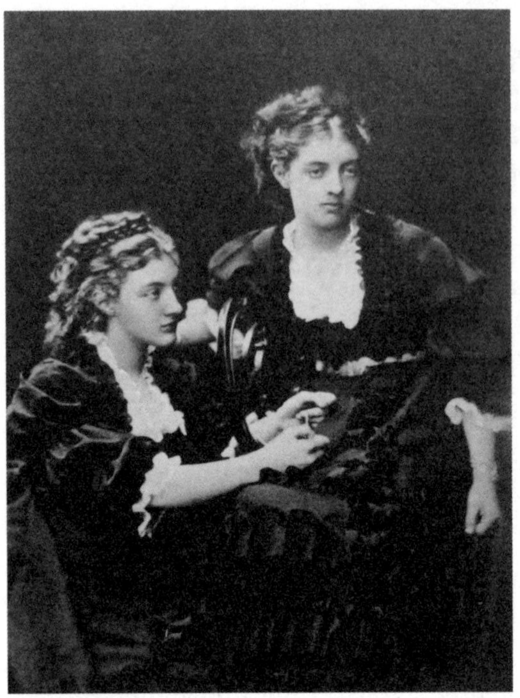

7.   *Frances and Amy Graham*

encourages an analytical understanding. Like her friend Mary Gladstone, Frances in childhood 'read furiously but inconsequentially'.[22] That said, she was soon tackling major texts. Once she spent all her savings on an edition of the works of Heine, only for her mother to confiscate it on the German governess's advice that it was 'not at all "*passend für junge Mädchen*"'.[23] Needless to say Frances was resourceful enough to secrete it back. But it brought home to her the separate spheres for which she and her siblings were being groomed. While she craved the intellectual stimulation and discovery open to her brothers (if largely ignored by them), for Frances and her sisters knowledge was little more than a civilising veneer in their preparation for marriage and motherhood.[24]

Even as a child Frances found this deeply frustrating. Intellectually curious and with a forceful personality, she would always ask the direct question and seek beyond the adult platitude, ever ready to engage with any who would listen. The first who did was her father. Though away on business most of the week, he would spend Saturday afternoons thrilling his children with chemistry lessons in the attic, especially as most of his experiments ended in an explosion. 'Amuse yourself with your latin' was admittedly a distinctly patronising response to Frances's desire for a classical education. However once he realised she was serious, he was urging her at his expense to get tutors in mathematics and latin 'if you like'. As a father, William Graham was sympathetic to 'all our fun, was our chosen companion (as we were his), and gave us the best of a wonderfully stored mind'. Plundering men's minds would become something of a habit with Frances. It began with her father whom she worshipped as her 'guide, philosopher and friend… a man of singular beauty and character.'[25] By contrast her mother, having 'played a much less important part in our lives', was largely written out of her childhood. Her siblings may well have thought differently. With one handicapped child[26] to look after and four other daughters to marry off, their mother had other priorities. Frances's denigration of her mother and adulation of her father was but the preamble to a greater claim: 'I always felt in my heart that I was my father's favourite'. Certainly she went out of her way to make it so.[27]

Admittedly, between father and daughter there was an instinctive rapport. Both were easily amused by the risqué and a quip about a Burne-Jones woodcut of Cupid and Psyche was couched 'in such frank biblical language' that it even shocked the artist. So crude was it that thirty years later even she balked at repeating it.[28] In all this she would be always egging her father on. He was only just able to stand up to her when they discovered that the butler had hung Watts's *Endymion* upside down. With the artist due to call she begged him to leave it but Graham feared the offence such a tease might cause. However naughty she was, 'it was easy to provoke a lurking smile or glint in his eye'. Although only eleven when they arrived in London, she soon picked up on her father's new obsession with art and how it was not shared by his wife. 'My mother wanted quite another world for us children, and we realised quite well how different her outlook was from his.'[29] Hence she seized every chance to accompany her father on his visits to the studios of his favourite artists.

No doubt, Frances appreciated the respect shown to a major buyer but these visits opened her eyes to a magical world. Most exciting was Rossetti's studio in Cheyne Walk. There she remembered the romantic and recently widowed Rossetti reading out his 'House of Life' sonnets a year before their publication. Then there was the menagerie of animals he kept in his garden – fawns, exotic birds, armadillos that escaped into neighbouring gardens, and peacocks in full display.

Soon new artists would be invited to the Grahams' Highland retreat at Stobhall, such as Fred Walker and William Richmond; the latter happy to flirt with the girls – discreetly reading them Tennyson's *Idylls of the King* on the Sabbath or provoking giggles during a particularly solemn sermon.[30] With Walker, Burne-Jones and Rossetti paintings on their walls – a revelation to many of their visitors – Frances first caught a hint of the distinctiveness of her father's imagination. With him as guide, she would, in time, become an astute judge. By her father's side she would come to meet all the great artistic figures of the day. It undoubtedly helped being the daughter of a wealthy patron, especially if in the early days she was little more to them than a fresh-faced child. In time some would come to appreciate her learning and quick turn of phrase. If she could be provocative and stubborn, it only amused. For the most part she was charming, respectful and, above all, watchful.

In 1869, when Frances was just fifteen, Graham commissioned Rossetti to paint her in an early version of *La Donna della Fenestra* (fig. 8). A year later Burne-Jones painted her as the young bride in his *King's Wedding* (fig. 9). At a time when artists' models were from the lower orders and presumed (often rightly) to be the artist's mistress, the use of a respectable girl, let alone one's patron's daughter, was highly unusual.[31] It was also odd (if perhaps in character) that Graham should be insensitive to this and indeed be the instigator. Admittedly, Frances was fully clothed, modelling only her face, but this was louche company for an evangelical to expose his daughter to and one only too likely to arouse her mother's disapproval. From a young age Frances was fascinated before she was shocked. Indeed she was not easily shocked, seeing, for instance, the beauty rather than the nakedness in her father's purchases. This became a symbolic battleground. Mrs Graham successfully put her foot down over her husband's acquisition of Rossetti's *Ligeia Siren*, 'even after the "unpopular central detail" of her pubic hair was masked by strands of flying drapery'.[32] As Frances neared adulthood, the balance of power began to shift. Bringing home a Milanese nude dressed in little more than her hair, Graham warned, 'I am afraid Mama won't like this'. Retitle it 'John the Baptist' was Frances's brisk response. Jane Graham was no fool. Yet sensing she was no match for this new alliance, she held her tongue.[33]

What had begun as a teenage revolt, had in adulthood became something more. With her father by her side, art became part of a shared rebellion, reinforced by a shared fascination with beauty and the momentum optimism brings. With her new position came new sensations of control: the excitement of being favoured; and an early appreciation of the power that comes with attraction and how to

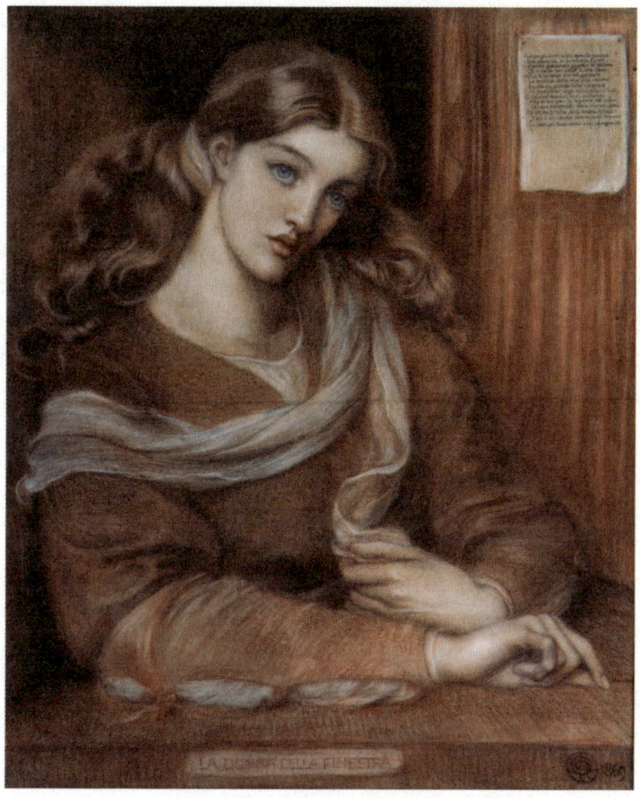

8.	*La Donna della Fenestra, by Dante
Gabriel Rossetti, 1869*

exploit it. It was Frances who increasingly joined her father in his dealings with the artists and who had the confidence to entertain them when they came to the house. As 'Panza', his nickname for her suggests, they were now a partnership. Yet while she respected his authority, she was a much more forceful presence than Don Quixote's Sancho. By the early 1870s he was willing to defer to her judgement. After finding Holman Hunt's *The Shadow of Death* (1873) 'distasteful and theatrical', they went together a second time for Frances to give her opinion. When serious illness struck Graham in 1873–74 and 1877, Frances became his secretary, learning much from his correspondence about the business of art, while adding mildly flirtatious postscripts to her artist friends. His world had become hers and she would be 'his companion in all his expeditions [buying in Italy] and friends with all his friends'. When still recuperating in 1874 Graham found himself in Madrid: 'You will wonder why I am here', he wrote to Rossetti. 'Of course a woman was at the bottom of it as of all other things. I didn't want to come abroad at all but Frances did and so I had to come.' When Frances heard that he had been to Rossetti's studio at Cheyne Walk without her, she was 'very disappointed' and made him promise to take her next time – as he wearily explained to the artist.[34] By the late 1870s he had come to depend on his twenty-five-year-old daughter: 'there are things you can do for me in town that nobody else can'.[35] When in 1879 her father finally accepted that their home was overwhelmed with his pictures, it would be Frances who would clear the decks; single-handedly arranging major loans to the South Kensington Museum[36] and other museums around the country. And at his insistence she alone would decide the rehang at Grosvenor Place. She could be quite critical of his purchases, dismissing the duds as 'Tuppies' (after Mr Jingle's worthless marriage licence in Dickens's *Pickwick Papers*). Yet such private jokes only showed how much she enjoyed the chase. 'Any dealer had only to murmur to him, "*Virgine – intatta – sulla tavola*" to lure him to any distance', she would recall in mock despair. Unlike most great collectors he found the pursuit of the bargain – 'smelling around for £20 Leonardos' – too tempting; to the benefit of many an unscrupulous Italian aristocrat.[37] To Frances this sport was a price worth paying as the muse became the manager.

By 1880 she was a figure in her own right. Decamping to Italy for the summer, Browning would be her guide in Florence and Venice. Her bible would be Ruskin's *Stones of Venice* – just as his letters bombarded her hotel ('My darling Francie'). But it would be Burne-Jones's declaration that 'you can't see Venice unless there is a little Venice inside you first' that she would never forget. This was a life that was exciting, carefree, even glamorous. It was not the life of her married sisters. But it was complicated – not least by the other great influence shaping her young life at that time, her father's favourite artist, Edward Burne-Jones.

❦ 2 ❦

BECOMING MY FRIEND

She combined a delicate sensibility to beauty with a robust, positive temperament that enabled her to get all the enjoyment out of life that she could. Burne-Jones found her … exhilarating [and his] relationship with her became, after his art, his chief source of happiness.

David Cecil[38]

'The new pet is Frances Graham from Glasgow', reported Ruskin in January 1878 'and she is a great pet of Edward Jones's'. Like all good gossip it was not to be spoilt by being hopelessly out of date. For Frances had known Burne-Jones for at least ten years by then. As a child she had been dragged around the artists' studios by her father. Rossetti was her favourite – raffish, romantic and entertaining – the artist in 'a sort of dressing gown' as he read his latest poem 'with a deep booming voice that seemed to come out of his boots.' By comparison the taciturn and tongue-tied Burne-Jones was something of an anti-climax (fig. 10). Though barely fifteen, she had already modelled for Rossetti and a year later she was the queen for Burne-Jones's *The King's Wedding* (1870; fig. 9). In both cases the driving force was her father, not the artists. There was nothing to suggest that very soon she would become the muse of 'Ned' Burne-Jones for the last twenty five years of his life.

Indeed in 1870 nothing could be further from the artist's mind, for his life was in turmoil as his affair with his model, Maria Zambaco, descended into high melodrama. Greek by birth and widowed, Maria was as temperamental as she was sexually alluring. Anyone less like his wife, Georgie, it would be hard to imagine. Quietly attractive, intelligent and fiercely supportive Georgie may

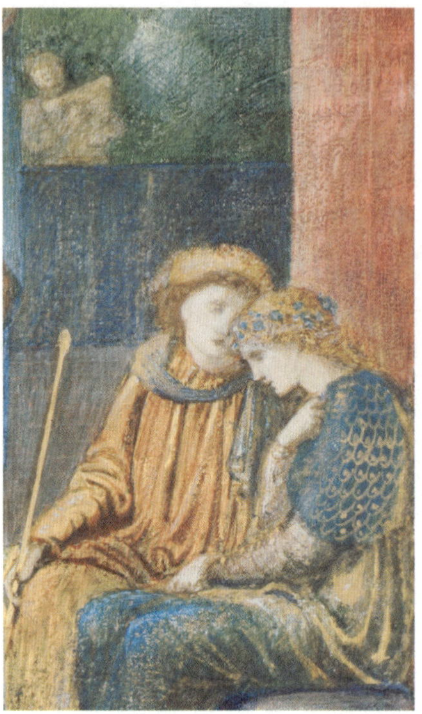

9.   *The King's Wedding (detail), by Edward Burne-Jones, 1870*

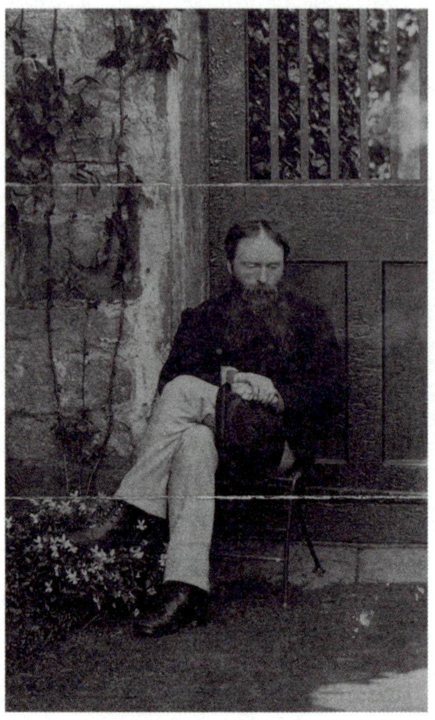

10.   *Edward Burne-Jones aged 'about forty' in 1874*

have been, but within her the Methodist strain ran deep. A touch earnest, she would have been better to have 'married a good clergyman' her husband would later claim (probably correctly). Moreover, she had for health reasons ended all sexual relations with him. When Maria lit on Burne-Jones, he was always going to be tempted.[39]

In 1868 a stray letter exposed his transgression. Georgie was devastated. Then, with Maria urging that they should run away to a Greek island, Burne-Jones's nerve failed him. 'How often I tried', he would later recall to Frances, 'with all the strength I could, years ago to be free – knowing there was nothing for me but pain, on that road – and I never, never could.'[40] Maria became hysterical, culminating in a theatrical suicide attempt in January 1869. Having brought enough laudanum for two, she then tried to throw herself into the Regent's Canal, with Burne-Jones grappling with her on the bridge. At that point they were apprehended by two passing policemen. Such a scene was deeply humiliating and public, with gleeful accounts soon doing the rounds among his rival artists. Yet just as he couldn't break free from his wife, so he couldn't give up on his mistress and for the next two years he oscillated between the two. Maria was still modelling for him in 1872. By that winter however she had waited long enough and left him for Paris. There she would marry and it would be another sixteen years before they would meet again.[41] If *Phyllis and Demophoön* (1870) was a defiant declaration of his love, his *Love among the Ruins* (1872) signalled its demise.

The affair would hang over his marriage for the rest of his life. After a brief separation, Georgie had chosen the route of stoicism. One of four remarkable sisters whose offspring would include Rudyard Kipling and the future prime minster, Stanley Baldwin, she was not about to give up her artist husband. Nor after his death would she resist the role of keeper of the flame, immortalising him in her two volume *Memorials of Edward Burne-Jones* (1904). 'There is love enough between Edward and me to last out a long life', she would insist and she would work hard to ensure that life at The Grange wouldn't lack conviviality.[42] But the chill of formality now gnawed away at their relationship. Polite respect and careful conversation spoke of accommodation – not progress and renewal. 'I have been a bad man and sorry for it', Burne-Jones would admit, 'but not sorry enough to try to be a good one.'[43]

As is often the case, this crisis did not strike alone. Along with the furore over *Phyllis and Demophoön*, Burne-Jones was mortified to hear that Ruskin, his great mentor and guide, was about to denounce his idol Michelangelo for his 'dark carnality' and 'fleshy imagination.' It was an attack that went right to the heart of Burne-Jones's artistic values and thereafter their friendship would never be quite the same. He fell out too with Ford Madox Brown, and in time even became distanced from Rossetti. Inevitably he began to lose confidence in himself as an artist. 'I walk about like an exposed imposter' he confessed to Watts.[44] Sinking into depression, he sought to escape to Italy in 1871 and 1873 and there to renew his faith in the Old Masters – those 'I now care the most for: Michelangelo, Signorelli, Mantegna, Giotto, Botticelli … Piero della Francesca.'

No one could have been more delighted at this than his leading patron who had long urged him in the direction of the Old Masters. Yet Graham was more concerned by the sight of Burne-Jones retreating back into self-absorption and loneliness. He began inviting him regularly to dine. For his youngest daughters, Frances and Aggie, his presence was something of a curiosity and no doubt encouraged by their father they took him up as a mission. Rejecting his choice of 'the quiet life', their solution was to bring him back into society – a strategy that was not without self-interest as their father much preferred the society of his own home. To win over their father they resorted to bribery; buying a small drawing by Burne-Jones for 7s 6d and offering this to Graham if he would agree to take them all out to the theatre. Graham was not the first father to accept the present only then to refuse the request. Still he couldn't refuse Frances for long, however much he disapproved of the stage.

'We went about with Burne-Jones everywhere, Aggie and I and my father; to picture galleries, to circuses, to plays', where they used to take a box for the great Shakespearean nights and afterwards Burne-Jones would introduce them to the stars of stage such as Ellen Terry and Sir Henry Irving. Quite quickly he would be dining with the Grahams twice a week. As he relaxed, so he began to sing for his supper. He was a wonderful conversationalist: 'without exception the best talker I have ever known', Frances would recall; 'no party could be dull or flat for a moment if he were there'. Ideals were held passionately. Nor was his imagination hampered by convention, and all delivered in a style that was lively, often hilarious, and invariably self-deprecating. Crucially, he had the art of being able to talk to the young; and to accept being teased by them too. When he got carried away and declared himself 'good like Fra Angelico', the Dominican priest and artist, the girls pounced, nicknaming him Angelo thereafter.[45] Soon trips to Burne-Jones's studio were much sought after. The Grange was a large red-brick house surrounded by high ivy-clad walls in the village of Fulham – fast becoming suburbanised by the arrival of the District Line. At the end of a long rambling garden with fruit trees stood the studio, racked high with paintings on the go. Pinned to the canvas that he was working on would be the letters he was writing and he would flick between picture and letter as he sought to catch the seven posts of the day. To Frances it was a treasure trove.[46]

By 1873 Frances was no longer a child. 'When I was about 18 or 19, Edward Burne-Jones, who was about 40, and living a quiet life, became my friend and poured in to my lucky lap all the treasures of one of the most wonderful minds that was ever created.' So began a relationship that lasted a quarter of a century. She had enjoyed an easy rapport with him since her first shy sittings for *The King's Wedding*. Greater proximity now provided opportunities to provoke and stir and, in time, the first innocent attempts to flirt. No doubt he was arbitrarily dragged in as an ally in her adolescent revolt against her mother. To Frances, Burne-Jones's notoriety was part of his attraction. Unexpectedly he would become an iconic rebel for the young, set against the meanness of an avaricious age – its industrialism, commercialism, imperialism, and political corruption. Instead of fighting these and becoming dangerous, he created instead a separate world of the imagination in which to escape, a world of longings, desires and unconsciousness. To Burne-Jones, each picture was 'a beautiful romantic dream of something that never was, never will be – in a light better than any light than ever shone – in a land no one can define or remember, only desire – and the forms divinely beautiful'. Frances was not the only one intoxicated by this vision. To 'the *me* that was when I was young', Frances reminisced, with her 'ardent nature' driven by 'some strange law of desire of what is beautiful… everything [was] romance.'[47]

For the child still in Frances, part of his early appeal was his brilliance as a story teller. With him, she and Aggie learnt of Norse legends, Arthurian knights or mystical tales from the East. Others would be more humorous and tell of Samoan cannibals eating an unsuspecting missionary or Don Juan's (successful) entry into Heaven.[48] With him they entered a world of good and evil, of High Romance tempered by cruelty and of innocence lost. Inspired by Thomas Malory's *Le Morte d'Arthur* (which he read in 1855 and 'would never [let] go out of the heart'), Arthurian romance was one of the fundamental settings of his artistic imagination. But the tales Frances would hear would be more of Lancelot and Guinevere, Tristram and Iseult, and less of the noble Arthur of Tennyson. As Malory's epic was bowdlerised for Victorian morality, Burne-Jones would instead seek not to judge but to speak sympathetically of intensity of feeling, of passion realised or frustrated, and the destructiveness that could follow in the wake of temptation.[49] With him as her guide and mentor, Frances would roam imaginatively into a world beyond childhood.

There was always a fantastical element to his imagination, which would enthral her well into adult life. Most famous was his exposition on jewels – their language and symbolism and the magical powers they held for him:

> Sapphire is truth, and I am never without it. Ruby is passion, and I need it not. Emerald is hope, and I need it…Amethyst, or as the little stone man I know called it Hammersmith, is devotion – I have it – and Topaz is jealousy, and is right nasty. Sapphires I make my totem of! Prase is a wicked little jewel, have none of him. I gave one to Margaret, and it winked and blinked and looked so evil she put it away.[50]

This 'fantasy life', often cloaked in self-mockery, would draw her in and offer a brief reversion to childhood. Just as magical for Frances, who had resented the paucity of her formal education, was to listen at his feet as he talked books. 'All the books he had ever read (and they were innumerable) remained clear and deeply cut in his memory and drawn upon at will'. All of Scott he would read every year and he could quote Dickens freely. To have such 'treasures' poured into her lap was beyond thrilling. And he made it fun too, for he had that 'rare power' not just to amuse but to make others amusing 'so that laughter reigned around him.' When she agonised over her lack of a formal education, he would reassure her 'your education is beautiful – you know nothing that doesn't matter and enough of all that does'. All of which goes some way to explaining why, instead of retreating lest she reveal her ignorance, Frances would thirst after the knowledge and the company of learned men.[51]

Predictably Burne-Jones began to nurture Frances's appreciation of art and once again through the medium of his inventiveness. 'It was wonderful to hear him talk of Italy, where he had been very little, and very seldom, but he could describe the cities and churches and treasures as if his life had been spent there – as indeed his spiritual life was'. When in Italy herself with her father in 1876, Frances would receive detailed letters with instructions of paintings they must see. Part of the wonderment was his mastery of many mediums (painting, stained glass, tapestry, furniture, clothes, jewellery, even shoes) and the sheer versatility of his designing. Everything was grist to his mill. Not only did he seek to educate her taste but he would take great care to encourage her own artistic ability, especially in needlework. From 1873 he was sending out designs for Frances and Aggie to embroider. Frances showed real aptitude, exhibiting her work in the fourth Arts and Crafts exhibition at the New Gallery in 1893 – most famously her *Song of Solomon* (1876) and *L'Amor che muove* (1880; figs 11, 12). The latter was a rendition of Dante's vision of Heaven with a mother surrounded by her eight children and with a bow symbolising her role as protector – 'the Love that moves the sun and other stars'.[52]

Events would see him assume the role of her protector in turn. In 1872 her elder brother Rutherford, whom she had hero worshipped as a child, died of diphtheria. It was 'my first great sorrow' and later she would claim that thereafter she was 'stained with melancholia of which I have never been able to be entirely free'. Worse was to follow with the death in September 1875 of her remaining brother, Willie. Willie was an extraordinarily good-looking, fair-haired boy with 'a sunny nature', who had modelled as a page boy with mandolin serenading Janey Morris in Rossetti's *Mariana*. Suffering from a heavy cold, he had drained a bottle of 'cold mixture'. Unaware that it contained morphine, he died in his sleep of an overdose.[53] At Hawarden, Mary Gladstone heard 'the pitiful news of Willy Graham's sudden death on Wednesday Morn – supposed to have arisen from accidental overdose of morphia, no consciousness, no goodbye, only the cruel wrench – 17 years old, a bright and lovely young life, such as it is hard to associate with death. Poor Frances.'[54] Poor Frances indeed. She and Willie were particularly close. Much worse, however, was the fact that her parents were away, leaving the children in her care. For two hours she had tried to resuscitate him before he finally died in her arms.[55]

Her father never recovered from the loss of his last son 'round whom all our hopes were centred'. The confident, vigorous subject of Rossetti's pastel of 1870 soon declined into 'an emaciated ancient man with staring eyes' of Burne-Jones pictures in 1880. Yet as was his way, he took refuge in his faith and suffered in silence. For Frances, riven by guilt as well as loss, this silence became unbearable. Only later did she comprehend the distress behind the facade. Unburdening herself to a friend, she confessed 'it is so tiring always having to try and be good too; one cannot sit down in a heap on the floor or be wild and selfish in one's own grief. It is such a dead stop in everything.'[56] With her father increasingly a spent force – buying less and less as illness and depression took hold, it is not surprising that Frances should look elsewhere for comfort and reassurance. And especially to one who earlier in the year had sent her a valentine. 'Frances got such a beauty from Mr Burne-Jones', Mary Gladstone noted a little enviously in her diary; 'a big picture

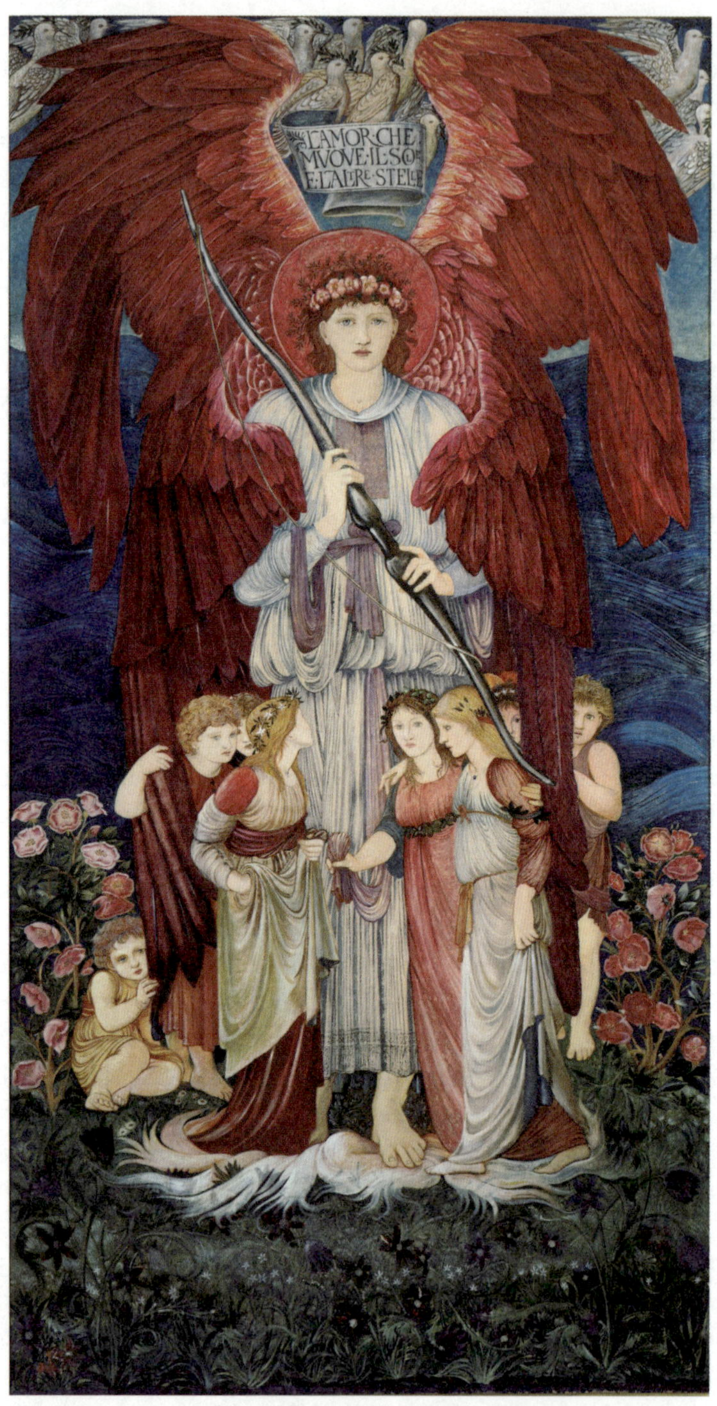

11.   *Cartoon for L'Amor che muove
il sole e l'altre stelle, by Edward Burne-Jones*

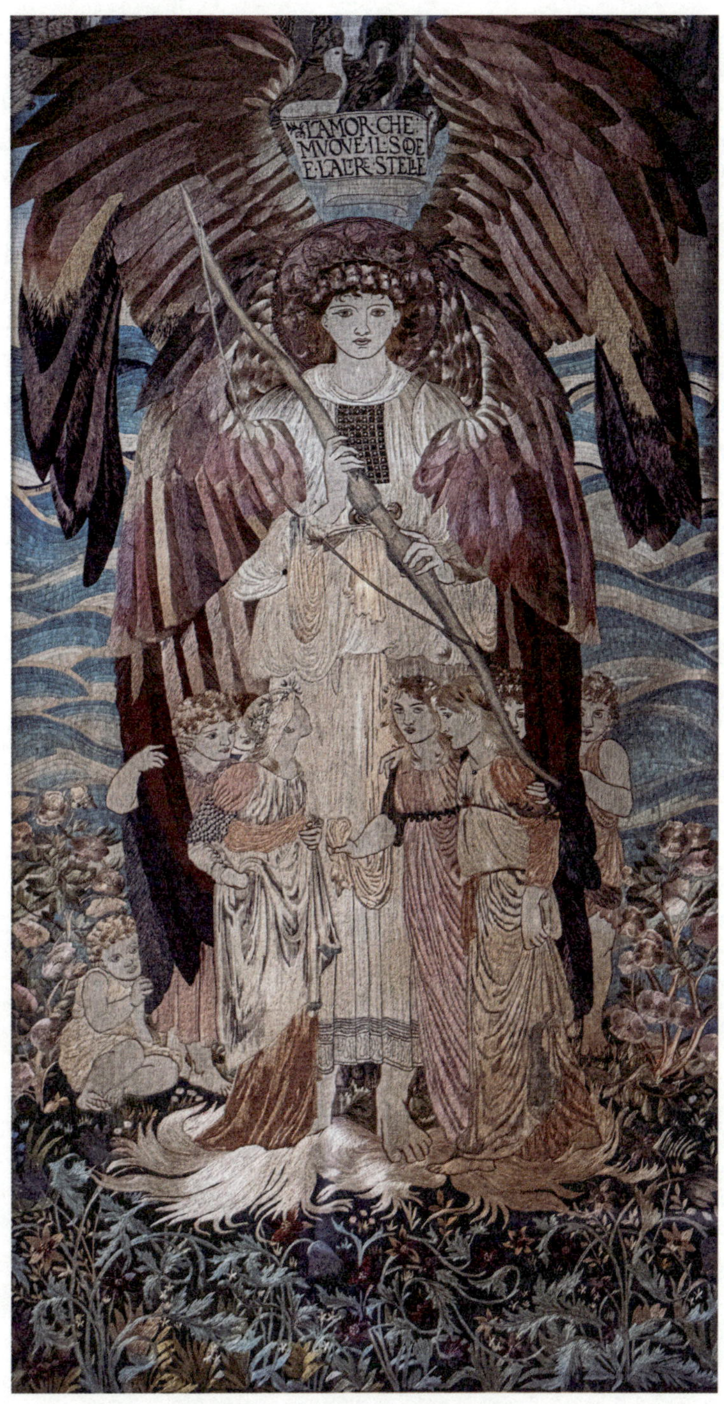

12.   *Frances's embroidery of L'Amor che muove il sole e l'altre stelle, c. 1880. She exhibited it in 1896 and it was later deposited in St Andrew's Church, Mells*

of Cupid dragging a maiden through all the meshes and mazes of Love.'[57]

It would have been very hard for Frances not to fall in love with Burne-Jones in 1875. At a time when she was deeply unhappy and isolated from her father, Burne-Jones was there for her. Yes there was an element of stargazing. Burne-Jones was artistically cool, tilting at the establishment, and producing pictures of Romance and longing, for which she would model. 'Part monk, part Puck', his company was mesmerising.[58] Vitally, for all that he was a celebrity, he took her seriously too. To the young and well-bred but long confined, this can only have been flattering and ultimately irresistible.

≈ 3 ≈

BECOMING LOVERS?

One with whom one has formed intimacies … and who was
my greatest friend for all my grown up life as long as he lived

Frances Horner[59]

At her father's death, Burne-Jones admitted to Frances that he had
loved her from 'when you were little'. His explanation that 'you were
so like him to me from the first, like a womanly form of him – and
that was why I so cared for you' has convinced few recent commentators. To them Frances was a victim, 'the muse of several of the
Victorian world's notorious "girl-lovers" – Burne-Jones, Ruskin and
Tennyson.' Whatever their motives, the worship of young girls was
in part a worship of innocence before the fall of adulthood. This
was a feature of mid-Victorian artistic culture, most famously with
Kingsley's *Water Babies*, Lewis Carroll's *Alice in Wonderland,* and
Julia Margaret Cameron's photographs. This belief in innocence
stretched to parents too and no one thought anything wrong in leaving children unchaperoned with middle-aged men and their friends.
Presumably, for the most part, there wasn't, but to the modern eye
such relationships appear disturbing and potentially far worse.[60] At
the least girls such as Frances could find themselves caught 'in the
fixed regard of famous men', not only as models but also 'psycholog-
ically' as the embodiment of 'powerful masculine projections of lost
childhood and [so] trapped in a state of prolonged adolescence'.[61]
Certainly Burne-Jones would often portray Frances on the cusp of
adolescence, her eyes cast down, vulnerable and trance-like in her
beauty. When he painted her in *The King's Wedding* (1870; fig. 9) she
is the shy, frail child bride – a picture of chaste virtue and domesticity

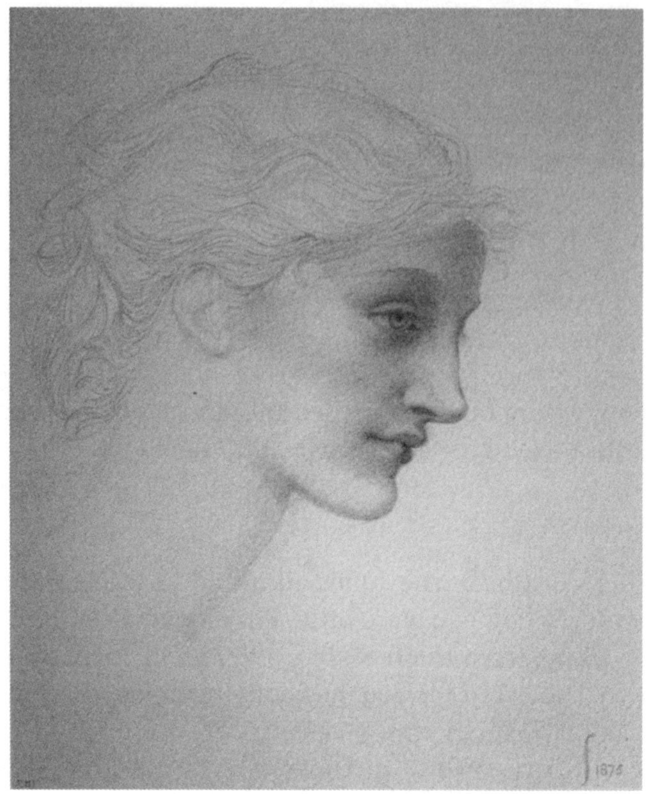

13.   Frances, by Edward Burne-Jones, 1875

under the protection of an avuncular king (Burne-Jones?) – a queen who had miraculously crossed over into adulthood with her childhood intact.

Yet Frances was almost sixteen by the time this was painted and nineteen when Burne-Jones became her 'friend'. The unintended consequence of her implying in her memoir that she was born in 1860 rather than 1854 was that later historians viewed her relationship with Burne-Jones as possibly paedophilic.[62] As it was, the age of consent was twelve and did not increase to sixteen until 1885.[63] Still to the modern eye there is something distinctly creepy about the faux-childish tone of Burne-Jones's early correspondence as well as the way the young Frances played up to it, with the looks to make herself younger than she was (figs 13, 14); unlike Georgie, his wife, who was no longer the fifteen-year-old girl he had fallen in love with.

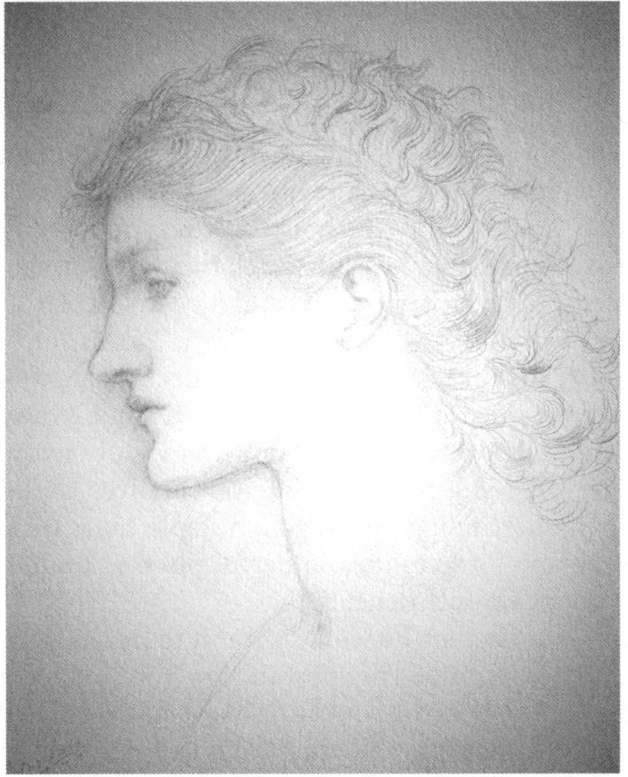

14.   *Frances, by Edward Burne-Jones, 1877*

However, that Frances at twenty should feel the need to pander to him in this way is striking. Nevertheless, one only has to look at the double portrait of Maria Zambaco in *Phyllis and Demophoön*, painted in the same year as *The King's Wedding*, to see exactly where Burne-Jones's sexual desire lay.

Nor was Frances as docile as 'girl lover' suggests. Although not above playing up to the role of *La Bambina* or the romance of courtly devotion, Frances was too smart and independent to be deferential. Indeed that was part of her attraction, for Burne-Jones soon realised that she could be stubborn 'as a young Spartan boy' and just as competitive. For all the delicacy of his sketches of her, she was quite a tomboy. When holidaying in the Swiss Alps in 1880 Frances and Aggie ignored their father's misgivings and climbed the Bernina. On their descent they met a party of undergraduate friends of Edward

Lyttelton and bet them they wouldn't make it. When later they heard that they had won their wager, Frances didn't hide her glee: 'they were anti-feminist in those days as all Lytteltons and Leighs and Balfours were.'[64]

Drawn to Burne-Jones's company, she took the initiative, determined to drag him out of his loneliness and in this she largely succeeded. Energising, remorselessly optimistic, and sweetly provocative, she proved unstoppable. With the clarity of youth, she embraced wholeheartedly his faith in which art and the pursuit of beauty sought to turn the tide of industrialised inhumanity. To this she brought 'an inherent purity of outlook, a sense of morality that answered Burne-Jones's fastidious work ethic.'[65] For one so mired in his own guilt over Zambaco, the religious certainties, however lightly worn, of father and daughter offered a haven of renewal. Frances challenged him too; for the unquestioning loyalty of a disciple came with a definite edge. In Penelope Fitzgerald's wonderful phrase, 'Frances, like the briar rose, wounded only to heal.'[66]

Even in matters of art he would submit to her judgement. Years later Burne-Jones reminded her how in 1873 'you stopped my picture of Tristram… solely because you didn't like it and thought the subject did not tend to edification – neither did it as I was doing it and you were quite right.'[67] She also offered something new. In contrast to the Pre-Raphaelite 'stunners' such as Lizzie Siddal and Janey Morris who had been plucked from obscurity, Frances came from the respectable upper-middle classes. As a 'young woman of great poise, originality and intelligence', she combined the attractiveness of a model with social cachet, learning and a capacity to empathise both with the art and especially the artist. From childhood she had learnt how to deal with the mood swings of the creative. Burne-Jones proved no exception, oscillating from the whimsical and bantering to bouts of melancholia when he would become withdrawn and evasive. To her this was just part of the price of 'the rather abnormal sensitiveness of genius – genius [when she first met him] which has not come to its full maturity'. That he was a genius she never doubted and no doubt too she played a significant part so that 'in later years he acquired calm and confidence and most of his nervousness seemed to drop away'.[68]

What are we to make of Frances's tortured description of Burne-Jones in her autobiography as 'one with whom one has formed

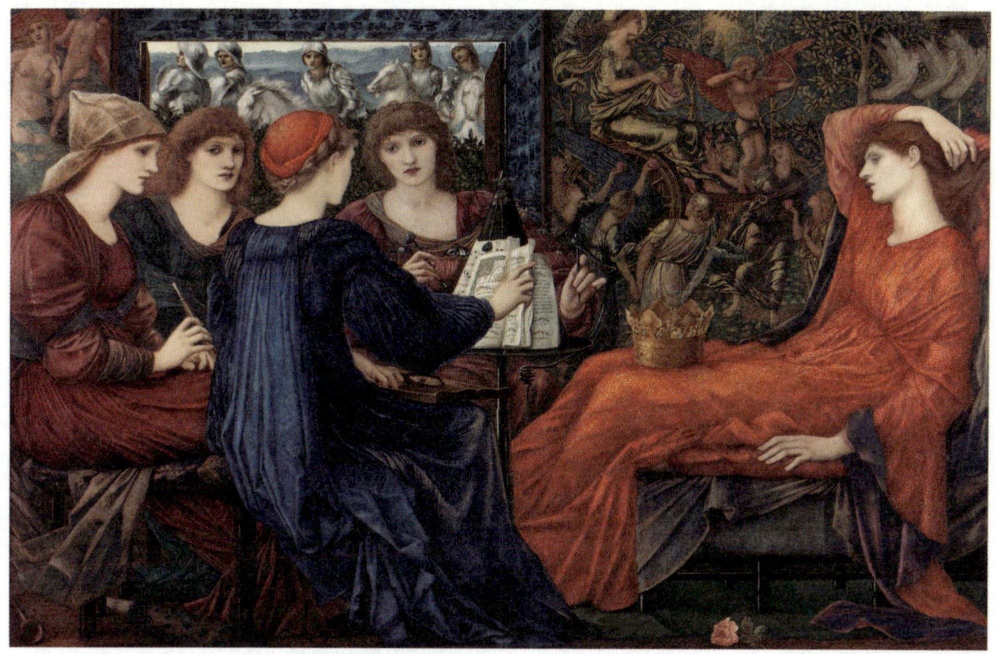

15.   *Laus Veneris, by Edward Burne-Jones, 1873–78.*
Frances is on the far left

intimacies …and who was my greatest friend for all my grown up
life as long as he lived'? Most biographers of Burne-Jones hold that
'Frances [simply] provided a platonic focus for many of his later
romantic yearnings and she reciprocated with an appreciation of his
art and benevolent humour'. Moreover she was just one of many.
For Burne-Jones had a number of similar sentimental relationships
with young girls, with 'Frances being the most important of these
Egerias.'[69] Yet for Burne-Jones, as his correspondence makes clear,
her physical attraction was beyond question.[70] He was not alone. All
her friends remarked on her beauty and would join her father in
dubbing her 'the Botticelli'.[71] Ruskin, on seeing *The King's Wedding*,
described her 'as least as beautiful as an ordinary Greek goddess'.
Hence her appeal to Burne-Jones who was always seeking his 'quintessential Greek ideal in an English woman'.[72] Yet for all her regular
features and high cheekbones, hers was a strong face rather than a
pretty one, her beauty arresting rather than conventional. Nor was
she necessarily the willowy, long limbed creature Burne-Jones drew.

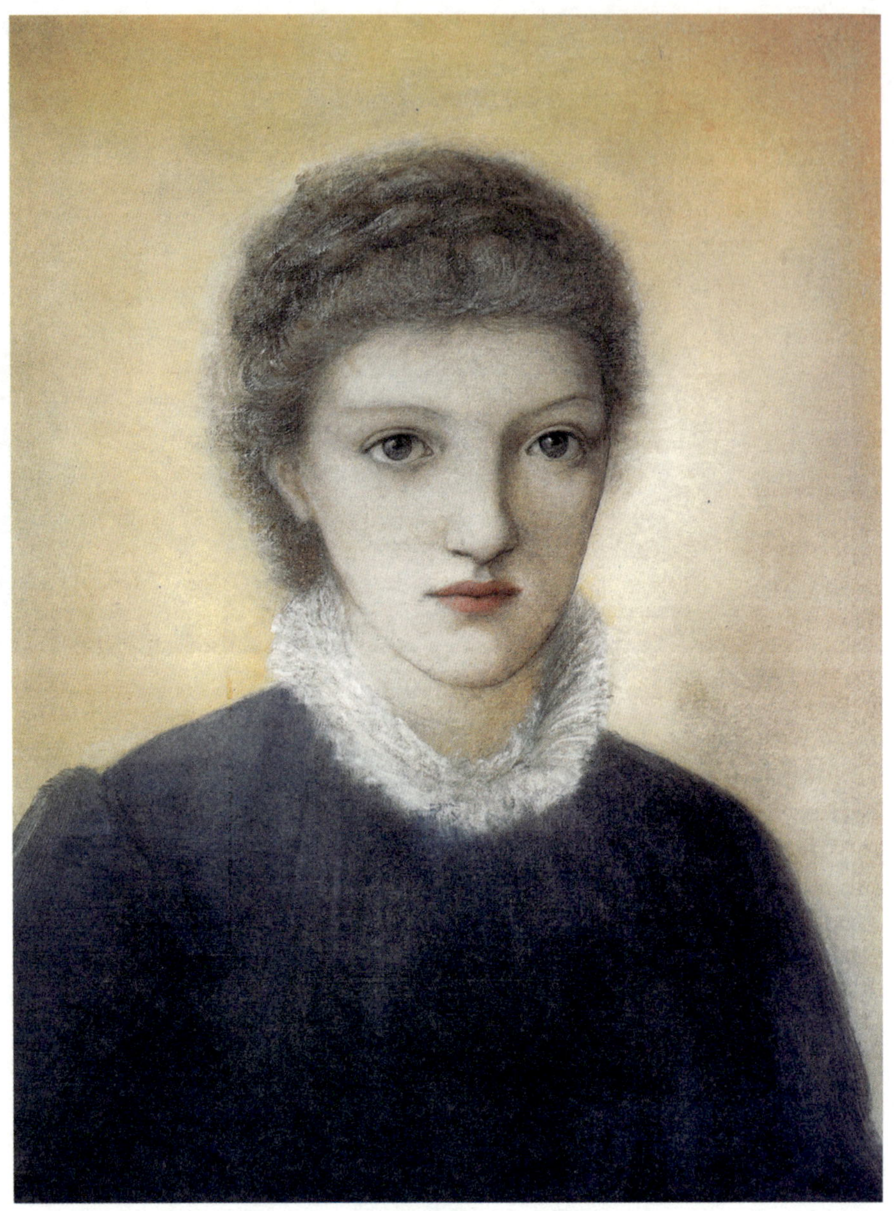

16.   *Frances, by Edward Burne-Jones, 1879*

Yet with a neat figure, an elegant neck, long 'golden' hair thick with curls, and full-lipped mouth she knew how to catch attention. What made her stand out though were her eyes – what Margot Asquith called great 'ghost eyes'.[73] With them, she stared out like a young fawn from Burne-Jones's 1879 portrait – vulnerable, trusting, but still curious (fig. 16). What his portrayals of her lack is the animation of her face, the youthful assertiveness of one vibrant and alive, that is so much a feature of a portrait from the 'early seventies'. Hand on hip, this younger Frances exudes confidence and a willingness to engage directly with the viewer. There is none of the vulnerability of the 1879 portrait or the submissiveness in the numerous sketches he made of her at this time in which character is sacrificed to beauty. As was his wont, he rejected a literal approach to portraiture, preferring to 'etherealize …his subject'.[74] Mostly drawing her in profile, he sought to capture a calm sensitive presence, languid in her otherworldliness and accepting. This was very much how he wished her to be. 'I do not easily get portraiture' he would confess; 'and the perpetual hunt to find in a face what I like, and leave out what mislikes me, is a bad school for it.' Or as Christina Rossetti noted, the girl in his pictures is 'not as she is but as she fills his dreams'.[75] And thus, perhaps, was a way of possessing her.

Did Frances feel possessed? She was well beyond the age of 'coming out' and if rarely chaperoned, being the patron's daughter offered considerable protection. On the other hand, in the early years of their friendship, for all her bravado she was very much under Burne-Jones's spell – in awe of his knowledge and experience. The treasures that he dropped on her lap and which so thrilled her also opened up a louche adult world where at times she must have felt out of her depth. Nor would she have been unaware of his feelings. The little displays of Spartan independence, the occasional refusal of his letters, the acting up the pre-pubescent, all suggest strategies of self-preservation in an unequal relationship.[76] Yet she would not have wanted to lose favour with the one person who brought such excitement into her life.

She may have looked naïve but she was not unaware of sexual passion. As a child being traipsed around the Pre-Raphaelite studios by her father she had seen at first hand its destructiveness. When Rossetti had a breakdown over his affair with William Morris's wife, it was the Grahams who had provided a refuge. Nor could she have

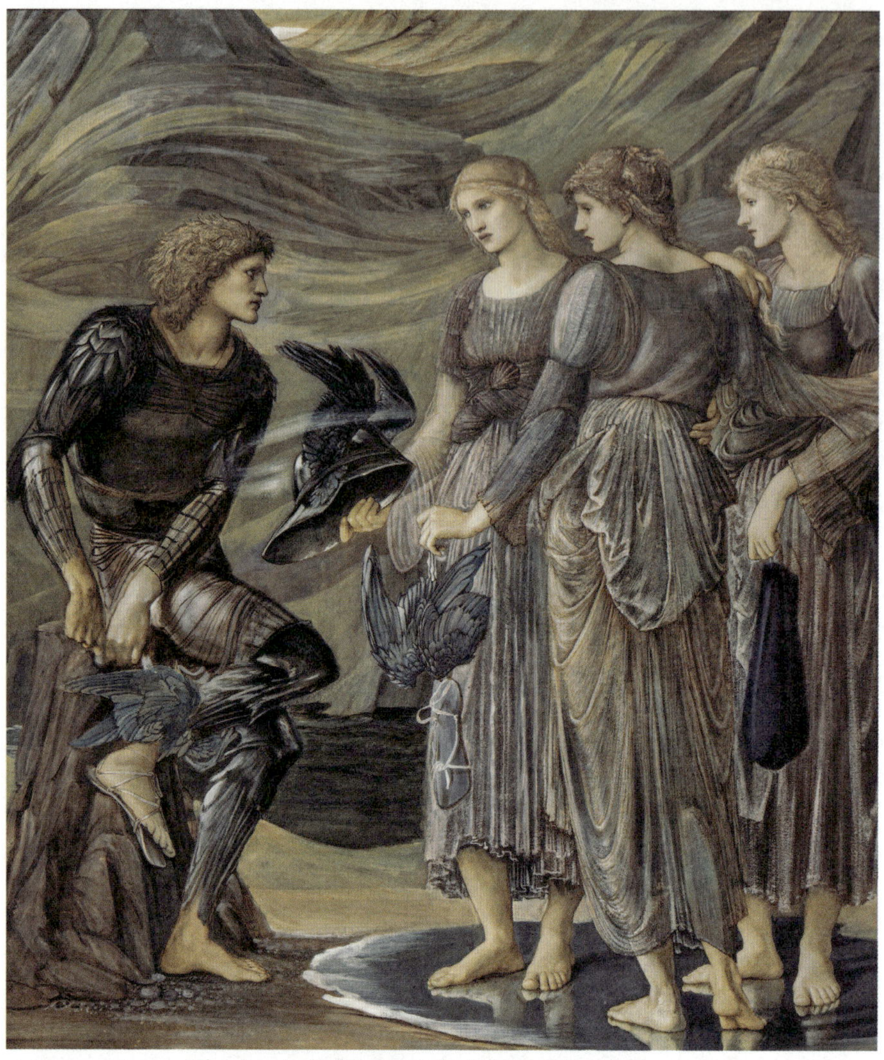

17.   *The Arming of Perseus, by Edward Burne-Jones, 1877.*
Frances is on the far right

not known about Zambaco. They had been in the same painting
when she was sixteen (*The King's Wedding* where Maria had modelled for one of the queen's dancing maids) and she was not sheltered from the furore over *Phyllis and Demophoön*. Indeed the
consequence was that Burne-Jones took refuge with the Grahams,
dining with them at least twice a week. She would not have failed
to notice in Morris's edition of *The Rubaiyat of Omar Khayam* that

all Burne-Jones's illustrations were of Zambaco. At the heart of her friendship with Burne-Jones was a willingness to understand – not an eagerness to judge (teasing aside). On the walls around her would have been some of the nudes she had smuggled in on behalf of her father. And as Burne-Jones gradually evolved a new artistic style, she would have appreciated the sensuousness in his work, of longings and tensions barely suppressed among the sumptuousness. To the modern eye familiar with so little being left to the imagination, Burne-Jones's women look silent and chaste, vacant trapped souls; unaware of the passions their beauty arouses. Yet the contemporary critic, W. H. Mallock, could declare of Burne-Jones's subjects that the 'only sorrow they know is the languor of exhausted animalism'. Ruskin was furious on behalf of his friend but the erotic charge in this new work was to Victorians undeniable.[77]

On 12 July 1865 Constance Hilliard – a particular favourite of Ruskin's – wrote in her diary: 'Drive into London to see Mr Jones the artist who is one of Cussy's [i.e. Ruskin's] friends. A nice petting and grave talks. Sweet run in the garden, tea and talks, and another nice petting before I went to bed'.[78] She was fourteen. Conventionally

18.   Jewel Casket, by Edward Burne-Jones

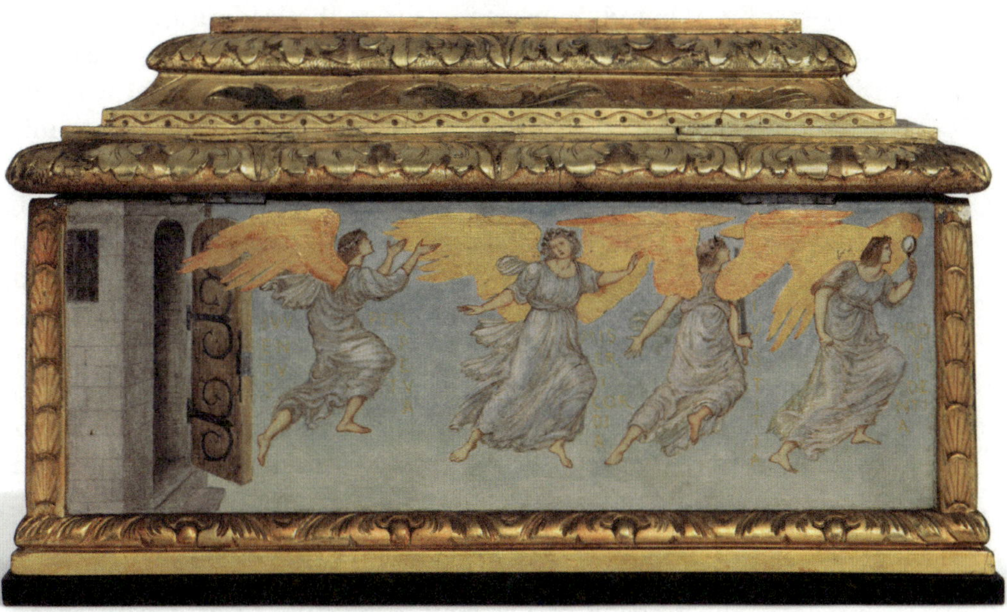

kissing meant intended betrothal. However it is clear that Frances's friends, such as the Tennant sisters, Margot and Laura, and well brought up middle-class London girls like Edith ('DD') Balfour went further, having quite physical flirtations with the likes of Peter Flower and Doll Liddell.[79] None of this would later shock Frances – indeed, when married, she facilitated Laura's assignations. Such activity was primarily explorative rather than emotional.[80] And there were limits. Doll Liddell would not be the only one frustrated at their refusal 'to go all the way'.[81] Few middle-class girls, no matter how advanced, were going to risk that. Still it would be surprising if Frances over their long relationship did not experience what Charlotte had with 'Mr Burne-Jones'. After all, as a teenager, she was a regular visitor to his studio at the foot of the garden. If this is only conjecture, so too are the implications to be drawn from her burning all her letters from Burne-Jones on the eve of her wedding.

By contrast, Burne-Jones, in his idolising of her, left little to discretion. First there were the mass of drawings of his inamorata. He would often sketch her in public; on one occasion while Mary Gladstone's sister, Helen, read aloud from Ruskin's *Stones of Venice*.[82] She would appear in his paintings: as the queen in *The King's Wedding* (1870; fig. 9), as a nymph carrying the pouch for the Gorgon's head in *The Arming of Perseus* (1877; fig. 17), as an attendant in *Laus Veneris* (1873–78; fig. 15); and, most famously, as the leading figure in *The Golden Stairs* (1880; fig.21).[83] The valentine of 1875 was a draft of what became *Love Leading the Pilgrim* (1877–1897, the last work he ever completed; fig. 3); but in 1875 it was a lover's gift with her initials pierced by an arrow from Cupid and possibly drawn for her to embroider. 1879 would see a rare formal portrait, for once front-on, wide-eyed and accepting. Gifts were showered on her: William Morris's edition of *The Rubaiyat of Omar Khayam* – gold tooled and bound in red leather and to which Ned had contributed six romantic illustrations (fig. 19);[84] a jewel casket for her birthday in 1877, elaborately decorated in gold with paintings of angels on the outside and on the inside with the Goddess of Hope (fig. 18); illustrated covers by him for her copies of *The Apocrypha* and the Book of Common Prayer (1879–80); and even delightful designs for her shoes.

Nothing however compared with the piano he decorated for her in 1879–80 (fig. 20).[85] The theme is the story of Orpheus and Eurydice. The tragedy of Orpheus, who fails to rescue his dead wife from Pluto's underworld after looking back on her too soon, is retold in a series of roundels on the outside of the piano. With Frances symbolising Eurydice, 'Burne-Jones himself is Pluto keeping her captive'. The colours of muted greys and ivory heighten the sense of 'desolation and dashed hopes'. This theme is extended to the lid with Frances portrayed as a celestial 'Raphaelesque muse' of his desires, straight out of medieval chivalric literature; one whom the poet adores but cannot approach. At his feet are his verses in her honour and a scroll from her inscribed *ne oublie* – 'do not forget', the Graham family motto. In stark contrast to the modesty of the exterior, on the inside of the lid there is an explosion of vibrant colour. At the centre of this seemingly lies Frances, startlingly portrayed as an Earth Mother (Gaia Omniparens), naked and fecund, surrounded by a riot of children. Gone is all pretence of restraint and

19. *Rubaiyat of Omar Khayam, calligraphed by William Morris and illuminated by Edward Burne-Jones, 1872*

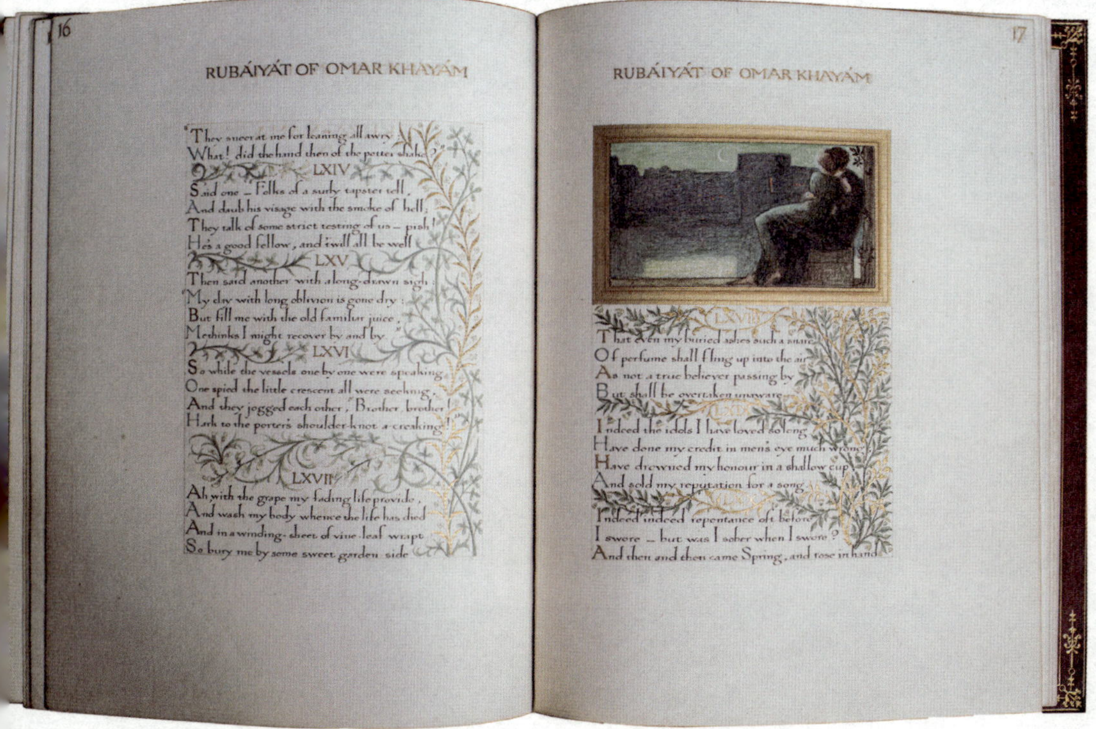

in an elaborate evocation of the 'luxurious self-indulgence of late Renaissance and Mannerist applied art',[86] he has produced a picture of passion triumphant. Typically all this is disguised as a practical joke, for it would only be seen when the lid was open and Frances playing the piano. Where, indeed, it would be very much in her face. Nonetheless, for all the tease, there was no disguising the two conflicting emotions raging within Burne-Jones in which Frances was both his ideal of virtuous purity and a figure of his desire and lust; emotions all the more torn as they fed off each other.

20.   *Piano, by Edward Burne-Jones, 1879–80, with details of the exterior and interior of the lid and side of the piano*

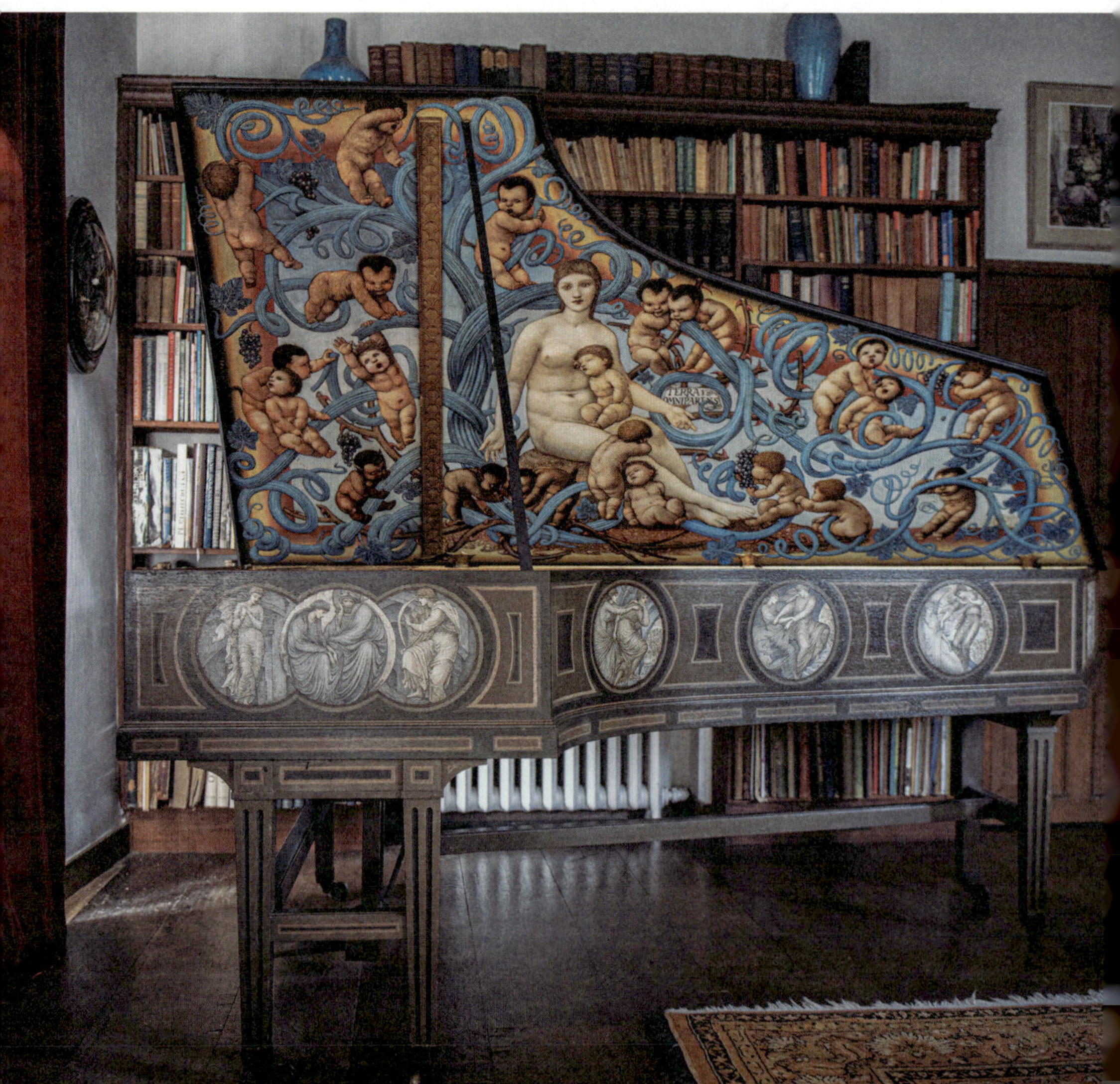

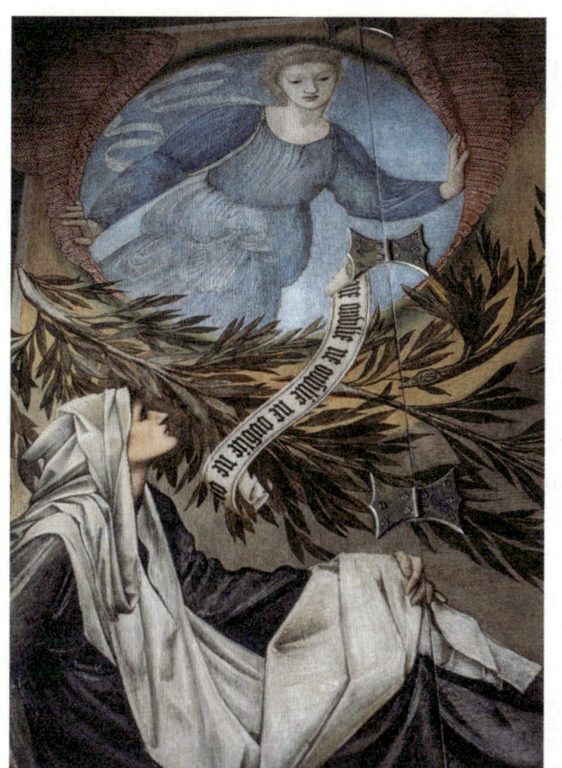

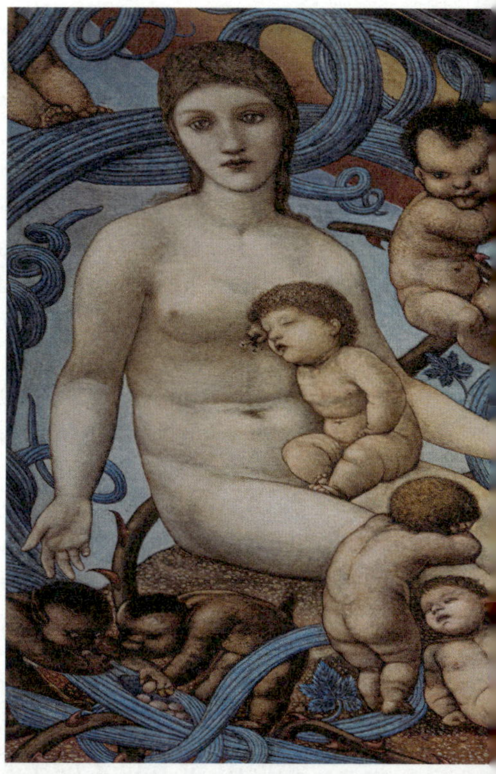

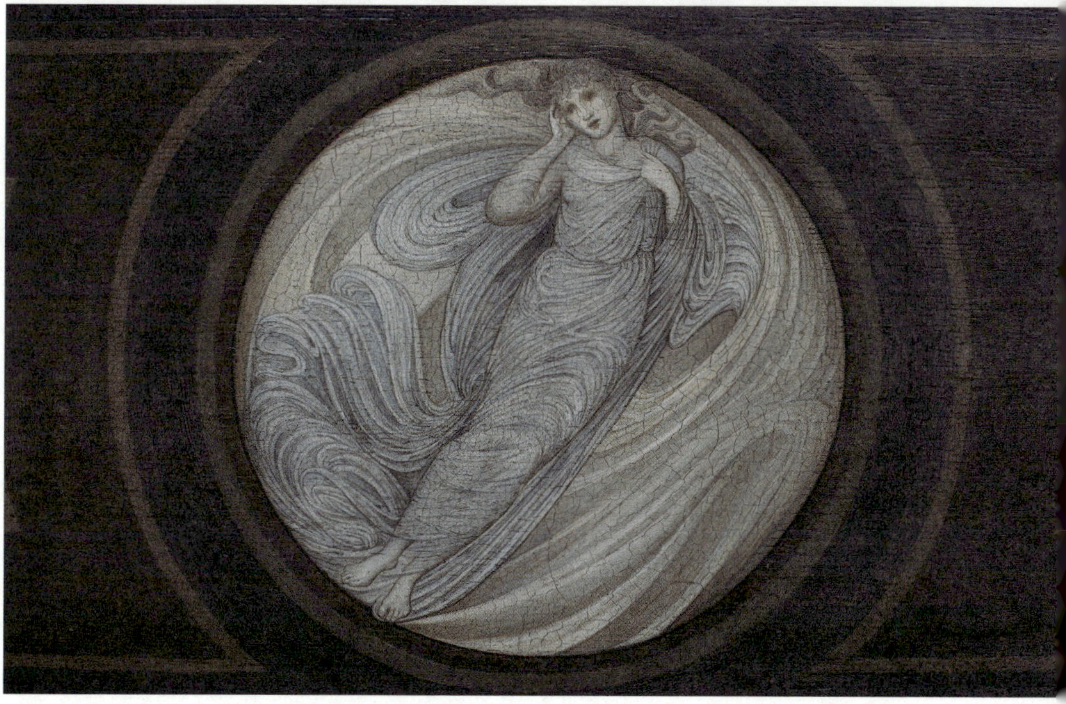

Perhaps the most unusual thing about this piano is that her father commissioned it. This was the latest stage of a long running game in which all knew what could never be; a love that could be indulged because it never would be consummated. Of course her father saw the tokens of love that came Frances's way. He seemed to enjoy the relationship as much as Burne-Jones. Certainly he encouraged it with his commissions. Nor does he appear to have felt pushed aside in his daughter's affection. One cannot conceive of his being so acquiescent if she had been the artist's mistress. Equally in being, in Burne-Jones's eyes, the embodiment of her father, she enabled Burne-Jones to love them both – but innocently. And be loved in turn. Hence too, both men dreaded the day she would be lost to marriage and saw in this love affair the delay of that evil day.

So paradoxically, this was a relationship fuelled by denial. To Burne-Jones, Frances inviolate was in part to be an atonement for past sins. Her innocence was to be a force for redemption and a barrier against base desire. But it was a struggle. 'Lust does frighten me', he confessed to Swinburne in the aftermath of the Zambaco affair. 'Did it not occur to you', he would later question Frances, 'that, if I had Margaret [his daughter reading in the studio] by me [when Frances visited], it might be for my sake that I might have protection from myself?'[87] In suppressing her vitality in his sketches he was suppressing his own desires for her. And with it, his own sense of inadequacy. To her amusement he was 'morbidly sensitive over his appearance', and would moan to her 'how blessed it must be to look in the glass and see you'. Fearful too perhaps of ridicule over his age: signing off letters a little defensively, 'Your Ancient Ned'. Such anxieties and the numerous sketches he would make of her in the 1870s told their own story. And part of that story was an implicit recognition that the twenty-five-year-old Frances, playing at the piano he had created in celebration of her, was by now very much her own woman.

*

Frances would later insist that she would have run away with Burne-Jones if she had been 'born ten years later'.[88] As with the piano, it was a running gag in their correspondence and never once taken remotely seriously. Part of the dance was a chivalric fantasy with Frances in the role of the liege lady, much desired but never to be defiled. Burne-Jones may have had the passion but not the courage. Nor did she.

Nevertheless that he was the love of her life she would never deny. Knowing him 'coloured the whole of my life'. What she liked was not just the adoration but also the claiming love, sure in the presumption that he would never claim too much: the shows of hurt when she hadn't called, the theatrical dismay at letters not promptly answered or the gift not enthusiastically appreciated. And to an extent she shared the frustration that underpinned their relationship. And yet it is revealing that in her memoir, she never offers any physical description of her lover. For her, what really attracts is his 'genius'. Just to be in his company was mesmerising and she was enthralled by the range of his knowledge and the excitement of his artistic passion. To Frances theirs was primarily a meeting of minds rather than bodies.[89] Above all, they shared a perspective on the world – romantic, fantastical and private; somehow protected from the sophisticated society they were both about to enter.

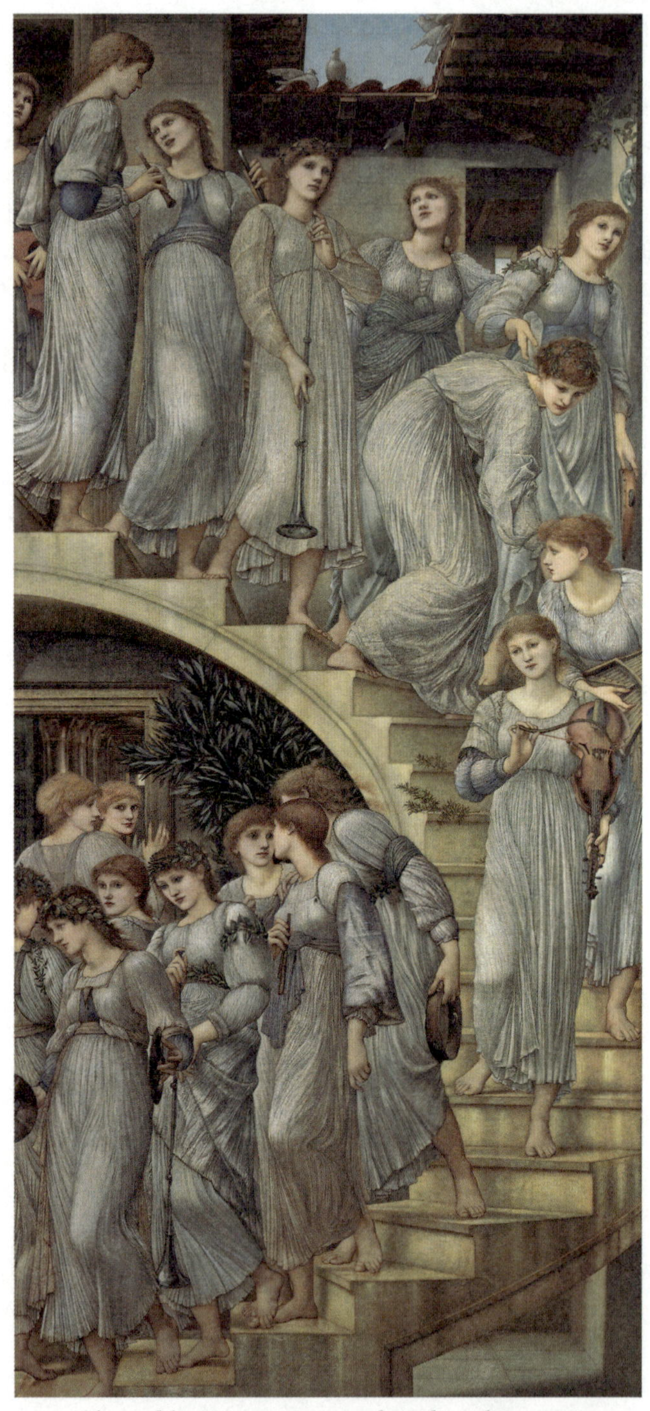

21.   *The Golden Stairs, 1876–80, by Edward Burne-Jones.*
Frances, with cymbals, leads the girls down the Golden Stairs.

4

TRIUMPH AND THE MUSE

Burne-Jones at her feet and Ruskin at her elbow

Margot Asquith on Frances Graham[90]

The opening of the Grosvenor Gallery in New Bond Street in 1877 was always going to cause a sensation. Although its founder, Sir Coutts Lindsay, denied it, it was widely assumed to be a challenge to the ascendancy of the Royal Academy. Then there was the flamboyance of its décor with marbled pillars, gilded ceilings and grand staircase giving it the appearance of a Venetian palazzo.[91] And lastly there was Burne-Jones, exhibiting for the first time since 1870. Tickets for the exhibition rapidly sold out and, within a week of opening, the exhibition had been graced by the Prince and Princess of Wales.[92] For Burne-Jones, emerging from his purdah carried great risk. Not only were all the leading Pre-Raphaelites (except Rossetti) exhibiting, but it had taken years for him to get over the brutal experience of public criticism seven years before. That he submitted eight paintings including *The Mirror of Venus* and *The Beguiling of Merlin* was a measure of his renewed self-belief. His new style caught the critics by surprise and stole the show. While *The Times* continued to decry the 'unwholesomeness', most, like Oscar Wilde, raved over his use of colour and others were fascinated by the ambiguity over meaning. Henry James became a firm supporter, praising the 'brilliant suggestive' portrayal of Merlin. He sought to tie down the essence of Burne-Jones's 'queerness'.

> It is the art of culture, of reflection, of intellectual luxury, of aesthetic refinement, of people who look at the world and at life not directly, as it were, and in all its accidental reality, but in the reflection and ornamental portrait of it furnished by art itself in other manifestations; furnished by literature, by poetry, by history, by erudition.[93]

Very soon the sensation had become Burne-Jones. As Georgie remembered wistfully, 'From that day he belonged to the world in a sense that he never had before, for his existence became widely known and his name *famous*.'[94] Her sense of loss would be Frances's gain. The Graham connection was manifest when the following year the highlights were two paintings William had commissioned, *Chant d'Amour* and *Laus Veneris* (fig. 15).[95] Later that year Frances would be in the public gallery of the High Court with her father supporting a very hesitant Burne-Jones giving evidence on behalf of his friend Ruskin in the famous libel action with Whistler.[96] As ever, she was fiercely loyal. He had not wanted her to come and feared that she was only 'there to laugh when I stumbled and I dare say I spluttered and was ridiculous.' Nevertheless, by 1879 their relationship had become more openly acknowledged. Not only was he painting her portrait and drowning her with gifts, but she was dining at The Grange when Georgie was away ('Fancy my being allowed')[97] and being introduced to his closest friends. This included a terrifying encounter with Mrs George Lewes, a.k.a. George Eliot and a close confidante of Georgie's. Frances found herself in the eye of a diatribe that ranged from deriding the Jews to 'the vulgar use [to which] people put their wealth – dinners and gowns and things'... 'She made me feel a minx, that was the worst', Frances fumed to Mary Gladstone. Actually what was worst was that this monologue was delivered with her hands on Frances's knees and 'her face quite close' and staring hard into her. 'I think she is much more like a man than a woman but Mr BJ says I am wrong.'[98]

Her association with Burne-Jones as he 'entered his fame' now gave her an aura among her friends: a magical quality that comes with attracting the love of a great artist. To be acknowledged as his inspiration inevitably excited onlookers and would stamp the perception of Frances for the rest of her life. So confident was she of her position that she would generously introduce Burne-Jones to friends such as Mary Gladstone, Laura and Margot Tennant, and May Gaskell who all in time would pay court to the celebrity artist. The only person she showed any resentment towards was his wife. Georgie was a touch serious but hard to hate (fig. 22). She had shown great dignity in the face of her husband's infidelity. Once again she was required to tolerate his latest fascination for a young woman. But it hurt. With the onset of children, Burne-Jones had banned his

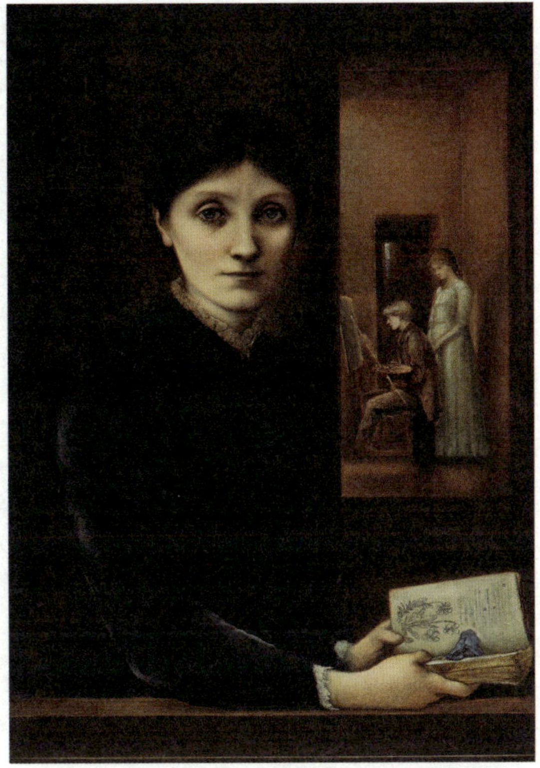

22.   *Portrait of Georgiana Burne-Jones,*
by Edward Burne-Jones, begun 1883

family from his studio lest they were a distraction. 'I remember the feeling of exile', recalled Georgie, 'with which I now heard through its closed doors the well-known voices of friends together, while I sat with my little son on my knee and dropped selfish tears upon him'. Yet as is the way with these situations, Frances was not sympathetic, making it clear how much 'nicer' her visits to The Grange were when Georgie was not there.[99]

By now the excitement generated by the Grosvenor Gallery was beginning to get out of hand. Burne-Jones had long subscribed to many of the values of what became known as the Aesthetic Movement. Reacting against the mechanisation and crass materialism embodied in the Great Exhibition of 1851, it emphasised the visual and the sensual over the practical, moral or narrative in art; holding that the pursuit of beauty – 'Art for Art's sake' – mattered more than the literal. By the late 1870s such beliefs had spread far

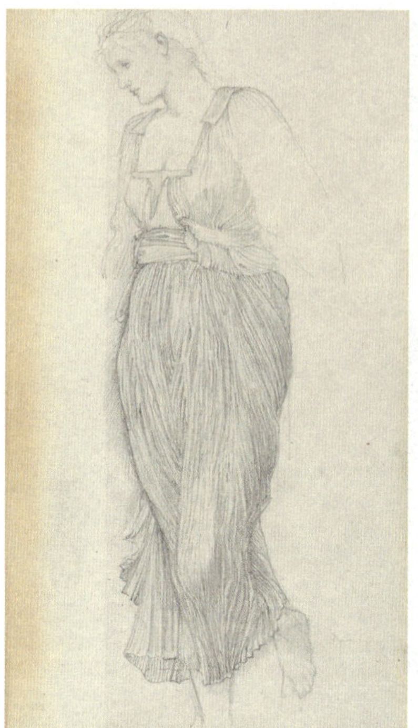

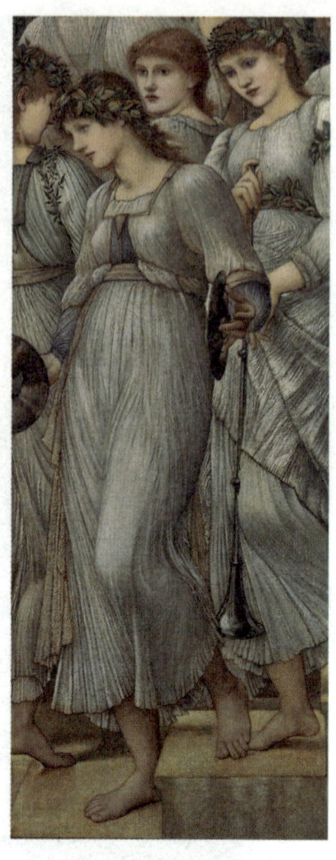

23. *Study for The Golden Stairs, by Edward Burne-Jones*

24. *Detail of The Golden Stairs*

beyond the world of artists and had diversified into a myriad of differing forms as artistic principles succumbed to fashion and swept through the cultural elites, be they aristocratic or from prosperous suburbia. To be true to one's feelings was all. As this 'craze' took hold, it would see Queen Anne Houses being built in Kensington and new interiors decorated across London, either imitating the medieval or indulging in the flamboyant as in Whistler's Peacock Room. Mid-Victorian clutter was thrown out in favour of *japonaiserie*, Persian pots and the latest fabrics from the new department store, Liberty's. Fashionable ladies were to be seen in free-flowing faux-medieval robes of dark greens and blues as seen on Pre-Raphaelite models. Soon a new language was developed ('greenery-yallery'; 'oh too, too utterly'), as aesthetes gave themselves over to competitive displays of affecting sensitivity and intensity of feeling. Much of this was hugely pretentious and found itself duly mocked by Gilbert and Sullivan and *Punch* as 'Passionate Brompton' – exhausted, effete and decadent. No one embodied this more than Oscar Wilde who in pursuit of celebrity arrived at the Grosvenor opening dressed in a suit shaped as a cello.[100]

All of this left Burne-Jones cold. As Mary Gladstone was glad to find, he was 'delightfully un-PB for such a PB artist'. And therein lay the problem, especially after the 1880 Grosvenor exhibition. For in his *The Golden Stairs* Burne-Jones produced what came to be seen as the iconic picture of the Aesthetic movement (figs 21, 23, 24). The portrayal of young girls, carrying musical instruments, descending a sweeping staircase sees Burne-Jones at his 'most abstract, neoclassical and moody'. With the girls so similarly dressed, collectively they represent 'Burne-Jones's quintessential dream picture' – a sublime study of youthful allure, innocently on the edge of adulthood. Without knowing where they are going to, the girls are seemingly caught in 'suspended animation', perhaps symbolising their being 'virgins descending into sexual awareness'.[101] The enigmatic nature of the painting defied explanation, which was unsettling for some but transfixed others. Aesthetically there was to be no overt meaning to distract from the beauty of the scene – as the artist intended.

Yet this picture operated on another level too. For the faces were not devoid of individuality but were recognisable and meant to be so. Among those identified are Mary Gladstone, May Morris, Laura Tennant, Mary Stuart Wortley, and Burne-Jones's own daughter Margaret – all Frances's friends – and leading them down the stairs was Frances herself.[102] There is nothing 'somnambulistic' about these girls as they cheerfully descend after their music lesson. For them, it was the cover shoot of the age. And for this brief moment few embodied this age more than Frances – the favourite muse of the favoured artist, with her golden hair, grey staring eyes, slim and graceful in Arthurian gowns of sage green and russet. Decades later Margot Asquith would remember Frances 'with the autumn desert in your hair and "soft shades" of Liberty velveteen.'[103] Such dress was decidedly counter-cultural, at odds with High Society increasingly in thrall to the strict etiquette of Court. By now, she was very much an independent lady. Dispensing with propriety, she at barely twenty-five was visiting unchaperoned.[104] To her contemporaries she exuded the glamour of one who had 'Burne-Jones at her feet and Ruskin at her elbow'; and who had become 'a leader in what was called the high-art William Morris school and one of the few girls who ever had a salon in London.'[105]

What makes a muse?[106] The word conjures up for the artist a human cocoon of sexual allure and worship. Part nurturer and inspiration, part lover and protector, to Freud the muse was 'the great understander'. In mythology, the muse offers still more – nothing less than that elusive alchemy of inspiration that draws out the best from the tortured artist. A staple of literary romance, muses have gifts once held to come from the gods, awakening rare, exhilarating, liberating moments of creativity for which all artists strive. To outsiders there is also the attraction of association with one whose intimacy with genius arouses both fascination and not a little jealousy (both appealing to the muse in their own way). Yet, at the heart of the myth of the muse lie some inescapable truths. Beguiling they may be, but it is a lucky few for whom the all-consuming romance survives the encroachment of domestication. From the outset most will have to sacrifice their artistic interests to the art of another.[107] However volatile and resentful this may make them, theirs remains a fundamentally passive existence, one of blank canvasses made flesh. And in Victorian England this was especially the case with the hierarchies between the sexes so firmly entrenched. So it is perhaps not surprising that the life of a muse to a Pre-Raphaelite artist was rarely a happy one: Ruskin and Effie Gray, Rossetti and Lizzie Siddal, Burne-Jones and Mary Zambaco – all were powerfully destructive relationships that ended respectively in divorce, death, and attempted suicide. The one who survived however was Frances Graham. Admittedly, she was protected by her father and his fortune. Class ensured that the world of Lizzie Siddal and Janey Morris was not her world. She was also unlike the classic Pre-Raphaelite model. Yes, she wore the clothes but she was not simply a creation of fashion: there were no flowing locks of red hair, no languid, ambivalent poses, no display of the submissive virtues of 'grace, delicacy and tenderness.'[108] Instead, she was both loyal and fiercely independent, intellectual as well as intuitive, energetic and ambitious. Looking back, Burne-Jones would describe the years after they had become 'friends' as the 'blissfullest years' and among his most creative.[109] A time Frances would proudly declare that would see him 'approaching his full fame.'[110] And in that she had played her part.

Then at the height of her triumph, she threw it all away.

Part Two

The Great Gamble
(1880–1883)

Aggie: Are you sure that you and Jack Horner are well suited to each other? What made you accept him?

Frances: I think it is because he is so big.[1]

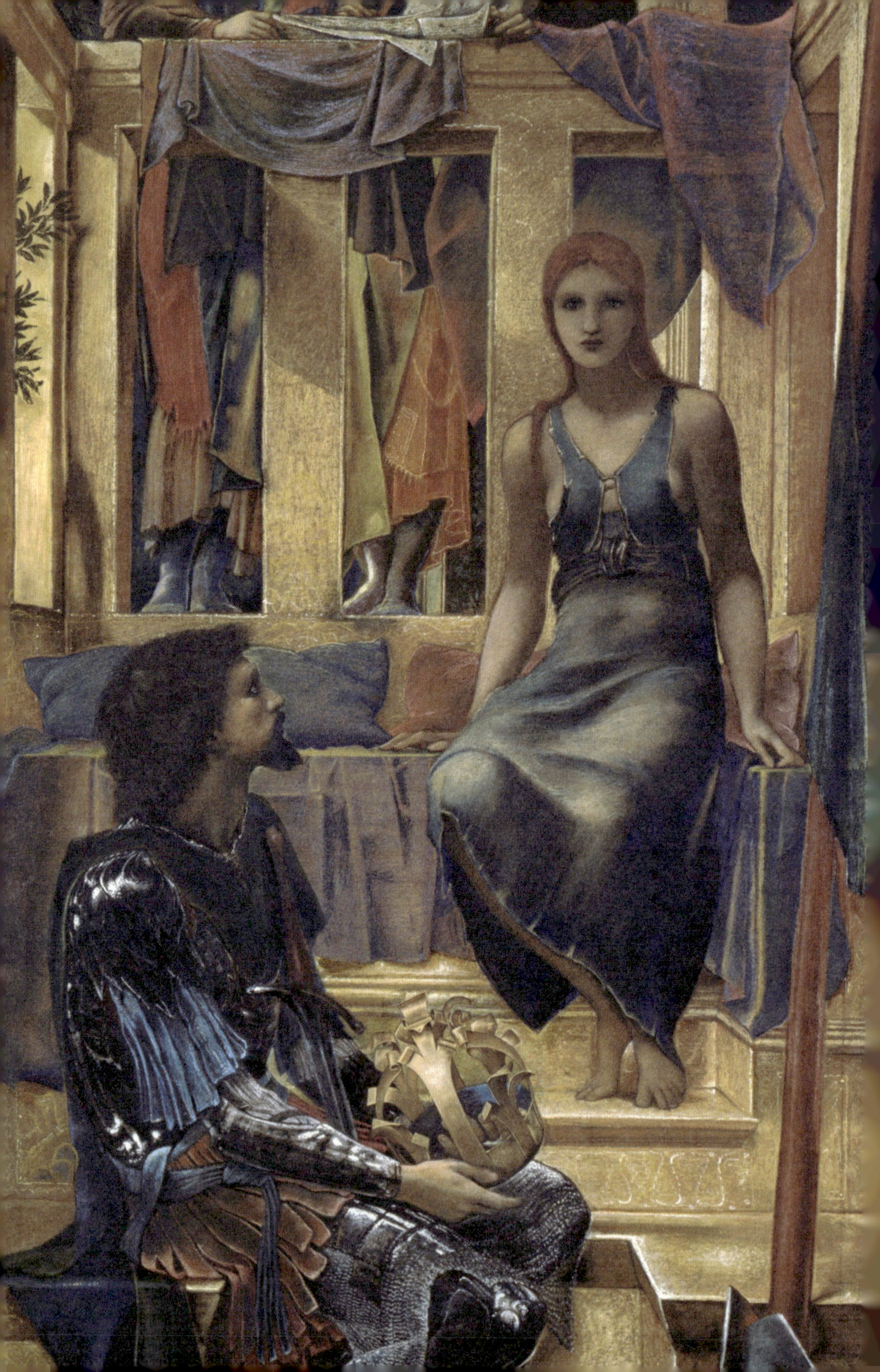

5

KNOWING ONE'S PLACE

We walked to church on Sunday morning and during the walk Jack asked me to marry him. He didn't do it very well; he said that he was a poor man and that he didn't suppose that I would ever look at him. I said that I didn't mind that. Then he said: 'You had better not marry me – you wouldn't like my home, or my people, or my life.' I said: 'I'll marry you whenever you like and live wherever you like.' He seemed very much surprised, and was silent for so long that I became uneasy, and I said: 'You might say you are glad.' Then he said, just like a child with a lesson, 'This is the happiest day of my life', and we walked on to church.[2]

Frances Horner

As they knelt side by side, she could only wonder at 'what big changes a few words can make in life'. After lunch they walked in the woods and he gave her 'a little seal ring that he always wore', before going to see her father. William Graham seems to have taken it all 'very quietly', despite Jack declaring that he 'never expected to get the best in life', his house was a barrack and he was not rich. But they had a roof and 'there should be something to live off'.

Her father's quiescence echoed his disappointment, as well Frances knew. When she had invited Jack Horner to join them at Armadale, a castle the Grahams had taken on Skye in September 1882, William had warned his daughter 'not to encourage him unless I meant to marry him.' Her protest ('How could I possibly know *until* I was asked') should have alerted her father. But it had never seriously crossed his mind that she would marry him. After all, she was fiercely independent, with her own salon among the artistic

25. King Cophetua and the Beggar Maid, by Edward Burne-Jones, detail of the cartoon

glitterati. Here she was exchanging a rich, cultured metropolitan life for a provincial, impoverished existence with a man she barely knew, who said little and was happiest shooting. No wonder Aggie took her aside: 'Are you sure that you and Jack Horner are well suited to each other? What made you accept him?' Frances's answer, 'I think it is because he is so big', did little to reassure. Her friends among the party were less surprised but just as depressed. 'With true human perversity,' reported Doll Liddell, 'everyone who had been wishing it suddenly became plunged in gloom …and there has been a funereal atmosphere over the house ever since'. For one or two, such as Godfrey Webb, their Oxford contemporary had killed off their own hopes. Even Frances caught the gloom, putting it down to 'the end of fun' for she was the life and soul of her father's house party. They were 'very fond of me', she acknowledged, 'and marriage is an end of things somewhat'.[3]

For none more so was this true than for Burne-Jones to whom the announcement was a bolt from the blue and a profound blow. Horner was everything Burne-Jones was not – younger (although still twelve years older than Frances), landed gentry with an ancient seat, and with seemingly little interest in art and beauty and new ideas. Bravely he tried to make light of it to his old friend Ruskin but the hurt of betrayal was plain to see:

> Many a patient design went into adorning Frances's ways. Sirens for her girdle, Heavens and Paradises for her prayer-books, Virtues and Vices for her necklace-boxes – ah! The folly of me from the beginning – and now in the classic words of Mr Swiveller 'she has gone and married a market gardener'…Oh these minxes! You and I will yet build us a bower and have our mosaics which none of them shall ever see.[4]

Despite being married and never intending to divorce; despite Frances being so much younger than him; and despite the fact that for many in her social circle marriage to the likes of Horner was something to be aspired to, Burne-Jones was devastated. She had modelled for him frequently, exchanged letters daily and had talked of running away with him (if not seriously). He knew his distress was comic to others but he could not help himself. It was not simply that he felt duped. Her engagement exposed the raw nerve of his possessiveness and the awful moment when dreams and reality collide.[5]

To modern commentators, Frances's decision represented the 'capitulation to the realities of life for women of her social world.' Marriage was the fate of one who at twenty-eight was running out of options.[6] By 1881 with all her sisters married (including her younger sister Aggie), Frances risked being trapped caring for elderly parents while her siblings led fuller lives.[7] Spinsterhood would be a humiliation, caricatured in Victorian novels as a life of loneliness, sexual repression and hysteria. 'Despair …Eight and Twenty! Living a life without hope', lamented Beatrice Potter in her diary. 'The position of an unmarried daughter living at home is an unhappy one, even for a strong woman.' One who did not escape this fate was Olive Maxse, who Frances later tried to rescue only to complain that lacking 'the fire of life… [Olive] doesn't rush to meet the unknown'.[8] Frances was never lacking the fire of life, nor one to stop rushing to meet the unknown. This is what attracted her many suitors. That eventually her choice should fall on Jack Horner was not therefore an act of desperation. Rather it had its origins in another engagement ten years before; not hers but her brother's.

*

Frances had adored Rutherford, 'my very handsome and rather wild' brother. And indeed loved him all the more so for being 'wild'. At Oxford, his friend Doll Liddell remembered him as 'strong and well built' but with the 'kind of recklessness, both as regards himself and other people, which possessed considerable attraction'.[9] Cutting quite a dash (at his father's expense), Rutherford made numerous aristocratic friends in the process. He would never be thought of as being in Society. Instead in his raffish appeal he was felt to be rather dangerous. Still the invitations that followed opened his eyes to new possibilities and ambitions – ambitions that also thrilled his young sister. But where she, an avid reader of Austen, saw Mr Darcy, others saw Mr Wickham – 'a charismatic and roguish interloper'. When May Lyttelton first met Rutherford, as she sheltered from the rain while out riding with Frances in Rotten Row in the spring of 1871, she was not blind to the danger: 'an odd attractive youth whom one instinctively mistrusts', she judged him.[10] Yet danger has its appeal. Soon they were dancing regularly at balls. Almost too soon, while others (such as Arthur Balfour) hesitated, Rutherford proposed.

Their engagement rocked May's parents. Quickly Lord Lyttelton went to Oxford where he found enough evidence to declare Rutherford 'slippery'.[11] As a committed Anglican, he also took strong objection to the Grahams' Presbyterianism. While behind these formal obstacles lay the unspoken injunctions of class. London Society was an exclusive and small network of related aristocratic families who preserved their status through intermarriage and accumulation of land. There were plenty of hangers on and 'entertainers' but it would not be until the mid-1880s before substantial wealth could gain acceptance in significant numbers. The Grahams were new to London. They were also cash rich and conspicuously so. Frances's bedroom in their house in Grosvenor Place overlooked the gardens of Buckingham Palace. With her father they would build up a major art collection and when in Europe they would travel with 'exceptional swank' in a private coach with six horses. As Frances admitted, 'we had everything we could have wished for'. All of which counted against them. So too the small breaches of etiquette that were eagerly pounced on such as riding too recklessly in Rotten Row or (apparently worse) riding with soft felt hats with cock's feathers instead of top hats. Frances was continually struggling between her instincts and the demands of convention. When Mary Palmer asked her parents for permission to write to her new friend, Frances Graham, the teenager was initially refused lest it took up too much of her time.[12] In this context Rutherford had pulled off a social coup.

May Lyttelton, Frances would recall, was 'tall, dark with wavy hair and a sort of boyish figure. She had great brilliance and was one of those people who were always criticised, always praised and blamed and talked of. Many people loved her'. But not all. She was a tremendous flirt with the vitality to charge a room, but when not the centre of attention she could wane into depression and 'nerves'. At her father's insistence, she reluctantly broke off her engagement to Rutherford. Her parents then went to great efforts to ensure the lovers never met, while at the same time promoting the cause of others more eligible. High hopes were raised for Arthur Balfour (fig. 26), nephew of the Marquess of Salisbury and his future successor as prime minister. All to no avail, for as one suitor put it, 'all her brooding is occupied with Graham'.[13] Even the best-laid plans go astray. Spying her at the Devonshire Ball Rutherford seized his chance. 'Won't you shake hands?' he asked her and with that he led her to the dance floor. May was delighted and her mother appalled.

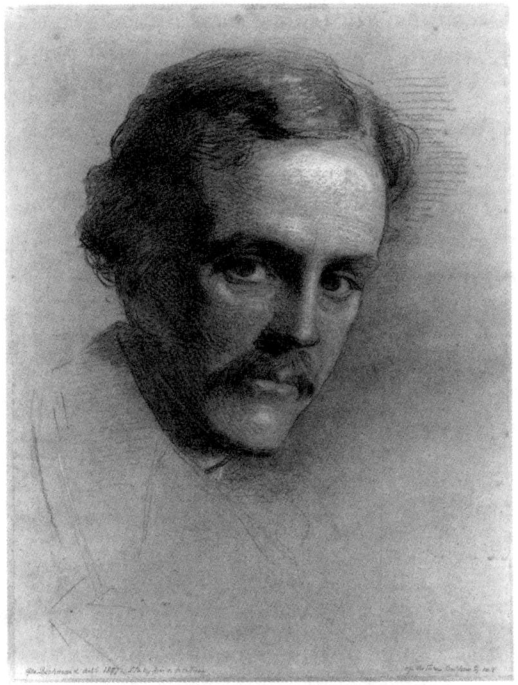

26.   *Arthur Balfour, by George Richmond, 1877*

Soon rumours (false) were circulating that Rutherford had crashed the ball. May now decided to take matters in hand. A meeting with Rutherford in Oxford left 'things settled as I wished'. She then persuaded her father to agree the engagement in return for a lengthy delay to allow Rutherford to prove his worthiness. Much to his son's disappointment, William Graham was equally determined that Rutherford would 'curb his spirit', but in the family business rather than the 10th Hussars on which he had set his heart (and his father's pocket). Thus he was sent to America to make his fortune.

As fate would have it, Rutherford never made it beyond Liverpool docks. Contracting diphtheria, he died quite suddenly on 28 October 1872. The relief of the Lytteltons was palpable. The depths of May's despair, however, took them by surprise. Only now did they concede that her love for him had been 'very real'. Belatedly they allowed her to write to Frances, though they soon came to resent the amount of time she spent with the Grahams when back in London. May's death from typhoid two years after Rutherford saw one last barb.

Her parents allowed a visibly distressed Balfour to place in her coffin the ring from his mother that he had hoped to put on May's finger. The ring that Rutherford had given May and which she had worn proudly when she was alive, was returned to Frances.

By such signals the Grahams' social position was made clear. To be fair, they had been caught out by Rutherford's meteoric advance and had no aspirations to Society. Their circle was happily restricted to William's two brothers, his artist friends, chapel and above all his own family. They would very occasionally give a grand dinner party (with eleven courses – two soups, two fish, two entrées, a roast, a bird, and three sweets) and on 20 June 1878 they even entertained Gladstone – with a crowd of admirers watching the Grand Old Man through the open window. Much more their style were small supper parties for close business friends and family. And all the more so during the long periods of mourning for their dead sons and the onset for William of illness and depression. So, apart from presenting Frances at Court in 1871, William Graham ignored the Season. His daughters' marriages were respectable rather than glamorous, their husbands notable for their public service rather than their birth. The eldest, Alice, married Quintin Hogg who made a fortune in his family's sugar company and then dedicated the rest of his life to philanthropy and the founding of the Regent Street Polytechnic (now Westminster University), outside which his statue still stands. Amy's husband, Kenneth (Muir) Mackenzie was a leading civil servant and for over thirty years Permanent Secretary to the Lord Chancellor. Ennobled later, he joined the Labour Party and was buried in Westminster Abbey. Herbert Jekyll, who married Aggie, was a captain in the Royal Engineers, progressing to become Private Secretary to the Lord Lieutenant of Ireland and latterly Assistant Secretary at the Board of Trade. The brother (and neighbour) of Gertrude, the famous gardener, he was knighted on his retirement. These men were not minnows but neither were they socially grand.

To the eighteen-year-old Frances, there was little romance to be found among technocrats and administrators. She had glimpsed what her beau ideal of a brother might have had and knew thereafter what she wanted. However, the world of Society, of town houses and country estates would only come through marriage and that in turn required being seen. The Grahams were sufficiently prominent to have gained entrée to most social events and indeed Frances's cousins attended many parties under the gaze of their mother. Rutherford's 'crime' had been to presume too high. In turning their back on the Season, her parents had significantly reduced Frances's chances. 'I longed to go to balls', she would later recall, 'but we were never asked to any'.[14] On a rare occasion when she was, she was only allowed to go in return for attending a meeting of the evangelists, Moody and Sankey. For her parents regarded such affectations as 'wrong and silly'. And potentially humiliating too, as Frances was to discover for herself.

When her younger brother, Willie, died in 1875, Frances received a letter of commiseration from Alfred Lyttelton, May's brother. He had befriended Willie at Eton, perhaps because he had noticed the young boy's sister ('P.S. Someone says your eyes are "full of subtlety and Passionate Resistance". Guess who? What does it mean?', her young brother reported to her).[15] She could not fail to have noticed him, for Lyttelton was the great cricketing hero of the school (and later England) at a time when the Eton–Harrow match was a highlight of the Season. He stood out as much for his manner as for his runs, displaying a winning combination of physicality, Corinthian spirit and *esprit de vivre*. In her reply to Alfred she admitted to having seen him 'from afar at Eton' and 'someday I hope to see you and know you perhaps'. Yet it was to this 'stranger' that she unburdened herself over the strain of a family in denial. And then risking all, she declared 'God knows how I loved your beautiful May – I think she was dearer to me (and to Papa too) than our own'. By the next letter she is calling him by his first name ('that is very unconstitutional, I know') and giving him her favourite books. When he went up to Cambridge, she visited him at least once and he took her with him to a party given by the celebrated (and notorious) don, Oscar Browning. She was the only woman: 'rather flattering to the female mind to have thirty undergraduates to hold one's fan ... Makes London seem quite flat.'[16] Invitations to join her family in Scotland would follow. Then the trail runs dead. Maybe it had nowhere to go; she was after all three years his senior. If his parents had heard of it, they would certainly have put a halt to this latest assault by the Grahams on their offspring. Possibly Frances, having been so forward, chose a tactical retreat rather than risk one of her few connections with London Society to which she aspired.[17] If so, it worked, as Alfred Lyttelton and his brother Spencer were to remain good friends all her life.[18]

~ 6 ~

INDEPENDENT LADIES

I was perpetually stumbling into friendships and intimacies –
not always wisely, and sometimes too well

Frances Horner[19]

By the late 1870s Frances found herself 'in the heart of a musical clique to which Arthur Balfour, the Lytteltons, the Austen Leighs and Gladstones belonged'. Moreover music was a passion as well as a connection. 'Our great social excitement' was going to the Monday 'Pops' or the Crystal Palace symphony concerts and 'all the Oratorios'. Yet what ensured her inclusion was her friendship with Mary Gladstone. Mary was an accomplished pianist and, as the daughter of the great Liberal leader, could attract the likes of Clara Schumann and Madame Neruda to private concerts in Downing Street. In return, Frances took Mary to *Lohengrin* at Drury Lane ('Oh how dreadfully I enjoyed it').[20] As was her wont, Frances's musical tastes – Haydn and Brahms as well as Wagner – were all a far cry from her mother's love of Mendelssohn and Liszt; and more disconcertingly, given her social ambitions, from Arthur Balfour's passion for Handel.

Despite Mary being seven years older, she and Frances became inseparable. Both were independent-minded, intelligent women unwilling to wait on marriage. Both became the private secretaries of their powerful fathers and entered fully into their public life. Mary's Christian faith strengthened Frances's and together they would 'go slumming,' under the charismatic guidance of a Father Eric Linklater, 'a very high churchman'.[21] He persuaded them to support his social missions once or twice a week in the East End (where Mary also shamelessly plugged the Gladstone name). And it was he who encouraged Frances to establish her 'cripples' home in the stables at Grosvenor Place. That such a controversial ritualist came to have such an influence is perhaps not surprising, given her

Romantic temperament. Still it marked a sharp departure from her Chapel roots.[22]

Both women shared a keen interest in contemporary art and Frances's introduction of Burne-Jones was a big 'break' for Mary. So too was meeting Ruskin at Herne Hill, where 'a great Froude-Carlyle talk' between Mary and Frances aroused the 'unfeigned delight' of the great man. But for the most part they were just confidantes. 'Dined most snugly with Frances' is a frequent entry in Mary's diaries when she was in London; 'we talked enormously'. In time she became 'My Frances' who 'looked beautiful' across the dinner table. Visiting late one evening she enjoyed 'a nice sight of Frances in her boudoir'. At most hers was an innocent crush if a protective one. What Mary would not do is launch Frances in Society, mainly because she had no interest in it herself. With seven siblings and twelve Lyttelton cousins she had less need for other company. But it was significant that, while Frances was invited to Hawarden (the Gladstone estate) most summers, she was not included when the Whig aristocrats came.

'Very odd how my greatest friends are all about fifty,' remarked Mary. 'But it is a pleasant footing because so delightfully safe'. Safety was the last thing Frances wanted. Nevertheless she also knew very few men of her own age. Summers in Scotland did offer the chance to invite the likes of Doll Liddell and Arthur Godley (from whom she learnt to 'love Clough and Matthew Arnold') – both Rutherford's contemporaries from his Oxford days. By comparison London for much of the seventies was for her a social desert. Her friends were her father's friends – artists and Liberal politicians of the stamp of Sir William Harcourt and John Bright who joined them in Scotland where both spoke more than they listened – unlike rare guests such as the Liberal, George Goschen, who sought out her views on German literature. Frances was naturally accomplished in entertaining her elders – a capacity to listen as well as to flatter, and all lightened with a dash of wit. Burne-Jones may have been considerably older ('Your Ancient Ned') but he offered much more stimulating and sympathetic company, the flattery of association with greatness, and above all engagement with one of the most creative minds of the age. With him she could enjoy an easy intimacy and much of the ritual of love. By comparison, no callow youths could offer the treasures that he poured on her lap.

Yet there were 'scrapes'. Frances once admitted that she envied her sister Amy's 'rather concentrated affections', never caring for anybody other than her husband ['and myself']. 'Whereas I was perpetually stumbling into friendships and intimacies – not always wisely, and sometimes too well'. Typical of these was her unwitting seduction of the influential art critic, Sidney Colvin. Having decided to exhibit much of the Graham art collection at Burlington House, including the Old Masters – then distinctly unfashionable – her father invited Colvin to lunch at Grosvenor Place to test the likely reaction. In Frances's eyes he was 'a very great person' and on hearing of his imminent arrival she prayed 'Please God, make Mr Colvin like me'. One suspects that it was not God who was responsible for Colvin's subsequent unburdening. 'I am not dumb where my feelings were concerned', he would write to her. 'May I hope that … we shall be friends in a fuller sense of the word than we have been yet?' At only nine years older, he was one of her younger suitors but to no avail: 'how right you are to keep your freedom at all costs, rather than give yourself away with the least doubt in your heart.' It was a dignified retreat of one who would remain a devoted friend. As for the reviews, they were all Frances could wish.[23]

More surprising was one who had treasures to match those of Burne-Jones: his long-standing friend and mentor, John Ruskin. It had begun as a tease. Ruskin was intrigued to meet Burne-Jones's 'new pet'. Achieving this in January 1878, he couldn't help enjoying the irritation of 'Ned' at the 'fuss' the Grahams made over Ruskin. Burne-Jones was always vulnerable to such irreverence, as he 'liked very much to have his friends all to himself and in a locked compartment of which he kept the key'. Frances was quite happy to join in the chaffing of her lover. More to the point, Ruskin was for her the leading authority of the artistic world. 'I was on my knees to him at once. I thought him the dearest company and the greatest man I had ever known.' Dragging him to the circus proved a major success; the first performance in England of Wagner's *Die Meistersinger* on the other hand left Ruskin cold, much to the Grahams' embarrassment. Nevertheless an invitation to his retreat on Coniston Water followed and 'to my great surprise I was allowed to go'.

By now Frances was aware that he was 'very fond of me'. Ruskin she quickly discovered was a 'strange, complex character'. What she found so captivating was the depth of his knowledge, the range and assuredness of his judgement, and his willingness to share all this with her. However, a sheltered upbringing had left him delicate in manner, emotionally disconnected, and inflexible in his opinions. Very likely she knew from artistic circles of the debacle of his failure to consummate his marriage to Effie Grey and her subsequent marriage to Millais. Quite possibly she would have learnt about Rose La Touche to whom Ruskin had proposed when she was still a child and whose death in 1875 had left him distraught. Still his insistence that Frances adopt Rosie's pet name for him ('St Crumpet' or 'St C') did not put her off. When they went out on the lake or the hills, he would be 'always making a curious sort of love to me, and I wondering if I could care for him enough to spend much of life with him'. On the downside, he could be 'rather unkind and loved power. He was not tender by nature and we quarrelled constantly.' Yet such was his conversation and courtesy 'that I always came back to his lure.' As he was being sculpted by Joseph Edgar Boehm, he promised her 'if you care, the clay that's in me is there for you to mould as you will'.[24] She was wise enough to know that this would never be true.

A month later, over dinner at the Mackenzies', Mary Gladstone learnt of Ruskin's mental breakdown in February 1878. Ever sensitive, she felt she could see it from 'the struggle on Frances's face'. Yet Mary had misread her friend. 'Don't be distressed, I am not in the least jealous', Frances assured Mary who had let slip her own attraction to Ruskin. 'It is a great disappointment to Mr Ruskin I know, only he doesn't believe it, but I am not [in love with him].' This did not stop him accepting Graham's invitation to Dunira in Fife that summer. Although in recovery, his behaviour remained distinctly odd: kissing a stone breaker by the side of the road who admitted he couldn't read; and 'apostrophising' a birch tree 'as if it was a woman'. Later he would claim that 'Francie was never more than a birch tree to me and it didn't always keep march-music time'. Still that autumn at Hawarden with Mary, he was still 'talking much of Frances'.[25]

Then a year later in 1879, there was the sudden return into her life of Father Linklater. The inspirational priest, who had encouraged her in her mission work, had always taken 'a fervent, devoted interest in my spiritual welfare which was rather excessive'. To overcome this infatuation with Frances, he had taken a drastic step, leaving for Oxford to train to become a monk. Plainly unsuited to that life, he eventually returned to his parish and in 1879, much to her

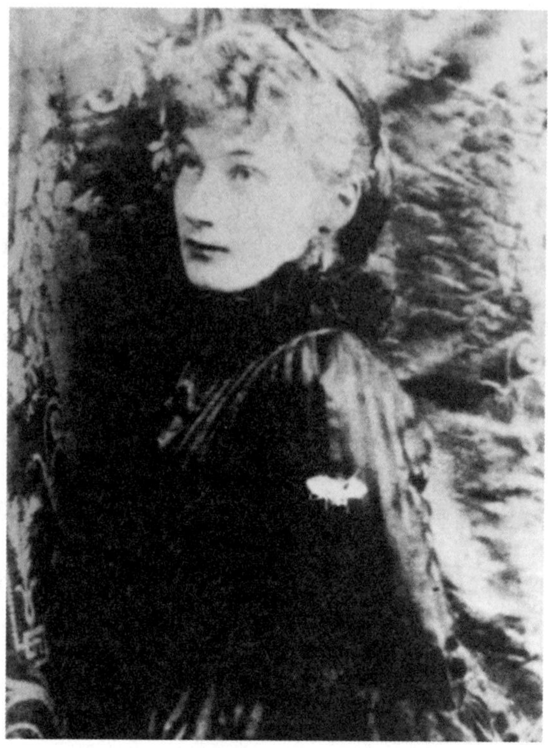

27.   Laura Tennant

bewilderment, was asking Frances to join him. Her mother was particularly excited at the prospect, judging that a clergyman of whatever description was just what Frances needed, and urging her to visit him. Clearly he retained his charisma for she admitted to being tempted. But by now, perched on the arm of the most famous painter in England, Frances's days of slumming were over.[26] Such flirtations with marriage had their benefits. A jealous Burne-Jones was an attentive Burne-Jones and 1878–9 would see a flood of presents and portraits. For now she was swept up in his fame and the next year would see the triumph of *The Golden Stairs*.

*

In 1880, while travelling with her father in Switzerland, she would meet three sisters who would offer her a very different world. Frances first saw Laura Tennant (fig. 27) while staying in the Hotel Klum in

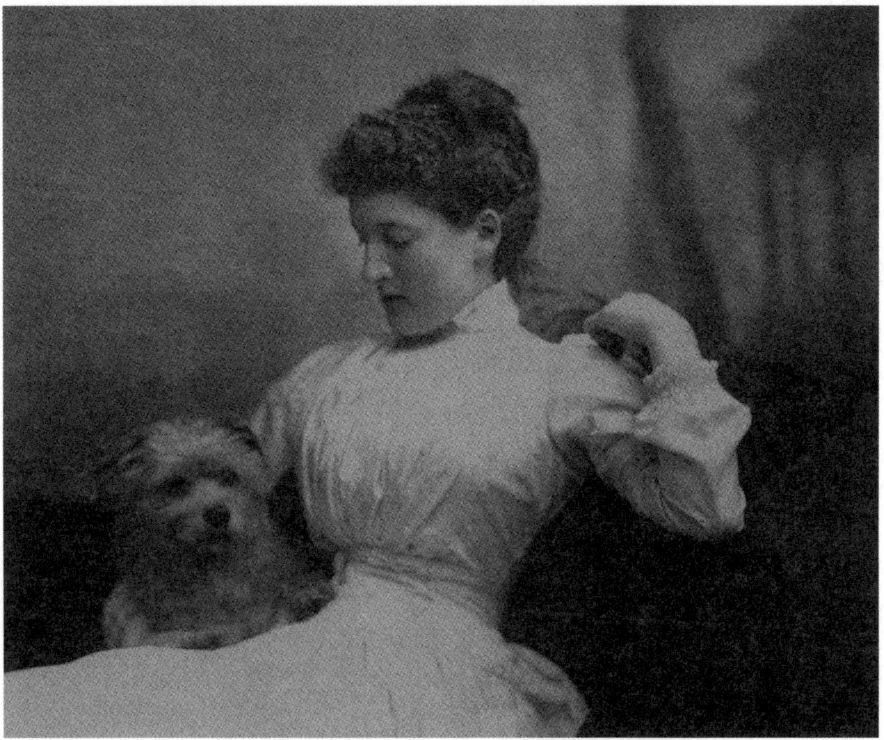

28.   *Margot Tennant*

St Moritz. Fascinated, she watched on as this 'enchanting flame-like creature' would mope around the hotel foyer with a large volume of Burton's *Anatomy of Melancholy* ostentatiously to the fore. Having made her mark, she would later that evening return to carry out the 'deadly execution' on the dance floor of the young students on reading parties. Frances and Laura hit it off straight away and she and her sisters Charty and Margot (figs 28, 29) became close friends for the rest of Frances's life. The next year they met up in Dresden for Wagner's *Tristan and Isolde* and Frances shared with them her love of Blake's poetry.

Like the Grahams, the Tennants were *nouveau riche* from Scotland – but much richer and utterly unconstrained by convention. Frances loved the devil-may-care exuberance with which they were already making their mark on Society, and she happily rode along on their coat-tails. They in turn were in awe of her friendships

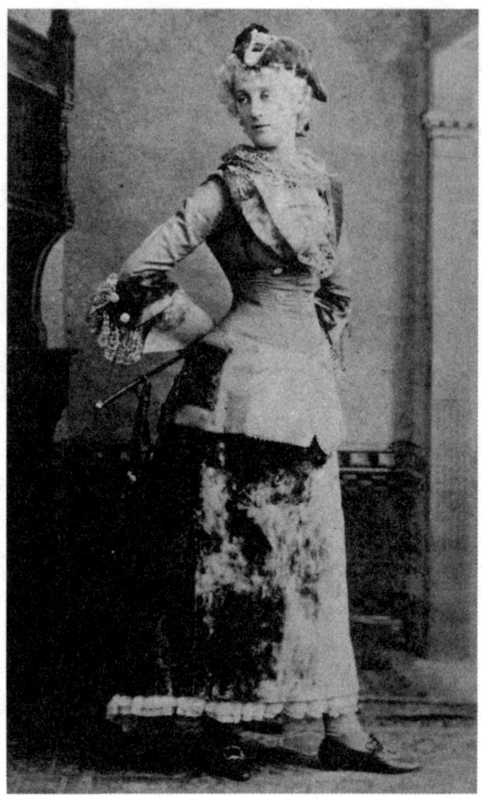

29.   *Charty Tennant*

with Burne-Jones and Ruskin; her counter-cultural dress sense with long flowing dresses (and no corsets) and hair piled up naturally, while they had spent fortunes at Worth's; and her passionate desire to use her artistic talents and not simply be decorative. Frances was eight years older than Laura ('my child') and offered her the friendship of a muse: warm, sensual and sensitive in judgement.

Francie has been with me the whole morning and I feel as if I had been to church. I feel so happy, oh! I feel as if her Love, her Soul, her eyes made me happy for ever. She loves me I know and I have the copyright in loving her as much as anyone in the world. She says so, she was so beautiful and good and kind and let me quite empty myself into her and only stroked my hair and told me what to do and she was so loving and *sympatisch*.

To them she was the modern independent woman free from the

hierarchical constraints of marriage and they became devoted to her. After one exhilarating ride in Scotland Margot poured out her feelings in her diary: 'Such a ride, oh such a ride Frances! … I thought of you my queen and wondered if the god of heather would ever let you care for me … I felt happy with a sort of glow of dimly acquired ambition and a love of Frances'. [27]

With Laura it became something more. 'If there is such a thing as love at first sight', she confessed in her diary after meeting Frances, 'if so, I felt it for her.' Hers was a teenager's crush riven through with emotional religiosity. Thanking God for sending 'my pale moonlit haired Francie', she prayed to Him as they knelt together at the communion rail, to 'seal our friendship and bless us, bind the ropes of love stronger than death around our women['s] hearts.' With Frances confined to bed with a chill, after being caught out in a storm, Laura seized the chance to nurse her. For all its innocence, theirs was an intense relationship with confidences shared on private drives deep into the countryside where 'we rolled in the hay and drank in the sky and the glory of the mountain tops.' After three weeks they parted, with 'poor white Francie in bed with her golden hair a halo on her pillow and her cheeks wet with tears'. Such affections are usually as ephemeral as the Victorian melodramas that inspired them. But not so with Laura. Three years on, as she was being feted by Gladstone and Tennyson on a Norwegian cruise, it was 'my Francie time' she remembered in her diary, her 'once in a lifetime' moment. It is a measure of her affection for her friend that in the company of some of the greatest men of her time, it is Frances who she remembers. A mutual friend, Edith ('DD') Balfour, would recall that as the friendship ripened, 'on Laura's side [it] grew into an ardent attachment which lasted all her life'.[28] What Laura would call 'an aethereal love for Francie'.[29]

With generous allowances and such intense female friendships, marriage with its submission and relentless childbirth seemingly held little attraction for Frances.

~ 7 ~

MRS JACK HORNER

A king among men

Frances Horner[30]

Hence the Tennant girls were so surprised to hear of Frances's engagement in 1882. After all, Frances and Laura had had long discussions into the night on the constraints of marriage: 'the White Burial' – what Mary Gladstone called an 'awful overwhelming change…[and the] goodbye to me-in-the-world'.[31] Laura was mystified that Frances of all people should succumb to what she derided as 'jam-pottism'. But Frances had no doubts. It is not clear where she and Jack first met but it was most likely through Doll Liddell (fig. 30), a mutual friend and a contemporary of Jack (and Rutherford) at Balliol. Kenneth Muir Mackenzie was another friend. It was Frances who had pressed her mother to invite Jack to Scotland in 1881, only for him to leave after a day on account of the death of an aunt. He must have made some impression for there is no evidence that they met or wrote until a second invitation in July 1882.[32] As ever with Frances, it was partly a case of necessity having to prove the mother of invention. Once again, she was in a scrape. A Rafe Leycester had laid siege and from early 1882 began a passionate courtship of Frances, crediting her with his renewed faith and pouring out his love for her in a torrent of correspondence. Somehow he came to believe that they had made 'a compact'. Frances did like him and the romantic in her was attracted to the mix of dramatic prose and literary allusion in his letters. But it was all too quick: 'our alliance was so sudden', she protested in June; 'I don't know you and you do not know me.' More to the point, if she was going to marry, she knew it wouldn't be to Rafe Leycester.[33]

Hence the invitation to Jack (fig. 32) and her prompt acceptance

of his proposal. Little correspondence before their engagement has
survived and all of it dates from
after the second invitation when
it primarily concerned complicated train times with no hint of a
courtship. Nevertheless, this was
not a desperate attempt to escape
Leycester. She had 'a lurking conviction' that she would accept Jack
if he asked but had balked at having to explain this to her father.
Possibly she had had her eye on
him for over a year but he was
too shy to presume to court her.
So she had taken matters into her
own hands. Outwardly, she found

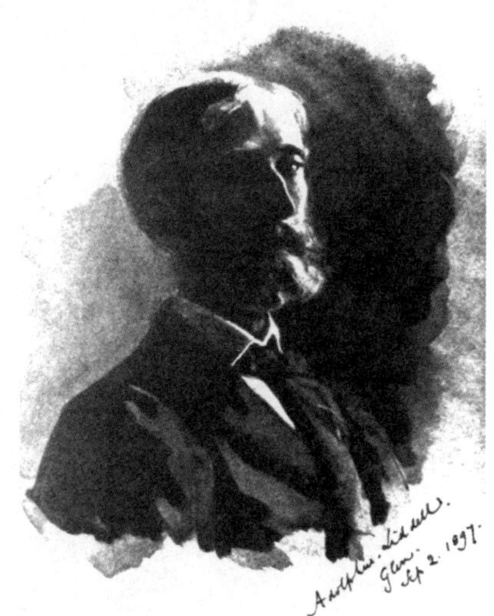

30.   *Adolphus 'Doll' Liddell, 1897*

him very attractive: extremely tall, good looking, with a golden beard
that was never cut. This together with his 'courtly manners' appealed
to her romantic side. 'Because he is so big' she had told Aggie and as
such protective. He had a presence – 'a king among men' – remembered his old Dame at Eton.[34] After 'rather stormy years' of 'love
affairs and entanglements', the prospect of marriage to Jack 'felt like
coming into a happy port after all the storms of youth'. Most significantly, the port in question came with long established roots in the
landed order and family estates held since the Reformation. With
him would come the setting to which she aspired. Like Rutherford,
she would have one chance and she determined to take it.

In truth she was tiring of being trapped in a hyper-sensitive,
often bitchy artistic world. 'What curious people who like you at first
and less afterwards', Leycester had written after she had shown him
some correspondence from Burne-Jones and Ruskin. In truth, she
was never a Pre-Raphaelite groupie. Rossetti, who had thrilled her
as a child, she 'hated' as an adult.[35] Rarely would she find herself in
the company of William Morris. By the 1880s her attachment was
solely to Burne-Jones. And even that had its place. She once, before
the artist became famous, 'drove [him] out in to the street uncom-
plemented' because Hubert Parry and his wife were due to visit. The
Old Etonian composer and his Balfour and Lyttelton friends were

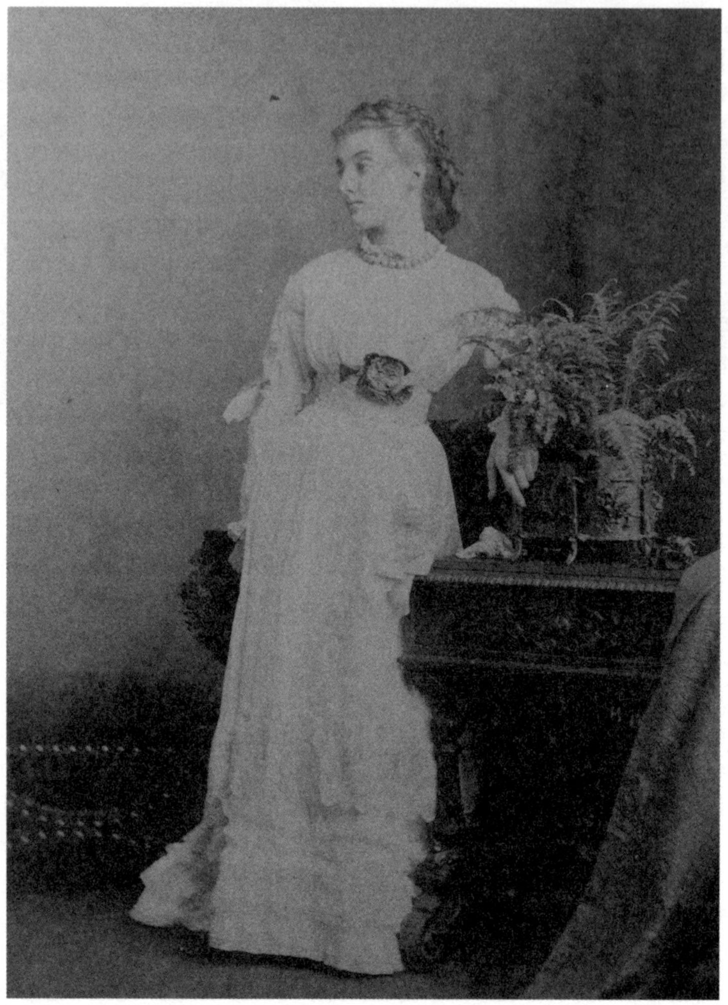

31. Frances

where she wanted her future to be.[36] She knew full well the impact her engagement would have on Burne-Jones. To a degree her marriage was a break for freedom, from his possessiveness.[37] It would compel a rebalancing of their friendship. So too her relationship with her father. Fifty years on, she would still remember a put down from her father ('Oh Panza, don't be such a donkey!') in front of her friends in 1882. Where once she would have laughed it off, now it stung. Perhaps after running his household at Armadale, it was time for one of her own.[38] Indeed for all her late night discussions with

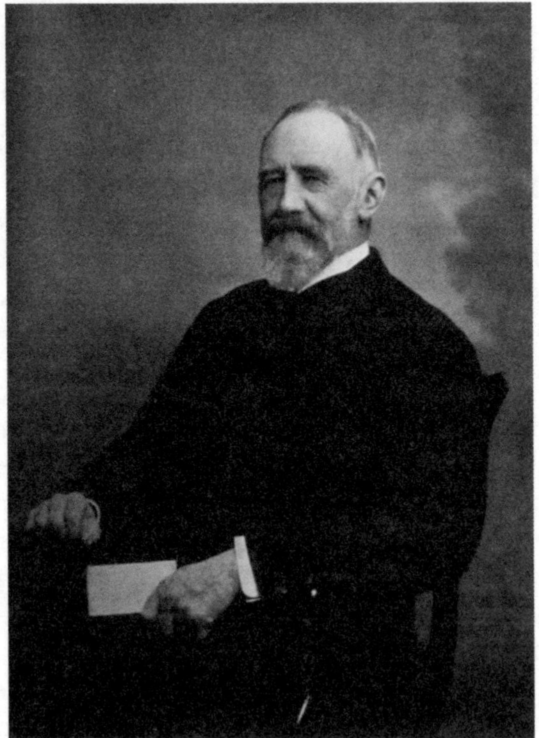

32.   Jack

the Tennant sisters, marriage in their circles could bring its own liberties and opportunities: one's own household and budgets, security of property and income under private settlements, a social position and personal freedoms, local responsibilities and the chance of public service. Spinsterhood, dedicated to her ailing parents, was not an attractive prospect. Frances knew that if she wanted a future, she had to marry.

Moreover, she chose Jack. Outwardly, Victorian families remained highly patriarchal but the reality often depended on the character of the husband and the capacity of their wives to manage them.[39] Jack was 'quite different from any of the men I had known before'. Intellectually she admired his 'extraordinarily well-stored mind … and his being a first rate historian and a good scholar' who was not only legally trained but a keen scientist too.[40] If she held him to be 'a thorough man of the world', crucially he was also 'a very modest one.' Thus his being a fount of knowledge did not become a constraint on her romantic imagination but a reassurance and resource. Similarly, her intelligence was a thrill, not a challenge, to him. After a long discussion of their favourite books, he wrote,

> It does seem so curious to be going to have somebody who will share every idea that one has got – because I have never had it, as all my friends and relations have been so different from me and I have always lived in a sort of fanciful world of my own, ever since I can reflect and now you are just what has been wanting to it, though I never imagined it would be you.[41]

Honourable, decent, kind and loyally devoted to her, he was not a husband who was going to crush her. Unlike the fate of her sisters, whose lives were dedicated to the service of powerful, difficult men.[42] Marriage would bring compromises but she had been managing older men all her life.[43] Indeed, in providing her with a platform of respectability and position she had arguably a greater range of opportunities for her independence than before. Such at least was the gamble she was taking.

By the time that Mary Gladstone arrived at Armadale in September 1882, Jack had gone. She had had a hellish journey via Greenock and Oban but as she saw the woods of Armadale, the weather cleared and there with the sun sparkling on the water came Frances and Amy in a little sailing boat out to greet them.[44] She found Frances very much in her element and boisterously happy. In insisting on Armadale for the summer, she had chosen romance over comfort. By now, she definitely ran the household. While her father sought to build up fires and cut out draughts, his daughter was for ever opening windows and urging everyone out into a landscape 'as if the Icelandic gods had been at play there'. Thus Mary found the next two weeks given over to crabbing and rock climbing and sailing and picnics and fresh air and ravenous appetites: a time for her 'oldest clothes, shortest petticoats, thickest boots'.[45] Frances's enthusiasm for sailing knew few bounds. As 'Captain of the *Pursuit*' she loved the rush of the elements, oblivious to her friends who were 'sick and cold and wet through'. And in the case of Mary, 'pretty well frightened'. Oddly the only reference in Mary's diary to the engagement was on the day of her arrival and then in a discussion with Kenneth Mackenzie. Presumably she was as surprised as anyone.[46]

$$\sim 8 \sim$$

THE HORNERS OF MELLS

The Horners were a very clannish family. They had everything in common and lived in an almost feudal way.

Frances Horner[47]

In 1874, three hundred and thirty one years after Thomas Horner acquired Mells, his direct descendant and Frances's husband to be, John Francis Fortescue Horner (known in the family as Forte), had entered his inheritance. He took great pride in being the eleventh generation in an unbroken succession of Horners since the Dissolution of the Monasteries that had seen them become one of the prominent families in the county.[48] For all the first Thomas Horner's commercial aptitude, it was marriage that really drove their advance. His nephew, Sir John Horner, had not only inherited Mells but also married Meriel Malte, the heiress daughter of Henry VIII's tailor. There are few better measures of social progress than extending the family home and together with his son, Thomas, Sir John transformed the farmhouse into a spacious Elizabethan and Jacobean manor house fit for a gentleman of means. With five gables on each of the long sides, mullioned and transomed windows, and a canted bay on the west end, its elegant, uniform front hid numerous extensions; by the seventeenth century with its various wings the house represented an H in structure.

In the eighteenth century a later Thomas Horner[49] decided to leave the manor house and in 1724 he built a dwelling befitting a family with almost 5,000 acres.[50] This, in turn, was redesigned, realigned and expanded, both externally and internally, into something much grander by Sir John Soane, in the first years of the nineteenth century (figs 33, 34). Set in a long-established deer park outside the village, Mells Park was now a substantial pile, with reputedly forty bedrooms, built on the edge of a high promontory overlooking the Mells river. By the time Forte inherited it, the house had endured many further 'improvements' including a fourth floor and two wings, each with high bay windows, and another bay superimposed on the entrance. On the other hand the woods of oak, lime and beech laid out in the eighteenth century were now at their finest. Mells Park may have been inescapably monumental but through it the Horners' standing in county society appeared assured.

There would be no lessening of ambition. Plans were drawn up for hothouses, follies, grottoes, temples, rustic cottages, hermitages, Turkish tents, lakes, plantations and 'eyecatchers'. Quite a few of these were actually built. So too was a major development of the stables in 1770, but this required the demolition of two wings of The Manor House to provide the stone. 'Half the old House is mouldering in ruins; the rest is occupied by a farmer' it was reported in 1794.[51] In 1850 it had been given over to an Anglican vocational school for craftsmen and thereafter was an occasional dower house. By then, however, the Horners' funds were becoming stretched.

Hence Forte discovered his inheritance was heavily burdened. With rents well below market value and agriculture in the throes of a twenty-year depression, he was always going to struggle on a gross income of £10,000 a year. With unfortunate timing, his clerical father took out a £55,000 mortgage on the estate in 1865 to provide for his ten children.[52] As a consequence of this provision, Forte's four sisters displayed little inclination to marry with their brother obliged to house and fund them at the Park. He was fond of his sisters even if they were a forceful tribe – not least Gertrude who continued to run the household as their mother drifted off into a religious old age. It wasn't ever thus. For much of her life Forte's mother, Sophia, was the affectionate, sensible rock on which her large family depended. Her husband, the Reverend John Stuart Hippisley Horner (always known in the family as 'the Prebendary') was a man of intellectual distinction. An early member of the Roxburghe Society, he was a learned collector who established the library at the Park. The family's clerical tradition was carried on by Forte's irascible brother, George, who from the pulpit imposed an unforgiving reign of moral rectitude on the village community. A brief flirtation with the ideas of the Oxford Movement aside, his was a very old fashioned Anglicanism. Indeed, by the late nineteenth century much of life at Mells was very

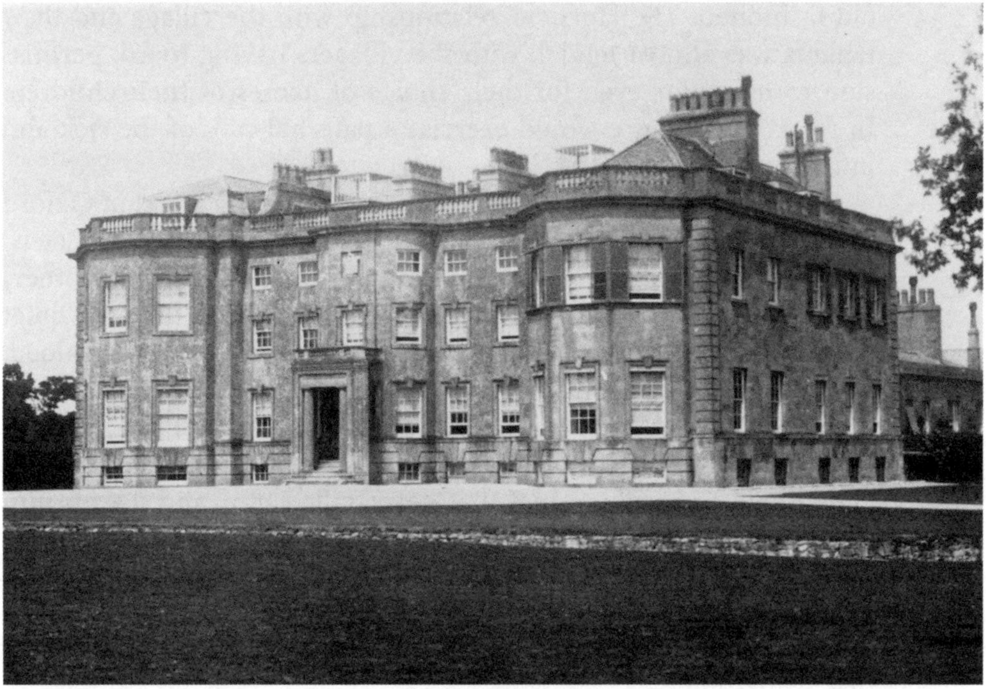

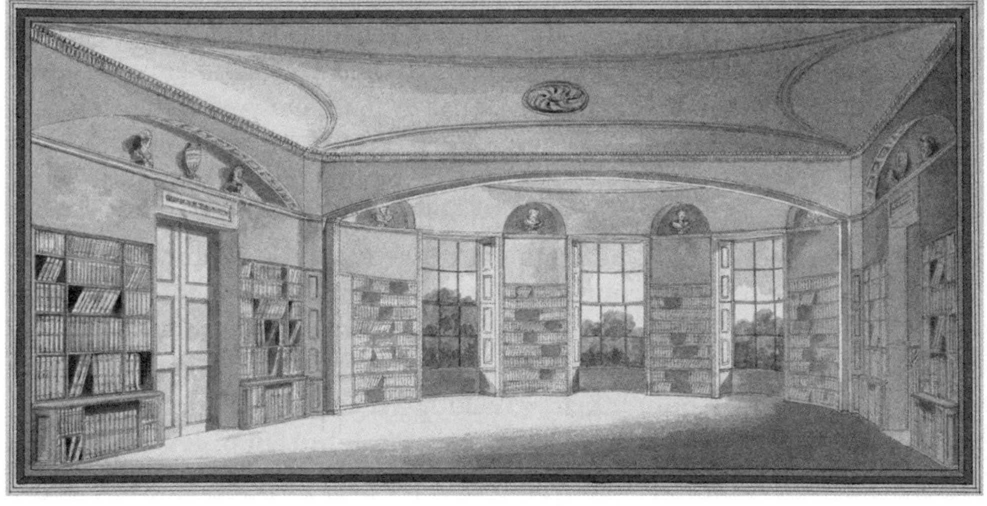

33.   *Mells Park*

34.   *The Library, Mells Park, designed by Sir John Soane*

old fashioned. The Horners' relationship with the village and their tenants was almost feudal, with the villagers having to ask permission to marry or even for their choice of names of their children. In return, the squire would exercise a paternal care of the sick and infirm and keep the rents low.

Forte continued the learned tradition, pursuing a first at Oxford in History and qualifying for the Bar. Despite his father, his scientific interests (and one sermon too many from his younger brother) had privately undone his faith. He was scholarly in his own quiet way and formidably knowledgeable. Facts were what he valued, whether scientific or historic – bulwarks against uncertainty, seemingly reliable and unchanging. 'His mind was not a very speculative or introspective one', his wife would later recall, 'but he had a high and simple code of conduct that never failed him' and it won him the affection of his tenants. Forte viewed this relationship as a sacred trust. Happiest as a countryman and especially a West Country man, he was 'wedded to habit and tradition. It was quite enough to say "it was always done so" or "it was always there" for [him] to insist on that as final.'[53]

Rarely had the outside world impinged. When it did, as in the English Civil War, it had almost proved catastrophic. While there were royalists in the family, the Horners of Mells raised the flag of Parliament in Somerset and led their tenants off to fight. During the conflict their estates were forfeited to the Crown and Charles I even stayed a night at The Manor House in 1644. Only with the victory at Naseby could Horners safely return. Even so, it was fortuitous that the Roundhead Horner died in 1659 allowing just enough time for his successor to pledge allegiance to the imminent Restoration and Charles II. Thereafter for the next two centuries nothing seemed to disturb the even tenor of Mells. True there were some Stuart links of which the family would be later become romantically proud; and even a Jacobite Horner MP who had to flee Mells disguised as an agricultural labourer before making his way to Westminster to clear his name.[54] More respectable was Sir John Hippisley who found himself in Paris in 1789 as revolution broke out and who was to play a key role in the tortuous negotiations to secure military supplies for the British Navy from the Papal States in the war against Napoleon – the first such co-operation since the Reformation. A significant continental figure, he would also negotiate the marriage of Charlotte,

Princess Royal and eldest daughter of George III; as well as serving as an MP and an active prison reformer. Ironically given the origins of their estates, the family were supporters of Catholic Emancipation in the 1820s and Forte's father and brother were strongly attracted to the Oxford Movement, but unlike Newman never so attracted as to convert. Still both were serious Biblical scholars, sustained by a wide-ranging correspondence on the religious issues of the day. Forte's own academic interests were historical and geological. More importantly, he was very widely travelled, not just in Europe but also in the USA, India and the Middle East.

Frances never really appreciated this cultural heritage. Many of the subjects of debate were too dry to hold her attention for long. Instead, to her, the Horners remained in spirit an eighteenth century family, learned certainly but fossils in a barely changing landscape. True, there was some industrialisation – an ironworks in the Mells river valley and some coal mining – but nothing on the scale that elsewhere was transforming the country. Nor much sign of the political issues that convulsed society in the nineteenth century – parliamentary reform, empire, Chartism.[55] Despite the faint air of retreat, her in-laws remained one of the leading families in the county as the first Thomas Horner had aspired to be. But the energy and radicalism had been lost. Thence she would portray the family tradition as Protestant, provincial, socially conservative (if politically Liberal) – one happy to be in a corner of England that the nineteenth century had apparently forgot. It would prove a backdrop that would set her off to perfection.

*

As it turned out the Horners were figments of imagination for others too. In the mid-century they found their family reputation the butt of a popular nursery rhyme – the tale of Little Jack Horner:

> Little Jack Horner
> Sat in a corner
> Eating his Christmas pie
> He put in his thumb
> And pulled out a plum
> And said 'What a good boy am I!'

A Jack Horner character had long frequented popular culture as a symbol of knavish practices and sharp opportunism. But it was the Victorian era with its romanticising of childhood and the mass-publication of literature for children that ensured that the rhyme would become so well known and a favourite to this day. Such prominence attracted interpretation and to the family's horror it came to be attributed directly to the Horners of Mells and their acquisition of the manor in the wake of the dissolution of Glastonbury. Thus much was made of Horner being the Steward of Glastonbury Abbey for twenty years. Someone who, as Cromwell's net began to tighten, was well placed to collaborate in the disgrace of the abbot. After all, the monks involved with the financial affairs of the Abbey were hung with Abbot Whiting. Horner would not have been appointed to the jury that condemned the abbot if he was not willing to do Cromwell's bidding. With the abbey destroyed, Horner was rewarded with the manor of Mells – the plum – in a victory for chicanery and nerve.[56] And as such it captures the interest.

Yet the evidence against Horner is circumstantial and for the most part supposition. As for his motivation, he could have been as much a religious reformer as he might have been a traitor seeking advantage. Equally he may have been under such pressure that he felt he had no alternative. One cannot tell. What one can say is that the nursery rhyme actually has nothing to do with Thomas Horner. After all, the earliest versions predate the Reformation. In all its various versions for the next 400 years there is no reference to Mells. Crucially, rather than stealing the deeds of Mells, Horner paid for the property and at a substantial price some years after the Abbot's execution.

Rather it was the revival of Catholicism in Britain after 1850 that changed perspectives. With churchmen of the calibre of Cardinals Newman and Manning and a major programme of church building to cater for the tide of Irish immigrants fleeing the Famine, Catholicism became more confident and assertive. In this climate old sores re-emerged and few were more painful and unjust than the Dissolution of the Monasteries. Inevitably attention turned to the destruction of Glastonbury, one of its most dramatic and brutal acts; so much so that Abbot Whiting was declared a martyr and beatified by the Roman Catholic Church on 13 May 1896. Biographies would be written in his memory. And much invented along the way – not least the scapegoating of Thomas Horner.[57] Thus Catholic Mells became identified with medieval England – a golden age of innocence and purity of spirit – lost in this case through betrayal and deceit.

Understandably the Horners were outraged at the calumny on their ancestor. The deed of Mells with Henry VIII's personal seal granting the Horners' legal right and confirming the price paid was now hung prominently for all to see. But, since most ancient estates owed much to nefarious ancestors, few people shared their sensitivity. The rhyme was too good and the story it told was too much fun to give up. 'You must, I think, call me by my home name' wrote Forte to his fiancée, 'unless you can invent a better one'. She could. She called him Jack.[58]

~ 9 ~

MARRIAGE

I wish I was a little richer for your sake

Jack Horner[59]

In September 1882 Jack was back with Frances again in Scotland and 'we had a divine time getting to know one another'. Such were Frances's high spirits that she had not been deflated by the banality of her fiancé's letters (filled as they were with cricket, fishing and conversations had on the train!). Or that it had taken him two days before he plucked up the courage to have 'it all out with my mother'. She may have been 'so pleased' but 'an unemotional letter as is her wont' from his sister Gertrude suggested that not all his family approved.[60]

As for Frances's friends, it was only natural, Jack reassured her, that 'the others should be a little annoyed' at her decision. And rather nobly, he suggested that her father come and live with them. Before that, there were the preliminaries to sort out. Financially the Grahams soon realised that the Horner estates were heavily mortgaged as well as funding allowances for numerous aunts and sisters. It is not clear how much Frances brought as a dowry but with six sisters to provide for it was unlikely to have been more than £10,000 (nonetheless the substantial sum of £1.19 million in today's terms). In return, Jack ceded 4,466 acres to a trust for Frances run by her family in addition to taking out a £5,000 insurance for her on his death.[61]

Frances affected never to care for money – as the offspring of the rich can afford to do. But talk of a celebratory ball being killed off on grounds of cost and Jack's opposition ('I hate and dread my fellow creatures') would have registered. She was just as startled by Jack's religion, which consisted of little more than 'a certain amount of observation' out of duty and 'from a sense of superstition'. Meanwhile his High Anglican brother was raising Graham hackles by trying to impose a pre-Reformation marriage service from the Sarum Rite of 1504.[62]

It was not until she visited Mells for the first time in November with her parents that she came to realise just what she had let herself in for. Fifty years on the memory was 'quite vivid to me still'. Mells Park was 'a great mass of building everywhere'. The front was largely Georgian with two low wings. To the rear was a courtyard with a proliferation of servants' quarters, outhouses, bake house, and laundry rooms to serve a main house with forty bedrooms. But most of these were unfurnished and some used as a store for china and redundant furniture. Indeed the only rooms lived in were 'a circular bow-windowed library full of lovely books'; a morning room 'with a beautiful old green Chinese paper'; and a dining room 'with red rep curtains', a Turkish carpet and a vast dining table with no silver to break up the expanse of white cloth. The walls were bare save for stern portraits of eighteenth-century Horners staring out into the gloom. The drawing room was almost empty. Beyond these rooms, there were very few curtains and carpets. Intensifying the gloom were the colza lamps, which let out a poor yellowish light but were declared safe; and more importantly were what the Marquess of Bath used at Longleat.

Jack's sister Gertrude (who had kept house for him) deplored flowers inside and offered nothing to break up the bareness of the rooms. By contrast 'there were immense collections of minerals in all the drawers; stuffed birds and stuffed animals on all the tables and shelves; collections of seaweed, bird's eggs and dried fish filled every corner, gathered by bygone Horners and housed in every kind of little Chippendale and Sheraton cabinet or nest of drawers.'

At least there were books: 'in lovely red morocco bindings' in the eighteenth-century library with its fine collections of English, French and Italian works. While the morning room had good collections of travel and history books and endless bound magazines: *The Edinburgh* and *Quarterly Reviews*, *The Gentleman's Magazine*, *Illustrated London News* alongside hundreds of volumes of scientific periodicals that took up whole walls. By contrast 'there was no poetry, no fiction, no literary books of any [i.e. modern] kind'. For 'the family were all mildly scientific', measuring the rainfall every day and setting the glass. Everywhere were telescopes, microscopes and a crude lab full of 'ancient chemicals, powders and specimens' (which she was later to throw out). No wonder 'this was all very surprising to me'. But worse was the realisation that 'all this was sacrosanct'. Her father, 'rather distressed at the pictures', offered to send down some of his own – a kindness that was quietly ignored.[63] Not that this stopped him from giving his daughter five paintings by Jacopo Bellini as a wedding present (fig. 5).

Gertrude was the only one overtly hostile to the interloper and perhaps the most threatened. More welcoming were Jack's mother, his other sisters, his brother George (the Rector), the latter's twin brother Maures (who often stayed) and an elderly Aunt Lily, who lived in The Manor House and who the sisters took it in turns to look after. What Frances hadn't taken in was that many of them lived in the house. There would be no escaping this tribe. When they went to church all the villagers stared at her – they too were part of the tribe. So it was a relief when before breakfast on their last morning Jack 'seized me' and led her through a plantation and past a holly hedge and onto a great terrace beyond which lay a long stretch of water: 'I thought it then and think it now, one of the loveliest surprises in the world; for the ground sloped steeply down across a green park to the water, and the view of wide sky and woods and shimmering water could never be forgotten'.[64]

Word spread fast. 'Frances just back from Mells, her new home', noted Mary Gladstone; '[the] first meeting: a conscious failure'.[65] 'I wish I was a little richer for your sake', Jack confessed, 'and cleverer and better'. Tea with Burne-Jones proved equally strained, however much Jack 'tried to behave well'. Compared to the subtle flirtatiousness and versatility of Burne-Jones, Jack seemed emotionally illiterate. Mary on the other hand 'loved Jack' on first meeting.[66] Still London must have brought home to Frances just what she was giving up: the company of artistic people, the galleries and concerts, a position in chic metropolitan society, the comfort of family and friends; and all for bleak rusticity in Somerset. Mells Park was no Pemberley. Nevertheless, she didn't waver from her intention and she married Jack on 18 January 1883 at St Peter's, Eaton Square. With an Anglican church in Belgravia, she was taking the first steps towards a future she had long coveted.

A year after the wedding Laura Tennant came to stay in Frances's new home. Conversation drifted onto how to tell whether a man was the one to marry. 'Well you know', explained Frances,

I think one talks to him and likes him and says to oneself 'if he worried me very much to marry him I might, perhaps' and then if he does, one marries him. It is so rarely that perfect ideal affinities meet … and then you know it is doing things for people every minute of one's life that makes one love them …[67]

Oddly, it was to be the basis of a successful marriage.

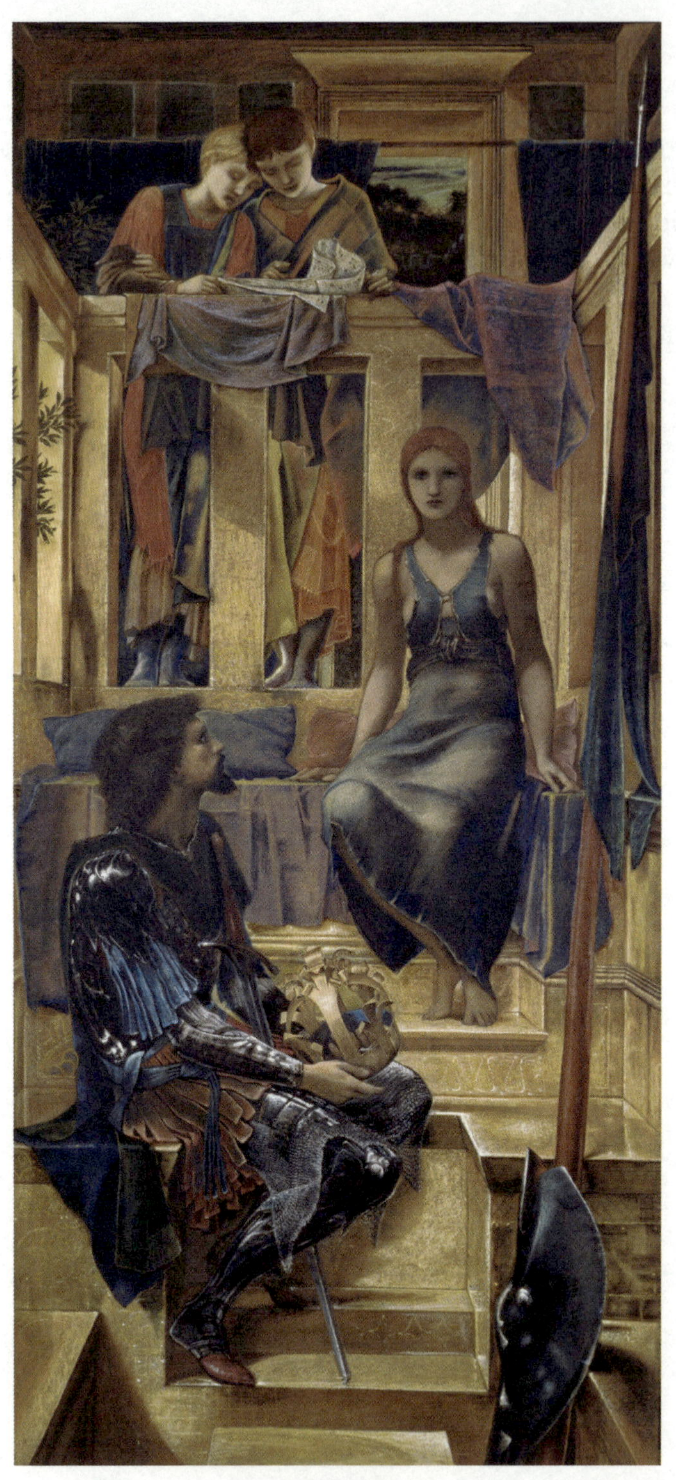

35.   *King Cophetua and the Beggar Maid, by Edward Burne-Jones: cartoon, 1880–83*

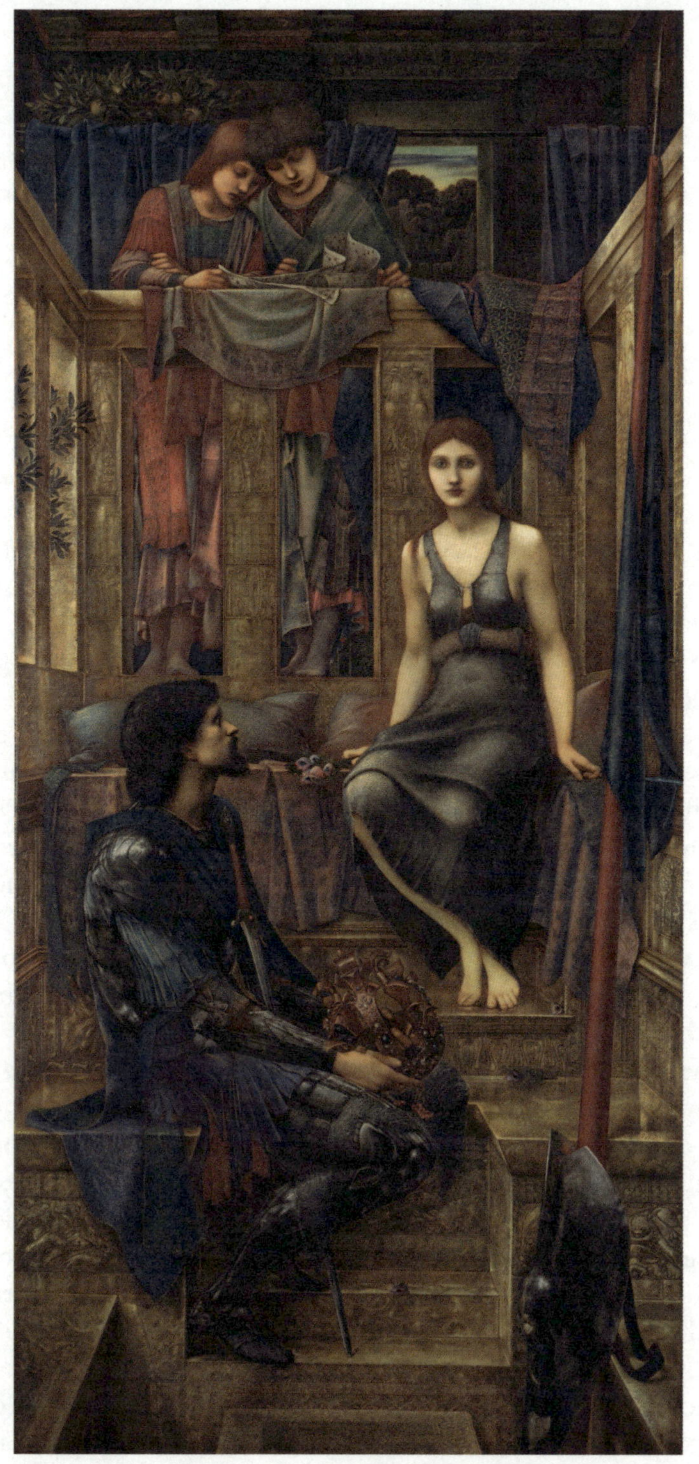

36.   *King Cophetua and the Beggar Maid, by Edward Burne-Jones: the finished painting*

~ 10 ~

BEGGAR MAID

'An end of things somewhat'?

Frances Horner, *Time Remembered* [68]

'Today is the wedding-day of my last unmarried friend', Mary noted in her diary while in Cannes with her father. However much she liked Jack, her sense of loss was greater: 'I was very glad to have that last glimpse of her.'[69] Burne-Jones too sought a last glimpse. Summoning Frances to Rottingdean, he painted her as he wanted her to be: demurely kneeling at his feet. He was still in denial on the eve of her wedding: 'I would sooner smuggle it into your hands secretly', he confessed of his gift of a drawing, 'than in the sight of Israel tomorrow'.[70] What he felt he had lost in Frances was someone who not only cared for him but crucially also for his art, who he felt understood him and to whom he could unburden himself. So miserable was he that he couldn't bring himself to write to her for nearly a year. Ultimately he needed his muse and, despairing over his latest work, he was writing to her again by October 1883.[71]

The painting that was tormenting him was *King Cophetua and the Beggar Maid* – held by many to be his greatest work (figs 25, 35, 36). It draws on the well-known romantic tale of a king who falls for a local servant girl. All ends happily when he marries her and makes her his queen. While some critics marvelled at Burne-Jones's use of colour: 'the dark rich golds and azures, black, bronze, crimson, olive, brown and grey, the tones and tints so subtly merging and beautifully graded',[72] others enthused over the contemporary political references to the emerging class divide in a fast industrialising society.[73] For unlike the fable, all in this picture has not ended happily. The crown that the king offers in homage is rejected by the barefoot girl, who looks very ill at ease amid the sumptuous wealth of privilege; so much so that she cannot catch his eye but stares silently ahead. Falling from her hand are anemones – symbols of a rejected love.

This in part reflected his growing loathing of the institution of marriage for reducing love to a base contract that legitimised the deflowering of innocence: 'a wicked mechanical device of lawyers for the sake of property and such beastliness.'[74] It was personal too. An embarrassed Burne-Jones had to concede to his assistant, Thomas Rooke, that the King's head was indeed a 'caricature' of himself. As for the Beggar Girl, Penelope Fitzgerald declares her gaze 'without question' that of his wife Georgie. Yet would Burne-Jones, so sensitive to public ridicule and scandal, want to publicise the state of his marriage so? As it was, he did paint Georgie in 1883 – an attractive portrayal but the lips are thinner and the face squarer than the Beggar Maid who is considerably younger than his wife. Frances on the other hand had the youth, the staring eyes and the shape of face. There is no suggestion that Frances modelled for this painting. Then she didn't need to. Nor did it have to be 'her'. Indeed in stark contrast to the Beggar Maid, Frances had seemingly deserted her (artistic) values for the wealth and privilege of a fashionable marriage. Yet therein lay the point, for her rejection of the artist and the emotional turmoil it stirred in him lay at the beating heart of this painting.[75]

Burne-Jones had begun work on the picture in 1880, eventually producing a draft cartoon in watercolour. Unlike the final picture the mood and context are light and the beggar maid full of vigour and glowing confidence and, for all the poverty of her clothes, looking 'a queen, as a queen ought to be.' Crucially there are no anemones. When, after Frances's marriage, he returned to the main picture in October 1883, it was in a spirit of creative frenzy and emotional turmoil. The mood is much darker, almost funereal. The maid shrunken and withdrawn, her eyes swollen with tears, as she refuses the offer of Romance. The outcome of his torment would win him lasting and wide-ranging fame: 'One of the finest pictures ever painted by an Englishmen' declared *The Times*. But Burne-Jones saw it almost as an act of exorcism – a cathartic release. 'I am very tired of it… I can see nothing anymore in it', he confessed to Madeline Wyndham, before adding 'It is like a child that one watches without ceasing till it grows up and lo! – It is a stranger.' Such is the creative process; but Frances could also have been that child. William Graham thought so and bought the original cartoon from Burne-Jones for his daughter. Time would tell whether it would prove to be their epitaph.[76]

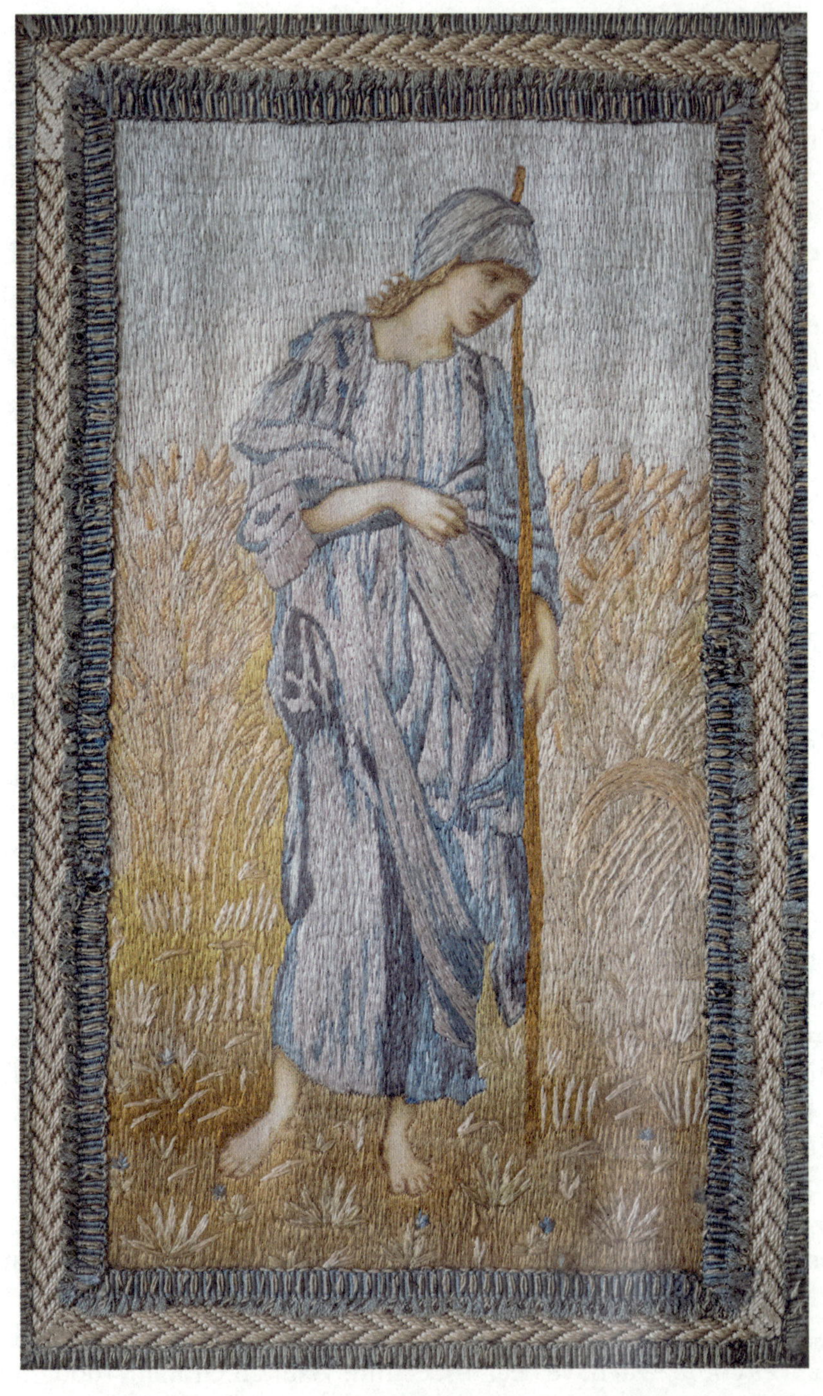

37.   *'Ruth in the Alien Corn', embroidery designed by Burne-Jones and
stitched by Frances*

Part Three

Married to Mells
1883–1891

All this was very strange to me. I felt a daughter of Heth amongst
them.

Frances Horner[1]

11

MARRIAGE AND
THE 'IDEAL SACRIFICE'

> I often think the very sacrifice of marrying a man must make one love him, unless of course one hates him.
>
> Laura Tennant to Frances, April 1884[2]

Not that marriage appeared to change Frances very much at first. The first three months were spent in 'a charming little house' at Chiddingfold, near her sister Aggie. Also there to keep her company were her two ponies and she would ride the Surrey hills with Jack, much as she had done the year before with Mary Gladstone. Soon her father came and stayed the night 'which touched me very much. He and I were the closest of friends', she would later admit, 'and at first he minded my being away a good deal'. Thereafter he frequently visited, so much so that the local rector mistook her father for her husband. This Frances acknowledged 'seemed curious, but not unnatural under the circumstance'. Since Graham was in his late sixties and with a shock of white hair, it can only have been the intimacy of their manner which misled the rector. Still, they had been playing these roles, if outwardly, for many years. What her real husband felt about this remains unrecorded. Their departure in April 1883 for two months in Rome – a city he knew well – can only have been a relief.

If so, it didn't last. Within a week Fanny, Frances's maid, fell ill with malaria. Worse was to follow as Jack went down with typhoid. Later Frances would liken her plight to *The Heir of Redclyffe* returning to England a widow as in Charlotte Yonge's High Church romantic novel. But at the time she found the situation terrifying. Not only was she herself two months pregnant with her first child, she was on her own without staff and any nursing experience. Meanwhile their hotelier, on hearing the news, pressed her hard to take her sick husband away.

As the disease took hold, Jack became violently delusional and intimidating. Wild accusations of 'her infidelity' poured forth. Thinking he was going blind, he had a black bandage tied over his eyes and railed if any light penetrated the curtains. More frightening was his conviction that the 'most wonderful old Scotch doctor' Frances had found was determined to murder him. Fearing for his own life the doctor refused to come into the room, sending in instructions from the corridor. Notwithstanding this, the hotel keeper was made to swear an oath not to let the doctor in and Jack kept the door locked and the key under his pillow. A nurse was found – a powerfully built Roman Catholic nun who vitally reminded him of an old nanny. She Jack 'adored'; only for the doctor in turn to declare the nurse a danger and compelling Frances to sack her while Jack was asleep. This stirred him to fury on waking and he now accused her of wanting to kill him too. Not only was she frightened, but having to wrap him in ice sheets for twenty minutes was physically almost beyond her, for he was such a big man to move. In time the abuse became more than she could bear. The doctor persuaded her not to leave and instead she telegraphed home. Within days an English nurse was sent out and soon Jack was on the mend. Even better, her father arrived and father and daughter spent an idyllic time in the hot deserted streets tracking down dealers and buying pictures – just like the old days.[3]

*

Eventually the young couple could put it off no longer and after recuperating in the hills north of Milan, they returned in June 1883 to the family seat at Mells. On arriving, they found all the tenants out to greet them. Releasing the horses, the farmers dragged their carriage through the village with the local schoolchildren throwing in flowers as they passed. Despite being well pregnant and looking anything but a virgin bride, Frances loved the traditional spectacle – 'very gay and pretty' she and Fanny thought it. Jack however 'didn't enjoy it', cringing at any display of public affection. It was the first indication of what was to come.

'The first few years were such a strange experience for me', Frances would remember.[4] The first shock had been the depth of isolation. Mells Park was only a mile from the village yet it might as well have been twenty. The most rapid form of communication was Jack's dog cart with a fast-trotting pony but he would be away with it sitting on the local bench or County Council. Even these commitments were largely within a twelve mile radius of the house. In this world 'a telegram was a heart shaking event'. Frances had never conceived of being so cut off. By contrast her new family were quite satisfied with the society within their four walls. The Horners were 'a very clannish family' holding 'everything in common' and Jack's immediate family continued to use Mells Park as if it were still their home. Then there were his aunts residing in the village who would expect to dine at Mells Park at will. Used to running the household, her in-laws viewed Frances as an irritant to a well-ordered *ancien régime*. 'I felt a daughter of Heth among them', she would recall. 'Everything I did or thought or said they thought vulgar and wrong'. Great exception was taken to Frances riding Jack's bicycle. Riding down from the Park she tumbled into the arms of a sister-in-law. '"I am so sorry", Frances stammered "but it is so difficult to get off". She looked at me with a pained expression and said "I wish it were impossible to get on".'[5]

The conflict was not generational. Jack's sisters were not significantly older and some would outlive Frances. Rather she was coming up against the smug certainty of a self-contained provincial world, largely untouched by modernity. For the Horners, while not of the grandeur of their aristocratic neighbours, were proud of theirs being a family whose roots stretched unbroken back to the Reformation. Agricultural fortunes may have been on the wane but the presumptions remained. That the Horners moved in the highest circles in the community – welcome at Longleat and Wilton – was felt most keenly by the Horner women. Almost possessively they made little attempt at first to introduce Frances into local society. Instead, her London ways were viewed with a mixture of awe and moral disapproval. A disapproval that knew few bounds since they even denounced the picking of flowers as a cruelty.[6] Frances's insistence on calling her husband 'Jack' and not by his preferred family name of 'Forte' also rankled; as perhaps it was intended to do.

Yet Mrs Horner, Jack's mother, set a gentle, if distracted, tone. 'A kind, rather retiring woman', with her life now centred around

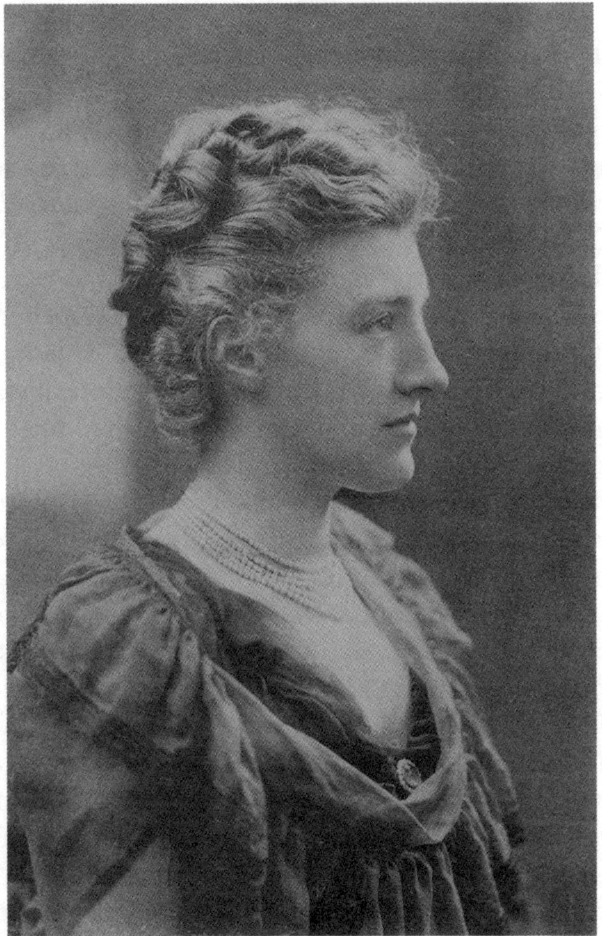

38.   *Mrs Jack Horner*

the Church and its daily rituals of services and saints' days. Rituals that as a Presbyterian often meant little to Frances. Much more difficult was the Rector – her brother-in-law, George Horner, 'who ran me rather hard'. Since he used to terrorise the parishioners into attending church regularly, he forbade her to enter the village during Vespers, lest it set a bad example. The example he himself set was unremitting as he sought to reform the parish: 'Celibate, vegetarian, teetotal, anti-sport, anti-smoking, anti-all amusements'. Combining clerical and familial power, he vigorously enforced a tyranny of virtue that knew few bounds: boys were not allowed to play marbles; nor was smoking allowed in the local reading room; 'no courting' was permitted and the sexes were separated in Church. Most repellent was the Rector's ordering the villagers to expel any of their children who got pregnant out of wedlock ('went wrong'). To Frances this was 'very wrong – but it was long before I could modify it'. More successful was her refusal to make her house guests attend church on Sundays. Other than disciplinary, George's 'influence in the parish was *nil* and the reaction to his rule was so great as to be unfortunate in other ways'. In time, among the casualties would be her own faith, for without humanity, it lost much of its purpose. This was a clash of values as it was of personalities. But for now, with Jack struggling to quell his brother (let alone his sisters), Frances had little option but to resent this '*odium theologicum*' in silence.[7]

In contrast to the vigorous pursuit of moral order, attitudes towards social improvement appeared 'extraordinarily feudal'. Nor did they stretch to concern over living conditions. Frances was horrified at the state of the tenants' cottages ('very old, very picturesque and very unfit for modern standards of life'). With leaking, badly thatched roofs, stone floors, damp walls and steep stone staircases, 'all this made me very unhappy'. And yet, she was astounded by her in-laws' and husband's 'calm indifference'. Though devoted to their tenants, visiting the sick, providing soup kitchens and clothing clubs, they viewed all improvements as 'a counsel of perfection' and, with the agents, resisted all her protests. Even more confusing were the tenants, who despite these conditions venerated Jack and the Horner family and showed little enthusiasm for 'my more sentimental sympathy'. Admittedly, rents were very low ('almost nil' at 1s. 2d and 1s. 8d per week; or about £9 at 2019 values). Yet the tenants distrusted talk of aid and Frances with it. All this was very confusing to one brought up on the fringes of Gladstonian circles. The Horners were themselves Liberal but as Frances discovered 'only out of extreme conservativism ... [and] no one could have been more wedded to habit and tradition' than Jack.[8]

Not that she was in any position to resist for Cicely was born in November 1883. For all that the birth went well, the long confinement afterwards and the anxieties that come with being a first-time mother and on her own only intensified her sense of loneliness. Jack was often away on county business. There were few letters from Burne-Jones to look forward to. Hence her joy when Laura Tennant came to visit in April 1884. With Laura came the opportunity late one night for Frances to unburden herself on the reality of her marriage:

Laura: I often think the very sacrifice of marrying a man must make one love him, unless of course one hates him.

Frances: Oh yes, it is often like that. It is horrid – one does it for him – and not for oneself – and then love covers the sacrifice, and the ideal love is the ideal sacrifice.

Laura: Do you never regret your marriage, darling?

Frances: No, never… at least… I can hardly explain myself … but of course moments come when … when I think it may be … well maybe I have refused the Highest … but … it is very very difficult to be unselfish.

Laura: Yes! I often think that if you had lived at [Wa…?][9] the whole face of History would have been changed … but this is wonderful – you settling down into a country house, being a 'county family' – much more thrilling than if you had done what we expected you to do – but you live here quiet always. When you leave alone pulling the tables and chairs about and moving the pictures and hawling [sic] down mirrors, you will come to London. Jack will go into Parliament and you will have a salon.

Frances: Ah! We can never afford it. We are too poor…But I am never dull. Could you be dull anywhere? Never.

Laura: Never, never.

Frances: I must go, darling. Jack will be up.

Laura: How wifely!

Frances: Do you think I am?

Laura: It must be so boresome when you want to read or talk – Jack comes up to bed. I should hate it.

Frances: Oh no! Jack's always awfully late. He has never yet gone to bed before me. I am always asleep first – and then he wakes me …!

Laura: Of course! My Dear! Goodnight, dear Darling

Frances: Good night, Bless you! What fun you being here.[10]

The sacrifice was partly other opportunities and other worlds, and partly the sexual submission of the inexperienced. Poverty (however relative) was another shock to one who had been brought up carefree on all matters financial.[11] Yet for all the wistfulness in these reflections, there is stoicism and no hint of regret: 'You know Laura', Frances would assert, 'I do think it is bad for a woman to live for ever at home …and withering on the family tree… It is not natural'. Even Laura had to admit to finding 'Frances… like a Botticellian Madonna with [Cicely] and hallowed domesticity'.[12] Nothing emphasised this crossing over to a new world more than the fate of her letters. 'I could not have buried my letters', she confessed. 'I had to burn them. I burnt Ruskin's and Burne-Jones's and Mr Linklater's and everyone's. If I had buried them, the flowers would have known and they would have told the grass; and the grass would have told the reeds and the reeds the water and everything would have known. So I burnt them – but it was very hard and hurt.'[13] May 1884 would see a visit by her parents which brought some relief and even more so their invitation to stay with them in London in June, with Graham arranging for Burne-Jones to hang the cartoon of King Cophetua (fig. 35) in Frances's bedroom for her arrival.[14]

*

When William Graham finally died on 16 July 1885 it came as something of a release. His suffering had been great but throughout his faith had not wavered. To the sustaining of his memory this mattered to her more than Frances expected (fig. 39). 'It was a wonderful passing to watch', she would remember bravely; 'the passage of one of the most saintly spirits to have ever been.' Other than family a few close friends including Doll and Mary were invited to pay their respects. 'The drawing room was arranged like a chapel' recorded Mary; 'the white coffin buried in flowers and a great beautiful Angel of Burne-Jones guarding the whole with tender gravity.' There they held a short extempore service, by 'the large window opening on to a terrace [with its] splendid distant view, and the sun flashing out into the solemn room.'[15]

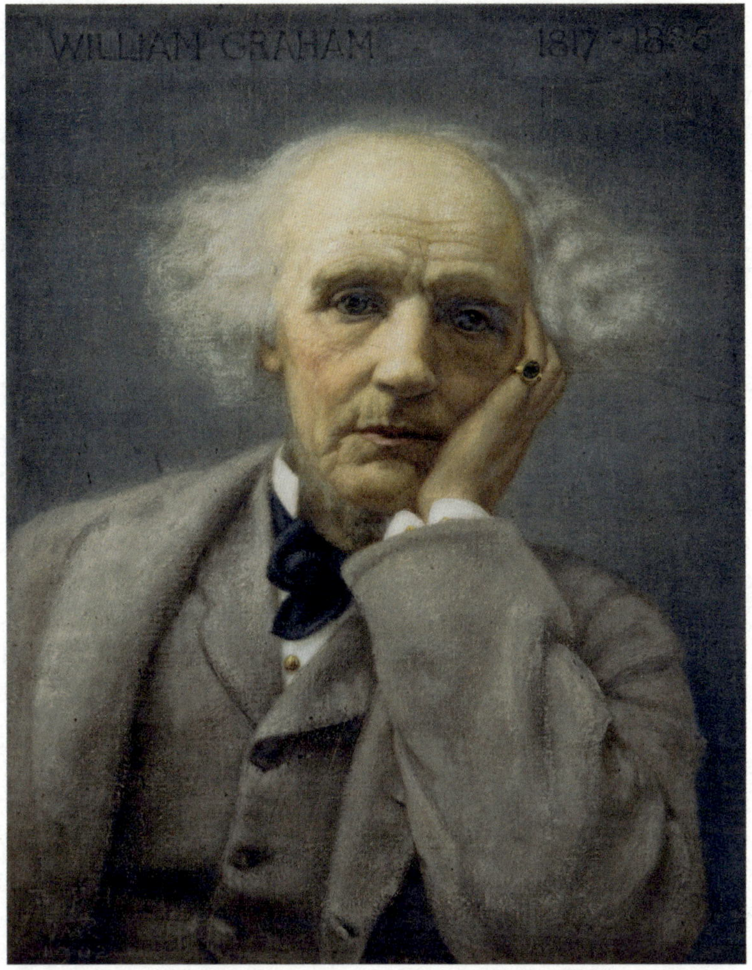

39.   Posthumous portrait of William Graham, by Thomas Rooke, 1902

Graham's death left Frances bereft. He had been her closest friend as well as a father, a lodestar in her early life. But his passing only illustrated how far she had moved on as she watched her father buried beside her two brothers in St Mungo's Cathedral, Glasgow. Amid all the embellished grandeur of the memorials of the great and powerful of industrial Glasgow, William Graham's head stone, designed by Burne-Jones, was 'a simple affair', set back into the hillside, looking over the city to the hills beyond.[16] Yet Frances saw only 'a place of natural beauty entirely defaced by climate, smoke and grime.' She was 'Francie from Glasgow' no more. Nor had she been for some time, as was made plain to her by an Oban baker in 1882. 'Are you English or Scotch?' he had asked. 'Scotch', she replied. 'May I ask where you learnt your English?' he inquired. Innocently she acknowledged that she had learnt it in England. After a moment's reflection came an enigmatic response: 'There will be a great many of my countrymen in England but …I'll tell you of aye place in Scotland where there are a great many English.' And where was that she asked. 'Bannockburn', came the reply.[17]

*

Determined now to lay down fresh roots, she set out to make Mells Park hers. The management of a large house and household was a substantial job – running the accounts, appointing, directing and cajoling staff, and organising the seasonal moves of the family to London and back. Fortunately Frances had years of experience of running her father's large and easy household, and especially the regular house parties they held in Scotland. Perhaps her ability to stand up to her sisters-in-law over this encouraged their departure from the big house, together with Jack's mother going to the Rectory where her son enforced a strict regime. None of this stopped them from calling but by now Frances was in control. Such victories came at a price. It would be many years before they accepted Frances's 'alien ways' and then only 'when Life had chastened me as well as them'. On the other hand they adored her children. And so she was left free to make Mells Park in her own image.

It was 'an old-fashioned house', recalled Doll, 'like a lot of packing cases set down side by side and joined with doors'. With little Horner money, the dictates of High Victorian fashion were beyond her means. Instead, Frances chose to clear the rooms and empty the packing cases and make of it what it was, 'a spacious, light and elegant eighteenth-century house of great charm'. The furniture was of the period and sound with enormous old-fashioned sofas and tables, while on the walls of red silk hung the remnants of her father's great collection (including a huge cartoon of Love with red wings, which she would turn into the tapestry that still hangs in the church). 'Wisely' she left alone the Library with its 'dim browns and gold'. Instead 'her personal books overflowed into the ante-rooms, passages and morning room, [making] every corner a model of comfort and charm'. Adding to this were casual arrays of wild flowers

– another stamp of authority. Informality was her touchstone. In her decluttering of the Victoriana and the opening up of the Georgian windows so that 'light poured in everywhere', Frances was also echoing the modern – symbolised by Clouds in Wiltshire, the new mansion of Percy and Madeline Wyndham completed to great fanfare in 1885. It was but an early example of her fast developing art of capturing the age on a shoe-string.[18]

So too was Frances's approach to landscaping. Being perched high on a rocky spur of the Mendips precluded formal gardens. Instead it allowed for an expansive terrace with spectacular views over two lakes, down to which ran a south-facing slope filled with trees and 'shimmering masses' of primroses and bluebells. Too poor to keep it smart, they came to love its 'untidy charm'. Similarly unable to afford to clear the lakes of rushes, they chose to take pleasure (before the onset of 'bird bores') in the moorhens, wild duck, and marsh birds that nested there. Trees were their main source of contention. Jack and his father were of the era when the conifer was a venerated 'rare specimen', 'however sickly or even dead'; Frances wanted cedars, oaks and thorn. In the end she succeeded with the last and produced a 'wonderful sight with scarlet and white thorn, and chestnuts, laburnums and lilacs, all in a riot of blossom together'. In keeping with this, 'what had once been' a formal three-fold avenue of beech leading up to the house had over time become a grove 'very fair in spring and glorious in summer' and home to vast numbers of rooks that would rise up at the bang of a door or a gun. Again informality was the key – what Doll admired as 'just the right mixture of nature and culture'. The effect was striking. 'A Dream of Arcady' was how one visitor described it as she was led by Frances onto 'the terraces overlooking the winding river and the woods and cliffs beyond'.[19]

Into this Arcadian idyll appeared her mother. Now a widow, she had unexpectedly taken the notion that she wanted to live in the country. Having just rid herself of her in-laws, Frances dreaded the arrival of her mother with whom she had fought for most of her life. That she of all her sisters should become her mother's companion and carer was not without irony. Yet surprisingly Mrs Graham proved her daughter's saviour. Firstly she was determined to make it a success. After all, it had been Frances who had done all the fighting. Her mother may have been independent minded and occasionally embarrassing, but she did not seek to challenge Frances's authority. Frances had assumed she could be farmed off with her in-laws only to discover they were 'mutually bored.' In fact she turned out to be 'an ally of sorts' in the daily engagements with the Horners, as well as a devoted grandmother to the children. Moreover, while she had been guilty of selling her husband's great collection, she did bring to Mells Park the pictures that she had retained, thus enabling Frances to create in Mells the Pre-Raphaelite haven she had always wanted. The art critic Julia Cartwright was not the only one dazzled by an array of Rossettis and Burne-Joneses looking down on them in a drawing room flooded with light. And there among Burne-Jones's cartoons of saints and angels and illustrated book covers was 'a beautiful drawing of Mrs Horner herself, a profile done in 1879 which is one of the best heads of her I know. It is the face which has so entirely taken possession of his mind.'[20] And of course the sale meant that her mother was now well off in her own right.[21] At Mells she had her own rooms, and came with her own books, piano, servants and a carriage and pair. Slowly but surely Mells Park was acquiring the Graham stamp. Not only was she generous in support of the running costs of Mells but she also enabled Frances to rekindle the prospect of a London life. Even so, such thoughts of escape would be forestalled by the incarceration that is motherhood.

12

'JAM-POTTISM'

There are odd things about having a baby which I can't quite understand. It is so common and almost vulgar in other people and so extraordinary and almost poetic in oneself – to oneself, I mean. When once you feel it is stirring and alive in you, it's a sort of mysterious secret existence away from the world which has a charm – and for a time I think your character changes or sleeps.

Frances Horner[22]

For all such sentiments childbirth in the nineteenth century was often a terrifying prospect for any young bride, pregnant for the first time and far from her family. Doctors were rarely at the birth and in the countryside chloroform rarer still. Instead most were reliant on the traditional arts of the maternity nurse. In an age without blood transfusions or antibiotics, miscarriages or difficult births could be fatal. Mary Gladstone (as Mrs Drew) almost died in childbirth in 1886 and in 1895 Margot Tennant's child was lost in order to save her.[23] Yet Cicely was born in November 1883 with barely a problem and indeed verged on perfection for 'she never cried, was always happy, and stayed where she was put'. Together they would drive out in the pony cart with a picnic for long days exploring the byways and woods in the neighbourhood. Frances would breastfeed Cicely while 'sitting on a heap of stones by the road side'.[24] Less happy was the arrival of Katharine in September 1885 with Frances already low after the recent death of her father.[25] The birth of Edward in 1888 and thus an heir to the Horner line was a cause of much celebration. Not for Frances. 'I was very ill. When I got better I felt an old woman and I have never forgotten the misery of that time, nor how long I took to recover'. So traumatic was the experience that she went prematurely grey – a bitter blow to one who prided herself on her youthful looks.[26]

Not surprisingly when she found herself pregnant again in 1891, 'the most remarkable thing about Mark is that I didn't want him.'[27] She hadn't realised she was pregnant until almost suffering a miscarriage. 'I don't mind so much now', she assured her close friend Edith ('DD') Balfour. 'The first incredulous despair is over and the philosophic side has got the upper hand again'.[28] But she did mind the enforced rest strictly supervised by her mother who 'flits in and out of my room like an uneasy insect'. And she resented missing a dinner at Wilton where Tennyson was to be a guest. Still it did get her out of church. So it was one Sunday that, with everyone at the service, she stumbled on a chimney fire in the morning room. Notwithstanding her condition, she and 'Marsh' (the butler?) climbed up onto the roof and poured '60 gallons' down the chimney. Such was the adrenaline rush that she hadn't felt the cold. Equally foolhardy, she would occasionally sneak off to skate furiously on the ice, returning covered in bruises from her falls.[29]

Yet soon there would be no denying what Katharine dubbed 'The Unborn'. Such was her size that Frances admitted to being 'alarmed about the number which the Almighty has most injudiciously entrusted to my case'. That she should emphasise the lack of a clergyman let alone a doctor in the village, suggests she was becoming fearful of the dangers ahead. Fears that only got worse with the baby 'miles past' its due date of 1 July: 'either it isn't a baby at all or there will be something phenomenal about it. It will come out full of strong oaths and bearded… You do not know how cross and horrid I feel or how I creep about – with what the children call "a cheerful bumpy sound"'. It would be another two weeks before Mark was born on 13 July 1891.

While the families celebrated the arrival of another son, Frances suffered 'the worst week – don't ever believe that there is anything nice getting well from a baby – it is almost as bad as getting ill of it.' As was common practice, she was incarcerated for up to six weeks 'lying in', together with nine months of breast feeding (much to the astonishment of her daughters who asked if the 'New Born drank blood'). In what was a hot summer, it took time to get 'over the gloom of convalescence' and she struggled to regain 'the spirit to go anywhere alone'. Even London for once lost its appeal: 'London and Londoners never sound the least attractive when one isn't in it. It needs the actual intoxication of drinking it to make the glamour – and when I am out to grass with a nice turnip peace creeping over me, it is just like seeing people dance without hearing the piper.' This was very unlike Frances and indeed after a short illness she 'went down into the depths.' 'I have got a long way along Recovery Road', she finally admitted, 'but I am not past Depression Corner yet.' With all strength gone she just wanted to sit down 'for good'. 'I can't think why it is. I am moderately well, nothing goes wrong, Mark is very cheering to me – and yet I do feel the world a greater Vale than ever. I think my nerves got all jarred and shaken and they won't come right again – and I am extraordinarily like Mama just now!'

Few Victorian men appreciated the nature of post-natal depression. After two months Jack, determining that sea air was the cure, took her to Westward Ho! to recuperate. Only for him then to disappear all day onto the golf course, leaving her behind with the baby and rapidly going 'mad'. Fortunately rescue lay nearby in the form of distant friends of his family, the Hamlyns of Clovelly, and there Frances met Con Manners, who would become one of her greatest friends.[30] Here in the Hamlyns' drawing room she would sit on the floor with Mark asleep on her lap. Or go walking in their 'park … of heather and gorse and gnarled trees looking like olives and steep cliffs down to the sea and tiny coves you can creep into'. Here slowly she began to recover. By November she had regained a lighter vein, able now to write proudly of her son: 'His name is Mark and he is delicious, always warm with vague smiles and fragments of an unknown tongue. I like him the best just now – because he is the child of my old age, I suppose.'[31] Still such experiences left scars.

*

> I hate the country – I always thought I did, but now I am quite sure of it – It is cold and you can't stay out, & when you are indoors you might as well be dead. Don't believe people who say they like living in the country they are silly, or deformed or offended with the world, or lying.
>
> Frances Horner to DD Lyttelton[32]

November rarely sees the countryside at its most appealing. And certainly not to metropolitan girls like Frances. Nor did such vehemence after nearly twelve years of marriage suggest she would be won over soon. However much she loved her children, the demands of motherhood had tied her to Somerset and the frustration of being incarcerated among the slow moving and easily satisfied was all too palpable. 'I have not even seen a pig killed or a gentleman buried', she lamented – 'but that is Mells all over'. Behind the berating of country living lay deeper issues. Not least reconciling herself to the constraints of marriage and 'the peace (which) comes when one has thoroughly accepted the convention that it [is] an absurdity to expect to do anything well and that one will never do anything at all, and one doesn't matter in the least and nobody cares.' The weather thus became a metaphor for a sense of entrapment and loss. Hence her admitting to Violet Maxse, 'it has rained here so much that I cannot feel properly sentimental about the country. [Instead] my thoughts keep wandering back to days behind me – and to what had been and what hadn't been.' Now others were taking her place. Early 1885 would see Laura Tennant modelling for Burne-Jones in his *The Depths of the Sea* (exhibited at the RA in 1886). Where once Frances had strode the salons of high art, now life consisted of tenant balls till 4am and visits 'to take jelly to sick people in the village, who I know can't bear it and give it to the cat.' Duty would prove a relentless taskmaster: 'Doing village entertainments most nights this week… The villagers sing songs – horrible ones – out of tune – and then we look as if we liked them – and then they don't look like they liked ours and then we all thank each other.'[33] Laura had a phrase for such a life – 'stuck in jam-pottism' – for Frances, a verdict all the more brutal for being true.[34] She would only be human to envy a little her closest friend and her liberty.

*

There was no danger of Laura suffering such a fate. She was too vivacious and unconventional a personality to be so confined. And too carefree, open-hearted and passionate not to win over even the most unlikely supporters. Mrs Humphrey Ward, the novelist, was entranced on meeting her: 'combined with this passion, this poetry, this religious feeling was first the maddest delight in simple things – in open air and physical exercise; then a headlong joy in literature, art, music, acting; a perpetual spring of fun; and a hatred of all the solemn pretences that too often make English society a weariness.'[35]

Part of the attraction was her apparent interest in everyone, whatever their standing. 'She could not be happy unless the crossing sweeper liked her, and unless she knew all about his joys and griefs and home life'. Many were taken aback by her openly expressing 'affection and pity with caresses and kisses'. Petite and doe-eyed with an air of ethereal vulnerability, she was quite capable of playing the *ingénue* – partly because she enjoyed the effect on others and partly from a desire to be loved. Once she had set her sights, she was hard to resist; 'she is up one's sleeve and round one's neck and inside one's heart before one has even looked at her'. Sometimes she went too far, coaxing a proposal out of a besotted Gerald Balfour, brother of Arthur, forcing her to seek refuge in an air of bewilderment. Her future sister-in-law, Lucy Lyttelton knew better. 'She had the naughtiness, the grace and quickness and mischievousness of a kitten…Nothing was safe in heaven or earth from the sallies of her wit…[for] she could strike sparks out of dead wood'.[36] This was just what Frances loved in her. Despite her marriage they remained as close as ever with Laura 'a child of the house' whenever Frances was in London. Caught in 'her spell' and her 'most glowing friendship to me', Frances admired how 'she always made straight for the heart of her friends'.[37] That her most ardent conquest should be one of Frances's oldest friends came as no surprise, not least because Frances did so much to engineer it.

'Miss Tennant – an able little animal, very smart and flirty'. As ever Doll Liddell went straight to the point. Frances had noticed their mutual attraction when they first met at the Grahams' dinner table, and by the summer of 1884 she had invited them together to Loch Alsh on the Isle of Skye for two weeks during which Laura was left with Doll unchaperoned. Frances was an enthusiastic match-maker rather than a subtle one. When the couple came to Mells in December she had her work cut out persuading Jack to be away and her mother to stay in bed just so Doll could lie with Laura until 3am. 'What a wonderful lover he was' Laura secretly confessed to DD Balfour, reporting 'how every nerve of her being was stirred by him'. What did this sexual behaviour involve? According to DD, there would be lots of hugs, arms around necks, sitting on laps, kissing and petting, visiting each other's rooms at night, ladies in nightdress and letting down hair, lying together. Everything but sexual intercourse. Hence Doll's frustration in November 1884 at Laura's refusal after much 'caressing … to go beyond'.[38]

Frances's goal in all of this was to promote the engagement of her best friend to her brother's best friend, despite Doll being sixteen years older. Yet Laura knew 'she could not marry him', not because of his age but due to his being a poorly paid lawyer without sufficient means. In any case she had made her mind up long before to marry Alfred Lyttelton – admittedly another lawyer but the son of a Liberal peer, a future cabinet minister and an English cricketing hero. Still, such was Doll's prowess that they continued to meet even after Laura's engagement. Indeed *en route* to Mells in May 1885 they had indulged in 'lover-like behaviour' on the train. But now Frances was furious with them, insisting on their returning in separate carriages. For, with the wedding weeks away, she feared for Laura's reputation. And her own too, lest the Lytteltons had cause again to wonder at the influence a Graham could exert.[39]

In the aftermath of her engagement in January, Laura issued (ostensibly on behalf of Frances and herself) what amounted to a manifesto on marriage.

> It has few attractions for either of us … the celibate life has more nobility near it I can't help feeling, though it is the most egotistical too. What we mean is that ANY woman would do for any man and that some women would do some other things if they didn't marry. I for instance might write, Frances might have done anything. I don't believe either Alfred or Jack would have died if either of us had refused them. They would have married some 'sweet girl' and been quite happy … Had I remained unmarried I might have worked for the majority instead of living for the very very minority.

And then ending on a note of defiance, she gave warning that 'Marriage … to some women is the end of womanism, to me it is nothing of the kind'. To emphasise her seriousness, she went public, sending it not only to her unfortunate fiancé but also to George Curzon and Mary Gladstone.

Alfred, along with most of his circle, put this down to Frances's influence over her impressionable intimate. Laura was young (twenty-two) and there was more than a hint of Frances replicating in their relationship the controlling guidance and inspiration that she had experienced under Burne-Jones. Laura made no secret of being a devoted follower. Seeing at Mells Frances putting such a brave face on the reality of marriage only reinforced her views. 'I am so sick of being told I shall have a rock and a shield – all twaddle… the fact is that marriage is a lower form of life'. Consequently rather than descending into the 'cellars of life', she preferred being 'a little Bambina' to Doll. In Frances's bedroom they would talk long into the night on the 'horrid sacrifice' of marriage. Tellingly, in his reply to Laura, Alfred emphasised his disagreement was with Frances and *her* creed that to be single was to be 'freer and nobler'.[40]

Did he fear that Frances was turning his fiancée's head just as Rutherford had turned his sister, May's? After all, her closest friend was marrying someone to whom Frances had once been attracted. Like Burne-Jones, Frances would prove very possessive of her girl-friends. Yet ironically, while the Lytteltons suspected the worst, Frances was actually trying to win her young friend over to the neces-sity of marriage. And was doing so in Laura's terms. For as Alfred acknowledged, 'the centre of [Laura's] religion was her recognition of the glory of sacrifice'. When Frances argued that 'doing things for people every minute of one's life makes one love them', Laura agreed: 'the very sacrifice of marrying a man must make you love him, unless of course one hates him.' As it turned out she was not to hate Alfred but rather came to worship him. From the depth of a 'divinely idle' honeymoon during which 'Alfred and I talk a great deal about you', the memories would be subtly different. Reminiscing on 'long talks in bed with you', Laura now recalled 'the spur that Jack's hoped for presence used to give our conversation… There is something very funny about not being angry with a man who gets into bed with you, isn't there? I do think it is very very funny but Alfred is the only man I would let do it.'[41] With her own sexual fulfilment there would be a greater understanding of how Frances could still write to Jack after seven years of marriage that 'I will never forget our nights together.'[42]

The world according to Laura had moved on. The language of sacrifice had become infused with the flirtatiousness of the coy mis-tress: if Alfred was her 'true Knight… my King', she was 'your little babe clad in white… [who] being so completely conquered I feel perfectly happy in my slavery.' And so she was. Their wedding in May 1885 in fashionable St George's Hanover Square, was the high-light of the season and they were hailed a golden couple, self-evi-dently enjoying the early pleasures of marital bliss and soon expect-ing their first child. Indeed so happy did they seem that their friends were utterly unprepared for the shock of hearing of Laura's death in childbirth on Easter Saturday 1886.[43]

'Poor Darling Francie. I am *so* sorry for you … she loved you so', wrote Margot Tennant on Easter Sunday. Brave sentiments from one who had just lost a favourite sister. But Laura's will left her attachment in no doubt. After her bible, 'my prayer book Frances gave me is what I love next, and I love it so much I feel I would like to take it with me', only in the end to leave it to Margot. To another sister she gave 'my Frances belt because a long time ago the happiest days of my girlhood were when we first got to know Francie, and she wore that belt in the blue days at St Moritz when we met her in church and I became her lover.' To Cicely, Frances's eldest and Laura's godchild, was given a 'bird brooch' – originally a gift from Arthur Balfour, designed by Burne-Jones. 'I leave my best friend Frances, my grey enamel and diamond bracelet, my first edition of Wilhelm Meister with the music folded up in it and my Burne-Jones "spression" drawings. Tell her I leave a great deal of my life with her and that I never can cease to be very near her.' Frances felt her loss very close indeed. In her wilder grief she even declared to Margot of her children that she 'would have let either of them die to save Laura.' A year on and Margot railed at how their friends had forgotten this grim anniversary – but not Frances: 'You who are the best of company in the world and understand more and quicker than anyone I know.'[44] Yet to an extent that few realised, Laura's death left an emotional hole that Frances would never quite succeed in filling.

~ 13 ~

'LOVELIEST AND BEST OF FRIENDS'

Hasn't ours been always a metaphysical friendship – independent of sight and touch?

Burne-Jones to Frances[45]

This period of her life often found Frances at Mells on her own, with only her mother and children for company, and thus ripe for introspection. Taking stock of her position, she broke her life down into three separate spheres.

> There is my own self-life, which somehow has never been really lived – the me that was when I was young…living for some strange law of desire of what is beautiful. The life that all young and rather ardent natures have and gets repressed by the world and by the inevitable squalor of life, till at last …it fades away – and in that life I dream that everything is romance…but remember, too, that I have no expression ever; that has been denied to me. I can never do anything that will give me the sense of completeness.[46]

However much she felt it crushed, this remained the essence of what she was and what she believed in. That said, she was not unhappy. 'Then there is the life I lead for Jack and the children – a real, happy, rather ordinary sort of life, full of all sorts of everyday aims and desires, and hopes, and fears – with nothing very big or noble in it, but just as human nature's daily food, and of course that is the life everyone knows and sees'. The antidote to such mundanity lay in 'the one other life I live [which is] in my friends'. If 'life is counted the greatest gift in the world, what we have to thank God for. And

113

if someone goes and gives you another [life] beside your own, it is putting themselves in the place of a very high person.' She knew of only one who could give her 'another life'.[47]

'After my marriage I didn't see Sir Edward Burne-Jones for a year or two and then our friendship renewed', Frances would recall in *Time Remembered*.[48] The melodramatic casting forth by the artist of his muse on her marriage was a myth too appealing to discard. Honeymoons, motherhood and Somerset were bound to set them apart. For all his despair, within months he was sharing with her his anxieties over *King Cophetua* and indeed over his talent as an artist: 'I torment myself everyday – every day I know it was a mistake for me to be a painter – Yet I would die if I wasn't one. I never learnt a bit how to paint – no former work ever helps me – every new picture is a new puzzle – I lose myself and am bewildered and it was all as it was at the beginning years ago. Are you sorry?' Soothing the intensity of the creative process was second nature to Frances but the apology hinted at something new. 'The present phase of the work is alarming', he admitted.[49] In his turmoil *Cophetua* had changed from a triumph of Romance to a much darker study of rejection (fig. 36). And in his keen desire that she should see it first, there was an awareness of the pain it might cause. His plaintive protest – 'this letter is in answer to the one you haven't written me' – suggests it was Frances who was keeping her distance. Alert to this too was her father. When he bought *King Cophetua and the Beggar Girl* to hang in Frances's bedroom in June 1884, it was the original full-size cartoon in which the girl eagerly anticipated the triumph of love (fig. 35).[50]

Graham's death the next year would begin the first tentative steps toward a rapprochement as they shared their grief for a man who had been a father to them both. Yet their meeting had the wariness of former lovers. 'I feel frightened of invading you', he confessed when she had invited him to Graham's bedside. There was an awkwardness too in the final scene as Burne-Jones, highly charged at the loss of his friend and possessive to the last, insisted that his little sketches that had raised morale during William's last days should be buried with him in his coffin. Later when all had gone, Frances quietly returned and from her father's open coffin took one of the little paintings for herself. For she was no longer one of the artist's 'pets'. If he was to rekindle her friendship, it would be on her own terms and in her own time. By contrast the loss of Graham 'destabilised' Burne-Jones

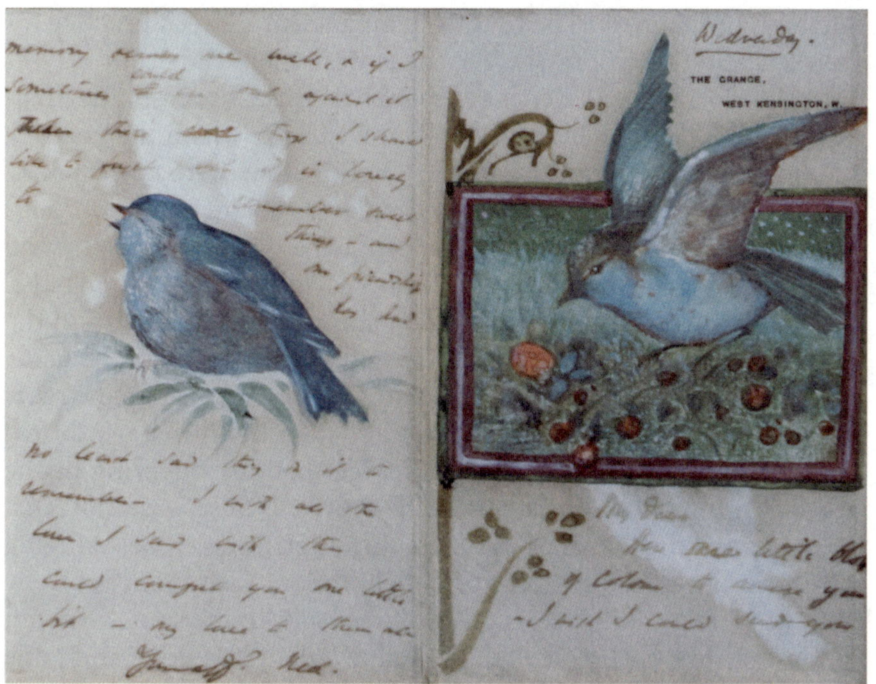

40.   *Illustrated letter sent to Frances, by Edward Burne-Jones*
'a little blob of colour to amuse you'

and intensified his desire for Frances: 'I wish you were back – I wish the old days were back – I want one more evening – just one'. Even he recognised that the rules of engagement had changed. 'I want to talk to you O so much but it was settled in heaven ages ago that that should never be'.[51] Still the sale of Graham's collection in April 1886 brought them closer. She shared his misery at the 'scattering of the pictures' and the loss of a remarkable artistic creation by patron, artist and muse. 'I want to mourn about it to you for a long time'.[52] And then later that month would come news of the death of Laura.

Now it was Frances that needed someone who would understand her grief. Determined to immortalise her dearest friend, she commissioned Burne-Jones to capture her spirit in a memorial tablet to hang in the church at Mells (figs 41, 42). Eight feet high, it would be a bas-relief in gesso – a new material for him and chosen for its permanence: 'durable as granite and enduring till Judgement Day'. Carving an effigy of a peacock with its tail descending flirtatiously to the floor, he claimed to be following an ancient Eastern practice for the deification of empresses. Peacocks were more classically a symbol of Immortality and hence reflected his refusal to accept the finality of Laura's death; hence too the laurel tree, on which the peacock perches, bursting out of the tomb.[53] By now they were corresponding regularly exchanging ideas and agreeing changes, almost subconsciously regaining the intimate language of friendship. 'It shall be as you say', he would promise; 'I won't do anything you don't like'. And he was quick to surrender when she corrected his Latin in the inscription. With Frances also resisting his desire to gild it, he had a rapid change of heart, claiming that, now 'I have worked up the relief of feathers elaborately … colour would flatten it, I think, my dear'.[54] Together they would laugh at his advice that any querying of the peacock motif should be quashed by a firm, if false, assertion that it was part of the 'Arms of the Lytteltons'. For Burne-Jones, longing to restore 'our ancient days', this collaboration, with Frances briefly assuming her father's role as patron, was balm to the soul. 'Oh I am so fond of this work and shall be hollow when it is done and gone away. I love doing it for you and for her but she won't come to me now'.[55]

*

As letters and sketches flowed back and forth between The Grange and Mells (fig. 40), Frances too came to appreciate what she had missed since her exile in Somerset. What emerged however was a very different relationship. For a start, marriage and distance meant that it would be predominately written and not face to face.[56] Moreover, for all Burne-Jones's longing for the *status quo ante*, their correspondence would not be plagued by the obsessiveness of love letters. On that Frances had been very clear. Such constraint freed up the full range of their mutual interests and over the next fifteen years Frances would – as muses do – inspire some of the artist's finest letters. Almost all the surviving correspondence is from him. After the Zambaco debacle he kept her replies under lock and key until he was ready to burn them. So apart from a few surviving letters from her, one has to read her thoughts from the regularity of certain themes and his reactions to her opinions. Still it is unlikely that he would have been so free with his thoughts and concerns if she had not been likewise. Together they created a private intuitive world founded on

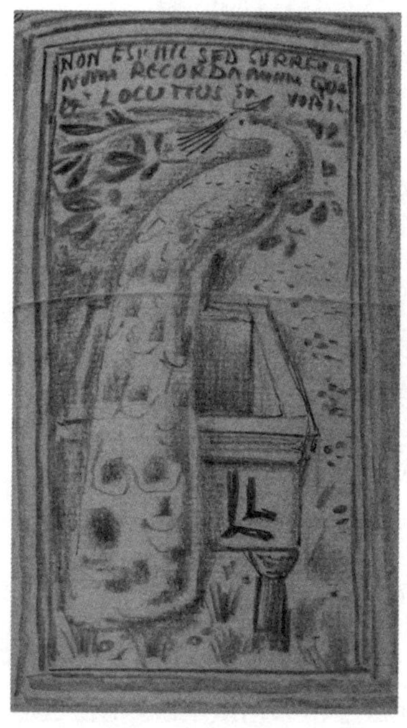

41.   *Burne-Jones's, preliminary sketch for the memorial tablet to Laura Lyttelton, née Tennant, inscribed 'something like this in plan, all gold except the peacock'*

42.   *The memorial tablet in St Andrew's Church, Mells*

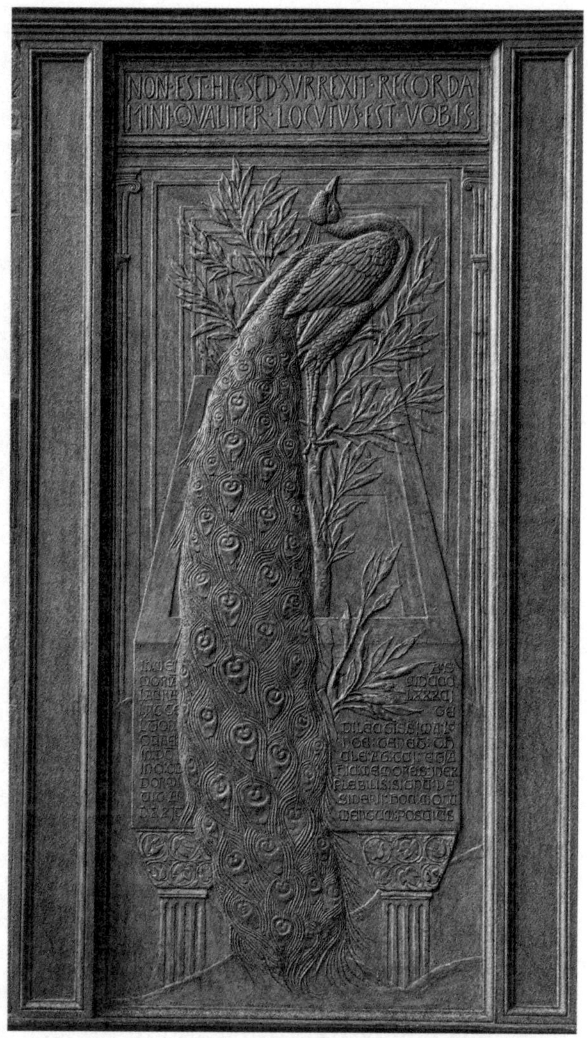

rock-sure trust and empathy. And, in the case of Burne-Jones, conducted in a flurry of thoughts, light and fast flowing 'like intimate breathless conversations overheard on the telephone'.[57]

What she wanted and got were the treasures that Burne-Jones had first given her back in 1873 – access to an idiosyncratic mind, fertile in its imagination, passion and human insight. If ever she bemoaned her lack of formal education, he would dismiss this out of hand: 'I never quite understood what you meant. Nobody is very much educated …and the encyclopaedic people are quite horrible'.[58]

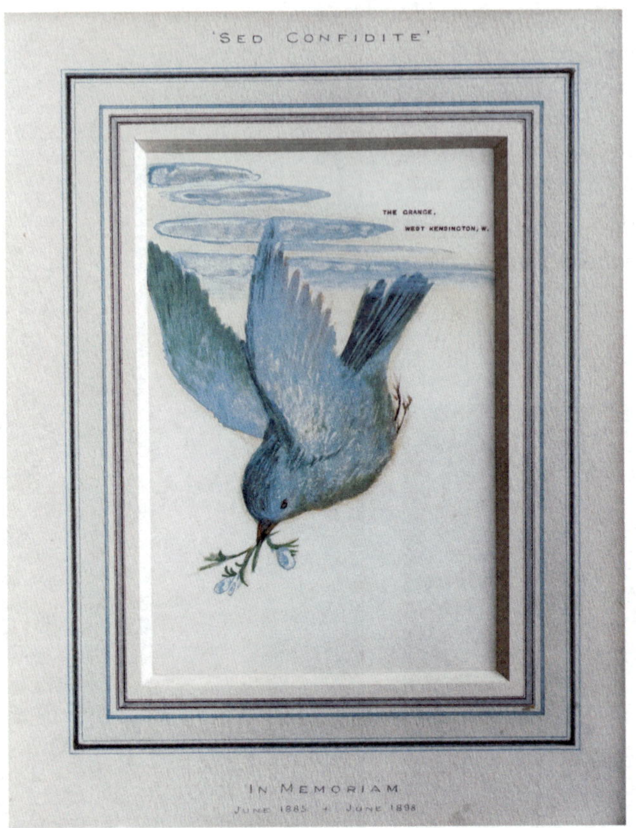

43.   *Illustrated letter from Burne-Jones to Frances,*
The mount, which Frances added later, reads 'In Memoriam, June 1885 + June
1898', the dates of death of her father and Burne-Jones

Then he would lead her off on another flight of fancy. They could talk about everything and nothing. The faces of sunflowers, the colours of days, the personalities of stones, and black poppies ('as handsome and terrible as Lucifer when the light he carried went out'). 'Do people act chemically on you?' he would suddenly ask. 'Can you talk to some people and be dumb before others?'[59] And all interspersed with vigorous discussions on learned matters such as the faith of the ancients that would see Burne-Jones talk of Damascus, Baghdad, and Iona in one breath.[60]

Not surprisingly, art figured prominently. Predictably they would discuss the latest exhibitions including his alerting her in 1889 to a new exhibition of 'Arts and Crafts' where among the 'nonsense are some beautiful things… [and the chance to] measure a bit the change that has happened in the last twenty years'. Two years later, he would be sharing her disappointment: 'so many poor imitations of me'. On a retrospective of his own work in 1892 he was quick to consult (and borrow from) her, partly perhaps because of her anger at his exhibiting of the cast of Laura's memorial without her permission in 1887.

To Frances he could let loose his despair at the developments of contemporary art and 'the rubbish ... about the beauty of unfinished works'. He would be no less sparing on his fellow artists: Holman Hunt was 'an Egotist [who] sees nothing but Hunt'. 'I can't make out why he ever wanted to paint or get up in the morning' was his dismissive verdict on his brother-in-law and President of the Royal Academy, Edward Poynter. Nor was much sympathy shown towards Leighton and his 'commonplace mind'. As for Sargent, 'the colour is often hideous [without] the faintest glimmer of imagination'.[61] Frances was well used to this. 'Of course anyone like Angelo never could live without fears and foreboding', she explained to a friend. 'But I think all artists must be like that. They hear the harmonies of life so to speak. But for us duller mortals it is given to be at ease sometimes in our hearts'.[61] Yet bolstering fragile egos didn't distract her instinct to judge. With an exhibition looming he asked her to London for her verdict on his latest work. 'If you say that they will not do, I must do them again' he declared bravely – 'but try to like them for I am very tired'.[63] In turn, he would find time to nurture her own artistic efforts, sending his assistant, Thomas Rooke ('the most timid, gentlest, littlest, meekest that ever didn't inherit the earth') to Mells to copy out his designs for her to embroider, along with much advice on colours and encouragement to use her instinct (fig. 44).[64] As Fiona McCarthy points out: 'they were not just friends but had for long been co-practitioners. An unbreakable bond lay not just in old affections but in the objects they had made together, Burne-Jones as the artist, Frances as his interpreter, embroidering and stitching, bringing his designs into tangible reality'.[65] Long unfashionable, needlework was nevertheless an art form that always attracted Burne-Jones and in Frances he recognised an artist of talent in her own right (figs 37, 45, 46).

All this was washed down with the tales she loved from the early days of the Pre-Raphaelites – of the heady excitements of Oxford, of Rossetti and Morris and how they later fell out over Janey. 'It was

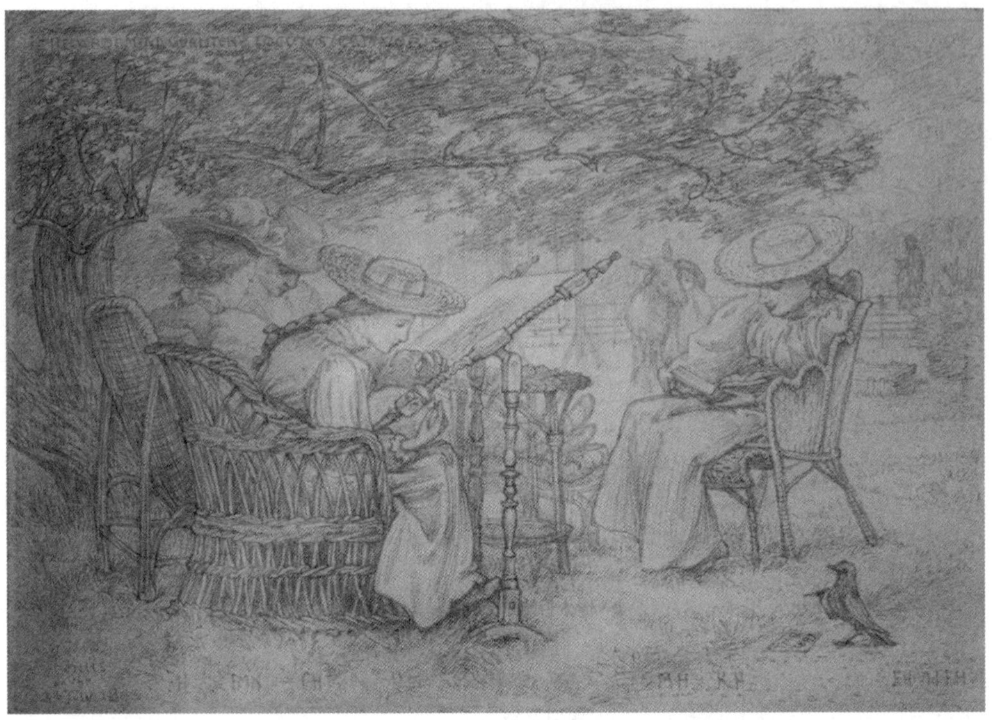

44.   'At Mells on 3rd July 1896, FH, [?EMN], CH, MH, KH', by Thomas Rooke

always G's [i.e. Rossetti's] fault, who loved to be unfair and next to a great love needed a great hatred', he would tell her. For all that Rossetti remained 'dear to me', 'Morris is too tied up in my past that I could disentangle'. Instead he related how they would meet for breakfast every Saturday and argue passionately all morning on matters as obtuse as 'why the medieval world was always on the side of the Trojans? [until late in the day when Morris] had to go his fat ways'.[66]

Just as passionate if less informed were Burne-Jones views on music. This was regarded as Frances's area of expertise. An early Wagnerian, she encouraged him to a performance of *Parsifal*. Despite the Albert Hall – 'it looked horrible' – being 'full of Bayreuth enthusiasts' – 'they were horrible. And yet I was conquered.'[67] Literature on the other hand was shared territory. This didn't stop him denouncing Tennyson for selling out. 'What abuse one used to hear of

Tennyson! What fights at college and school to get the least hearing. Till the *Idylls of the King* came they pretty well hated him. He wrote what they wanted and then they fussed.'[68] On her reading he could be quite proprietorial, directing her towards Le Fanu's *Uncle Silas* and the novels of Henry James, though he was forced to agree with her that while 'the execution is about perfect … it is all about infinitesimally little.'[69] As for his suggestion of the *Letters of Edward Fitzgerald*, who had made his name with the translation of Omar Khayam, she judged it 'a faint life, a mere ghost of one' and neither of them had any time for his famous aphorism that 'taste is the feminine of genius'.[70] That said, her enjoyment of *Tom Jones* was marred because 'it is much better than the novels that ladies write these days.' In turn her enthusiasm for Tolstoy's *Anna Karenina* exposed a raw nerve with Burne-Jones and later he would plead with her 'Don't send me Hardy's *Tess* because it ends miserably and I won't have nice girls hanged'. At such moments he would take refuge in Scott: '*Rob Roy* is perfect, perfect, PERFECT'. Scott was 'amongst the assured immortals and beyond criticism' because he captured an ancient nobility of language, ideals, humanity and setting and uncorrupted beauty that would be his lodestar. She grasped this too but she was open also to the romance found in Goethe. 'On Goethe, I salute but I pass on', was all he could manage in return.[71]

Just occasionally, among the comfort and complacency between old friends, was the capacity to surprise. Thus Frances was quite startled by his admission in 1890 that 'I wish I was a Catholic, I do'. The inspiration was a 'divine happy speech' by Cardinal Newman: 'two minutes long but ten centuries lovely'. Frances's evangelical roots ran deep, however much she would later pretend otherwise. Gradually she reined him back. Even so, the appeal remained strong. 'I have thought many times of what you have said about Newman and perhaps you are right…He might not affect me now; it was different when I was fifteen or sixteen and he taught me so much I do mind – things that will never be out of me. In an age of sofas and cushions he taught me to be indifferent to comfort; in an age of materialism he taught me to venture all on the unseen'; and all 'in a way that touched me – not scolding, nor forbidding nor much leading – walking with me a step in front'.[72]

As with many friendships, theirs was filled with the latest gossip and events – particularly treasured by Frances for whom Burne-Jones

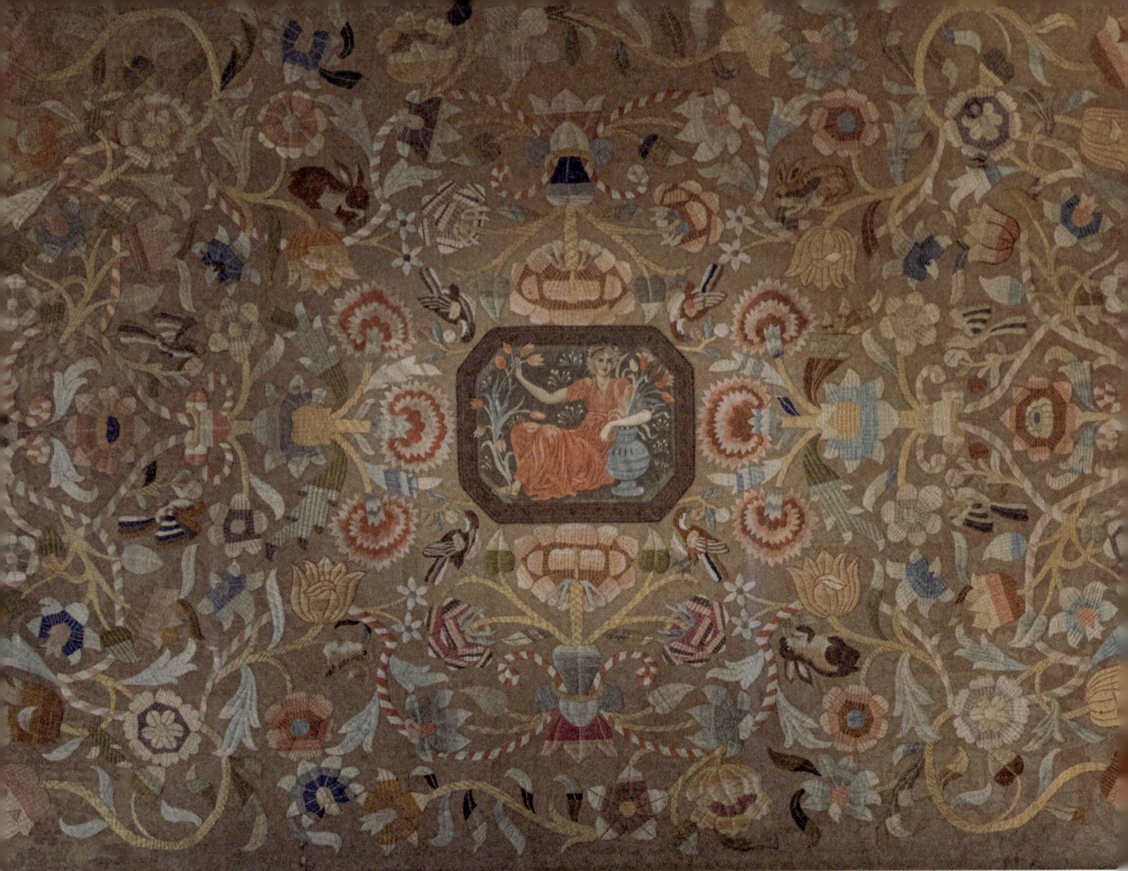

45.	*Embroidery for the drawing room overmantle, 'Flora', designed by Burne-Jones and stitched by Frances*

offered a rare lifeline into the world she had left behind. It was only through Rooke and his master that Frances heard some ten days afterwards of the destruction by fire of Clouds – the Wyndham house that had so caught the imagination on its completion barely four years before. Belatedly Burne-Jones filled her in on her child-hood friend, Mary Elcho's, frantic search for two of her children and their discovery safe and well. And how Mary's mother braved the flames to rescue the Old Master painting that they had bought at the Graham sale.[73] And then there were the great public occasions which Burne-Jones would attend 'under protest' such as Browning's funeral in Westminster Abbey.

People said to me 'How impressive'. I said, 'Yes indeed' – one has to in the world, but it wasn't, it was stupid, no candles, no incense, no copes, no nothing that was nice – placards all about saying 'Seats for The Press', 'Mourners', … I would have given something for a banner or two [or] a chorister [to] come out of the triforium and rent the air with a trumpet – how flat those English are … Why couldn't they leave him in Royal Venice?[74]

When reality failed to entertain, they would happily drift into fantasy. Burne-Jones liked to dream up 'map journeys' where 'I sleep often at Baghdad and Damascus and am to be found in Morocco'. These flights of fancy would soon include Frances. 'When we betake ourselves to the East I will do all the geography if you will do the cooking…I have a route already. We meet in Constantinople, and after there is one necklace of wonders till we come back to Damascus, the abode of peace. … Would this be a nice plan?'[75] Frances would indulge such escapism despite their implicit retreat into the past when she was still single. It is there also in the way he seeks to attribute to her his desire for the return of the child.

> Don't you a little bit wish you lived in a little house – and it was sweet and tiny, and didn't take any thought or waste any time, and were rather poor – only with pocket-money for books and toys – and no visitors – all friends living in the same street, and the street long and narrow and ending in the city wall, and the wall opening with a gate on to cornfields in the south, and the wild woods on the north – and no railways anywhere – all friends and all one's world tied up in the little city – and no news to come – only rumours and gossips at the city gate, telling things a month old and all wrong.[76]

But he was capable of more practical emotional support – understanding when she was in the throes of post-natal depression ('I knew you were worn out with the baby'). Ready too to listen when melancholy set in and left her railing against her rustic exile.[77] She in turn would lift him out of periodic gloom by saying 'something so funny and so merry and beguile me out of these pathetics – you would tease me out of it in three minutes and I should be screaming with laughter.' And she would be there for him too as his old friendships eroded. Having drifted apart from Morris over politics, at their breakfasts 'we are silent about much now and used to be silent about nothing'. He hadn't spoken to Ruskin for over a year. The marriage

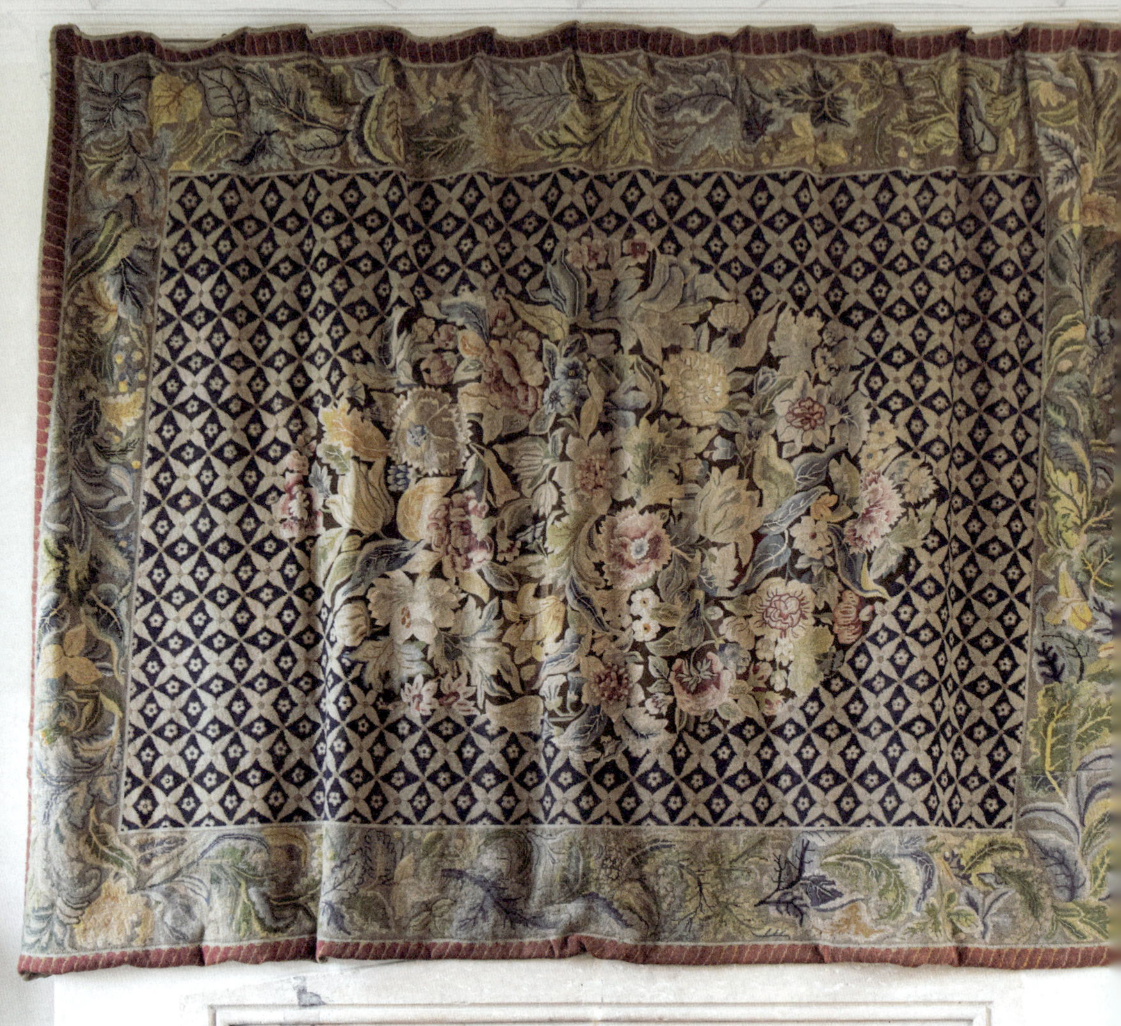

46. *Tapestry for the study overmantle, designed by Burne-Jones
and stitched by Frances*

of his much-loved daughter Margaret in 1888 rekindled old hurts of
loss and sacrifice. 'I wish you were here…I feel wild and crazy and if
you talked to me a bit of that happiest of times I [could find] peace
perhaps…I have had a bad time'. In need, she remained his 'sweetest
and dearest of friends'.[78]

*

'Hasn't ours been always a metaphysical friendship – independent
of sight and touch' he would claim – not very convincingly – as they
renewed their relationship. In 1884 he designed her 'a Magi picture…
if you like old men', before hurriedly adding '(and you can't, no you

can't and you are right)'.[79] The new arrangements did not come easily to him. Before her marriage 'I was so crazy and jealous of everybody; now [November 1886] I am quite good and can see the merits of people left and right – of Parry, and Benson, and all the Lytteltons and Liddell and Mony Mackenzie… and what work it took to train me, wasn't it?' Yet that same month he was writing to her how 'I long for you pretty much always'. And again: 'I think of you constantly – yes in spite of my vow to think of work only'. Nor did he fail to tell her whenever she appeared in his dreams: 'I cried myself awake the other night about you'. 'I would never misuse you in a dream – never', he would protest. Rather she was 'always divine' and untouchable – 'quite beautiful, and always right and always splendid and celestial' – to be 'worshipped completely'. This in time gave way to more disturbing behaviour. He admitted to suffering 'silent tortures' over her 'men friends'. So desperate was he to see her, 'will it bore you', he asked, 'if I come then [at 7.30pm]? Shall you be "dressing"? I would sit on the mat outside and talk to you most discreetly'. Once he sought to meet her train on its arrival in London only to lack the courage to speak and so watched in the crowd as she was driven home. When particularly gloomy, he would go to the Horners' old house in Grosvenor Place and 'look up at the bower window and grow sick at all I have had and lost'.[80]

What did Frances think on the apparent return of what Burne-Jones called his 'ancient troubles'? Seemingly very little. Distance allowed her to view such extravagance of phrase and sentiment as a pastiche of courtly love and very 'BJ'. And no doubt it remained very flattering to be so wooed by the leading artist of the day and in her eyes a genius. It is possible that she indulged his fantasy a little and played the game. Why else would she fear in 1890 lest one of her replies – lost in transit – should fall into the hands of the press?[81] Yet she was never remotely serious. Much more telling was that in November 1891 Burne-Jones discovered that she had been in London for two weeks and had never contacted him.

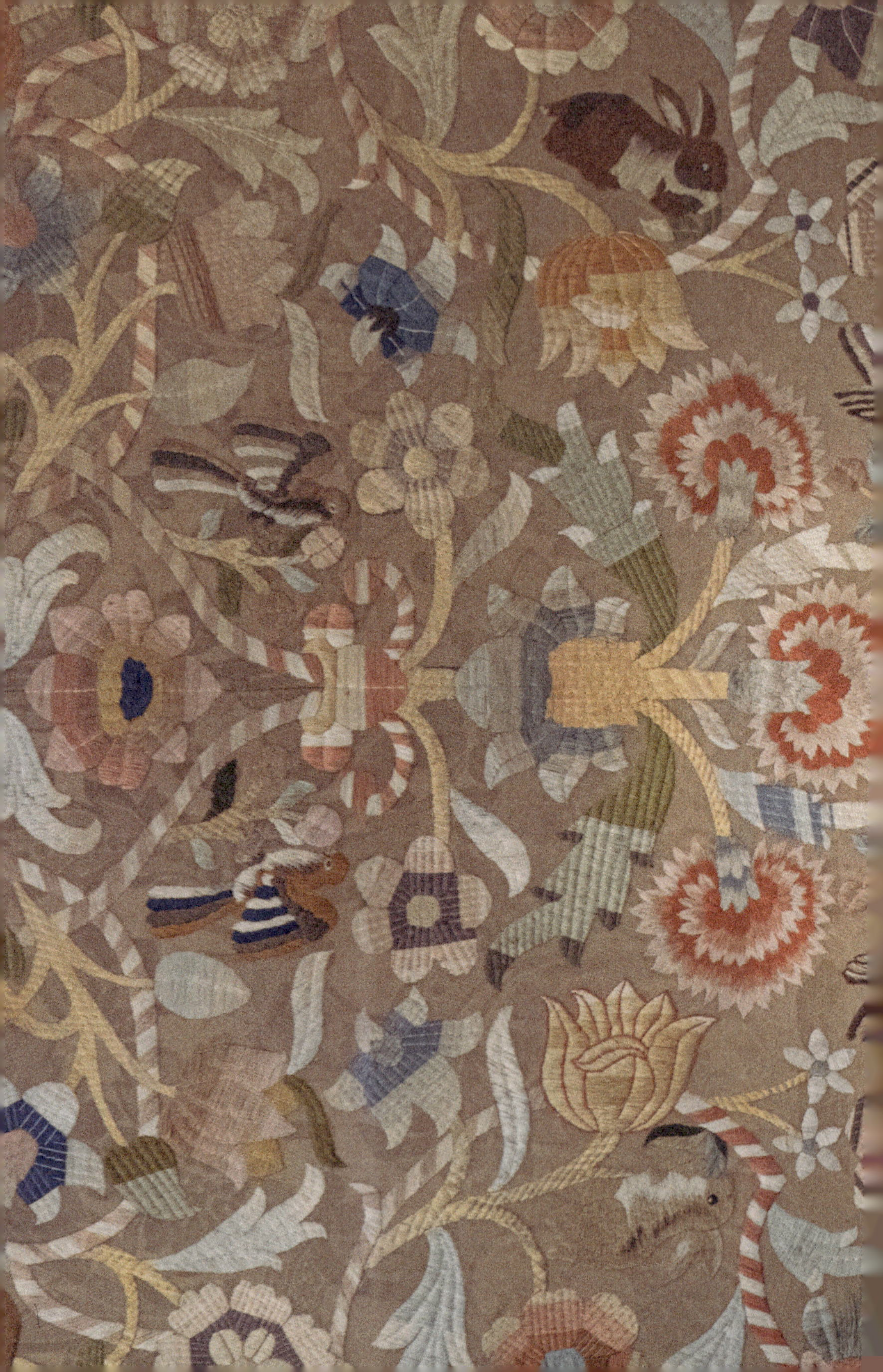

Part Four

Making an Entrance

Women like [Margot Asquith] or Frances Horner were able to disregard conventions, which men accepted as laws of nature, to break down the barriers that separated the various groups, and being, as they were, more flexible and therefore more adventurous than their male contemporaries, they introduced new ideas, new books, new activities and even new and rather pretentious pencil games after dinner – above all they provided an infusion of new life and new blood.

Mark Bonham Carter[1]

It is so strange to me how I have emancipated myself from ancient allegiances – here are both Doll and Ken [Mackenzie] whom I used to slave for and yield to, and mind instantly what they thought or did – and now I just smile to myself and let them pass and I really don't much mind whether they approve or disapprove – this sounds horrid and fickle.

Frances Horner to DD Lyttelton[2]

47.   *Detail of the drawing room overmantle embroidery, 'Flora'*

MAKING HER WAY AMONG SOULS

There was no reserve, no restraint, no holy places kept sacred

Mary Gladstone[3]

In late 1892, Burne-Jones received a telegram from the celebrated actress, Ellen Terry. To his chagrin, she was not after him but Frances, or rather her address. 'Why does she think I should know?' he bristled. Then teasing Frances, he claimed to have written back 'that tomorrow you will be at Mells and on Sunday at Longleat, on Monday at Panshanger, and Tuesday at Cavendish Square and Wednesday at Ashridge, and Thursday at Green Street and Friday at Bracknell and Saturday at Sloane St and Sunday at Wilton, Monday at Mells and Tuesday at Clouds... Was that right or have I misled her?'[4] As a tease, it was not without its truth. Frances was soon making her mark on local society, winning over the grandees such as the Earl of Pembroke. 'I could like Pembroke if I was not jealous of him', lamented the artist, as the proximity of Wilton to Mells provided Frances a lifeline of entertainments and people 'before the days of motors'. Ironically, it was her connection to Burne-Jones that was opening aristocratic doors in rustic Somerset. Even George Horner was briefly won over.[5] Soon the autumn would be dedicated to shooting parties at Longleat, Ashridge, Wilton and Stanway, the Elchos' house in Gloucestershire. Then from January until the end of May she might escape to London where her mother would take a house, before returning to Mells for the summer and numerous house parties. What would transport her however to the height of fashionable society would be The Souls.[6]

Numbering barely three dozen, they were a group largely of aristocratic young people, with four landed families (Wyndham, Balfour, Charteris, and Grenfell) supplying over half the membership. While

George Pembroke and Arthur Balfour (fig. 48) were wealthy, most (like George Curzon and George Wyndham) had yet to inherit and some like Alfred Lyttelton and Harry Cust had to work for their living. What they all had in common was what Balfour called a 'natural affinity' – a shared outlook on the world, a quickness of humour and the camaraderie of good friends. But what brought them together into an identifiable set were the Tennant girls. As with most things, it all began with Laura – or so Margot claimed. Laura's death in May 1886 so shocked her friends that 'none of us were keen

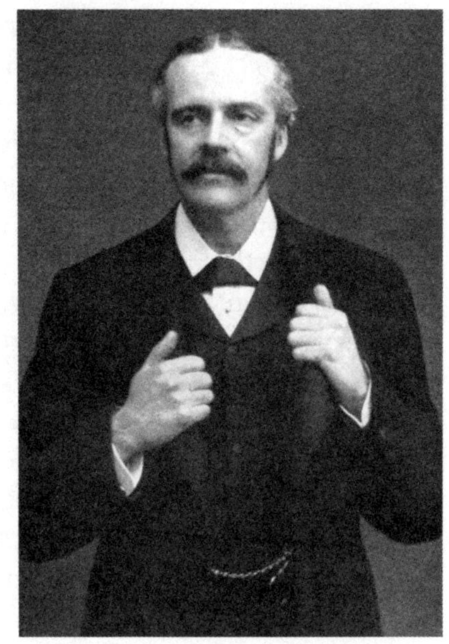

48.   Arthur Balfour

about going into Society after she died. But being devoted to one another we constantly met'.[7]

This devotion had earlier roots, not least in the 'tremendous commotion' of Laura and Margot's arrival in Society. 'They were quite unlike anyone that London had ever seen before – many were startled and most were delighted', remembered Mary Elcho, for 'the two girls were astonishing'. Still it would take two years and much 'social courage' (including brazenly catching the Prince of Wales's eye at Ascot) before the girls were accepted.[8] The issue was not that they were daughters of commercial wealth, but rather what Frances called 'the strange surprisingness of the Tennant lives and ways'. Mary Gladstone was equally taken aback, when visiting Glen, the Tennants' house in the Borders; but was enthralled too at 'the reck-lessness of manners and talk. There was no reserve, no restraint, no holy places kept sacred…at meals you tore through subject after sub-ject with the rapidity of lightning; retort, repartee, contradictions, capping flew across the table with a constant accompaniment of shrieks and peals of laughter'.[9] At the same time, two of the Souls, Mary Elcho and Ettie Grenfell (fig. 49), had acquired grand houses in which they all could gather. Edith ('Ettie') Fane, who became Lady

Desborough in 1905, gained Taplow through her marriage to Willie Grenfell in 1887 and later in 1913 Panshanger through her grandfather, 6th Earl Cowper. Vitally the expansion of the railway now made weekending from London viable.[10] Nevertheless, it was Margot who was the catalyst and whose energy, *joie de vivre* and determination forged them together into 'the Gang'.

None of this would have registered beyond the fragmentation of London Society that was already well in train as it numbers approached four thousand.[11] At its head remained the 'smart set' around the Prince of Wales, where the higher aristocracy and raffish plutocrats could mingle at Marlborough House.[12] Here the traditional rituals prevailed. Week-long shooting or racing parties, immensely formal dinners, regimented conversation, giving way in time to card games on which vast sums would be wagered and lost; and all washed down with the occasional full-blown scandal. By comparison, most Souls viewed such displays of wealth as vulgar, preferring to value intelligence and wit over social class and gender. Their houses could be quite frugal both in their furnishing and their table. As for dress, 'The Souls dressed with a kind of aesthetic smartness all of their own'.[13] Rather than racing, they preferred hunting, and even more so tennis, cycling and golf in Scotland at North Berwick.[14] Instead of baccarat and bridge they preferred talk on art, philosophy, poetry and literature and being open with their feelings, if entertainingly so. Literary tastes included contemporary novels by Edith Wharton and especially Henry James, as well as the classics of the nineteenth-century novel. While everyone could quote Shakespeare, with most of the men classical scholars, there was great admiration for Gilbert Murray's translations of Greek drama.[15] In art, their enthusiasm for the avant-garde would see Balfour commissioning Burne-Jones's *Perseus* series and Percy Wyndham John Singer Sargent's *The Wyndham Sisters*. Likewise the Souls would patronise modern architects such as Lutyens[16] and Detmar Blow, while the Wyndhams' Clouds was the iconic home of the age.

Above all, they like to talk and debate themes, great and small. For them the art lay in 'general conversation' – whole table talk rather than whispered discussion with those to your left and right. The dinner table became a stage. Scathing of anecdotage, they preferred the fast interchange of wit and argument. Harry Cust, editor of the *Pall Mall Gazette*, was held 'the unchallenged leader of the dinner table. Quip, retort, repartee, quotation, allusion, epigram, jest – all flashed with lightning-like speed from that active workshop, his brain'.[17] This was quite revolutionary in High Society, not least with women participating as equals. At Wilton, when not flirting with Charty Ribblesdale, the retired Indian administrator, Sir Alfred Lyall, set a debate running on whether a man lost or gained by marriage. A 'splendid conversation ensued', recounted Frances in which 'Charty

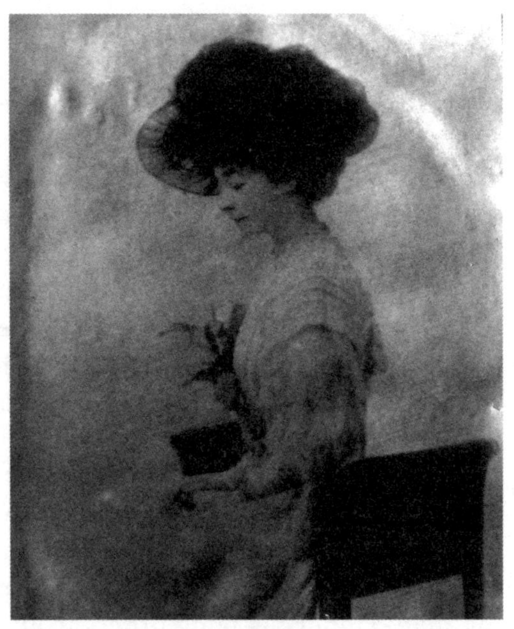

49.   *Ettie Grenfell*

and I sustained against the table that he gained'. Alongside the cut and thrust of debate, which she clearly relished, was also the thrill of participation and a nascent sense of liberation.[18]

Another distinctive feature of gatherings of the Souls was their obsession with after-dinner games: Charades, Telegrams, 'Clumps' were general. Others were more specific to houses. The Tennants liked essays on X in the style of Y; and more embarrassing character sketches which could get quite pointed. This could be very competitive company. Speed was the essence at Taplow, and general hilarity at Stanway. But all of these games required considerable intellectual confidence and knowledge of literature, history and languages – a version of Scrabble was played in French and German. 'It is such fun staying here', wrote Laura Tennant from Stanway. 'We quarrel about everything – we talk up to the top of our bent… We play games and the piano. We none of us open a book or write a letter. We scribble and scrawl and invent words and language and reasonless rhymes'. Such prowess among women as well as the men made this intimidating company for most. It wasn't easy for those who were shy or self-conscious; or simply young and inexperienced and fearful of appearing foolish. The character games were 'more dangerous', Margot admitted, and once out of hand required 'fine training' and control of temper, especially on subjects that were sacred. Mary Elcho's maxim was that 'light subjects should be treated seriously and serious subjects lightly'. Again this was easier among friends.[19]

None of this would have mattered if the Souls hadn't been so prominent politically. Ironically they rarely discussed politics. At the height of the Irish Home Rule controversy with political debate ugly, even violent, the Souls prided themselves as being cross-party where Liberals such as Asquith and Haldane could mix freely with Balfour and the Tories. Ideologically they were pragmatists, offering little beyond a complacent acceptance of the landed order and belief in Empire. Yet in an age when political office was regarded as the highest accolade, George Wyndham spoke for many of his friends in confessing to be possessed 'by that monster, ambition'. In the 1880s, as Irish Chief Secretary, Balfour had established himself as the coming man. Under his wing others would come into office and by the time he became Prime Minister in 1902, his cabinet included five Souls and another, George Curzon, had been appointed Viceroy of India. All of which made the Souls public, glamorous and ripe for criticism.[20]

Balfour resented the charge of the Souls being an exclusive set as 'ludicrous', maintaining that they were 'a spontaneous and natural growth, born of casual friendship and unpremeditated sympathy'. Their visitors' books were filled with an array of writers, artists, actors, and others of the moment – none of whom were Souls. Yet the impression of exclusivity was reinforced when a mock exam paper on 'gang language' was leaked to the press. It was resented that they made a virtue of not following 'the rules of the social game'. They also revelled too obviously in their intellectual superiority over a philistine and staid Court – to whom the Souls appeared insufferably pretentious. Notwithstanding this, Daisy Warwick, one-time lover of the Prince of Wales, was particularly generous in her verdict: 'they were clever and well-read, and exercised a great influence on London Society for five or six years. I think they sent us all back to reading more that we would otherwise have done, and this was an excellent thing for us'.[21] Her prince was less impressed, dismissing Balfour as 'an effeminate creature mixed up in the Souls'. Asquith's daughter would later confront such hostility: 'thanks to the Souls,' she declared, 'it was no longer fashionable to be dull'.[22] Through them, it became acceptable to talk about serious things – history, art, literature – frivolously. Yet therein lay their flaw. It was all too much of a game to make an impact beyond fashionable Society. Admittedly it was not a role they sought. As Beatrice Webb in 1892 judged, the Souls 'were good to look on … with the exquisite deference and ease which constitutes good breeding' but with a 'vain restlessness of tickled vanity. One would become quickly satiated'. The one who did stand out for her was 'Lady Horner'.[23]

*

In the charmed consanguinity of the Souls Frances was at the outset an outsider, but not completely. She had known Mary Wyndham, later Elcho, as a child through their parents' shared enthusiasm for the Pre-Raphaelites. Having been denied the Season, the connection had withered with time. It was music and Mary Gladstone that had brought her into contact with Arthur Balfour and the Lytteltons in the 1870s. However Rutherford's wooing of May Lyttelton had left Balfour ever wary of Frances. A decade on and Laura Tennant would be startled to hear Balfour include the philandering Sir Charles Dilke and Frances in the same sentence on the frailties of men and women.[24] Without her marriage to Jack she would never have been acceptable in the aristocratic core of this circle. However poor they were, she was attached to an ancient landed family with estates dating from the Reformation, and had a house to entertain in. And it was the Horners' long-standing friends such as George Pembroke who would first include her in events at nearby Wilton. Thereafter it would be in the slip-stream of her close friends, Laura and Margot Tennant, that she would eventually secure her entrée into what became the Souls.

On the other hand, Frances had much to offer. Crucial to her appeal was a lasting fascination among the Souls with the muse of Burne-Jones. He was the artist that they all admired. Their houses had Pre-Raphaelites on the walls and Balfour commissioned the *Perseus* series for which Frances had indeed modelled. The artist's passion for Frances thus gave her an aura which belied mere prettiness and undoubtedly attracted the Souls. As they quickly learnt, Frances's appeal was not just decorative. In company that placed such store on intelligence and learning, she was more than capable of holding her own. For all her lack of formal education, she was as well read as any and at home as much with the canon of English literature as she was with Goethe's verse and the works of Schopenhauer. Clever, learned minds she found 'fertilising' and would seek them out, even if, like the historian J. A. Froude, they had ' a very cold, grey mind'. Nor was she a 'blue stocking', too intellectual to relish the light-hearted, often heartless 'badinage' of the Souls. Once inside, she led from the front. 'Frances is with us, fresh and vigorous as ever and so splendid to look at,' Margot was soon reporting back to Harry Cust, and already 'a great success at Panshanger'. In turn she would now have to make a success of Mells.[25]

Mells Park was far from convenient – the night train making weekending from London only just possible. On the other hand the house was big enough and with Soane's library (fig. 34), the drawing room and dining room boasted rooms of considerable grandeur, even if the fittings were distinctly shabby. More worrying, it relied on a 'beastly old well' and Doll was not the only one to complain of stomach bugs.[26] Nor could it match the Jacobean attraction of nearby Stanway or the latest luxury of Taplow Court or the historic grandeur of Panshanger which Ettie would inherit. Yet the Souls could be quite disparaging about Ettie's extravagance. Stanway was a favourite retreat despite being famously uncomfortable and cold with ancient furnishings on which the dust lay thick. By contrast, Frances would betray her roots by making sure her house was clean and the food good (a rarity in Souls households). For she and her sisters had been well trained by their mother in the arts of running a household – a skill she held vital if they were to marry well and in the case of Frances a skill well-honed on the Grahams' annual excursions to Scotland. Frances was never in doubt that it was 'the host or hostess who make or mar [a party] – not what is on the table, nor even the chairs and certainly not what is on the walls.'[27] Although, discreetly she would pay close attention to all three.

More importantly, she had a clear idea of what appealed to her guests. After 'plunging into all the best that London had to give – art, politics, and society', coming to Mells would be 'like taking a deep bath in the country, remote, old-world and feudal, with all the charm that lack of wealth can give a place'. Consequently, making a virtue out of a necessity, she kept things relaxed and informal with very few servants. 'What mainly distinguished the atmosphere at

Mells', remembered one guest, 'was the extraordinary nonchalance – Frances Horner had a wonderful capacity, while appearing herself a rather busy and slightly worried hostess, of inducing the rest of the household to take things as they came'.[28] In a class-ridden society rigid with hierarchy and protocol, Mells became to its devotees a release. Invariably such a carefree atmosphere took considerable planning behind the scenes, from whom to invite to the invention of the latest game. But it was her ability to relate to anybody that put everyone at their ease. 'I was quite prepared to detest Mrs Horner and I have ended up loving her' wrote a young Emily Lytton, terrified at the cynical company she found herself in: Mrs Horner [is] 'a perfect hostess, so kind, so natural, so amusing and altogether delightful'. Her great friend DD Balfour declared her 'one of the world's best companions, witty, gay, provocative, social. She had a strange kind of Pre-Raphaelite beauty which was not for all tastes, but her charm was felt by all kinds of people'.

In such a competitive gathering, many felt they could confide in Frances. Margot called her 'more like a sister to me than anyone outside my family'. 'Few women as well endowed with heart, head, temper and temperament as Frances Horner. With most women the impulse to crab is greater than to praise, and grandeur of character is surprisingly absent from them; but Frances Horner comprises the best in my sex'. She had always been good at making girl-friends and much experience at dealing with difficult men. Vitally for her it was an interest and not a duty. Thus at Panshanger in a debate on what gave the greatest pleasure, while Margot said hunting, Frances simply said 'people'.[29]

Hence she was willing to work at relationships, seeking to understand as much as to judge, even when pushed to the edge by some of her friends. Charty Ribblesdale, sister of Laura and Margot, with whom Frances went on numerous expeditions on the continent, was certainly attractive company: tall, willowy, with 'gleaming golden hair', vivacious, often outrageous and fun-loving. Yet she could be utterly self-centred and unreliable. Frequently Frances found herself having to bite her tongue. 'Dear Charty: I believe that unconsciousness is part of her charm – only sometimes it makes one sigh for [her] coldness'.[30] Her sister Margot, one of Frances's oldest friends, could crash through the sensitivities of others in the name of candour. Some of her utterances ('Margots') were too (unintentionally) comical to hurt: 'Ettie is an ox, she will be turned into Bovril when she dies'; of Henry James, 'his mind went to his head'. More often her tactlessness would cause 'a good many jars and jangles'. Frances loved the exhilarating independence in her friend but winced when Margot and Violet Granby[31] entertained country house parties with 'skirt dancing'; otherwise known as the cancan that had thrilled Margot when she saw a performance at the Folies Bergère in 1893. Loyally she drew a comparison between the Margot living 'eagerly in the glare of publicity' and the private Margot with her 'splendid generosity…and absence of all mean or jealous thoughts'.[32]

Frances would be just as loyal when Harry Cust found himself facing public disgrace. Nor would she join in the mocking of Ettie's relentlessly 'sparkling, radiant side,' which Frances chose to take at face value: 'She has much finer and rarer qualities than most of them, I think'. As a result of such generosity, all felt happy to dwell under Frances's spell. 'You are one of my most precious possessions', acknowledged Margot, one 'who has never been vexed with any of my failings'. In a doggerel celebration of the Souls delivered to an exclusive gathering at the Bachelor Club on 9 July 1889, Curzon gave the formal declaration of approval: 'If the Horners you add/Then a man must be mad/ Who complains that the Gang is a wrong sort'.[33]

Just as well because for some reason the Horners were not present at the feast. For all her popularity, Frances never quite lost her insecurity amid a world into which she had not been born.[34] 'I love her', she admitted of Charty, 'so dearly I always want to feel her hold me tighter – but I think I am morbid about that – I'd rather be squeezed to death than be let go of'. Therein lay the rub – a constant fear of being dropped.[35] That it was not her natural world she noted on a hot afternoon at Panshanger when strolling the grounds with the retired Indian administrator, Sir Alfred Lyall. She liked him exceedingly: 'He is rather a spectator now but has a good storing background of action and work in his life which gives the interest that sometimes is a little lacking in this highly aristocratic society – delightful as it is'. The hurried afterthought could not quite disguise her middle-class disquiet at the idle complacency of the leisured classes. Later, after falling in with Curzon, she owned to 'I'm not a great admirer of George Curzon… I never much care for the cast of his mind or his way of looking at things, but he is very light and easy'. Yet he was not above loudly querying whether the Souls were getting infiltrated by the middle classes, or in his dismissive name, 'Cosquiths'.[36] His targets may have been Asquith and Haldane, two young Liberal lawyers and her good friends, but this was a vulnerability she shared. As when a gleeful Blanche Dugdale regaled her sister-in-law, Betty Balfour,[37] on what can only have been an excruciating scene for Frances:

> Lady Ribblesdale [Charty] talking of a Peacock said it was a voluptuous bird, at which old Mrs Graham [Frances's mother] took exception and said 'that word beginning with a V ought not be mentioned'. I stood up for it and said it is what we would all be if we knew how, on which the old lady nearly fainted, and Lady Ribblesdale screamed with laughing, and asked the dear old soul if she would like to be [it] if she knew how, and then there was a rapid proposal that a class should be formed and a Professor found (Lady Ribblesdale proposing Swinburne) to teach us the way in which to walk. Wild nonsense but so refreshing I felt inclined to walk around the room on my head.[38]

Other insecurities, however banal, exposed raw nerves: such as her age and the anxiety as she approached forty over her declining 'Pre-Raphaelite' looks. Not only were many Souls women ten years younger, but Frances's hair had gone grey after the trauma of Edward's birth.[39] Spiritually too her foundations were being eroded by the agnosticism of her new friends. After all even Balfour had struggled to defend the faith in his *In Defence of Philosophic Doubt* – 'King Arthur' who all Souls looked upon in awe, but who in Frances's revealing phrase, would never be more than 'the very close friend of all my friends'.[40]

Nevertheless when in Scotland she would draw upon what Margot called 'social courage' to call in on Whittinghame, the Balfour estate in Scotland, to pay homage. Such anxieties were, after all, but the price she paid to have the life she had set her heart on. Now 'a sudden brilliant company' could descend on Mells. They 'talked all at once all day and all the next day' before driving through fog to Longleat where they found Pembroke and four Wyndhams: 'Four Wyndhams! I think four is a little too much, even of the best'. Now too she could escape Mells after the Tenants' Ball and dine the next night in London with Burne-Jones and Charty. The following afternoon would see her at a private concert with Wyndhams, Pembrokes,

Trees and Beerbohm,[41] before going on later to the Opera: 'the whole house lined with countesses and duchesses in tiaras and everyone a bouquet … and talking just a little loud which is the inevitable effect of London, I think'. Later she would reminisce: 'many were the feasts we attended. We were young, we were merry, we were very, very wise; all sorts of celebrities were guests, but Charty Ribblesdale, Margot Tennant and I were amongst the women at most of them'. 'So you see I am not stagnating', she would write to her husband after a play with Arthur Balfour and Burne-Jones as companions. On another night, after accompanying Harry Cust to the theatre, she admitted 'London is rather delicious: full of delicious little notes and cards and people wanting you and I have enjoyed even this peep'. But 'it will be fun to give you a hug again and I hope you are missing me'. Rutherford Graham's little sister had arrived.[42]

~ 15 ~

'NEW MORALITY', NEW WOMEN?

It is a theory of the 'Souls', and a delightful one, that the two sexes can associate without any thoughts of earthly sentiments or any social danger.

'The New Morality'[43]

It was only a matter of time before the Souls became a highlight of dinner-table gossip and newspaper columns. By 1888 Lord Charles Beresford's famous jibe was doing the rounds: 'You all sit and talk about each other's souls. I shall call you the Souls'.[44] The name stuck and the hunt was on to reveal the secrets of a sect 'as liberal in its views as it is exclusive in its composition'. Inevitably there was mockery of their self-importance and much play on what made a Soul. This title the Gang happily embraced (despite later denials) and did not shy from holding ostentatious dinners in their name. Frances, however, could not resist taking up the challenge of definition. With DD Balfour, she produced 'The New Morality', a parody penned anonymously in 1890 and strictly for internal consumption. Some like Pembroke were quick to recognise Frances's hand (and indeed many of his ideas) as well as her purpose. For all that it was intended to entertain, 'The New Morality' was a manifesto for the Souls as she wanted them to be.[45]

Like a true Pre-Raphaelite, Frances first posed the Souls as a reaction against 'these days of rank materialism'. Then, rejecting the charge of exclusivity, she insisted that they would 'welcome prose-lytes from every class, for stupidity is the only disability'. Admittedly the Souls were 'a chosen band, a peculiar people' combining 'the spiritualism of Augustine with the apolausticism [sic] of a Rubilius'; as if that made them any more inclusive.[46] Predictably, all critics were dismissed as 'disappointed aspirant[s], to their ranks'. Denying any 'lofty ideals', Souls shunned the traditional vows of poverty, chastity and obedience. Instead they were as 'moral as their neighbours', even if atypically their dinner parties were devoted to 'mundane ethics such as: the morality of infidelity, the intellectual disadvantages of monogamy, the existence of the soul'. In these, wit would outplay wisdom, and 'frankness [carried] almost to excess'. Then pandering to the suspicions of conspiracy, she confirmed they were a secret society operating 'under the thin disguise of reading-classes, as feminine and mysterious in their character as ancient rites'. An elect band, moreover, who 'have invaded many of the statelier houses of England', on a mission to 'raise the tone of an aristocratic society'. Already 'useless conventions' are discarded, nothing is done 'for the sake of appearances', chaperones 'abolished', and 'shooting parties [made] intellectual'. By their heroic efforts 'they have rescued us from the dullness of respectable society and from the depravity of [the] fast life'.

Written very much tongue in cheek, 'The New Morality' was froth and nonsense to tickle the self-esteem of her friends. The Souls were far too pleased with themselves to bother with reforming others – respectable or otherwise. Nevertheless, for someone like Frances – merchant class married to country gentry – the Souls were unusual because they opened up opportunities for clever women that class would normally have denied. This would be true for many of the women in the Souls – Laura and Margot, and DD Balfour were all offspring of businessmen. Because it mattered, they would turn what might have been a casual gathering of friends into something apparently more substantial and influential. And this explains why they seemed more concerned over exclusivity than some who were born into it. It is they too who make the Souls 'feminine and mysterious'.

The public focus on Balfour and his male acolytes disguised the fact that the Souls were almost entirely run by women. They determined the parties, designed the entertainments for the weekend, bonded the group with their correspondence, set its rules and kept its rituals, arranged its assignations, and where necessary supported their friends in their public life. It is they who discovered the new writers and artists, and embraced the new cultural fashions. On them fell the task of devising the parlour games and not surprisingly they encouraged activities in which both sexes could partake. At their table there would be no segregation of sexes, no men staying behind with the port. They even considered establishing their own paper, to be entitled 'Eve' (Frances had suggested 'She') to be subtitled 'A Woman's Journal for Men', Nor was it a surprise that Frances should be the driving force behind 'The New Morality'. 'Lady Horner was a woman of great gifts, having the brains, energy and high spirits which are essential for anyone if they are to hold a central position among a group of men and women', wrote one observer.[47] More than that, she cared. Widely regarded as the 'High Priestess of the Souls', she was a keen guardian of its rituals (and some of its secrets too).[48]

To appreciate how unusual this was, one needs to recognise the obstacles women had to overcome to participate in Society, which was male dominated, preferring its women to be beautiful, sensible, loving, loyal and largely silent. What passed for humour was 'crude and heavy chaff' which could degenerate into bullying and humiliation. In this intimidating atmosphere women's lives were governed by a host of conventions designed to keep their reputation intact. Not speaking until spoken to, always being chaperoned, not referring to a man by his first name or putting a hand on his arm, not drying newly washed hair before the morning room fire in case men walked in, no mixed swimming. Loud laughter was frowned upon. Dinners were formal, ritualised and with no general talking until the ladies left. This is what the Souls broke down. At table conversation was general and after dinner, 'games' were riotous, 'openly funny and intellectually competitive'. More to the point here was company in which women 'interrupted, laughed gleefully and capped men and each other'.[49]

Frances revelled in this role. At Wilton she once led a discussion on which of the traditional virtues should be eliminated. 'Truth was done for as a virtue which no moral being attempted to practise. Hope was declared a tiresome weak-minded thing. Faith followed as a gift you either possessed without effort or were wrong to cultivate. Charity was left grudgingly. Mrs Horner wanted to do away with Justice but Lord Pembroke clung to it'. For Frances the key to the New Morality was the validity of freethinking women. For her, 'independence of mind … [was] a gift from the Gods'.[50] But how far did that relate not only to society at large but to the institution of marriage? How far could independence of the mind translate into independence of action? As a young woman Frances had been fiercely protective of her freedom. The constraints of marriage, however well known, had still come as a shock. 'Frances might have done anything' declared Laura in her open letter on the eve of her wedding. And both had been determined that marriage would not be 'the end of womanism'.[51]

*

'We have almost given up going about together this year!' Frances confessed to DD. In addition to escaping to London, every September she would leave Jack and the children to join Pembroke on his yacht sailing in the Western Isles. In 1890 she also went with Charty on a continental jaunt ending in Bavaria with Oberammergau. Frances did invite Jack but at a time she knew he couldn't do, for she was determined that they should have no male escorts. This would be a girls' trip, very independent for the times, with much laughter, the occasional scrape and even a proposal. On her return 'I hardly dare look Jack in the face', she confided to DD: 'I feel such a light woman, for I have got to join the yacht next week.' Guilt had its limits. Because Jack is 'very angry', Pembroke noted, 'She thinks he really doesn't mind much, which is subtle.' While Society may have deemed such carefree behaviour a dereliction of duty, it was 'a theory of the "Souls", and a delightful one, that the two sexes can associate without any thoughts of earthly sentiments or any social danger'. That men and women, whether married or not, could be very close friends – sharing thoughts and feelings and secrets without succumbing to sex was certainly 'novel'. To pull this off would take mutual respect, considerable restraint and occasionally things left unsaid. Still it was hugely attractive to women surviving in a condescending and predatory male world. In the same spirit it allowed women to lunch, shop, attend concerts, visit men [and vice versa] without their husbands.[52]

The advocate for such thinking among the Souls was George Pembroke. Very tall at 6′6″, he was striking, scholarly, and the heir to large estates. To Frances, he looked the beau ideal of an aristocrat. And yet, after a youthful expedition to the South Seas and a desultory stint in parliament, his public life disappeared amid the chains of his inheritance. He was never robust. He suffered in health 'from his great height', was Frances's quirky assessment 'but he had personal beauty and charm and was a wonderful friend.' His appeal was more than the attractiveness of the frail. For many his 'personal beauty' was moral and not just physical. Either way, he was 'a human

142

sirenometer… Someone with the scientific property of attracting charming people to himself and making his home their playground'.[53] It is an odd phrase, partly for its femininity and partly because sirens were temptresses who in Greek myth would lure seafarers onto the rocks. Pembroke was complex. 'I confess' he once told her, 'I take pleasure in a way when people don't like my friends. One likes them less for being popular – there is a sort of innate, intensely vain, I suspect, fastidiousness inside one that resents it.'[54] This was sophisticated, self-centred too, with shades of Burne-Jones and Ruskin in its possessiveness – a trait to which Frances was always drawn no matter how much she resisted. In this she was not alone. Pembroke's company was 'very much loved and sought after' by the women of the Souls, who vied for his attention; the Tennant sisters would regularly cut each other to be with him. He in turn 'clung very much to his friends', living 'a great deal in his correspondence', which Frances put down to his lack of children but perhaps reflected more his concept of 'friendship'. In an intensely private letter to Frances ('what I have said to you in this letter I could not have said to any other friend in the world'), he rejected 'love in the man and woman sense'. The carnality of a Cust or the promiscuity of Pembroke's sister, Gladys de Grey, stung and embarrassed him. Yet he insisted that 'my friendships are very like loves'. Into them he would pour his life and soul and, in Charty's hands, would suffer a broken heart for his pains. 'Can you understand at all, I wonder?'[55] He knew Frances would, for on people 'you are nearly always right.' As with so many, she became the trusted confidante – 'Dearest Donna', whose letters convey 'such a feeling of living spirit and fun and warmth – and all that is nice- with pen and paper'.

In turn, Frances was rarely happier than when she was sailing with Pembroke on *The Black Pearl* in the Western Isles: 'Most delicious time… out all day sailing and fishing and caving and walking on the hills (which sounds an odd way of yachting)'. Together, 'in a great mean swell' they shared the exhilarating power and beauty of nature in the raw. 'Oh it is such Paradise to sail up the Sound of Mull and see the marvellous, serrated shape of Rum lift itself out of the water… and to feel the whole land is full of story'. It was to him that she would first show 'The New Morality' and also a rollicking account of her and Charty abroad. More tentatively she sent 'a Vision of Maya' – a short story later published anonymously in

Temple Bar – safe in the knowledge that only he would recognise the portrayal of Laura.[56]

'I don't suppose you court him when she [i.e. his wife] is there', Margot chided Frances. 'You darling scoundrel – he likes you ever so much.' As so often Margot had crash landed some way off target. Charty wasn't much the wiser. 'Lord Pembroke', she alerted Harry Cust, 'wrote a panegyric about Frances Horner that she had "high spirits verging on devilry!" [only to end] up with, "she is nice , isn't she?" Flat don't you think?'[57] But that was the point. It was because he offered a loving friendship and not a love affair that Frances would declare 'If I could get heaps of Pembroke I should be quite satisfied. Let's get hold of him by both wings', she urged DD, 'and make of him a constant companion.'[58] The only person she talked openly of loving was DD.

*

'Miss DD: tall, fair, pale, quiet in manner…Lovely long lashes, altogether an attractive girl' recalled Daisy White on first seeing her at Stanway.[59] Edith "DD" Balfour (fig. 50) was the only daughter of a London merchant, trading in Russia, and some eleven years younger than Frances. They met at Lords in June 1883, recalled DD, when Spencer Lyttelton 'told me I must be friends with her.' Frances was just back from Rome and enjoying being the young wife of the moment, and 'with her big, rather mocking eyes, [she] frightened me.'[60] Yet cool and self-possessed, intellectual, lively in conversation, fluent in French, unmarried and unchaperoned, there was plenty in DD to attract Frances. Very soon they were fast friends and after Laura's death increasingly devoted to each other. 'Love to have a baby playfellow?' wrote Frances. 'You silly darling to think you could love me – Just try'. Such was DD's affection for her that Frances admitted she 'trembles a little. It is neither the Frances I know, nor the one God made, but the one you think me, and what a fragile and elusive abstraction that is. But it is the only thing in life I care about really'. Writing from Longleat, 'this poor country mouse is rather tired of creeping about strange houses and longs for the quiet and seclusion of Hereford Gardens'. Two years on and she was still writing, 'it is dear of you to have held out your arms to me – I can't help loving them that love me, can you?'[61] It is easy to read too much into such sentiments. Certainly there were hugs and caresses, kisses and late-night confessions, but the spirit is more Pembroke's, where 'friendships are very like loves'. Clearly there is a pattern for Frances attracting much younger and adoring girls under her wing – Laura, Margot, DD; and others would follow. These relationships would be emotionally intense – and all the more so for not being sexually driven.

This idyll was threatened in June 1888 when DD was seduced by Doll Liddell. Over forty years on, DD was still surprised by the strength of physical attraction he aroused

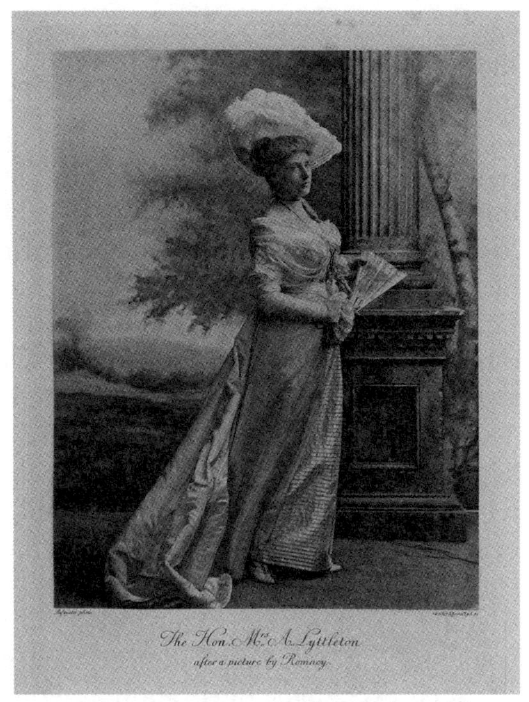

50.   *DD Balfour*

in her. Still for all the pleasure she felt, she was racked with guilt as, like Laura, she felt no love for Doll. So much so that she couldn't tell Frances 'already my greatest friend'.[62] Inevitably Frances found out when Doll in despair showed her DD's latest effort to break it off. 'She thought it almost crazy', DD remembered. 'I was sitting down on the hearth with my head against her knees – [Still] she kissed me when she went to bed and said she was sure I should have happiness'. Two weeks later at Panshanger Frances was persuading Doll to step back. Twice the lovers separated and twice desire brought them secretly together again before finally parting in 1890. After which DD retreated to Mells for the summer where she 'cried most of the time'. Gradually Frances re-established control, ever protective of 'more fragile textured little creatures'.[63] That Christmas with DD abroad, she would 'miss you dreadfully and hate to feel how much is flowing between us: – *Zwei Wasser wohnen zwischen Mir und Dir – das eine sind* [?] *Thrähen das Andere ist das Meer* [Two waters lie between me and you – one are tears, the other is the sea]. You will find the Portico Room waiting'.[64]

For some reason theirs was now to be a secret relationship. Indeed Frances took delight in no one 'know[ing] anything about the love between us. Oh fancy, Lord Bath said to me, "Well there is one person that you have made an enemy of". "Who?" "Miss DD Balfour"…He couldn't make out why I laughed so.' But plainly something about this friendship had aroused concerns among her circle. Margot bristled at this replacement of Laura. More worrying, Lord Elcho wrote confidentially to DD warning her of Frances's 'influence'. Presumably the corruption suspected was not sexual but moral, especially her view of independence within marriage? Frances protested to DD that she never wanted to influence her but to love her. 'I would gladly die tomorrow to give anyone I really loved a real happiness in their lives'. As for Elcho, theirs had always been a frosty relationship. 'So [at dinner] I hardened my heart and had it out with him but it was no good. He was awfully taken aback – but of course never suspected you – I only said "don't you think we might be better friends?" And he said, "Aren't we good friends?" And so I said "No, not a bit." But unluckily I didn't do any good'.[65]

Such exchanges illustrate how Frances remained something of an outsider on the inside as far as the Souls were concerned. And how far the Souls were less radical than 'The New Morality' might suggest. Certainly few adhered to the restraints of Pembrokian love. 'I had a very funny talk with Gity [Pembroke's wife]', Frances reported to DD. "Tell me are you a cynic?" Gity had suddenly asked. 'I said "No except sometimes at a party." Then she said "what do you think of marriage?" … which was so comprehensive and soul searching that I was floored. Then she said: "I want very much to ask you – are you happy about Mary Elcho and Arthur Balfour? Are you happy about Lucy [Graham-Smith, née Tennant] and Harry Cust?"[66] Balfour and Mary Elcho maintained an *amitié amoureuse* for thirty years but were so 'inseparable' at Clouds as to upset Gity. As it was, Mary's husband had a string of mistresses, while she had a brief fling in the desert with Wilfrid Scawen Blunt. The resulting daughter was simply absorbed into the family.[67] Violet Granby did the same on at least two occasions, with one daughter, Diana, being fathered by Harry Cust. Similarly, Curzon's pouncing on DD after breakfast at Stanway was more in the spirit of *droit de seigneur* than Pembroke and New Morality. Indeed in terms of sexual ethics the Souls could not have been more traditional.[68]

On this Frances was not judgemental, holding that part of a hostess's role was to 'smooth pillows'. She was very relaxed on grand flirtations. Yet she could still be quite coy. House hunting in Mayfair with Aggie in the 1880s, she was rather startled on being shown into a bathroom to find the lady of the house in the bath: 'Please come in. I don't mind in the least and I hope you won't'. Blushing they made their retreat (and didn't take the house). Like Gity she did draw the line at marriage. 'When I married', she told Violet Cecil, she 'sat straight down and in the flesh at least have never moved from my appointed path'. Despite later describing Cust as the 'Rupert Brooke of our day. Gold-haired, well-born, a poet, irresistible', yet resist him she did – if rather enjoying his attention nonetheless: 'He always called me Attila, the Scourge of God, when I refused, generally on ethical grounds, to do anything he wanted'. She would remain her father's daughter and indeed her class for longer than she would later let on. But was there even the desire? Margot and Frances once fell into a vigorous discussion on the Pre-Raphaelite view of human beauty. Where Frances saw perfection in such figures, for Margot 'they are too lacking in vitality'.[69]

Looking back from the 1940s Violet Bonham Carter argued that the impact of the Souls was 'liberating and civilising [for women]… How much of our fun and freedom was a direct heritage from them'.[70] If so, this liberation was immediately limited to those with independent means and personality and restricted too to seeking freedoms within the existing structures of marriage and Society. Nor was there any getting away from the fact either that these very able and well-read women were pouring their creative artistry into devising games rather than books or good works. Or that the purpose of the games was to entertain men who, after the demands of Westminster, wanted diverting, not challenging. Ultimately, Frances's feminism was about asserting oneself within the existing system – a pre-revolutionary perspective and important for that. But it would be the next generation – that of DD Balfour (deemed 'too modern' by Margot) and Frances's youngest sister Aggie – who would seek power as well as liberty and embrace the cause of women's suffrage. The advent of the 'New Woman' was imminent and it threatened to leave Frances in its wake.

RUBÁIYÁT OF OMAR KHAYÁM

OF NAISHÁPÚR

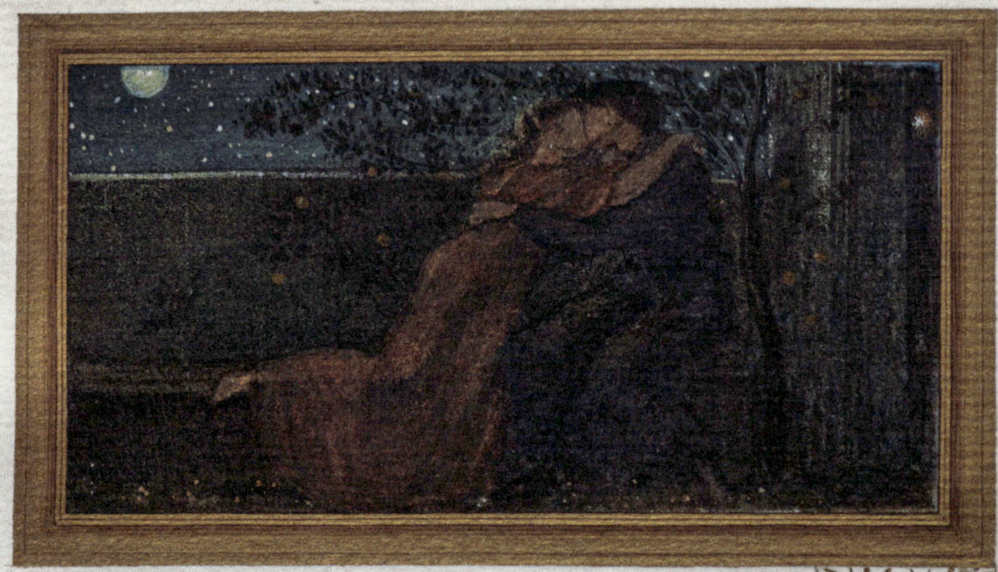

Awake! for Morning in the bowl of Night
Has flung the stone that puts the stars to flight:
And lo, the Hunter of the East has caught
The Sultan's turret in a noose of light.

Dreaming, when Dawn's left hand was in the sky,
I heard a voice within the tavern cry,
"Awake, my Little-ones, and fill the cup
Before life's liquor in its cup be dry."

And as the cock crew, those who stood before
The tavern shouted, "Open then the door!
You know how little while we have to stay
And, once departed, may return no more."

Part Five

The Year of Living Dangerously
1892

After dinner I talked to Asquith and asked him to tell me the full innermost story of the late summer and autumn of the year 1892. And when he asked me if I was sure I could bear it, I said that I had reached such a pitch of philosophy that I believe I could. He warned me that it would pain me very much, but I couldn't go back after that vaunt and so he straightforward began [the rest of the letter has not survived].

Edward Burne-Jones to Frances Horner[1]

You know what I feel about Mr Asquith and to have had a life like you two have had together makes all other things seem small.

Frances Horner to Margot Asquith[2]

51.   *The opening stanzas of the Rubaiyat of Omar Khayam*

~ 16 ~

BY THE HAYSTACK AT MILFORD

The proper answer to men about women and women about men – it is only now and then that the inexplicable happens – suddenly it does and one can't make out why but each will do something inexplicable to each other.

Burne-Jones to Frances[3]

Margot began 1892 in a role that came only too naturally to her – that of a 'bludgeoner'. The cause was (for her) the shocking news that DD Balfour had become engaged to Alfred Lyttelton – once husband to the blessed Laura. But the honour that she sought to defend was that of another sister, Charty. Despite being married to Lord Ribblesdale, Charty had on Laura's death quickly assumed the role of companion of Alfred, even looking after his sickly child while the baby lived. That her love was unrequited did nothing to deflate an open friendship and the pleasures and standing that came with it. Now distraught at the marriage she had long dreaded, she nevertheless behaved with dignity. Not so her sister, Margot. To her face DD was denounced for betraying Charty, while to Alfred she criticised DD's looks, intelligence and health. It was bitchy and vindictive and ensured that DD would never trust her again. Not surprisingly, given the furore, the Lytteltons chose to marry in Italy in April and later avoided the Season by decamping to Wimbledon.[4]

'Clapham or Peckham Rye would have been quite enough', teased Frances. Had she felt betrayed too? At least it hadn't come as a surprise and Alfred 'had always been one of her special friends'. It was always accepted that girls like DD should aspire to a good marriage. Frances certainly believed this. They would remain good friends and confidantes; Mells would remain DD's 'second home'; Frances would be godmother to DD's first child, who would also carry Frances's name. Nevertheless the sense of loss was palpable; both in her feeble excuse to avoid the ceremony and in a letter she wrote DD on 'your wedding day – almost unbelievable… You must pretend I'm there … even in the carriage and four and you will certainly find me standing on the threshold of the first home'. The sense of possession, of a deep friendship threatened, can be seen in her begging DD to call on her immediately on her return, where they would draw the blinds, light the candles and gossip: 'and you must tell Alfred that one very large room is mine, not his at all, and I don't intend to give it up. Your very loving Frances who belongs to you both with all her heart and loves you as she loves Laura – I couldn't send this letter without her name being in it as a benediction'. For all the emotional turmoil, the incantation of Laura was calculated.[5]

And as such, spoke of desperation. There would indeed be a room for her (in yellow wallpaper to her liking) in the Lytteltons' home; 'but I don't intend to sit in my room much'. Such sentiments only stirred in Alfred fears of Frances's 'influence' that he had first experienced on the eve of his marriage to Laura. Her sharp rebuttal to DD ('Don't pretend I tire of you') did little to calm him. Nor her follow up: 'I am considered most restful, tell Alfred, a sort of secular and moral sedative – a kind of bromide really'.[6] Yet she knew that things would not be the same and it hurt. Her wild claims to DD exposed also a raw vulnerability in her. Still to shake off fully the lingering depressions after Mark's birth, she had become physically quite frail. 'You are very thin, about to be too thin', warned DD with Frances's sisters, Aggie and Alice, joining in the chorus. And not without reason. Frances was frequently bedridden with temperatures of 104° and on one occasion losing all strength in her legs. 'Isn't bed odious, all holes and crumbs' was a plucky response to the enveloping gloom. The onset of her forties when so many of her friends and rivals were considerably younger didn't help. Nor did her social success bring the fulfilment her younger self had imagined. 'You were living, as you say, thirsty and caged and never quite satisfied, but at any rate drinking deep of the stream', one close friend reminded her.[7] Her closeness to DD had left her open to criticism [usually from men denied the company of a pretty girl] and more isolated that she liked.

How far was Jack part of the cage? Although respected by her Soul friends for his integrity and learning, he didn't have the alertness of mind to join in and anyway was becoming increasingly deaf. Imperceptibly, they had begun to socialise separately. As Frances's recent breakdown showed, while he cared for her, he lacked the sensitivity to connect with her. Consequently DD's marriage left her emotionally bereft, vulnerable and alone. 'She does love you that is pretty certain', Burne-Jones tried to reassure her after meeting DD. Before offering an image of Frances sitting 'opposite a glass, so that you can see DD's face when she is brushing and comforting you'. Such was balm to Frances, as once again she sought comfort from her oldest confidant.[8]

*

On 11 May 1892 Frances and Burne-Jones were walking the countryside near Milford, the country home of Bob and Barbara Webb, when they became detached from the rest of the party. 'What I told you by the hayrick at Milford',[9] he later reminded her, remains elusive but the consequences would be momentous. It would seem that declarations of love were made. Burne-Jones made these incessantly. This time, however, Frances appears to have responded. There may even have been a kiss.[10] What is certain is that the effect on Burne-Jones was transformative and left him ecstatic – convinced that they were lovers again as they had been in the 1870s. They were he told her 'Back to the old days'… 'and back came all the old feelings…so like twenty years ago'. The next night she accompanied him to a supper given by Mary Elcho at which everyone was invited with their lovers ('such overcoupling'). 'Did I talk folly last night?' he wrote the next day. 'You looked tired – were you sorry about anything?'[11] Seemingly not, as she was soon vigorously defending his reputation. 'All my life I have known him and admired him,' she declared to a friend; 'when I was fifteen we used to see much of him and he was the first man of genius I had ever met and that flung open the world'[12]

There was no doubting his renewed ardour for her. 'It is hard to write unless I may say all the wild loving words that come first to my heart…How strange it all is to me and yet so familiar…I am living in a dream – is it a month ago? How unpremeditated it all was….O never say those things to me, that it would be better if you had not crossed my path – never say them – you are so glorious in my eyes and have always been – you are romance and beauty.' Later he would claim 'you have knocked all my work on the head this summer. I

152

have done nothing…it is funny to have a pencil in my hand and not be drawing. They are jealous these Muses.'[13] For she would be his muse now: 'The old stammering times are done with – when I could never talk to you or before you or in your presence but felt muzzled always – now I can begin at once talking quite intimately about everything and you can help me in a million ways.' Very quickly he is seeking to remould her into the Frances he wanted her to be – the muse he always wanted: sweet, deferential and devoted to him. Behind all of this lay his instinct to control, chiding her when she didn't comment on his Launcelot picture or his latest 'Chaucer plan'. It is there too in his fresh desire for her to sit for him again, possibly as Brunhilde, or for another portrait, this time 'life size'. He even bought back from Ken Mackenzie 'that painted sketch of you I made ages ago that Walter Crane said was the exact portrait of your spirit'.[14] Back too came his possessiveness: 'Mr Haldane, … I must say, does come pretty often… [He] mustn't go too far'. For all that he would plead 'Let us praise jealousy a little – it is of such modest an origin' – it was still ugly and repressive.[15]

At first Frances didn't fully appreciate just what she had unleashed. Very soon after Milford she had left for Mells and then Scotland. Highly charged declarations of love from Burne-Jones were nothing new and quite conventional in an age of Walter Scott – sentimentally satisfying but rarely of significance. 'My Sovereign Lady, My Mistress', he would address her. High in the Perthshire hills overlooking the Kingdom of Fife, ('a romantic country full of legend'), such emotion could be thought fitting.[16] With her self-esteem dented, it is easy to appreciate how easily she might have been overwhelmed at Milford. In July Burne-Jones did briefly 'dread that you were saying more than you quite meant'. If so, she didn't press it, preferring to put her faith in the maxim: 'If you live in London, people discuss you; if you leave it, they forget you'.[17]

By August it dawned on her that things were not as she presumed. He was now bombarding her with letters, three to five a day. When she asked him to restrain from writing so many, he resisted for two days before sending one of thirty-two pages. Belatedly she sought to stem the tide, declaring this emotional torrent as babyish. All to no avail: 'the day you cease to be exacting, I shall dread what has happened', he replied almost joyously.[18] Admittedly she had often been quite sharp with him – yet for him this was part of her appeal. Equally, he frequently resorted to innuendo in his letters, which perhaps blinded her in turn to the intent behind his insistence that she held the key to his innermost feelings: 'you won't lose the key will you? I know the pocket where you put keys now and I want to lie there for ever'. Another letter brought a long confession of his affair with Maria Zambaco, and a conviction that with Frances came redemption. '*All* the romance and beauty of my life means you, and my days are ending in splendour through you'.[19] And then there were the note books. She had asked him to write up his thoughts and especially the early stories of Rossetti and Morris and the early Pre-Raphaelite days (fig.52). These tales he provided [some later reproduced in *Time Remembered*]. But he also sent (by special delivery for security) the first two volumes of his thoughts. Others would follow. 'I think volume 2 is warmer still', he warned her, 'and 3 must be destroyed – it must be'. That same day he was making plans for Frances to visit when Georgie was away: 'We won't look at pictures – we won't lose a moment on them – never – that can be done when Charty or Daisy come with you'.

Frances was horrified. But her protests only met a howl of rejection: 'I do not understand women at all', he protested before concocting a self-serving riposte – 'it may be because I have so clearly understood myself about you that I have felt I understood you…It doesn't matter so much in your case because I love you'.[20] Blind now to any feelings she might have, he persisted in his fantasies of seduction: 'In the world that need never be overcome, I shall be at your side, or nestling between your feet – so move them gently or don't move them at all'. The prospect of meeting her had him 'tingling, trembling all day long' thinking of her with 'some funny mingling of awe and worship and wantonness'. Days later he was writing of his 'savage hunger for you … Absolutely all my life hangs on you… I am terribly in love'. When she protested at such new feelings, he insisted he had always felt like this for her. Hence his keeping of his daughter Margaret 'by me' when Frances had visited his studio because he couldn't trust himself to be alone in her company. Again and again he returned to what was said at Milford.

> Now tell me, tell me true, if you had ever wanted something
> with all your soul and knew for years you never could have it;
> and the desire of your heart was far removed from sight even;

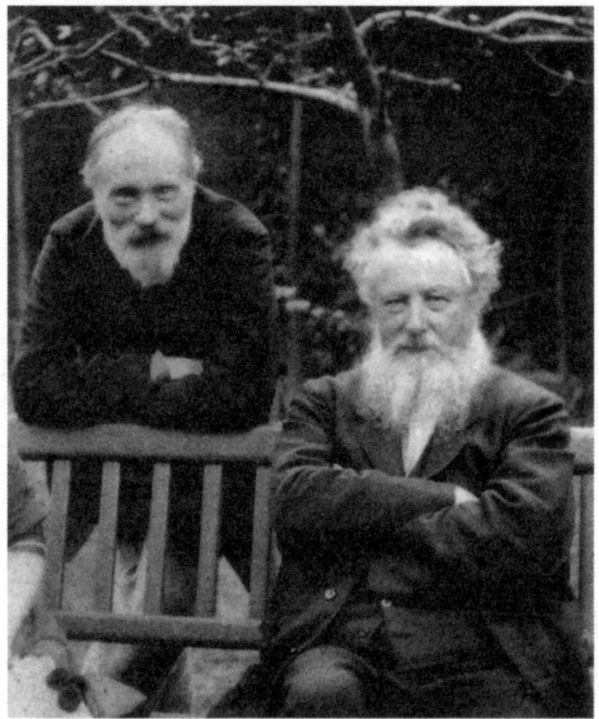

52.   *Edward Burne-Jones and William Morris, 1890*

and so long had gone by that it was 20 years … and then suddenly after some strange sentences were said, all you had ever wanted was given you, how would you behave?[21]

Had she led him astray or was he in thrall, as he put it, to 'Love and his overdriven steeds'? For Frances, guilt now mingled with a real fear of scandal. As Burne-Jones's imagination careered wildly out of control, how she had come to dread what she had said or done by the hayrick at Milford. Still she had protected her independence for too long to become the deferential muse he sought to make her. Nor had she any desire to be the next Maria Zambaco. Physically Burne-Jones at fifty-eight held no attraction for her – 'a funny little thing that glares' was how he described himself. Determined to regain the initiative and restore their friendship to normality, she invited him to Mells in October. Not without trepidation – for she hated scenes; but also because matters were more complicated than they seemed.

'MUST I LIKE ASQUITH?'

It is strange how one comes gaily and carelessly to meet the influences which are to be the dominant ones in life…I did not guess then how intimately – nor for how long – our lives were to be associated; nor did he.

Frances Horner[22]

'Must I like Asquith?' protested Burne-Jones at Frances's suggestion that he might join them at Mells. 'I certainly don't unlike but …we are poles apart in the world and could only meet at dinner.' Yet for Frances, when she had first met the young lawyer in March 1891 over dinner at the Northamptons, the attraction was instant (fig. 53). They were 'sitting far off on the opposite sides of the table'. She had raised the subject of a tale written about a village idiot. Asquith immediately challenged her: 'I think he criticised it in order to draw me. I thought it great fun to enter into a heated literary controversy with a distinguished stranger across the dinner table'. The next day she was regaling DD on Asquith: 'I liked him very much – very keen and quick and with more acidity in his favour than Mr Haldane'. The intellectual purist in her still held Haldane 'a superior man,' but after a visit to an exhibition it was Asquith's company she enjoyed 'enormously'. Soon afterwards she departed for Mells and the birth of Mark. They would not meet again until Spring 1892. It was during this time that Frances was enveloped in post-natal depression. But Asquith too was suffering with the sudden death of his wife and it was with Frances that he chose to share his grief. Thanking her for her letter of condolence, he 'recognised the tones of one who is acquainted with sorrows; they come from the heart and go to the heart'. He in turn would bolster her as she sank into gloom: 'I was dyed melancholy early in life', she would say, 'and it is a stain that

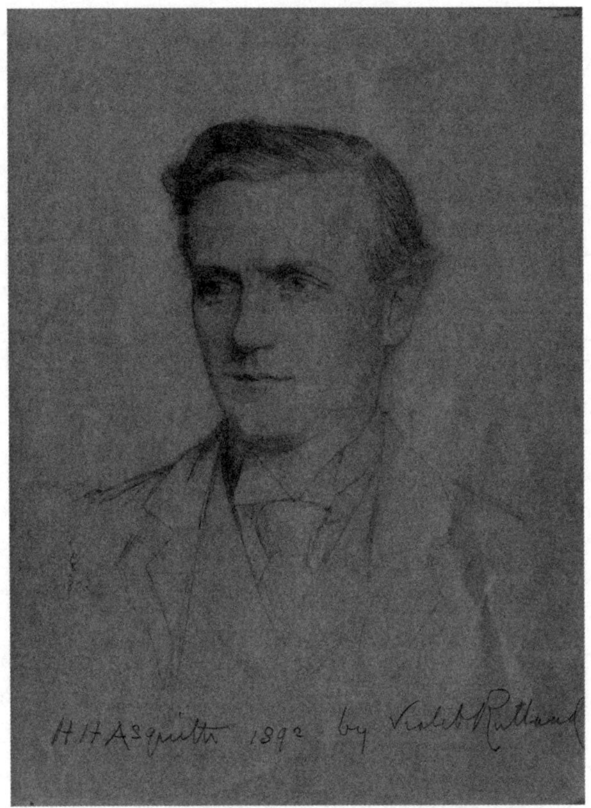

53   *H. H. Asquith, 1892, by Violet Granby, later Duchess of Rutland*

doesn't easily come out'. For all that, she willingly distracted herself at his request, finding someone to look after his children.[23]

By February 1892 Frances was well enough to brave London. Encountering Asquith again at Charty's house in Munster Square, they were soon meeting regularly for dinner and outings to the theatre. March would see an invitation to Mells and by May he would be frequently calling on her. As ever with Frances their friendship was first and foremost a meeting of minds. 'Asquith', she enthused to DD, 'was delightful, agreeable and interesting and very sympathetic – a mind that errs on the side of lucidity and hardness but very tolerant of haze in others and the sort of person you know will understand whatever you say to him'. His letters were full of literary and classical allusions and the cleverness that she loved. In her excitement she would press on him her latest reading: Balzac's letters, Ibsen,

Rosebery's *Pitt*, and Balfour's continuing philosophic doubts in his Rectorial Address at Glasgow. From the depths of Gibbon came his plaintive admission that 'I have not got to the end of your list'. On her recommendation, he had now seen *Hedda Gabler* twice, benefitting from 'the more excellent way into which you first guided me'. He even endured her brief passion for Romanian folk songs.[24] In all of this there is a hint of an improving mission and she seems to have become a mentor on matters of Society and etiquette. Unlike some of her country house set, she held to the middle-class virtues of 'work' and 'action' and admired how her lawyer friend had worked his way up. If all this sounds rather austere, their correspondence was laced with a shared sense of humour, mostly at the expense of Asquith's Liberal colleagues and in particular a 'Mr Roundell'. 'I used to know him when he was in search of a wife,' gossiped Frances. 'I never could understand on what principle he proposed: he was refused so often and by such different people; but I am inclined to believe it was alphabetical'.[25]

As they 'walked back' one night from the theatre to the Mackenzies' house (where Frances was staying), Asquith attempted to kiss her – only to be firmly resisted. Unbeknownst to him, five days earlier there had been the incident by the hayrick at Milford. Yet Frances was startled rather than appalled and if Asquith was duly rebuffed, he was not rejected. She enjoyed his company too much to let him go. Agreeing that there was 'not much wisdom in "thinking too precisely on the event,"' they continued to meet up almost every night and even wrote mildly flirtatious letters to each other. 'Do you become a pagan in the summer?', wrote Frances from Mells. 'I do…I want no better earth than this and only a little better climate. But these green field rhapsodies are not to your taste… Jack's off to Oxford for a few days and I shall be here alone. I wish you were attainable: we could settle our account so nicely'.[26]

This was little more than sport – not least because of Margot Tennant. Even before his wife had died in 1891 Asquith had become infatuated with Margot. She, on the other hand, was perfectly frank that she couldn't return his feelings. By June 1892, as he was screwing himself up to make another bid, he had recruited Frances to advance his cause. Always fancying herself as a match maker, she leapt at the challenge. Her first report wasn't very promising. Whether Margot 'will ever take courage enough to fling herself into the unknown, I do not know. To some people it is sufficient bliss to be out of their depth … but Margot I think likes to feel the bottom – and I don't think she can ever be stormed as most women can be through the heart… but I wish she could be.' Two weeks later she was even less encouraging. Given that Margot 'does not seem to want for marriage at all', she now urged delay. After all, in terms of his political career, 'it is not a very bad thing for you to start at this precise moment with the horizon free.' With the elections likely to return a Liberal government in August and the opportunity of advancement, she advised him to focus on 'making your political life so independent and so far reaching.' For to speak plainly, 'it is true that women like best to look up and that you cannot really win them on your knees'. Other than that all she could suggest was that 'I think if Margot were very much with you she would not easily consent to do without you – so that I should always feel glad when I know you are together'. So half-hearted is this that it is hard not to read into Frances's advice a degree of self-interest. And how far were her concerns entirely for her friend when she made this promise: 'if I thought I could cure you [of his desire for Margot] tomorrow by …charm, I would try; I'm cynical enough for that – [for] caring passionately means suffering deeply and I dread it for a friend'. And what is one to read into her offer: 'I have a great deal about the Art of Making Lovers Happy. Come and stay with me and you shall see'.[27]

July brought no joy for Asquith. True he won his election handsomely with 20,000 gathering to cheer the result. Beside him on the platform was Margot who was called out to make a speech in celebration of their MP. Still not yet forty, he would soon be invited into Gladstone's last Cabinet and as Home Secretary hold one of the great historic Offices of State. But at this moment of great personal triumph, Margot's latest rejection left him despondent. 'I suppose, as you say, I ought to feel satisfied and happy'... with 'the chance of bringing off this dream of young ambition', he wrote to Frances. 'Still – still – I have not, and I know I am never likely to have, what I really want'.[28] Frances would have none of this. Although he presumed otherwise, she was thrilled by the drama of the election and later by the gossip in his letters from Westminster as the parties jostled for office. 'The Arena', they called it and she would write how 'I love a vicarious existence in it through my friends.' Like him, she agreed that 'Personality is still the most potent factor in the world'.[29] And with the election leaving her friend the coming man of British politics, she saw that this was not the time for a wobble over his unrequited love of Margot. 1892 she insisted would prove his 'annus mirabilis'. Down though he was, it is inconceivable that Asquith would have turned down office but significantly, on his appointment, the first person he told was her; 'are you glad?' he asked. She was now a trusted confidante for politics as well as love. Her letters he kept in his pocket and when in 'need of inspiring companionship, I turn to you!' She not only stiffened resolve but crucially she added 'a real zest to what is called success'. Rather oddly in the wake of Margot's rejection he reassured her that 'there is plenty of room and whatever happens to me there is no fear of your falling out at the edge.' By August she was, he declared, his '*very* great friend'.[30]

A measure of her new importance to him came the following month in the form of a 'confession' written on the first anniversary of his wife's death. Frances had teased him over his natural reticence only to provoke an outpouring of candour. His wife was 'an angel from Heaven'... A figure of 'soft grey tints' rather than 'strong colours, [who] cared little for Society, ... hardly knew what ambition meant, [and was] not the least anxious for me to "get on." She was the gentlest and best of companions, a restricting rather than a stimulating influence, and knowing myself as I do, I have often wondered that we walked so evenly together.' Sometime before her death 'I became an intimate friend of Margot... It did not trouble my wife'. And with her passing he quickly convinced himself he was in love with Margot. 'It may seem strange but ... I never [was]... conscious of any disloyalty to the memory of the dead... Do you smile?... I know too that she does not love me, at least not in the way that I love her. I am under no illusions, but I love her and my love for her is the best thing in my life'. Such admissions took courage. Frances had a mocking tongue and he could quite imagine the fun she could have over 'a man's faith in the eternity of his passion.' In fact she recognised his confiding in her as 'a tribute' and unexpectedly responded with one confiding in him; 'epoch-making in a friendship' he called it and Frances was now 'my friend in a special sense'.[31]

Quite what did that mean? Similarly his praise of their 'secret and instinctive sympathy'; why secret? And then there was his tantalising aside: 'Margot was right in what she said to you about you and me'. 22 September saw another milestone in Asquith's rapid rise as he stood to move the address in the new Parliament. Before heading out for Westminster, he had breakfasted with Frances. 'Let us always be as we were today' he urged, trusting that she won't be 'jealous' of Margot. But why did he think she would be? A week later he was at Mells. 'Well, how do we stand?' he challenged her on his return.

> I shall remember Sunday as a red-letter day: will you? Don't let there be a reaction! ... Do you repent? No good. It is too late. But you don't and won't repent. ... A word unspoken, a room unentered, and uninvited visit not paid, who can say what a difference 'accidents' such as these may make in our lives. Don't let me be a disturbing element. No one knows better than you to whom my heart is given. But what I said to you last night is all true and I will keep my word.

Seemingly, as at Milford, something had happened. His quip that she had given him 'a latch key by which I can let myself in at all seasonable hours' was presumably metaphorical. In Asquith's eyes at least their friendship had moved onto another level.[32] Frances was undoubtedly attracted to Asquith and, with Margot showing no interest, the way was clearer. And unlike Burne-Jones, Asquith appreciated the rules of the game. Would she have contemplated an affair with someone open in his love for another? Still, with desire and opportunity, 'accidents' can happen.

Four days later, Burne-Jones would arrive for his first and only visit to Mells. For one so acutely attuned to the risk of scandal, Frances had found herself by the end of September in an extraordinary position of being pursued by two very different men at the same time. Just as extraordinary was her management of these parallel lives throughout the summer. Admittedly this was a situation thrust upon her and one that caused her much anxiety. Not that she was helpless. Both Burne-Jones and Asquith could be 'rather afraid of the flickering of her semi-cynical smile'. Yet she had no wish to hurt them. By the end of September she could no longer hide in Scotland. With Burne-Jones now a risk, even she saw that matters could not be left to drift. Faced with a choice however, she decided to choose neither of them.

∽ 18 ∽

SHOWDOWNS AND SOFAS

I said [to Daisy White who had asked why he had not visited Mells before] that as long as I didn't see Mells, I refused to believe you were married or had children.

Burne-Jones to Frances Horner[33]

Burne-Jones could barely contain his excitement. Letters poured forth from Clouds where he was staying before coming on to Mells the next day. Now on the eve of the culmination of all he had desired for so long, he was trembling with expectation.

> It is so strange – and I vowed so long and loud I would never go to you…I shall be dumb I know – I shall never know what to say to you. Will you lead me about by the hand?... May I sleep on the mat outside your door? It made me heart breaky to think of you… If I saw you daily I couldn't worship or love you more.

So he was 'rather disappointed' that she wasn't at the station to meet him. Instead she had stayed at Mells to greet the arrival of her children. It was the first sign that matters were not as he had imagined. So too was Aggie's presence; much as he liked her, she was a complication. Still his spirits soon recovered as he took an 'infantile delight' in seeing the 'many things of my hand in your house'.[34] On the walls were paintings he remembered from her father's collection, while in the music room was the piano with its fantasy on the love of *Orpheus and Eurydice* – so fitting to his hopes. They lingered over the embroidered panels that she had faithfully completed to his design (fig. 54), his stained glass designs and the little *Rubaiyat of Omar Khayam* which William Morris had written out and illuminated with Burne-Jones's miniature paintings (fig. 51). Eventually it could be put off no

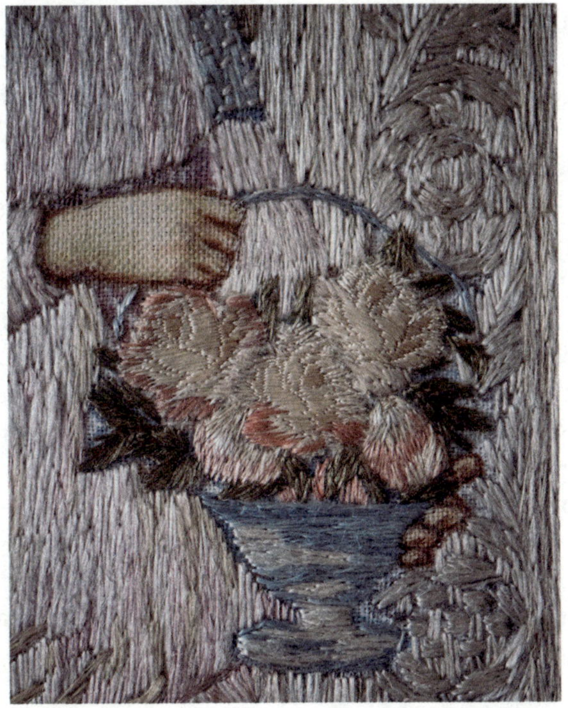

54.   *Detail of St Elizabeth of Hungary. Embroidery
designed by Burne-Jones and executed by Frances*

longer and finding themselves alone briefly in the Library, he seized his chance.

Years later he would chide her: 'And you dare (when do you not dare) to ask me if I remember the Library – when you cried – I sometimes wonder if I really remember anything else…I wanted to cry too and couldn't because I was a man'. Such was his emotional outburst that Frances was genuinely frightened: ('I was wicked to make you cry'). And yet her rejection (despite her numerous hints at restraint) came as a complete shock for him. What he had lovingly visualised as a knightly pilgrimage to his liege lady was, in the cold light of her denial, little more than the tawdry infatuation of an elderly man for a much younger and married woman. Having wound himself up for six months to hope, he was left humiliated and bereft.[35]

But not of his manners. He told his stories and entertained the children; and even went to church, passing the old Manor House on the way to which he insisted the Horners move immediately. His thank you letter was uncharacteristically anodyne. 'Most beloved mistress, … it is so nice now to know where you live and all the ways of the day'. Others that followed wallowed in regret. 'Oh how I repent me of the notebooks… I have blundered terribly about you and misunderstood and mis-seen many things – but my love for you has been the best thing I have ever done'. Bravely he insisted 'you are to feel no entanglement, to feel free and out of doors always with me'. And soon they were back to old ways discussing art, tales of Rossetti and Morris, and his latest thoughts on Avalon.[36] Seemingly Frances had regained the companion and confidant she loved instead of the lover she didn't want. Back intact too was the relationship on which her standing and reputation had long depended. 'Yes actually he came over from Clouds and stayed Sunday,' she gushed to DD, 'and we had divine talks'.[37] By such slight of memory Burne-Jones's visit had become a social coup and something of a triumph – as indeed it appeared to be. Only her aside, that his visit had left her 'as sterile as a golf course', hinted at how emotionally drained she was. And now for Asquith.

*

> What do you mean? No, I won't 'put away' – where to I wonder? – and you couldn't 'give me back' Sunday if you wanted to… Why should I want it back? The memory of it has been with me all through this week, not only as a memory but as a hope and a promise… the still vivid impression of what we thought and felt and said… Don't let us slip back: I won't if you won't.
>
> H.H. Asquith to Frances Horner[38]

Frances's attempt to stand Asquith down by 'Pembrokian letter' was doomed to fail. Not least because her heart was never in it, however much conscience and the Pembrokian ethos of Platonic love and friendship urged a calmer engagement. Finding his company captivating, she offered little resistance. Shyly she offered to meet. 'Oh yes I am quite sure I have "nothing else" to do on Thursday night' he quipped, 'and I should "like to", if you don't mind. I am "not to hesitate to say if not quite convenient"? How polite you are!... Drop once and for all your Pembrokism.'[39] Symbolically, this meeting with Asquith involved standing up Burne-Jones ('I can't see what you have to say to Asquith that is so important as all that').[40] That night after dinner she took Asquith to a performance of *Orfeo*. His memory of that night was less elevated: 'The sofa looks empty and gaunt: at this hour a week ago it was very different. Do you remember?' Thereafter she was no longer 'Mrs Horner' but 'Frances' in his correspondence. Seeing each other every night, privately or with friends they soon began to adopt the little deceits that come with an affair: 'our hurried departure' one day, opera glasses mislaid on another, a mythical engagement on the next. 'Did you enjoy your "party" as much as I did? Au revoir until this evening.'[41]

The following weekend saw them at Mells and the establishing of some ground rules. 'We had a nice Sunday – don't you think? I won't say that you were "kind", but you said many things which I shan't forget… You will remember your promise – that it should add and (if it may be) enrich your life and not take out of it any bright or good thing that was already there. Then I shall be happy'. Not for the first time, when on uncertain emotional ground, Frances took refuge in being demanding. Nevertheless she had come to hero-worship him. 'It is still rather a mystery to me', he confessed,

> and I am afraid in many ways you idealise and magnify and transfigure what you think you have found, but what you really create. I am well content that it should be so, if only you will always be the same, and not some fine morning awake and bring the naked light of your critical lamp to bear upon me and say to yourself "So! It was a dream". Am I safe do you think?... You said to me once that the gods had been good to me. So they have and never more good than this last month.[42]

Such was Frances's devotion that she idly speculated on the possibility once of their marrying. If Mackenzie, of all his friends, had brought Asquith rather than Jack to the Grahams' Scottish holiday, would things have been different? 'But I belonged to the very middle-classes' he retorted. 'I don't suppose you would have looked twice at me, would you?' Her sentiments were different now and she admired his tenacity as he recounted his struggle as a young lawyer in search of a brief: 'the chilling, paralysing, deadening depression of hope deferred and energy wasted, and vitality run to seed'. Now with 'the great and charming' smiling on him, his hour had come. [43]

And in a sense, hers too as she began to emerge as a political muse. She not only attended debates in the House of Commons but would also advise and occasionally contribute to his speeches and articles. On issues such as the payment of MPs he would seek to justify to her his vote. His letters would recount the gossip from Cabinet meetings ('Rosebery in particular was at his gloomiest') and details of his interviews with the powerful, including Lord Cromer on Egyptian affairs. His press cuttings he would send her ('Don't you think that I am getting on?') and she would be mobilised to host political dinners for him, including one for Beatrice Webb ('not more prickly than I had expected'). Frances was both flattered and fascinated by her introduction into the political world and especially by being on the arm of the coming man.[44]

For all that, Asquith remained very open on his love for Margot. After accompanying her to the station, he confided to Frances 'She was sweet beyond words (you don't mind me saying this – I tell you everything)'.[45] On another occasion, he recalled 'there have been moments when we were almost more than lovers, and then a cloud sweeps down out of the blue and she seems separated from me by the whole width of heaven.' With his quest seemingly hopeless, he had turned more and more to Frances. 'And then, when the light turns low, you suddenly flash into my life, radiant, helpful, smiling through your tears, and you tell me that you will be with me and surround me with your love – and I am content.'[46] Content too with assignations in beech groves and 'culs-de-sac' and visits to Mells crackling with 'an atmosphere of electricity... not perhaps associated with the best regulated hearths'... 'I wish I were in my bedroom at Mells. Can you guess why? Goodnight'.[47]

On such scraps she chose to gamble.[48]

~ 19 ~

BLAME GAMES

Oh my dear, my dear, what a thing you have frivolled away that can never be got back.

Burne-Jones to Frances Horner[49]

It had been too good to be true. A month after leaving Mells distraught, Burne-Jones finally exploded. 'I shall never make you understand I know – that is my despair – it is clear that you can hurt me to the quick and have not the least suspicion... Oh no one ever [gave?] fuller and sweeter love than you – but for all that you have never been in love... I cannot bear it. I feel tired, worn, old and wasted.' Nothing symbolised her rejection more than her request that he burn all her letters, which at last he had done ('and it hurt').[50] Gone too was the chance to be the muse he had always wanted,

> a companion who identified with everything I did... I have waited and waited saying 'I wonder if she'll care for this or ask about that'. O Dearest, it sounds so little – but it wasn't little to me, it was everything – it was what I had been wanting all my life – a woman to be by me for whom I worked and who inspired and rewarded everything.

But Frances was never going to sacrifice her life to him or his art. Ever since she was a child traipsing around the studios, she had seen at first hand the plight of those who had. 'I will not be like every other woman' she retorted. If she was to be his muse, it would be on her terms.[51] Nevertheless, in his aspiring to more, something of the trust between them had been lost, an awkwardness that left him too 'frightened now to draw from her'.[52] That 'we see things so very differently' he blamed firmly on her desertion of him for the glamour of the Souls and Society. 'You are in the thick and swim of a world that I can't like or rest in for an hour; a world of restless pleasure and unreal brilliancy and it fits you and you like it and would be dull without it and the thought of it chills me and makes me angry and stony'. This was a betrayal of his values as much as his company. 'Can you imagine an artist born at Panshanger or Hatfield? I can't'. The previous Sunday he had laid out *The Golden Legend* on the table for her. Hoping that 'she'll look and wonder at it a bit – everybody else has, everybody has a pretty word to say about it'. Presumably she didn't? And so with an arch display of self-serving regret, he cast her forth. 'And now the worst is you can never ask me about my work again for I shall feel so silly if you do... Oh my dear, my dear, what a thing you have frivolled away that can never be got back'.[53] Frances's response to such melodrama hasn't survived but it plainly was sufficiently ferocious to have him scurrying to apologise. 'Forgive me …I believe every word you say …Love me again dear, I can't part from you – it is such an old story – I haven't a corner of my life or my thoughts where you are not, so you haunt me everywhere. I want you all to myself … [a] hopeless desire that has never known & can never know fruition … Pity and forgive, Angelico'.[54]

*

It is quite possible that Frances had unwittingly brought his tirade upon herself by a comment two days earlier which 'dreadfully hurt' Burne-Jones. Or perhaps she knew exactly what she was doing. The subject was a Mrs Gaskell (fig. 55). May Gaskell was an accomplished singer and pianist, who frequented the fringes of the Souls and gave elegant small dinner parties in her flat in Marble Arch. She had long been a friend of Frances who in 'early Spring' 1892 had brought her to The Grange to meet Burne-Jones. 'Beautiful in a girlish piquant manner', May was also very vulnerable, trapped in a brutal marriage with a bullying military husband. She quickly brought the chivalric out of the artist and in turn became the devoted follower he had long desired: deferential, adoring, and with no upbringing in art, eager to learn from him, as arm-in-arm that summer they sauntered around museums and galleries. In short, she was everything Burne-Jones felt he wanted and Frances wasn't. He was soon confiding to her his frustrations over Frances. At a reception 'Fifty people ate her up... She looked bright and well and is always kind, but I always feel she

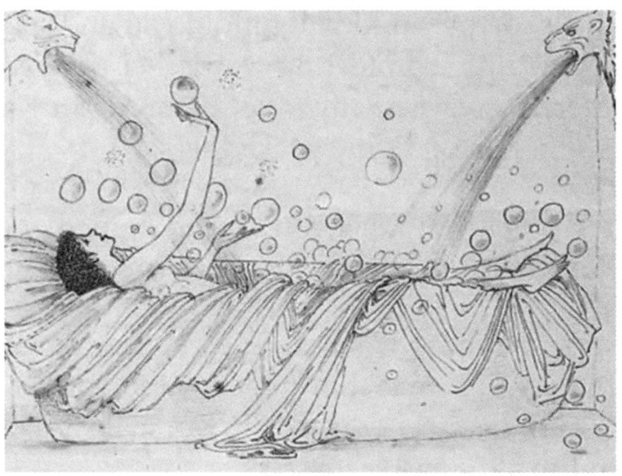

55.   *Sketch of May Gaskell enjoying a bubble bath,
by Edward Burne-Jones,*

sails along in the blue very far out of reach – and I potter along'.[55]
Frances, he declared, would want 'many friends', not one. Instead of
'one desire fulfilled [she] would want to add kingdom to kingdom – I
cannot share and am made to be jealous'. By contrast, May, thrilled to
have such an exalted champion, could not have been more attentive.
By August, he was declaring to her, 'I love you beyond all reckoning,
beyond all measure – you are quite perfect – body and soul you are
perfect, perfect'. That said, he was using similar language to Frances
at the same time: 'You are a brave girl and quite perfect, always and
always'. Burne-Jones would claim that he loved May at first sight. If
so, such feelings coincided with the hayrick at Milford. In effect, he
was running these relationships 'concurrently' through the summer
and autumn.[56]

As with the letters to Frances there was no shortage of expres-
sions of physical lust – if anything more so and seemingly some
action.

> O my God how I love you – it is terrible that one creature
> should have such power over any other – and I lie under your
> feet – and have no will or strength against you.

> But I should like to eat you; yes I really mean eat – set teeth in
> and chew up as I can't see how I shall ever have you all to myself
> in any other way.

Fly to me in all sorrow and I will unfold you and spoil you and pet you and say little comforting words… I gave you a heavy time this afternoon sweet lady – yet before I sin I am sure of forgiveness – so I go on in my wickedness.

Two or three times yesterday you looked pained and troubled at me – did my hands hurt you? Or were you sorry for me?

I know I pain you with my letters and yet they are as tame as I can make them – of course they pain you but you are so patient and sweet – and the nicer you are the worse I get – but give me time – I can learn to master myself.[57]

Not that she was keen sexually. But, having been long abused by one controlling man, she was not going easily to resist another. On the other hand, in her torment of a marriage, 'his friendship to me was like a benediction through the storms of life – his love a safeguard – his influence a continual help to the present hour'. For that she was willing to put up with his demands.[58] And there is no doubt that she represented a significant shift in his affections. While he continued to correspond with Frances, over the next two years he would send almost seven hundred letters to May; and it would be her children he would paint – most famously his portrait of her daughter Amy.

'A profound secret I want this to be', insisted Burne-Jones, 'a most holy compact.'[59] May was only too willing to assent as she feared scandal as much as Frances and hated going behind her friend's back. But very soon Frances sensed something was up. Writing to May on 26 October, Burne-Jones admitted, 'as Frances won't be there (I suppose), I should commit no indiscretions of speech as I did the other night – but should speak guardedly as becomes my years – she lays pitfalls for me and I fall into them invariably'. Trying to reassure May (and himself) on the charge of disloyalty he insisted that 'she [Frances] has no right in the matter at all – nor do I so much as matter to her as that…If I was necessary to her she had a splendid chance, only her own hands destroyed that chance'. By early November he was alerting May: 'she knows I am sure'. Frances seemed to have proposed an evening with just the three of them. This served neatly to flush him out and in his embarrassment sparked off his tirade.

At the same time he reassured May 'my mind was estranged and free before I ever told you – else I should never have been moved by you – I have never been untrue – never – never – nor once lied about love – nor will I ever.' Was he deluding himself or simply being deceitful? Fiona MacCarthy generously chose to describe him as 'a creature less of sexual treachery than of peculiar emotional elasticity'.[60] Others have attributed it variously to the male menopause or to the loss of his mother at his birth and thereafter his constantly seeking the maternal love denied to him. But it was also in him to want both Frances and May; for he couldn't resist the controlling game. Hence the repetitive phrases in his letters over the summer. It is there too in his request for a photograph of her – not just any photograph but the one in Frances's drawing room ('I want it. I want it now'). When in May's presence he left a letter from Frances lying prominently on a table, she chided him at his casualness as being unfair to Frances. He claimed that he had left it out 'on purpose' to see if she read it – 'beautiful of you to refuse…when you wouldn't look at it I compared you to others and said "she is perfect – there is none like her" – there is none like you'.[61] In April 1892 both Frances and May were vulnerable and needy, seeking refuge in the protection he offered. It was a role EBJ could never resist playing. One he had painted all his life.

*

How shall we ever get comfortable again?

Burne-Jones to Frances Horner [62]

'Do you know that years ago St C [Ruskin] said to me "Tell her", meaning you, "she can't hunt with the hounds and run with the hare"'. It was one of those barbed comments that intimates descend to when falling out – all the more hurtful for its shard of truth. For she too wanted both. Unlike Burne-Jones, Frances had not been deceitful. She had never wanted an affair and after much resistance he had eventually come to realise this: 'I have always been frightened that you were hurried that 11th of May and that you would never allow it – but it is so, I see it is all true'. However, she hadn't expected him to turn to someone else. First she was very angry – 'broken down' and 'troubled' he called her – as if somehow it was her fault. Yet she worried more that she was going to lose the friendship that had defined her life. As it happened, he too feared such a loss. 'Yes I am frightened of you leaving me', he admitted.[63] Encouraged, Frances took matters in hand and came up to London to see him. Burne-Jones was thrilled: 'you look so pale but wonderfully beautiful', he cooed; 'no face is like it or will be for centuries.'

Quickly he sought to reconstruct their 'bargain'. Claiming no longer to be 'jealous' of her new friends, he insisted 'I want you to play with Mr Haldane and Mr Asquith'. Ironically with no idea how close she had become to Asquith, he sent her many instructions to persuade him not 'to waste his heart' on Margot. 'She'd be a horrible wife…The Siren from Glen'.[64] As late as 24 November he was still protesting 'I haven't, I haven't being doing without you lately – it is true. If you could only see into me – it is you day and night'. Frances knew better but knew also now not to push. 'You are merciful to me and understanding how I love', he wrote in gratitude. Only a month later was there an admission of sorts, acknowledging that he was calling on May 'for I like her much'.[65] By then they had entered into a new compact: 'And you must defend me always and always be on my side – as I am on yours – in big things and little'. Typically their relationship was to remain a 'sacred secret'. From whom? May? Still secrecy suited Frances too. She had no sexual jealousy of May. When he promised that 'I am much tamer now', she was greatly relieved. What she gained was the return of the Burne-Jones with whom she had always enjoyed 'gutsy talks' on Balzac, Voltaire and Rousseau. And with the delivery of the Mells piano for his major retrospective, outwardly her standing remained undiminished. For Christmas she gave him a ring with A on it (for Angelo, their childhood name for him): 'I haven't used A since I was naughty', he wrote, returning to the childish banter of earlier days. 'How could I ever hurt you as I did – I was mad, I think – but I do love you so my dear, my dear.'[66] Yet he would never quite lose the madness. At a reception in early December, after he left and gone outside,

> it was so hard to leave that I didn't quite leave you – hoping you would come out of the house and walk back home. So I waited a bit and then another bit. [But Frances was] so late [in leaving] that they sent for a hansom for you and you drove past me. But I saw the tip of your hat – a man went in and I envied him…

It was like things I used to do 20 years ago and I haven't learnt better. Isn't it silly of me?[67]

*

What a strange year it has been.

Burne-Jones to Frances Horner

While Burne-Jones mused over the tribulations of 1892, Asquith looked back exultant in his triumph.

> Do you remember a midnight walk we once had together through the streets of London? In the days when you were very stand-offish… How haughty you were! And unresponsive – moving yourself in your well found port (with which you were so well contented) and refusing to budge an inch when I timidly suggested that you might – at least on a voyage of experimental discovery – 'put out to sea'… Every step on the road I took alone and unsupported, up to the point when I pushed open the door and forced my way in. Are you sorry? Do you repent?... Or do you feel that you and I are a little richer than we were twelve months ago. … And then I forced my way into Mells where there was no butler (except a female) and for ought I know, no bodies. Very bold and unmannerly – wasn't it? And …and…enfin! Would you have it otherwise?[68]

Almost certainly not. In the innocent days of the summer, she had declared 'I can't live in the future, can you? I would buy one day with a thousand years at any moment if the Angels were open to such bargains'. And in a sense she had. For however 'delightful' was her affair with Asquith, her position would always be emotionally precarious. 'As for the "long run" ', remarked her lover a touch breezily, 'we don't know how long it may be or how fast it may run'.[69] There would be only one winner from this.

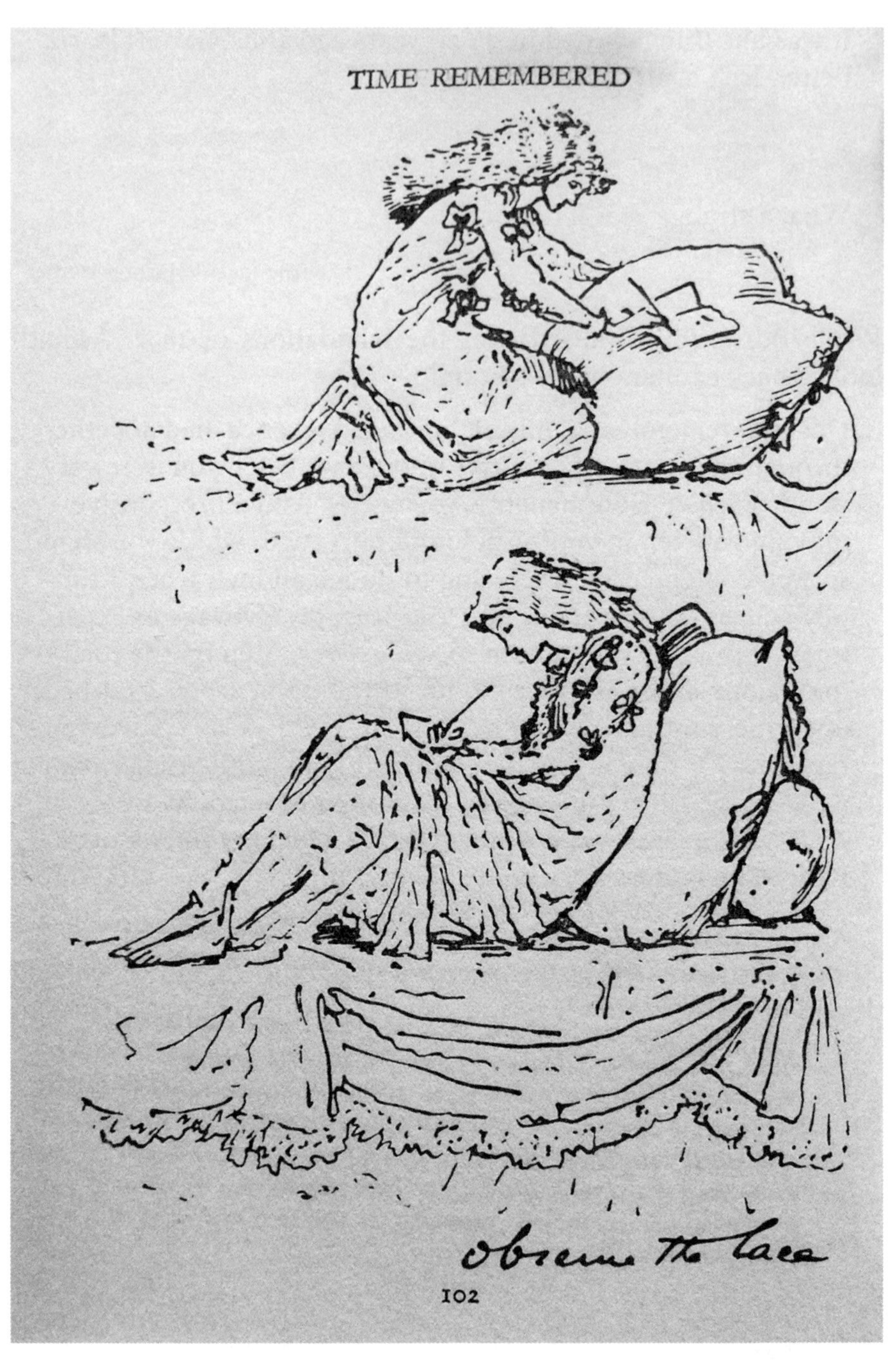

56.   *Sketch by Burne-Jones of Frances writing a letter to him,
reproduced in 'Time Remembered'*

Part Six

Dream Endings

For you fit me through and through and only to look at you is
to live splendidly.

Burne-Jones to Frances Horner[1]

~ 20 ~

CULS-DE-SAC

To Frances: a dancing shape, an image gay, to haunt, to start,
and way lay.

H.H. Asquith to Frances[2]

The new year found Asquith in jovial form, relishing the conspir-
atorial thrill of their liaison. 'Screens are excellent things in their
proper place – Mrs Gaskell's drawing room for instance – but they
are not needed in a self-contained and secluded flat. But even there
a [mirror?] has its uses.' Perhaps too there was the frisson to be had
in the drawing room of a rival. Then there was the excitement of
office and his immersion in government business, especially the var-
ied fare that landed on the Home Secretary's desk. This he shared
quite freely with Frances, from a dynamite explosion in London ('a
commonplace affair') to agonising over whether to commute the
death sentence on a murderer due to hang in the morning: 'someone
must decide these things'.[3] Politically these were exciting times with
Gladstone embarking on his last mission in the cause of Irish Home
Rule. Asquith and Frances dined together regularly for an update
before setting off for the next round of debates. She continued to
host little political dinners for him in which the Gerald Balfours and
Alfred Lytteltons would break bread with Irish Nationalists such
as Dillon and leading Liberals including John Morley.[4] Inevitably,
with Asquith 'submerged' under departmental business during the
day and defending the government on the floor of the House every
night, they didn't meet as freely as they would have liked.[5] This
was particularly frustrating as Frances had just taken a lease on a
house in Stratford Place. On the other hand, in early March, with
Margot insisting again on 'a parting of the ways', Asquith was soon

176

weekending again at Mells. Then on 16 May he very dutifully remembered the anniversary when 'we went to the theatre and walked home'. And though she had resisted his advances then, he recalled finding her letter the next day when she wrote of 'new opportunities and interests [that] keep coming in the most surprising way if one only throws the doors open. Has not this been so, both with you and with me?'[6] They were never to be so close again.

For by now, Frances was no longer in London, having succumbed in April to 'a relapse': 'Influenza or Typhoid, I don't know which'.[7] Not until July was she fit enough to return to London. There had been no let-up in their correspondence and at his request she had sent him roses from Mells. Yet on her return political controversies over Ireland meant that he was cancelling engagements quite frequently: 'I am hideously pressed on both sides right now', he would plead. To little avail, and for his sins he found her 'rather haughty' at a recent wedding. Later a visit to Mells 'suffered slightly from a lack of sun and an excess of Wyndhams'.[8] But far more so for what was unspoken – the Dodo affair.

Or, to be precise, *Dodo: a Detail of the Day*.[9] Published in May 1893 by E. F. Benson, the younger son of the Archbishop of Canterbury, it told the tale of the fast set in decadent London of the 1890s. Something of a publishing sensation, what caught the eye was its hilarious portrayal of a young socialite, giddy and shameless in her advance through Society. With her shallow ambition ('All these people must know who I am'), she was the amoral adventurer of cliché. Much fun was had over vulgarity denouncing the vulgar. But beyond the frivolity and gaiety and displays of seemingly open emotion, was the cold selfishness of someone who did what she wanted and ultimately betrayed everybody. What gave this lampoon its vicious edge was that it was unmistakably based on Margot, down to her turn of phrase and unintended witticisms. This was a ridicule long in the coming. Seemingly a carefree spirit, she was frequently to be found in the papers. Society gossip in 1891 had revelled in Margot's audacity in attracting the Kaiser's attention in the Royal Enclosure at Ascot. Keen to follow up on this triumph, she had moved heaven and earth to get an invitation to the ball in his honour, only for him to ignore her all evening. Then Frances had felt for her friend: 'Any stick is good enough to beat Margot with. It is a warning against ever trying and succeeding in outshining others.'[10] However, *Dodo* was brutally unfair in its characterisation, exaggerating all her worst features and not penetrating through the froth to the vulnerable and constant friend of many. More to the point, it was public and so much more damaging to her reputation. Margot was mortified when at a ball the Princess of Wales addressed her as Miss Dodo.

By this stage Asquith's hopeless devotion to Margot was widely known and a source of some ribaldry. To his intense embarrassment, senior Liberals such as Rosebery were writing heavy handed hints advising him to read *Dodo*. In similar vein, when he came to Mells in July, Frances left a copy by his bed. Possibly she felt it was a delicate way of letting him know what he might be in for.[11] Still it was quite a betrayal of a long-standing friend. Nor was she without motive – emotionally certainly, but politically too. Bound up as she was in Asquith's political ambitions, she would not be the only one who felt Margot would be a liability in a role that Frances could have fulfilled with distinction. Either way, it proved a catastrophic error. On seeing the book by his bed, Asquith angrily tossed it out of the window into the garden.

Quickly Frances sought to repair the damage. September would see him back for some 'Delightful days at Mells. I never regretted [the lack of] the Wyndhams for an instant! Indeed I think Mells is best when one is encamped there alone'. Afterwards he would return to London to find 'a beautiful piece of work which you have done for me… When I think of the time and thought and taste and deft labour … I feel that you have "given yourself with your gift"'. As indeed she had and perhaps too much so. Meanwhile over the summer letters and roses and bunches of lavender flowed out from Mells: reminding him of 'beech woods and well-meant "walks", and frequented culs-de-sac and bank holiday revelries and all kinds of fragrant memories…'[12]

These euphemisms had grown decidedly stale. In trying to act as if nothing changed, Asquith only confirmed that everything had. His striking refusal to join in the denunciation of Margot marked out that his resolve wasn't going to falter. Unlike Margot's: at her lowest she now saw the virtues of his loyalty. So while friends of Asquith were trying to dissuade him, friends of Margot were advising her to make the pragmatic choice. Curzon, Balfour, Blunt, even her lover, Peter Flower – all urged marriage to Asquith. Lord Dufferin, recently retired Viceroy of India, called on her in Grosvenor Square with some avuncular advice not to marry for love: 'You should marry in spite of being in love, but never because of it'. Perhaps this was just as well for, much she as admired Asquith, to someone as passionate as Margot, he fatally lacked 'this power of making love'.[13] And then there was his name. Her social insecurities would insist that he drop Herbert – the name he had been called all his life – for his second name Henry.[14] This would be 'a duty marriage' driven by 'strong approval more than by love' she confided to DD. With melodramatic flourish she declared 'I hope, if I marry Asquith, I shall die with my baby; then I shall have done the right thing'. And so in May 1893 she seemed at last 'to re-open the door'. In October with Asquith a guest at Glen, the Tennant estate in the Scottish Borders, she met his latest proposal not with rejection but with a request for three months' grace to consider it. Only then to insist that he was not to write to her until she gave her answer.[15]

If for Asquith this was progress of sorts, for Frances it felt more like a stay of execution. In no sense did they fall out, but after his return from Glen, their correspondence gets a little tetchy. In his diary she has returned to being 'Mrs Horner'. She still went to support him in the House and held small dinners for him. And so understandably she was a little hurt when on 5 December he pulled out at the last minute because of 'another guest whom, at this moment, it is not convenient that I should meet'. Over everything hung the shadow of Margot's imminent declaration. There was a valedictory air to Asquith's review of the year past in which Frances's 'constant friendship and affection' was a boon that will 'master time. Let us always hold fast to it'. She in turn commissioned Burne-Jones to draw (and sign) a portrait of her as a memento. 'Your magnificent present came last night', he wrote, 'and wherever I pitch my tent I shall keep it near me as a perpetual feast for the eyes and the heart'.[16] But not near enough. On 9 January 1894 Margot wrote to accept Asquith's offer.[17]

Asquith seemed genuinely surprised at the 'tone of farewell' that marked his next visit to Mells. To him 'there need be no break in the continuity of the story; and no change …could possibly blot out… such a friendship and affection as ours. So let us remain as we are.'[18] This was impossible. Frances had no desire to lose a friend but propriety dictated that she should step back. Here would begin the myth of her triumphant matchmaking that would enjoy its fullest expression in her autobiography forty years later. In this, her close relationship with Asquith is fast forwarded to Scotland and late 1893 where 'soon he became a close personal friend and I promised to help him in the attainment of his desire – to marry Margot Tennant'.[19] That she was in a position to do so is unquestioned. Along with only Con Manners and Ettie Desborough, Frances had long been one of very few in whom Margot confided over her love affairs. Yet Frances had done everything in her power to prevent the marriage – something Margot never once suspected.[20] With the die cast, Frances now made a great display of endorsing the wedding, with her daughter Cicely to be a bridesmaid and offering Mells Park for the honeymoon (which Asquith accepted without a moment's hesitation).

Privately she grieved her loss. The speed with which Asquith absorbed himself in his new situation was both natural and hurtful. The realisation that he viewed their time as 'a pleasure and a refresh-ment', something that left him 'ashamed but unrepentant', was no less painful for being inevitable from the outset. Belatedly he realised her plight: 'I don't know if you are of a forgiving disposition – for I don't remember ever testing that side of you before!'[21] Undoubtedly she was jealous that the opportunities that she had glimpsed and for which she was so much better suited, were now Margot's. As she reminisced, they had met as he was 'just entering on that brilliant career which led him to 10 Downing Street' and she saw the chance to bring him on, as twenty years earlier she had supported Burne-Jones at the outset of his fame. It was a role she loved to play and one she could play very well. No doubt too she was envious of the money Margot could bring to his cause. Worst of all, she would no longer feel at the centre of things.[22]

All of these were secondary to the loss of Asquith himself. 'Never was better company than Henry Asquith in those days: keen, cour-teous, giving you always of his best', succeeding at everything he put his hand to. No 'party [was] complete without him'. Theirs was an intimacy of minds – a rapport that meant 'I grew to enjoy things in proportion as he shared them'.[23] And then largely at his instigation, it became something more. Back in the summer of 1892, as Frances was escaping the hayrick at Milford, she had written to Asquith: 'it is rare as you say for people to get both sides of their life perfect. Persons and things are so ill-sorted that one sometimes wishes for a general reshuffling'. With Jack drawing up a list of her friends to whom he attached 'a black mark', she was more than ready for a 'reshuffling'.[24]

Asquith offered a liberation – emotional as well as intellectual – and one all the more exhilarating for being so precarious. Briefly with him she enjoyed the life she had ever wanted. Tragically she let him come too close. They remained friends and Frances would never forget his birthday. He in turn would occasionally visit Mells, was briefly their lodger in 1898, and as late as 1910 was writing scraps of a poem entitled 'To Frances: a dancing shape, an image gay, to haunt, to start, and way lay.' Yet Asquith had quickly moved on. 'Nice talk with Asquith', she reported to Burne-Jones. He 'is happy and has got what he wants and doesn't want what he hasn't got, [un]like all the rest of us'. As for Frances, his marriage soon sucked the life out of their friendship and left her adrift. 'I used to agree with you', she admitted to DD, 'saying that the more one knew and saw Mr Asquith the more one loved him – but I hardly know him at all now and I don't find it makes much difference'.[25]

FREE FALL

Oh Harry Cust! Harry Cust! I was wrong to like you so much.

Edward Burne-Jones[26]

I don't mind Harry Cust being immoral or Violet Rutland lying or Pamela [Wyndham] intriguing any more than I mind dogs barking. The shock is when people do something one could never have believed.

Frances Horner[27]

Burne-Jones's lamentation signalled that Harry Cust's philandering had at last got the better of him (fig. 58). Though none would admit it, his string of affairs among the willing had only added to his lustre – not least among the women of the Souls. Violet Granby (fig. 57) was not the only one to have borne his child (in this case the future Diana Cooper). There was also his long-standing relationship with Margot's married sister, Lucy Graham Smith, which in turn did not deflect him from a courtship of Pamela Wyndham, apparently with an eye to marriage. Many sought to dissuade Pamela, to no effect. Then in September 1893 had come word that Miss Nina Welby-Gregory (fig. 59) was pregnant. Nina was the pliant acolyte of Violet Granby, very beautiful and utterly silent. Frances found her a complete mystery: 'her extreme calm, and absence of all emotions, good or bad, and her utter indifference to any consideration except that of what Harry's feeling towards her for the moment may be, are very disconcerting'.[28] Enigmatic, 'ornamental' and tragically dull, Nina was the last person Harry would want to marry. But she adored him. So, seeing an opportunity, Violet Granby had thrust them together in the hope that her lover would marry Nina – someone she, in turn, could manage. With Harry now hesitating to do the honourable

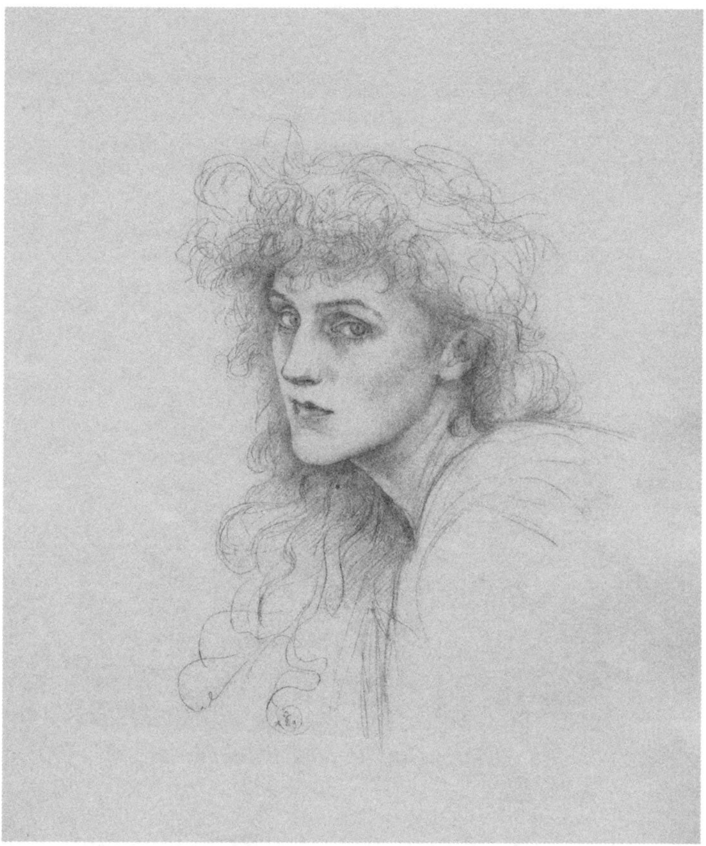

57. Self-portrait, by Violet Granby

thing, Violet spread the news of Nina's pregnancy among the Souls. Having always prided themselves on being morally superior to the louche Marlborough Set, for the first time the Souls now faced the prospect of a public scandal. Ultimately, Balfour was compelled to adjudicate and, threatening social and political exile, ordered Harry to marry Nina on 11 October. To complete the melodrama and avert any gossip, both Lucy and Pamela were dispatched to India (on separate ships!).

And then, a child came there none. Had she lost the child? Had there ever been a child?[29] For those who couldn't believe Nina capable of such deceit, the blame lay elsewhere – on the manipulative Lady Granby; and on Harry for his cold rejection of Nina after their marriage.[30] Burne-Jones was one who feared for Nina. But his

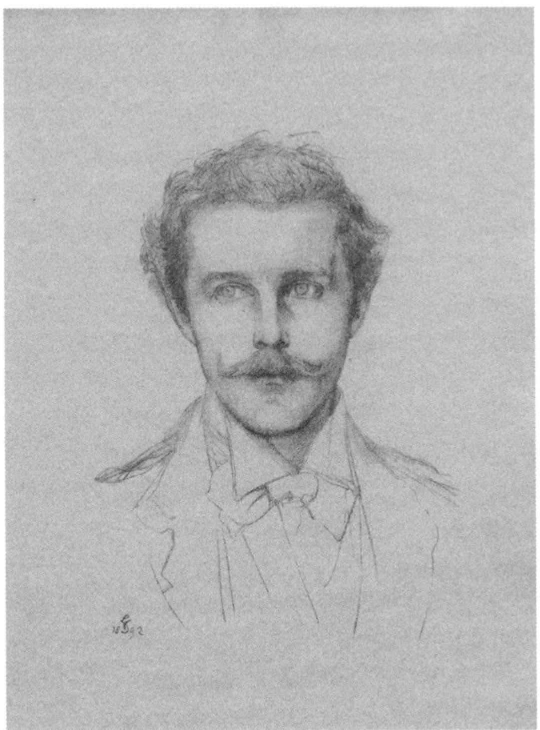

58.   Harry Cust, by Violet Granby, 1892

'the other ladies must be men and get over it' illustrated where the strength of feeling lay.[31] For those for whom Harry was a 'godsend' in a house party, Nina was the evil siren. One who showed no mercy was Mary Gladstone as Frances discovered:

> It is dreadful having Mary and Nina here together. Mary said she could not smile in the same room! And that she hated everything Nina did or said. I think she expected her to lie on the ground with her hair loose all the time – and I don't believe she ever did really. Mary … is harsh… and always wanting to make out that other people are sinning.

But because Mary was 'stimulating in so many ways… I love her still' and so 'cowardly I avoided combat'.[32] Even generous friends like DD felt that Nina would be better off dead than live with the shame: 'I don't want her to [die], though I generally feel it to be the only solution'. As for Frances, she still welcomed Nina to her house. Nevertheless, what really concerned her was saving Harry's political

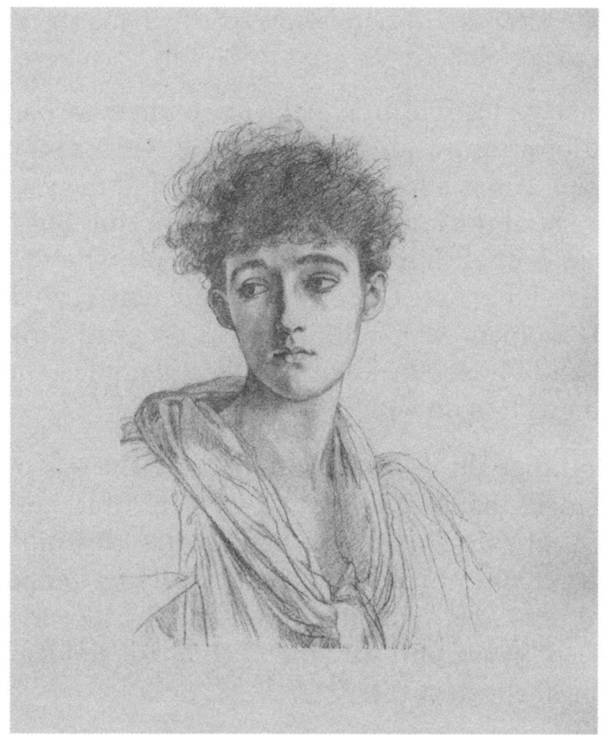

59. *Nina Welby-Gregory, by Violet Granby*

career, bravely accompanying him to meetings with Asquith and Balfour in September 1893. There were always going to be limits to his rehabilitation and although he left parliament at the 1895 election, to return in 1900 his reputation was forever tarnished.[33]

For some this event broke up the camaraderie of the Souls. Others attributed the decline to another marriage in 1894 and the loss of Margot who had given their gatherings such life force. While 1895 would see many of them in office for the next ten years and so less ready to play. Thus Curzon's departure for India as Viceroy marked their final (and very glamorous) hurrah. For Frances though, it was the death of Pembroke that marked the end of an era. Never in robust health, for two years a mysterious intestinal disease had slowly and painfully devoured him. A sad flow of letters from health spas in Gibraltar and Germany (where Frances had travelled out to see him) offered little hope to his friends. For all that he was a modest, private man, when he died in May 1895 they would gather in force at Wilton along with two thousand mourners to bid him farewell. Although women rarely attended funerals save of their family, Frances was determined to go. 'Yesterday I went to Wilton', she wrote to DD.

> It was like some terrible dream: the place where we had been so often just for pleasure, all decked out with sail – a strange pageant of grief. It was a lovely, hot blue day and the grave under the horse chestnuts looked pretty and peaceful. But it was all terribly sad… The Church was full of people who really loved him: Charty, Ettie, Kate C, Betty [Balfour] Kath [Lyttelton] and I the only women except the family. I dropped a rose down from you and I hoped he knew that we did not feel the strange scene had much to do with him.

Jack and Doll thought it 'beautifully done'. Yet it was precisely the triumph of form that Frances found 'very terrible' and upsetting. Afterwards 'I sat with Doll on the bank by the clear little stream… and we talked of him which I liked. Betty [Balfour] too such an angel to me [with] her sweet sympathetic ways'. Still DD was wise not to go: it had been 'so sad and so unlike Pembroke and such a strange end to all our happy days there'.[34]

*

That autumn Frances was sailing but not on the *Black Pearl*. Instead of Mull and Skye, she was in the Mediterranean en route for Constantinople. Nevertheless, 'I have been haunted all my time here by Pembroke – I never am on deck without fancying he will come up looking more darling at every hour of the day. I never sit in the evening watching the stars come out without remembering the happiness of his companionship'.[35] Her new host, Lord Llandaff, could not have been more different: 'manlike, he was a slave to routines and could not enjoy impromptu joys'. Still she had a good friend and ally in Mary Crawshay and together they 'haunted the bazaar, drank sherbet and listened to the bulbuls in the hanging gardens, and felt they were living with Omar Khayam'.[36] With 'divine …skies and sympathetic blue sea' – into which she dived every morning, this was just the restorative tonic she needed. Admittedly, Athens was a disappointment 'except for the Acropolis' and Broussa 'more easternly wonderful' than Constantinople. 'Stamboul', she reported back to Jack, 'is all so squalid and mean':

no bazaars – earthquakes and massacres have done for them; the mosques all done up in vile taste; I cried for their having painted over the mosaics at St Sophia. It *is* a lovely church but so spoiled… only there was worship going on and The Koran and it was very impressive.[37]

The massacres were of two thousand Armenian Christians who the week before had marched in protest at the Sultan's stalling on agreed concessions to them. Their violent repression had sparked pogroms, led by Muslim fanatics and supported by the Turkish police across the Ottoman Empire. The full extent of the horror was not yet clear when Frances witnessed the Sultan's weekly progress to prayers. 'Never seen anything more glittering as a spectacle': 10,000 picked troops in green and blue uniforms with 'white-veiled women' lining the route, as 'great fat wicked-looking pashas…and enormous black wickeder-looking eunuchs' passed below their balcony followed by carriages of wives and 'some darling little boys in uniform…his sons'. Finally 'a carriage with a hood up and cowering inside, harassed, furtive-looking, a man who looked like a Jew and so the Sultan drove by and everyone bowed down'.

Thanks to their friend the ambassador, Sir Philip Currie, they were granted a brief audience with the Sultan, 'a little man dressed in a soldier's overcoat down to his feet…with an interpreter beside him'. Fascinated to see one whose duplicity and evil was a staple Liberal belief, Frances couldn't resist the opportunity and 'tried to say, "Sire, we have been horrified by the cruelty and injustice of your government". To such little effect that she felt sure that the interpreter translated their greetings as "the strangers bow to the dust before the Refuge of the world and their eyes are blinded by the glory and splendour of the shadow of God, and the benevolence of his reign"'.[38]

The next day they saw the reality for themselves. Calling in on the British Embassy on Bosphorous, they found dragomen from the British and Russian embassies preparing to go out and stand guard over Armenians sheltering in churches. Joining them there Frances heard terrifying tales of massacres by Turkish troops: 'a heart rending scene… all the women had lost husbands and children. They threw themselves at our feet, clung to our dresses and kissed our hands … all sobbing and shaking'. Outside the Turkish police were waiting for them. Rumours abounded of Turkish theological students, aided by police, 'breaking into a church and massacring all inside – women and children – heaps of them thrown into the Bosphorous … I shall be glad to go from this place. It is vile in every way'.[39] By the time order had been restored, up to three-hundred thousand Armenians were dead.

*

On her return she found 'long arrears of mothering to do'. But not just for her children. The marriage of her latest 'Laura' was in trouble within months. Staying with Aggie in Dublin, Violet Cecil[40] had been determined to meet Frances and they had hit it off on first sight. Fresh faced, exuberant, and free-thinking, Violet at twenty-two was eighteen years younger than Frances but 'she spoke most lovingly of you', Burne-Jones reported with some glee. 'She says she slipped in to your [bedroom] and talked for four hours.'[41] Youthful adoration was just what Frances needed in the aftermath of Asquith's wedding. 'So sweet and natural, with lots of fun and interest – and no spirit of competing or wanting to be anything you aren't which is very soothing, I thought her delightful', Frances admitted to DD.[42] And they had much in common. Both were ladies of spirit, without fortunes, marrying well (in Violet's case very well with Lord Edward Cecil) if not for love, and sharing a bond in 'BJ'. 'There is a spirituality of Passion', Frances would claim on the eve of Violet's marriage, 'which seems to draw us closer together' and she begged her not to forget 'this wonderful time'.[43] A year on and she feared her young friend was getting restless.

'The longer I live the more I feel convinced that happiness is an art not a condition', Frances confessed to DD. Not without reason. 'Lady N [not identified] is quite nice and I think people like her but she is the sort I could never take *inside* the house … Jack is supposed by the others to carry on violently with Lady N which I fear must be a symptom of senility, as I noticed she always had great success from the aged'. It was clearly time to regroup.[44] And, as ever, she would look to Edward Burne-Jones.

~ 22 ~

TRIANGULAR COMPANY

Oh dear one, you are so deep in my life that you are a part of the
air I breathe – are you jealous of my surroundings? … You said
yourself that triangular company was perplexing and anxious
work.

Burne-Jones to Frances Horner[45]

This was never going to be easy. Frances now had to come to terms
with what Burne-Jones rather coyly called 'the friendship between
Mrs Gaskell and me'. In fact, he was increasingly open with Frances,
sharing his fear of 'kitchen talk' and discussing his plans for sketch-
ing May.[46] If truth be told, Frances was a little more jealous of his
'surroundings' than she expected to be. And, while she had no
desire to adopt the deferential role that Burne-Jones craved and May
offered, she did indeed find 'triangular company … anxious work'.
Emotionally she had long been bound up with Burne-Jones and
so too her identity. Still, when the test came she didn't fail him. In
August 1893 news arrived from Paris that *Love among the Ruins* (1872)
had been destroyed. A photographer in Paris, not appreciating that
it was a watercolour and not an oil, had poured egg white to bring
out the colouring. Its loss left the artist 'sickened, and stunned and
staggery'.[47] For this was no ordinary painting. With Maria Zambaco
to the fore, it embodied the height of their affair, just as it was about
to come crashing down. Frances, who had known him for so long,
understood this in a way May could not. She was as distraught as
he at this 'terrible loss... I feel as if someone had died … If only it
hadn't been that one … if only I could put my arms around you and
comfort'. But with her sister Amy at Mells ill and very 'frail', Frances
was tied. 'I can't bear to think of you so far off and alone. I do hope

189

rather that you will go away. Go to May, she is soft and gentle and she loves you so'.[48] Such generosity of spirit hit its mark. As the awkwardness ebbed away, Frances and May would occasionally call on him together and even arrange dates to ensure that he was not left alone for long. 'I had a delightful time with BJ last night', Frances divulged to DD: 'he seemed to put aside all the things that sometimes come between the closest of friendships'.[49]

Nevertheless Frances was not walking away. She could always make him laugh but now with a purpose, as she reminded him that theirs was a friendship with ancient roots – instinctive, telepathic and not easily discarded.

> You know exactly how I feel about things always without my telling you; just as I know, or think I do, what you feel without your even saying a word to me… And I know you might and do always say to yourself 'there is one woman in the world (I'm afraid there's more but that is not my fault) who thinks that there is nothing ever good enough for me and no one fit enough to black my shoes…and she lives rather a solitary life in spite of an impression to the contrary and she has hardly any friends and those she has she would serve up as relics…And I can't help being very fond of her for I have known her so long – though perhaps Mrs ****** and Lady ****** and Nun **** are more easy and delightful to me in many ways'.[50]

Theirs remained a relationship distinctive for being a romance of imaginations. 'What', he asked her, 'did you mean once by saying to me that you didn't care what I did but only what I thought?' As she confessed to DD, 'I wish I had the inside of some people's brains'.[51] This was true but as she was discovering, only partly so. With Asquith married and Pembroke dead, in her gloom it would be Burne-Jones to whom she would turn for solace.

> Darling you were so sweet to me the other night and you will never let me get far off from you, will you – because the world would be a very grey one to me without you. I don't think I should want to stay in it – you are so bound up with all in life that means romance to me. But when you are proud… I am easily discouraged and so we might come to be separated in the crowd – and I always say to myself, 'he will never tell you the

day he ceases to care – he will never say for people don't – one has to find it out and not be stupid and blind about it'. How you will scold me for that but you know it is true, isn't it?[52]

Lest he felt tempted to move on, she looked to make herself indispensable. She was always adept at raising morale. 'As I growled at my fate', he acknowledged, 'your letters are always bright to me – always – you have learnt how to live and are much clever at it than I' (fig. 56). She sensed too his anxiety as his popularity appeared to wane. With the Grafton Gallery 'crammed with fashion' to see some 'flimsy Romneys' and so few to see 'heavenly things at the New Gallery', he would despair, 'Oh what is to be done with these people? Forget them is best and go one's own way'. As if he could. 'Tell me when was my prime? Did I ever have one?', he would fish and she would be quick to reassure.[53] It would be to her he would turn when old friends – especially Morris – died. Soon they were seemingly back on old terms. 'Only when I write to you', he confessed, 'a thousand madcap follies come into my head and I spin away…I am your longest friend that ever was…Come and take me to a play tonight. I feel reckless and daredevilish'. Frances's relief was palpable: 'I saw BJ a little' she told DD. 'It was very free and I feel as if I had taken breath for ever so long and needn't come up to the top again for ages.'[54]

Still reconciliation required acceptance of May. 'I do love her very much and will tell her so', would prove a constant refrain in Frances's letters. At his request she agreed to write to May 'who is ill and bullied', assuring him that 'I really am deeply pitiful for that poor little spoiled life'. Waspish certainly, but it reflected her suspicion that May rather overdid her plight. Rallying to one desperate cry for help, Frances had arrived to a scene of domestic harmony with May 'bright and alive'.[55] However, Frances determined to absorb May rather than challenge her, relying on her rival's acute sense of guilt. May would soon become a regular guest at Mells. She had after all been a long-standing friend and would remain so. But Frances had always been the more forceful personality and was now not shy of asserting a pecking order where Burne-Jones was concerned. 'I am glad for you she went to you', she told him bristling with condescension, 'because she is very, very nice and she would appreciate the honour she was having'. 'I love her with all my heart', Frances would protest, 'and she knows a little of what you are and that is a great big tie'. In all of this May happily acquiesced, even to the extent of writing to apologise when walking out with Burne-Jones they had unexpectedly met Frances. While Frances insisted to Burne-Jones that 'there is nothing to explain', she could not help 'wish[ing] it had been me who had been walking with you'.[56]

Stealthily Frances reasserted possession. Thanking Burne-Jones for his latest 'little note…'

> For it touched and gladdened me as any proof of your love and thoughts must always do…Believe me it is in no one's power to cast a shadow between you and me… in my heart … I always say to myself – oh yes he may love this and that … but those others are all different and he belongs to me and I to him… That is my little private credo. So you see not one of them could really hurt. You know every fold of my nature and love me in spite of my every weakness and pride, so why should I fear what woman could do'…. 'Though I always have pressed you to have men-friends! They are so much better in heaps of ways.[57]

It helped that from 1894 May was often away for months on end taking cures in Switzerland and Italy, when not at Beaumont, the family estate near Lancaster. 'May out of sight of all people, trying a rest cure, I suppose', reported a forlorn Burne-Jones. With May 'an invalid for many a month'… 'Of course I should fall in love with you', he jested. Soon they were on old territory. 'Do you know I haven't the faintest idea how old you are', he admitted. 'I think of you always as three and twenty [actually she was forty-three] – but how sweet it is that I have known you so long – and how safe it is – Beyond the reach of Fate'. Or indeed anyone else. Flattery aside, Frances too would reinforce these 'ancient ties' by calling him 'My Darling Angelo' – the nickname of her childhood. 'I thought with a tightening of the heartstrings how I loved you', she would declare. 'There was never anyone like you in this world – the only bother is that so many people have found this out'.[58] Nor was she above a little coy flirtation. With Georgie away, 'I could come and stay' was more of a temptation than a prospect. So too was her desire to 'slip away and go and live dishonoured in lodgings for a bit. Will you come? I know you won't, but if you were me, you would'. As ever, he would push matters to the limit. When her letter arrived unsealed, he teased: 'I remember a good twenty years ago observing how delicate you were, as becoming a princess, in the matter of moistening your envelopes'. This was as nothing compared to the letter from Miss Anderson, the artist's over-eager secretary. Asked if there was anything else he needed writing, 'for fun I suggested, "Yes, write for me to Mrs Horner" and to my amazement she set to work. I have no idea what she said'. What she said (and what he dictated?) was 'Sir Edward… bids me say to you that when a whole fortnight has passed in toil without a word from you he begins to think that a little or a good deal of distraction ought to be administered to him in the shape of "petting". I think that was the word he used'. It was not long before Frances was reappearing in his dreams.[59]

*

> And often and often I thought of you – for it was as if you and I
> at the end of life were chatting together over the past.[60]
>
> Edward Burne-Jones to Frances Horner

For Frances, it was the restoration of an old conversation that she most treasured. Burne-Jones was of course for her a vital, if not wholly reliable, source of London news, whether of ribald gossip or vivid descriptions of great events, such as Tennyson's funeral ('so flat and flattening') or the 'going out of Gladstone' after the rejection of his second Home Rule Bill.[61] Humiliation was also the fate of their friend Henry James. To the Souls he was the greatest author of the late nineteenth century. Play writing was a recent departure and, as with his novels, so his plays made few concessions to the back stalls. *Guy Domville* was certainly a demanding play, in which the hero renounces his vocation to be a priest to secure the family fortunes, only for him to revert to the priesthood at the end. Burne-Jones was at the St James's Theatre on 5 January 1895 to support his friend on the first night. Describing the scene later to Frances, he told of how

> It began beautifully – far away above the heads of the audience
> I feared. Yet it went on, bless him, as many of his stories do, so
> that nobody did anything…Some people wouldn't stand it and
> roared and hissed and it was so horrible, so that nothing will
> induce me ever again to go to a first night… Nor have I written
> to Henry James – nor do I know what to say – he is too good

for the stage – it is coarse work – I am always sorry Shakespeare stooped to it.[62]

After barely thirty performances, the play was pulled and replaced by *The Importance of Being Earnest* – a sure fire hit by Oscar Wilde, then at the height of his fame. On 5 April however Oscar Wilde was arrested for 'committing unnatural acts.' To Burne-Jones, Wilde's fall was 'like a nightmare. Sometimes I am so sorry for him … and sometimes I say it serves him right and let justice do its full – he has shamed and hurt the best things so wickedly'. What really offended him was not the homosexuality, nor even the spending '£50 per day on rent boys' while leaving his wife impecunious – though he deplored this. Rather it was the cynicism of the 'hideous' Yellow Book crowd who in their ridicule corroded all faith and values.[63] 'I am sick of wit and want never to hear of paradox again… How he has sullied and hurt the sweetest and best things …so I curse him… No ideal of life can stand against these cataracts of wit and mockery'. With Wilde 'wiped out', the 'air will be cleaner'. Frances was no cynic but for her the trial and the public fascination it aroused was 'like looking on at an execution and one turns away sick'.[64]

As ever books were topics of fierce discussion, as each tried to educate the other. Despite Frances, Burne-Jones continued to despair of the late nineteenth century's penchant for the brutal, unforgiving ending. She in turn, on moral grounds, deplored his enthusiasm for the 'full and unrestricted Pepys'.[65] They managed to agree on the works of Le Fanu, with Frances conceding that they were 'curious and uneven but full of wandering genius, I think'.[66] She was more sure in her support of Burne-Jones's nephew, Rudyard Kipling. 'When I read "The Recessional" this year, it gave one that sudden start and throb that means something of the first rank – at least so it seemed to me'.[67]

What they never lost was their Romanticism and especially their love of nature in the raw. 'What a summer!' he exclaimed. 'It rains and blows and thunders – there was a thunderstorm the other day, the very wickedest thing I ever saw. The sky cracked like a shivered looking glass and the thunder …snarled…and the roads ran white like devil's milk'. Frances may have decried the boredom of the countryside but not when the weather ran wild. 'Storms sweeping over the land,' she in turn would recount. 'And the tree going and quite a hot uncanny air – as if full of portents… But you know I am a rather restless being and if I am not sitting beside the person I love best … then I like to be meeting the wind on the hill, or sailing or running about or feeling alive somehow'.[68]

His work remained their closest bond. With her, he continued to share his struggles with epic portrayals of *The Fall of Lucifer* (1894) and *The Dream of Launcelot* (1896). Burne-Jones's last years were frantic ones – a race to the last. 'I vow it keeps me sane', he would insist. 'Though it tires me to bits to stand all day, it staves off madness…I love it – I love its tiredness…the bad body beaten and crushed for a bit'. Despite working on many paintings at once ('Perseus, at a portrait or two, at Avalon'), by the end 'Nothing matters but Avalon. And to think you are only a drive from it'. She knew its significance to him: 'Glastonbury, it's holy ground isn't it?' she would offer up.[69] In the meantime she loved his illustrations for Morris's Chaucer ('delightful, the most lovely book that ever was made'). And he took time to praise her 'beautiful' embroidery' exhibited in Oxford Street, triggering a long debate on the background and framing.

Fellow artists remained a rich vein. Frances invited Sargent to a house party at Mells. She found him 'very nice and simple and … very shy and not the least like an American and he wasn't very like an artist either!' Among the guests was Margot at her most overpowering. Sargent proved 'very frightened of Margot…He hated discussing all his Great Friends, and having his coat collar stroked and talking about his pictures, and he hid behind Violet [Cecil] and me in a way that made me feel quite hysterical.' Burne-Jones claimed to like Sargent personally but 'I never want to see anything he does'. Frances found this professional jealousy hilarious and she chose to rile him further by admitting 'On Sunday we had two art critics (!) here'. Including 'one called Berenson who lived in Florence. I am afraid you would hate him: he was *exactly* like a man in Ibsen, you know what Ibsen's learned men are like – but he knew a lot'.[70] On modern developments in architecture they were as one, railing against slate roofs and red-brick houses. Or what Frances, finding herself in Westgate-on-Sea in Kent, denounced as 'an Awful Place…with little hot red villas swarming with dreadful young people and every now and then these…culminate in worse places called Margate or Ramsgate or Hell's Gate'. Plainly it had not been the most successful of family holidays but then as Burne-Jones pointed out to her, 'how sweet it is to live in a land of stone as you do'.[71]

Lightening these exchanges was the gentle teasing that was the mark of old friends who knew each other only too well. 'So horrid my life is compared with yours', he would insist when he wanted to provoke her. 'With you it is all peace, ordered duty, voices of children in the glades, buttercups, daisies, milking pails at eventide, rumours of an outside troubled world, sleep and delicious wakings'. Charged with being a country bumpkin, Frances never failed to rise. That he was writing three letters to every one of hers was another constant complaint ('Are you busy? Are you bothered?'). Instead, he claimed, she would be skating all day long at Wimbledon or on the Serpentine by torchlight 'while I am gnashing my teeth at the darkness when I am so busy'. Before quickly parrying her likely response: 'And you will say I ought to be thankful at my age that I have teeth to gnash'. Occasionally such banter would hit home. The 'timid' Rooke adored Frances but Burne-Jones couldn't resist passing on his assistant's inadvertent comparison of her to Marie Antoinette. 'Quoth Rooke: "she was very like Mrs Horner in many ways. She had the same devouring interest in things that were alive and happening, *and in all men that were notable and making time famous*"'.[72]

In January 1896 Burne-Jones was in Upper Brook Street watching Frances's children act a short play. 'When in the epilogue, I was brought into that beloved circle of you… and thought of many years, I felt a tear coursing down its way, for in a moment I saw all the past – ancient loved evenings and many a loved time and one whom I never forgot – so my heart was full and tender.' She too was drawn back to the past. Declaring herself 'so stupid and empty … yet I hunger and thirst after wisdom. I think it is because I got to know you early in life and have never been able to be satisfied since, so it is your fault after all darling.' Time had brought them full circle.[73]

*

This was a relationship that would end as it began – with a picture of Frances. Started in 1892 and never finished, it had a variety of provisional titles including 'The Maiden and Necromancer picture', 'The Sorcerer picture', before acquiring *The Wizard* after Burne-Jones's death (fig. 60).[74] Conceived and then abandoned in the emotional heat of 1892, he would return to it in 1896 and be working on it to

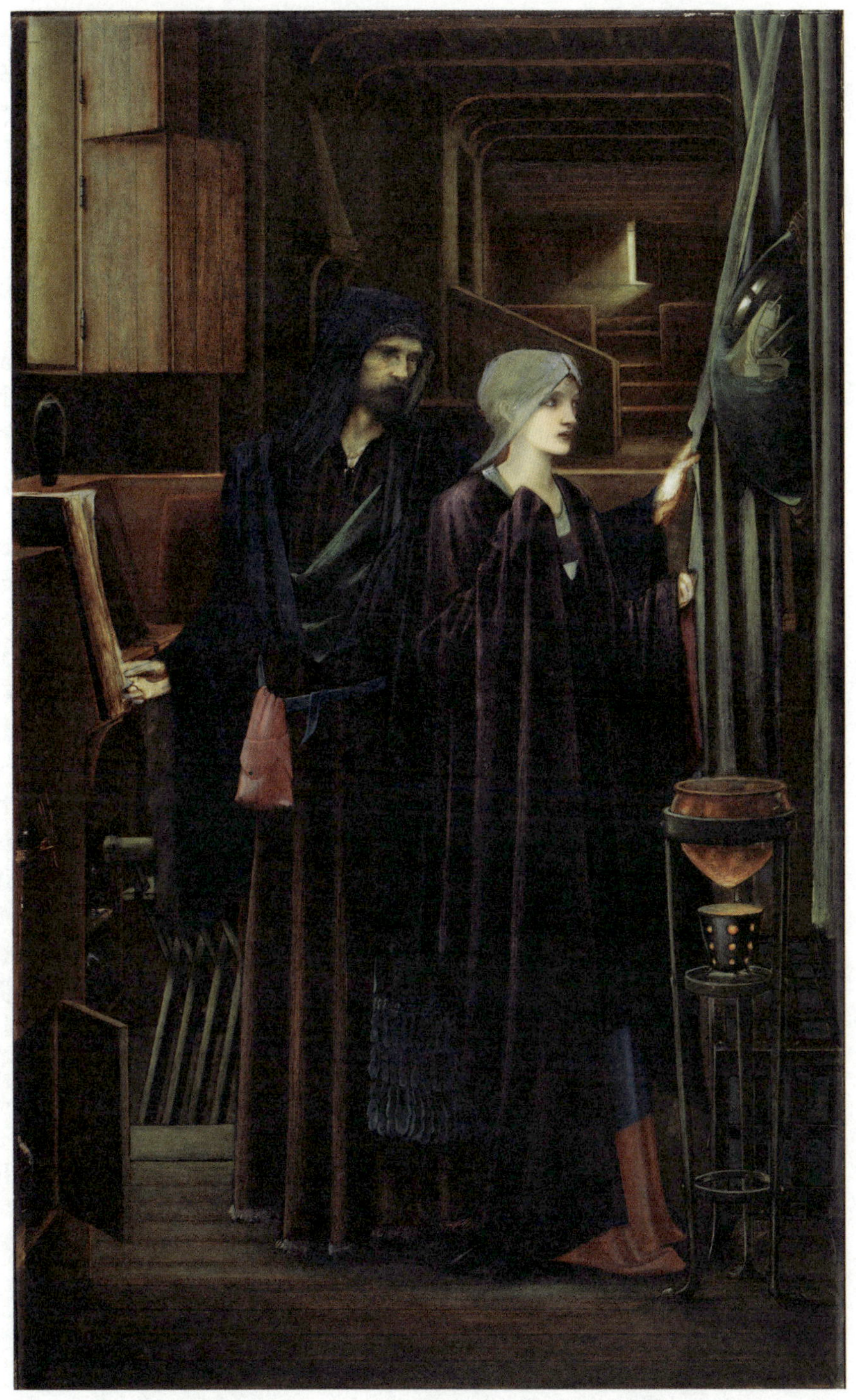

60.   *The Wizard, by Edward Burne-Jones, 1892 and later*

the last.[75] Quite possibly its origins were even earlier. 'The work I brought down', he wrote to her in November 1897, 'is something I began just twenty seven years ago – if I may have time I will pay all my debts – and you were a girl of ten'.[76] This was probably more a tease than being precisely accurate. Still it would place the picture starting in 1870 when she was sixteen (but playing much younger) and he had just painted her for the first time in *The King's Wedding*. In both pictures she is the impressionable, fresh-faced young girl, sweet-natured and eager to learn – a Frances that he had known at the outset and for which part of him continued to long.[77] Either way, *The Wizard* is a profoundly nostalgic piece, reflecting not simply the tumults of the 1890s but also the vicissitudes of a friendship lasting nearly thirty years.

In it, Burne-Jones has Frances, on the cusp of adolescence, as she stares out of a window at an image of a shipwreck conjured up by the wizard. She is transfixed by the display of the elderly magician's power, just as she had been mesmerised by Burne-Jones's 'treasures' in her youth. Their being together in the privacy of his darkened studio, lit mainly by the coals of a brazier, highlights their trust and closeness. Behind her, however, and out of her sight, the Wizard stands, looking on longingly at the young girl. His frustration is palpable. Yet for all her vulnerability, she is inviolate. It is she in her innocence who is in control. Burne-Jones is the wizard and this picture captures the sexual tension ratcheted up in its intensity by the necessity of denial – 'a tense unspoken narrative' last seen in *Cophetua* and building up in Burne-Jones until, at last, it exploded by the hayrick at Milford.[78] And yet at the outset, he had sought out Frances's innocence and purity precisely as protection from the destructive lust that had overwhelmed him with Zambaco. Part of Frances's attraction for him had been the very morality that denied him. Thus, his desires, as in the picture, would remain unfulfilled. In returning to the picture in 1896, he was, through his restraint, finally acknowledging that their relationship would be on her terms.

~ 23 ~

YOU ABOVE ALL OTHERS

He never let me go for more than two or three days silent, then he would scold me a little, and I loved that sort of constant, claiming love so.

Frances Horner[79]

June 1898 and in the fading light of his studio at The Grange, Burne-Jones was up a ladder making one last improvement to *The Last Sleep of Arthur in Avalon*. This monumental work – it measured 24 by 9 feet – depicted the king mortally wounded on his deathbed, still in full armour with his head resting on the lap of his sister Queen Morgan le Fay, and surrounded by scenes of great mourning. This was a painting that drew on ideas that had inspired him all his days. 'Nothing', he had once declared, 'was ever like "Morte d'Arthur" – I don't mean any book or any one poem – something that can never be written, I mean, and can never go out of the heart'. To him the Arthurian legend revealed a lost age of feeling and nobility of mind, of man at one with his world, and as such offered a moral rejection of the crass materialism and trite selfishness of the present which, in headlong pursuit of industrial progress, was crushing all he held to be human and beautiful.

Art had been Burne-Jones's sword in challenging the brute folly of the age. Now at the last this painting had become more of a refuge, a world apart that had come to absorb him completely. 'I am at Avalon – not yet in Avalon', he had told her. There had always been one last improvement since he first worked up the painting in 1881. Now he was so beset with ailments that he could barely stand all day, let alone climb the ladder. Still climb he must. For nearly two decades this work had dominated his studio. Now, aware his powers were declining, he sought desperately to complete it, determined that this was to be the best of him, the masterpiece that would encapsulate all that he had held dear. Yet it wouldn't come. A detail altered, colours remixed, frantically he sought satisfaction. But still it wouldn't come. It never would.

'Angelo is ill', Frances had warned Violet Cecil in February. But no more than usual she discovered on arriving at The Grange, braving 'the angry glare of other ladies who straggle round his sofa'. Anxieties over his health were a constant refrain of his correspondence. So when he actually died on 17 June from an angina attack it caught her by surprise. At sixty-four he had become increasingly frail but there had been no diminution of his passion to paint. Only three weeks before Frances had been in his studio (fig. 61), marvelling at 'the unfinished picture of Avalon… shining like a star in the room'. On hearing of his death, she rushed to his studio, 'for I wanted to see all the things and get them by heart before they scattered'. The prospect of their dispersal, of course, rekindled the distress she and Burne-Jones had shared over the break-up of her father's collection. More than that, in the privacy of his studio surrounded by the art that meant everything to them both, he was still a presence. Here too were the last echoes of their life together. Burne-Jones's reluctance to declare a work finished meant that 'there were not many strangers on the walls' and in their company she made her farewell. 'I don't know if it was mostly pleasure or pain seeing them so', she admitted to Jack, 'but I wouldn't have missed it for anything.'[80]

By the time she returned 'on Saturday,' much to her irritation The Grange was awash with tears: Nina Cust and Lady Granby – 'all clinging together till their own husbands couldn't have told which was which' – before being upstaged by Ellen Terry who 'hugged indiscriminately all around'. If Frances found their emotion intrusive, she didn't deny May's request to come to Mells. 'Of course we talked nothing but Angelo all day… and half-forgotten things rise up'. That May felt she could turn to Frances in her sadness says much of Frances, particularly at this time, even if she couldn't resist one last assertion of seniority. 'I like to have her for she loved BJ', she assured Jack. '[But not] nearly as much nor not nearly as long as I did. I know you will be glad she is here'.[81]

Burne-Jones had told her once that she was not to come to his funeral but she was never going to obey that. By contrast and befitting

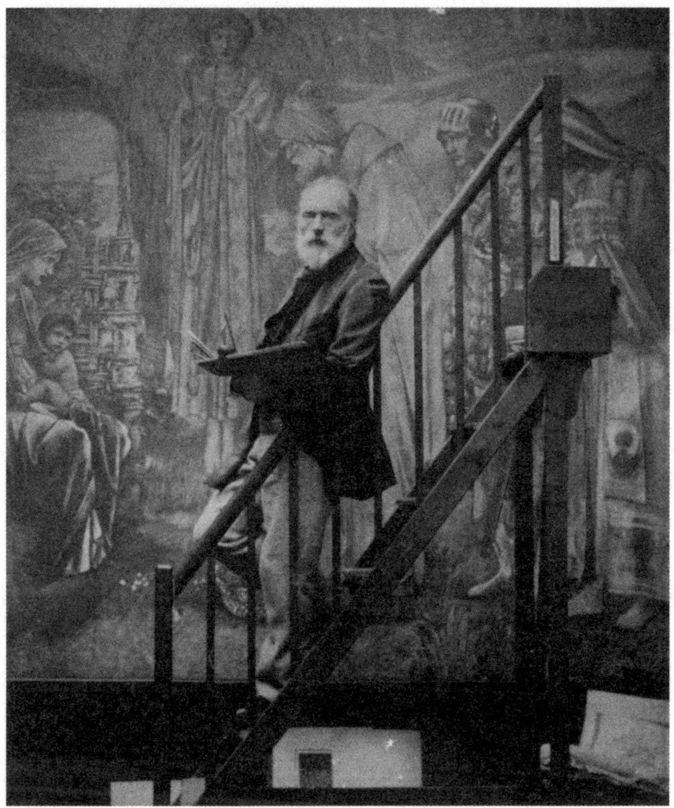

61. *Burne-Jones at work in his studio*

their 'secret' relationship, May stayed away, sending a wreath of lilies as a private symbol of their love. So on 21 June 1898 Frances travelled down from London to Rottingdean to see Burne-Jones buried in a simple country ceremony with, in Kipling's words: 'no mobbing; no jabber; no idiotic condolences'. No one wore black. Among the family and friends were a few aged remnants of the Pre-Raphaelite past – Val Prinsep, Holman Hunt, George Howard Earl of Carlisle, Charles Hallé.[82] Frances found herself standing by Henry James. 'I am glad we stood together in the strangely mingled crowd' he would write afterwards. 'What your missing must be, you who have known him so much longer and seen him more closely.'[83] The next day saw a memorial service in Westminster Abbey – the first ever for an artist in the Abbey. St Paul's had been considered but Burne-Jones had long made his loathing of that ornate church plain. Nonetheless, with the full Anglican fare and Sir Hubert Parry on the organ, it was everything the funeral wasn't. One suspects Burne-Jones would have bristled at the sight of the great and good filling the Abbey to overflowing. As his acerbic nephew remarked, 'The best of Babylon had turned out'. And then as is the way of things, the world moved on leaving Frances behind in her grief. 'I think the suddenness [of his death] is so shattering, but I dread the future most, when the crowd closes up again and the dust begins to lie on one's mind and heart'.[84] For as she confessed to DD,

> I think I got to depend on him as a kind of background for life, and he had grown so spiritual and good and yet so human that I took everything to him. Do you remember our time at Wimbledon together? Ever since, these last few years he has drawn me closer and closer to him instead of ever letting it slip at all, and that is such a lovely end to the story. He never let me go for more than two or three days silent, then he would scold me a little, and I loved that sort of constant claiming love so… I got so used to it I daresay perhaps even you hardly knew how naturally and happily I lived in his love – it was the most unfailing thing I ever knew. And now at home I can't move or look up without seeing him: a picture on the wall, or a photograph or books which he gave – everything in my life seems to have been steeped in him … It is twenty four years now since he came into my life.[85]

'What a dreadful feature of separation silence is', she would lament as Burne-Jones's August birthday passed without a letter. Seeking distraction, she summoned Rooke just 'because I want to talk to him'. And she would while away the evenings with Aggie reading Burne-Jones's old letters laughing and crying over them 'until I felt as if Time had slipped away'. Such temporary reliefs could not quell feeling 'so purposeless'. Admittedly 'there are still the children and Jack and Mells'. But they would struggle to fill the void.[86] 'I just want to be quiet', she made clear to Jack.

> I dare say, my beloved husband, even you hardly realise what a key note he was in my life; it's been so many years: 25 years since he first came into it, and, though I was quite happy living as I did and seeing him and writing to him constantly and freely,

now it's gone I feel so terribly bereaved. … And you must draw nearer to me yourself and help me more for I shall want more. You must try and not be impatient with me and so will I – I am glad to be alone just now.

It had been to Aggie that she retreated in the wake of the funeral and it would be Aggie who took over her hosting over the summer 'as people washed in and out'. Not for a while would she be ready to face 'the dusty world' again and get back 'into the inevitable groove'.[87]

*

What would raise morale was that 'all sorts of people' had written to her on Burne-Jones's death. On hearing the news, 'my thoughts at once turned to you', comforted Asquith. 'I can hardly imagine anything that could tear a greater gap in your life or create such a breach between the present and the past. He gave you always his best and it must be some solace to you to remember that up to the end you above all others lightened and enriched his difficult life'.[88] 'You above all others' – how she must have enjoyed that. Burne-Jones's last letter on the night he died may have been to May but their relationship was 'a profound secret', not to be uncovered for a generation or more. Thus the way was seemingly clear for Frances to assume her status as the keeper of the flame. 'There are some people who have *no* shadows in their natures', she later declared to Sydney Cockerell, 'idols who are pure gold all through … one or two men, of whom BJ was chief. You will smile and think this the folly of friendship…'[89] He did not and would have expected nothing less from Frances. 'Such a rare and perfect relationship as yours and his',…Asquith pronounced, 'was one of those gifts of the gods which they bestow on few…' She would have toured the New Gallery's retrospective exhibition of 235 of his works in December 1898 with her reputation secure. And she sent Jack to protect her interests 'at the BJ meeting' seeking to find a picture of his to buy for the nation, finally settling on *King Cophetua*.[90]

She was not to have it all her own way. In early 1900 she bumped into 'Lady BJ the other day. I believe now, which I did not at first, that she will leave out of the book the Angelo we loved and put in the one she and Margaret loved only and they are not the same'.[91] Publication of *Memorials of Edward Burne-Jones* by Georgie in 1904 confirmed her worst fears. Other than recognising that Frances's regular correspondence 'touched on most of the subjects that interested him', she is almost completely written out of the story. Thus, Frances is excluded from the account of the Laura Lyttelton tablet despite commissioning and agreeing the design. Even its location ('put up in some church') is rendered anonymous. Georgie does include the 'Sirens for her girdle …' letter to Ruskin in full in which Jack is dismissed as a 'market gardener' and Frances a minx who didn't appreciate all the gifts Burne-Jones had brought to her.[92] Needless to say, there is no reference at all to Maria Zambaco. To be fair to Georgie, few wives would give much space to rivals who maimed and almost destroyed her marriage. It would only be natural to resent another with whom her husband had flirted for so long. Moreover she was dependent on others returning BJ's letters and Frances was necessarily circumspect in her selection.

Even Frances recognised the book's excellent insight into the painterly life – establishing the artist within the domestic and emotional context of his family and the wider social scene. But for Frances she missed the essence of his art and pointedly would quote Burne-Jones in her defence: 'The lives of men who dream are not lives to tell, are they? My life is what I long for and love and regret and desire'. Turning the screw further, she declared that this would be beyond the understanding of those driven by 'long familiarity and loving comradeship'. To bring it to the fore 'needs another dreamer'.[93]

She had always seen herself as a fellow dreamer, happy on one level to indulge his escapism from the modern world – the chivalric faux medievalism and even the fantastical world of fairies and spirits. The opinions and stories that once held her in thrall were as much about colour and an imagination in free flow as he painted pictures with words. She would never quite lose that childlike understanding, nor how he could make the world magical. For her he had been a loving, protecting force as much as an inspiration. And demanding too. Throughout their deep affection, there was a continual struggle over what she was to be. While they were strongly attracted to each other's company, sharing values, enthusiasms and intimacies, theirs was a relationship that was marked and paradoxically sustained by two tensions. The first involved the nature of a muse. After Zambaco, Burne-Jones convinced himself that he sought a muse who was modest and pure, devoted, artistic, sensitive to the Romantic values that so shaped his work. In truth he wanted more. Not that Frances was acquiescent, even at the outset; although the 'little Spartan' in her had only added to her appeal. For all the passage of time, he would always see her [and draw her] as she was when a young girl of seventeen and the playmate of father and artist. In time, she would resist this, asserting her independence to become a muse on her own terms, wanting his mind and his love but not his body. Likewise, while she admired his dedication to his art (and himself) she had other social ambitions that he despised.

For all the exhilaration of Romance, to Frances, people and good company mattered more. 'Oh if you were here', she would write. 'What's the use of summer except to be with those you love – a summer's day alone in the country is absurd – it's a paradox – & the people who pretend they enjoy it are poor cold blooded Wordsworthians with cocoa in their veins'.[94] Twice these tensions pushed them to the brink – in 1882–3 and 1892 – only for both to step back, neither quite ready to let go. Thus throughout, their relationship was constantly shifting, its dynamic subtly redefined. Ironically, for all his attempts to mould her, in the end, it is she that moulds him. This came at a price. But not at the cost of the excitement experienced when as a teenager she had such treasures poured onto her lap. 'You haunt me everywhere' he had cried in 1892. Now, with his death, it would be he who would haunt her for the rest of her life.

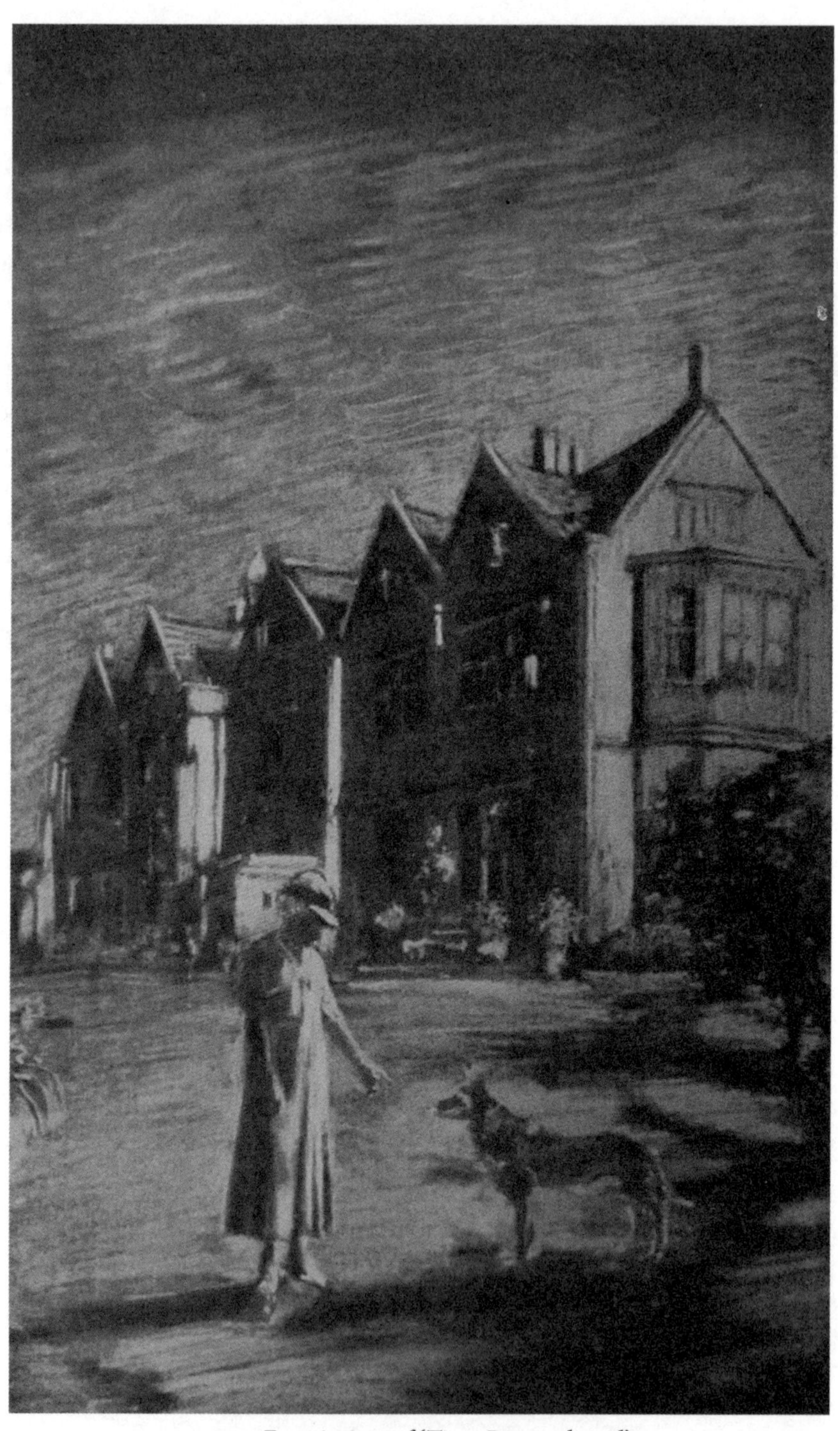

62.   *Frontispiece of 'Time Remembered',*
Frances in the garden at Mells, by William Nicholson,

Part Seven

========

Halcyon Days
1899–1914

We were very much in the political world. My dream had come
true – Asquith, Haldane and Grey had more and more power
in the State. I used to think that if Asquith were Prime Minister,
Grey Foreign Secretary, and Haldane Lord Chancellor, all
would be well with the world, and so it was for a time, before
the shattering years broke on us.

Frances Horner[1]

∾ 24 ∾

NEW BEGINNINGS

[Must] try very hard to make my life a more respectable one!

Frances to DD Lyttelton[2]

Never shy of the melodramatic, Frances once declared that 'Death walked into my life when I was eighteen and ever since has been a familiar presence'.[3] Yet in the wake of Burne-Jones's death, Frances was to suffer two further blows. The first was long expected. Her mother at seventy-nine had been ill for some time. Caring for her had not come easily to Frances, not least because her mother's only comfort was to be read the works of the sentimental novelist, Ouida. So much would it grate on Frances that her voice would get 'hard and unsympathetic' as she read how the hero 'bounded onto the stage – over the heads of the stupefied throngs – and gazed with a hungry glare on the snowy loveliness of her form palpitating beneath the shimmering gauze'. And yet on looking up Frances would see 'mamma's eyes wet with tears'. 'He is very noble, dear' she explained; 'what I admire in Ouida is that Vice is Vice and Virtue is Virtue'.[4] Having rather dreaded her arrival, Frances had become much closer to her mother at Mells, and not least through her children – by whom as 'the conventional, white-capped, pleasure providing, elderly grannie', she was adored.

Her death on 13 July 1899 was, however, a 'deliverance' after three months of suffering had reduced her to such 'a tiny pathetic figure beside us'. To the shock of the 'village people', Frances resisted the 'pomp and expense' of the traditional Victorian funeral in favour of a 'beautiful simpler ceremony'. Thus her mother's coffin was drawn on a farm cart to the graveyard in Mells, with the grandchildren and their Graham cousins, dressed in deep black, walking behind. To her surprise, Frances took the death of 'Our Darling little Mother' very hard: 'The rooms are so ghostly and I feel as if I have lost half a child and half a parent'. Nevertheless, she chose to move herself into her mother's old quarters. And without Burne-Jones to turn to, she spent long hours obsessively designing a cross for her mother's grave. 'Memorials are so difficult aren't they?' she insisted to DD, 'and yet the Greeks managed them alright – but our churchyards are a terror'. This time Jack saw the old signs of gloom pressing in and took her away on a cruise to Stockholm from which she would return 'in the rudest of health'.[5] That summer came the second blow. Frances was at Mells entertaining a flurry of bishops when she got word that her sister Amy, to whom she had always been close, had , while on holiday in Mull, suffered 'a curious attack'. A sudden 'swoon' had left her prostrate and unable to move her head. Frances set off for Scotland that afternoon and nursed her sister for three weeks until she was well enough to return to London. Despite the latest medicine Amy died some months later in December 1900 and was buried at Mells.[6]

*

In her memoir, *Time Remembered* (1933; fig. 62) Frances made great play of the fact that she and Amy, in comparison to the rest of their siblings, were '*not* religious'. Yet to the amusement of her metropolitan friends, she fought hard in the 1890s to retain a faith that ran deeper than she admitted. Supporting her fashionable actress friend, Mrs Patrick Campbell, in her latest play, Frances was nevertheless appalled at the burning of bibles, hostility towards marriage, and the 'cheap cynical dialogue that made me feel as if I should go back to the moral sentiments of my youth'. In turn, Asquith had been amazed to hear that she had spent a Sunday in London 'flitting about from Church to Church, in close attendance upon some Yankee pulpit orator. Were you edified? I almost hope not'. Her mother would undoubtedly have been the compelling force. But that same year would see Frances attending St Paul's, leaving Burne-Jones to 'wonder if the Church crushed and depressed you as it does me – and if you could pray in it… and if you had any hope that a prayer could get past the cornices'. As ever with Frances, the attraction of St Paul's was as much personal as theological. Declaring herself 'devoted' to Canon Scott Holland, she would regularly go to hear him preach. He was 'the only clergyman I like at all just now'. That it should be for his 'breezy quality' suggests that she had come to wear her faith quite lightly.[7] By now too her beliefs were very much Anglican and Establishment and often she would take guests to nearby 'Wells to see bishops and palaces and cathedrals and images'.

Back at Mells, the departure of Jack's brother George to Oxford in scholarly pursuit of the Hittites should have brought relief. His replacement, the Reverend Lear and his powerful wife (a relation of Millais) were soon at loggerheads with the Horner ladies, not least over access to the Rectory now that their brother had departed. 'There is really so much friction between the Rectory and the Lears that it is really uncomfortable', Frances complained to Jack. 'You feel quite guilty if you speak to them'. All this was very wearisome. There was nothing breezy or inspirational on which to feed a faith in need of sustenance, and especially after three deaths among those to whom she was so close. With the onset of the new century, she was confessing to Violet Cecil how 'I like the new religion ... of a humanitarian church and intellectual equipment'.[8] She was beginning to wear her Anglicanism very lightly indeed.

*

An afternoon in late April 1895 saw Frances cycling through the surrounding lanes by Mells with Cicely racing on ahead, her mother looking on anxiously. Her concern however was not for her daughter but for her husband as she awaited some news of which he had not an inkling. At his appointment as Commissioner of Woods and Forests, Jack was duly 'quite stupefied with surprise – so grateful and humble about it and yet really much excited'. Frances had long 'wanted something for him so much, not for the money nearly as much as for a sense of worth and responsibilities'. She was certainly aware (if indeed she hadn't instigated it) that her Liberal friends, Haldane and Asquith, had been pressing Jack's case. Hence her relief when Rosebery's letter finally arrived. For very soon the Liberals would be out of office and the chance gone.[9] Despite Jack's lack of ambition, she knew that this post would interest him too much to refuse. As a role it was hardly one of political importance, but it was public office and with it some status and the need, as she giggled to DD, for her 'to try very hard to make my life a more respectable one!'

As she and her young friends were quick to note, Frances now had far more excuse to be in London.[10] Jack's salary of £1,200 a year

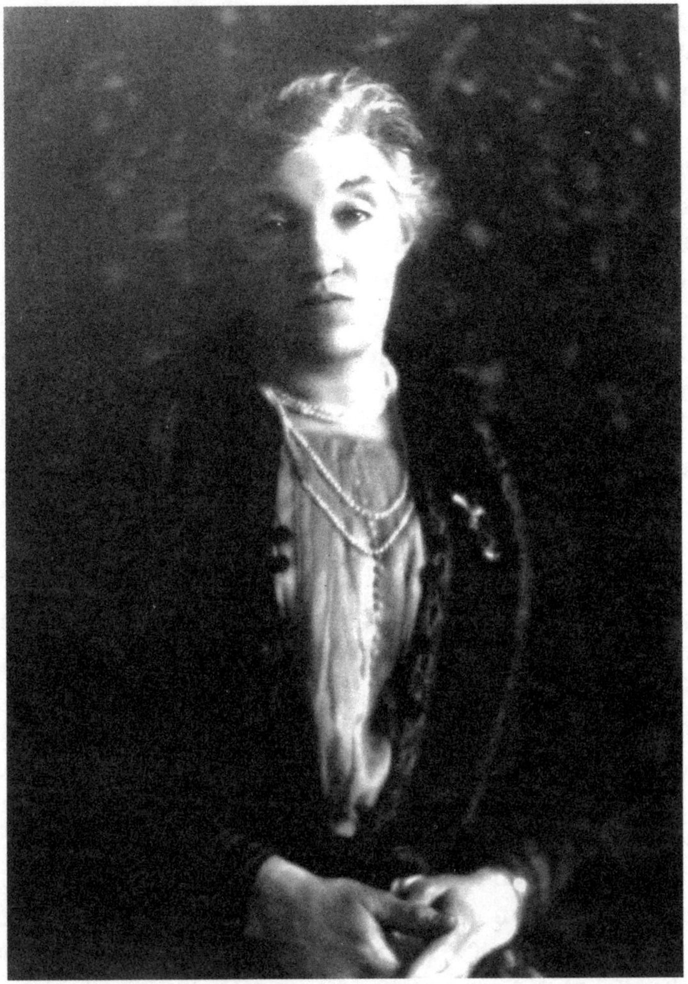

63.   Frances in 'respectable' middle age

(equal to £145,800 today) opened up the prospect of owning their own London home in addition to Mells Park. The house they chose was 9 Buckingham Gate. Proximity to Buckingham Palace gave it a cachet among her friends, especially at times of royal occasions such as the Diamond Jubilee and Queen Victoria's funeral. It also was easy to rent out – when the Horners were at Mells – to visiting royal dignitaries such as Archduke Franz Ferdinand of Austria (whose assassination was to launch the First World War); and Pertab Singh, the Maharaja of Idar (whose clothes were 'covered in diamonds' and who was so thoughtful to the staff).[11] Indeed Buckingham Gate had originally been built by Prince Albert with just this in mind.

What Frances had in mind saw Buckingham Gate depart from the prevailing fashion for vast extravagant receptions in favour of small private dinner parties. Exclusivity ensured that invitations were much sought after. So too was their hostess. As art became socially more respectable, so the enigmatic allure of the muse of Burne-Jones retained its pull long after his death. Added to which was the social distinction of being a leading Soul; well read, learned, artistic, she carried off an air of gentle learning with just a whiff of cordite – enough to attract as well as intimidate. Yet she was also drawn to 'what Ruddy [Kipling] would call "the fun and riot of life"'.[12] And this was reflected in her enthusiasm for bringing together groups that didn't meet socially – politicians, painters, writers, and wits on the make. Into the mix she would drop in a celebrity or two. The American comedienne, Ada Rehan gave her first private party performance in Frances's house. She was a major star at the time, which ensured that this private event secured a gushing review in the *Westminster Gazette* (21 March 1902). At another of Frances's parties the ballerina, Miss Angela Vanbrugh, danced – at a time when ballet was just coming into vogue. But the real stars were from the stage. Sarah Bernhardt, of whose fame Burne-Jones had once written 'Like Napoleon, she has enlarged the borders of glory', came twice to supper. Mrs Pat Campbell didn't just come to dinner, she stayed for two months, keeping them up half the night as she rehearsed *Pelléas and Mélisande*. 'We thought it all very exciting, but so tiring [too that] we nearly died of it,' Frances would recall. That such celebrities came was in part because Frances was a figure of fascination in her own right. Thus Ellen Terry, the leading actress in her day, kept offering Frances her box at the theatre and was effusive in her thanks when Frances took her out for a drive.[13]

Such entertaining required Buckingham Gate to be made fit for purpose and so began Frances's long friendship with a young architect called Edwin Lutyens (fig. 64). They became very good friends as he 'beautified every house I had anything to do with.' She would reminisce on his 'happy laughter [and] loving disposition', but what she really admired was his 'great resourcefulness' – that ability to come up 'instantly' with another design when the original one 'did not please one'. One can imagine the budding architect attentively paying court with Frances enthusiastically changing her mind at every corner; and how his young wife, Emily, became 'dreadfully jealous' of 'Mrs Horner …whom I think can help you when I can't'. Frances's commission and especially the network she offered would launch his career among the wealthy and powerful and he was not going to miss out.[14] 'Throughout Lutyens's career', writes Jane Brown, 'especially at its most frenetic and frustrating periods, there seemed to be a leavening, soft and gracious, emanating as the mists along the Mendip valleys, wreathing out from Mells'. And in its chatelaine he found someone who 'always understood him and brought forth the best in him'.[15] Here he was at ease with his surroundings. As for Frances, no longer the muse, she now energetically assumed the role of patron – if vicariously through the pockets of her richer friends.

*

Frances's own extravagance finally took its toll. In truth, as she admitted to DD, both Frances and Jack were hopeless with money. In any negotiation with his tenants, Jack was quite happy to be exploited. As for letting out Buckingham Gate for the summer he was infamous for wooing prospective tenants with the warning that 'you better wait and see how beastly the back stairs are'. As befits one brought up in comfort, Frances preferred to ignore the subject of money 'in spite of mankind' – with inevitable results. As early as 1894, 'a financial crisis' meant they would be wintering in Mells and not London. Hence the following year her excitement over Jack's appointment (and salary). However, this was to prove a brief respite. Her mother's death and the loss of her support quickly brought matters to a head. The decision to let Mells Park and not sell Buckingham Gate suggests Frances's influence. Jack's family were outraged at the loss of the ancestral home and George led a campaign in the village against letting of the house to an amiable Mr Francis and his very wealthy American wife, ostensibly on the grounds of her divorce. 'Of course we minded letting Mells fearfully', Frances insisted but the rent was good. Bravely she declared to DD (herself fresh from the splendours of Blenheim), 'I don't much want to live in palaces, I would rather live in a garret and have pocket money'. And there was always the illusion that they would return. 'We thought if we could manage to economise for a few years, perhaps by the time the boys were of age we might be able to live in the Park again'. It was never to be.[16]

The Manor House, to which they moved in 1902, was to Frances 'a small Elizabethan house in the village'. Yet for all the downsizing, this was hardly a garret. And it was far more the ancestral home of the Horners than the Park. Admittedly building the latter had seen The Manor House greatly reduced. But the surviving southern wing, with its impressive Elizabethan five-gabled façade through whose great windows light streamed into the rooms, had the potential to be both comfortable and exhilarating. Aesthetically Burne-Jones was in no doubt which was the finer and on first sight in 1892 he had insisted that Frances should abandon the Park for The Manor House 'that very afternoon'.[17] For Lutyens too, it was inspirational. Here his early enthusiasm with Arts and Crafts could mingle with Tudor and Jacobean traditions to create an Old English Vernacular. A triumph of imagination, it would be realised in a series of country houses over the Home Counties that would make his name. With their vaulted and beamed ceilings, small-paned windows, finely crafted interiors, panelled walls and expansive fireplaces, they spoke of a romantic England rooted in an ancient landscape. And, as such, an architectural complement to an age of Elgar. If 'Mells today is one of the places where the spirit of Lutyens's particular Englishness lingers', it was less for what he built there than 'for its influence upon the pattern of his building, and the people he encountered there'.[18] For in The Manor House the past still lived on.

Nevertheless, moving in December was foolhardy. 'Indescribable mess and discomfort… and bitterly cold – no windows to keep out the air, all the chimneys smoke… and all the woodwork painted yellow! [I am] tired of building nests', Frances protested. [On the other hand it is] 'rather nice being really so near the church – the bells almost ring under the rooms but they are such lovely bells'. With four boisterous children, they were soon very much on top of each other. 'There are certain houses which are good for a large noisy untidy family like mine – Mells [Park] was. And certain ones which are dignified and require doors shutting … a quiet tread on the carpet… the furniture set carefully in an appointed plan – this is that and Mark bangs and Katharine litters me to distraction'.[19] Inevitably Lutyens was called for, although, along with some alterations, he was primarily involved in laying out the walled gardens and a loggia. Later a music room was built for the Burne-Jones piano. Inevitably what money there was was spent on kitchens and bathrooms.

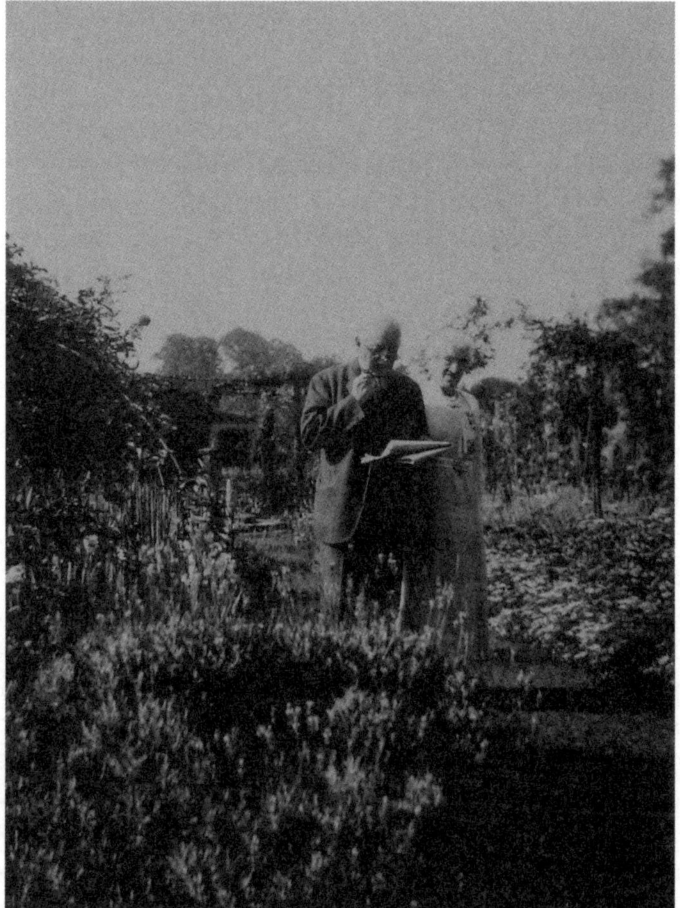

64.   Sir Edwin Lutyens and Frances in the garden at Mells

Together they enhanced the main entrance, designing stone piers topped with Talbots, that led from an avenue of lime trees and wild flowers, through tall wooden gates opening into the forecourt and its spectacular juxtaposition of house and church (fig. 65). Frances was no gardener but faced with the 'bare surroundings, with no shining magnolias clothing its walls, no herbaceous borders brightening its green courts, no rosemary spreading around its pavements', she called in a friend, Norah Lindsay. The outcome was a walled garden 'so intimately joined to the house that one seems hardly to exist without the other….[with] lupins and tall Henryi lilies nodding in at the windows of the sitting rooms'.[20]

By now the children were of an age when they were happiest sleeping outside and gallivanting by the pool Jack had built 'for Edward'. Frances would remember 'delicious rides' with Edward with 'the days slipping by silently'.[21] Not too silently. With their parents more London based, Mells became a place of space and freedom, a time for holidays and friends. 'Mells is heavenly now – warm and green and delicious' and with 'a great party of children'.[22] It would be to The Manor House that they would bring their friends from school and university and it became established as their idea of home. When another financial crisis in 1906 saw Frances propose letting The Manor House and retreating to London permanently, her children rebelled and some of her father's Old Masters were sold instead, along with Buckingham Gate.[23]

Nevertheless, The Manor House was not well suited to grand country-house living and the large weekend parties that Frances had enjoyed at Mells Park. By comparison The Manor House was so small that there was hardly room to fit the family in and often when their parents had visitors, the children had to double up or overflow into neighbouring cottages. Equally, there wasn't space for anything more than a skeleton staff. All of which made life much cheaper. More importantly it shaped the way Frances entertained. As she had attempted at Mells Park but much more so, the atmosphere was very relaxed and informal, with 'young and old friends crowding in'. The intermingling of the generations, the living at close quarters, the merging of garden and house, a well-worn comfort, the being drawn into fierce debates punctuated by peals of laughter – all created an easy intimacy, a sanctuary from a frenetic yet still rigid Society. So appealing was this that her friends continued to visit in droves – whatever the discomfort. Haldane was a regular as were numerous Asquiths. One pool party for 'mixed bathing' would see Augustine Birrell and Herbert Paul swimming 'furtively amongst the rushes' and Millicent, Duchess of Sutherland looking glamorous in a lilac bathing suit. On another occasion Mrs Patrick Campbell joined in. Finding herself suddenly out of her depth, she 'seized Jack around his neck and clung so hard that they both slowly sank before her eyes'. Frances quickly came to the rescue, not wholly convinced that the actress was in any danger.[24]

This was a neat reversal of jealousies.[25] But Frances and Jack were much more settled now they were together more. On their

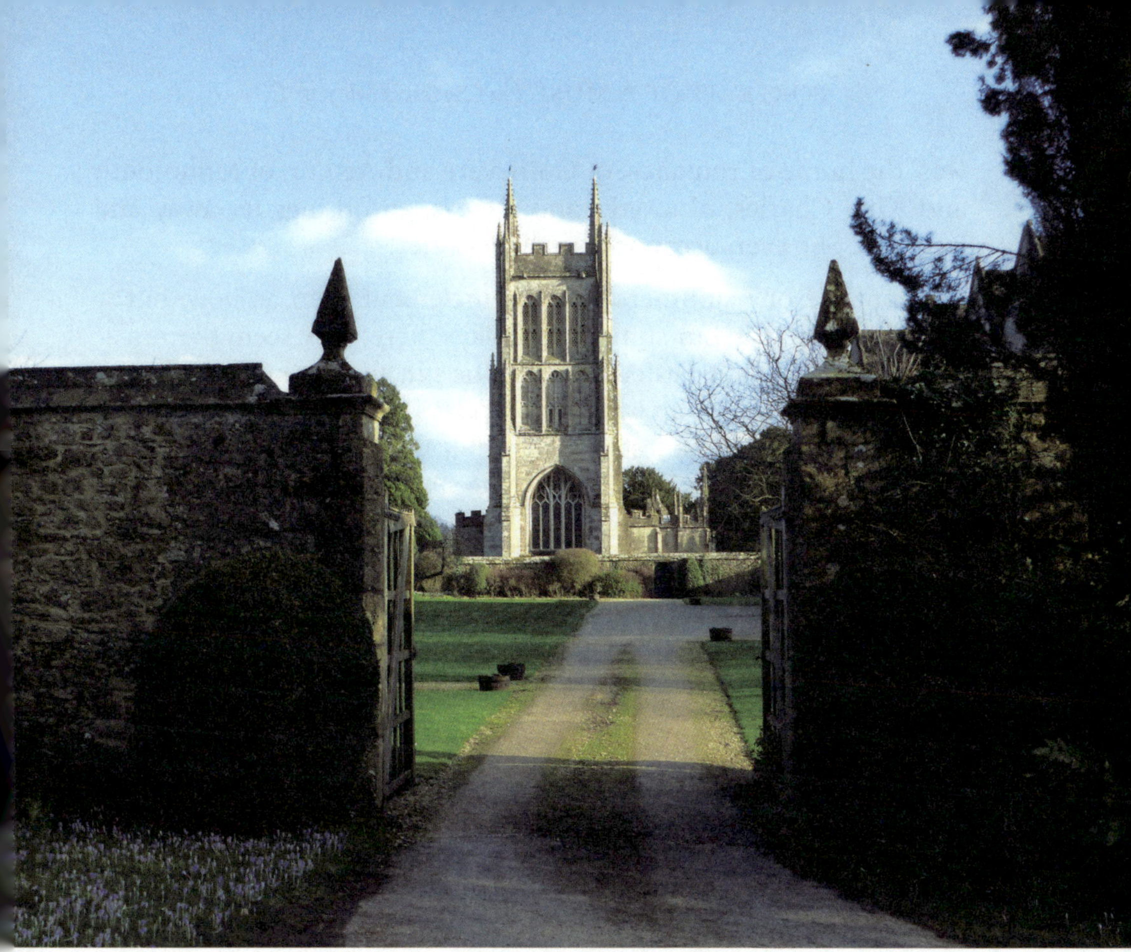

65.   *Mells, the view through the gateway, redesigned by Lutyens,*
to the church beyond

anniversary in 1898, she would write, '15 years happy together and it has been very happy… I know in many ways I have come very short but not as regard love and sympathy… and you have always been an angel – even when you were a furious one like the other day'. By now she was well able to cope with his occasional explosions, relishing instead the grounding 'My Dear Old Darling' gave her. That they remained something of a mystery to each other was probably no bad thing.[26] Frances was also becoming much more appreciative of Mells. Proximity brought greater engagement and understanding of village life. The appeal of London was beginning to pall. 'I actually have not a whiff of London longing', she would protest to DD. Now she begins to acknowledge – as Burne-Jones had long taught her – the beauty of 'a stone county, rich in beautiful old Manor Houses, stone tiled cottages, in thatched barns and grey walls'. And how it was 'the home of romance, of Guinevere and Arthur, of Monmouth and King Charles, of monks and abbeys, and things far away and long ago'. She even began to like the weather!

> I suppose our summers were as inclement then as now, but looking back on our summer holidays there, they seem to me a vision of constant garden life, as if the sun always shone and the wind never blew – a vision of long days and moonlit evenings when we sat out and strolled among the scented borders, or slept out in the loggia and watch the stars till darkness brought sleep and silence to us at last.

Thus were fresh roots laid that would last her the rest of her life.[27]

~ 25 ~

'PLATONIC MARRIAGE!'

No, you don't want me to find a wife for Mr Haldane, I'm sure.

Burne-Jones to Frances Horner[28]

In July 1900 Raymond, Henry Asquith's eldest son, visited Mells Park for the first time. There by the lake below the house he saw a sight he would never forget.

> A vast white mass with the brain of Socrates and the shape of Nero executing his absurd antics from a thin plank that bent double under his weight and sporting fantastically in the water with a divinely beautiful girl [Cicely] no whit abashed, recalled the sunniest days of the Roman decline. Finally he came out and, after lurking coyly in the bushes for a few minutes, reappeared clad in nothing but a bath-towel and a panama hat and joined us at tea on the lawn where he was soon explaining the theory and history of Buddhism – its superiority to Christianity and its weakness as a practical religion – to a host of local spinsters who had flocked in for the food and gossip. It was magnificent.[29]

'It' was Richard B. Haldane, an austere, serious-minded Scottish lawyer, a formidable continental intellectual and a sometimes radical politician and Liberal MP (fig. 66). That he should also have fallen in love with Frances was for her something of an occupational hazard. Men did. For Haldane it was her intellect that most appealed, finding her 'one of the cleverest women I have seen and as full of insight as she is clever.' Inevitably her celebrity was part of the draw, having grown up 'under the guidance of Ruskin, Rossetti and Burne-Jones, all of whom were attracted to her'. From them she 'possessed a great sense of the beautiful' and the art to bring this instinct out in others – not least him. Much of this was fanciful but such was his obsession that he was even willing to forgive her early levity towards the sacred mysteries of philosophy.[30] More importantly, she 'did much to enlarge my outlook on my fellow human beings, and to diminish the angularity of my views of life and society.'[31] To see the 'good as well as the bad' in people. His admiration remained undiminished even when he realised she was more fixated on his friend Asquith.

Admittedly he was difficult company to like. Physically he wasn't attractive. Rotund with soft high-pitched voice and odd hand gestures when speaking, 'in figure, features and demeanour there was something about him of the old-fashioned family butler'. In terms of personality in these early days there was much that grated. To many, including Harold Nicolson who was not close to him, he could seem 'an aloof and rather inhuman little person'.[32] In argument, he could in his younger days at the Bar play the intellectual bully. Not least towards his sister-in-law who railed against 'his omniscience, his self-satisfaction and his sneers at people who disagreed with him'.[33] Frances was not sheltered from this side. 'When first I knew RBH[aldane] and Cyril Flower asked him to describe me, he said I was a woman of pleasure which I thought pleasing but misleading'. For which read patronising. In his autobiography published posthumously, he was quite tart in his dismissal of the Souls who were her friends and their worship of Balfour; provoking her in turn to declare that he 'never really did belong to our group though [he] liked to think [he] did!'[34] As his first visit to Mells made plain. Walking through the house, Alfred Lyttelton heard peals of laughter coming from the morning room. There he found Charty Ribblesdale and Frances reading Haldane's translation of Schopenhauer's principal work, *World as Will and Idea* 'where he describes the efforts of the unborn children to enter the world through the medium of lovers' meetings!' 'The Metaphysics of Love were most diverting', quipped Frances to DD. Soon afterwards while she was pregnant and confined, she did make a more concerted effort to read Haldane's book only to conclude 'I do not feel quite sure that we should really [grip?] as friends. He would have to alter a bit – I expect – for I am too old to'.[35]

Yet when they had first met, at dinner at May Gaskell's house, not even the very attractive diplomatist on her right, Sir Philip

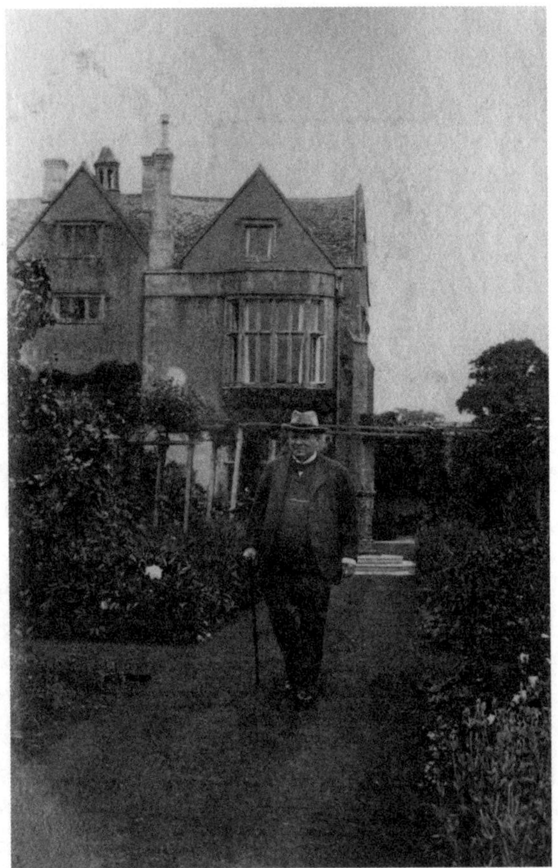

66. *Richard Haldane in the garden at Mells*

Currie, could distract her from Haldane. They bonded initially over Germany –'his spiritual home. His God was Goethe, mine was Heine'. Goethe may have been substantially the more important literary figure but at least Haldane had taken her seriously and Frances ⁓i⁓oved the challenge of his intelligence and the entrée he offered ⁓ld of ideas. Staying with him once in Scotland she would b⁓ ⁓cover 'an orgy of professors'. From the off they had a rap⁓ ⁓as and arguing the difference.

⁓ was the range of his knowledge, the lawyer's re⁓ ⁓ent and most of all his respect for her intelligence. Sh⁓ ⁓ find him 'always stimulating and interesting, and ⁓ightened up by a keen sense of humour ... [especially] if it glanced obliquely at himself'. She admired the courage of his thinking and laughed at the odd absurdity that went with it. What particularly appealed was Haldane's readiness to collect information from everyone he met, irrespective of their standing. Thus on holiday in Ireland she looked on amused as he talked 'to everyone he meets – car drivers, fishermen, priests, hotel guests. I hear him in long political discussions with them all – I love that quality because I live with people who have so little of it, I suppose'. Even if he left many of his audience bemused in his unforgiving pursuit of complexity, that too, for Frances, was part of the fun.[36]

Haldane also cut a rather unlikely figure as the jilted lover. Engaged to the beautiful Val Munro-Ferguson in 1890, Haldane was humiliated when she suddenly broke it off on the eve of their wedding. In the spirit of Victorian melodrama, she offered no explanation and refused to meet lest he should undermine her determination. Soon rumours were flying of a lesbian relationship. Thereafter she lampooned him in a series of novels – *Betsy* (1892), *Music hath charms* (1894), *Life again, Love again* (1897) – before dying insane in 1897. Few would have read any of these novels but the possibility only added to his embarrassment and hurt. Inevitably his plight aroused the prurient interest of Frances's friends. Doll Liddell's dismissal of Val ('She drank beer, was flat chested and wouldn't fizz') hardly helped. All this Haldane bore 'with extraordinary sweetness and dignity'. 'After some years the wound closed … [but] it shook his confidence for a very long time'. All of which made him ripe for rescuing. Socially too there was work to be done. 'Mr Haldane's touch is heavier [than Lyall's], Frances admitted to Ettie. 'He is much less accustomed to the bewildering mazes of female conversation – but in some ways that increases his interest – he is rather *terre vierge*' [virgin territory].[37]

By 1895 Haldane was such a regular at Mells that he would join the Horners on Christmas Day. To the children he was a source of ghost stories and overly generous presents. Seemingly, Jack was accommodating of this odd arrival who in turn respected him as 'the most perfect gentleman I ever knew…a considerable scholar who studied under Freeman the historian'. For all that Haldane liked coming to Mells, he had no interest in country pursuits other than walking. 'Heavy in build and slow in manner' he may have been, but, fuelled with vigorous conversation and with Frances for compan he would tramp the hills for hours. He also endeared himself to the others by being a willing figure of fun. 'His spherical figure, his twinkling benignity and pneumatic bulk' was seen at its most absurd when tobogganing down the hill at Mells on a tray, 'looking like a large Sunday joint'. In time he would join Frances and the children on holiday in France – the first of many such expeditions together. While in London she advised on the décor of his flat at 28 Queen Anne's Gate and would often act as hostess for dinners as he sought to advance his fledgling career in politics. In 1909, when Haldane was in denial over his declining sight in one eye (what proved to be the onset of diabetes), it was Frances who took matters in hand: 'The Haldanes are so frightfully *un*-humble, they back their opinion against God's any day'. Backing hers, she moved into his flat to nurse him, blithely assuring her daughter Katharine that it is 'much easier for me being here'.[38]

Were they lovers? There is little evidence of much physical affection on either side. After Val's rejection Haldane settled rather easily into the role of jovial bachelor, devoted to his centenarian mother to whom he wrote every day, and quite happy to be looked after by his younger and unmarried sister, Elizabeth, to whom he was very close. On the other hand, the fact that both women loathed Frances suggests some threat to their possession. When Jack was close to death with scarlet fever in 1908, Haldane's mother was 'terrified' lest Frances became free to marry her son.[39] She needn't have worried. Frances recalled a conversation in the library she had with Haldane on his first visit to Mells. After he had left, Daisy White and Charty Ribblesdale rushed in to hear what gossip Frances had uncovered about Haldane's jilting. 'He is the *most* extraordinary person and we've just had the most extraordinary conversation', declared Frances, milking it for all it was worth. 'What about?' cried they. 'Platonic marriage!' she replied. Yet there is a sense of restraint too in Frances's memory of their relationship.

How can we describe the quality that draws us to some human beings? We say a man or a woman is lovable and words fail to illuminate; we are conscious of the unexplained, the ineffable. A great personality evades our touch. A nature like Lord Haldane's, both very simple and very complex, still keeps the secret of it attraction, felt, but unrevealed.

Both had other friendships. Frances wrote of Haldane being one of 'the two or three friendships' after Burne-Jones she was 'fortunate to enjoy, above desert and beyond requital'. Similarly when Lady Tweedmouth [sister of Lord Randolph Churchill] died young in 1904, Haldane wrote to his mother of the loss 'of a tie that has lasted for years … she and Mrs Horner have in different ways meant very much to me'.[40]

What Frances meant to him wasn't always clear. Mary Belloc Lowndes who would later know them both well held that Frances 'fascinated Haldane', opening up to him a sophisticated artistic society of which he had no ken; but mainly through her personality as with wide-eyed innocence she flitted between the serious and the frivolous, a sharp teasing wit counter-balanced by unexpected generosity and heart.[41] Frances's fortieth birthday party and 'having you very close to me' marked for Haldane a shift in their relationship, an anniversary he never forgot. That night, as a present, he gave her a pocket edition of Goethe's *Faust*. Inside the front cover were photographs of Goethe and one of the Terrace at Mells, while on the flyleaf was an excerpt from another text written out in his own hand. Translated it reads:

> You know every feature of my being,
> Saw the purest tremor of each nerve,
> With a single glance you could read me,
> Hard as I am for mortal eye to pierce.

However such understanding is not the prelude to lust. If Frances had looked out the rest of the stanza, she would have learnt that he saw her as a bringer of peace: comforting, healing, restorative – a refuge from the humiliations and uncertainties of the past.

> You brought calm to my heated blood,
> Guiding my wild and wandering course,
> And in your arms, an angel's arms, I could
> Rest as my ravaged heart was restored.[42]

That was in April 1894. Frances had her own memories, remarking in spring 1895 that soon it would be 'a year since that day we walked together in the discreet places of Hyde Park'. Even so, she still wasn't certain what he felt 'about it all'. She however was ready to declare her hand.

What is it that I have loved in you? What draws us together? It was, on my side at least, the recognition of a rare and noble nature … one who could not live without the stars any more than I could … Only I have felt, perhaps wrongly, that that was not the side of your life that needed sustaining by me and that I could be more help to you on the working side so to speak: And most of all by the warmth and reality of that close affection you had missed before I knew you. Perhaps I was wrong …

The defensive tone reflected that they were actually in the middle of a blazing row – over his political future – one she would quietly steer, as she felt best.[43] These were early days and there is a hint that, to Frances, Haldane needed training in matters of the heart. That said, Frances could be very possessive. Never more so than in a spectacular bout of jealousy over the 'ghost' of Val Munro-Ferguson. As late as 1897 Beatrice Webb could note of Haldane that despite 'the beaming kindliness of his nature…there is a pathos in his personality …he is a restless, lonely man, in his heart still worshipping the woman who jilted him seven years ago'.[44] Matters came to head in September 1897 when he heard that his erstwhile fiancée was dying. All the hurt and love he had repressed for so long overwhelmed him and he longed to 'hold her hand once more'. For a week he waited for the summons to her bedside but none came. Confiding this in Frances may have been naïve if understandable. Her fury caught him completely by surprise. Only his response has survived:

Last night I had a dream that was very vivid. I was in a strange house and knew that you were living there & I had come to seek you but I could not find you. And at last Edward appeared & came up to me & said 'You have hurt mother, & she is very sad'. I awoke and Kennedy came and put your letter in my hand.

The thought that was most with me was that her death had robbed me of you. I felt hard & angry. When I read that letter I put it straight into the fire. There has not been a moment in the past three & a half years when, if you had both come before me, I should not have gone straight & unswerving to your arms. I thought you should have known this. Why did you not understand? It was right that I should tell you all I did. It was right that I should feel it … Why would you not have faith when I asked you? Yes indeed – what is there to compare with your record – nothing! I owe the best I have to you … Did you think that I had forgotten this? … Sometimes it seems to me that you never understand how unlike we are in our speech, or make allowance for difference of language when we talk.

No, you must never doubt again. Think of your supposing that what has been built up so firmly since 1893 could be swept away like this. … I shall write again tonight and tell you news of [Asquith's visit] … Although I found it out from him, I am not in the least jealous that you have invited him to stay at Buckingham Gate![45]

Plainly Frances had overstepped the mark. But it was also a measure of how much she valued the 'great gift' of his companionship. True she had moved swiftly on Asquith's desertion.[46] Still, as before, she could inhabit the political life vicariously; this time through Haldane's career. Two years younger and long devoted to her, he offered a relationship over which she could share some control. Nevertheless, for all that it was an *amitié amoureuse*, their attachment was no less passionate and would last until Haldane's death in 1928. Crucially for both, it was to complement her marriage rather than threaten it. It wasn't just for form that Frances would insist that 'Jack and I and all the children were devoted to him'. It was Haldane that they would make the guardian of their children 'if something was to happen to Jack and myself'. As for wills, Jack's was at Buckingham Gate and she alerted her friend that 'mine is unsigned somewhere but I leave you [Haldane] full power over everything of mine'.[47] At the heart of such trust was a marriage of minds, established right from the 'blessed day it was when I first came to know you at Mrs Gaskell's house & when we sat in the back drawing room and talked. Since then there has been no slackening'. What had begun as an intellectual attraction deepened into a friendship that was instinctive, comfortable, and enriching. 'More & more as life goes on with me', declared Haldane, 'I feel that our relationship is the largest & deepest fact in my life.[48]

26

A POLITICAL MUSE?

Are you deep in politics?

Burne-Jones to Frances Horner[49]

By his later years, Burne-Jones had developed a deep distrust of politics and politicians. So when in November 1897 Richard Haldane had called in with 'a great deal of political table talk' about Lord Rosebery [the erstwhile Liberal leader] and others, the artist was quickly bored and a little perplexed that Frances should be so fond of him. 'Do you remember the days', he protested, 'when you and I used to sit in the boudoir at Gros[venor] Place scorning their politics and wondering how any reasonable person could take an interest in the daily press!' She did and in return reminded him of a dinner engulfed in fierce political debate over the Church or the role of the press when all turned to them and 'asked what you and I were talking about? [And] I said Justinian – now isn't that wonderful'. 'Those were the years of arrogant youth' and now he feared that she had succumbed to the fatal attraction: 'are you deep in politics?' he confronted her after she had sent him a speech of Rosebery's.[50]

In truth, youthful rebellion aside, she always had been excited by the political drama. Behind her social advance was a hunger for the company of the best – people who made things happen. Inexorably this led her to the world of politics. The Horners were Liberals but by the end of the century more for ancestral than ideological reasons. Frances was much more committed. Indeed, she had been so since she was eleven when her father had first entered parliament and they moved to London; and fourteen when in 1868 her father held on to his seat after the recent Reform Act had doubled the electorate. Adoring her father, Frances would have been caught up in the excitement as the Liberals swept the board in Glasgow. Moreover, her father's friendship with Gladstone saw invitations to Downing Street and Frances's close companionship with Mary Gladstone. Together they would go canvassing for Mary's father and later be courted by young Liberal MPs. Predictably, her political creed was firmly Gladstonian – with its belief in moral conscience and individual responsibility, and rooted in the evangelical faith and charitable good deeds that had been the hallmark of Frances's upbringing. However much fashions would change, these instincts would remain with her far longer than she would admit.[51]

Burne-Jones had no truck with such conventionalism. Gladstone, having stirred him up over the Bulgarian Atrocities in 1877 only then to become distracted (in Burne-Jones's eyes by the pursuit of office), was now an arch hypocrite. His later bombardment of Alexandria and the annexation of Egypt in 1881–2 (apparently in the interest of bankers and high finance) only compounded his original sin. Eventually he got his just deserts in the humiliation that followed the death of Gordon.[52] 'What do you think of *your* Mr Gladstone', Burne-Jones chided Frances, 'and his divine nemesis?'[53] Admittedly, his friend Morris's adoption of Socialism offered no alternative. Dismissing socialists as 'angry, malign, ugly', Burne-Jones enquired, 'Have they reached remote Somersetshire? I dare say I agree with all they want – indeed I know I do – it isn't that…I hate the atmosphere about them, and the tone.'[54] Consequently, he abandoned political activism and focussed on improving society through beauty and art. This was the creed Frances had learnt on his knee and she too would shun activism while longing with him for 'victory to be on the side of loveliness.'

In another way too Burne-Jones would shape her political imagination – namely in the Romantic admiration of Great Men; heroic figures who straddled the age, guiding society beyond the petty aspirations of the small-minded and the pen pushing. Even here Burne-Jones's faith was wearing thin. The death in October 1891 of Charles Stewart Parnell exposed a raw nerve. The Irish leader's advocacy of Home Rule for Ireland had transformed British politics in the 1880s. With the Irish MPs under Parnell's leadership holding the balance of power in Parliament, Gladstone and the Liberals took up their cause. Ireland became the central issue of British party politics with the Irish plea for devolution also stirring up very English concerns over the morality of Empire, the role of democracy, and the rights of property. Yet, at the last, the revelation of Parnell's affair with Mrs Kitty O'Shea saw him brought down by the priggish and moralistic among the Liberals and the Irish. Burne-Jones was incandescent. 'I want vengeance' he raged to Frances … I want vengeance. I want the Liberals not to get into power again – no not for fifty years' after Parnell was thrown into the 'adders' pit of…English middle-class conformists!!!' His death roused Burne-Jones to apocalyptic language:

> Today about noon came it seemed the world's end – sudden black, and out of the blackness a flash like the opening of Hell's mouth, and after a flash, a roar like Doomsday – and after the roar a lull and then a wind before which all things bent and broke … and a big poplar lies across the garden wall. All these signs are because Parnell has gone…Such shattering thunder are the salute the Gods make when a brave man goes out and I think that was a very brave man.[55]

Surprisingly (and in more measured tones), Asquith had written to her in similar terms. 'Did you know Parnell? I did…I was a Parnellite – latterly in a sneaking kind of way – up to the end'. In spite of his 'limitations …and incredible stupidities in calculation and conduct…I think that he will be reckoned as one of the great personal forces of this century…Personality is still the most potent force in the world.'[56]

Therein lay the fascination of the political world to Frances. Burne-Jones's pleading – 'Though you have forgiven and even learned to like and admire, and I am afraid a little to love some politicians, we need never change our views but still hate politics with all our hearts'[57] – suggests that his pupil was no longer listening. And understandably so. In the late Victorian era parliamentary politics was at the heart of social ambition and the celebrity culture. Indeed the ambitions of her Souls friends focussed on little else. And before them she had glimpsed the thrill that comes with proximity to power through Mary Gladstone. Living life in the slipstream of her famous father Mary 'love[d] being in the mainspring of history, and all the stir and stress and throb of the machine is life and breath to her'. Through Asquith, Haldane and Sir Edward Grey (fig. 67) Frances would enter this world in her own right as a close friend of the coming men of the Liberal Party. With them she would meet the men of the moment and debate the issues of the day – in 1891–3 largely Home Rule for Ireland.[58] Burne-Jones would tease her for only liking ministers in office but, in truth, she was much more broadminded than that and would exploit the fluidity of Liberal politics in the 1890s to meet with those whom the more tribal would abhor. Burne-Jones was not the only one to distrust Joseph Chamberlain and in Liberal circles he was reviled as the architect of the party split over Home Rule. But the artist's aside that, 'I don't think I care for clever talk half as much as you do', explains just why Frances couldn't resist the chance to engage over dinner with this most prickly of politicians. The fascination was as much personal as political and ran the risk of her independent eye giving way to the complicity of understanding, as she freely admitted. 'Under the same roof… I know I should get to like Judas Iscariot or Cecil Rhodes. Isn't that a sign of a contemptible character – I never can resist propinquity'.[59]

As well as being a regular theatre goer, she frequently attended Parliamentary debates from the Speaker's Gallery, thanks to her friendship with the Speaker's daughter.[60] She could get the same buzz in the Ruritanian court of Dublin Castle where Aggie's husband was an Under-Secretary. Among its exotic mix of viceroys, harassed ministers, intemperate generals and scheming academics and lawyers, she relished the sense of being at the centre of things.[61] As with all theatre, this required considerable suspension of judgement. But the appeal of politics as theatre was to her irresistible. 'On Tuesday I went to a big [political] meeting and it was rather exciting as crowds always are. Lord Rosebery spoke and afterwards I went to see *Julius Caesar* and it was rather the same sort of thing – Lord R and Beerbohm'.[62]

This was politics seen from the grand circle. By now, others were questioning whether women too should have a part to play on this stage. Discussion over how women should contribute to the political process was increasingly a matter of public debate, raising issues of justice and loyalty for Frances that she would find highly conflicting. Many of Frances's friends supported women's suffrage, and with the vote the chance to reconfigure the political debate for the wider benefit of society. Frances Balfour and Maud Selborne were suffragists in the Women's Liberal Federation. So too was Mary Gladstone from 1884. Betty Balfour, DD and Aggie were strong advocates across the dinner table. As were most of the male Souls, including Arthur

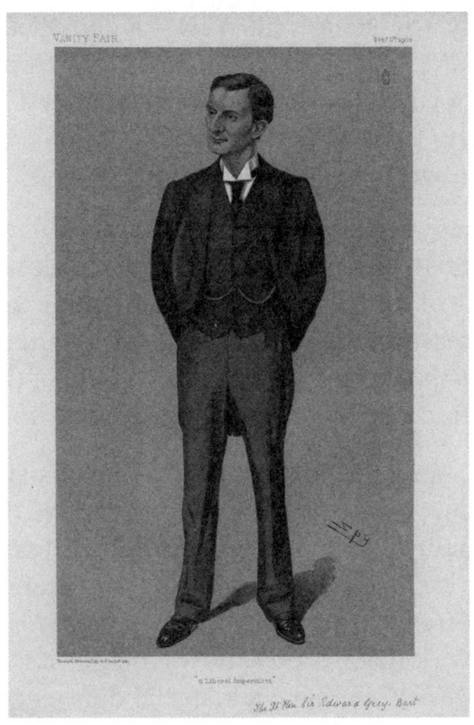

67.   *Sir Edward Grey, drawn by Spy for Vanity Fair*

Balfour. As a child, Frances had resented being denied the educational opportunities provided for her brothers and later had published 'The New Morality' to trumpet the talents of women in a male world. To men like Elcho she could seem dangerously radical in the matter of gender relationships. Even Burne-Jones would protest that 'I can't sympathise with you on the subject of women'. Only in time to be worn down by her, conceding

> Still the more I live, the more I am on the side of women. I don't care what women do to men or how they hurt them – a long cigar is full compensation to most men – … so count me in on any platform you take. But women shall be spoiled a bit for a time, I think.[63]

Yet when Haldane proposed a Women's Suffrage Bill in 1891, Frances confessed that 'I am rather sorry he is associating himself so tremendously with that – but I supposed it cannot be helped'.[64] Such disengagement should be seen in the context of the hostility shown to the reform by the senior Liberals – Gladstone, Rosebery and Harcourt[65] – and perhaps more surprisingly from the Asquiths, especially Margot who was virulent on the matter. On hearing about 'your Sunday party [where] you seem to have fallen out over Women Suffrage', Asquith wrote to stiffen Frances's resolve:

> there are so many channels and avenues through which you can make yourself felt, and some of them lead so close to the centre of things, that of all the women I know there are few, if any, who has less reason to turn their eyes backward and renounce the future. *You* don't want the suffrage, or any of the impostures which are offered you by the 'emancipators' of your sex.[66]

It was April 1892 and she was coming under his sway. However, it was also her traditional world view – a perspective that valued influence over an equality that in her position she did not need.

As ever, it was Burne-Jones who got to the heart of Frances's dilemma. 'Do you envy men because they can work? It is very few of them whose work matters one straw whether it is done or not'.[67] It was precisely to 'work', to make a material difference in society, that Aggie, DD and Elizabeth Haldane sought out responsibility and local authority to advance their causes. Few men could match the contribution to public life of Haldane's sister. A published philosopher and biographer in her own right [with books on Descartes, Hegel, and George Eliot] for which she was awarded an honorary degree from St Andrews, from 1892 she was a major participant in the Poor Law debate, while all the time managing Edinburgh Infirmary. In addition, she was a member of the 1912 Royal Commission on the Civil Service, the first woman to be a trustee of the Andrew Carnegie UK Trust and a JP in Scotland. For her public contribution she was made a Companion of Honour in 1918. Alongside this, there was no escape from traditional duties such as hosting for her bachelor brother and caring for their one-hundred-year-old mother. None of this would have appealed to Frances. DD was continually trying to arouse her interest for the latest cause: 'Personal Service, Maternal Mortality, The White Slave Traffic, Empire Marketing, Entertaining for the Colonies, The League of Nations', Frances would recall but all to no avail. For, as she openly confessed, while DD 'cared for politics more than for politicians, … with me it was the other way around'. Thus Frances would never have been found, as DD admitted, 'reading up things generally on the Voluntary School Question – in order to keep abreast of Alfred [Lyttelton]'. There was too much of the blue stocking in all of this for Frances. Once when Phil Burne-Jones called her clever, she smartly denied it: 'I am not clever – very, very good natured but not clever please'.[68] A joke certainly but it illustrated how Victorian she could be at times. It is there too in her admission to Katharine that she couldn't be 'a public philanthropist like DD or Elizabeth', preferring instead to 'do things in the small which alleviate human misery'.[69] For her it had to be personal, supporting 'oure poor' (i.e. local needy) than confronting national ills.

The summer of 1900 found Frances at the Paris Exhibition, where the Jekylls were leading the British delegation. This Frances 'enjoyed immensely'; not least for the sight of Herbert 'reluctantly escorting' the king's mistress, Mrs Keppel. There she was compelled to acknowledge that her little sister was now 'a person of considerable prowess' with 'very remarkable powers of organisation'. Only then to dismiss the diplomatic life: with lots of 'entertaining… It sounds quite vile as a life to me. But [Aggie] is so much younger and has such vast energy!'[70] Ignoring the competitive streak between two close sisters, Frances's rejection of the life of public service for women reflected her preference for the advancement of the right men over measures and that would require a different, less overt approach.

Frances's instincts were more traditional, wanting influence through people, inevitably men. She lacked the wealth and social position to run an aristocratic salon in the classical sense. But through the Souls and latterly her liaison with Asquith, she was developing a network which would give her access to the soon to be powerful in both the main parties. A more fundamental concern was that in Jack she lacked a political career to promote. Her time with Asquith had shown her what might be done, but Margot had taken that opportunity. That her choice should fall on Richard Haldane suggests that this was a friend in need rather than the pursuit of ambition. He was never going to be Prime Minister. A philosopher turned politician, he valued the rational and sweeping over the human and the petty too much to build up the necessary power base. Moreover he revelled too obviously in intrigue to be trusted. Yet to his friends such as Asquith and Grey, he would be fiercely loyal. And with the Liberals adrift after the 1895 election, Haldane was a creative force leading the way in the development of

'New Liberalism'. This would see him challenge the old Gladstonian creed of individualism, nonconformity, and moral crusades such as Irish Home Rule. In its place he looked to work in co-operation with early Fabian socialists such as the Webbs to explore the openings for progressive social reform including welfare, housing and employment law and how one might use the state to provide a safety net for the extremities of self-help. A vital element of 'national efficiency' was the modernising of public education and the expansion of universities. In tandem with the Webbs he would see their efforts realise the founding of the London School of Economics (1895), the passing of the University of London Act (1898) and eventually the creation of Imperial College (1906) – all while in opposition.

Such dynamism appealed to Frances but it was leading her into distinctly unfamiliar territory. Her 'slumming' in the East End and later her frustration at the complacency over the housing in Mells all demonstrated an active social conscience but ideologically it was quite a leap from charity to state welfare. Similarly she thought his aspiration for 'educating the democracy a flat impossibility!' That didn't stop her going with Haldane to hear the Fabian Graham Wallas and George Bernard Shaw speak: 'great fun… people asked foolish questions… very amusing'. Charles Trevelyan there 'with rather odd females… I enjoyed myself immensely'.[71] Here was another form of political theatre and Frances is back in the stalls, even if viewing the event with an almost anthropological eye. This is not to say that she didn't take matters of social injustice seriously but that most of what was being proposed she viewed as impractical, even faintly comic. Nothing infuriated Haldane more than Frances's attitude to the new women. As Frances recalled, he was

> very serious minded then – too much so and I had many early quarrels with him, steep ones which seem so absurd to look back on – always on the subject of Mrs Webb or Mrs Green [the historian and later Irish nationalist] whom he regarded as the pattern of womanhood…R thought we always antagonised them and failed to appreciate their worth.

But then she held his Fabian friends as people 'who held the view that children interfered with lives dedicated to the service of the State and that married companionship should be based on common interests and a partnership in work'. In other words a rejection of all she stood for in a woman.[72]

Matters came to head in 1894–5 when, with Rosebery in Downing Street, Haldane found himself again passed over for office. Declaring that his life was at a crossroads, he determined to abandon the Liberals, 'call myself Progressive' and dedicate his life to 'helping the masses'.[73] Supporting a life of Fabian opposition had no attraction for Frances. She never saw the point in talking at the powerful when you could walk with them. 'You must not let it cast you down or make you feel that you have failed', she would insist. 'That would be absurd – remember how much younger than all the others you are and how large a future there is open to you.' And then to cheer him up she reminded him that at least 'the big one [Gladstone] is gone and you are all glad'.[74] But it was 'You', not we. Anyway Haldane was in no mood for placating. His letter does not survive but her response was masterly.

> I am going to try and answer your letter. No I wasn't hurt by it, though it was very cold and very hostile, which sounds absurd from you and me. I was deeply moved by it. If you think I am going to let religion, or politics, or pride or anything else come between me and anyone I love, you are mistaken in me. Our views on the conduct of life may be different, no doubt they are, but so long as neither of us hold anything unworthy we need not be afraid. Do what you think right and I will help you all I can.

Urging him 'not to be impatient with me', she asked for a 'chance to understand what you are striving for and caring about [for] much of the political detail is unfamiliar to me'. Equally he mustn't assume that her pragmatism (what she called 'a hopeless Sanity'] meant she didn't share his ambitions. And then with a tug on the heartstrings she reined him back in.

> Perhaps it is true that another woman might have helped you more. I have never felt that our relationship was a very lucky one for you … but my only desire for your future has been this: that you should use your great and exceptional powers in a way that is most worthy. For that I should stand aside at any moment.

Safe in the knowledge that would not be asked of her, she then returned to her theme, urging caution ('sanity') and for him not to burn his boats: 'I mean there is no actual choice pending here, is there?'[75] This would not be the last time she would rescue his career.

Thereafter she would take her role more seriously, seeing it primarily as a facilitator. Mells became a political home for the Liberals. Asquith, Haldane and like-minded journalists such as Massingham[76] were regulars. 'The press is too much with us', she would complain to Burne-Jones – as if she hadn't invited them! Other guests included Winston Churchill, who would climb the Mendip Hills and, surveying the valleys below, seek to imagine the carnage of a modern battlefield. 'I wish I could have come to Mells', wrote John Morley. 'It is as familiar in my ears as Hawarden and Hatfield. My best friends all speak of it as if it were their house'.[77] As she had done for Asquith, so she hosted political dinners for the bachelor Haldane. One such in 1902 illustrated how she sought to further his cause. It was a small party, made up of family (Jack and Cicely) and close friends (Mary Elcho and Arthur Balfour). Into this private gathering she invited Beatrice Webb. With a Tory Education Bill due before the House, Frances placed Beatrice beside Balfour, the Conservative leader in the Commons, urging her to 'make as much use as possible of the one and a quarter hours he had free from the House'.[78] It is not clear if Balfour knew this was coming but almost certain that Haldane was the instigator. At a more basic level Frances offered support, joining him occasionally on the platform when he was on the stump in the West Country or raising morale when reshuffles passed without the call. And all the while she kept an eye to the future, awaiting the moment when Asquith would be Prime Minister and Haldane in office.

27

POLITICAL INTRIGUES

Lady Horner was a political intriguer, but her bias was born of friends, not convictions.

Edwin Lutyens[79]

Not that she had expected that this future would emerge in the midst of a war. But then, the Boer War would challenge the British political system to its limits and indeed Britain's identity as the world's most powerful and beneficent empire. To this, Frances was not immune. As her father's daughter, Frances had learnt to abhor imperial conquests and the jingoism it aroused. Imperialism was only justifiable as a civilising, Christian mission. By the 1890s the tone of the language was changing – becoming more intolerant, arrogant and supremacist. Burne-Jones attributed it to 'the bombast of the newspapers'. And when the mining giant and political adventurer, Cecil Rhodes, began scheming to form a continuous band of British colonies the length of the African continent ('from Cape to Cairo'), Burne-Jones denounced it to Frances in vitriolic terms. 'Let's have no more dominant races, we don't want them – they only turn men into insolent brutes'. In so far as she thought of Empire (as opposed to Europe), he was preaching to the long-converted. Hence, amid the Jubilee celebrations of 1897 and the serried ranks of Empire marching by, Frances was so keen to promote Kipling's *Recessional* among her friends – a hymn to humility for a nation 'drunk with sight of power'.[80]

And yet, she was also a child brought up on the Arthurian legend that venerated the knightly ideals of a chivalric society. It was when she was staying with Aggie in Dublin Castle that Frances first encountered the military world. Placed beside General Sir Garnet

Wolseley, who regaled her over dinner with tales of his spectacular victory at Tel-el-Kebir in the annexation of Egypt, she glimpsed a fantasy of heroes where the values of courage, honour, and decisiveness prevailed. Empire too was a theatre providing in drab industrial Britain a splash of colour and dash, where men of action overcame seemingly overwhelming odds, and all against exotic backdrops. It was hard not to get excited at tales of derring-do. Indeed after months incapacitated by depression following Burne-Jones's death, what drew her out was the visit of Violet Cecil, anxious for her husband on the eve of a battle at Omdurman (1898) against the Mahdi. 'We kept the telegraph office open all Sunday and about 7pm all the telegrams poured in – one actually from Omdurman. It has been very Mellish', Frances reported to DD.[81] Omdurman was a turkey shoot with maxim machine guns against 52,000 tribesmen armed with spears, 95% of whom were killed or injured. But such details did not stir the telegraph office at Mells. Instead the mood was one of exultation: 'What a time it has been – a time of heroisms and tragedies. The sounds of Trumpets in Heaven'. Similarly she wrote to Jack, 'Isn't it thrilling about Fashoda?' after the French had backed down following a stand-off in the Sudan.[82] So perhaps it was no surprise that with the outbreak of the war against the Boers she should be an enthusiastic volunteer. 'I am afraid Jack is too old and Edward too young, so I shan't be able to speak with my enemies at the gate'. But that didn't stop her getting her children on a local stage to raise funds for the war. In this she was far from alone.[83]

Early hopes for a swift victory soon gave way to 'the bitterest anxiety'. 'Rumours appalling …no one thinks of anything else', she informed Violet Cecil, now out in South Africa with her husband. 'Black Week' in December 1899 in which Britain suffered three defeats in the field only confirmed her worst fears. Such national humiliation left her furious ('I can hardly keep my temper') at such 'abominable generalship'.[84] The coming months would see the position rectified and the relief of Mafeking saw a spontaneous outpouring of national celebration. By now, however, she was repelled at the revelling over 'a big nation crushing a small one (which gives me a kind of twinge)'. After the debacle, she hoped 'we shan't hear too much of that weary word Imperialism which in some mouths is merely inflated jingoism… [Instead, we should] think on our splendid courage, patriotism, unity of national feeling – great chaps our

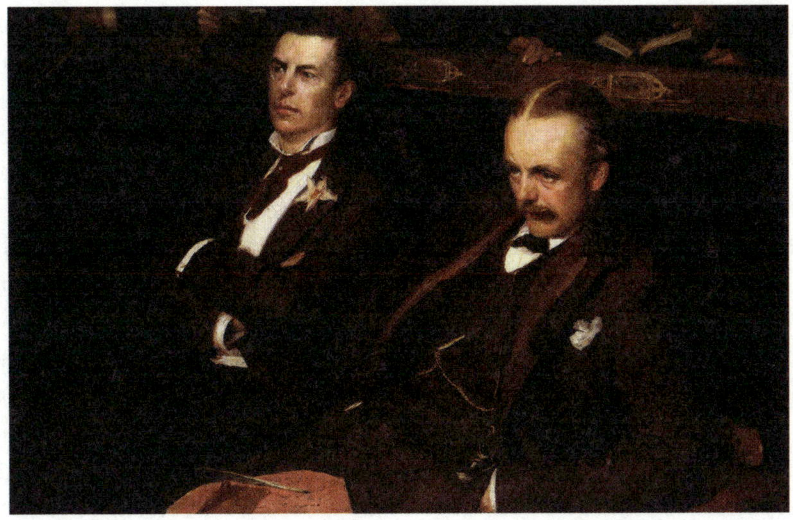

68.   *Joseph Chamberlain and Arthur Balfour, by Sydney Prior Hall, 1903*

soldiers! Their lives deserve less squandering'.[85] This was not a change of heart, for Frances was always a patriot, never an all-conquering Anglo-Saxon imperialist. The distinction had become blurred, but no longer.

Such beliefs left her unexpectedly isolated among her friends. Violet Cecil (soon to embark on a lifelong affair with Sir Alfred Milner, the architect of British policy in South Africa) and DD were fiercely committed to the imperialist mission. So too were all her Tory friends among the Souls. More disturbing were her closest friends in the Liberal Party – Asquith, Haldane and Grey – who under Rosebery would become Liberal Imperialists and, with their formation of the Liberal League threaten to split the party. Updating Violet, she admitted that 'The Liberals are somewhat divided: all our particular friends supporting the government strongly'.[86] Despite this, she would often invite to Mells Herbert Paul, a former Liberal MP and now Pro-Boer journalist who was sacked from the *Daily News* for his views. For one who declared that she valued her friends over her political opinions, these were testing times.

The conflict also challenged her romantic notions of Great Men. For, if anything, the war exposed a failure of leadership – the revelation of an empire being led by pygmies. With many others, she felt misled over the war by the Colonial Secretary, Joseph Chamberlain, 'with his cad side turned uppermost' (fig. 68).[87] But her disillusion went further than this. With the Tory press acting like a vigilante mob seeking out critics of the war among the Liberals, few politicians called out for a spirit of unity in the national interest. Looking on from the Ladies' Gallery, she was left 'miserable' by the tone of the parliamentary debate and its abdication to forces outside: 'The interest seems to be far more in the headlines of the newspapers than in the House of Commons now.' She came to see this as symptomatic of a wider moral decline: 'I hear the season will be at Cape Town!' as many of her class went out to view the sport. Of course there was much virtue signalling, such as Margot's giving up her horses for the war. 'She will ride other people's horses instead', remarked Frances tartly. Nor in war time would there be any let up in 'Belshazzar's feasts' *chez* Tennant, to Frances's disapproval after one extravaganza. There she found Balfour and Asquith, 'both rather sick, the one of office, and the other for office'.[88] 'It is Ichabod!' she declared (echoing the 'glory' departing Israel after the capture of the Ark of the Covenant by the Philistines).[89]

The Tories' cynical exploitation of the public euphoria, following apparent victory in the field, by calling a General Election in 1900 was only to be expected in such shameless times and left her 'profoundly depressed'. Admittedly, the Liberals were hammered. But it was the triumphalism and the division it engendered that appalled her. 'It is dreadful in Frome: such bitterness and such rows; of course, it is full of breweries and tied houses, I daren't go near the town this week'. 'I feel quite glad', she wrote to Violet, that 'Angelo did not live through this black year'.[90]

The failure of leadership that hurt most came from within her own party. Haldane's ambition to use Liberal Imperialism to purge the party of the old guard and pave the way for a centre party focussing on social reform and national efficiency had come to naught. Relations with the Fabians had cooled and Balfour's Tories with their large majority had no need to collaborate. However before this, the position had been undermined by the leadership of Lord Rosebery. Rosebery was an odd choice to be the leader of 'a revolution in our party'. It was less that he was an aristocrat of enormous wealth and glamour who had made his name by winning the Derby three times. Rather his spell as leader and Prime Minister in 1894–5 showed him to be both egotistical – hypersensitive to any perceived slight – and lacking in the fighting qualities required of a leader; especially one out of office.

Frances, who was a natural enthusiast of cross-party collaboration, was willing to believe in Rosebery, whom she had known since 1880, despite the fact that he could be 'not at all Christian or forgiving in his temper' towards others. His sudden resignation in October 1896 while speaking in Edinburgh shocked her, not least because it had been 'sprung on all his colleagues', some of whom were on the platform with him. Frances too had been there, riveted by a drama 'fraught with human emotions', with Rosebery seeking to justify his actions as if in the dock on trial. Nevertheless she condemned his 'quite an unjustifiable action towards his party' – self-centred, spineless and selfish. Especially so as Asquith and Haldane had 'burnt their boats' in support of him.[91] Returning that night to Whittinghame, she found Balfour 'awfully nice and kind and seemed pleased I had come' – still up at 11pm and for once eager for her news.[92]

By 1902 Frances had become increasingly frustrated as the party drifted away from her gang. Sir Henry Campbell-Bannerman was 'our so called leader' oscillating between the warring factions.[93] He was of the old guard with little appetite for the New Liberalism that Haldane was preaching. Yet for all his apparent weakness, he had skewered Liberal Imperialism with his 'methods of barbarism' speech (1901). Joining with the radical wing of the party, he denounced the concentration camps and burning homesteads as the Army brutally extinguished the last Boer resistance, two years after the premature celebration of victory. Still amid the disarray, she sensed opportunity and in an extraordinary letter urged Asquith to act. 'How close your interests are to my heart', she declared. 'For 10 years now your friendship has been the thing I have treasured most and that I have been proudest of in my life'. Then asking his forgiveness for the 'impertinence' of what follows (it should have been the King or the Archbishop of Canterbury urging him, she protested), she pressed on. 'The premiership of the Liberal Party is going begging'. She claimed from her contacts (and not just Haldane) that the party, having waited 'patiently for the hour to strike', was losing faith in Asquith. 'The idea that you are failing the party seems everywhere in the air' with confidence passing to Sir Edward Grey. 'You are the natural leader', she insisted. 'I feel certain that this is the great chance of your life and that it is not too late… if you could make them feel that you really care…[It is] a great and splendid thing when power and opportunities fall into hands like yours'.[94] Asquith resisted the challenge and perhaps was in no state to take the risk. About this time Beatrice Webb found him 'simply dull. He is disheartened with politics, has no feeling of independent initiative and is baffled by Rosebery, snubs and is snubbed by Campbell-Bannerman'… Eats and drinks too much [and] … is resigned to missing the leadership'.[95] It is a measure of Frances's ambition that she never gave up on her desire to see Asquith in Downing Street, and perhaps too of her naivety in believing that power would gravitate to 'natural leaders'. Just how extensive were her 'contacts' within the party? How far had she appreciated the risks of a coup? The fact remained that Asquith was naturally a very cautious conspirator.

Unlike Haldane, who revelled in conspiracies and subterfuge and whose reputation as an intriguer had probably contributed to his twice missing office. By 1905 he was back on manoeuvres. Joseph Chamberlain's call for Imperial Preference or protection (1903) not only split the Tory party but challenged Free Trade – a central tenet of the Liberal creed. With Arthur Balfour privately alerting Haldane that his government's resignation was imminent, the gang around Asquith sought to seize the initiative, firm in their belief that the party needed a changing of the guard if the Liberals were to be able to defend Free Trade in the coming election.[96] The outcome was the 'Relugas Compact', a private agreement drawn up that September in a hunting lodge at the village of Relugas on Grey's Scottish estate.[97] In this, Grey, Asquith and Haldane committed to not accepting office in the next Liberal government unless all three were offered the key senior posts (of Foreign Secretary, Chancellor of the Exchequer, and Lord Chancellor respectively). Furthermore, by insisting that Campbell-Bannerman would lead the government from the Lords, *de facto* power would pass to Asquith in the Commons. Essentially, they calculated that any Liberal government without them would be too weak to survive. If this was not audacious enough, Haldane, using his connections with the King, had primed him to raise the possibility of the Lords to the Prime Minister at Balmoral in October.[98] Haldane kept Frances fully abreast of the plan. Her main concern was the need for secrecy especially of the King's involvement. 'Yes' Haldane agreed. 'I dread Margot. She is so easily pumped. But HHA [i.e. Asquith] promised me not to tell her. Only I don't quite rely on him…I have written a further full letter of suggestions for the K[ing]… I wish I was in HHA's shoes for a month to do this, but he certainly showed no lack of zeal when I saw him'.[99]

On Monday 4 December 1905 Balfour resigned and the game kicked off. Quickly it became apparent that all was not going to plan. By Wednesday they learnt that Asquith, who was supposed to be leading their negotiation, 'had not been resolute' – as Haldane had always feared. Indeed he had accepted the Chancellorship of the Exchequer without any pre-conditions. Weakened by this, Haldane and Grey still stood their ground and the next day Grey refused to serve if Campbell-Bannerman remained in the Commons. All Haldane had been offered was the Attorney General in the knowledge that he was never going to give up £20,000 a year (£2.4 million in 2019) at the Bar for that. With Asquith on board, the Prime Minister now had the whip hand over the plotters and could await their return to the fold.

Regarding the matter 'finished', Haldane called in on 9 Buckingham Gate where Frances was entertaining some women friends. They left almost immediately and Haldane and Frances went downstairs to the schoolroom. What followed would change his life for ever. Frances read the letters Haldane had received from Campbell-Bannerman and Asquith urging him and Grey to accept. After a brief reflection, she passed judgement: 'From your point of view and that of Grey this may be right [to stay out], but you told the King that you would not leave him in the lurch – besides you are making a real risk for the Free Trade cause'. Predicting 'a very heavy reaction', the 'weak' government would need all the help it could get if Free Trade was not to 'perish'. When he protested how anyone could join a government 'weak … and discredited from the beginning', she snapped back 'The better for you to be a member of it – the worse for the King and the public who cannot escape from it [if you are not]'. This was a blunt reminder of higher responsibilities than personal ambition – of his duty to party and nation, which had got lost from view amid the delicate subtleties of conspiracy. There was no instant recanting and Grey and Haldane met up again that night at the Café Royal for dinner outwardly resolute in their defiance. But slowly what Haldane called the 'ethical question' made 'a great impression on me', worming away at their certainties. With Haldane the more desperate of the two for office and Asquith urging acceptance, Grey and Haldane changed tack. Campbell-Bannerman, appreciating that Haldane at the War Office was a small price to pay for securing Grey in the Foreign Office, did not play on their embarrassment. He was, after all, still Prime Minister in the Commons and firmly in control.[100]

Very quickly Haldane was reconstructing events. Beatrice Webb caught him in exultant mood.

> Asquith, Grey and I stood together, they were forced to take us on our own terms. We were really very indifferent...But it was a horrid week – one perpetual wrangle. The King signified that he would like me to take the War Office; it is exactly what I myself have longed for...I shall succeed. I have always succeeded in everything I have undertaken.

Beatrice saw through this bravado. 'Merely the foam of his excited self-complacency, in the first novelty of power,' she judged.[101] In truth, Campbell-Bannerman had seen off the young men. Identifying Haldane as the leading plotter, he thought the War Office after the Boer War a suitably poisoned chalice. 'We shall now see how Schopenhauer gets on in the Kailyard'.[102] As fate would have it, the general election in January 1906 – much to the surprise of most Liberals – gave them the greatest landslide victory in British electoral history (and crucially one that left them for the first time in twenty years not reliant on Irish votes). If Haldane had stayed aloof in December, he would have been in the political wilderness for a decade, if not for ever. In a memorandum dictated to Frances at Mells on 3 June 1906, he acknowledged that his critical change of mind was 'wholly due' to her. 'The whole week was one of the most miserable I have ever spent in my life', he recalled. 'The one illuminating hour in it was that of our talk, and the new light that came. I have never for a moment regretted the consequent decision or the vast change which your influence made in the course of my career'.[103] He would become her devoted follower for the rest of his life. She, once the inspiration of artists, was the muse of politicians now.

As it turned out Haldane proved a major success at the War Office. Not only did he embark on a programme of modernisation but he also created a properly trained 'reserve army' of a quarter of a million men, amalgamating the various volunteer elements into a Territorial Force. Crucially all this was achieved without conscription and perhaps more remarkably on a reduced budget.

The rationalisation of military command around his creation of an Imperial General Staff required deft political handling. So too did the development of a continental strategy. Haldane twice went on 'missions' (1906, 1912) to Germany – including a long interview with the Kaiser – in an effort to improve relations. But with Germany rearming rapidly, Haldane and Grey had ensured by 1914 that Britain had an expeditionary force ready to prevent the war being lost in the crucial first months of a German offensive. This required considerable secrecy and the careful management of his opponents in Westminster – both in as well as outside his party – to the extent that the Army was briefly taken 'out of politics'. This would cause trouble later but there could be no denying that when war broke out in 1914, Britain was uncharacteristically ready for battle.[104]

Haldane's achievement was remarkable and it is tempting to think of the consequences of a few words said in private in the schoolroom of 9 Buckingham Gate. Not that Frances would have seen it that way. For her what mattered – as it always had – were the politicians and not the politics. And by 1908 the Relugas plotters had realised their goals. Following the death of Campbell-Bannerman, Asquith finally assumed the leadership of the Liberals. Grey's control at the Foreign Office was such that he ran policy largely independent of his cabinet colleagues. And in 1911, his work at the War Office done, Haldane was appointed to the Woolsack as Lord Chancellor. The years before the First World War were tumultuous ones with cavalry charges on strikers, civil unrest in Ulster, suffragette violence, arms races and international crises; while in parliament, the Lords and Commons were at loggerheads in a battle for supremacy. Amid the political heat, old friends among the Souls, such as Balfour, Curzon and Asquith would now divide. Others such as George Wyndham, who dreamed so high, would see their careers disintegrate in a parliament out for blood. Under the pressure Asquith succumbed increasingly to drink. Yet for Frances her memories were of halcyon days: 'we were very much in the political world,' she reminisced. 'My dream had come true – Asquith, Haldane and Grey had more and more power in the State. I used to think that if Asquith were Prime Minister, Grey Foreign Secretary, and Haldane Lord Chancellor, all would be well with the world, and so it was for a time, before the shattering years broke on us.'[105]

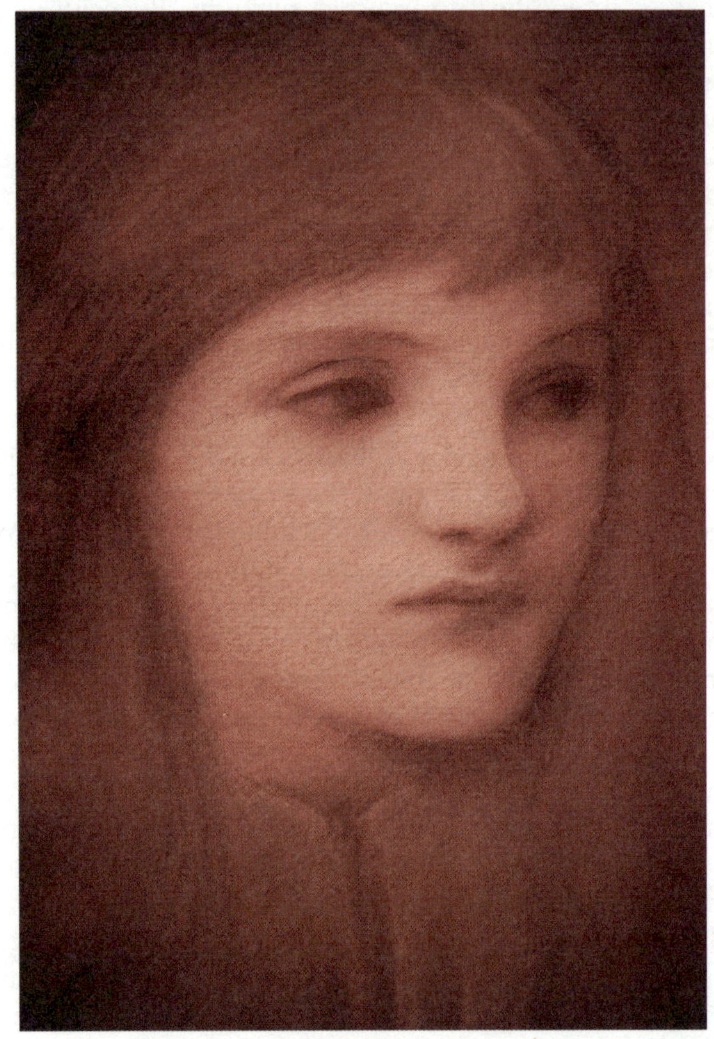

69.   *Detail of a preliminary sketch of Cicely Horner, by Edward Burne-Jones, c. 1891–2*

247

Remote Operators and Callow Youths

[I hope] the younger generation… will still tolerate me as a sympathetic, if remote, operator.

Frances Horner to DD Lyttelton[1]

28

PRE-RAPHAELITE CHILDREN

Frances lived in a *very* immoral world in her youth, I suppose a rich Glasgow world, yet she adored moral Burne-Jones. She once told me that had she been born 15 years later, she would have run away with BJ. I said, 'No, your children would have held you back' and she agreed.

Mary Belloc Lowndes[2]

Rather to her surprise, Frances proved a more enthusiastic mother than many of her generation.[3] That would cause trouble in the years ahead. But in her memory, her children enjoyed an idyllic childhood. And none more so than her eldest, Cicely (fig. 69). Although not the brightest, she learnt to read quickly and like many first born, she went out of her way to be helpful to her mother. Even her doll was named after Frances. A natural country girl, she was easy to please with a succession of ponies and dogs and an aviary built for her in the garden. Together she and Frances would race on bicycles round back lanes, which rose like 'the waves of the sea'. Such energy and daring appealed greatly to Frances. So too, if not more so, did her beauty. For Cicely 'entered into her beauty when she entered the world, with large eyes and a complexion like Red Rose and Snow White'. What made her artistic mother so proud would in time come to haunt her daughter. For now mother and daughter shared an easy rapport, a capacity for certainty and a readiness for action.[4]

By comparison, Frances never felt quite as one with her next daughter, Katharine. That she was 'an unhappy baby at first' possibly reflected that she was born while Frances was still grieving her father. Nor did it help that as a child she lacked the looks of her elder sister – something Frances made more of than she should. True

Katharine was 'much quicker at lessons' than Cicely but conversely less practical. 'As a little thing she was constantly in trouble' – not in the sense of being naughty but of not seeing the consequences of her actions. She almost drowned when tiny after falling into the deepest part the lake and was only saved by Hetty the nursemaid, diving in and pulling her out. Later when she was older and the incident long forgotten, she walked into the nursery bath with her best pelisse on. To Frances, such behaviour was of a piece with other oddities including 'many of the sayings that we treasured in the family'. Nor did she ever want a doll. Unworldly and detached, Katharine took refuge in books, quietly losing herself in a discreet corner, no matter how 'dull' (in Frances's eyes) the tome. 'Oh, mother', her serious young daughter would remind her, 'one always has to push through a little with books, and then it gets all right' – a first hint of the austere judgement that would from time to time catch her mother by surprise. As it did in 1901 with Frances thrilled over a triumph of match making, which saw the Liberal Chief Whip, Herbert Gladstone, finally propose to his future wife on the terrace at Mells. 'Two walks and two moonlight walks did it! I must say I was rather out of breath', Frances confessed to DD. But looking round, she sensed her fifteen-year-old daughter 'shining eyed but thinking us all rather too frivolous'.[5] By contrast, Katharine felt closer to her scholarly father (fig. 70), even if both rarely expressed their affection. Nothing emphasised the difference between mother and daughter more than the sudden arrival of Aunt Lily. One of Frances's older sisters, she had dedicated her life to missionary work in China. She and Frances had never got on and would not now. 'Lily is here from China', Frances wrote in despair to Burne-Jones:

> My dear, I can't believe she and I can be children of our parents. For she is *happy* there. She loves what she calls the heathen … I should die there and of the life. She had photographs – groups of heathen – heathen of all ages – and whenever I saw a photograph of an Englishman…she admitted to one as having been "a valued helper". I think that is a very good phrase. I am always going to call them valued helpers in future. But I don't think Lily's was any good – in fact I think he was dead. She is good but so dreadful that it is almost pathetic.

Still, the virtue that so exasperated Frances only inspired her

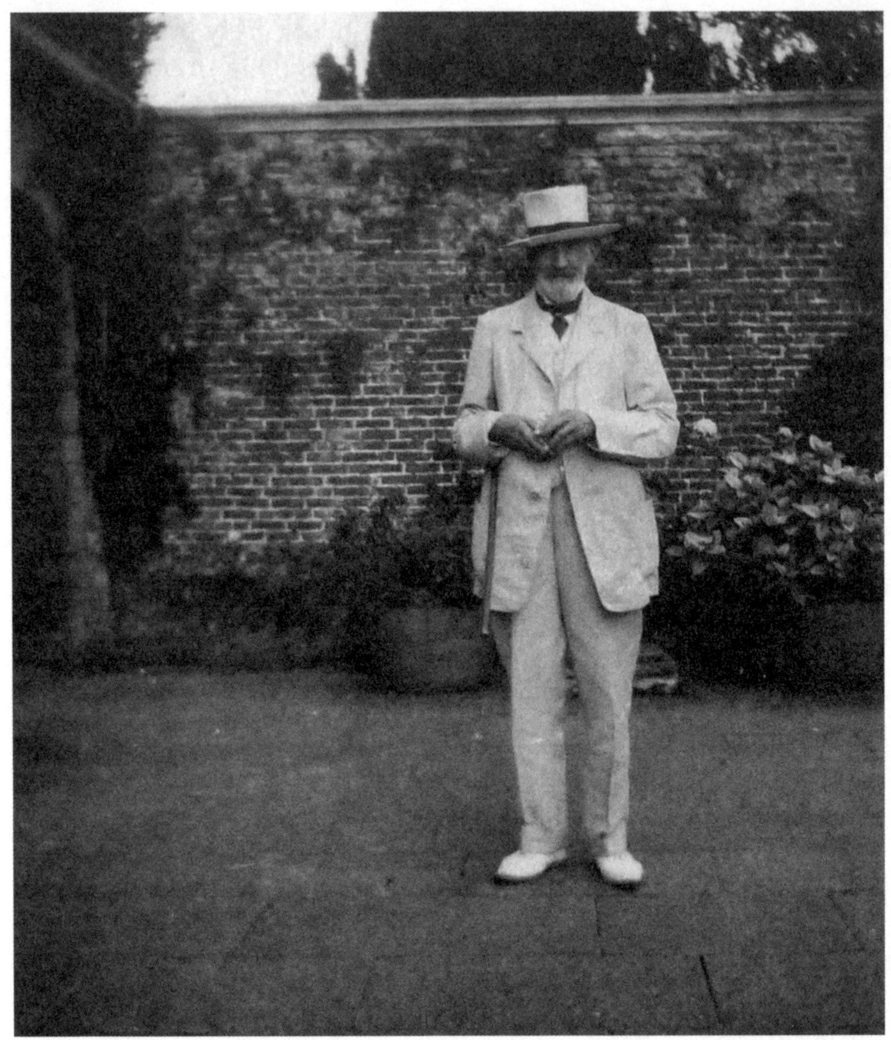

70.   Jack

daughter to become obsessively religious. Apparently fearful that she had sinned against the Holy Ghost, Katharine determined to sleep on her bedroom floor to mortify the flesh in preparation to becoming a missionary. On another occasion, she was discovered at 2am crying 'at having to go to China'. 'Katharine is getting rather a strange little thing, full of religion and mysticism', Frances shared with Burne-Jones. 'I want you to have a talk with her someday. Isn't it strange how my father seems to shape their little characters still.

I'm sure she didn't get a morbid conscience from Jack or me!' By now Frances's faith had declined into little more than social convention and in that light she ensured that Cicely and Katharine would be confirmed in Westminster Abbey. Nor was Katharine destined for China. Yet her interest in matters religious would never wane.[6]

The boys on the other hand were in their different ways spoilt by Frances. For all the trauma of Edward's birth which left her 'an old woman', the arrival of a son and heir was a cause for celebration. As important for Frances, 'Edward was a beautiful child, as indeed he always remained' (fig. 72). Clever too, which Frances valued highly. Although he was to grow up to be fearless (on horseback 'his courage was reckless'), as a child he was timid and precious. He had a keen sense of style and from an early age was 'very particular' about his clothes – for which he was nicknamed 'The Popinjay' by his sisters. His manner too was ostentatiously chivalric. Unlike rougher contemporaries he had 'charming manners [and was always] very friendly and courteous', if lacking their drive.

Was it his future as the Horner heir that sucked any ambition out of him? He was certainly aware of his destiny. The young boy was quick to remind his mother whenever her conversation became outrageous to 'think on the honour of the Horners'. When his father was away, 'Edward pretends to be you in church and crosses his legs and tidies his books as like as he can'. He 'cuddles your letters', Frances would write in an effort to get Jack to respond.[7] Instead Edward became dependant on his mother: Edward has been 'a perfect angel' all holidays Frances pronounced proudly to DD. 'It is a great happiness to me that he is growing up sweet and delightful and his intimacy with me increases every holiday'. Conversely when she packed the children off with their nanny to Felixstowe before leaving for a cruise in 1897, Edward immediately went down with a mysterious illness – everyone deciding 'it was too bracing a place for him'. A serious infection that left him briefly blind in one eye and bedridden for six weeks was milked for all it was worth. Even Frances felt him 'rather pathetic in his excessive politeness'. On the other hand she loved his possessiveness: 'Mother, aren't we happy without dear Cicely?' he would say when he had her to himself. 'So angelic' she declared him. Blind to his faults, she would pin on him all her hopes.[8]

Mark couldn't have been more different (fig. 71). Right from his christening he was his own man. As the holy water splashed on his face 'he gave some little sobs of departing guilt [before relapsing] into his usual state of philosophic doubt', while behind him stood Edward 'chanting amen whenever he had a chance'. What was unusual, however, was that this was not a private service but shared with 'a dear little brown farmer's baby'. Yet this was fitting for it would be among such folk that he would be most at ease; 'whether it was Granny's maid, Rowthorne ('Don't go on washing her – come and let's talk secrets on the stairs'), or the housekeeper's room where he would often as a child take tea. There he once piled all the chairs in a row and, pretending it was a train, he sat in the front as the driver. Suddenly he leaned over and spat on the floor. When asked why he replied, 'of course, engine drivers always spit over the side'. After Edward went to school, 'Mark was left in undivided possession at home: family, servants, stables, estate. All were under his rule, and he maintained his supremacy among them throughout his life'.

It was no different in London. Mark soon got to know all the bus drivers and cab drivers – they called him 'Lord Roberts'. He was even allowed to go to tea (and bacon) with one of them. He made great friends with the footman (later their man servant) Albert Maxted, who Mark dubbed 'Crock' and was called 'Blight' in return. The flip side was that he was less able to engage with his own. When Violet Cecil asked if she could bring her much younger son George, Mark (who found this tiresome) threatened to teach him how to spit and swear – much to the mothers' amusement. 'The Mark Fiend is dominant', Frances would warn her guests.

A country lad through and through, he would say things as they were. Mark 'very filibustering' calling Cicely 'an idiot', Frances recounted to Burne-Jones. Only then for him to defend himself by saying that it was just what his father had said to the driver. To her amazement, he 'could not see that the analogy was not close'. But perhaps it was and that is what made him so loved. So too his openness and integrity, laced as they were with a touch of rural cunning. Not for him joining his siblings and mother in deriding Granny Graham behind her back. Devoted to her, every night he would find his way to the East wing where she lived to join her in prayers ('including loud petitions to God for objects he most coveted, which then Granny delighted in procuring for him').[9]

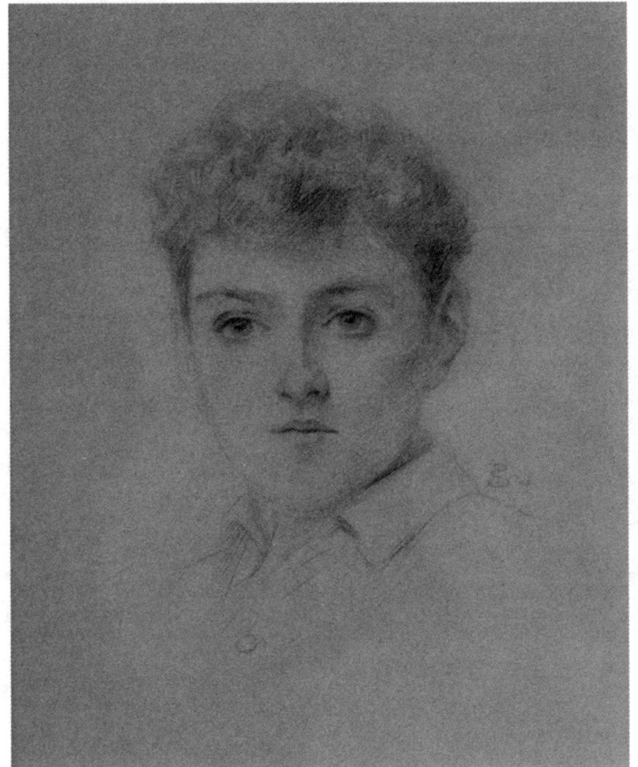

71.   *Mark, by Violet Rutland (formerly Granby), 1908*

*

Escaping to Sweden in the aftermath of her mother's death, Frances was relieved to receive 'a dewdrop' from DD on the behaviour of her children. 'I never feel as if one is really responsible for praise or blame. It all seems so irrespective of one's efforts'. Fomenting such doubts would be her brother-in-law, George, always quick to judge some misdemeanour. Admittedly Frances was often away in London, or visiting friends in the country or more occasionally on trips abroad with close friends. The reception on her return would see a 'tempestuous welcome' from Cicely, while the boys were generally 'cheerful. They did not resent it like Katharine'.[9] Still it was also a measure of how much (and unusually so for the times) she was central to their lives. In this Jack was not much help. She would have to remind him how much their children look forward to him being there 'though I know you [would] rather

72.   Edward and Mark

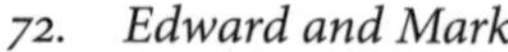

be in other surroundings'.[11] With the children careering around, he quickly became 'irritable', and retreated back to his study. Then there were his explosions: 'forcible vocabulary that belonged to a past generation' was how Frances would describe them. 'Oh my God! Where the Hell are you going to?' he yelled at her as she stalled 'the motor' at the brow of a hill and began to slide backwards. Yet none of this was taken remotely seriously and was often imitated to great dramatic effect by his offspring, who recognised that for the most part he was gentle, kind, loyal and quietly enjoying being the butt of their humour.

Thankfully for Frances, she had Nanny Day who stayed fourteen years until Mark was ready for school. 'Gay, energetic, religious and sensible', she was crucially 'a very good playmate nurse', ever ready to go bird nesting, flower hunting, or on picnics. With her 'even going to bed was fun'. Still Frances frequently had them on her own and rather relished the mayhem. 'Mells is heavenly right now – warm and green and delicious' and with a 'great party of children'.[12] Here, loosed from the constraints of London, the children could run free, bicycling, pony carting, and riding. The summer holidays were for Frances sacrosanct as 'children's time'. There would also be long family gatherings with her sisters on Mull – exhausting certainly, but a boon to realise that 'my own little girls feel like two fresh sweet poems after the others!' Indeed, away from her high-spirited cousins, Katharine would 'write mystic verses all day'. Occasionally they would holiday abroad, such as to Austria in 1904. When Jack was not available, she would seize Haldane as a companion and take the children to Brittany or Ireland ('this country is like the most interesting

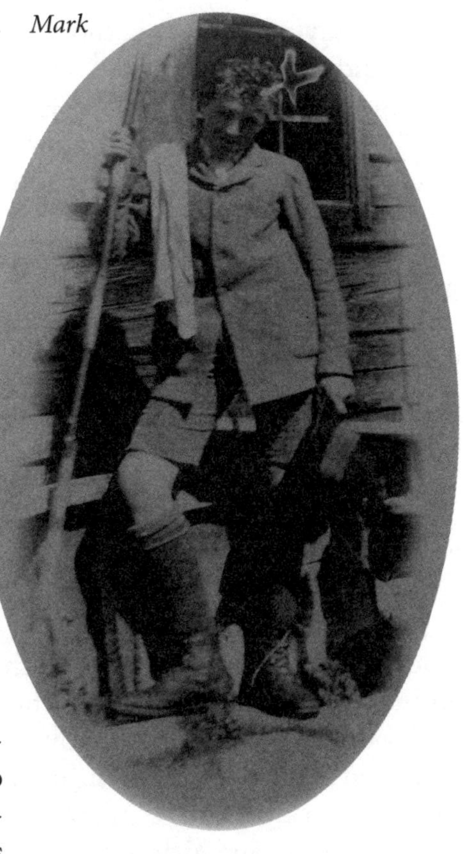

73. *Mark*

person. It has an extraordinary temperament, and never gives you two consecutive hours alike – I like that').[13]

'Can you bear the family', she would enquire of impending guests: 'they are rather ebullient at Mells?' Yet to Frances's credit they were a happy gang and especially when she was around. With them, she was fun, lively and a touch anarchic. From her they inherited (and often displayed against her) the teasing wit and outrageous argument that she so loved. But it was their innocence she adored, capturing this in a series of pen portraits drawn of them for Burne-Jones. It is the summer of 1896. Cicely, the eldest, was still only twelve and already as tall as Frances:

> To look at her you would think she had been born hundreds of years ago and had known all the love and all the sadness in the world- [when] really she is thinking of her canaries and whether the cat will get at them. Katharine is mightily excited over ancient history or whether she likes Keats as much as Shelley and what is a fine sounding name for a knight. Edward is never in disgrace but always tidy, punctual and beautifully dressed. He refuses to wear anything that is in the least soiled or even rumpled. As for Mark…the whole conversation below stairs is of his doings and sayings. And he has been very busy, for haymaking has set in and no cart can be loaded without his superintendence.[14]

Yet such idylls were not without purpose. Beautiful, literary, precocious and high-spirited, they were – as they were intended to be – unmistakably children of the Souls. And for this they were much admired. Thus at Stanway, Arthur Balfour gazed on as 'the children, beautiful and godlike Charteris and Horners ranted, and roared and pianola'd in the drawing room'.[15] Staying with the Horners, Charty was 'very struck by the licence of family conversation and manners'.[16] At the same time, Frances ensured that they were from very young well versed in Souls' sport. Visiting Mells in 1892 Emily Lytton found the Horner children 'very precocious and already playing intellectual games'. Riddles were obviously popular: 'I am black and white and very spoiling', offered Mark on his widowed grandmother.[17]

Underpinning this from early on was Frances's insistence on education. Finding a suitable tutor proved far from easy. First Frances chose a poet from a neighbouring farm, who she saw as an 'embryo Chatterton' but who turned out only to be submitting jokes to *Punch*. A French tutor followed and was 'much inspiring'. But not academically, preferring to teach the children perilous circus tricks on their ponies and scaling up the outside walls of the house. The next disaster was a German governess who proved of the 'larmoyante kind'. Finally Frances hit on 'a treasure'. Miss Nora Neroutsos from Cambridge was young, able, and critically for Frances, good with both boys and girls. Her daughters would not go to school but she was determined that they would enjoy a full literary education. Similarly, Frances dreaded her sons (especially Edward) becoming hunting and fishing bores. Thus Miss Neroutsos brought out a keen interest in history in both Katharine and Edward. Katharine's literary verse began to win critical acclaim among Frances's friends, much to her mother's delight. 'You are blessed amongst women to have a child who could write those lines' acknowledged Georgie Burne-Jones, if then to query how Frances would keep her 'unspoilt'.[17] Only with Mark's 'book knowledge' did Miss Neroutsos fail – much to his frustration and almost certainly, the result of a learning difficulty never diagnosed.[19] On the other hand, Edward won a scholarship to Summer Fields primarily on account of being so well taught by her. This was just as Frances had imagined it would be.[20]

Not that her imagination stopped at academic prowess. Her children were to look the part too. And that part was Pre-Raphaelite.[21] 'I am writing this on my knees in bed,' she warned Burne-Jones in July

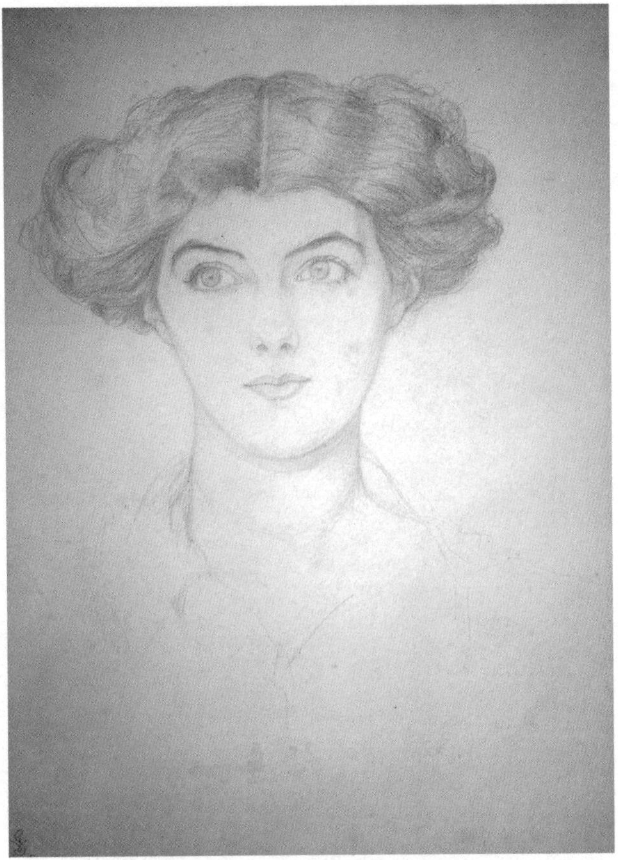

74. *Katharine, by Violet Granby*

1897. And with 'a high sense of moral superiority over all those people who are at Bayreuth with everyone else's husband and daughters'. Instead, fleeing the racket of the boys, she had taken the two girls to Brittany to swim 'in heavenly little bays in none of the guide books'. As 'Katharine's eyes shone out of her head' (fig. 74),

> Cicely looks very bonny …in a pink bathing gown; and when a bathing gown is wet, it is only the honour of the thing, as you know. And she picked up a great long gold-brown sash of seaweed a yard long and danced on the edge of the sea with it; and I thought she had walked straight out of a picture of yours to comfort me. There is a mother's vanity.[22]

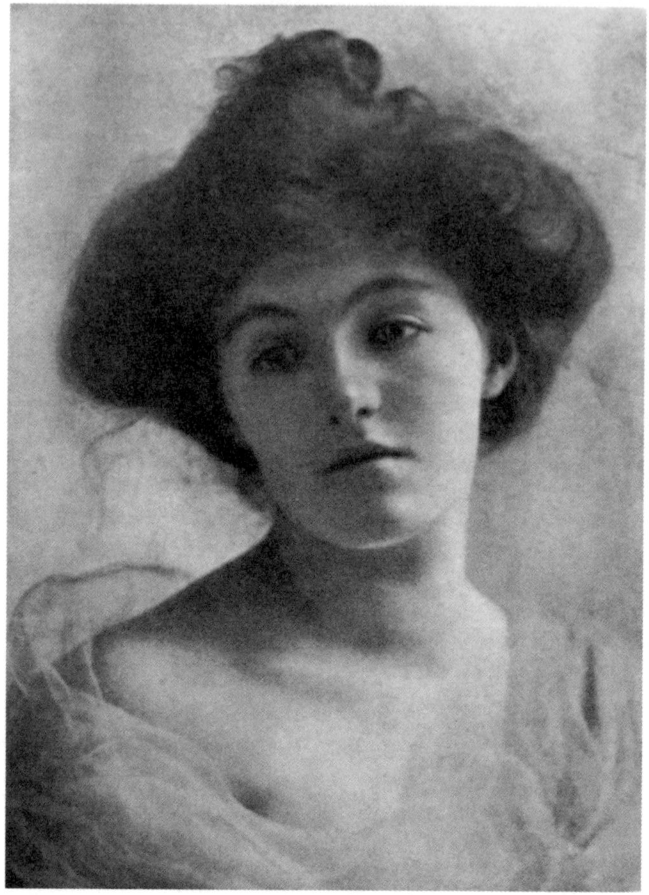

75.   Cicely

More than that, it was her ideal – that her children should be the embodiment of Pre-Raphaelite beauty, as she had been in her youth. And none looked so promising as Cicely (fig. 75). Soon the artists were circling. 'She looks quite as old as you were when I first knew you', Burne-Jones had purred as if that gave him possessory rights. Frances had been almost sixteen when first he had painted her. Cicely was only thirteen; but he had already, as a gift for Frances, made a large chalk drawing of her when she was barely eight. 'Oh Cicely won't love her beauty', he had written then. ' I think she will grow up to be a miracle…I wish Millais will paint her – he draws so beauti-fully'. Instead, he had kept her to himself. Hence his rage on hear-ing of Sargent's picture of *his* Cicely ('who is mine – who was made

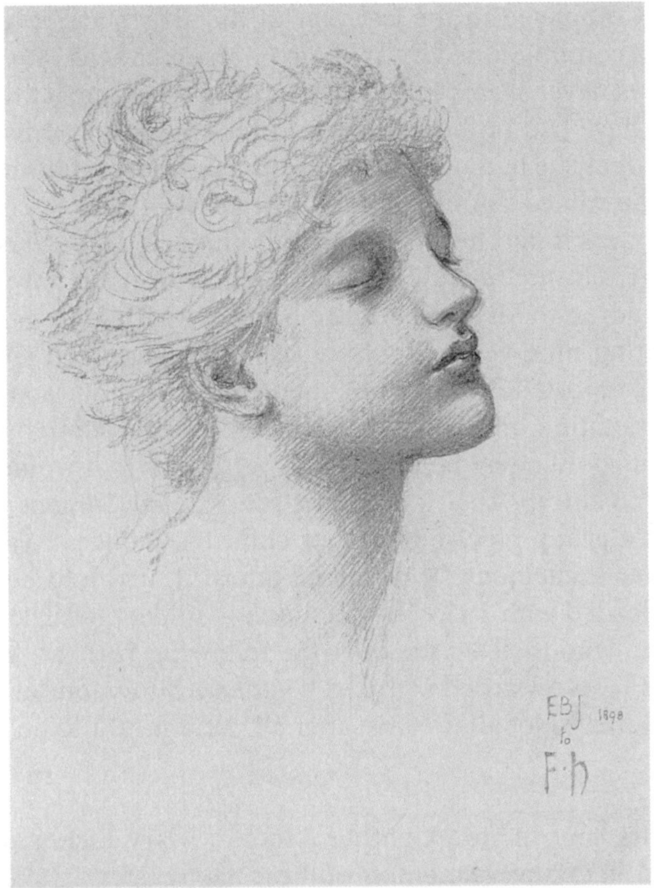

76.   *Study of Edward for*
The Prioress's Tale, by Edward Burne-Jones, 1898

to fulfil a dream of mine and who is my vindication'). Frances was quick to pacify him: 'Of course Darling she is yours – not Sargent's or any others – yours'; revelling once again in his possessiveness – if vicariously through her daughter. Soon his son Philip was in on the act. Declaring 'little Cicely the most beautiful child I have ever seen... It is simply *wicked* that no record should be made of her during these wonderful years.'[23] Not that Frances needed any encouragement. By now attention had also fallen on Edward. 'Edward's face keeps its pure goodness, and beauty, free and fresh, untouched by ... great sin' judged Canon Scott Holland, virtues – at least visual – that were soon dubbed 'Pre-Raphaelite'. This association was sealed when he modelled for the martyred boy in Burne-Jones's *The Prioress's Tale* (fig. 76). Completed in the last year of the artist's life, it had originally been commissioned by William Graham back in 1865.[24]

Frances never seems to have considered what impact this attention may have had on her children. After all, she was only wishing on them what she had once had. And Burne-Jones embodied much of what she valued. Bumping into Georgie soon after Burne-Jones's death, Frances found her 'very good and kind and we talked of him a bit – she told me how dear she thought it of us to have brought up the children to love and admire him so, which is true'. However at one sitting nine-year-old Cicely seems to have been spooked; a 'sad scene', reported Burne-Jones, involving 'hellish whispers' of The Devil, temptation and sin. More generally, expectations would be raised that could never be fulfilled; expectations that would in time fade only to entrap. That was for the future. Now Sargent was talking about a group picture of all her children. Frances could barely contain her excitement. 'If we could afford it, it would be delightful', she pleaded with Jack. They couldn't – unlike their friend Percy Wyndham, who took up the offer the following year (at the cost of £2000) and was rewarded with *The Wyndham Sisters*, one of Sargent's finest pictures.[25] Not all dreams, after all, were meant to be.

*

Many years later in 1952 Cynthia Asquith, Mary Elcho's daughter, composed an evocative memoir of these happy days.

> As I write the years fall away and I am back at Mells in a room full of books and of reminders of the Pre-Raphaelites, by whom Frances Horner was so greatly admired... Frances, perhaps the most accomplished needlewoman of her day, sits stitching vigorously at a large embroidery frame. From time to time, she lays down her needle to study a catalogue of bulbs. She is also listening, and intermittingly talking to Lord Haldane, a constant guest, who is puffing at a large cigar [and] speaks on the Infinite in his queer guttural whisper. Cicely, the eldest of the family, with looks straight out of a fairy tale, is painting a watercolour of the view of the garden through the window. Mark the youngest of the family, an extremely handsome boy of twelve or so, is poring over the Army and Navy Stores List, which for him, no one quite knows why, holds all the romance of Arabian Nights. A large dog lies at his feet.

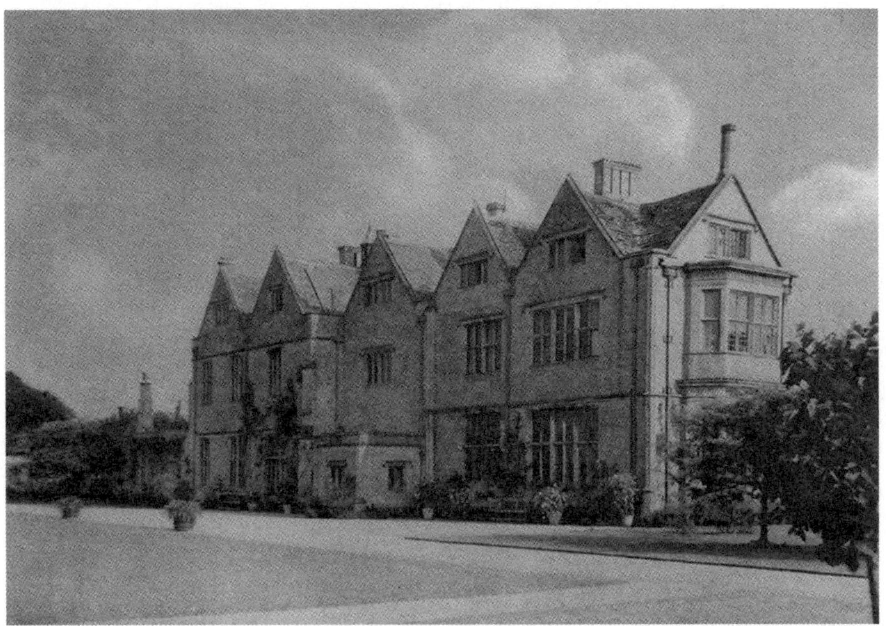

77.   The Manor House, Mells

Katharine drifts into the room, wearing a pale-blue sun-bonnet. In her hands is a volume of Yeats's early poems... Perched grimacing on her shoulder, sits Fluto, a little monkey that Raymond [Asquith] has given her. This creature is very dear to her, but not to all visitors, some of whom he is not too particular to bite. Edward comes in superbly dressed all in white for riding.

The three Miss Horners, who live in the village, suddenly appear to remind their sister-in-law – quite unnecessarily – of some parish function at which she is expected. They are visibly horrified to see that their niece Katharine is smoking a cigarette... They depart.

I am asked to read aloud from William Morris's *The Earthly Paradise*. As so often happens, this has an immediate Pentecostal effect. Everybody bursts into conversation. Some argument springs up. It may be about Yeats. It may be as to whether or not the monkey is to come to luncheon. It may be – very likely is – about why on earth the So and Sos have been asked to stay, for Frances's children do not by any means share her gregarious taste in human beings. Excited by the raised voices, the monkey starts to gibber and chatter. This sets the big dog off barking. Sir John comes in, and asks a little plaintively if there need be quite so much noise, and why not go into luncheon, which has been ready for ages?

We enjoy an unforgettably good meal, for our hostess has made her home as famous for food – both its appearance and its taste – as for stimulating talk. In the afternoon we ride or bathe.

After tea we sit in the lovely walled-garden and talk. I love making a third with Edward and Katharine. Edward, receptive, responsive, is always a fluent eager talker. Katharine can be silent, seemingly far away, rapt in her own thoughts. She never speaks for the sake of saying something. She has no small talk, but at any moment may kindle – and then how one listens! – into lively speech; even flare into brief flame. And whatever her mood, one always wants so much to know her point of view, and enjoy the climate of her mind.

To remember Mells is to be reminded of so much – the discovery of Yeats – budding friendships, quickening interests; in fact of a lovely sense of widening dawn.[26]

~ 29 ~

MARRIAGES AND JEALOUS GODS

I think I am happier than anyone has a right to be and I am only afraid of some jealousy of God.

Katharine Horner[27]

That her unworldly younger daughter would marry before Cicely took Frances completely by surprise.[28] After all, Katharine was not in Frances's eyes particularly attractive, 'only coming into her share of beauty later on'. In public she could be painfully shy and unforthcoming. 'Shake hands Katharine, shake hands', her father would have to remind her. No doubt Katharine did feel in the shadow of her noisy sister and no doubt too resented Frances's barely disguised favouritism for Cicely.[29] Still there was no escape from the driving force of her mother. Nor in truth did Katharine seek one. For all her independent spirit, she would still bring her writings to Frances, seeking and receiving her mother's acclaim. Hence her declared intention to marry a Labour leader smacked more of teenage provocation than a revolt. For all her steely resilience, Katharine was not a natural rebel. The product of a childhood hemmed in by a forceful mother, her instinct was to disconnect behind a shield of self-composure, retreating into a private imaginary world of her own. Outwardly she remained the dutiful daughter steering clear of confrontation. Only to a treasured few did she reveal her frustration. 'I am afraid of drifting' she raged to Edward,

And the only thing I care about has been denied to me. I have a vision of myself 'come out' and living in London ever as the rest and I loathe it at the bottom, and myself too, and I think everyone ought to make their own lives and I can't make mine.

This is all hidden away and at the top I am happy and pleased with everything but I can't forget the other side and nor do I want to… I feel it is years since I have spoken to anyone who understood me or whom I understood. I wish I could write. I wish I could understand things. I wish – and this is a condition of real life – that I could be myself.[30]

Ironically, just as she craved to be left alone, she developed into 'a lovely, tall creature, large-eyed, long-lashed, with a magnolia complexion' that would win her many admirers (fig. 78). As with her mother, it was her eyes that mesmerised. 'I have never seen any eyes like hers', reminisced one friend. 'Too expressive to be blue, too lovely to be grey, flecked with lilac, they had a rapt, considering, intent, yet far-off glaze.' Just as unnerving, Katharine's beauty could ambush, 'sometimes going into abeyance only to break out afresh'.[31] 'She has the power', wrote another, of looking very sad and very beautiful at the same time which is fearfully moving'.[32] Blinded by the outward allure of diffident manner and quick wit, none saw a shy, restless soul seeking perfection and fearful of seeing only failure in herself. Later to cover this she could be recklessly gay or just a little too sharp before retreating without warning into silence.[33] So, while much loved, she remained nevertheless elusive. 'All girls, like all men, long to know you well because you are so beautiful but are puzzled how to do it because you are so uncommon and remote', protested one of her friends. To Katharine's unease, this only added to her attractiveness.[34]

When in 1900 Raymond Asquith first visited Mells Park, Haldane's *tour de force* in the swimming pool had not been the only memory. As ever there was the intrigue at seeing a hostess who had modelled for Burne-Jones, and her elder daughter who was 'about as perfect a specimen of female beauty as I have ever seen'. In the face of this he barely noticed Katharine, then only fourteen, with her dark hair and her mother's eyes and their intense far-off gaze – eyes, he would later recall, that 'would draw a limpet off a rock.' A year later at Clovelly (home of Con Manners's sister, Christine Hamlyn) Katharine was almost sixteen and more interesting: 'a low broad brow, a delightful nervous voice, and that lively and significant eye which one usually misses in a woman. She is really very clever, both by instinct and knowledge. She is also something of a poet herself.' Also impressive

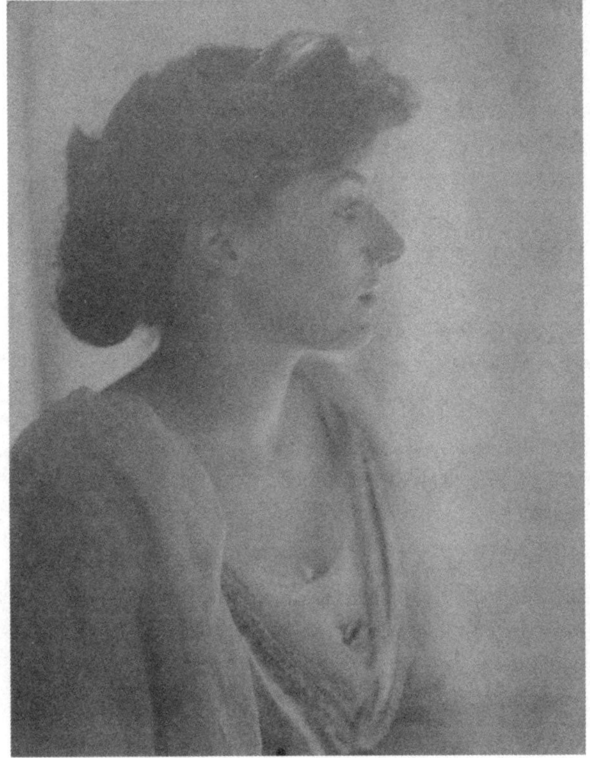

78.   *Katharine*

was her finding 'two serious Homeric errors' in an essay on the classical element in Tennyson; 'I really became rather friendly … finding in her many of the qualities I admire in boys – especially a combination of purity and vivacity'.[35] Their meetings were occasional and fleeting. Frances seems to have taken a shine to Raymond ('who we all think a most delightful person'). He was formidably good looking: tall and erect, with deep grey eyes and aquiline nose, looking every inch the coming man in the Roman senate. Dazzling too was his extraordinary academic achievement: a scholarship to Balliol (to the delight of his father), was followed by the prestigious Hertford and Ireland Prizes, and capped by a First in Greats. Even the dreaded law studies saw another First and election to an All Souls Fellowship (1901). All done so effortlessly it seemed and laced with an insouciant air and a wickedness of wit that amused Frances, occasionally against her better judgement.[36] There was perhaps a hint of flirtation

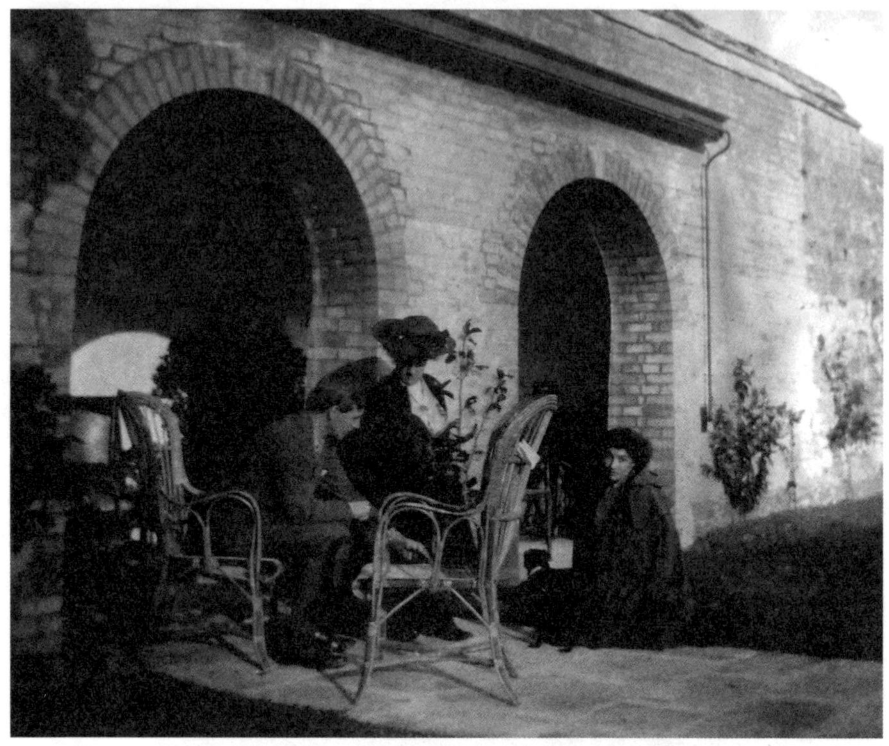

79. *Raymond Asquith, Frances and Katharine by the loggia at Mells*

in his denial 'that I look on you as a mocking friend but a laughing friend is what I like … and I don't care how often you laugh at me'. Such was their rapport that she came easily to rely on the advice and support of Katharine's talented suitor (fig. 79). That he brought fresh connections with Henry Asquith was an added boon. Conversely, for Raymond, Frances and Mells offered a haven to one who had cast himself adrift emotionally after his father's second marriage: 'I turn to Mells when I say my prayers and also when I don't'.[37] As Frances began to take matters in hand, Raymond found himself invited on Horner holidays to Austria, Venice and Ireland. By 1903 he and Katharine had fallen 'fathom deep in love': 'You know how I would like to give you the whole world if it were mine, and the sun and the moon and all the stars'.[38]

Yet it was not all plain sailing. The Society that Frances paid homage to, Raymond held to be vacuous and tedious, and perhaps a little daunting too. Likewise to Katharine, for all the thrill of being courted by a Fellow of All Souls, Raymond was intimidating company intellectually. Especially for one who so doubted herself. The austerity of the pure Classical mind could be quite challenging to her self-schooled preference for 'your dear Celts' – especially W. B. Yeats. Too easily she would retreat into herself. 'O Katharine, Katharine how can you be so hard and wicked and unkind to me?', Raymond would write partly in jest. 'Oh why, why don't you write to me…Just one paragraph of scolding, with leave perhaps at the end to write to you again?' A rare meeting in London meeting saw her 'more beautiful than ever, but more than ever inexorably yourself – remote, elusive and unattainable'.[39] In truth, both were very inexperienced. Raymond admitted that until her, he had 'little inclination to have a solitary talk with a woman' and so didn't know the 'tricks'. In the long periods of silence when they were apart fears would arise that her heart had gone elsewhere. After a 'midnight ramble with Ego [Charteris] – who was indeed himself in love with her – Raymond would protest that her story was 'shockingly thin'. In fact she never looked at anyone else. In time he would resign himself to the fact that 'there will always be a strange uncaptured element within her which rebels a little against any authorised alliance – I am not sorry for …it will prevent me ever growing lazy … in my love'. Finally in 1906 Katharine had agreed to marry him, wooed by letters like this:

What a lovely night now – the moon on the snow – what a night for wolves and chestnuts – O Katharine, if we were only in our mountain shanty! I can see you very clearly kicking the snow off your foolish little shoes on the threshold and crouching on a cushion by a log fire, wet and glowing, the pure bright blood in your cheeks and your great eyes shining like silk. And I would get you a brown blanket for your skirt, and pull off your drenched blue stockings and bathe your beautiful feet in a basin of hot water and verveine, and all the air would thrill and quiver with the radiance of your loveliness and the stars would cluster round the lattice to look in upon the divinity of you, just as they stood over the inn at Bethlehem and Orion would draw his sword to keep guard over your door…[40]

At which point Frances suddenly changed tack. While she relished the romance of young love, marriage was quite a different matter. Money was an obvious concern; as a barrister starting out, Raymond earned barely enough to support himself and he was much too proud to ask his father to subsidise him. Relations especially with his step-mother were anyway distinctly chilly. And then there was the cynical air of 'anti-cant' which Frances had presumed at first was a joke but now was not so sure. Whether weighed down by the expectation that followed academic success or the loss of his mother ('the only person for whom I have ever felt… love'), Raymond took refuge in a rejection of all he had achieved and an outward disdain for ambition.[41] Not for him running the Empire or entering the Cabinet. But such responsibilities – 'greatness' – were just what Frances expected from her Asquith son-in-law, who she held to be the leader of his generation and one with the opportunity to create a dynasty. More prosaically, she feared his cynicism might affect her daughter. 'I put a very high value on her opinions', he protested; 'though it is true I hardly ever speak to her except to mock them'. To which she insisted that Katharine 'deserves the finest note of passion'.[42]

On the other hand, Raymond's melancholic streak ('I have done nothing worth doing, and know nothing worth knowing, feel nothing worth feeling, and am nothing worth being') was one she recognised in herself even if she covered it differently. Nevertheless, under the guise that at twenty-one Katharine was too young to marry, she urged a separation so that Katharine might see others before committing herself – what Raymond in 1906 dubbed 'the compact of divorce which Frances wanted in the summer'. Nor was she the only obstacle. His closest male friends were appalled at the prospect of 'losing' him to marriage. Harold 'Bluetooth' Baker, an old friend from Winchester, was probably a little jealous. Another devoted contemporary, Conrad Russell, on the other hand 'wouldn't dream' of congratulating him. 'It is dreadful to think I can't dine with him again without that dull white-faced girl with a face like a rabbit sitting opposite. I can't believe I should ever like her; and I know she won't like me'. Interestingly it was her latest religious enthusiasm that he most deplored. Taking the drastic measure of going abroad to avoid the wedding, he warned his friend: 'Don't become a Roman Catholic'.[43]

Any opposition to the marriage quickly faded and in 1907 Raymond and Katharine became formally engaged (fig. 80). Crucially Margot had come up with the money – £400 a year (£48,400 in 2019); not a fortune but enough and importantly it was

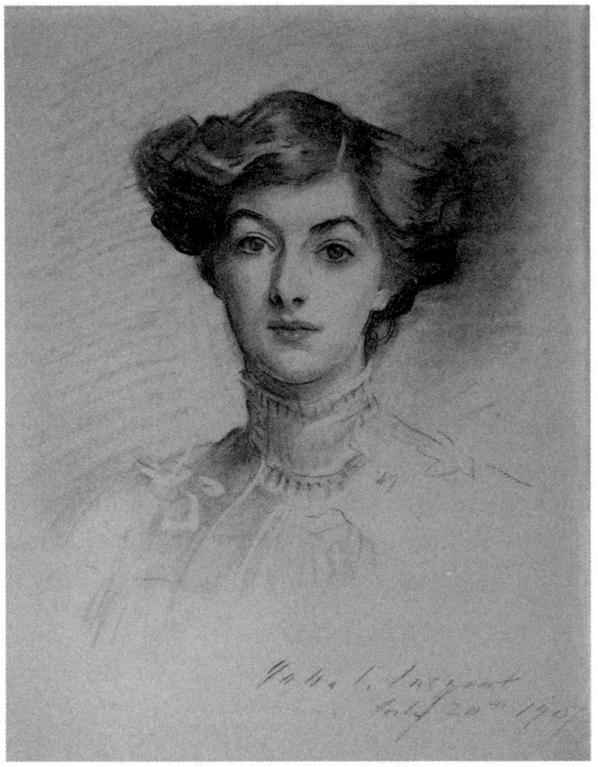

80.	*Katharine, by John Singer Sargent, July 20th, 1907,*
three days before her marriage

deemed a gift rather than a request. Raymond correctly judged that by now Katharine would 'enjoy the freedom and independence more than she minds the discomfort'. Not least because Frances once again turned full circle. Eager now to revel in the news, she was frustrated by Raymond's determination to keep it secret, ostensibly to spare Katharine 'the coarse felicitations of maiden aunts when they speak of the great happiness that is in store for her'. He pursued this to such an extent that at parties, to maintain the pretence, they barely spoke to each other.[44] Still nothing was going to deny Frances the Society wedding she craved. Not least because, on Jack's retirement with a KCVO, Francie from Glasgow was now Lady Horner.

On 23 July 1907 at St Margaret's Westminster, Katharine, wearing an ivory gown with pearls and sequins, was led down the aisle by her father, accompanied by eleven bridesmaids and two pages. At the sight of the bride there would be no stiff upper lips among the Horners. 'Cicely her sister, was shaking with sobs like an elephant (they are all very tall)', reported a gleeful Katharine Shaw Stewart to a friend. 'Mrs Horner was weeping copiously and steadily and "Old Jack" was striding up and down gulping down his sobs'. The reception was held in the garden of 11 Downing Street, the official home of the Chancellor of the Exchequer and father of the groom. A former Prime Minster, Arthur Balfour, proposed the toast as befitting a marriage of Souls.[45] Afterwards everyone repaired to Cavendish Square for dancing – Asquith leading the way until Lady Desborough drew him away (as he was by now quite drunk) to Margot's bedroom where they found her 'arrayed in a kimono and having a little invalid's supper (just like the powders you give dogs, Lady Desborough said)'. 'How delightful the wedding was' Raymond wrote to Frances from Italy. 'I confess that I thoroughly enjoyed it', somewhat to his surprise. 'Both of us owe a great deal to you for putting the idea into our heads'.[46]

*

For all the glamour of being feted by Society, Frances knew from her own experience that her girls' future would depend on marrying well. She was romantic enough to want them to marry for love but not so much so if it meant living in 'a garret', as she had once feared for Katharine. By contrast, she had always held out much higher hopes for Cicely. Yet what did 'well' mean? 1892 saw her with Cicely staying at Dunrobin Castle on the Duke of Sutherland's Highland estate. This was living on a grand scale. With its striking combination of Scottish Baronial and French Renaissance style, it was a chateau of 189 rooms, situated on a spectacular site with terraced gardens descending onto the shores of Dornoch Firth. 'It is the sort of beauty I love', she would confess. 'Wild melancholy, while inside the *ne plus ultra* of luxury'. But the latter led her to ponder whether those who have 'every joy piled onto their knees' are really happier than 'all the ordinary people we know with perhaps one or two nice things to colour life'. Before concluding 'perhaps it is the kingdom of the mind that matters most'.[47]

The kingdom of the mind was never going to woo Cicely. For all the opportunities her famed beauty could provide, she was too self-possessed, opinionated, high spirited, with a shrewd sense of

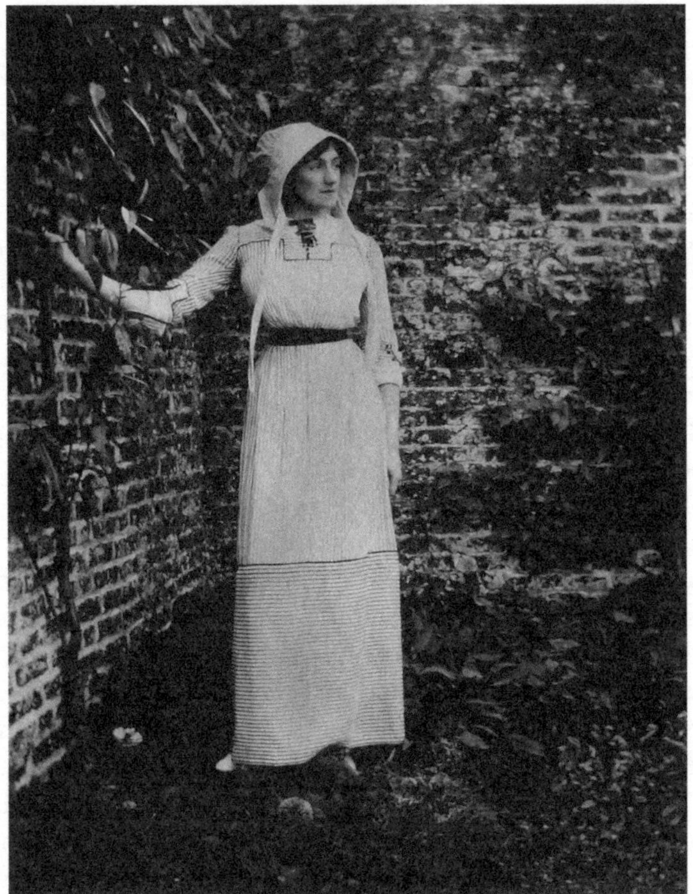

81.   Cicely

humour and above all very sporty – swimming, golf, tennis and horses – to give sophisticated society much of a glance (fig. 81). Not that she was short of proposals (including one 'out of the blue – we don't even know him!') but she preferred the company of her female friends.[48] When she finally did settle on a suitor, he came from the very un-Soul territory of the race course.[49] George Lambton was the fifth son of the 2nd Earl of Durham and so came with little inheritance. Nor was horse-training regarded as a suitable profession for an aristocrat. Ominously George could only finance himself initially through gambling. But by the 1890s racing had become hugely popular, earning a new respectability among the upper classes, without really losing its raffish appeal. George, training for the Earls of Derby, proved to be hugely successful, winning all the major races including the Derby. Handsome, elegant in dress, and charming, he became an idol of the racing world. Despite his being nearly eighteen years older, in Cicely's eyes he was a catch and one with whom she shared a passion for all animals but especially horses.

'No wonder you were a great deal shocked at first', sympathised Raymond. Indeed so shocked was Frances that he had to warn her against an 'egotistical' attempt to 'force her taste'. As if she could. Yet this engagement was a 'terrible disappointment', dashing all her hopes of a grand match. It also made plain how detached she had become from her once favourite daughter. As Raymond was quick to point out 'Cicely has always been as frankly bored by politics as you are by racing'. What Frances viewed as vulgar and brash, Raymond preferred to call 'another case of Cicely's "call of the Wild"' – all part of 'the constitutional twist in the direction of the debonair and horsey, which no amount of poulticing with politics and Pre-Raphaelitism could ever iron out of her [Cicely]'. As for reassuring Frances over the so-called 'Beckett Affair', the best he could manage was that at forty-eight a man was bound to have had affairs and better with 'a pretty and attractive woman of breeding [than] some silly actress or nameless slut'.[50] Money would remain a concern throughout their marriage, as Frances feared. But with Cicely unstoppable, Frances gave way to celebrity, proudly declaring Lambton 'a man who is more universally beloved than anyone of our time' and 'perfect' as a son-in-law.[51] And so in 1908 they were married.

*

As it was, by then Frances was in no state to hold out against her headstrong daughter. For in March she had been overwhelmed by great tragedy. Everybody loved Mark. He was the country lad at heart who knew all the farm-hands by name, knew too of their girlfriends and even how they liked their tea during the hay harvest. When he was sent away to school, he would take a Somerset paper. Back home he loved nothing better than to ride and hunt, charging around the countryside chanting his favourite refrain: 'Over the hills and far away rode Mark the hunter'. 'Mark is running loose in the garden all summer', Frances recounted to Jack. 'It is so different from London: he has not been a tormentor for an instant since he came down'. What made Mark special, however, was a generosity of spirit: 'an inexhaustible sympathy for everyone and everything', whatever their class or politics.[52] As a child he was often in a world of his own imagination, looking 'full of plots and plans and impudence' Burne-Jones had once remarked.

Always happiest with practical mechanical things such as engines and trams, Mark was less well suited to the competitive world beyond Mells. Academically, his school years were always going to be a struggle. It didn't help that his head master at prep school took a 'great liking to him and used to put his arm around Mark and kiss him'; which the boy loathed and for which he was 'often chaffed'.[53] Nor would Mark prove an easy fit at Eton – he was too eccentric, too in his world to make lasting friends. Without thinking, he would find himself regularly in collision with the authorities. Many a riot in Mr Impey's house would have Mark at its heart. And no boy was beaten more – a point of honour in Mark's eyes. Frances could see where this was heading and when in 1907 Mark developed an inexplicable 'lameness' so that he spent the summer on crutches, she seized the opportunity to withdraw him.

For all his rumbustiousness, Mark's health wasn't always the strongest. Frances was often worried for him, be it a period of deafness or a throat operation: 'most upsetting, expensive, gory and of remote benefit'.[54] On 22 February 1908 Mark woke up with a sore throat and headache.[55] Two days later he was diagnosed with scarlet fever, sufficiently serious for him to be transferred to the London Fever Hospital for specialist nursing. A week later his father went down with the same illness and was transferred to the same hospital. That night Mark's disease appeared to have spread. Typically he sought to reassure his mother: 'Well you see, Mother, of course we can't expect improvement everywhere at once'. The next day hopes were raised as his temperature dropped. Later that night Frances wasn't so sure. As she left promising to see him in the morning, he asked plaintively

'Will you be able to stay a long time?'

'Oh yes', she replied, 'as long as you like'.

'That's a good job for then you can read to me.'

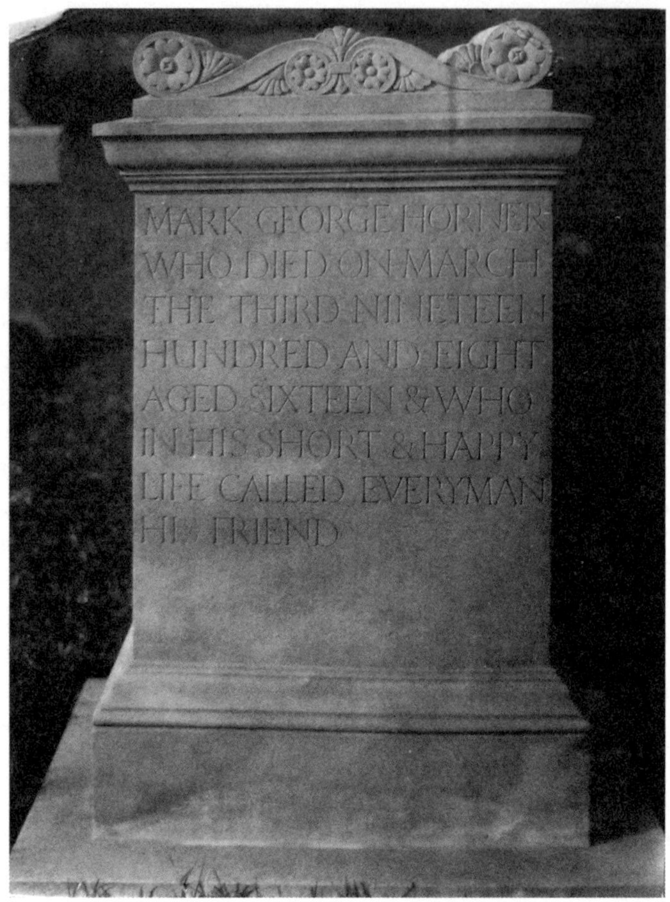

82.   Mark's tombstone in the churchyard at Mells

That night he became delirious, calling out 'Mother, Mother,' only by
3am to quieten again, leading the doctors to feel it safe to leave him.
But soon after 'a change came' and by 5 am Mark had died. Rushing
to the hospital, Frances arrived too late and found him 'lying looking
like a lovely Greek statue, with his shining close curls tight round
his head, and his loving, eager, busy little heart stilled for ever.'
Grief overwhelmed her – brutal, unforgiving and isolating. There
would not be a day when she didn't think of Mark. Guilt too that she
hadn't nursed him herself, that she hadn't been there when he died.
Memories flooded back of her sixteen-year-old brother dying in her
arms; she had been unable to save him – just as now she couldn't
save her sixteen-year-old son.

With Jack still in isolation (but recovering), Frances had to face the funeral on her own. 'Frances has shown the most glorious courage', Raymond reported to Jack. 'She is heroic; and, though she is quite heartbroken, she continues still to be quite charming to everyone'.[56] However, as Frances confessed to Jack, she felt 'so bewildered' as she arrived at the church to take her place by Mark's coffin. 'It looked so long – just like a man's and I always see him as a child. I felt quite stupid of course and kept being sure it had nothing to do with Mark'. The Church 'packed with weeping poor people all in black and all feeling not for us but simply bereaved and astounded… Oh my darling we have lost a most perfect possession'.[57]

The next day she endured a memorial service. Once again the church was 'crammed with peasants from the outlying villages prepared to sob at the simplest eloquence', recounted Raymond Asquith. Only for the local parson, Mr Lear, to choose this occasion to hector the packed congregation on their failure to attend church in such numbers more often; that life was short and that they should lose no time in mending their ways. ('You have had a warning. Profit by it'.) Frances 'got so choked up that it prevented me from breathing'. The villagers 'stupefied and bewildered just like we were'… Lear's sermon 'so dreadful – you know egotistical – scolding – horrible'. Her family were furious. 'Poor Edward cried with disgust and indignation' and Raymond would have 'dearly liked to have kicked Lear around the parish'. Usually so detached and unemotional – Raymond found himself in tears for the first time 'since my own mother died'.[58]

As for Frances, she resented the prolonged loneliness as the doctors continued to refuse her access to Jack lest she infected her remaining children; a frustration he no doubt shared. But one he couldn't express. Once he was out, they escaped to Deal and there in wild weather, 'Daddy and I walked and walked and I cried and cried because he did not know what to say'. Instead she took 'comfort' in her remaining children who had been 'as passionate in your sorrow as I have'.[59]

Mark's death, along with his sisters' marriages, represented a breaking up of her family. It also put much into perspective. 'Last Easter we were with you, weren't we?' she asked Ettie. 'Raymond and Katharine were pretending they didn't know what engaged meant and Mark hadn't begun to be lame and I sometimes used to *fancy* I was unhappy'. Now she would draw hard on Ettie's 'divine compassion'. That the very grand Lady Desborough should be the one Soul to rally was unexpected. 'I don't know how it is [that] your sympathy is so tender, Ettie', Frances wrote, 'because you have never known sorrow yourself'. 'It is fear, I think, [that] makes me understand', she replied. A brave answer from one who lost both her parents when young.[60] In commemoration of Mark, Frances decided to offer clean water to Mells village from the Manor's own supply and predictably Lutyens was summoned to design two well heads, alongside a three-cornered stone shelter at the heart of the village. Eric Gill would carve the inscription. Such schemes soothed to some degree the loss she felt. So too her husband now: 'Jack Horner is deafer than ever', noted Lutyens, 'but a dear and so cheerful and nice to Lady Horner, it is rather touching'.[61] That said, she chose to place her trust for the future on her remaining son. Edward, she declared, would be her 'rock'. This would prove a courageous choice.

~ 30 ~

SIPPING HONEY

Such a safeguard in life [sons], … I should like mine to have brains – but they won't and will grow up bully boys and never be heard of in this world and the next.

Frances Horner to Henry Asquith[62]

Frances could not help it, but the greatest pressure she imposed was on the child she loved most, her elder son, Edward. It was not simply that he was the heir to an ancient line stretching back over four hundred years. Frances sought in Edward the embodiment of the Pre-Raphaelite knight she had so adored in Burne-Jones's paintings: honourable, courageous and valiant, selfless in the cause of others, both independent and a leader of men. It was wildly Arthurian and an impossibly tall order. Yet he had the looks and the manner and with his mother beside him gave early substance to the fantasy with his inclusion in Burne-Jones's *The Prioress's Tale*. In the chivalric tradition, cultural learning was as valued as martial prowess. And in Raymond Asquith, Frances held that Edward had his role model. In Raymond's glittering record she saw the preparation for future political triumphs as a new Liberal generation inherited the mantle from Asquith, Grey and Haldane. It was a future she wanted for her son and for now she did not doubt her ability to achieve it.

As it turned out, Edward was never a bully and did have brains, even winning a scholarship to his prep school, Summer Fields in 1898. Rather than prove a 'safeguard', his early success would nearly break him. Despite at the age of ten being rather late to go to boarding school, he was nonetheless 'so unhappy and long for you and home.' He was teased too: 'my name is already a curse to me' (presumably over Little Jack Horner).[63] In time he was able to stand his

277

ground. During the Khaki election of October 1900, Edward found himself one of only four Liberals; when 'the cock of the school' insulted the Liberals once too often, Edward challenged him and 'I licked him wonderfully'. However, the academic pressures he found much harder to shake off. Summer Fields was a leading feeder for the main public schools and the head master took excessive pride in his honour board of Eton scholarships. In the nursery at Mells Edward had been free from such competition, being largely ignored by his older sisters. Frances too had indulged him, even if there would be no doubting where her ambitions lay. Always so anxious to please his mother, Edward began well: top in Greek and French, second in Latin and winning an 'orange' for top scoring in history. But he froze in exams and soon his confidence fell away. By 1900 Frances was hiring tutors for the holidays and Edward began to suffer from asthma attacks. All to no avail. There would be no scholarship when Edward entered Eton a year later.[64]

The Eton that awaited him was epitomised by the Head Master, Edmund Warre, an advocate of muscular Christianity – a moral code of courage and honour, learnt through sport and ultimately demonstrated in patriotic duty on the battlefield. Intellectually the school blended the classical with the gothic revival and a Pre-Raphaelite fascination with the chivalric code. All this was embodied in the chapel with its windows and plaques to the Etonian dead of the Crimean and Boer Wars. On one wall hung G.F. Watts's heroic painting of Sir Galahad inspiring boys in turn to 'a pure form of knighthood'; while above the altar hung a tapestry by Burne-Jones, of 'The Star of Bethlehem' guiding them to Christ and their holy mission.[65]

At least Edward continued to look the part: 'Edward grown so tall and handsome'.[66] But in Impey's Edward found himself in 'a most terrible house', its housemaster emotionally cold and self-centred, engendering an atmosphere of cynicism and bitchiness – and perhaps worse. 'I am sorry to say the chaps here, at least most of them, *are* beasts', Edward alerted his mother, 'although no one has molested me at all yet'. Edward was able enough but, away from Mells, once again he crumpled in the face of competition – both academic and sporting. Very soon between mother and son there began a conversation of the deaf, with Frances quick to remind him why he was there.

I want you to turn your mind to the serious part of your life at Eton. Now you are really equipping yourself for life both mentally and morally. You know it is not easy to send you to Eton. I mean it is a big expense, but neither your father nor I shall ever weigh that as long as you are doing your best to take advantage of it in every way and get all the good and happiness you can out of it…Ever your mother who loves you and thinks of you a good deal.[67]

This call to arms almost reduced him to tears at breakfast on receiving it. It didn't help that Ettie's son, Julian Grenfell, was thriving, leaving his mother exultant: 'Is it wonderful? He is above *Horner* and the other scholarship boys'. Edward would promise his mother 'Oh, I will try so hard and you shall be pleased with me again'. But to no effect and Frances would soon be on his back again.

Making your way up the school and getting all the good you can from your education: it is the only thing your father and I ask you to do in return for our trying at any cost to give you the best chance… Those donkeys who despise work will simply remain in the ruck all their lives. Look at Mr Asquith, Lord Milner and Mr Haldane and all the friends we are so proud of: if they had been 'saps' where would they be now, I should like to know.[68]

Under fire from a mother, who had previously sheltered him all his life, left Edward quite depressed. 'School is a beastly invention', he raged to Katharine:

I want sympathy awfully, as I'm not happy. I can't help it, but it is true and tonight I am feeling rather wretched. I don't know why. It isn't exactly homesickness that I have but an indescribable feeling of almost forlornness sometimes…partly because there is no one here [at Impey's] whom I love and can tell things to…What a bad idea school is! I do wish I were one of those people who are always contented and happy.[69]

Even when Frances did appreciate just how 'unsettled and unhappy' he was, her ambition was still remorseless:

I can't quite understand it – as, if you are unhappy in a good

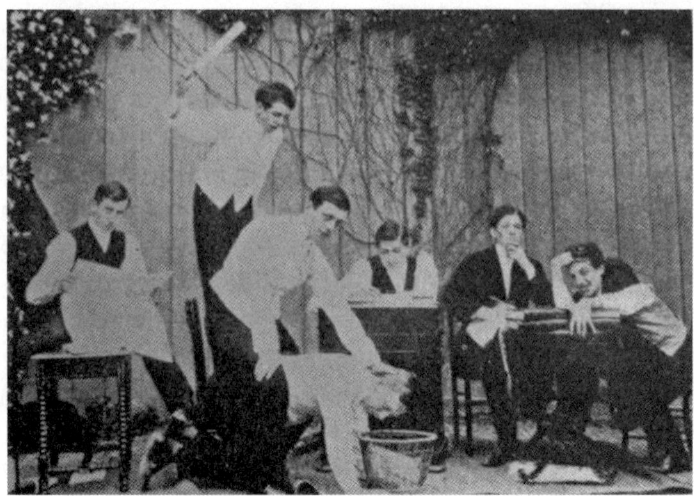

83.   The editorial board of The Outsider
Edward is seated at the desk

Oppidan House at Eton at your age with lots of friends, I can't think where and how you would be happy…You see, you are at Eton not just only to enjoy yourself, you are there to get equipped for life intellectually, morally, physically, and if you can get that once into your head, it will make you vastly independent of all the little ups and downs of life…This is not a vexed letter, it is really full of sympathy, only I just want you to pull yourself together and not give way to being unhappy…I wish you would get some joy and happiness out of your Eton life – if your youth there slipped by without it, it would be such a pity.[70]

By now such diatribes left him, he confessed to Katharine, 'inclined to commit suicide'. There is no evidence to suggest he was serious or whether, on learning of this, Frances reined back her strictures. Without ever letting him off the leash, Frances remained in her eyes supportive, being more bewildered than angry in the face of Edward's inertia. True, as one prone to depression herself, she might have been more attuned to the warning signs; even if in herself she had viewed such symptoms as weakness. And yes, they could ill-afford the fees. But the fact was she had built him up impossibly high, indulged him – loved him perhaps – too much, and had come to live too much of her own life in him for his own good.

Eton had one last humiliation. Put up for Pop – the self-electing prefect body – by his friends, his bid accrued the ignominy of twelve black balls. Still, his last year was not all gloom. He was invited to become a member of the prestigious Shakespeare and Essay Societies. He also joined the editorial board of *The Outsider* (fig. 83), a rival magazine to the official *Chronicle*. It proved hugely popular, with Edward producing a serial story, articles and some poetry. More importantly, it was through *The Outsider* that he would make the friends who would last the rest of his life. Together they would form a close band – Julian Grenfell, Ettie's son; the extremely bright Ronnie Knox; the even brighter Patrick Shaw Stewart; and Charles Lister, Charty's son. Yet for all that, while his friends feared that life would prove too dull after Eton, Edward was 'longing to get away from this place'.[71]

*

Frances could be forgiven for hoping that Oxford offered a chance for a fresh start. To one denied a university education on account of her gender, Oxford was an opportunity for the mind not to be missed. As for the future, she had that already mapped out. Like her friends Haldane and Asquith, Edward would be called to the Bar before entering parliament and a glittering career in government. That he lacked independence and initiative mattered not. With honest endeavour on his part, she would make it happen. As she explained:

> I shall feel very thankful if you set your teeth and work [hard] at Oxford and really make a fine career there but I know how insidious the *ease* of the life is – how strait is the gate and few that seek it. I am very ambitious for you … I think if once I got you started there [at the Bar] I could push you into success. But don't let anyone divert you from the idea of hard work.[72]

Hence her disappointment on discovering that Balliol alone had taken seventeen Etonians and Edward was in with all his old friends. More than she should, Frances loved the Etonian cachet and took pride in her son being part of the fashionable 'Eton Push' at Oxford; for many of whom she would turn Mells into a second home. Yet she knew these were not the role models her son needed – being very able but not 'grinds' willing to work hard towards academic success. Oddly the one she deemed the worst influence was still at Eton – Charty's son, Charles Lister. Lister was certainly unconventional (not least in being an active socialist). But what concerned Frances was his capacity for wild frivolity and high jinks, and the way he drew others into his escapades. 'The theory that he led us all at Eton is quite groundless and invented for dear Charty's satisfaction', Edward explained. 'I love him dearly and think him a better companion than almost any of my friends but at the same time am constantly roaring with laughter at him – so you may make yourself quite easy on that score'.[73]

Much more influential was her future son-in-law. Raymond's return to Oxford as a Fellow of All Souls would see him acquire the same authority over Edward's circle of friends as Arthur Balfour had exercised over Frances and the Souls. Like Balfour, he was considerably older than his acolytes; like him too he was idolised. His ridicule of hard work, ambition and convention, often delivered with a polished sarcasm, intimidated and thrilled in equal measure. 'There is an insidiously corrupt poison in their minds – brilliantly distilled by their inspiration, Raymond', noted Cynthia Asquith. 'I don't care a damn about their morals and manners, but I do think what – for want of a better word – I call their anti-cant is really suicidal to happiness'.[74] Of none would this be more true than of Edward. Frances did spot the danger but in truth she idolised Raymond as much as anybody. And the early signs were not unpromising. Eddie Marsh – lawyer, networker and recently appointed secretary to the up and coming Liberal minister, Winston Churchill – found Edward at Mells 'leading a simple and well-ordered life. I saw him at Stanway, the Sunday before last, where there was a large juvenile party and Mr Balfour. We had a romantic midnight walk with bare feet in the dew and the nettles under the moon. Except for the nettles, which kept us tossing endlessly for hours afterwards, it was most enjoyable.' At Oxford in his first year, if Edward had made his mark at all it was for his dress. As Marsh spotted, Edward had always known that he was good looking – tall, 'a perfect Greek forehead', fair curls and bright staring eyes – and he liked to dress. Liberated in Oxford, he indulged himself with 'stocks and large-brimmed hats, sticks with ivory knobs, folded ties and pins', and looking more like a Regency buck than an Edwardian gentleman.[75] As such, he seemed guilty of little more than youthful affectation.

However, by his second year Edward was in free fall. 'Very decadent … fat and bitter and very splendid', reported Julian Grenfell. For the most part this rarely got beyond the level of misbehaving at dining clubs, where the drunkenness was only exceeded by the arrogance. If the degeneration of her adored son was heart-breaking to Frances, his gambling debts and wild extravagance – double those of his contemporaries and on such a scale that the College alerted his parents – astounded her, since he knew well that they would struggle to pay.[76] Frances duly descended on Oxford. Julian provided some cover during lunch, but afterwards Edward 'was catching it thick now I have gone', Julian told his mother.[77] 'I am ostentatious and need applause', Edward confessed to a friend. And there were plenty willing to applaud. 'For all

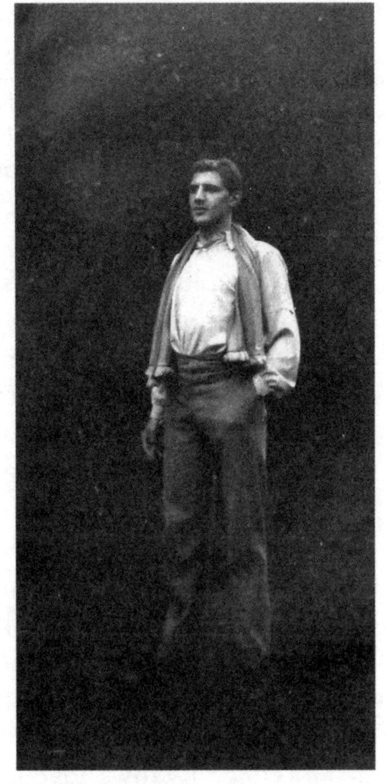

84.   Edward

his Pre-Raphaelite good looks, and much charm', remembered one contemporary, 'it was impossible not to be angry with him as to be angry with him for long. He came back after each scolding with the affectionate eyes and caressing ways of a faithful dog who has been beaten… He had no ambition but to sip honey'.[78]

By now Edward was wildly flamboyant in language as well as dress, often hilariously so – avoiding seriousness because he feared ridicule and inadequacy (fig. 84). 'Nothing was ever quite worthwhile' he would protest. For him 'the joy of living descended into a craving for excitement'. Ultimately, this riotous life saw him arrested for drunk and disorderly behaviour. On being named in the press, he rang Raymond in a panic who advised him to do nothing. As he told his sister, he was to trust that Frances hadn't seen the report. Of course she had and even managed to get the report 'corrected' in the Westminster Gazette and Daily Telegraph, but too late to prevent publication. Frances was in no mood to excuse youthful indiscretion because Edward's 'behaving as a common cad disgraces everyone'. Whereas '15 years ago… no one minded', she acknowledged, 'now-a-days public feeling has so changed… it is never forgotten'.[79] Such parental concern for reputation rarely resonates with the young. Nevertheless, it was 'an additional little disappointment' on the ever-growing charge sheet.

That the list of his vices made little reference to girls reflected a lack of opportunity. With few female colleges at Oxford, Edward and his friends kept predominately male company. Those girls they met would be sisters of friends, rigorously chaperoned by their mothers. That didn't stop Edward, along with all his contemporaries, falling in love with Diana Manners, the Rutlands' daughter (fig. 85).[80] Despite being only fifteen when she first fell among his crowd, she mesmerised them all, not just for her beauty but for her vivacity and a wild streak that made her seem fearless. Well-read if not well-educated, she was fresh, different and energising, brightening up any party. Edward would love her for the rest of his life but to her he would never be more than a very dear friend. Easter 1908 would find Edward with Patrick Shaw Stewart and Charles Lister in Florence. 'Really I love girls', insisted Patrick to Katharine 'but I haven't the courage of Edward, who "jollies" one after another with the dispatch and impartiality of a barber'.[81] A combination of 'Greek good looks' and effortless charm would always play well. In his own way, Edward was excellent company, radiating a youthful exuberance and freedom from responsibility. Or as one put it, 'his characteristic and contagious conviction that life should be lived, not only lavishly but resplendently'. Knowing Edward wrote one friend 'was as great a luxury as one could possibly enjoy'.[82] However, this would never provide the emotional support he needed.

Edward's last year at Oxford was always going to be a testing affair. Aside from the looming exams, he was missing some of his best friends – literally in the case of Charles Lister who, predictably, had been sent down. Also away was Julian Grenfell. As it turned out, the pressure for academic success applied by Frances was as nothing compared to that endured by Julian from his mother.[83] Ettie was unforgiving in her competitiveness and as Julian began to struggle, he ricocheted between worshipping and hating his mother. Soon he was exhibiting wild mood swings and occasional violence, almost

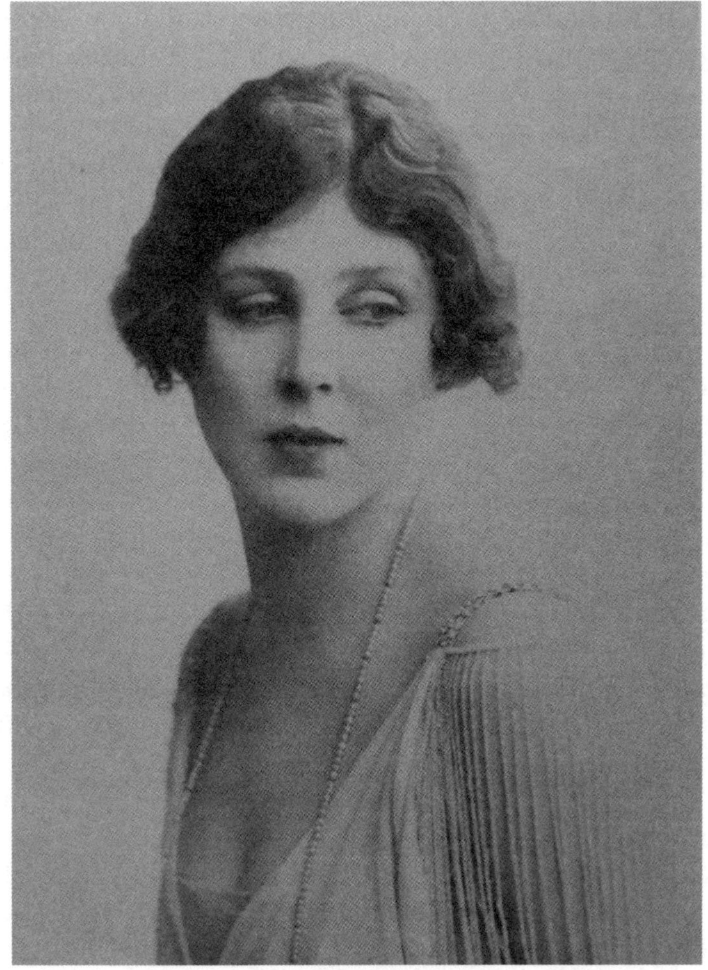

85. *Diana Manners*

killing a taxi driver over a fare. To make matters worse, Ettie began to flirt quite openly with Julian's friends, most notoriously with Archie Gordon, whose death in a car accident in 1909 saw her open in her grief. When she later turned to Patrick Shaw Stewart, Julian finally cracked and left for Italy.[84]

Much of this fell on Edward to deal with. Indeed for many of his friends he became the shoulder to lean on. And, as he would inevitably turn to Frances for help, she would turn Mells into a bolthole for recuperation for his friends. 'I think Edward is one of *the* nicest people and his philosophy of *dolce far niente* and the primrose path is dangerously enticing', wrote one after a stay at Mells. 'I am sorry Mells is over', wrote Patrick to Diana Manners. 'It was extraordinarily good and Edward was an angel to me, only work clouded it'. As for Julian: 'I do want to thank you most frightfully for various things. For being so jolly to me all last term. For wanting me to come to Mells trailing my clouds of melancholia. For writing me two very jolly letters'.[85]

There would be nothing jolly about exams, especially as Edward had signed up for Greats, the toughest test of all, involving papers in Latin, Greek, Ancient History and Philosophy. He had always presumed that the outcome would be disaster. But sharing digs with Patrick Shaw Stewart saw him being caught up in the slipstream of his more cerebral friend. Patrick even enticed him to Devon and 'the grimmest of reading parties' with 'a gutter-snipe of a tutor'. By May 1910 Patrick was insisting that 'Edward has done a lot of work' as if it was a point of surprise: indeed 'he is confident now – rather too much so, I fear'. What Edward himself recognised as 'the extraordinary egotism you encourage in me'.[86] All to no avail. When the news came of Edward's third-class degree, Patrick was at Mells, with both Edward and his mother not due until the next day. 'It is a terrible blow. I can't bear to think what his mother will feel…or he himself'. As it turned out 'it was hair-whitening, though Katharine was a darling and Edward took it brilliantly'.[87] His mother did not. Katharine tried to stir her husband to pacify Frances. Despite confessing that 'I do not see any plausible line of consolation', he dutifully went into battle. Arguments that 'academic distributions are all rot' and Greats was technically such a challenge that 'very hard to get even a Second', got short shrift. So too the line, Edward 'is bright and beautiful (which I never was). Why not be content with that?' Teasing her went spectacularly flat: 'Anyhow Edward has done much better than Cardinal Newman who had to work 14 hours a day for his Third. If only he would become a Roman like Laura [Lovatt?], I don't see how he could avoid being Pope someday. I believe you would like that. It is a big position'.[88] The problem (not to be acknowledged in Frances's presence) was that even if Edward had worked throughout, he would never have got a First. Instead, 'she seems to feel his lack of industry as a personal grievance', Raymond explained to Katharine.[89] Yet for Frances, gone in her eyes was the dream of greatness. Edward was one of a gilded generation, who she had always seen ruling the country as their parents in the Souls had done before them. What she was facing now was the realisation that, while 'superficially resembling them in habits and catch words and so forth', Edward's own 'moderate and less disciplined wits' would leave him the jester and not the leader.

Still at least he was loved by them. Interestingly his contemporaries placed greater value on the manner with which he took the news than the degree itself. 'Most wonderfully calm…Your example will remain at Oxford as an influence towards aristocratic thinking and high living', commiserated one. 'I should like to be with you at Mells weeping and cursing the unjust judges' declared Diana Manners. 'I swear to not being a success snob. I have never liked you so well as now when you are sad'. Flirtatious and comforting, she provoked an honest self-assessment from Edward:

> I could forget Greats easily with you. I am not actively miserable for the reason that I have half expected this. I am not really very clever you know, and my wares, such as they are, least of all marketable in the examinations room. But of course I am ostentatious and need applause from a certain kind of gallery rather badly, so that a failing of this kind gives me the sort of feeling that I suppose committing a crime would be to a very moral person. And my mother minds – that is the worst bore – and there is nothing on earth to say. I can't even apologise.[90]

Even so, there would be no split, no falling out. Both mother and son were too emotionally intertwined for that. His letters to 'Dear Darling Mother' remained affectionate, breezy, caring and gossipy; and in the face of everything, supremely optimistic. In January 1910, the Mells estates were settled in both Jack and Edward's names – itself an historic statement of trust. But no longer spoken, there could be no denying that something had been lost.

~ 31 ~

COTERIE

Sometimes I feel we have more of youthfulness than these callow birds, whom we feed and lodge, but who seem so much less responsive than we were (and are) to the sun and wind, and the infinite possibilities of un-travelled space. They have so many things that at their time of life you and I never had or dreamed of – in particular measureless freedom to make of their lives in their own fashion. And yet, somehow, I am not sure that we did not make more of our caged and cabined opportunities than they do of their uncharted liberty. Perhaps after all, the modern parent is not an improvement on our own, and we may see a return to the rigid, restraining traditions of the old regime.

Henry Asquith to Frances Horner[91]

'Edward is reading law', Frances informed Patrick Shaw Stewart. 'You know the pathos of that situation, don't you?' No one appreciated this more than Edward himself. With the help of Haldane and Raymond, he had secured a place in a top chambers under the eye of F. E. Smith – a leading barrister and Unionist MP who had a fondness for aristocratic charm. Far from the 'measureless freedom' to make his own life, Edward felt utterly disengaged – so much so that he forgot to attend his first legal exams in 1911. By 1914 he was no less bored. 'No briefs come and I can't face repetition of this last term at the Temple', he confessed to Patrick (then thriving in the City). '*Nothing* to do except lunch well and sleep after it and I am getting fat'. 'I can't see him in a solicitor's office', joked Charles Lister, 'unless he was there to borrow money or sell the family estates'. Another friend judged that Edward was only fit for patronage and 'ought to be hereditary posset-bearer to the King at £10,000 a year'.[92] Edward rather played up to this, adopting the affected pose of an eighteenth-century Whig grandee down on his luck. As such he would be fearlessly extravagant in coin and conversation and a slave to nothing but the highest fashion. As self-parody it entertained his friends and enriched his servants and tailors. But it also nurtured a sense that the professions were beneath him, further encouraging him in his idleness. 'I doubt if I have the imagination to counteract my natural love of pleasure', he would protest. Irresolute (even as a child) and now in London on his own without his mother to drive him on, he shamelessly conceded that 'it is so fatally easy to spend the time between the sofa and the bath'. As a result, he confessed 'The only thing I am good at is introspection. I believe my mother is right and self-centredness means hell but one can't alter it by founding a boys' club.'[93]

This last idea reflected his mother's social work in the 1870s but Edward showed none of her religious or social responsibility. The years before the First World War saw the London Season at its most ostentatious, with a visceral mix of plutocratic wealth, aristocracy and numerous chancers on the make. It was also a time when revolution seemed in the air, with national strikes, civil war in Ulster, suffragette violence and growing international tension. Some of Edward's friends were vaguely attuned to this: Charles Lister and his advocacy of Fabianism; Julian Grenfell not wanting a 'swagger' regiment; Diana Manners and being 'anti-snob'. All of them (except Patrick for whom it was all so new) despised the flaunting of wealth at Ettie's Taplow and Panshanger. For all that, in the years before the war Edward and his friends came to symbolise hedonistic excess and the ugliness of privilege. They called themselves the Corrupt Coterie as a tease of their parents and the Souls; but also because, as Diana put it, 'Our pride was to be unafraid of words, unshocked by drink and unashamed of "decadence" and gambling – Unlike Other People, I am afraid'. Their antics quickly became the staple for celebrity gossip columnists and paparazzi and they featured regularly magazines such as *Tatler, Globe, The Bystander,* and *Sphere.* Their clothes would set the latest fashions of the day.[94] In their desire to shock, they occasionally shocked themselves. Their gambling often got out of hand. Diana would later excuse this by arguing that at least the money stayed within the Coterie. But not always. 'There was a horrible poker floater here', Ego Charteris told his mother. 'Edward lost £181 playing at a table with Diana, Iris Tree, … and I am ashamed to say, Letty. Bouch – the Belvoir MFH – took most of it off them.

George lost £120. It sounds like Bedlam. It has wrecked my holidays. I can never feel the same about Edward and Diana again. Diana is going to the Devil'.[95]

It is hard to imagine that the youngest of the gang should have such influence. Yet vivacious, beautiful, flirtatious and wild, Diana was quite capable of egging everyone on. And none more so than Edward who would carry on a forlorn courtship with her until his death: 'Oh what a wonderful *ease* there is in relation to you altogether', he wrote. 'You are the only thing I care a damn about in the world. I love you better than my life, but I don't care much about the latter'. Many of the others were sexually driven in their pursuit, but for all her allure, she was more chaste than she appeared. In truth, Diana loved Edward but was never in love with him. They were the closest of friends – teasing yet devoted – but nevertheless unbound. 'Faithless Diana', he would chide her. 'The truth is that I can't – no, I won't love you unless you love me. There's the rub'.[96] None of which dissuaded him from being her willing partner in crime.

By 1913, their generational revolt was in full swing. Over a series of 'jollies' they would cock a snook at convention. 'We had become an even closer Coterie', recalled Diana, 'very irritating to others and utterly satisfying and delightful to ourselves'.[97] Two events in particular caught the spirit. In September the Coterie decamped to Venice where George Vernon – hedonistic, childish and crucially very rich – was holding a party in the Casa Capello on the Grand Canal. Edward was driven out by his host, along with Denis Anson (the son of the Warden of All Souls and a particular dare-devil) – a carefree expedition across lands that would be convulsed by war in a year's time. There was no let up on their arrival.

> There was dancing and extravagance and lashings of wine and charades and moonlit balconies and kisses, and some amateur prize-fighting with a mattress ring and seconds, and a girls sparring match and, best of all, bets on who would swim the canal first, Duff [Cooper] and Denis Anson, and in their evening clothes. I can see Duff now, jacket flung to me, miraculously climbing up one of the great posts that moor the gondolas at the entrance steps … Denis I had no eyes for, but I heard him plop and saw them both breaststroke to the other side. Duff won. What fun we thought it![98]

Such 'jollies' were fast becoming unaffordable for Edward. He had been mired in debt for as long as his friends had known him. His income from the law was no match for such unabashed extravagance. While his friends revelled in the bravado (Edward 'delightful and has just embarked his last £1000 on a bogus mine', Billy Grenfell recorded after a stay at Belvoir), in 1911 the bank refused Edward any more credit. To his shame, he had to pull out of a planned jaunt with Patrick Shaw Stewart to Spain; though typically he sought to find honour in destitution: 'I think of trying to feel like a Whig nobleman who has lost in London at cards'.[99] By 1914 his debts were so great that once again they could no longer be ignored. This time however salvation came in the form of Thomas Beecham, the conductor and heir to his father's patent medicine fortune. They met through parties that the Cunards[99] gave at their Cavendish Square house rented from the Asquiths: 'I like the little man quite immensely', Edward reported to Patrick, while sailing with Beecham on the Dart. The little man was just as enamoured with Edward's *ancien régime* charm – to such an extent that he cleared Edward's debts! If Diana is to be believed, this was part of a wider scheme to purchase honours. She told Duff that when Thomas Beecham's father, Joseph, was made a baronet in 1914, he had to pay £10,000. Four thousand went to Lady Cunard, five hundred to Diana and rest [i.e. £5,500 or the equivalent of £624,000 today] to Edward to pay off his debts.[101] Edward could hardly believe his luck and with lessons unlearnt, he was quickly back on the razzle.

In July 1914 with Europe on the brink of war, Edward and Constantin Benckendorff – son of the Russian Ambassador – organised a small boat party on the Thames with a lavish supper and a quartet of Thomas Beecham's musicians from Covent Garden. Katharine and Raymond were there along with Claud Russell,[102] Duff Cooper and his sister Sybil, Iris Tree,[103] 'a lovely Swiss girl call Jacqueline de Portalès', Diana Manners and Denis Anson.[104] Amid the high jinks and drunkenness, at 3 am Diana encouraged Denis Anson – then half cut – to jump in and swim to the Embankment (in a repeat of the Venice escapade).[105] Anson handed his watch to Diana and dived in. Almost immediately he was in trouble with the strong currents. The captain stopped the boat and Benckendorff and one of the musicians dived in to rescue him. Only Constantin survived. The next day the papers were full of the irresponsible smart set and of a life (as Julian pointed out) that had been 'chucked away because he could find nothing exciting enough to do in the ordinary things'.[106] Anson (who had just inherited a baronetcy) was a fool who was quite capable of getting himself killed. Revealingly none of the close group dived in to the rescue. Admittedly Raymond was a very poor swimmer.[107] Duff Cooper, who was a strong swimmer, was held back by Diana as he tried to get out of his jacket.

What followed was an Establishment cover up. At the inquest top lawyers including F. E. Smith ensured that most of the party did not have to testify as witnesses. In Diana's case it took the intervention of her mother, now the Duchess of Rutland, who simply descended on the coroner's office in advance of the hearing. Instead, it was left to 'Iris Tree who volunteered to step into the breach, [and] distinguished herself (they say) both by the manner and the matter of her evidence'.[108] The verdict of 'death by misadventure', though accurate, caught nothing of the context. Anson, after all, hadn't just fallen in. The press took up the fury of the Covent Garden orchestra over the loss of one of their own for the sport of the 'idle rich'. In Society Diana, after one outrage too many took most of the blame. Yet she was not alone. Margot Asquith spoke for most of the Coterie's parents at the callousness of the group: 'the young people afterwards showed no real feeling; they ran about bickering, ballrooming – to parties, operas, and felt martyrdom because they were criticised'.[109] Diana so hated confrontation that she persuaded Edward to return Anson's watch to his family rather than face them herself. Even in the 1950s, writing her memoirs, she dropped in that the bandsman 'was a consumptive and due to die'. As if that mattered.[110]

Edward at least was 'still in rather a low key', having taken refuge at The Wharf, the Asquiths' Oxfordshire retreat. Not that Margot would have cut him much slack. Never one for holding back she pronounced judgement on the Coterie.

> The clever group of nowadays is very inferior to my clever group called 'Souls'. They are sexless and soulless, and so disloyal that they only hang together by a thread of mutual love of gossip and common capacity to say bright things, read bright and blasphemous novels, modern and very moderate poems (which crop up like weeds every day); and an impulsive, uninspired, dry desire to go against authority under the name of anti-cant.[111]

She regretted that the old moral disciplines of hierarchy, faith and self-help had been eroded by largesse. More worrying she couldn't understand their world. This is brilliantly captured by her amazement at her stepdaughter Violet's social success:

> Violet is not pretty but everyone is in love with her. Somehow her wits and vitality, her wonderful manners, keenness and sweetness of manner all triumph over torn and dirty clothes, not a very good complexion and not pretty teeth, just as if they were unnoticeable trifles… What Violet has really got is brains and kindness – the right things appeal to her but she has an insatiable love of pure amusement.[112]

Frances was equally despairing: 'I had a young man here… quite dressy and had a moustache and didn't read books or newspapers or that sort of thing'. She in turn was struck

> at the amazing position now attained by young unmarried girls. [It is] as if men valued youth to a very peculiar and exceptional degree, far more than was the case, say thirty, forty or a hundred years ago. Then the affairs, which married people in society had, were with one another – the girls played no part at all. Now men both married and single, no longer quite young, delight in the society of girls. They like their conversation and their fresh point of view.[113]

An observation fuelled no doubt by Henry Asquith's new passion for Katharine's close friend, Venetia Stanley.[114] And by the cruel advances of age. With her face declared by Cynthia Asquith 'a scene of savage grandeur', she could seem quite formidable to the unwary.[115]

However, the Coterie shared far more with the Souls than they let on. For all that they felt overwhelmed by the expectations of their parents, they never really challenged their class assumptions or their belief in patriotism and Christian duty. These manly values of honour and loyalty, first learnt on their mother's knee, had been vigorously reinforced by their schooling and when the call came the younger generation would not be found wanting. Nor were they in a position to rebel. 'There is no fear, believe me, of the older generation being trodden down. They have their feet to firmly on our necks, what with references to the beauties like Duchess of Leinster, and living genii like Lord Curzon.'[116]

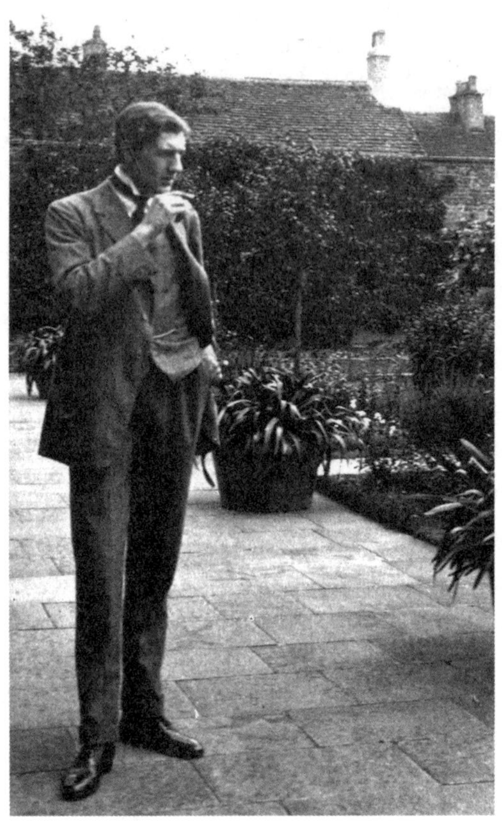

86.   Edward in 1913

The antics of the Coterie were more a desire for space from the competitive pressures of their parents' world rather than a rejection of it. In fact, other than with Margot,[117] the Coterie got on well with their parents' generation. Many of the leading lights were offspring of the Souls. They had been brought up together on the grand circuit of Mells, Stanway, Gosford, Belvoir, Taplow, and Panshanger, the childhood home which Ettie had inherited in 1913. Raymond, who found himself golfing and talking a good deal to Arthur Balfour (then Prime Minister) and Lady Elcho, noted that they 'have an extraordinary charm for me – both singularly, and particularly in combination – she is worn and faded but I think one would always jump among lions to redeem her glove...' When in Venice for the Vernon party, they discovered the older Asquiths there for the PM's sixtieth birthday. The parties quickly merged. After days spent arm-in-arm with Diana Manners exploring the sites with *The Stones of Venice* in hand, Asquith was 'dressed up as a Doge and [they] hung the *sala* with Mantegna swags of fruit and green leaves and loaded him with presents, tenderness and admiration. I think he was ecstatically happy that day'.[118]

At Mells, Frances hoped 'the younger generation… will still tolerate me as a sympathetic if remote operator'.[119] Not remote enough for Edward perhaps but she went out of her way to provide a home for his friends (fig. 86). 'Exceedingly pleasant at Mells', Raymond wrote in thanks. 'Forgive us for basking in the sunshine of your plans without helping to make them. But you have an unparalleled fertility in plan making'. She would remember them as 'a most brilliant group of young men'. In time they would become 'the golden lads and girls who filled our lives with joy and laughter'. At their head stood Raymond, 'very distinguished and good looking and endowed with astonishing wit… a leader in the young world of those days'.[120] Memory plays tricks but given what was to come, the era before 1914 inevitably became in time a golden age. In keeping with this, Frances saw her role as one in which

> She made a golden tumult in the house,
> Like morning in the hills.[121]

This informality was rare and greatly relished by the young. [122] Not that Frances was a push over. 'A forceful character [with] a vigorous mind and salt-like sense', recalled one regular to Mells, and with more than enough energy to match the young. No doubt, what most found invigorating, a few found intimidating; but all were attracted to her 'robust unfastidious love of life and of human beings'. That said, she didn't always get her own way. A 'good domestic Mells', reported Patrick to Diana, 'with autumn tinted tennis and arguments on economy in which Edward plus me defeated Lady Horner'.[123]

Another attraction of Mells, perhaps unexpectedly, was Jack (fig. 87). Not that he said much amid the cacophony of youthful debate.

> In the background, [was] Mr Horner, seldom visible out of his study, and then nearly always silent; until all of a sudden, reliable information would be in demand during one of the

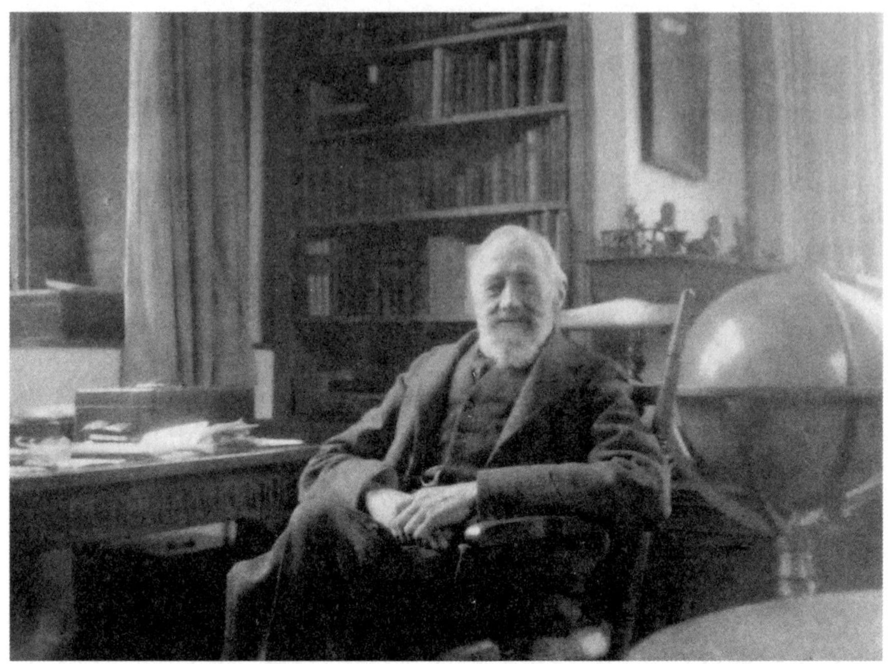

87.   Jack in his study at Mells

interminable discussions which, day and night, occupied the minds and tongues of all the inmates of Mells. He was then the person who in answer to a direct question would come out of his daydream, look up muttering 'Let me see', disappear for about ten minutes into his study and return to deliver a little lecture on any point under the sun, full of the most precise and relevant information.[124]

Rather than thinking him a bore or a pedant there was respect for his formidable erudition and authority. Moreover, looking like a 'tall bearded figure out of a Paul Veronese picture,' he had a presence, intensified in turn by his deafness. Crucially from time to time a vein of 'silent good humour' would break through the detachment. 'Though aloof [he was] ready to bend and, when unbent, [was] charming and humorous'. Above all, he had integrity in which even the most cynical could trust. J. M. Barrie once came across Duff and Diana debating what was worse – being called a bore or a cad? 'It depends on who called you that' said one. 'Suppose Sir John Horner called you a cad,' said another. 'Oh, my God! That would do for you,' they all cried out.[125]

What did for Edward was that his friends so liked his parents. To him, even at twenty-two, they could be a huge embarrassment. Much to Patrick's amusement as he recounted to Diana:

> The dignified silence of Sir John, the somewhat resentful radiance of Lady Horner and the unplumbed despair of Edward as he contemplated his actually very happy guests. I believe he would like his parents to take porridge in their rooms on the occasions he may entertain there, on the ground that there is no room large enough for them to look merely incidental in. Everyone who has ever known parents knows the feeling but few give way to it so mournfully as Edward.[126]

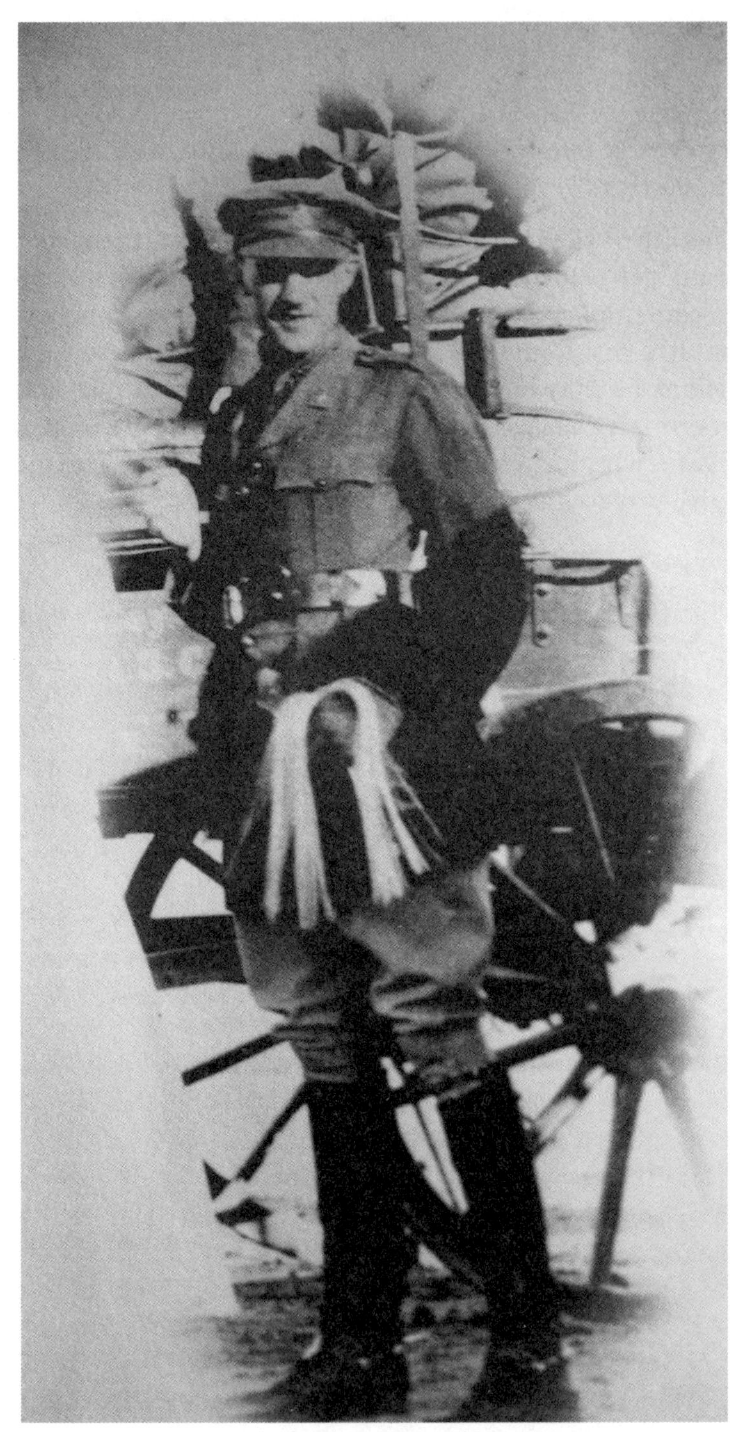

88.   *Edward in uniform*

Part Nine

The Shattering Years

To look back on our Venice party now, only four years ago, is to recall only the dead …

Duff Cooper, 23 November 1917[1]

~ 32 ~

'OH DARLINGS, THE FUN OF IT'

I think it's up to the Coterie to stop this war.

Diana Manners[2]

I loved the first and hated the last part of the night in a way to make other times hardly seem to have existed…the experience both good and bad was so vivid.

Edward Horner[3]

It was only to be expected that the outbreak of war in 1914 should coincide with an enormous party at Mells. 'There is a Hell of a crowd here this weekend', discovered Raymond. 'People sleeping not only in one another's beds but in flower-beds and cony-burrows and places where you would hardly dream of putting the Son of Man'. Venetia Stanley was also there and amused the Prime Minister with her 'picture' of the jarring sensibilities between mother and daughter: 'that kind of strained strenuousness which Frances shows in emergencies (and which is quite effective) does not appeal to Katharine's rather pulseless, though not superficial, temperament'. Raymond had caught this too and found it hilarious.

> The atmosphere here is appalling. The crisis has brought out all that is best in British womanhood. Katharine still keeps her head. But Cicely Lambton and Frances Horner have sunk all political differences and are facing the enemy as one man. They have cornered all the petrol … and turned Perdita's pony-cart into an ambulance. Cicely thinks that everybody ought to give up everything except racing, which (she tells me) has ceased to be a sport and become an industry, and that every-one should enlist at once except George because the whole of

300

Cambridgeshire depends on George continuing his industrial career at Newmarket, and where (she asks) should we be at a time like this without Cambridgeshire.[4]

Quickly the reality of war imposed itself on even this quiet corner of Somerset. Stirred by the chance of adventure, the young labourers in Mells caused 'great havoc' by enlisting (many never to return). In one of the first battles, Col. Hogg of the 4th Hussars and Frances's nephew died of his wounds. September also saw the death of George Wyndham's son Percy and Con Manners's son John. Such losses shook Katharine. 'I live in a shiver of fear now.'[5] As would her generation for the next four years. The party was over.

But not for Edward. Initially he had taken his lead from Diana who railed against 'war lust', asserting that 'it is up to the Coterie to stop this war'. Yet Edward couldn't resist the popular euphoria and within a week was ordering a 'special pair of boots for riding into Berlin' (fig. 88). For him, as for a surprising number of his friends, the Great War came as a salvation. After a few desultory years at the Bar waiting for briefs that never came, the war offered action and excitement. More importantly it brought honour, responsibility and, vitally, a sense of purpose – and one appealing to an ancient heroic intuition. If such Romance had set them on their way, the horrific reality, for all that it hit hard, would never completely quell such notions of duty and destiny. To be fair, Edward did have a clear sense of the *casus belli*. As he explained to Diana, the German government had 'forced the war [and] had planned it ages ago and made the Austrians send their ultimatum to Serbia – [they] are mad but couldn't be stopped [until] now ... Also they must be beaten, must in the sense that there will be no help for the world until they are and their Government altered'.[6] The instinctive values of patriotism, class loyalty and chivalric romance nurtured from the cradle kicked in too. As he told his mother, 'getting out is the point beside which nothing else matters'. Typically he was far less certain how to go about it. It says something about the tempo of Asquith's management of the war that within three weeks of the outbreak of hostilities, Edward would be lunching at least twice with the Prime Minister at Downing Street. 'He is full of zeal but poor fellow, rather feckless', judged Asquith. Hence his verdict that 'Poor Edward Horner is not likely to get nearer the front than Winchester'.[7]

Edward's first thought was to join the North Somerset Yeomanry – appropriate as landowner leading his tenants and appealing to the romantic in him. Less appealing were his brother officers who were likeable if 'so stupid that it is dull to a degree never dreamt of'. Raymond was perhaps closer to the mark: 'Poor old E went off to the North Somersets last week with Cicely's two best hunters, [a cook and] a body servant… But all these conveniences have been confiscated for the use of the regiment and old E sleeps on bare boards, rises at 5…It makes one's heart bleed'. As ever his mother came to his rescue. Mobilising Haldane who contacted Kitchener, she got Edward transferred to the regular cavalry and by September he was with the Royal Horse Guards in Forest Row in Sussex. When he then determined to get a regular commission, she came up trumps again procuring through her contacts a commission into the 18th Hussars: 'You have been marvellous about it and I am continually ashamed to be giving so much trouble', he thanked her. Yet behind her endeavours lay great anxiety. Initially she, like him, only saw the honour in it, but very soon she was doing her best to delay his dispatch to France; in part encouraged by Haldane's crumb of hope that the war might not last the year. But by February 1915 she could do no more and became almost fatalistic as she saw him off:

> I would like him to go and be useful and with all the conditions in his favour that I can make for him – that is all … Edward is very unlikely to come back. No-one knows that as I do: he is very *conspicuous* – very reckless of danger: carried away by excitement. I feel him in rather a different position to a regular soldier posted to a regiment … Edward has no tie of comradeship or responsibility or any relationship to any superior or inferior – I hope he may do well to be useful and serious but we can none of us shape events.[8]

On 5 March his regiment was unexpectedly ordered to the front line near Ypres in support of the 2nd Dragoons who were seeking to recapture some lost trenches. There a mine intended for the Germans went off prematurely and 'I found myself underneath trees, sandbags, earth, with sprawling men, thinking I was dead – also a pain in my side'. With the explosion and the deafening machine-gun counter fire from the Germans, Edward had to work hard to keep his men from escaping down the communications trench ('curses righted this'). Once over the top Edward sought out the dragoons and found them clinging to the edge of a crater sixty yards across and twenty feet deep. Soon he was also taking shelter on the slippery side of a crater while overhead 'the never to forget marvellous sight [of gunfire] lighting up the place like mid-day'. Eventually (hours late) the French attacked and Edward could get back. By now badly bruised he had to hobble back five miles to Ypres 'in the light of a sniper's moon.'[9]

As described by Edward, his first action read like a *Boys Own* adventure – full of adrenalin, exhilaration, fear, excitement, noise and colour; one where everyone got back. 'I am very happy now, on the whole more than I can remember being except at moments'; even if conditions were 'devilish uncomfortable'. That said, Edward had no intention of letting war deny him his comforts. A complaint over the food saw his mother sending out 'heavenly parcels': not just food but also Balkan cigarettes, cigars, tobacco, chocolate, French novels and a riding whip. There was his sartorial independence to be maintained too: 'Would you order me a pair of *brown* (instead of the regulation green) puttees, extra-long, from Grant of Piccadilly?' he ordered his poor mother. The point of absurdity was reached a month later when he asked Raymond to send out a gold tiepin for his servant. Raymond was suitably sardonic in reply:

> May I send you out an emerald ring for his nostril? And some attar of roses for your charger, and a Degas for your dugout, and a sheet or two of Delius for the gramophone – or would a little something by John Sebastian Bach be more seasonal in Holy Week? And 'some precious tender hearted scroll of pure Simonides' for use in the latrines? It seems very horrible that you shouldn't have got these things long ago: but you know what our War Office is like…[10]

Out of the blue Edward received an invitation to dine with Sir John French, Commander in Chief of the British Expeditionary Force, at his headquarters in Saint-Omer. French was an enthusiastic player on the fringe of High Society and an acquaintance of Frances. At the dinner Edward was surprised to learn that French 'wanted to send me home with a message so as to avoid the trenches'. Oddly the tone was more of an offer than an order. 'But I couldn't do it, could I?', Edward explained to Diana Manners. With a great offensive imminent, Edward was clear where his duty lay. Diana's reply was enigmatic: 'French says he can't sleep when you are at the trenches'.[11] It turned out that at this time French was also trying to get John Granby, heir to the Rutland dukedom and Diana's brother, out of the line before the major offensive at Neuve Chapelle due on 10 March. John's mother, Violet, Duchess of Rutland, was desperate to get her son away from the fighting and was seeking to reach French through his very close friend George Moore – an American businessman of much wealth and dubious connections, but crucially with a very influential hold over French. Moore was distinctly creepy, with a sexual obsession for Diana Manners despite being generations older. She found him utterly repellent and hated it when he attempted to kiss her. Yet such was her mother's desperation, she virtually pimped her daughter, persuading Diana to 'coax this boon out of Moore'. Unknowing, Diana's friends looked on appalled at her flirting with him. Yet when Violet found Moore in her daughter's bedroom at 3am, all she recorded in a note was 'Oh dear'. Other strategies included getting doctors to fake medical assessments and pulling strings with French, who needed little persuasion. Eventually she succeeded in getting John back to Britain and keeping him from the front for the rest of the war, despite recruiting many of their tenants to their deaths.[12]

Seemingly French was keen to do the same for Horner. Had Frances attempted something similar? In an undated letter to Haldane Frances protests her innocence, perhaps too vigorously. 'I never asked you to write to French, never ever suggested it. It was your own proposal to me – for which I felt most grateful and perhaps even jumped at! My only difference was that I thought it was better to be done now – and now when Edward goes out … because just now anything could happen at any moment at any minute.' Ironically it would be the virtues of patriotic duty that she had long drummed into him which would prevent him from seizing the opportunity. Unlike John Granby whose conscience ate away at him for the rest of his life and who in 1940 would spend his last days trying to burn the evidence.[13]

The Neuve Chapelle offensive proved a failure ('we hear the worst news of casualties and incompetence'). However as a cavalry-man Edward was safely behind lines waiting for the breakthrough. Indeed even a German counter attack on 22 April (including the first major use of poison gas) didn't seem to cause him much anxiety. Suddenly, on 7 May, he was hit by sniper fire. For all that there was a battle going on, Edward would later recount this action to Patrick as if it was a rude interruption on a hot summer's day

> I was rather enjoying my part in the war, long rides and always sleeping in different parts of the country – a lot of support and not much first line work except for a little shelling sometimes. It didn't seem dangerous and one was alone with one's troops a good deal…Mine thought me very good at getting them food which made up, in confidence, for my frequently having to consult *them* as to the points of the compass. Well, there came my knock out – just a shot as we were walking back to our horses one night after cutting down hedges near Ypres.

This was the genial bumbling Edward his friends knew and loved; and, as with all his scrapes, there would be no shortage of melodrama: 'O Patrick I have hardly had a moment not hellish since. My kidneys must in future be referred to in the singular'.[14] That night, 7 May, French personally telegrammed Sir John to warn him that his son was wounded. A second telegram gave more detail: 'Horner suffering from a penetrating abdominal wound, serious nature – doing as well as can be expected'.

What followed was a remarkable triumph of personality and indeed privilege over protocol.[15] For Frances was determined to get to France to save her son. The next morning she stormed into Downing Street and within minutes Asquith had retreated to the Cabinet Room to write to Cambon, the French Ambassador, to secure passports. Margot meanwhile had left for King Edward's Hospital where the leading surgeon, Sir Arbuthnot Lane, was operating, and persuaded him to join the Horners with a nurse on the night sailing. Diana claims that it was she who, through the ubiquitous Moore, secured the necessary transport: 'He would do all I asked', she recalled, 'and he had extraordinary power – power great enough to arrange transport for Sir John and Lady Horner'. So it was that Frances, Jack and Katharine (and Diana too) set out across the Channel that night, wearing Gieves jackets in case of U-boat attacks. Landing at Boulogne, they were picked up by a GHQ car travelling at full speed to the front-line hospital.[16] It was still dark as they arrived only to discover a 'never stopping row of ambulances, dusty and weirdly slow-moving, [while] processing in other directions, occasional funeral cortèges – Union Jack affairs with bowed heads and rifles'. Racing around with only 'searchlights' to guide them, they could not find Edward initially. Eventually they discovered him in a dressing station in the nearby town of Bailleul, amidst a long line of 'stretchers' at the Convent of the Assumption. In contrast to the suffering around him, Edward appeared to Diana as if out of a Burne-Jones painting:

> Drunk to serenity on morphia, lying crusader-like with long curling hair falling on a fair white pillow, a décolleté cream silk shirt, long white arms dégagé but weak in the extreme. When he saw us, he smiled the smile of the drowned woman and said 'O darlings, the fun of it'. They laid him down on the ground, the crowd by then having become infected by worship of Edward's beauty.[17]

Lane's diagnosis confirmed the wound to the kidneys. Having got him transferred to the base hospital at Boulogne, Frances's irresistible determination to bring her son home then met an immovable object in the form of British military pride as Lane was refused permission to operate. Instead, the military doctors deemed Edward at first too ill to be operated on, let alone removed to England. As they waited, Frances sought to sustain morale by reading to him (pandering eventually to his preference for Fielding's *Tom Jones* over Victor Hugo). Neither could distract from the 'awful' scenes of gassed soldiers and 'terrible suffering' she now witnessed first hand. It was 'a time of black depression', she would recall: 'that month was the most vivid of my life'. After ten days they risked the operation and the kidney was successfully removed. Still it was not until 1 June that she got Edward transferred to a hospital in London. It would be another month before he was safely home.[18]

Edward had been the first of the Coterie to be shot. But days later Julian Grenfell was brought in to the same Boulogne hospital with a head wound. It soon went sceptic. He died with Ettie and family beside him on 26 May and was buried in a cemetery high on a windy hill outside Boulogne. 'Ettie very calm', Frances noted, even writing to Frances to express her delight at Edward's recovery. It was the first glimpse of her 'stubborn gospel of joy', which would be greatly tested in the years ahead.[19] For the Coterie and their parents the war was no longer a game.

FIGHTING ON THE HOME FRONT

I cannot write. My grief over Haldane is too great.

Margot Asquith[20]

Beb[21] came in looking rather queer and said he had broken a vase. He had smashed an inoffensive vase in Edward's room, because it 'wasn't pretty'… I felt alarmed. I believe the desire to smash is a recognised symptom of nervous strain from Artillery work, and I do so understand it, only one *must* drastically discourage it for there is nothing it mightn't lead to, and his arguments when scolded were rather unhinged. 'Gallant and wonderful soldiers were being killed, so why should ugly things survive?' Such arguments might lead to the smashing of Lady Horner's face.

Cynthia Asquith[22]

As fate would have it, it was while she was out of the country nursing her son that Frances first heard of Haldane's fall from office. Since the beginning of the war he had come under sustained and vicious attack from the right wing popular press led by the *Daily Mail* and Leo Maxse's *National Review*. With the war effort stuttering, the hunt was on for traitors and scapegoats. Haldane became a target as 'pro-German'. Not only was this grossly unfair but the evidence on which it was based was pitiful: an off-the-cuff remark at a dinner of German professors in 1913 that Germany was his 'spiritual home', his two 'missions' to Germany in 1906 and 1912 (including an interview with the Kaiser) to improve relations. That Britain was in a position to fight at all owed everything to his reforms at the War Office but this now was being used to explain failures by others in the field of battle. It didn't help that he lacked the popular touch. He was too odd, too philosophical, too convoluted in expression. What followed was vile, with journalists and Tory politicians eagerly awaiting 'when the plump body of the Member for Germany swings in the wind between two lamp posts'. When in May 1915 Asquith decided to form a national coalition to fight the war, the Tories made Haldane's dismissal a condition of entry. Or so he said. In fact the Prime Minister had offered up his friend first. Asquith had become tired of Haldane's capacity to ruffle feathers (most recently over conscription). Moreover, unknown to Frances, Haldane had offered his resignation twice. Asquith knew he would go without a fuss.[23]

Not so Frances. She found it 'incredible that a campaign of misrepresentation could have been deliberately carried on by men of high character, but it was'. What she found worse was the sight of her friends Asquith and Grey feeling 'the gale too strong to do anything but let Haldane swing in it'.[24] Her natural instinct was to fight. Declaring it 'all wrong to let yourself be driven out of the government at this moment', she berated him for not allowing 'the decision to remain absolutely with Asquith'. Resigning 'leaves your reputation undefended' against these 'unfounded attacks' and ensures the 'absolute triumph of your enemies… and that can never be obliterated.' She urged him to reconsider this 'fatal step'. 'If I could have been there I could have made you see this and I am pretty sure that I am right.'[25] But she had misread her man. What made him convinced that he was 'no more use to the country' was not right-wing press barons and hard Tory leaders such as Bonar Law and Carson. These 'little things don't matter', he assured her. 'The blow to all my hopes for peaceful development which this outbreak of war has caused is the really serious fact, & it is that that affects me.'[26] Yet while he looked on his fate with equanimity ('oddly enough I do not feel depressed'), for her Haldane's fall was a bitter blow. 'It is not because I care for you to be there', she expounded, 'but I care passionately for your public life and I don't feel that this is the right way to shape it'. For his public life was her public life and she had dedicated the previous twenty years of her life to 'the right way to shape it'. An occasional lunch at Downing Street could not make up for the loss of influence. Margot understood just how wounded Frances would be. 'I cannot write. My grief over Haldane is too great', she exclaimed. 'We ought to have kept him and gone to the country … Poor darling I know too well what you feel!'[27] Actually what Frances felt was never to be quite so sure of the Asquiths again.

*

By way of distraction in Spring 1916 Frances got involved with a canteen programme for munitions workers in London run by Clemmie Churchill (wife of Winston). A new canteen capable of feeding a thousand at a sitting opened in Hackney Wick to support three thousand munition workers and operating day and night. This opened Frances's eyes to a whole new world of mass crowds passing through and the crashing 'clangour of iron and steel'. Roped in by Frances to help on the night shift, Cynthia Asquith described huge, dark buildings towering overhead, sparks flying out of the chimneys – a 'real Nibelungen noise and atmosphere'. Frances's role seem to have been supervising the cooks and volunteers and helping too to find entertainers (theatre stars and generals mainly). She was also recruited by her niece, Pamela McKenna, as a VAD (Voluntary Aid Detachment) nurse and worked for six months on a soldiers' ward at St Mary's Paddington before deciding that she was 'too deeply pledged' to the canteens.[28]

As for Edward, his injury took a long time to heal. Not until the autumn of 1915 was he up and about. A stay with the Elchos at Gosford in the Scottish Borders refreshed his spirits (despite accidentally almost killing a game keeper when out shooting). It was there that Beb Asquith,[29] so traumatised by his war experiences, smashed the vase. Meanwhile Edward was proudly showing off his war wounds to Letty Manners: 'Edward is very sweet and awfully well. He showed me the wound in his back the other day. It is an awful thing – 11 inches long – it has only just healed. I expect he will be passed for home service'. Home service was the last thing on Edward's mind. Hence his fury when a medical board in December declared that he would never be declared fit for active war service on one kidney. Raymond assured him his injury was 'a sufficient oblation upon the altar of patriotism'. Even this seal of approval couldn't overcome the sense of drift and, worse, guilt, as the war began in 1915 to take its toll among the Coterie. In July Billy Grenfell was killed very close to where his brother had fallen months before. August saw Charles Lister succumb to gangrene at Gallipoli. When at Gosford, Edward had seen Yvo Charteris set off to the Front only to die in almost his first attack. By November George Vernon was dead too. Soon Edward was confessing to Diana how he couldn't meet his friends still in service when in London 'in the old comfortable way'.[30] Eventually a post was found for him in Egypt training ANZAC troops and where the climate might help the asthma attacks, which had worsened since he had been shot. There was good company too in the form of Ego Charteris and his new wife Letty (née Manners) who were stationed at Cairo. But the work was desultory and he spent his time 'tearing around … searching in vain for adventures'; or writing letters 'all whine and struggle and longing for home'. Raymond understandably was merciless: 'True he may be shot by a bow and arrow by a seditious Copt on the horizon or pelted with camel's dung by a drunken donkey boy…'.[31] And then on 23 April 1916 Ego was killed in a surprise Turkish assault on the Suez Canal.

*

The day before, Katharine gave birth to her third child: a boy in addition to her two daughters, Helen and Perdita. He was to be called Julian after Julian Grenfell but typically Raymond nicknamed the greedy babe Trimalchio (or Trim) after the gluttonous host of a dinner party in Petronius' *Satyricon*. By now Raymond too had joined up, despite Katharine's extraordinary efforts to protect him from the fray. In the first instance she assumed at thirty-six he would be too old. She also encouraged his political career – indeed he was the prospective Liberal candidate for Derby – but Raymond saw through that ruse and anyway had little interest in politics. In March 1915 she arranged a meeting with the Prime Minister (her father-in-law), the Foreign Secretary and the Cabinet Secretary (Grey and Hankey) – and almost certainly without Raymond's knowledge – to plan a transfer to a staff post with the Dardanelles campaign. All to no avail, as patiently Raymond explained 'the loathing and contempt' with which the staff officers were held.[32] There would be no stopping him now: 'poor love so unfit and so pathetically keen' remembered his old Oxford friend, John Buchan. In October 1915 he travelled to Mells to say goodbye to Frances and the children. Violet Asquith (Raymond's sister) who was convalescing there, observed the stark contrast of Katharine in 'abject despair… she might as well have just

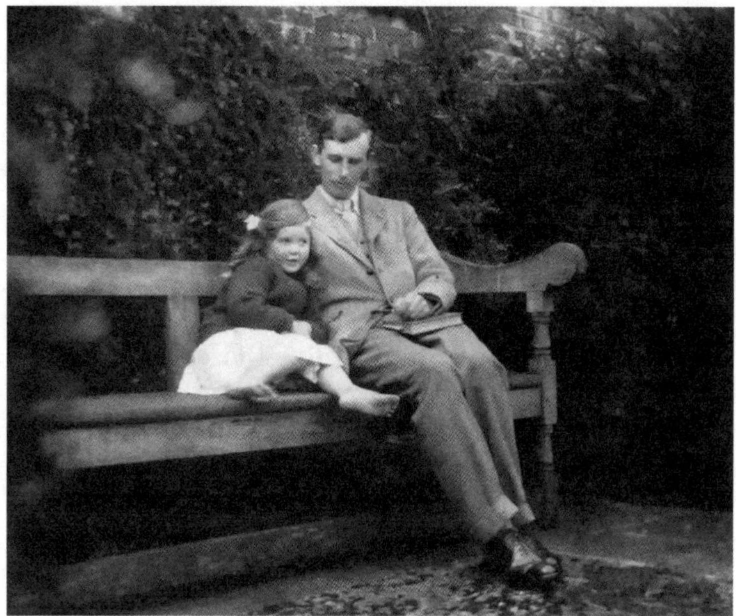

89.   *Raymond and Helen*

seen him in his coffin', and Raymond 'happy and excited'. Around them Mells remained as

> lovely and lulling as ever – the garden flaming with hollyhocks, red-hot pokers, Michaelmas daisies, dahlias, and that delicious half-rotten autumn smell in the air – the lichen peacefully creeping on over the old stone churches and walls. It is all so calm and normal and undisturbed, it is almost impossible to imagine the horror that is shaking the world'.[33]

In his letters home Raymond initially did not stint them the horror of trench life including the rats crawling over his face as he slept ('fortunately I am a lover of animals') and the terrifying experience on being under fire – be it shells or bullets ('I don't know where we should be without them'). Such irony soon gave way to a bitter, harsh tone, angry at 'these damned attacks' which were both extremely dangerous and utterly useless. In December 1915, he had just missed a bullet by three inches and in one twenty-four hour period his men had been heavily bombarded four times. While he just about kept his cool, such was the terror that he saw men face down in the mud scrabbling 'idiotically with their hands like moles trying to scrape their way into the side of the trench'. Yet he was furious when in January 1916 he was transferred to GHQ at Saint-Omer. Katharine had managed to get him to promise to go if he was ordered. It would prove a brief respite for he made it clear he would return to the regiment once the fighting season returned.[34]

Before doing so, he was given ten days' leave in order to see his new son. Leaves from the Front produced their own pressures, a frenzied selfish determination to live life to the full – seeking thrills to blot out the inevitable return. 'You were sweeter than honey', he wrote to Katharine after an earlier leave in January when she was heavily pregnant. 'And I suppose I was rather a brute to make you spend so much time in flashy company. But somehow a good glass of wine and the sight of Dottie's [Diana] hard eye and dazzling skin, gives me the illusion of living fast and brilliantly which one rather needs under the circumstances'. Katharine was remarkably forgiving of his fondness for Diana but her trust in both paid off. Raymond remained loyal and loving and Diana her closest friend.[35] In turn, Raymond was very relaxed over Diana and Katharine's drug-taking, as they gravitated from 'Jolly old Chlorers' to injecting themselves with morphine. After which they would lie 'in ecstatic stillness through too short a night…Strange to feel so utterly self-sufficient – more like a Chinaman, or God before he made the world or his son and was content with or callous to, the chaos'. Summoning Diana to Mells, Katharine would insist 'it is about time for another night of oblivion, although I've oddly refrained since you were last here'.[36]

Part of the reason why Mells continued to have a pull for the Coterie was that Frances and Jack proved quite unshockable. At one dinner, conversation had got round to a tale of an officer buggering his batman in a shell hole in No Man's Land. Jack, by now quite deaf, asked what all the laughter was about. Edward tried to steer the conversation elsewhere but Diana boldly repeated the story. After a moment's silence, Jack replied, 'he must have been an uncommonly handy feller'. Stories about Jack were much treasured by the Coterie. Not least his reply to a policeman who had ordered him to take cover during a bad air raid: 'I shall do nothing of the kind – I am going to my bed'.[37] Raymond's relations with his parents on the other hand only worsened with the war. 'If Margot talks any more bosh to you about the inhumanity of her step-children', he fumed to Katharine, 'you can stop her mouth by telling her that during my ten months exile here the PM has never written me a line of any description. I don't see why he should. He has plenty of other things to do; and so have I…' In fact, Asquith, for all his formality with his children and what another son called his 'excessive belief in the powers of the unspoken word', was devoted to Raymond. As for his stepmother, between them lay a chasm of misunderstanding. After Frances had spoken up strongly in Raymond's defence, Margot did write. Raymond replied assuming she would never read it. He would never know that she had copied his letter into her journal.[38]

Raymond returned to the Front with none of the sense of adventure shared by Julian Grenfell or Edward. He had come to Katharine's view 'about the utter senselessness of war'. He hated the fighting: 'we are all living so entirely on the edge of doom.' But he was trapped by the code of honour. 'Without the glamour of the winding sheet I have no *locus standi* in the world', he protested to Diana. By now too even he was looking for a Blighty wound and grumbled when a nearby mortar failed to do its job. From Katharine he sought distraction: 'Tell me about your mother's "cracking row". I always like to hear about rows'. Food parcels and hams from Mrs Gould at Mells raised his spirits along with photographs of the children and of The Manor House and its Church. Income tax bills were a less welcome preoccupation with Katharine only getting by with the occasional cheque from Haldane. 'You are sweeter and more lovely even than you were then, my Fawn', Raymond would write on their wedding anniversary, 'and I adore you a million times more and I am not sorry a bit'.[39]

The Battle of the Somme had raged since July and every day Raymond waited with his men for the order to the front line. Suddenly on 6 September he was summoned – not to the Front as it turned out but to a crossroads on the road to Fricourt. After waiting an hour two cars drew up and out stepped his father on an official tour. It was the last time they would meet. A week later and Raymond was in the front line. The next morning, soon after leading his soldiers over the top, he was shot in the chest. Knowing he was dying, he calmly lit a cigarette in an effort to reassure his men – a courageous last act in a sacrifice all the more poignant for being so insignificant – as he would have been the first to point out.

*

Frances took the call from No 10 and having broken the news to her daughter summoned Diana to Mells. 'Before I went I was frightened for Katharine', Diana would later recall.

> Her energy even when stimulated by Raysie [Raymond] was so slender a thread held by him; he taught her to breathe and articulate. I found her crouched in a dark room over the fire, too dead a thing to seek death. She has a fear that living she will deteriorate into a woman that Raymond meeting would not care to know and an agony of being a duty to *us*. Poor angel. Thank God I felt competent and strong. I tried hard to sink my misery and think only of holding Katharine up as we all must…I wonder if Raymond knew that Katharine would inevitably be irreparably broken by his death – did modesty close his eyes to the staring fact or did he keep them shut intentionally; seeing he could not have returned to the regiment.[40]

Frances wrote in similar terms to Ettie. 'I honestly feel there is no recovery or future for [Katharine]. She was a being so lightly anchored to this world and [it was only] through Raymond that she held'.[41] The Prime Minister drove down to Mells to comfort Katharine and found her inconsolable ('I have never seen anyone so stunned and shattered. All she wants is to die'). Bravely she rallied for the memorial service and endured the grieving of his friends. Helplessly she looked on as others wove him into the myth of a Lost Generation whose potential the war had denied and who now, serene above the common fray, were joshing with the gods. 'Dearest Katharine, I feel his death to be the most triumphant of all his brilliant achievements', wrote Maurice Baring. Though none would gush more than Churchill for whom Raymond was one of those

> gallant charming figures that flash and gleam amid the carnage – always so superior to it, masters of their souls, disdainful of death and suffering – [who] are an inspiration and an example to us all. He was one of the very best. He did everything easily – I never remember anyone who seemed so independent of

physical and worldly things and yet he enjoyed everything and had an appreciation of life and letters and men and women, and manners and customs refined and subtle to the last degree. Oh how unbearable for you to have lost him![42]

And then there were those like Conrad Russell, who in their own grief sought in proposals to Katharine to recover something of what they had lost.[43] Katharine preferred 'stolen' to lost and, long disenchanted by the war, had little truck with the chivalric embalming of her husband.

Six months later, she was still inconsolable. 'Cicely comes in here and looks at me helplessly, silently but not unsympathetically and I feel the tears slowly welling up and trickle down my face. Now I hate crying in front of C ... it gives me a greater feeling of demoralisation than anything in the world'.[44] In time, she would seek refuge as a nurse at the Duchess of Sutherland's military hospital near Newmarket. 'It is wonderful to be numb to all physical sensation for eight or nine hours on end'. Also numbing were the drugs. 'I have a sweet doctor who orders me a hypo full of something new whenever he sees me and none of your 6ths or 8ths but a glassy [gloosy?] ½ grain'. When the doctor was replaced, she suffered severe withdrawal symptoms ('the after effects of twilight sleep'). 'My nerves were all over the place', she confessed to Diana. 'I couldn't endure and I cried and screamed and raved and wouldn't stay in bed'. Cynthia Asquith found her weeping so uncontrollably that her tears would 'have watered the desert'. A year on and seemingly more settled, Katharine, she felt, had nevertheless changed for ever. 'Regards the rest of her life as a debt to be discharged'. Without Raymond she was but 'a haunting thought'.[45]

~ 34 ~

ENDGAMES

It is a little rash to say so but I think that I'm rather happy here.

Edward Horner[46]

'Coming Home at once', Edward had telegrammed from Cairo and with it Frances's 'plaintive' spirits fell. Egypt, she had hoped, would prove a safe posting from which Edward could see out the war. His return would mean a revival of the games they would play, he to get to the Western Front while she would discreetly lay obstacles in his path. Neither was blind to the other and Edward appreciated too the love that drove his mother's strategies. But nothing would stop him. When he complained that life at the cavalry holding station at Tidworth was 'so monotonous', she seized the initiative drawing on her contacts to arrange for Edward to attend a six-week course at Clare College, Cambridge before joining the staff at Army Headquarters. Only for Edward to conspire to fail the course. Eventually he found a military board willing to pass him fit and by February 1917 he was back with the 18th Hussars in France. Exhausted by her war work and distraught at Edward's relentless desire to risk all, Frances lost the will to fight on. As she admitted to Haldane

> I feel sorry for him; somehow the War seems to have no use for so many and one doesn't know how to keep them and it seems a choice between doing nothing and being killed! But whenever I have moved in any way, it has turned out wrong for him, so I don't like to even if I could now.[47]

Why was Edward so determined? Survivor's guilt to a large degree. By 1917 six of the leading members of the Coterie had been killed, with only Edward and Patrick left. Nor was it what it had been in other ways too. From the trenches Raymond had issued a stirring defence of the Coterie and their disdain for the old enemy, the Souls.

> We do not hunt the carted hares of 30 years ago. We do not ask ourselves and one another and every poor devil we meet 'How do you define Imagination?', or 'What is the difference between talent and genius?', and score an easy triumph by anticipating the answer with some text book formula, originally misconceived by George Wyndham in the early eighties at Glen, and almost certainly misquoted by Margot in the late nineties at the borrowed house of a Frankfurt baronet, not because it was either true or witty or even understood, but because it was a sacred obligation to respect whatever struck the late Sir Charles Tennant as a cut above what he had heard in the night school at Paisley when they taught him double entry – we don't do these things – but don't be discouraged my Diana, for all that. The game is not up. There are brains and brains.[48]

But with most of their friends dead, this has an elegiac feel. In their place came an older, richer, more raffish set and in the forced gaiety of wartime the Coterie had become very fast. Edward wrote to Katharine of 'sensational' developments: 'huge gambling, sieges, seductions and the Coterie enlarged'. Edward craved such excitement and very quickly became victim to its temptations. Eddie Marsh caught a glimpse of this frenetic, destructive life when joining them at Duff Cooper's flat after the opera.

> They began to play *chemin de fer*. I've never seen real gambling before. It was like a Drury Lane melodrama, £100 in the bank, Banco etc. Edward made me sit by him as his mascot, and I was a very good one as long as I'd stay. He was in uproarious spirits and very amusing but infinitely touching and pathetic behind it. I felt it was an *echappée* from the terrible sadness of his life. When I went away he came into the hall and kissed me, which he has never done before – there was such a mutual consciousness of everything between us.[49]

Unlike the pre-war days, he was playing now with people who expected to be paid and soon he was mired in such debt that Diana feared for his honour. In addition to well-tried sources such as Beecham, he prostrated himself before old friends like Patrick, openly admitting that repayment was 'unpayable in Sir John's lifetime'. If this was not humiliating enough, George Vernon's executors were chasing him for unpaid loans. 'I am penniless and gradually becoming a melancholic maniac' he confessed to Patrick. 'I am looking forward to the Front again, as soon as I'm passed fit, as it is better than this life'. Only the army offered an escape from his debtors and the addictions that beset him. It offer him discipline and respect, a chance to break out of the vicious circle of self-loathing that privately ground him down. Within days of arriving, he was rejuvenated by the return to war. 'It is a little rash to say so', he confided to Diana, 'but I think that I'm rather happy here'.[50]

*

One night in early October, Frances was woken to hear that Mells Park was on fire. Despite the pouring rain, the blaze had taken hold (fig. 90). By the time she got there, colliers and farmers from the village were braving the flames to rescue what they could. For three hours 'our people' held back the flames until all their water ran out. The house might have been saved if the fire-brigade from Frome hadn't taken four hours to arrive – and then prove 'quite useless'. Still fourteen thousand books were saved, only to be damaged as they lay on the grass all night in the rain. More successful was the rescue of the Italian pictures; the portraits of Jack's grandparents also 'survived, smelling horribly – nothing will ever destroy them.' Surveying the ruin the next morning, Frances was numbed by the desolation: 'The whole thing has gone and I wonder if we shall ever rebuild? … The house was *too* terrible – an empty blackened shell with fallen keystones and inside piles of debris, like the pictures of the Cloth Hall at Ypres, I can hardly bear to look at it – we feel quite bewildered'.[49]

'I think Mummy and Daddie [sic] will die of it', Katharine reported to Diana. 'Entangled with experts' and with the insurance proving hideously complicated, to say nothing of the well-meaning neighbours visiting to offer redundant opinions on how so much more could have been saved, it all had left her parents at their wits' end. 'Daddie was marvellous for a week but now I think he is a little off his head'. Not so Cicely. 'Old C. had a good effect', admitted Katharine. 'She was so unsentimental that it was quite a relief, though it shocked me a little'.[52] As for Edward, Patrick felt 'it is ghastly for him – he is so ancestral'. Indeed, on reading of the fire in a newspaper Edward laid bare his despair to his mother.

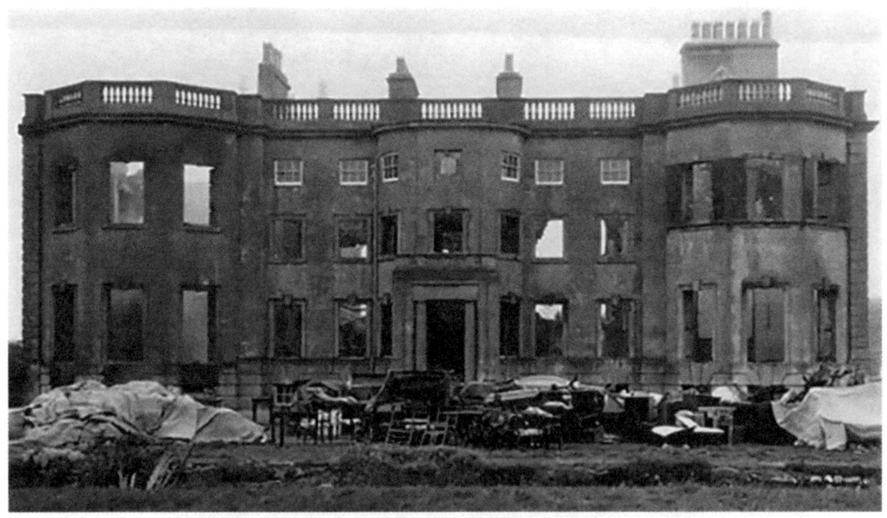

90.   *Mells Park after the fire*

It is the crushing summit of our troubles. Curiously, I used to think of two things as so impossible to bear if they happened that they surely wouldn't. One was Raymond's death and the other was this. It seems wrong to couple them, but somehow I did. There is nothing to say. We cannot contend against our luck. I am glad, you and I, from telling each other lately, know how much we both adored that house.[53]

But he was talking about The Manor House. On hearing that it was the Park he was 'not so dreadfully sorry' and was much more interested in the insurance.

For Frances the Park had meant far more than an insurance cheque. Since she was a young bride, the Park had been a symbol of her identity, sustained in later years by the possibility of their return. And now it was 'gone'. Never would they have the funds to rebuild. So Edward's attitude pained her. Still she was a survivor. Barely a month later a reporter for *Country Life* had been summoned to write a full-length article on 'Mells Manor House, the seat of Sir John Horner'. In this, the ancient roots of the Horners would be entwined with descriptions of a house that was 'an excellent relic of an Elizabethan age… [and] a delight to the antiquarian eye'. There was barely a mention of the Park. For all the shocks of the present, an ancient Mells

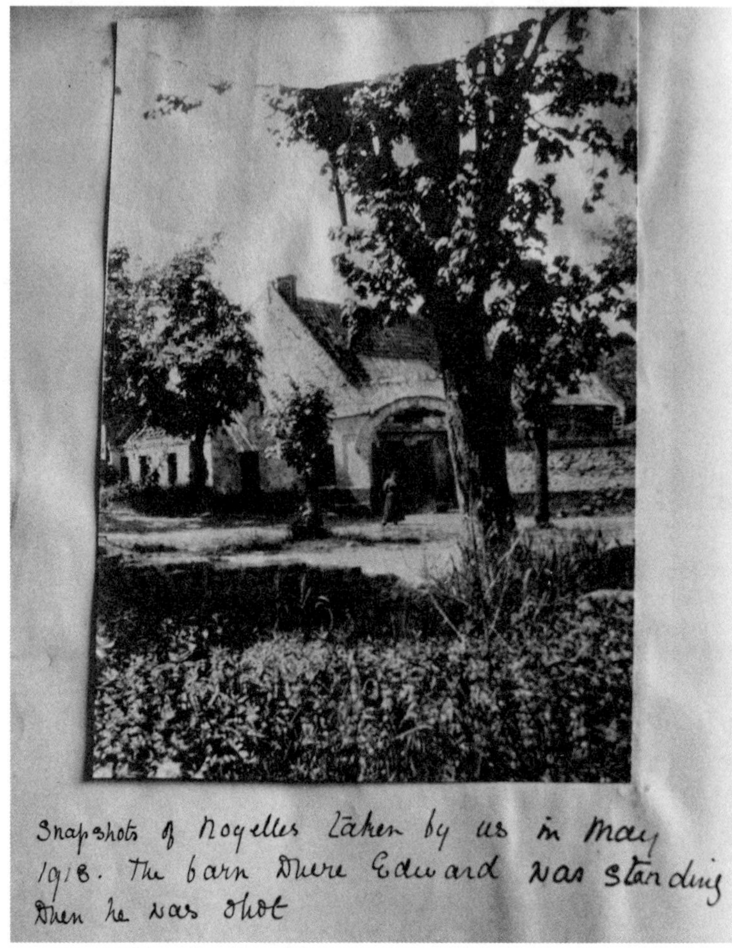

91.   Noyelles, the barn where Edward was shot

still stood strong and unmoved. And with this, Frances, in public at least, would appear unbowed.[54]

*

So too Edward, who, having been granted ten days leave in the aftermath of the fire, had returned to France. By now, in a battlefield dominated by the machine gun and the tank, the cavalry were used as additional infantry. So heavy was the fire he came under as he cleared roads and battery sites that there was talk of Edward getting the Military Cross. At last he seemed to have found his metier.[55]

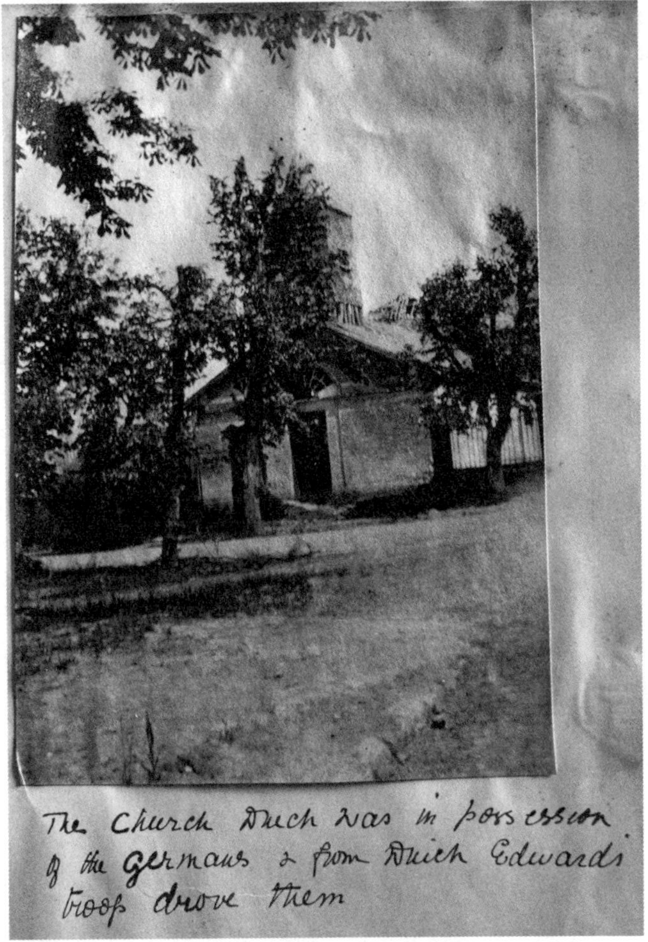

92.   Noyelles, the church

Three days later saw the first attack by tanks *en masse*, in the wake
of which Edward was sent with his squadron to clear out some
Germans holed up in the village of Noyelles (figs 91, 92). The village
was made up of a small square and two parallel roads leading from
it. On the other side lay a Church backing on to the river Scheldt
and the Saint-Quentin canal. With reinforcements due, Edward was
trying to hold the square with a Lewis gun in the face of increas-
ing German numbers. For the most part it was a desultory affair
with spasmodic bursts of gun fire throughout the day. Late in the
afternoon a great cheer went up as the Germans fled the church.

Almost immediately, as Edward stood on a doorway giving orders to his soldiers, a sniper hit him with a single shot to the stomach. He was rushed to a dressing station, but too late to save him. He died just before 8pm on 21 November 1917 and was buried nearby in a roadside cemetery outside Etricourt.[56]

To help her break the news to her parents, Katharine summoned Diana, who rallied despite finding the news 'overwhelmingly dreadful'. For Jack, the loss of his son and heir was a shattering blow. Months later Cynthia Asquith would find 'the poor old boy look[ing] bowed down and stupefied with grief'. Haldane tried to call only to be turned away by Cicely and Katharine as their mother was 'having the opiate'. When Frances recovered she wrote to Ettie with the news. Yet all she could manage was 'There is nothing to say, is there?' That Edward had been at Mells only ten days before intensified the sense of loss. 'I don't believe I realised quite how much my life was colonized, indeed built on the thoughts of Edward's presence and Edward's future', she admitted to Haldane. 'I never conceived that Jack and I would be left outliving him – and with no particular meaning in the future and Mells having gone too, which I didn't mind when Edward was there to raise a new Mells ... but now it all seems so futile. I really can't seem to live at all ... anyhow you have been a beloved angel to me always and even when I say "d___ your self-righteousness"'.[57]

Such flickers of spirit Frances had to draw on as she faced the community around her. 'The people here are frightened of me', she told Diana. 'I know so well what they feel and how relieved [they are] if I look the same'. Without a body to bury she had to endure 'a horrible service'. She could sense nothing of Edward in the church. Instead she would seek him out in the red court, the bath and the loggia – 'all of them seem to be full of his splendour'. And then there was Katharine 'who is so thin and has so much on those young shoulders'. Her return to London left Frances lonely and even more so when Katharine moved to a hospital in Saint-Omer (fig. 93). Hence Frances's extraordinary request of Diana: 'I wish you could come and be my daughter, I should be very happy darling'. In a subsequent letter she declared

> I do love you very much – and with a love that has its roots
> in depths that can never change. Besides you know and

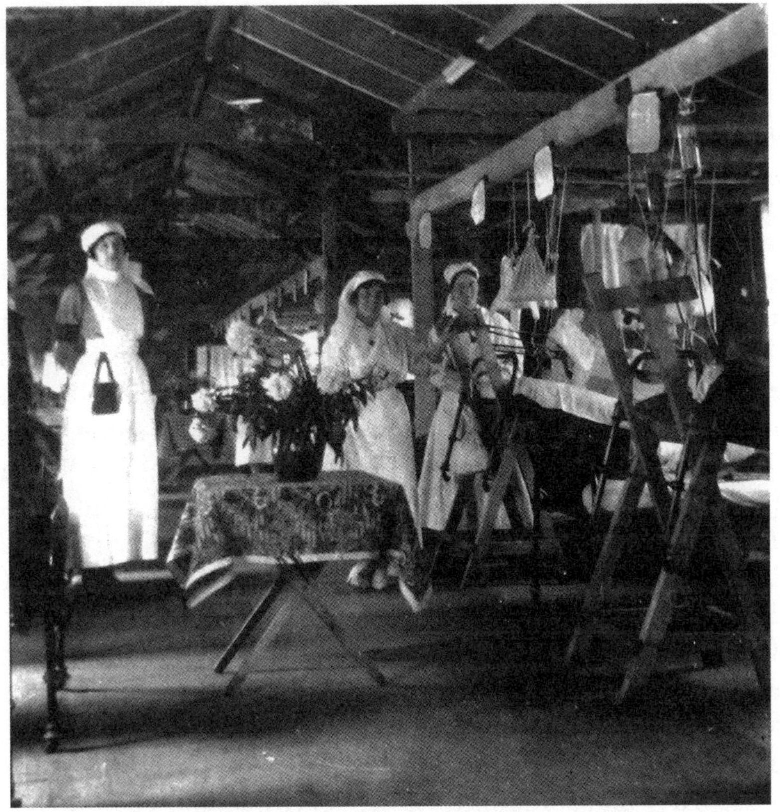

93.   *Katharine, on the left, nursing at Saint-Omer*

understand – so few people do – and Mells is to you as well as
to me so soaked and permeated with those beloveds... I have
hardly been able to bear it this time and yet the homing instinct
is so strong that I cannot bear to be anywhere else. I am afraid I
have grown to be a very old woman in one year.[58]

For all her despair, this was a return to old habits.

'Oh God, the unutterable cruelty of it!' wrote Cynthia Asquith
in her diary on first hearing the news. 'Katharine's one anchor in
this world, and he has been so wonderful to her since Raymond's
death!'[59] In departing for France Katharine was not trying to escape
her grief for Edward. Rather, like her mother, she was seeking him
out; not in rooms at Mells, but in the battlefield where he felt so
alive. So one night she was taken by Duff in a car almost to the Front

Line: 'Drove along rain washed roads and stars and the guns making flashes like summer lightening all over the sky. There were Verey lights and great noises in the distance – we were only a little way from the trenches … seeing … what R and E must have seen every night… Then I broke down'.[60]

His friends preferred to seek Edward in myth. Vain and weak he may have been but not in public memory. Diana, who knew him as well as any, would note that 'he had a lot of melancholy woven into his *joie de vivre*. He could not bear to be humdrum. He thought life could do more than it can, and that it had not given him much except a loving family and friends.' The wallowing in self-pity, the impulsive acts, his emotional dependence on others: these would all be forgotten. Instead, the Edward that survived was his Romantic free spirit, the exuberant stylishness, the self-parody amid the recklessness and scrapes, and the charm and good looks that rarely failed to disarm. There was decency too and a generosity of spirit (and pocket) as well as the loyalty of a trusted friend. Nor did it matter that in Eddie Marsh's sad verdict Edward had 'no achievement other than his gallant death'. Edward was in Duff Cooper's memoirs 'a glorious relic of a glorious past' whose death represented an end of an era. Some twenty years later Viola Parsons reminisced on the Coterie: 'They had something of the versatility and vigour, and also the fate of the Young Elizabethans, or King Charles' cavaliers. They were the most dazzling of the lost generation who would now [1937], had they lived, be at the head of the country…Edward Horner the real glory of the lot'.[61]

Part Ten

Resurrection

[The war has not] left us maimed and broken… Since then a
new generation has sprung up with new hopes and gifts – young
life is all around us with its wonderful freedom and energy, and
all the possibilities the future holds for its children.

Frances Horner[1]

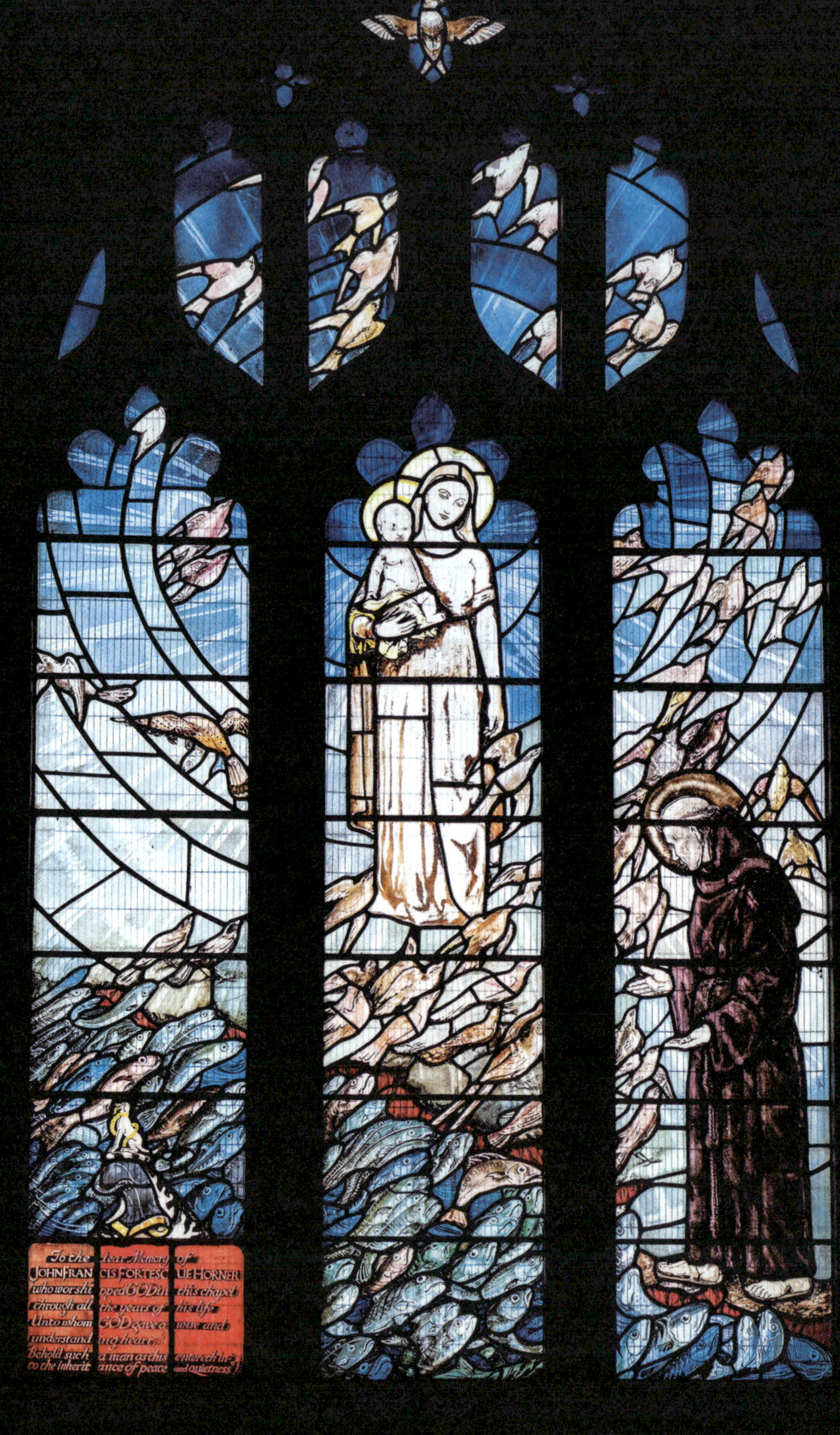

To the dear Memory of
JOHN FRANCIS FORTESCUE HORNER
who worshipped GOD in this chapel
through all the years of his life
Unto whom GOD gave a wise and
understanding heart
Behold such a man as this entereth into the inheritance of peace and quietness

35

THE OLD ORDER PASSETH AWAY

I had not remembered the charm and beauty of this place… the house is full of the heavenly fragrance of stocks, tobacco plants, lavender and roses – a delicious house to rest and dream. Full of comfort, beautiful things, sweet smelling flowers, peaches ripening on old walls, gentle flittings and hummings & pretty grandchildren [bathing with their grandmother, as Brutus, the Great Dane, looked on]. But under all this, the sadness & melancholy of it all – Both the sons dead, one lying in the little churchyard next to the House, carried away at sixteen by Scarlet Fever, the other sleeping in France as does the husband of the best loved daughter of the house, Katharine Asquith – Both their swords are hanging in the beautiful little Gothic Church beside inscriptions of long dead Horners who died in their beds.[2]

So Clemmie Churchill found Mells, as the last great decisive battles were raging on the Western Front. Yet behind this idyll of fortitude lay despair and anger, not least at the silence expected when grief was universal. As Katharine admitted, 'A more decrepit trio that Mother, "Daddie" and I it is hardly possible to imagine'. In particular she was 'in a state' over her mother, for whom depression was taking traditional form. 'Death walked into my life in a very real and terrible way when I was eighteen', Frances was reminding DD, 'and I think ever since has been a familiar presence to me. One after another of those I loved most in the world were struck down and some in such a terrible way. … Mother's death, old as she was, was so terrible –and so

94.   Window commemorating Jack in St Andrew's Church, Mells, commissioned 1927, designed by William Nicholson

was Amy's and so were my boys'.[3] Katharine in turn was downcast at her prospect of 'asceticism and domesticity'. Inevitably, they got on each other's nerves. 'I had a slight argument with Mother during the afternoon which always upsets me. She was testy because C[icely] had come up for the day. That always spells Trouble'.[4] For Frances too. Cicely's world was not her world and Cicely's assertiveness wearisome. 'I long for you to be sitting in the garden and just pottering about' was addressed to Katharine. A little to her surprise Frances developed an easier rapport with her younger daughter – founded on shared cultural values laced with the latest gossip and given energy with frequent visits from the grandchildren. Instinctive differences would remain to trip them up occasionally. 'I might seem to fail in the sympathetic and emotional side', Frances admitted after one spat, 'only because I want to give you the best of my brains'.[5] As she would find out, her daughter was quite capable of finding her own solutions. Save for one as over everything Raymond's death hung in the silence. Friendships too were strained by the conflict. Katharine had long been a good friend of Cynthia Asquith and in the early years of the war she had joined Cynthia on visits to D.H. Lawrence for soliloquies on mines and miners ('punctuated by intelligent, listening remarks from Katharine …Katharine loved him'). But Katharine disapproved of Cynthia taking lovers while her husband, Beb, was at the front and in turn by 1916 Cynthia was lamenting the loss of the 'lovelorn, moonlit, remote Yeatsy' Katharine of her youth.[6] After the war, they would rarely meet up.

For Frances nothing symbolised the loss of the old pre-war world more than the ruin of Mells Park – looking now 'as desolate as Ypres'. Sitting among the destruction, she could only ruminate on 'the vanity of all human desires'.[7] London Society too had lost much of its allure. In many ways, in its elaborate artificialities and hierarchies, it was a bluff waiting to be called. But *entrée* into it had been a driving force of her life and one to which she had dedicated her children. She would have to adjust to a world of democracies in which the likes of Jennie Churchill (Winston's mother) were no longer celebrities. Or indeed alive. In a gruesome twist of fate, Lady Churchill, while staying with the Horners in 1921, fell down the polished stairs at Mells, breaking her leg. For the vanity of too-high heels, she would pay a terrifying price. Developing gangrene once back in London, she died soon after the amputation of her leg.[8]

Economics too had returned to wreak havoc with Frances's dreams. The war had hit Jack very hard. 'The poor dear old man is very aged', noted Conrad Russell. 'When I was here last he could walk ten miles and went shooting in the snow. Now he suffers from his heart and hardly stirs out. I cannot want him to live much longer'.[9] However, before Jack died he was determined to remove the burden of debt he had inherited on the estate and could never shake off. There were Edward's debts to pay off as well. Hence, more of William Graham's Old Masters were sold at Christie's in 1919. So too some of the Horner library, there being no room for all the books after the fire. Eliminating the family debts would take something more drastic: the sale of 4300 acres and twenty-two farms – all in all, two thirds of his estate. There had been a brief boom in estate prices after the war and by 1921 over a quarter of England had been sold. Jack delayed his sale until 1923 and the price suffered accordingly. He also sold off mineral rights. Much later, several huge limestone quarries were developed on this land. Warning sirens from these quarries sound out over The Manor House to this day as a reminder of the cost of this economy. More immediately, without land their rental income fell sharply. Still Haldane, whose lawyer brother Willie had overseen the sales, was much more upbeat.

> You have now a small but compact Mells Estate, with all the mortgages, which have drowned the old property, paid off. Your own mortgage of £2000 will also be provided for and paid off & there should be a small surplus. You should all be – with care – better off and free from anxiety. It has been – this plan – as far as can be seen a real success, & the thing is to keep within the new margin, & avoid anxiety for the future.

And while Jack insisted that Katharine was being profligate ('Calculations with Daddie a few days ago which seemed to prove that I could never, never, possibly live on my income! I know calculations are misleading…'), Haldane was more reassuring. As he explained to Frances:

> Anyhow, you may feel comfortable about the future of your two daughters, so far as worldly affairs are concerned. All the debts are paid off, & the value [remaining] is £170,000 to divide between them after your time, about £70,000 of it independent

of land altogether. Your modest £2000 per year of income only seems restricted because a lot of domestic charges are provided from it. You will have to dip, but you may do so – for there will be a great surplus of capital left. You are better off than I am, & yet I do not worry.

Frances nevertheless did continue to worry, even after 38 in his will left her £5000 (the equivalent of £290,000 today). She in turn would leave £40,000. She was not a hoarder but having been born rich and then suffering decades of precarious finances while living in a world of rich friends, it was not an anxiety that would ever leave her. And her security came at a price. For with the loss of land on this scale, the Horners' status as great landowners in the locality was in decline. Without an heir and great estates, 'an ancient order' was disappearing fast.[10]

To the sadness of who and what had been lost was added anxiety of what was coming. Accelerated by the war, the old world was all too quickly giving way to the new. Frances, for so long the advocate of reform in Mells, ironically had, post war, given in to nostalgia. 'Up to a few years ago', she recalled

> the village was in happy oblivion of the nineteenth century – its ugly buildings, its cheap economies in iron and slate, and all the vulgarities of speech and thought; but schools and telephones and district councils and all that we dignify by the name of progress, have begun to make themselves felt, and though no doubt the standard of living has been raised, the beauty and simplicity of life and thought and surroundings have been much impaired.

This was partly generational. Frances deplored the impact of the motor car and dreaded driving Jack. Katharine on the other hand adored her car, 'the Albert', which she would drive in all weathers with enthusiasm if not expertise. Somehow she managed to hold up 'the whole traffic of Piccadilly [causing] a block which I believe lasted until dinner time.' Not that this daunted her. That winter 'much against Mother's advice', Katharine set off from London for Mells. Amid 'storms of unprecedented violence', floods, rain that 'blinded me' and wind which hurled us from side to side', she made it through triumphant.[11]

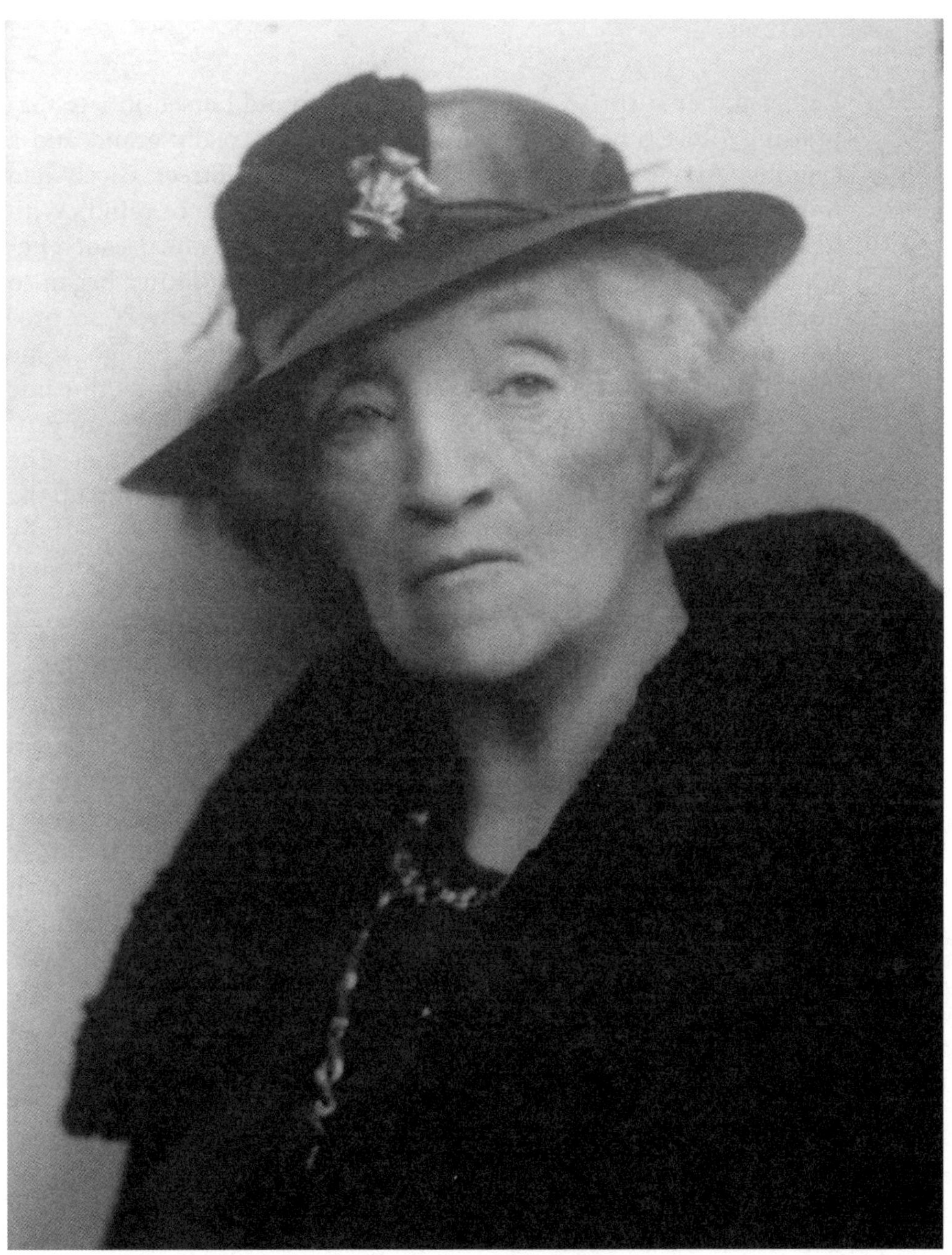

95.   *Frances, her face now 'a scene of savage grandeur',
according to Cynthia Asquith*

*

Rather to her surprise Katharine (fig. 96) found herself in late 1923 praising 'old C's behaviour' and declaring her 'really grand and a standby'. Arriving 'by chance' at Lower Berkeley Street, Cicely had missed Katharine's letter warning of 'Mother's state of mind'. With her sister something of an unguided missile, Katharine dreaded her reaction when she heard the news. 'After dinner Mother began to unfold the tragedy. Unfortunately her preliminaries were so prolonged and impressive that C formed the notion that I had got some unmentionable and mortal disease. When the hideous truth came out, she burst out laughing, partly from relief and partly from genuine amazement. Nothing could have been better for Mother'. The sisters met up the next day in Selfridges and, while weighing up the merits of suitcases, 'she touched lightly and I must say quite tactfully on the subject, pluming herself a little that her behaviour without priming had been all I could have hoped for'.[12]

The subject that caused Frances such distress was Katharine's reception into the Roman Catholic Church. What had taken Frances by surprise had, in truth, been long in the coming. From childhood Katharine had held a keen religious interest. As early as 1906 Frances and Raymond had joined forces to dissuade her from converting to Catholicism. 'Frances is profoundly right not to let you become a Papist', he had pronounced. 'A priest meddles with your life infinitely more than a family … Still I would rather have you a Papist than an actress'. This flippant aside suggested that he thought her motivation primarily one of youthful rebellion against a controlling mother. Yet four years later, finding himself in Chartres, his lighting of 'a candle for you before the shrine of the Black Virgin' suggested her interest had lingered.[13] Spending Easter 1915 with her in-laws, she engaged in a discussion with Asquith on the Resurrection, admitting that her own ideas on it were 'rather fluid' and wanting to crystallise them into something more robust. She had long ceased to attend the Anglican offering at Mells; indeed her parents attended only rarely and largely out of duty.

The war, of course, changed everything and yet nothing. Yes, without Raymond Katharine felt rudderless, but if anything the war damaged her faith rather than sharpened it. Her immediate resort was to the goddess of morphine and the promise of oblivion: with 'morphia… I get so dizzy with staring into myself. How awful thinking is or talking or anything that involves an activity of the mind'. Music was a healthier solace. Toiling at the piano every day produced little improvement but 'all the fun of the novitiate' together with the occasional 'moment of rapture and escape'. She sang Parry's *Blest Pair of Sirens* in choirs conducted by Vaughan Williams (with the rehearsals attended by Peter Warlock – and occasionally by Holst who proved a disaster). It was not a great step but a revealing one for her to 'believe one might approach religion in the similar way'. One 'gets the certainty of its being right because it is so beautiful that there is no question about it'.[14]

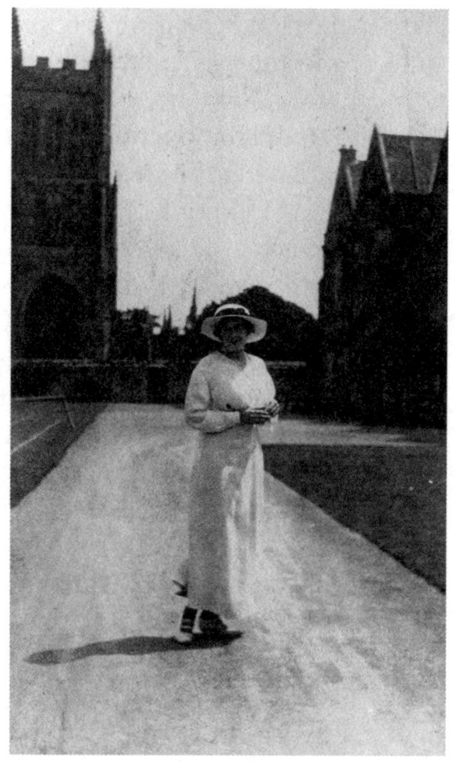

96.   *Katharine outside The Manor House*

Providing certainty of a different kind was Hilaire Belloc. Academic, journalist, writer, Belloc was both polymath and polemicist, most especially as a vociferous champion of the Catholic faith. In his company conversation would range far and wide – politics, religion, history, literature, and social reform – in which he would irritate and inspire in equal measure. Intellectually attractive he may have been but Katharine found him daunting too. She had met him through Edward before the war, but it would take a car crash to break through her reserve. Belloc was at the wheel driving Katharine and her daughter Perdita in May 1919 when the extravagance of his argument distracted Belloc from the cyclist in front of him. Luckily the cyclist survived. As for the damage to the car, it was, Katharine quipped, 'an expensive and dangerous way to get to know your friends'. Soon they were inseparable – not as lovers but as companions who instinctively understood each other in their sadness.[15]

With the loss of his wife and of his elder son Louis in the war, he was 'unhappy in the way I am', Katharine would explain. Interestingly the only other person who she felt appreciated her was her mother 'but even she understands more by sympathy and making comparisons than from having the same personal experiences.'

Crucially talking to Belloc brought 'relief' and made Katharine 'less desperate – partly because you are so sure of certain things'. Much as (though in a different way) Raymond too had provided her with certainty and security. Amid the destruction and despair of a broken Europe and with the prospect of more chaos to come, 'dogma alone remains' declared Belloc. Faith, not reason, would provide shelter and a home for the spirit, in the form of the moral authority provided by the Catholic Church. He would even promise that faith with its belief in eternity ('we are not creatures of pain and loss but their victims for a time') would see her recover the company of those she had lost. 'All will be restored to you.'[16]

However Belloc did not press her. Explaining that 'faith is not taught. It is inhabited and breathed in,' he left her to take the plunge.[17] Other friends were more assertive. The early decades of the twentieth century witnessed a remarkable number of conversions especially within the social and literary elites, among them Eric Gill, G. K. Chesterton, Ronnie Knox, Compton Mackenzie, Maurice Baring, Graham Greene and Evelyn Waugh. They would help to make Catholicism not just the religion of the Irish working class or the exclusive terrain of the few Old Catholic families that had hung on after the Reformation. Instead, Belloc saw the opportunity to make Catholicism 'chic', 'aristocratic and not suburban', a giddy world to be immortalised in *Brideshead Revisited*. By the 1930s there would be twelve thousand converts a year in England alone.[18]

Converts were much more active proselytisers than those, like Belloc, born in the Faith. As Katharine discovered at a 'picnic dinner' with her friend Maurice Baring: 'Ah by God he very nearly succeeded in converting me. I wavered.' If it hadn't been for the imminent arrival of other guests, 'they would probably have got me. I am like a shuttlecock'. A walking holiday in the Pyrenees with Diana saw her in Lourdes praying for a conversion, as if hoping for the decision to be made for her. Katharine hesitated for so long that her eventual conversion took many of her Catholic friends by surprise. The decisive factor was her introduction to Father Vincent McNabb

– vigorous advocate of the simple life, denouncer of industrialisation, and crucially a great friend of Belloc. He became her latest 'great standby. I worship him' wrote Katharine. Under his 'instigation', she steeled herself to tell her family of her 'Catholic intentions'.[19]

Frances took the news as anyone (except Katharine) would have predicted – badly. Reluctant to worry her ailing husband, Frances got Asquith to summon his daughter-in-law to The Wharf. As it turned out, they were both spared this ordeal, Katharine discovering as the children piled into the car that Helen had succumbed to measles and a temperature of 104 degrees. The next morning her father had a fall and Mascot the dog became seriously ill. For Frances there would only be one cause. 'My Mother is weeping to Haldane over my conversion', wrote Katharine in despair to Diana, 'and will arrive here soon after dining with him and say I am mismanaging both Helen and Mascot and attribute it somehow to the priests'. With her mother insisting, lest it kill him, that Jack should not know, Christmas was spent as if nothing had happened and Christmas Day would see Katharine accompany her mother to Westminster Abbey. Hurt and surprised by her mother's reaction, Katharine sought to take stock.

Mother is sweet too. It is very genuine and bred of affection for me. It's so awful that one only hurts the people who love me… Truly it never crossed my mind when I embarked on it [Catholicism] that anyone would mind or take any interest. Possibly a faint scorn from one or two friends …It is Mother who has derailed my common sense.

The fact is I have made my peace with God and I am going to be a Catholic & Mother regards it as an awful tragedy and treats me as if I was committing a really shameful crime. She talks about 'your father' (always the worst sign) and altering of wills and complete separation between us…. I have committed myself pretty far, so it is difficult to draw back. Besides I don't want to.

It really might be incest. What did the Victorians do to their brains – and how, how, how does it affect her relations with me as she knows I love her. She might become a Mormon if she liked. I wouldn't be different to her. I didn't reckon with this complication with Mother.[20]

To a degree, this is disingenuous. Frances's reaction to such a prospect had been clearly demonstrated in 1906. And if Katharine really felt her mother wouldn't mind, why did she keep it so secret? What she couldn't have foreseen was the scale of Frances's upset.

'Yes it is true about K and I won't deny that it was a great blow to both Jack and me', confessed Frances to Ettie. 'I think it such an extraordinary back movement. Can't imagine how Katharine with her clear mind and her historical knowledge can have found any attraction intellectually in that religion'. There can have been no greater measure of Frances's embarrassment than that Ettie should have only heard five years after the event. Some seventy years later Helen would view her grandmother's response as 'conventional prejudice… pretty common in those days… Catholicism was un-English, superstitious, the religion of servants, not of educated sophisticated people. It did one harm socially … These disadvantages really did exist [but were] not catastrophic'. For one who had fought so hard to make it in Society, it was only to be expected that Frances would be 'very sad at Julian's religious *handicap*!!' As if to emphasise the point, Beb and Oc Asquith, as trustees of a fund established after their brother, Raymond's, death to support the education of his son, refused to pay for Julian's education should he go to Ampleforth, the leading Catholic boarding school. Worse, they threatened to make him a ward of court: 'this can be done at once' wrote their father. After sharing the legal advice with Frances, Henry Asquith sought to play for time. Frances, fearful of a scandal and a 'rupture' pleaded with Katharine 'don't force this on him'. Agree to Winchester and 'I will agree to it and get HHA to – and then this needn't happen'. Then ratcheting up the pressure on her daughter, she wrote

> You know I've never let it [her conversion] make a difference though of course I minded it but I felt I had no right to interfere. [Yet now Katharine is denying Julian] the *best* education… then I feel that I should have to go against you, to the anguish of us both.

Two weeks later she and Asquith met with the Cardinal, who was a little too 'suave' for Frances's liking but quite flexible on Julian's schooling provided Winchester provided access to priests as at Eton and Harrow. Yet in the face of all of this, Katharine still held her ground.[21] Sanity was only restored when Asquith finally stepped in on her behalf and Julian was sent to Ampleforth. Asquith seems to

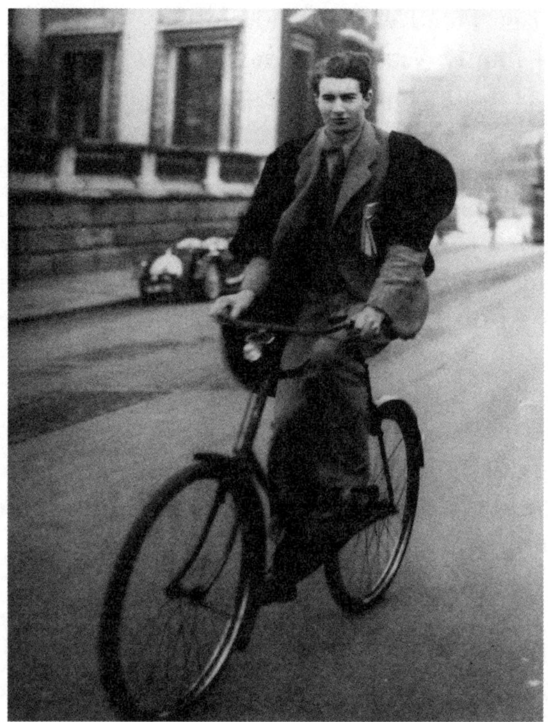

97.   *Julian as an undergraduate in Oxford*

have been won over after a private meeting with the Headmaster of Ampleforth who assured him that Julian would be prepared for Oxford and Greats – to Asquith the more important family 'tradition'. Ironically, the Headmaster immediately hired a top Winchester don to secure this – which he did (fig. 97).[22]

With the loss of an heir and the Horner name, the prospect of Mells becoming a catholic house was, in Frances's eyes, a mortal blow for a family tradition dating back four hundred years to the Reformation. One could, of course, argue that local tradition preceded the Horners and that this represented a return to an older past. Nor were past Horners immune. In the seventeenth and eighteenth centuries there had been considerable support for the Stuart cause, symbolised by the icon of the veil that Mary, Queen of Scots had worn on the scaffold and which was later given to Sir John Hippisley by Pope Pius VI. Nearer in time, Jack's father had been an enthusiastic supporter of Tractarianism. But such subtleties passed

Frances by when faced with social embarrassment. In this matter she remained firmly Victorian, viewing the flurry of conversions of the young as modern parents might fear a cult. At the heart of it she placed Belloc. He had always been a figure of hate in her eyes. Invited to Mells before the war, he was barely in the door before he had denounced his hosts for 'stealing' their estates from the Abbot of Glastonbury at the Reformation and thereafter he would refer to Frances as 'hag Horner'.[23] Both she and Asquith took grave exception to Belloc's presuming to put up memorial plaques to Edward and Raymond in the Catholic cathedrals of Cambrai and Amiens (although Frances in 1925 did travel with Katharine to see them; fig. 100). Belloc's brash triumphalism stirred up long discarded evangelical loyalties in her. While she lived, she was determined that Mells would remain firmly protestant. As for Belloc, he would be *persona non grata* at Mells until her death.

Nevertheless, her closest friends urged reconciliation. 'Katharine's going over [to Catholicism agreed Haldane] has something tragic about it – a doubtful act of judgement as regards both time & eternity. Now that it is done the wise thing to do is to make the best of it'. DD went further:

> I can imagine what you and Jack must have felt about it from different angles. I suspect you mind what I should – shackles on thought, priest's influence, the bar to intercourse; and yet, and yet, I think even with that I should feel glad for her. It is so awful to live without the spirit; and it comes in many different ways. I feel so intensely that no religion and no philosophy and no science can interpret the absolute truth and that all forms of belief are fragmented visions. But the great thing is to have *some* vision … She is nearer the truth now.

Frances promised to 'try not to be unreasonable about it: she is a child of such love and such close ties to us, it amazes me! But I want to prevent it being a war between us if I can'. Katharine saw this too. At the height of the row and with her children all ill with measles, she distinguished between 'Mother so hostile to my preoccupations and so very sweet too about my maternal troubles'.[24]

Then there came another sweetener. Conrad Russell was with Katharine when the news came through that Asquith had accepted an earldom – a title her son would now inherit. While she made a show of disquiet ('Raymond would have stopped this – he didn't like being ridiculous'), she was more amused by the reactions of others. 'Conrad treating it as a disgrace through which I must be supported… The Russells have such a stratum of snobbishness it is funny to see it come out so perversely'. Alongside this were the Horner aunts, dismissive of a Liberal being ennobled: 'too much good fortune' and somehow a point of shame. Not so Maurice Baring who couldn't resist stirring: 'what fun to be the mother of a Papist peer'. Overriding all of these, however, was her mother's 'frank pleasure', as the girl from Glasgow became the grandmother of an earl.[25]

*

In March 1927 Jack finally died. He had been ill for three years and before that depressed since Edward's death. As their marriage began, so it ended, with his suffering 'bad fits' and physically he was often beyond Frances to manage. Katharine, who loved him dearly, found him 'quite frightening' by the end and she marvelled at her mother's stoicism and courage.[26] It was left to Conrad to recapture the man who had been lost:

> He had a perfect disposition and character. He didn't like people like Violet, Duchess of Rutland and said before ladies she was a bloody old bitch and he hoped she would break her neck. It was only the truth, and people who disliked the truth thought him rough and discourteous. But his character was essentially sweet and kind and he was a scholar and a gentleman – both rare things.[27]

With him an old order passed away.

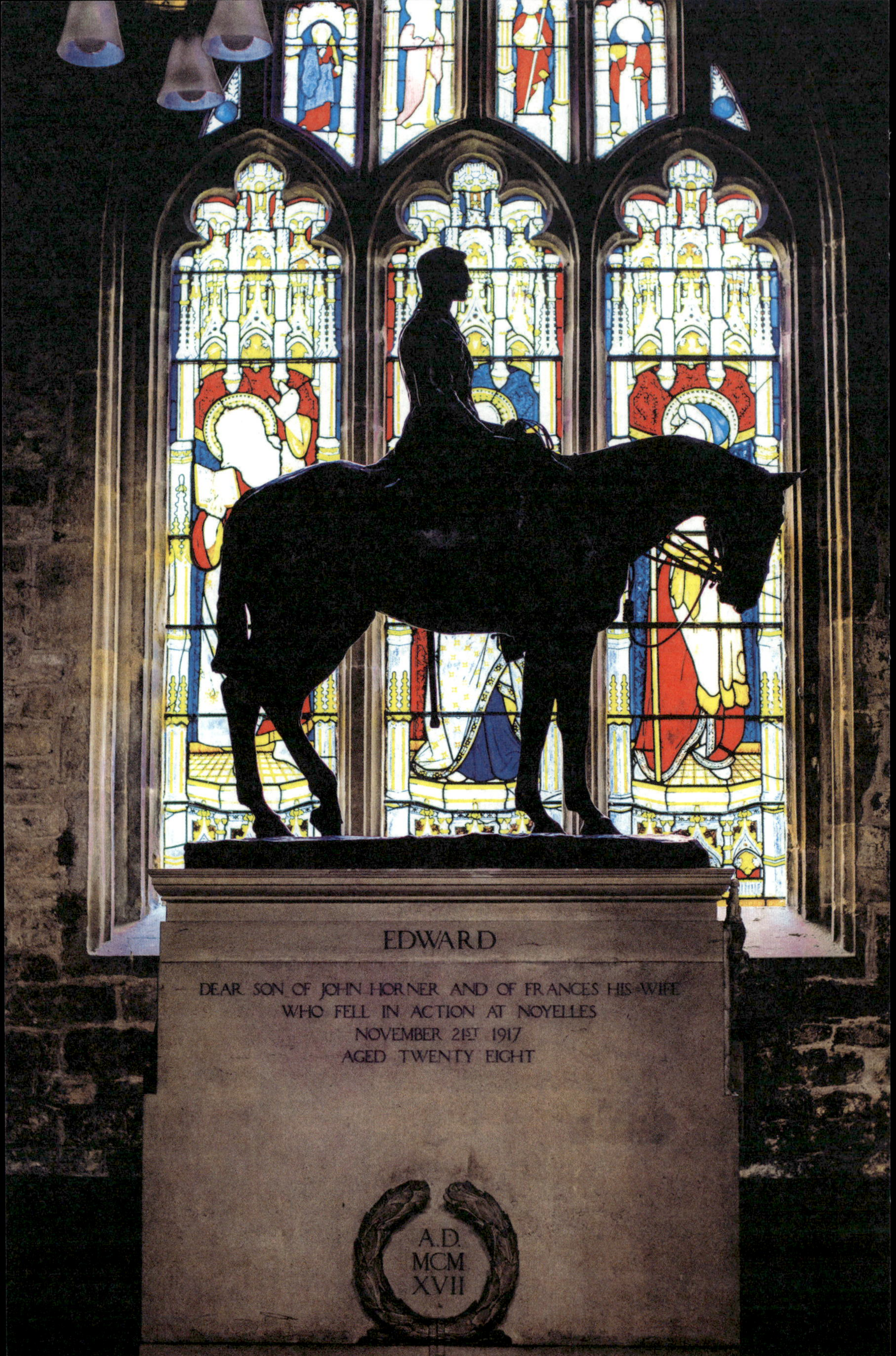

EDWARD

DEAR SON OF JOHN HORNER AND OF FRANCES HIS WIFE
WHO FELL IN ACTION AT NOYELLES
NOVEMBER 21ST 1917
AGED TWENTY EIGHT

A.D.
MCM
XVII

36

COUNTER ATTACK

Mells has cast such a spell of memories about me I cannot accli-matise myself elsewhere! I have become very creep mouse.

Frances Horner[28]

With a certain amount of artistic and literary culture [Frances Horner could] manage society, friends, a family, garden and household with ease and success [while having] few doubts; perhaps at times she has wondered what life comes to, but whatever the results of her questioning, she has faced it bravely, and although she has had great losses… she remains unsub-dued and undaunted.

Ottoline Morrell[29]

Frances was never one for decay and despair. Defiantly she would insist that the war has not 'left us maimed and broken… Since then a new generation has sprung up with new hopes and gifts – young life is all around us with its wonderful freedom and energy, and all the possibilities the future holds for its children'.[30] Moreover Frances was determined that she and Mells would be part of that future. First though she wanted to secure the memory of the war on her terms. Unlike her daughter, she had no time for the notion of the war as a waste or pointless. Edward, his friends and the villagers in Mells had through their shared sacrifice, nobly faced, won victory for civ-ilisation and humanity. Relief from the horror and loss would be sought through public memorial. So, fresh from his triumph of the

98.   The Memorial to Edward in Mells Church: the figures by Sir Alfred Munnings, plinth by Sir Edward Lutyens; lettering by Eric Gill

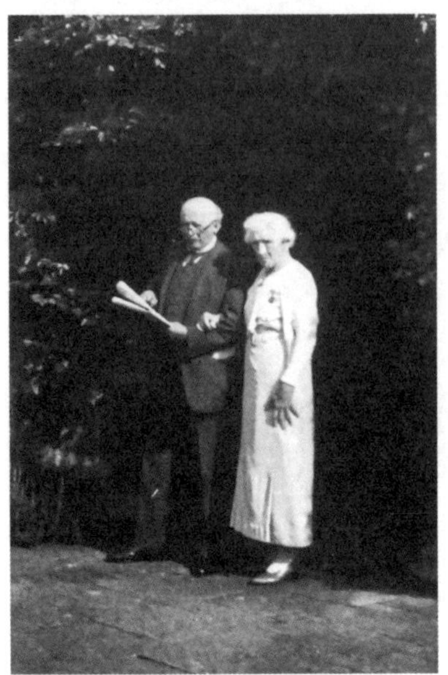

99.   *Lutyens and Frances
in the garden at Mells*

Cenotaph, Lutyens was summoned down to Somerset to commemorate the dead of Mells (figs 99, 101). With St George slaying the dragon surmounting plaques bearing the names of those killed, the themes of heroic sacrifice and patriotic duty were echoed in the public epitaph (composed by Robert Bridges and carved by Eric Gill).

We died in strange lands
Facing the dark cloud of war
And this stone is raised to us
In the land of our delight.

From the Church of St Andrew rang out again the eight church bells and their carillon of chimes, which had lain silent during the war. With their restoration and repair Frances declaimed not just the return of peace but victory.[31]

As for her personal loss, the war had allowed Edward to become immortalised as her Pre-Raphaelite knight (fig. 98). To seal the memory, she commissioned Sir Alfred Munnings to sculpt a life-sized bronze of Edward on a charger, standing on a plinth by Lutyens. On the plinth lay Edward's gauntlets – icons for veneration – and an inscription from Shelley's elegy on the death of Keats: 'He hath outsoared the shadows of our night'. Seeing it for the first time reduced her to tears. But she quickly recovered to demand why the rider and horse had their heads bowed. She wanted them upright and eager to embrace the day: 'I want it to be the morning glory', she told Munnings and so it was. Every inch the triumphant warrior, a knight errant for modern times, Edward's monument dominates the church at Mells just as it in turn dominated The Manor House, where he had been so loved and where she felt him still.

Edward's death and the imminent end of the Horners' hold on Mells after more than four-hundred years saw Frances adapt the church to sustain the memory of an ancient familial tradition – becoming a public record of private griefs. In memory of Jack, William Nicholson designed a window portraying St Francis. Opposite the peacock memorial to Laura, Eric Gill carved an austere inscription, suitably in Latin, to Raymond. While by the door is Frances's striking tapestry of an angel whose huge red wings stretched out in protection of her young. Drawn for her by Burne-Jones, it remains one of Frances's finest pieces, if long after its completion also one of her most poignant.[32] Given their shared love of Wagner, it is not surprising that a performance of *Parsifal* in 1920 should stir memories of Edward.[33] That drive to possess the memory is there too in her response to Belloc's presumptuous memorial tablet to

SOUVENEZ VOUS DE EDWARD WILLIAM HORNER, DE MELLS dans la Comté de Somerset Lieutenant au 18ème Regt. de Hussars Anglais. Tombé au champ d'honneur en defendant Noyelles, le 21 Novembre, 1917. SON CORPS ENSEVELI À FINS REPOSE LOIN DES SIENS MAIS EN TERRE AMIE.

100.   *Memorial plaque to Edward, installed by Hilaire Belloc in Cambrai Cathedral*

Edward in Cambrai Cathedral (fig. 100). Dutifully she went in 1925 with Katharine (and Lutyens and Haldane) to see it, but afterwards sought out the village of Noyelles where Edward had been killed. This was the site which counted for her. 'I was glad I had gone for I loved seeing the little village, every yard of which I knew'. Here she could imagine the 'troops clattering up and down' the paved roads and Edward very much in his element at the last. The relief this pilgrimage brought led her to a remarkable admission: 'I often feel about Edward as if he were [now] safe – I never felt him very safe in this world'.[34]

Back in the world of Mells, after Jack's death she found herself taking on the responsibilities of the squire and immersing herself in the affairs of the local community – in a way that her pre-war self could never have imagined. By the 1930s she was decrying modernity and its assault on ancient ways, much as the Horners had when she first descended on them with her 'new' ideas in the 1880s. Fearing not the 'jam-pottism' that Laura once decried, Frances threw herself into reinvigorating the morale of the village. She proved tireless in

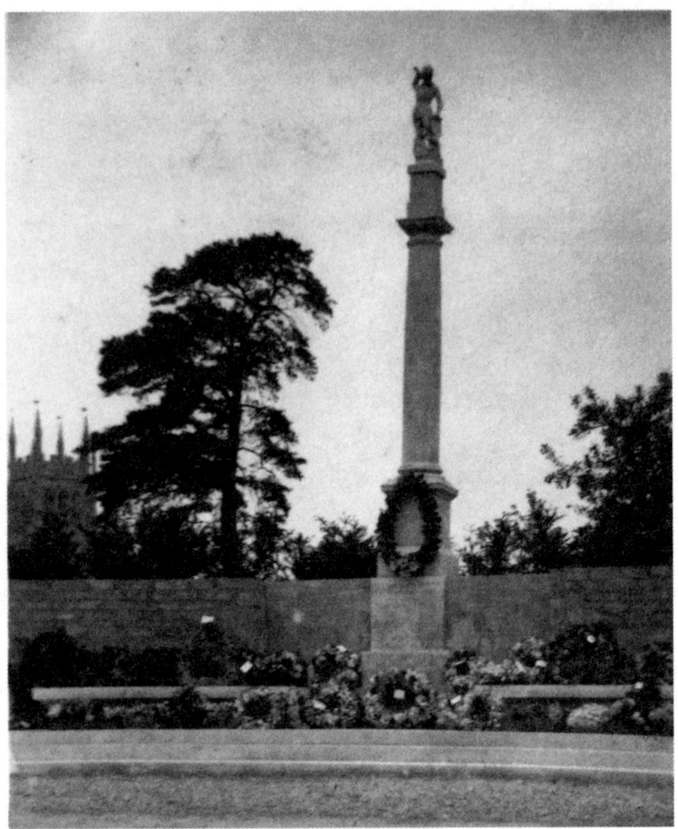

101.   The war memorial at Mells, designed by Lutyens

her support of local events and herself contributed occasional lectures – mainly historical in which enthusiasm outstretched veracity but entertained nonetheless.[35] The war with its equality of sacrifice seems at last to have broken down the mutual suspicion that had dogged her relationship with the village, making her more appreciative as well as more appreciated. Together they drew on that timelessness of Mells which 'sustains and consoles'.

Nothing would symbolise the return of pre-war Mells more than the restoration of Mells Park. As ever, Frances turned to Lutyens. He proved unusually reluctant; recognising privately, 'they will never pay'. Salvation came in the form of Aggie's daughter, Pamela, who had married the rich Liberal Chancellor of the Exchequer, Reginald McKenna. Together they would rebuild the Park in 1923. Yet, for all Frances's talk of the McKennas 'coming to our aid in rebuilding it',

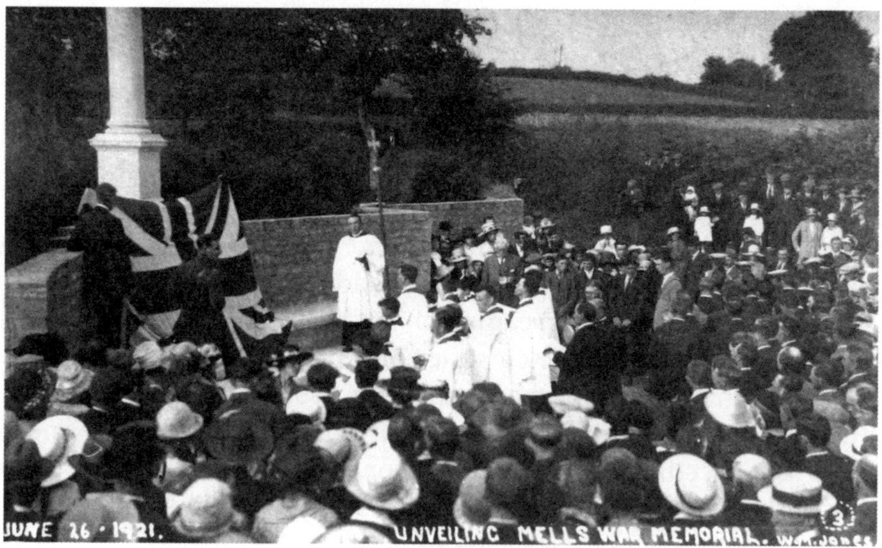

102.   *The unveiling of the war memorial at Mells*

this would be very much on the latter's terms. True, Lutyens was retained but instead of the stone roofed French house that she had dreamt up, McKenna insisted on 'a plain square box'.[36] The Horners had been 'all rather skiffy coffy over the Pamela McKenna marriage', and, as befits former owners, were quick to deem McKenna's design 'monstrously ugly'. Conrad was more sympathetic to McKenna than most, admiring his 'very advanced' views on Germany and his 'jolly' manner. 'But at heart he is a common commercial-minded man who worships efficiency and money. He and Sir John are as the poles and Sir J. cannot conceal his dislike of him'. Pamela, however, was musical. She was also 'extravagantly whimsy, whamsy' over animals and was discovered in the village by Katharine 'with glowing eyes and flushed triumphant cheeks' after a set to with the butcher on the subject of 'Humane Slaughter'.[37] Pamela was at least family (if not a Horner) and thus through her Frances could maintain in Mells Park the fiction of a restoration of former glories. And the McKennas brought a cachet to local social life with the Neville Chamberlains and John Maynard Keynes and his ballerina wife, Lydia Lopokova, frequent guests. So too came Aggie, her youngest sister and now a regular visitor where once Frances had held sway.[38] To her credit, Frances continue to believe it was a price worth paying.

345

*

Just as she had brought in the McKennas to restore Mells Park, so she looked outside to revitalise the local church in the wake of Katharine's conversion to Catholicism. Lear had never been popular. By comparison Canon James O. Hannay was quite a catch. Originally an Anglican clergyman in the West of Ireland before the war, he had been an advocate of the nationalist Gaelic League until hounded out in a sectarian campaign led by the local Catholic priest. This had been provoked by a series of political satires on Irish life, which Hannay had published under the pseudonym of George A. Birmingham.[39] Searing in tone and often very funny, he was merciless in respecting neither unionists or nationalists, with the result that he had few friends left in Ireland by the time he signed up to serve as a padre on the Western Front.

On the other hand, he had developed a reputation in England for writing light comic tales that sold extremely well. To the reading public he was a name and even Haldane was 'curious to hear about him'. Hannay proved to be tall, purposeful, and vigorous in opinion and debate. In company, he was a witty, stimulating conversationalist, if one who could let his irritation show in the company of dullards. And he never quite shed the occasional prickliness of the exile. Unconventional and independent, he was just the person in Frances's eyes to revitalise Protestantism in Mells. Like her's, his faith was instinctive and elemental rather than doctrinal.[40] Lady Helen Asquith remembered his sermons for being 'literary rather than spiritual. He was moved by words, by poetry and by drama and also I think by visual beauty'. As indeed was Frances. As to be expected, on Catholicism he was deemed sound. 'Of course for Ireland, mixed marriages might be the great solution', he once admitted, 'but for me it is like a knife being turning round and round in my heart'; not least when his own daughter married a Catholic. While his novels spared few, the political Catholic priest whose faith acted as a dead hand on progress was a staple character. No wonder Katharine reported nervously that 'the Hannays are very powerful, masterful people but quite nice'.[41]

Hannay, however, didn't come to Mells to fight again the Reformation. For in Mells he discovered 'the realisation of my dreams': a fifteenth-century church of 'rare beauty, rich in ancient memories', dominated by a tower that 'haunted' his imagination.[42] For him, it symbolised the timelessness of faith, a heroic redoubt that had withstood the ravages of centuries, a symbol of an ancient and, above all, inclusive tradition. Having spent most of his life fighting the turf wars of the Reformation in Ireland, pre-Reformation Mells offered a haven from the hatred. So too the Church of England, with its aesthetic 'superb abundance' and broad-church Anglicanism in which 'everyone could find a home'. Hence free from political censure, he reintroduced a pre-Reformation Sanctus bell and a Sanctuary lamp he had found discarded in the church. Much to the fury of George Horner, alive and vitriolic still, but Hannay was more than a match for elderly angry correspondents.

The other appeal of Mells for him was more concerned with the eighteenth century and the ideal of the Protestant Ascendancy. For the first time in his life, he was free to feel part of a majority, with rectory and manor house standing side by side and the squire holding paternal sway over a loyal community. The snob in him greatly enjoyed the company of the great and the good who gathered at Frances's table. What mattered far more was the opportunity to escape the modern and recapture an ancient order. Reflecting this was the gathering of the families of the squire and priest for the ringing of the bells on New Year's Eve. The village team of bell ringers would ring out the Old Year with muffled bells as the two families crowded into the belfry. Just before midnight one of the ringers would climb into 'the torch lit darkness of the bell chamber' to remove the 'mufflers'. He would then strike the hour by hand – the clock didn't work when the bells were 'up'. When he was down there was much handshaking and wishing of Happy New Year before they were deafened by the joyful, unmuffled peal of the bells, as the party climbed down the steep spiral stairway and on to the Rectory for hot rum punch. 'It was exactly like a scene out of Hardy', reminisced Katharine.[43]

*

Frances's own literary interests had moved on from Wessex tales. When Ettie was convalescing after an illness, Frances urged her to 'plunge' into Proust's *À la recherche du temps perdu*. Recommending the recent English edition by C. K. Scott Moncrieff ('really rather a treasure I think – full of such wise sayings and such beauty'), she couldn't resist a little one-upmanship: 'I read it first in French but it is easier in this excellent translation'. Thereafter she was relentless, suggesting some 'Russian Novels' to be followed by a collection of 170 Chinese poems: 'they are very queer and a touching flavour of extreme modernity in the far gone past'.[44] By now the muse had become an established patron. Lutyens and artists such as William Nicholson and Rex Whistler among others were devoted to her.[45] So too the inveterate political gossip and close friend of Raymond, Harold 'Bluetooth' Baker.[46] The arrival of Conrad Russell – aristocratic, wise and cultured – to manage the farm was another boon to Mells society and he became a sensitive mediator between Frances and Katharine (fig. 106).[47] Not that he was much of a farmer and, punctured by the war, his ending up in Mells represented a retreat from shadows of the recent past. Russell was a distinctive even eccentric figure, with his check suit, the turned out toes, and the stoop of a tall man, one indeed whose hair was cut by the ploughman with the help of a pudding bowl. An astute if occasionally acerbic observer of human foible, he was attractive company, noted for his boundless curiosity, integrity and gossip. And, since Raymond's death, he had been devoted to Katharine.

There would be no let-up in the social whirl of The Manor House: with visitors as eclectic as Eric Gill, J. M. Barrie, Norah Lindsay (the garden designer), Augustine Birrell (Liberal politician and *litterateur*), and Lytton Strachey fresh from his debunking of the Victorians. Grandee poets such as Walter de la Mare and Robert Bridges (the Poet Laureate) mixed with young academics such as John Sparrow (fig. 104) and the fledgling novelist, L. P. Hartley. From Westminster Abbey came Dean Inge. A prolific author, three times nominated for the Nobel Prize for Literature, his freethinking, often quirky opinions sustained a regular column in the *Evening Standard* for many years. The literary critic Desmond MacCarthy was another acquisition.[48] So too, Edmund Gosse, poet and promoter of Ibsen. He was a devoted lover of cats whose stay at Mells was not apparently blighted by the Horner cat choosing to bite him.[49] And then there were the student sons of old friends, including a shy Donald Maclean down from Cambridge (fig. 105.

Hosting a small private party for Albert Einstein was a particular coup. Einstein was an international celebrity, even if few understood his concept of Relativity. Haldane (whose guest Einstein was)

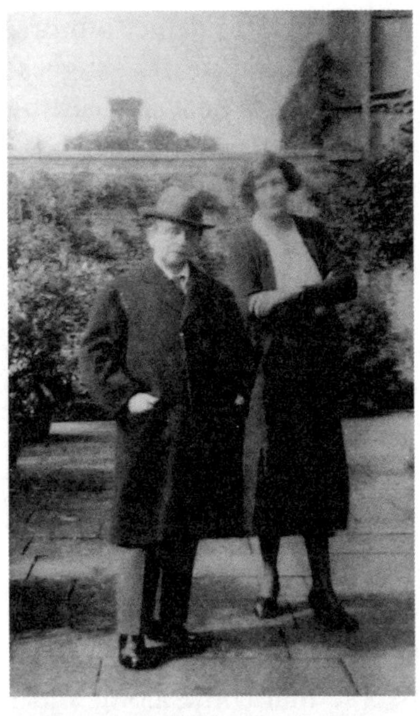

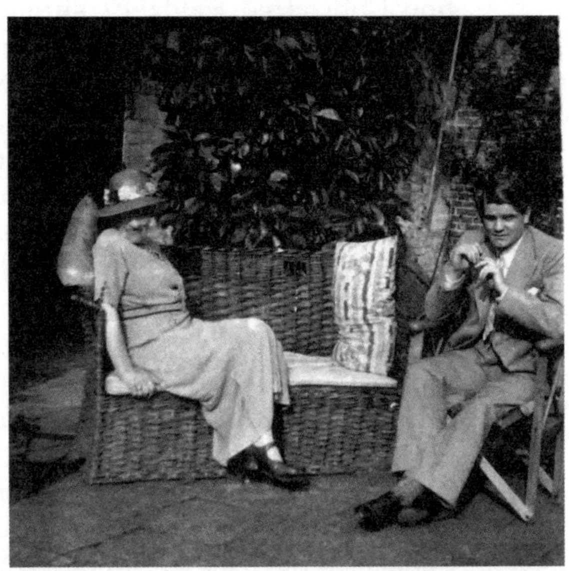

103. *J.M. Barrie and Katharine*

104. *Frances and John Sparrow*

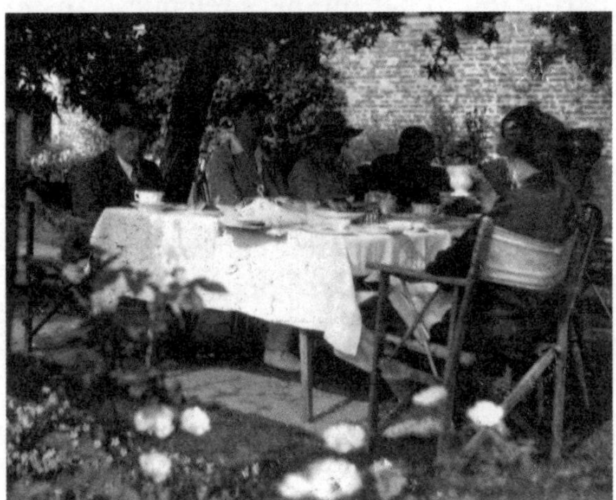

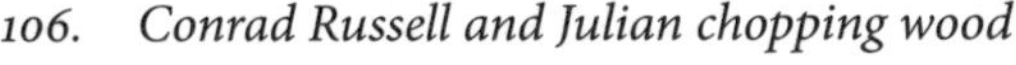

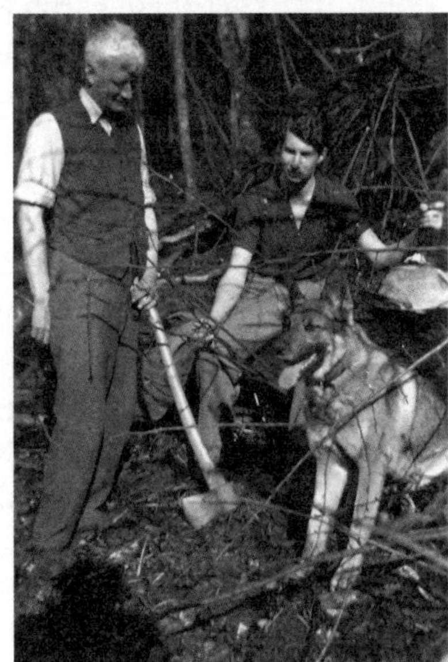

105. *Breakfast in the garden: J.M. Barrie, Julian, Frances, Donald Maclean, Katharine*

106. *Conrad Russell and Julian chopping wood*

of course believed he did; indeed going so far as to detect a moral dimension. Unfortunately, the scientist looked askance at the suggestion. Undeterred, Haldane continued to promote the cause, insisting that there was 'an unhallowed interest in Relativity among the people'. Needless to say, Haldane's lecture on the subject at the opening of the reading room Frances had built for the miners in neighbouring Vobster had left the audience utterly bemused, not least Frances and the Canon. By the night of the party Einstein's lack of English was becoming a strain. Frances not only spoke German but she also had a piano on which Eilona Derenberg could accompany Einstein on his violin.[50] With love of music providing a universal language, the evening proved 'too extraordinary but a huge success'. Frances may have found his science incomprehensible and 'wish[ed] my outlook was more intellectual!' But she would always remember the artist in him, adding him to her Romantic Pre-Raphaelite pantheon: 'Einstein had the head of a musician with wide dreamy eyes and gentle manners'.[51] Typically she felt frustrated that she hadn't 'enough to offer the new interesting people that come along and I can't get them early'. Katharine found her mother's relentless hospitality overwhelming at times and the company of Barrie and his ilk a crashing bore.[52] However, she did spot that Frances much preferred her friends, including the remnants of the Coterie such as Diana and Duff Cooper, as well as new faces such as Siegfried Sassoon and Evelyn Waugh – but *not* Belloc.[53] All in turn were drawn to the Elizabethan Manor House to which Frances brought a very special magic. 'It is a hot evening in July or August', she once wrote…

> We dine in the garden, at a table spread on the stone terrace on the south side of the house. The scent of flowers fills the air – the Church Tower seems to be brooding over the scene, and a mixed company sitting around are talking – talking – the light wanes and we sit as the moon rises and we can just see each other's faces dim and white in the twilight. What do we talk of? Politics – art – personalities – a good deal of personalities.[54]

*

One person who combined personality and politics was Haldane. By the end of the war their relationship had lasted twenty-five years but had declined with the restrictions on travel. Peace would see him

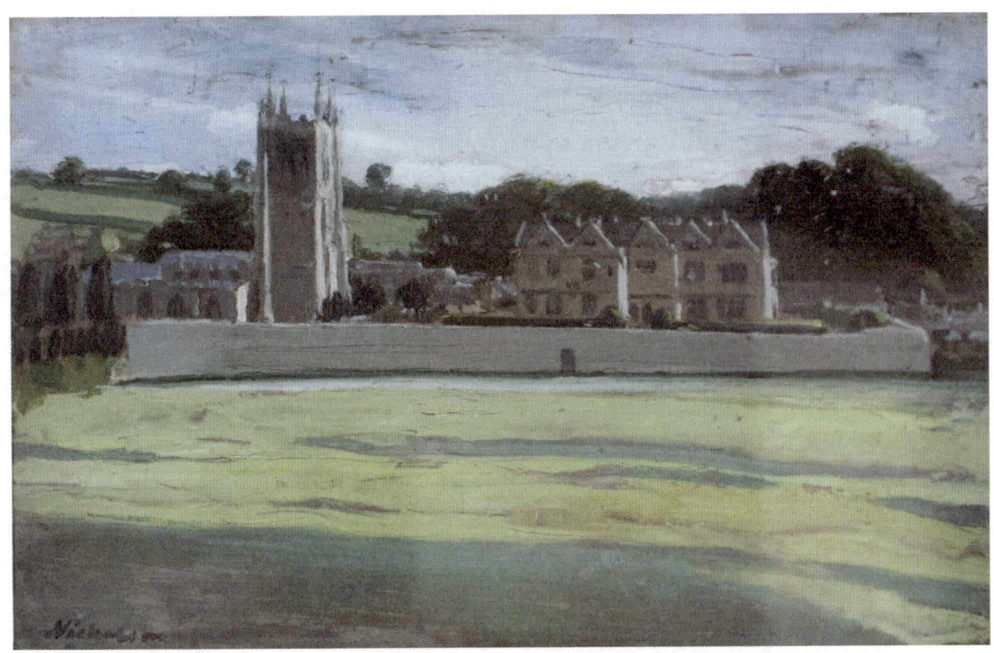

107.   The Church and Manor House at Mells, by William Nicholson

once again at Mells. 'Richard pilgrimages here', Frances reported to Katharine, 'full of committees and general staff and the infinite – a queer mixture which makes him what he is but very beloved by me anyhow'. Not least he was a vital source of political gossip: 'From Paris [the Peace Conference] I hear privately bad accounts', he alerted her. 'They want to cripple Germany permanently. There would be something to be said for it were it not that 45 million people cannot cripple 70 million. But they can lay the seeds of war in the future. I am apprehensive of what is likely to happen twenty years hereafter' – prescient indeed.[55] In turn, he would confess 'I love my communion with you. How strange is it that you and I, so different, should so completely belong to one another. But so it is – a great elemental fact…' That said, 'How much better a correspondent I am than you' suggests that he was making the running. On this occasion his rebuke worked. 'Missed you …today', she reassured him.

I have thought a great deal over our walks and talks. You said this morning that I never said very much … Half shyness I believe: but every now and then when I am with you I have felt deeply moved and I was so last night. I am ashamed at the unselfishness of your love for me. I seem to be taking so much from you and giving you so little ... by putting my hand into yours I have condemned you to walk the best years of your life alone ... It was very horrid of me but it came partly from my habit of seizing on the life of the moment – no one has taken less heed of the morrow than I have.[56]

She did enjoy the stimulation of their occasional 'walks and talks' and the emotional base his loyalty gave her but he would not have been the first of her courtiers to have wanted more.

Admittedly, their common bond of politics had withered with the split in the Liberal party following Lloyd George's wartime ousting of Asquith. As war gave way to peace the divide became terminal. With horror Frances looked on at the public denigration of the Asquiths, especially Margot, 'a terrible end to what might have been such a wonderful career'. Nevertheless, Frances remained loyal even after Asquith had lost his seat in the 1918 election. Defiantly she would summon her grandchildren to Parliament to witness his 'triumphant [re] entry' after a by-election in 1920.[57] On 6 December 1923, with Britain in the throes of another election, Frances, together with Katharine, attended an election night party in Selfridges – with two thousand dancing while a man with a megaphone bellowed out the latest election results. Despite the spectacle, it was a grim night with a neighbouring table cheering every Labour gain as another nail in Asquith's coffin. Winston Churchill joined Frances's party, defiant in the face of the abuse but utterly exhausted and in despair over the results which would see the emerging Labour party overtake the Liberals. He nevertheless spent two hours teaching Katharine and Ettie Mah-jong: 'There is something very grand about Winston' declared Katharine.[58] By November, he had jumped ship, joining the Conservatives in the face of the rise of the Labour Party and their threat of 'socialism'. He was not the only one to desert the party. So had Haldane. He on the other hand had joined the Labour Party. Thus in the wake of the election he found himself again in the Cabinet – this time in the first Labour (minority) government. Any conflict of loyalties Frances may have felt was swiftly forgotten as the old times returned: 'I enclose a Cabinet document, which please burn when you have read it', he would write. On re-entering office, he faithfully reminded her how 'you…have made all the difference to my career as well as my life. And here I am again, an aged Lord Chancellor, for the second time'. Amid the regular updates on Cabinet meetings there would be frequent assessments of the 'curious' Ramsay MacDonald, the Labour leader – the illegitimate off-spring from a Highland bothy who was now courted by aristocratic ladies.[59] By the end of the year, the government had fallen and the Conservatives were back in office. Crucially Labour remained in second place, thus displacing the Liberals in the two party system. The once great Liberal Party was left with little more than a rump of forty MPs.

Class conflict now overtly became the *leitmotif* of British politics. In 1926 the challenge of labour gave way to open conflict with the General Strike. Led by the miners, the Trade Union Congress attempted to close down three major industries in what became over nine days a struggle for ascendancy between the economic power of the unions and the political authority of parliamentary government. Katharine's spirits fell as her mother took a 'fervent interest' in events, even installing a large wireless in the drawing room. 'O my God what an invention', Katharine protested. 'It booms away incredibly boring details about the numbers of special constables enrolled and yet one cannot help listening to it. I never have the strength of mind to leave the room'. Such engagement inspired the Canon to deliver a 'passionate' sermon to 'his congregation of solid farm workers, miners, quarry men and housewives, that however just one's cause, violence, rapine and murder was *always* wrong'. A tirade greeted with bemusement by his congregation for whom such revolutionary horrors seemed a far cry from the timeless tranquillity of Somerset village life. Even Frances was 'immensely amused'. Still as an indication that change was afoot, the time would come when tea parties for the Conservatives would be held on the lawns of The Manor House.[60]

*

Nostalgia was very much to the fore at the Burne-Jones centenary exhibition held at the Tate in 1933. Prime among the objects on display was Frances's piano. Yet for all the eloquence of Stanley Baldwin – thrice Prime Minister and nephew of 'Uncle Ned' – the private view was a desultory affair. 'A little crowd of forlorn old survivors

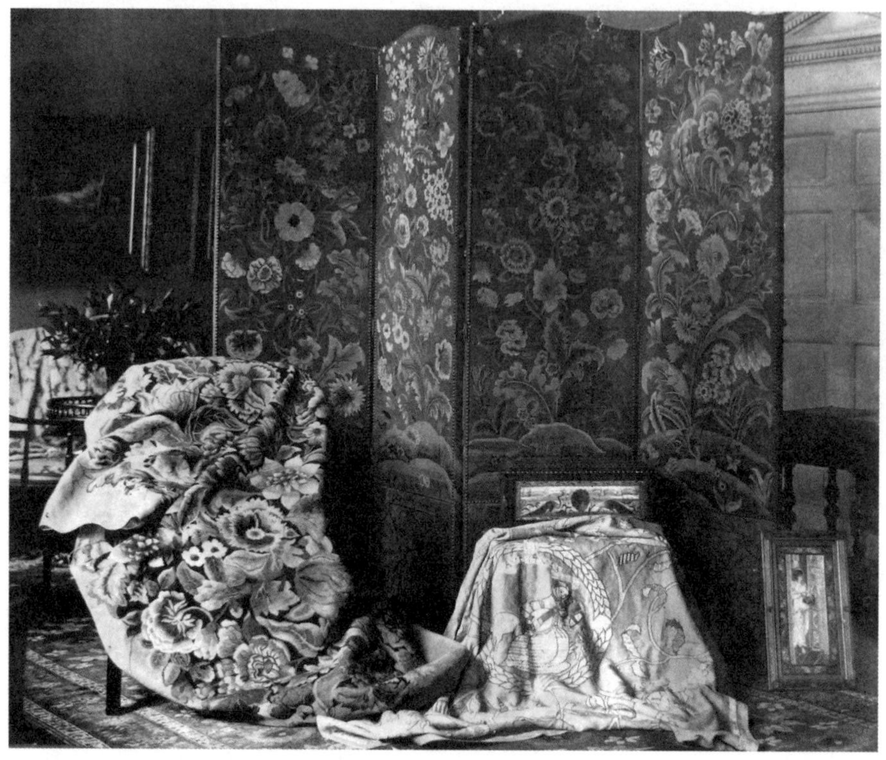

108.   *The embroidery exhibition organised by Frances at the London home of the Duchess of Sutherland, February 1935*

paying their homage to the beauty and poetry now utterly scorned and rejected', observed one devotee of Burne-Jones. Another spoke of 'a gathering of tender ruins'.[61] Admittedly Burne-Jones's reputation had been in decline since his death (if not a little before) with the rise of Impressionism. The later modernists regarded his work without mercy. True the onsct of the War had revived the chivalric ideal and with it a renewed interest in Burne-Jones; but the exposure of 'the Great Lie' in the late 1920s took the artist down with it. Hence *The Times* generously saw the exhibition as a guilty indulgence 'for what he meant in our youth' – something presumably one had grown out of. Frances characteristically sought to fight back and with her friend Violet Milner talked of curating another exhibition, making more of his drawings, stained glass, cartoons, books and boxes, only then to balk at the cost. Just as well, for as Sydney Cockerell warned, 'the tide of feeling against BJ is high'.[62] As if to make the point, *Love and the Pilgrim* which had started out as Frances's valentine and was later sold in 1898 for £5775, fetched just £21 at auction in 1940.

Yet survivors have their appeal. With both Georgie and Philip Burne-Jones long dead, Frances had the field to herself. The aftermath of the exhibition saw numerous of the young, (including a 'very charming' Noel Coward) track her down, eager to meet the artist's muse. Mary Belloc Lowndes was another who found her 'fascinating', as with coy hints of an immoral youth, Frances would pedal out again the elopement story that never was or would exchange gossip on Asquith's latest lovers (all false but it was revealing that this still stirred her to the last). 'It is a surprise when the young seem to be drawn to the old, and exquisitely flattering', she would admit to Sibyl Colefax, her latest best friend: 'when anyone loves Mells (and me!), it goes straight to my heart'.[63] Also cheering was the exhibition of Frances's needlework in 1935 that the Duchess of Sutherland hosted in her honour (fig. 108). By now she had come to see the opportunity such retrospectives would bring.

Having frequently denounced 'lying memoirs, always full of "letters we had better burn" and naïve conversations and false history', Frances overcame her scruples later that year to publish *Time Remembered* (admittedly at the behest of Virginia Woolf, Lytton Strachey and Desmond MacCarthy). Unlike Margot's candid and shamelessly vain *Autobiography*, Frances is a much more elusive figure in her memoir. Writing was for her 'like giving a dinner party. It is the guests who make it a success as it is the stars that glitter in my pages'.[64] And prominent among 'the stars … shining on its pages' are Rossetti, William Morris and especially Burne-Jones. Having been written out of the Pre-Raphaelite story by Georgie Burne-Jones, Frances now sought to restore the record. Nearly a third of the book is given over to her reminiscences of 'BJ', with each letter and anecdote reinforcing the intimacy between them. Thus she sought to have the last word and take possession again of the myth surrounding the artist and his muse. Similarly, her friendships with Asquith and Haldane are drawn into the spotlight to bring out the political muse. Of course, much is left out: 'Time remembered is grief left out' was her text. There is barely a reference to her Glasgow roots and a complete denial of her early evangelism. Not surprisingly, there is no mention of Milford or her affair with Asquith. As for her children, there is no place in the Pre-Raphaelite idyll for Edward's

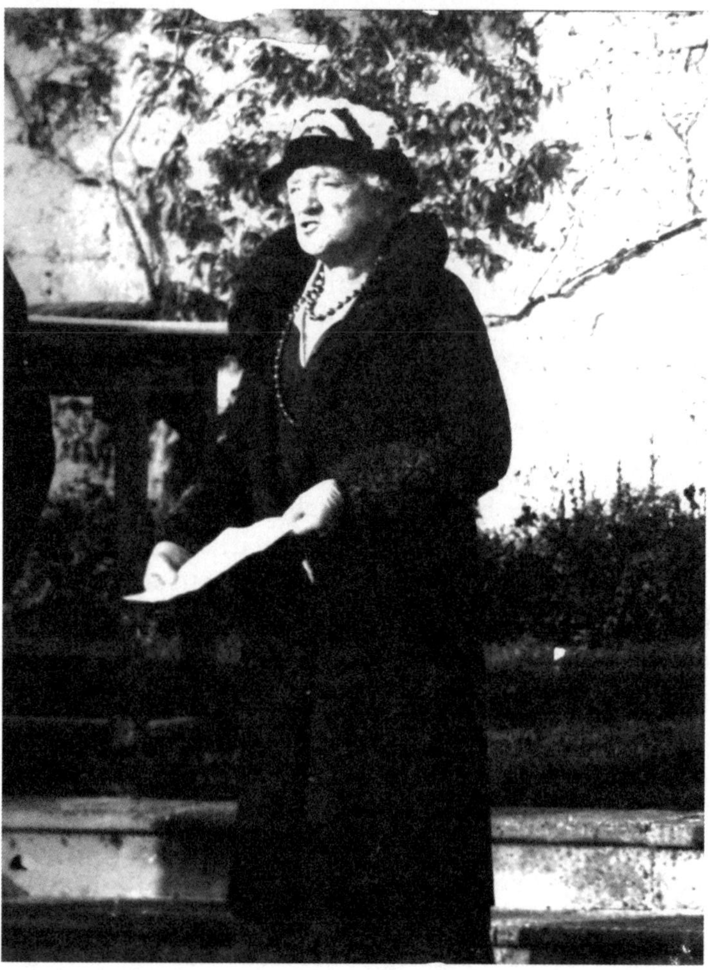

109.   Frances delivering a speech

failings or Katharine's conversion. She is equally reticent about herself, preferring to be portrayed as one who experienced life through
other people. By such myths lives are lived. Those that knew her well
knew better.[65] Even in her eighties she remained a remarkably energetic force – still encouraging and inspiring others, and brooking
no doubt or despair. In the face of post-war gloom and with few
resources she had galvanised Mells again, restoring it to its pre-war
vigour.

37

CANON FIRE

You recall silly Canon Hannay, he *adored* her.[66]

Nevertheless there came too the first hints of mortality. A fall had left her 'pretty well on the whole', she insisted, 'but I don't soar with wings or even run but only crawl!'[67] By now most of her closest male friends had died. She was at Asquith's bedside as he lay dying. Ever possessive, she would claim that only 'I could pierce the cloud' that divided him from the rest of the room 'even for a few minutes'. Haldane too died in 1928, though distance and later infirmity seems to have kept them apart for a number of years. Frances had rarely been without a lover or devoted companion and into the vacuum strode the Canon. She admired his 'brisk and purposeful services' and promoted 'my Canon's sermons' among her friends. Finding herself responsible for the welfare and social life of the village, she came to rely on his support. Hannay threw himself into the community – from the cubs and guides, and the District Nurses to the Women's Institute and the village cricket side. This was not natural terrain for Frances and she found him 'a stay and strength…most of all to me, to whom he has given so much of help and counsel and companionship'.[68]

What ensured that their working relationship would blossom into deep friendship was that Frances found Hannay fun. With him she could argue over the latest novel or play before debating vigorously the to and fro of high politics. Of course, their rapport was based far more on what they shared – even writing a joint letter to *The Times*.[69] Allied to their strength of opinion, both instinctively sought the path of action. Every summer they would disappear together on long holidays abroad. Initially Katharine would be 'a dutiful if slightly reluctant third' (fig. 110). But Frances was a seasoned traveller, having visited Austria and Italy with her father, Rome and Scandinavia with

Jack, and with numerous sorties to France and Germany in between. Katharine marvelled at her mother's 'power of making hotel friends'. With Hannay she travelled as far as Yugoslavia. There she relished the crisp air and the picture-perfect scenery, and (despite being in her eighties) the view of the pool below her window where:

> all nearly stark, swimming beautifully and diving from heights – mahogany coloured so I have lost all sense of decency. The only thing wanting to one here is a youthful body! I never want a new heart but I should like new legs.

Her description of their tour of Hannay's old haunts in Ulster (where their car got stuck on Magilligan Strand) was straight out of one of the Canon's novels.

> a very beautiful, very desolate country … wilder than Cornwall or Caithness and such a hard iron people, whose politics entirely defeated me. They were so passionately loyal to England and dislike the English so much and were so violently anti-Catholic it almost [nullified?] my attitude. Then that absurd Free State… like being with Alice in Wonderland – the signposts in Gaelic which no one can read, customs every few miles – passionately disloyal and yet most friendly to the English.[70]

As with Haldane, this was a relationship of 'walks and talks' but much more easy-going and equal.[71] Hannay was besotted but far too prim to get carried away. Neither did she. Her granddaughter, Lady Helen Asquith, was closer to the mark in her description of 'a very solid friendship originating in mutual admiration and esteem, cemented by a number of common interests and concerns (literary as well as parochial), which ripened into strong affection and dependency on both sides'. When Frances died, Hannay would promise Katharine to burn all her mother's letters to him – there were 'hundreds' of them. Nor did his replies survive at Mells. Both of which suggest that this was an *amitié amoureuse* and one that sustained her for the last fifteen years of her life.[72]

Yet in 1933 Hannay resigned from Mells. Sixty years afterwards Helen still found it 'odd'. Admittedly, brought in to staunch the flow of Catholicism, he had proved powerless as first Helen and then Perdita converted. Actually Hannay doesn't seem to have put up much resistance. Ordered to see the Canon by Frances, Helen found him

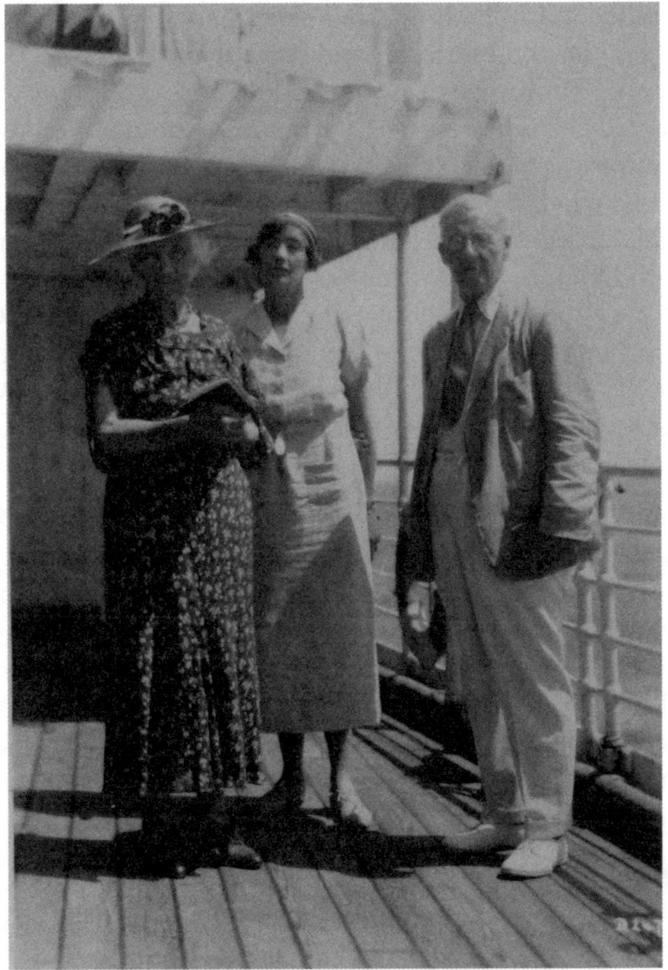

110.   *Frances, Katharine and Canon Hannay,*
holidaying on board ship

'very nice indeed' – merely pointing out to her 'rather laboriously' that 'going over to Rome' meant 'surrendering one's judgement' – something that, 'however agreeable', was ultimately her decision – not her destiny. An argument he used also with Perdita and with similar results. Perdita's conversion while engaged to Billy Joliffe, the heir of the nearby Hylton estate, predictably caused uproar among her in-laws and gave Frances a local ally in Lady Hylton. Frances had long hoped that her two grand-daughters (fig. 111) would prove sufficiently independent to resist the calling but seven years of what

Conrad called 'Catholic Bogie Talk from Lady Horner' proved ineffective: '[she] fears the Priests, who seem to me to be good, amiable, well-meaning but rather tiresome middle class old footlers'. Frances also resented feeling 'deserted' in her own home.[73] Yet what was really at stake was made plain by Helen's 'rough up with Lady Horner about whom you'll marry'. Ironically, at university in Oxford the person she felt closest to was Hannay's son Seamus. Helen thought him 'rather good looking' with 'deep set dark blue eyes' and she came 'to like him very much'. But when she was received into the Catholic Church in her second year he denounced her in a 'very bitter and angry letter'. 'Surprised' and hurt she responded in similar vein and she never saw him again.[74] As Conrad reported, worse was to follow at a ball at Cliveden.

> When all the young people were putting on their wraps in the hall, Lady Astor screamed out before everyone: 'Helen, Helen what made you do it? I shall never rest until I have won you back. Was it Maurice [Baring] did it?' It gradually dawned on the wretched girl that her change of religion was in question and she remained silent and confused. 'Was it that drunkard Mr Bellock?' yelled Lady Astor. 'You don't think Mr Bellock seriously tries to follow Christ do you?' She screamed, but I imagine got no answer.[75]

As it turned out, not only was Hannay losing The Manor House to Catholicism but he was losing the Anglican grandees too – something 'he minded terribly'. 'We could hardly realise', explained Conrad to Helen,

> I think the appalling sadness of the poor Canon's situation. The ablest and most thoughtful of his Parishioners – I mean myself – never sets foot in his Church. Reggie [McKenna] the great Panjandrum attends fitfully and scoffs, one young McKenna steeped in Socinianism and now the only three does with a veneer of culture all gone over to Rome – and after giving him a fair trial too. And now we have Inge – the ablest and most learned of our divines – writing a great work to show the failure of the Church and the harm it has done in saying quite openly he isn't surprised the best and ablest and most honest people never go to Church at all. Poor old Hannay. It is a tragedy and I wish I could console the old boy.[76]

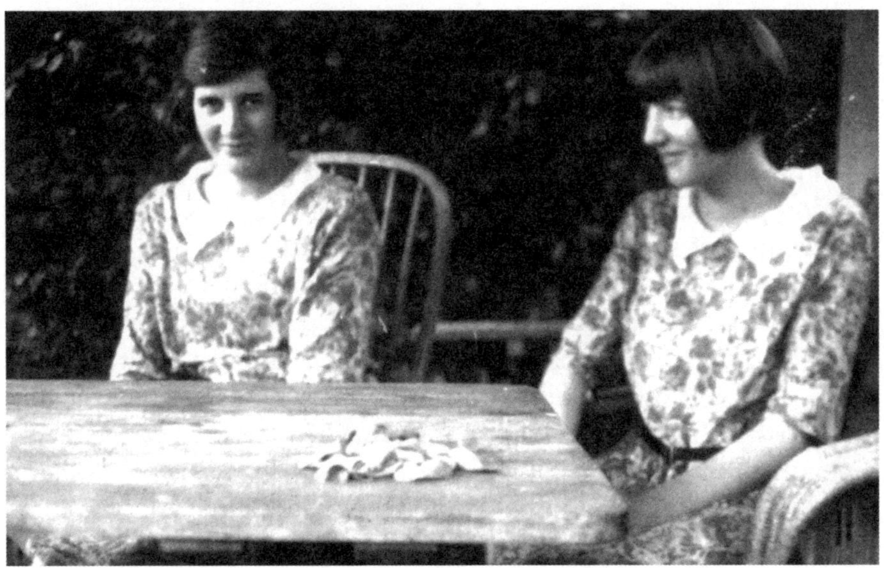

111.   Helen and Perdita

The official reason for the Canon's departure was 'loneliness'. 'Stricken into numbness' after the death of his wife, Ada, in 1933, he found himself rattling round an empty rectory and with Frances in London for most of the winter. However, the drive to leave came from his daughter, Althea. Both she and her mother had long come to resent the patronising manner with which they were treated by Frances. How their father took her side, even adopting her grand manner and what they saw as the sybaritic life. To be fair, Helen remembers Althea as 'dumpy' and 'no fun' and how 'we Asquiths were inclined to mock [Ada] mildly'. Ada who loyally typed up Hannay's novels was deeply hurt when in *Fidgets* (1926) a thinly disguised portrayal of Frances ('Lady Wenlock') kisses the unnamed but easily recognisable narrator. His daughter, Althea, would later write that 'the mutual attraction felt by Lady Horner and father is rather distasteful to me and my brothers and was very much so to my sister', pleading to a biographer 'not to make a cess-pit out of it'. Hannay, who was not particularly close to any of his children, treated with contempt their suspicion that the English were 'profoundly immoral with the sexual habits of a rabbit warren'. Nevertheless, with both Frances and Hannay single, Althea saw the chance to reclaim him by playing on the risk of an impropriety that never was. To her, bringing him back to live with her in London offered her father 'a new start and I think he knew it and made a great effort to redeem himself, which he did'.[77] There is no record of what must have been an extraordinary conversation between Althea and Frances. Yet the outcome was that Frances arranged through Dean Inge for Hannay to be offered a London parish, Holy Trinity, Prince Consort Road, Kensington. By the summer of 1934 he had moved in with Althea.

Twenty years later Althea, whose resentment of Frances had barely abated, nevertheless acknowledged that her actions were 'a mark of the greatness of her character that she did it although it was against her own interests, her own wishes'. Had Frances feared local gossip? If so, the message hadn't reached Hannay. In his memoirs published in late 1934, Hannay wrote openly of his relationship with Frances and of how Ada's death had proven a release: 'the coming of my great sorrow rent the veil that still hung between us and perfected the last and greatest friendship of my life'. Ironically for Althea, there would 'not [be] any interruption of the steady strong flow of the best of all my friendships'.[78] For all Althea's prim morality, her father saw no need for redemption. Indeed, with Frances's support, Holy Trinity became a redoubt for the fashionable and the Liberal old guard. With respectability secured, they would see more of each other in London, while in the summer he would be a frequent guest at Mells, before they disappeared for a jaunt abroad. In truth, much of the mischief of this affair springs from the embarrassment of youth at aged parents – one over eighty and the other a devoted admirer eleven years younger – having a blast in old age.

Katharine was not immune to this either. Naturally she resented Hannay's 'fann[ing] the flames of prejudice', assuming that he was winding Frances up over, for instance, letting cottages to Catholics. Yet for all their religious differences, what mattered more was that she found him deeply 'uncongenial'. His brusque manner and loud presence jarred 'the more complicated and sophisticated spirits among us such as my brother and sister and my mother', remembered Helen. Not least when he would walk across to The Manor House of a summer evening and 'lure Lady Horner out to look at the tower in the light of the setting sun or by moonlight'. Mid-dinner party he would be heard outside calling out to her, 'Come out and look at the tower, Lady Horner'. At which Frances would rise and 'we would all troop out obediently'. It never crossed his mind that those who had lived by the tower since birth might have preferred not to be uninterrupted over dinner. Yet Hannay always felt Katharine was a friend. For 'on the surface', her daughter noticed, Katharine got on with him and thus 'he really liked and respected her'.[79] Frances was not fooled. Another reason perhaps for moving the Canon on.[80]

With the departure of the Canon, relations with Katharine certainly became easier. Frances's enthusiastic engagement with her grandchildren had always been appreciated. But now the balance was shifting. University and marriage were claiming the young; while with each fall came a new and unspoken dependency of mother on her daughter. ('Katharine such an angel to me').[81] Perhaps as part of this, Frances became more accommodating of Katharine's friends, who would in time form the bedrock of the Catholic intelligentsia that was now gathering around Mells. Very much on their mettle, they would spar with the 'witty, vivacious and sharp-tongued' chatelaine. Although quite intimidating, she won over the young such as Evelyn Waugh by being 'at the same time informal, illustrious and affectionate.' Indeed he felt welcome enough to retreat to Mells to complete his biography of the Catholic martyr, Edmund Campion (1934) and later his novel *Scoop* (1938).[82]

Still, Frances's keen support in 1934 for the building of Campion Hall, a Catholic private hall within the University of Oxford (fig. 112), struck all who knew her as bizarre. Campion Hall was the brainchild of Father D'Arcy. A charismatic Jesuit priest at the heart of the literary Catholic post-war revival, D'Arcy's passionate conviction sat alongside being 'essentially English, deeply traditional and nostalgic with a real passion for the Stuart cause'. Waugh used him as the model for Father Rothschild SJ in *Vile Bodies*. With a penchant for the aristocracy, D'Arcy was determined to be the first priest across Frances's door, in part to defuse some of the tension between a mother and her daughter.[83] How they met is not recorded (presumably through Katharine or her children) but for his purpose it was well chosen; for D'Arcy came to ask Frances's advice on the building plans for his project. Predictably, she urged consulting Lutyens, who having dismissed the existing plans as 'Queen Anne front, Mary Anne behind', offered to design it instead. Fr D'Arcy accepted – reassured apparently, 'that I had Lady Horner to check extravagances … She had given him the chance as a young man and so could control him.'[84] At a final cost of £34,000 his faith may have been misplaced.

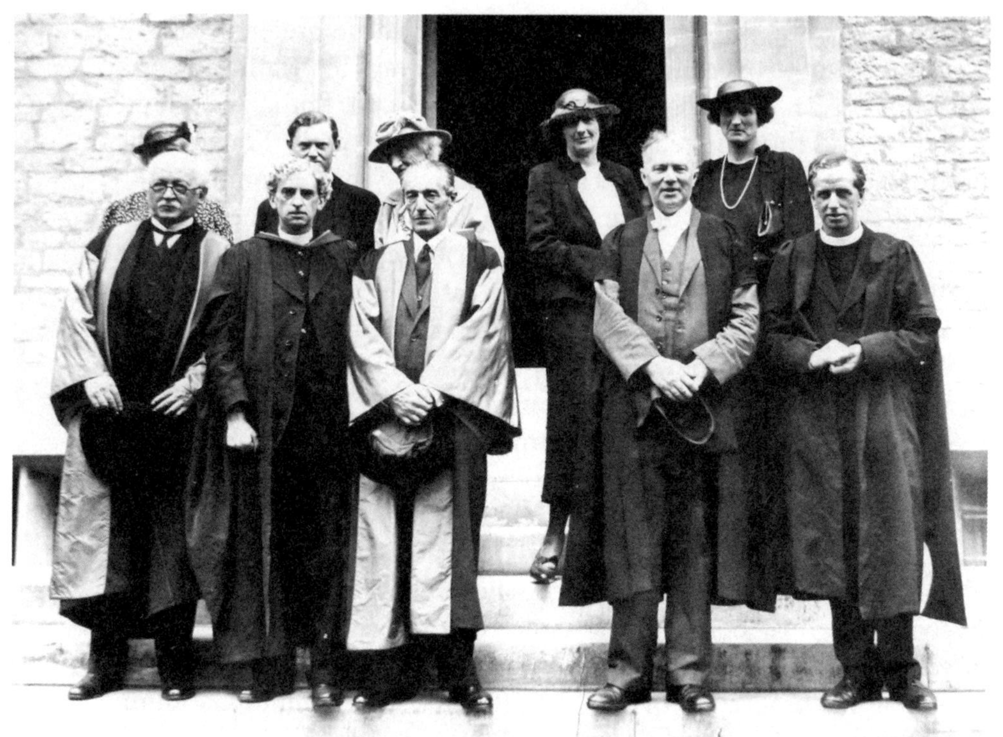

112.   *The opening of Campion Hall, Oxford, 1936*
FRONT ROW L TO R: *Lutyens, Fr D'Arcy, the Spanish Ambassador*
(the Duke of Alba), the Master of Balliol (A. D. Lindsey), Father Ronald Knox
BACK ROW L TO R: *?, Evelyn Waugh, Frances, Katharine, Mrs Aubrey Herbert*

Still Frances was hooked, as she and her protégé embarked on one last adventure. As ever for Frances, this seemed a case of people before principles. Yet to those who thought they knew her well, they could only explain it in terms of the mesmeric powers of Jesuit priests. 'Lady Horner has struck up a friendship with Fr D'Arcy SJ in Katharine's absence' (fig. 113), Conrad gossiped to his sister.

She went to see him (ill) in bed at Farm St, taking him flowers and now she's asked him if he can recommend a clergyman for Mells Rectory!! He says he knows the very man. Well I've always heard Jesuits were very clever at getting around old ladies and it seems to be true. But isn't this very funny?

Nevertheless, Frances's commitment to the project never wavered, watching on proudly as her grandson, Julian, laid the foundation

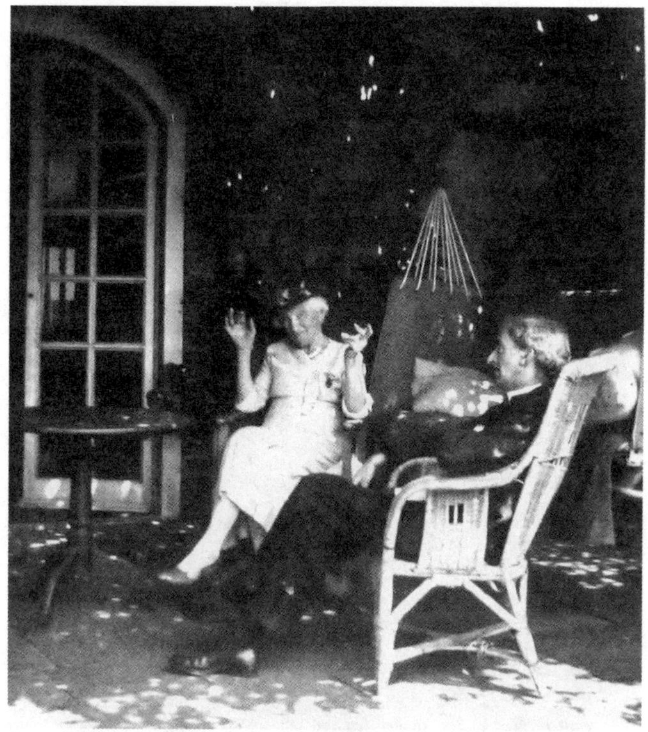

113.   *Frances and Father D'Arcy*

stone in 1934. At the opening ceremony in 1936 she was to be photographed (looking a little dotty alongside an earnest Waugh) with the committee on the steps of the hall. Conrad found it all very odd 'as she thinks Catholicism a poison to souls. I suppose she prefers it to staying at home'. At eighty-two, why not?[85]

In truth, little had changed. She just chose to ignore Katharine's Catholicism. When Katharine went on retreat or as in 1936 made an uplifting visit to Lourdes, it was frustrating for her that she 'can't talk about it at Mells as none interested'. Another rebuff came with Frances's refusal to let Katharine open a fête for the nuns at Frome. When Helen protested to Conrad that Grannie should by now be 'inured to Catholic activities', he explained that 'you will never "inure Grannie" to anything. You will only make her miserable'.[86] Frances made it perfectly clear there would be no catholicisation of Mells in her lifetime. This for the most part Katharine bore silently. The

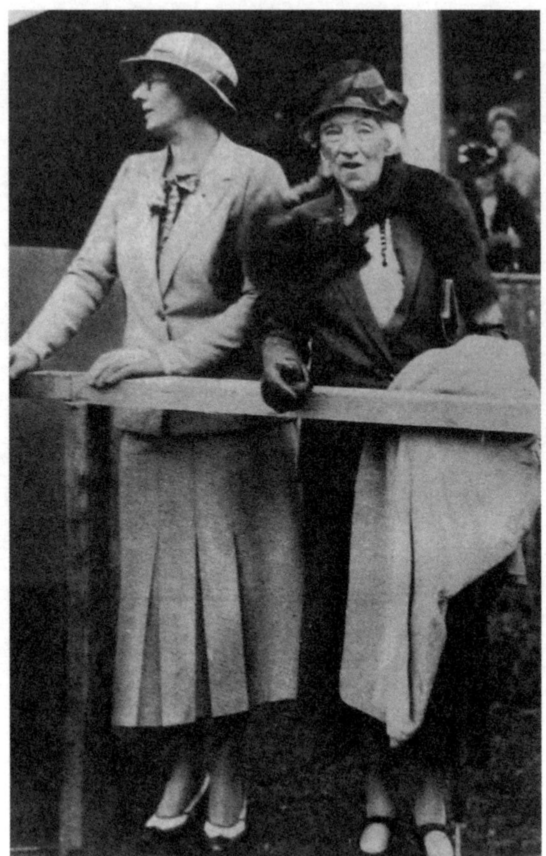

114.   *Katharine and Frances at Frome Show, 1933*

early years of 'religious uncertainty' ('I am strangled by superstition') in the aftermath of her conversion had given way to the warmth of conviction and a moral certainty that would shelter her against a muddled, broken world.[87] Seemingly reticent, she did not lack for steel. This, after all, had been a rebellion long in the coming. In the battle for the soul of Mells, she could afford to wait.

38

MUNICH AND MELLS

One reason why I warm to Winston is that he loves his country; and lately I have been disturbed and astounded by what seems to me an indisputable discovery that, today, the aristocracy and the rich put *their own class* before their country – he is an exception. Though he hates the Bolshies and rightly, he puts the power and dignity of his country first and that is wisest too from a Conservative point of view.'

Desmond MacCarthy to Frances Horner[88]

Miss Gamble, who runs the village shop, has said to Mr Hoad that she thinks Hitler is in the right. It has deeply shocked Mounty and he said darkly it wouldn't surprise him if Miss Gamble found her windows broken one morning. So minorities are persecuted. And Mrs Baker (aunt to Miss Gamble) said she believed the Second Coming of Our Lord was at hand and he would appear as soon as the first bomb fell on England. Lady Horner sent Mrs Baker a message telling her not to talk such rot.

Conrad Russell to Diana Cooper[89]

Nothing would divide the country more than the policy of appeasing the European dictators in the 1930s. Yet on this issue, Frances and Katharine were as one. For Frances the prospect of another world war so soon after the Great War was too horrible to contemplate. Both she and Katharine feared for Julian – just returned from travels in Italy with a beard and looking 'very handsome and 35 with a touch of Bloomsbury about him'. With his good looks and a first in Greats, he was everything Frances had wanted in a grandson. War threatened to rekindle the hurt of their previous losses. For Catholics there was also preservation of the Faith. With the Left massacring priests in droves at the height of the Spanish Civil War, for many Fascism in the 1930s seemed the only bulwark against the spread of atheistic Communism on the continent.[90] Matters came to a head in the autumn of 1938 over whether to defend the peace settlements of 1919 against impending German aggression or to concede the Nazis' demand for the transfer of the German-speaking Sudetenland from Czechoslovakia. Fearful of sliding into a war with Germany, the Prime Minister, Neville Chamberlain sought to find a compromise, flying three times to Germany to broker a deal. 'I think NC's was a fine gesture and quite right', Frances confessed to Ettie – both ardent appeasers. 'But I am almost sure we shall now let Hitler have his way and what about next time? And yet, I'd rather fight for a better cause if fighting there had to be… how furiously the nations rage'.[91] Such sentiments echoed Chamberlain's notorious justification on the eve of his final meeting with Hitler: 'How horrible. How horrible, fantastic, incredible it is that we should be digging trenches and trying on gas-masks here because of a quarrel in a far-away country between people of whom we know nothing'. Two days later on 29 September he returned from Munich, waving an agreement with Hitler and promising 'peace in our time'. For this, he was greeted like a saviour, with crowds filling the Mall to cheer him on the balcony of Buckingham Palace. Yet his triumph had required compelling the Czechs to dismember their legitimate state and its defences against future German invasion in order to save British and French skins in the short term. Even its supporters like Christopher Hollis recognised it was 'a miserable balance' and justifiable in terms of 'craven relief' and the need to buy time to rearm.

However as Hollis arrived at a party Frances threw to celebrate Chamberlain's success, he was greeted by the news that Duff Cooper (Diana's husband) had resigned from the government in protest. Hannay too couldn't stomach Munich, refusing to hold a celebratory service on Chamberlain's return and suffering a boycott by some of his parishioners as a consequence. Back in Mells, Conrad, who cheered Duff Cooper's rejection of 'the peck of dirt old Chamberlain has brought us from Munich', resented being 'asked to hail Mr Chamberlain as the greatest of diplomats'.[92] Munich quickly became so divisive, cutting across old loyalties, that people were often caught

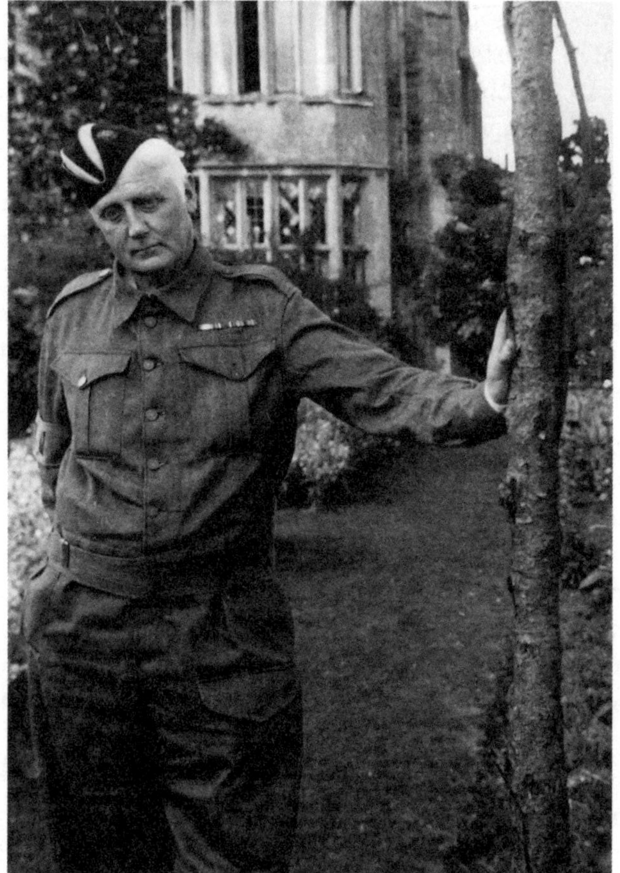

115.   *Conrad in Home Guard uniform, August 1940*

by surprise to find their friends in the opposite camp. Thus Conrad was startled after ringing Katharine to discover that she was 'going to remain loyal to the Coroner [i.e. Chamberlain]. He is her King and he can do no wrong'. So too Frances who wrote in support to Mrs Chamberlain.[93] Privately Frances was hopelessly bewildered about the situation:

> I just can't judge it. Ought he? Ought he not? Is he right ethically, or the others? I suppose Time will show. But I hate all the clichés – Czechoslovakia betrayed! Czechoslovakia having nobly ensured the peace of Europe!! *Balderdash.* ... worse – wild and whirling words – but one must keep silence.[94]

One who was not going to keep silent was Diana Cooper. Knowing full well that her hosts were 'very strong Chamberlainites', she arrived at Mells on 18 October, eager to defend her husband. As she 'talked "crisis" the whole evening, Lady Horner and Katharine listened in hostile silence. They think Duff mad or inexplicably silly', noted Conrad who didn't, relishing instead Diana's cool, clear challenge.[95]

Throughout the autumn the matter was left to simmer, avoided rather than forgotten. It was six weeks after *Kristallnacht*, the Nazi pogrom against the Jews in November 1938, before Conrad dared to raise it again. On New Year's Eve Katharine had called round to share a glass of crème de cacao and a 'political crack':

Her admiration for Chamberlain is unbounded, greater than ever. I said: 'Do you think it was nice of Mussolini to raise [an Italian annexation of] Tunisia only three weeks after signing a pact in which he promised to maintain the status quo in the Mediterranean? Do you think that a straightforward way to treat Chamberlain?' She refused to answer and I repeated my question adding: '*You must answer*'. She said: 'Perhaps Mussolini had good reasons for doing it that way which we do not know'.

I asked her: 'what do you expect the situation to be at the end of 1939 after further concessions?' She looked at me, puzzled by my stupidity and said: 'Of course it is bound to improve. Each time we make a concession the situation improves. In time (when we have conceded enough) we shall be able to live quite happily with the Dictators.'

We spoke of the Jewish persecution. She does not defend it of course but she did say: 'You never hear the other side. You only hear what the Jews say. Violet [Bonham Carter, Raymond's sister and great supporter of Duff Cooper] believes everything'.

Naturally, Katharine thinks Duff quite awful. She is not a pacifist and does not think you should turn the other cheek *ad infinitum*. She still thinks of the Munich agreement as one of the most splendid episodes in English history'.

The tension rippling through this conversation continued through the usual rituals of New Year:

A silent, sticky dinner... Lady Horner and Sir Almroth Wright [eminent physician and absurd anti-suffragist] silent mummies…Katharine's three children a silent wedge of non-talkers… Per next to me. She makes no effort at all. If you start a subject, it is a dead baby, killed at birth… Billy [Jolliffe, Perdita's husband] spoke politics all dinner – but sotto voce for fear of explosion. I could just hear 'League of Nations' and 'Appeasement' faintly whispered as if they were kinds of buggery, which they feared might be overheard… Billy's for Chamberlain out and out.

Later 'according to tradition' some went up the Tower as the new year was rung in:

Lady Horner strolled out into the north court (coatless on mild drizzly night) and stood waiting for the iron tongue. I had my hot punch in hand and healths were drunk. Katharine said: 'Conrad thinks 1939 is going to be one of the worst years ever experienced' and I said nothing as I think it may be.'[96]

As the family (along with Bluey and the Canon) had gathered on 28 March 1939 to celebrate Frances's eighty-fifth birthday, Conrad's prediction appeared ever more likely. Two weeks before, Hitler had marched into the rump of Czechoslovakia in blatant contradiction of the Munich Agreement. 'I try to stop my ears when they talk of evils ahead', Frances confessed to Sybil Colefax but it would not be long before she would be asking her friend, 'How do you feel about the Nazis – surely they must disappear into *Hell*.'[97] Characteristically, with war imminent and ignoring all advice, she and the Canon escaped in late August to Brittany for one last jaunt. From her hotel she looked out on little boats with white sails darting playfully about in the bay. She and Hannay walked the beaches in weather so glorious she even swam in the sea twice. And they talked: 'but gravely, sadly, for over us hung the shadow … of war… Why should all this innocent and joyous life be suddenly brought to an end?'[98] What was incomprehensible was now unstoppable. The lifeblood of an old world in which she lived and played a part was visibly draining away. Every day guests fled, fearful of the coming conflict. Hundreds more passed through *en route* for the ports. 'Pandemonium here! Douglas Fairbanks in the hotel!' Frances gleefully reported.[99] Yet soon all was silent and she and Hannay had the hotel to themselves. Nevertheless, they hung on until their week was up. Then they reluctantly made their way to Saint-Malo to join hordes scrambling to get home to England.

By the time Frances reached home, Mells was already bearing the imprint of war. As refugees poured out of London, a hundred families had been settled in the village, including two in The Manor House itself. The next day on 3 September 1939 the family gathered to listen in resignation as Chamberlain broadcast the declaration of war. Naturally thoughts drifted to Julian. When Raymond was killed in 1916, Winston Churchill had urged Katharine 'to think of the days to come when your little boy will revive his image and carry into the forefront of his country's service the name that all will honour'. It was no comfort to her then and certainly none now. Katharine, Frances wrote to Ettie, is 'very good but very unhappy and who isn't – except Winston I suppose'.[100] Otherwise, little was said and life took shelter in long established routine. Like an old record Cicely repeated her opinion from the outbreak of the last war: 'the worst of the Cabinet is there is not one person in it who knows about racing, and the King hates racing, so you see anything may happen'. When Evelyn Waugh arrived on 21 September he found little going on and 'Mells looking supremely peaceful and spacious'. Inside he discovered Frances rehanging the pictures rescued from her London house.

That same day Julian was called up.[101] The heroic effort to restore Mells after the destruction of one world war was imperilled now by the advent of another.

Arcadias
(1940)

English Perfection realised: a thinking man's Arcadia[1]

With war looming there would be one last hurrah for the old order in the form of a visit by Queen Mary to The Manor House.[2] Having been postponed the year before because of the risk of war, it was not to be stopped a year later despite the declaration of war the week before. So at 3pm on 10 September 1939 Queen Mary drew up outside The Manor House in 'a huge royal motor' – the first royal visitor since Charles I. Dressed all in white, the Queen greeted the two hundred refugees Frances had arranged on the lawn. Then they went on a long tour of Church, gardens and house (which with half the staff away Frances felt was looking 'just horrid'). At which point Queen Mary called for tea. Served by Mrs Gould, they had a 'good tuck in'. However 'it was still (only) 3.45!' As Frances and Conrad frantically considered what next they might do, 'Queen Mary asked for a cigarette. (Contrary to her reputation) she was highly affable at tea. No one was shy. At times it was a regular "wa wa"', recalled Conrad.

'The Queen then said in the firmest manner possible that there must never be any question of making peace with the Nazis – "dreadful people"' (to which there was now vigorous agreement). Spirits revived, Queen Mary asked to see upstairs. 'We were all exhausted' recorded Conrad who took refuge on a sofa with the Duchess of Beaufort, Queen Mary's niece and lady in waiting. '"Isn't the Queen extraordinary?" declared the duchess. "She never sits down." When the Queen came down she duly rebuked her niece for not coming up to the bedrooms, "You've missed the quilts", she said.' Finally at 5pm 'we bowed and curtsied her away and Katharine and I gave Lady Horner a stiff brandy and soda'. It was a fitting finale for the remarkable progress of one 'Francie Graham from Glasgow'.[3]

Within a month she would take to her bed never to rise again. The optimism that had driven and sustained her throughout her life was now fading fast. 'I feel so cold and unsanguine, which is wrong. Everything seemed so long ago and far away… If the Canon were here, church would be a comfort: that's wrong too – indeed nothing is right with the world'. And perhaps this had been so for some time. The striking of the Horner miners in 1936, however politely conducted, had been a startling revelation that paternalism no longer held sway in Mells.[4] The loss of the village school that she and the Canon had fought so doggedly to protect struck another blow to the social order. And then in 1938 McKenna sold Mells Park to a timber merchant, giving Frances only two weeks to match the price. 'One can't help minding [but] we were all away and too scattered to oppose it'. Nevertheless, it was the war that finally punctured her. 'Lady Horner no better' reported Conrad to Diana. 'The war is killing her wish to live'.[5]

The immediate cause of her illness was the breaking of her finger in a door – painful but not terminal. But soon she was 'terribly ill' with bronchitis, almost dying – until 'I thought better (or worse) of it' she would joke. 'Her vitality is extraordinary', exclaimed Katharine.[6] Yet Frances was bemused to find herself with 'no more strength left', putting it down to a year that had been 'so tiring, and frightening and disturbing'. Uncharacteristically she found herself in retreat from the world: 'I lie in bed in a big window here and watch the trees and all the past that floats past me'. Forlornly she would remark 'it is odd how people disappear silently at these times'.[7] With black outs and rationing she wondered if she would ever see Ettie again; both knew the answer to that. The Canon however made it to Mells and stayed for a week 'to my great pleasure more than Katharine's'.[8] Conrad too was a regular visitor. On one occasion when having tea with Katharine

> Lady Horner sent down to say that she had a message for me. I went up to her bedroom and there she was in a chair and looking like a very old man dying – somehow she looked like Voltaire or Goethe. I suppose it is the dressing gown. She then

told me Lady Lansdowne is going to marry Colum Crichton Stuart and, my word, wasn't I surprised. I was quite stunned… She is only old physically – very old. In conversation, she is like talking to someone of 30. As quick as a weasel and quite undeaf. When I saw her yesterday I made a rather smutty joke (about me being a sodomite) and she laughed delightedly for five minutes.[9]

The new year however was bitterly cold and eventually it proved too much for her. At 10pm on 1 March 1940 Frances died in her sleep, a month short of her eighty-sixth birthday. Katharine was very distressed by her going, declaring herself 'blessed' in their 'long companionship' – as indeed it had been. The funeral on 5 March was held on a 'bright, sunny, very cold day. The scene was one of simple rustic piety. Dreadfully moving'. The villagers had turned up in force and their children with snowdrops in hand provided a guard of honour. Conrad was surprised to find 'quite a lot of people who remembered her arrival as the Squire's young bride – among them the two Miss Horners, Jack's sisters; both in their nineties and still up to 1am every night. (Not all battles were won.) Fittingly the Canon led the service. 'He was terribly shattered poor dear', recorded Helen in her diary that night – though 'in the same ways still very like himself'. Fittingly too Lutyens would design (and Gill carve) her memorial stone as she was buried beside Jack in the peace of the little graveyard set among calm undulating fields. Behind her loomed the great tower, standing sentinel over her and the house that had come to define her. Diana Cooper was in Gibraltar when she heard the news. 'Well, well, she was like a fine tree, strong and beautiful in youth, and in age magnificent, a great shelter… and now is a good time to be cut down'.[10]

*

I wonder greatly about the future here… It'll be Catholics only. A private chapel in the house and good Father D'Arcy installed as domestic Chaplain. Will Katharine take the veil? I mean to keep the old flag flying at Little Clavey's 'And ever upon the top most roof the banner of Voltairian scepticism flew'.

Conrad Russell to Diana Cooper, 6 March 1940

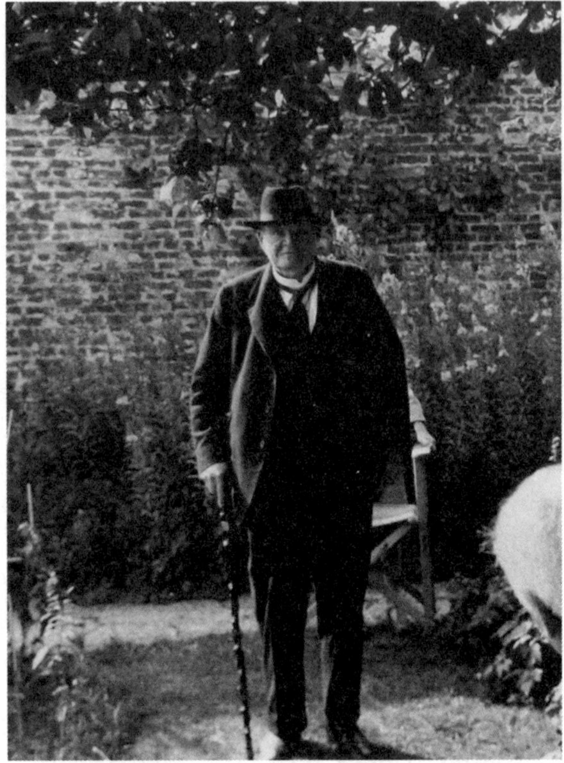

116.   Hilaire Belloc in the garden at Mells, 1940

Belloc is at The Manor House – fancy that!

Conrad Russell to Diana Cooper, 18 July 1940

While Conrad pondered the imminent revolution, Katharine was swamped by more prosaic concerns. 'Poor Katharine', noted Diana, 'what a lot she will have to shoulder. How desirable the convent will look to her as she flounders through wills, trusts, mortgages, mortmains, mergers and all the insane laws that follow on death. Only you [Conrad] will be of help'. Very quickly Mells began to change. Sir John's will had, on Frances's death, divided the land between his daughters with Katharine retaining The Manor House and the village. Cicely quickly sold off her share.[11] The compact estate that Haldane had exalted after the 1920s sales was now very compact indeed. As had happened after her father's death, so her Burne-Jones pictures began quietly to disappear. Admittedly Frances donated in

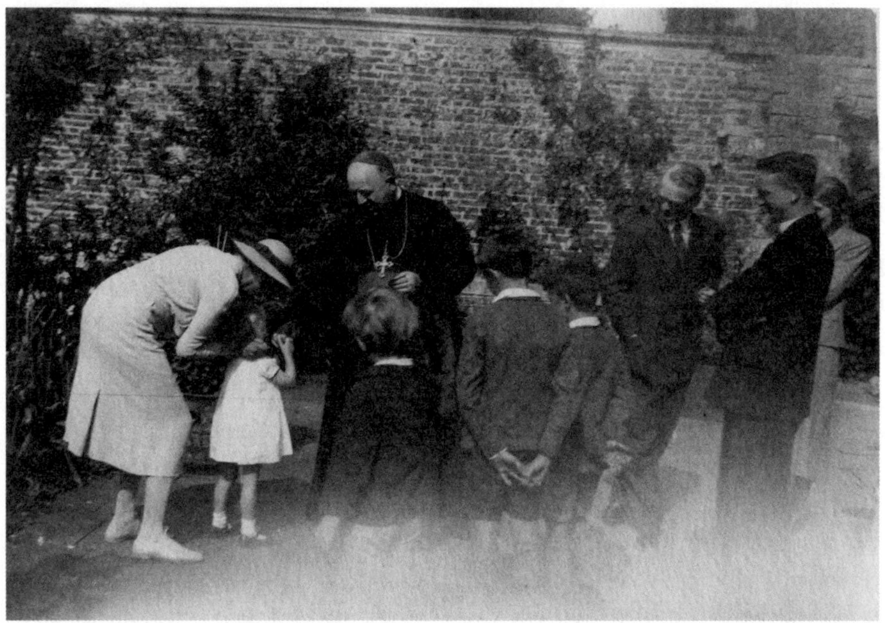

117.   *Katharine presenting children to the Bishop of Clifton, August 1940*

her will Burne-Jones's *Frieze of eight women gathering apples* (which her father had bought for £200 in 1879) to the National Gallery (it was later transferred to the Tate). More ominous were 'the Lady Horner sales' at Christie's in 1943 and 1949 with *Briar Rose: The Briar Wood* the most notable casualty.[12]

Yet by far the most striking development was a counter-reformation launched by Katharine that would define Mells until the present day. By July a chapel had been constructed out of the kitchen maids' quarters, and consecrated by the Bishop of Clifton. Matteo di Giovanni's painting of the Crucifixion was taken from the house and hung over the altar; while Stations of the Cross were inherited from Maurice Baring. Otherwise it was a modest, unpretentious setting with 'plain oak benches' reflecting the piety of its patron. Emphasising the new order an outside bell would ring out at the Elevation of the Host. Looking on from beyond the garden wall the church of St Andrew with its ancient tower lay becalmed. For the family it had become little more than a mausoleum.

Things now moved on apace. Priests from Ampleforth were recruited to say Mass. 'I believe the presence of a Priest in the house just makes the whole difference in the world to Katharine', conceded Conrad. 'One can see her recover her spirits and blossom out as soon as one is there'.[13] None more so than the arrival for Christmas of Ronnie Knox – convert, priest, scholar and one of the foremost Catholic populists of his day. Knox had been a friend of Edward's at Eton and Oxford and in 1909 had stayed at The Manor House. With him came memories of times when Katharine was genuinely at ease with the world. One picnic on the lawns of Balliol stood out. Katharine and Raymond had just become engaged. 'It was the hottest summer and we sat in the quad eating strawberries and some played poker on the grass and I can see Ronald now slightly detached sitting on a low wall with a book smoking a churchwarden pipe – I thought it slightly affected – but I loved them all and was happy'. After the war (October 1947) he would come to live permanently at Mells where he would complete his famous translation of the Old Testament. Symbolically he would retire to the study that was once Frances's with its mullion windows on three sides and a large open stone fireplace on the fourth. Another marker for change was the resonating tones of Hilaire Belloc; now welcome and, if increasingly immobile and declining fast, still able to shock the pristine piety of the converts 'with jokes about the resurrection and visions of Christ'.[14]

Around her Katharine began to attract a coterie of like-minds and converts, many of them leading lights of the Catholic intelligentsia. A gathering of the faithful at Mells provided a sense of belonging – 'an elect drawn together by religious mystery'.[15] Many of them would be buried in the family graveyard nearby including Siegfried Sassoon, Ronnie Knox and Christopher Hollis.[16] For them, the calm of Mells gave some protection from the cultural storms raging outside. Even Conrad was shocked when, alone with Lord Hylton after lunch, 'I said something about a [stray wartime] bomb falling on Mells and he said, "except for you, my dear Russell, I should welcome the destruction of that plague spot of Jesuit intrigue".'[17] Such prejudices only stiffened resolve. More disturbing were the ravages of modernism. To converts such as Sassoon the appeal of Mells was that it offered 'a survival of a vanished civilisation'. Amid its historic surrounds, an ancient Catholic past was resuscitated, resilient against the advancing chaos of populism and mere fashion. With Evelyn Waugh, Christopher Sykes and Christopher Hollis in the surrounding neighbourhood, Mells under Katharine became a hub of an aristocratic Catholic renaissance and a haven for those like its chatelaine seeking a refuge from the world.[18] For one seemingly so pulseless, Katharine proved the beating heart of this community. Among these trusted friends she would lose her natural reticence and become a warm, lively conversationalist, making her point with unexpected ardour and often very funny. With them too, she was serious, placing in discussion great store on spiritual reading, sermons and retreats, less from an intellectual pursuit than the ever-present path of moral and spiritual growth. There was a simple integrity to her faith that set the tone. So too her capacity to drift out of range when confronted by what she disapproved. 'What struck me most as a boy, observing Waugh, Sassoon and many others with her, was that … you just didn't play the fool with Katharine; you got nowhere trying to play games with her or be …clever, clever. It was not the least that she was forbidding: you just didn't get anywhere… And I think that was enormously refreshing for someone like Waugh.'[19] And it gave her an unsought authority in her own kingdom.

For Mells this was the greatest revolution since the Reformation. At the traditional Christmas Day dinner, Conrad was struck by the transformation Katharine had wrought in a matter of months.

> Katharine sat at one end of the table and the Black Monk at the other. Grace said by the Father and a lot of muttering and crossing by the Faithful. How queer it is – and I thought of all the old Ghosts – Sir John and Edward, Raymond, Bluetooth, … and of the poor Canon on whom the dread sentence 'never to return' has been pronounced. To me it's just stunning.[20]

Hannay's fate was hardly surprising. By now he had finally recognised 'the veil' that hung between him and Katharine. Rather pathetically, he wrote the day after Frances's funeral to thank Katharine for treating him 'not as an intruding stranger but one who has some right to share your sorrow'. Presumably at her request, he had spent the night burning Frances's letters. All to no avail. Hannay would only return for McKenna's funeral and his own.[21] Conrad survived because he was an old friend and good company on whom Katharine could rely for practical advice and the management of the farm. Still he resented an exclusion that on occasion could catch him by surprise: the secrecy with which the chapel was established, the eager discussing of the Mass at tea as if he wasn't in the room, and the obsession with the Rosary at 6.45pm when previously he would call in for a drink. 'In The Manor House the saying of Rosary at 6.45 is announced and advertised *ad nauseum*: "do stay till Rosary", "tell Per Rosary is in 10 minutes", "Were you at Rosary yesterday?". Everyone is nervous and jumpy. It might be the start of the Grand National'. At other times, he would find Katharine's silence impenetrable. It would upset him when she appeared so immersed in 'religious melancholy' as to be fit for a 'nunnery' (something that actually had no appeal for her).[22]

Even so, they remained close. When he fell ill, it was Katharine and Perdita who welcomed Conrad into The Manor House and nursed him back to health. 'I am in clover,' he wrote to Diana. From his bedroom, 'I can both hear and see the outside bell which wobbles and tinkles at the Elevation of the Host. And I was able to cross myself in bed just like the wicked old Peer in Evelyn's book'.[23] Two years later in April 1947 he was dying and back in The Manor House under Katharine's care. To his family his death bed reception into the Roman Catholic Church was a complete shock (or more euphemistically 'an enigma'). His quip to his sister that he 'wanted to know if there was anyone at the other end of the telephone' was a tease meant to stir. On the other hand, his continual provoking of Katharine over her faith had always hinted of protesting too much. He wanted to belong, and to belong especially to Katharine. 'A convert at the last to the Catholic faith', remarked Diana on hearing the news and pleasing that 'Katharine was there to reverence his parting soul. No one better could he have desired'. Katharine saw it differently. 'It was a miracle', she told a friend. 'I should have had more faith'.[24]

*

For some though, this Catholic revival at Mells was more a continuation than a revolution. After all, anyone less revolutionary than Katharine it would be hard to imagine. Hence, she continued to invite the rector to dinner every Sunday night (where he and Ronnie Knox got on famously). Indeed, the return of the spirit of Abbot Whiting distracts from how much the new order had in common with those that went before. Catholic Mells was just as socially conservative as the 'feudal' community of the Horners. And again, to Hannay the appeal of Mells was pre-reformation and lay in its being 'where tradition was the only guide of life'. Spiritually, Jack's Tractarian father shared Burne-Jones's love of Newman and the appeal of ritualistic, visual Catholicism. Even the sternly Protestant George Horner admired Burne-Jones's stained-glass windows in Oxford. For both Knox and Waugh conversion was preceded by a 'love affair with the Pre-Raphaelites'. For Frances this affair lasted a lifetime. Similarly, Burne-Jones and Fr McNabb, idolised by Frances and Katharine respectively, actively rejected industrialisation in favour of promoting the traditional crafts and a *faux* medievalism. Each of these perspectives involved romantic visions of an ancient England conjured up in the face of the relentless advance of brute modernity with its industrial revolution, empire, war and most recently class. In their different ways, they sought to protect and nurture a lost world of their imagination. For all their creativity, these boltholes of the mind were rear guard actions against the future – exercises in nostalgia. Still, few would have predicted that, in the end, it would be a return to the oldest tradition of all that would win out. Certainly not Frances.[25]

Nevertheless her stamp on Mells remains to this day. Most obviously in The Manor House where her design has recently been lovingly restored. Despite all the picture sales, many of the works so vital to her story remain in place: Burne-Jones's portrait of her father; the sketches of her and the Pilgrim Valentine; the blue angel that comforted her father in his last hours, and Rosetti's portrayal of her as *The Donna della Fenestra*. Throughout the house are Burne-Jones's needlework designs and the many gifts and mementoes he gave her. Wander through the village and it is her commissions by Lutyens that stand out: the war memorial, and the triangular shelter in memory of Mark. It was Frances too who, by enhancing the entrance, brought out again the sheer beauty of the setting and the timeless juxtaposition of house and church. More importantly, she and later Katharine would make Mells a place of books, pictures, of ideas and thinkers: a Mells of John Hippisley Horner and Ronald Knox; of the scientific Horners as well as Frances, the Pre-Raphaelite interloper. It was she who opened up a private world to the society of politicians and newspaper editors, artists and writers; to the *haute monde* of the Souls and the *jeunesse dorée* of the Coterie. Hence the irony that over an achingly beautiful cover of The Manor House in a recent edition of *Country Life*, the title should read 'English Perfection realised: a thinking man's Arcadia'.[26]

*

She is a social climber and has had personal success, a patron of arts would describe her, and a political intriguer. She is political, her bias born of friends and not conviction. That side of her leaves me cold, but I like her artistic intuition, leanings. It is very funny her grandchildren calling her 'Frances.'

Edwin Lutyens to his wife[27]

We will never see anyone like her again, with her extraordinary breadth of understanding and outlook, her love of the young and comprehension of people and things which others of her age failed completely to recognise... I don't think I ever knew anyone who inspired more *personal* affection.

Osbert Sitwell[28]

She grew greater as she grew older. A very unusual thing.

Bongie Bonham Carter[29]

Lutyens's judgement in 1911 was distinctly uncharitable from one whose own ambitions had benefited so much from her artistic instincts and active promotion. Nor would it stand the test of time as their friendship blossomed in the decades that followed. Perhaps it took one 'climber' to recognise another having to make their way. As 'Francie Graham from Glasgow' she had been born without the connections or spectacular wealth that allowed a few women to escape the hierarchies of her time; but she had been close enough to want these opportunities for herself; and later to break free from the constraints of a muse to realise her own artistic and political dreams. What followed was a demonstration of how a woman might get on in Victorian England through personality and a mastery of the arts of influence. Yes, she could flirt and plot; but behind such conventionality lay an enthusiastic, effervescent mind that was instinctively challenging and independent. This was what made her such a distinctive hostess, able to mix at her small dinners politicians and aristocrats with writers, artists and the up and coming, be they Oscar Wilde or Albert Einstein.

Along with being the muse of the most successful artist of her day, Frances had soon been hailed as the 'High Priestess' of the Souls

– the aristocratic elite at the forefront of Society who counted future prime ministers and viceroys among their number. In time, she had become the confidante of two Cabinet ministers. She was attracted to achievers, be they prize winners and leading writers, political power brokers, cultural icons, social titans and renowned wits – but especially to the coming men. Their company brought excitement, not resentment of their youth. She understood too the vulnerability and the craving for support that was the flip side of apparent confidence, talent and ambition. It was what made her so attractive to Burne-Jones, Asquith, Haldane, Lutyens, and even Hannay. Intuitively, from an early age, she knew how to manage and sustain such fragile egos; but also how this offered opportunities for one brought up before the emergence of the 'New Women'. Meanwhile at Mells in Somerset, the ancient seat of her husband, she created a Pre-Raphaelite haven lauded to this day. When the First World War brought death and the destruction of all that she had achieved, she found the will to rebuild the world she had lost and the imagination to engage with what was to come. All this took great courage in a male society, particularly in the face of her own insecurities. Thus in a discreet, subtle, human way, her life was a study in power – artistic, social, political, familial, local – and all the more fascinating for operating from a perennial position of weakness in an age on the cusp of modernity.

Of course, she was flawed and in later years she could be distinctly formidable; for all her good intentions she left casualties in her wake. Younger generations would mock her for being dazzled by duchesses, forgetting how much they, unmuddied by the struggle, had later benefited from her social ambition. Conversely intellectual snobs would make play of her being largely self-taught. Yet this is to ignore what made her so appealing. For she never lost that magnetism that would win over friend and foe alike – the provocative, teasing wit and the gentle shy smile that would then disarm; the sheer energy with which she lived life; her passion for new ideas and people – especially people – that won her followers of all ages; the generosity of spirit of a loyal friend keen to share in the dreams of others and make things possible; the laughter she could arouse in the most serious of souls; and behind it all a restless, irrepressible intelligence – always questioning, always hoping.

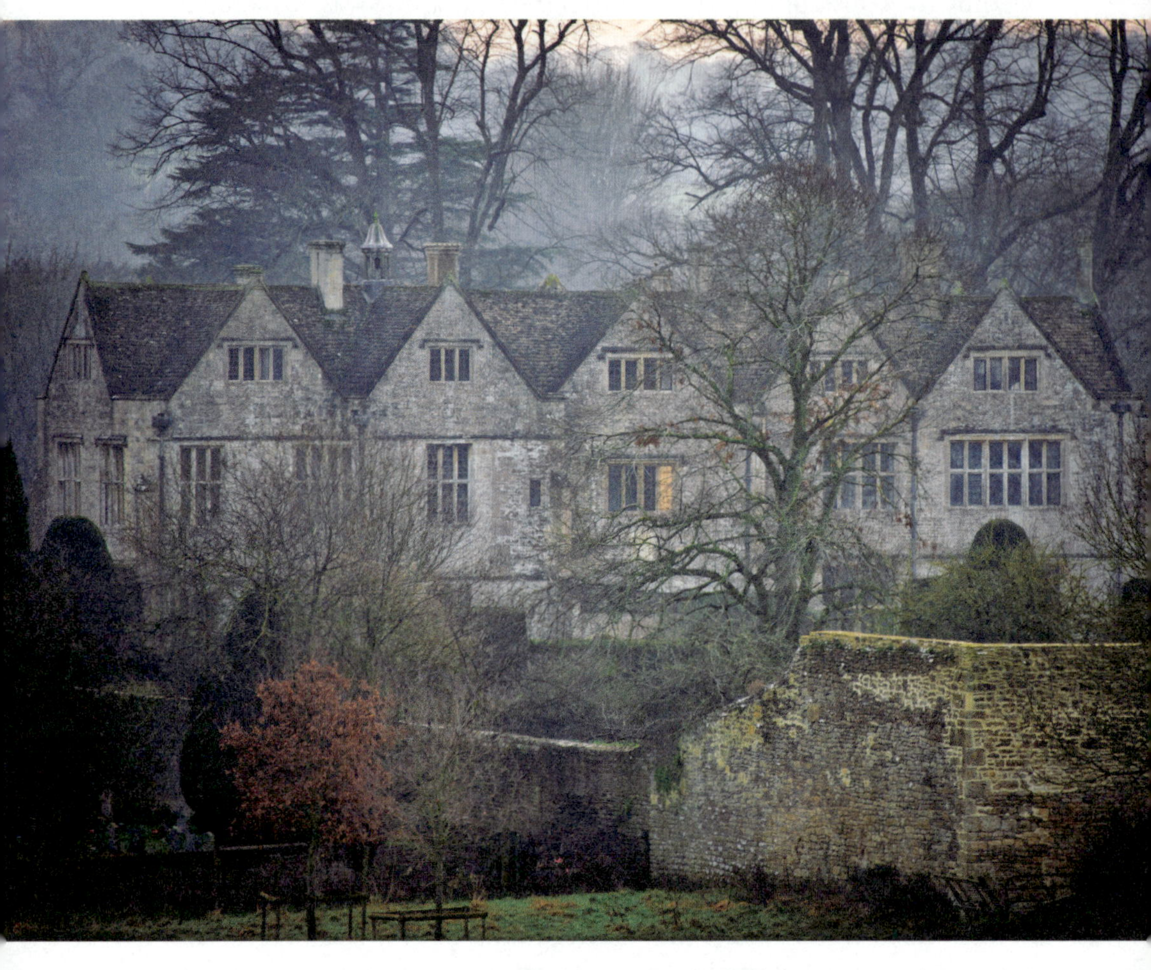

118.   *The Manor House, Mells*

NOTES

What will your biographers be able to do with a letter headed 'Tuesday 16th?' All the resources of the 'higher criticism' will be exhausted in the effort to discover from internal evidence in what month or year it was written. You should be less exacting in your demands upon posterity.'

So Asquith chastised Frances Horner but sadly to little effect (HHA–FH, 22 August 1892, MP, M/01/1270). To the despair of her biographer, Burne-Jones was equally as negligent. Where a date can be determined, it has been included. Where it has been suggested the date has acquired a ? For the most part one has had to rely on the order in which Frances collated the letters in her eleven volumes of correspondence with Burne-Jones. This order can prove more arbitrary than reliable – an irony that would not have been lost on Asquith.

After being initially expressed in full, the following names are abbreviated as below

HHA	Henry Asquith
KA	Katharine Asquith
RA	Raymond Asquith
EBJ	Edward Burne-Jones
DD	Edith Balfour (later Lyttelton)
FG	Frances Graham
WG	William Graham
EH	Edward Horner
FH	Frances Horner
JH	Forte ('Jack') Horner
KH	Katharine Horner
RBH	Richard Haldane
MP	Mells papers

PROLOGUE

1. EBJ to FH, n.d., quoted in FH, *Time Remembered*, p.112.
2. Francis Aidan Gasquet, *the Last Abbot of Glastonbury* (1895).
3. *Country Life*, 10 November 1917.
4. Watkins v Horner, C 1/1275/39, National Archives Kew.
5. William Graham [henceforth WG]–Frances Graham [henceforth FG], n.d., MP, M/04/1342–4.
6. WG–Edward Burne-Jones [henceforth EBJ], 17 May 1885; 'early June 1885', Oliver Garnett, 'The Letters and Collection of William Graham – Pre-Raphaelite Patron and Pre-Raphaelite Collector', *The Walpole Society*, 1999–2000, pp. 265, 273.
7. WG–EBJ, 30 June 1885, ibid. p. 278.
8. EBJ–FG, [August 1885], MP, M/04/1341/1.
9. Frances Horner [henceforth FH], *Time Remembered*, p. 112.

PART 1 'The Blissfullest Years' (1860–1880)

1. Fiona MacCarthy, *The Last Pre-Raphaelite: Edward Burne-Jones and the Victorian Imagination* (2011), p. 275.
2. FH, *Time Rememberd*, p. 6.
3. They toured Britain in 1873–5.
4. EBJ–Frances Horner, [1892], vol. 4, MP, M/05/1353
5. Stephen Wildman and John Christian, *Edward Burne-Jones: Victorian Artist-Dreamer* (1998), pp. 167–9.
6. EBJ–FH, July 1892, FM Cam, EBJ papers, xxvii, 13. MacCarthy, *The Last Pre-Raphaelite*, p. 188. Admittedly he bought many of Burne-Jones's pictures! As with any private collection, there would also be a few duds.
7. EBJ–FH, '1892', vol. 4, MP, M/05/1353.
8. Margot Asquith, *Autobiography* (1926), p. 8.
9. Wildman, *Victorian Artist-Dreamer*, p. 100.
10. A.G.W. Liddell, *Notes from the life of an*

Ordinary Mortal (1911), p. 78. Wildman, *Victorian Artist-Dreamer*, p. 109. Garnett, 'William Graham', p. 146.

11. Garnett, 'William Graham', p. 146.
12. Frances Horner, *Time Remembered* (1933), p. 5. Mary Wyndham [later Elcho] remembered going with her parents to a concert at the Grahams' and being overwhelmed by the pictures. Her father would later buy some of Graham's collection for Clouds. Caroline Dakers, *Clouds* (1993), p. 76.
13. Rosalie Mander (ed.), H.T. Dunn, *Recollections of Dante Gabriel Rossetti and his Circle* (1984). Garnett, 'William Graham', pp. 159–60.
14. MacCarthy, *The Last Pre-Raphaelite*, pp. 188–9.
15. On WG's collection, see Garnett, 'William Graham', pp. 152–71.
16. In his will Graham directed 'my Trustees to allow my wife the life rent use and enjoyment thereof or of any such portion thereof as she should desire to retain.' Garnett estimates that the family still retained up to two hundred pictures and a few were bought back. But these were the lesser works.
17. Only Nancy Ellenberger suspects Frances's real age. *Balfour's World: Aristocracy and Political Culture at the Fin de Siècle* (2015), p. 312. In her memoir, Frances continually underestimates her age, *Time Remembered*, p. 64.
18. Garnett, 'William Graham', p. 168.
19. Frances's siblings were Alice, Florence, Rutherford, Amy, Willie, Lily, Agnes. She was the fifth child.
20. Frances would claim that she paid for it entirely out of her allowance and dressed shabbily as a result. It lasted three years until the matron she had hired was found drunk. FH, *Time Remembered*, pp. 53–4.
21. FH, *Time Remembered*, p. 1.
22. Patricia Jalland, *Women, Marriage and Politics* (1986), p. 12. Mary was the daughter of the Liberal politician, W.E. Gladstone.
23. 'Not at all suitable for young maidens'. FH, *Time Remembered*, p. 39.
24. Jalland, *Women, Marriage and Politics*, pp. 7–17.
25. FH, *Time Remembered*, pp. 2–3.
26. Florence who eventually was placed in an asylum.
27. Her mother was often the butt of Frances's jokes. Once when her mother was recruiting a governess for Aggie, Frances impersonated an applicant. 'I professed to share her favourite theories and said all the things about religious teaching … which

I knew would appeal to her. Poor darling, she thought she had found her dream at last, and engaged me with a proviso that "Frances" must see me first.' When exposed, 'I was scolded of course but I think it was disappointment rather than anger which filled her mind'. *Time Remembered*, p. 43.

28. FH to Sydney Cockerell, 3 November 1904, Cockerell Papers, Add MS 52726.
29. FH, *Time Remembered*, p. 26.
30. He had been summoned north to paint Frances and her two sisters, Florence and Amy. The sketches were 'lovely'; Amy had just come out and had 'wavy brown hair and large starry eyes'. The final picture was called *The Music Party* and dated 1867. A.M.W. Stirling, *The Richmond Papers*, p. 240; and in S. Reynolds, *William Blake Richmond, an artist's life, 1842–1921* (1995).
31. On the life of a model, see Jan Marsh, 'Pre-Raphaelite Models', in Jan Marsh, *Pre-Raphaelite Sisters* (2019), pp. 16–20.
32. Jan Marsh, *Dante Gabriel Rossetti* (1999), p. 469. Garnett, 'William Graham', p. 161.
33. FH, *Time Remembered*, p. 6.
34. WG to Rossetti, 3 April 1874, 19 July 1875, in Garnett, 'William Graham', pp. 221, 226.
35. WG–FH, n.d., MP, M/04/1344.
36. To be renamed the Victoria and Albert Museum in 1899.
37. FH, *Time Remembered*, p. 45. Garnett, 'William Graham', p. 150.
38. David Cecil, *Visionary and Dreamer* (1969), p. 179.
39. Though note his later assertion: 'You ask me if I have ever found temptation irresistible – no never – if I have given in, I have given in with my whole will and meant to do it.' EBJ–Mrs Gaskell, 18 January 1893, Penelope Fitzgerald, *Edward Burne-Jones, a biography* (1975), p. 183.
40. EBJ–FH, 13 September 1892, Vol. 5, MP M/05/1353.
41. But see MacCarthy, *The Last Pre-Raphaelite*, pp. 249–50, who speculates that they had met briefly in Siena in 1873.
42. MacCarthy, *The Last Pre-Raphaelite*, p. 214.
43. EBJ to Olive Maxse (nd 1890s, Penelope Fitzgerald, *Edward Burne-Jones, a biography* (1975) p. 130.
44. EBJ–G.F. Watts, January 1874, Fitzgerald, *Burne-Jones*, p. 155.
45. FH, *Time Remembered*, pp. 106–8.
46. MacCarthy, *The Last Pre-Raphaelite*, p. 214.
47. EBJ–Helen Gaskell in ODNB, 'Edward Burne-Jones', by Christopher Newall. FH, *Time Remembered*, p. 185.
48. FH, *Time Remembered*, pp. 136–44.

49. Mark Girouard, *The Return to Camelot: Chivalry and the English Gentleman* (1981), pp. 180–96.

50. MacCarthy, *The Last Pre-Raphaelite*, p. 321.

51. FH, *Time Remembered*, p. 26 EBJ–FH, nd [1892?], vol. 4, MP, M/05/1353.

52. It now hangs in St Andrew's church, Mells. See also his designs for a purse in the mid-1870s for her to embroider with her birth sign, Aries. Charlotte Gere, 'Portraits', in Alison Smith, *Edward Burne-Jones*, Tate Britain exhibition catalogue (2018), p. 152.

52. Burne-Jones was commissioned to 'ornament' a brass plaque for the wall by the North Door in Eton College Chapel in memory of Willie Graham. FH, *Time Remembered*, pp. 45–6. Garnett, 'William Graham', p. 158.

54. Mary Gladstone's Diaries, 14 September 1875, Add MS 46257.

55. F.H. *Time Remembered*, pp. 45–6. MacCarthy suggests that a nurse may have been responsible for an accidental overdose. MacCarthy, *The Last Pre-Raphaelite*, p. 360.

56. FG–Alfred Lyttelton, n.d. Lyttelton papers, CHAN1/2/7/22

57. Mary Gladstone's Diaries, 14 February 1875, Add MS 46256. The Valentine was an early sketch for *Love and the Pilgrim* with Frances in the role of the Pilgrim. Originally it had been devised as part of a series of three tapestries drawn from Chaucer's *Romaunt of the Rose* with its 'quest of the perfect love symbolised by the mystical heart of the rose'. Although he started to paint it in 1877, it was not until 1895 that he returned to it. By the time it was exhibited in 1897, the Pilgrim had become a man! Wildman, *Victorian Artist-Dreamer*, pp. 182–4. MacCarthy, *The Last Pre-Raphaelite*, pp. 478–9.

58. David Cecil, *Visionary and Dreamer* (1969), p. 180.

59. FH, *Time Remembered*, p. 105

60. See the example of Alice Liddell, the model for Alice in Wonderland. Francine Prose, *The Lives of the Muses* (2002), pp. 1–2, 57–98.

61. Catherine Robson, *Men in Wonderland* (2003); Nancy Ellenberger, *Balfour's World* (2015), pp. 52–3. MacCarthy, *The Last Pre-Raphaelite*, pp. 190–1.

62. Throughout *Time Remembered* the differential varies between four and six years: p. 64.

63. And then only after W.T. Stead's exposé of child prostitution ('the Maiden Tribute of Modern Babylon') in the *Pall Mall Gazette*. At nineteen Frances could quite respectably have got married. Pat Jalland, *Women, Marriage and Politics, 1860–1914* (1986), p. 79.

64. FH, *Time Remembered*, p. 31. Edward Lyttelton captained Eton and Cambridge at cricket and much later became Head Master of Eton. He was forced to resign in 1916 after being falsely accused of being pro-German.

65. MacCarthy, *The Last Pre-Raphaelite*, p. 276.

66. Fitzgerald, *Burne-Jones*, p. 158.

67. *Tristram and Iseult* was abandoned in 1872–3 and not properly attributed under its correct title until 2012. It shows Tristram kissing his wife while his former lover tries forlornly to pass him a letter. Given that Burne-Jones was attempting to escape from his own love triangle, Frances's objections may have been pragmatic as much as moral. *Daily Telegraph*, 9 September 2012.

68. FH, *Time Remembered*, pp. 104–6.

69. Wildman, *Victorian Artist-Dreamer*, p. 196.

70. FH, *Time Remembered*, opposite p. 40. One of the few surviving photographs of the young Frances is reproduced in her autobiography, *Time Remembered*. With her sister Amy beside her, she looks heavy of build and jaw and far from the slender Pre-Raphaelite ideal. However, she is not the figure attributed to her. The photograph has been titled 'Amy and Frances Graham'; yet Frances is clearly the more attractive figure on the left.

71. Mary Gladstone diary, 24 March 1877, Add MS 46257. FH, *Time Remembered*, p. 64.

72. Finding her of course in Maria Zambaco, a real Hellenic living in England! MacCarthy, *The Last Pre-Raphaelite*, p. 189. Eliza Korb, 'Models, Muses, and Burne-Jones's Continuous Quest for the Ideal Female Face' in Birmingham Museums and Art Gallery, *Hidden Burne-Jones* (2007), p. 29.

73. Margot Asquith, *The Autobiography of Margot Asquith*, ed. Mark Bonham Carter (1962), p. 134. Her brother Willie thought a photograph taken in 1875–6 not only 'divine' but also much more realistic that EBJ's sketch; though both captured 'the Crescendo of the eyebrows'. Willie–FG, nd, MP, M/04/1343.

74. Abdy and Gere, *Souls*, pp. 128–30. Korb, 'Models, Muses and Burne-Jones's Continuous Quest, pp. 28–33. Wildman, *Victorian Artist-Dreamer*, pp. 144–5.

75. Wildman, *Victorian Artist-Dreamer*, p. 314. Anne Anderson, 'Life into Art and Art into Life: Visualising the Aesthetic Woman or "High Art Maiden" of the Victorian "Renaissance"', *Women's History Review*, 10, no. 3, 2001, p. 447. The 'unself-conscious pencil portraits' – preliminaries to working

up the ideas in the major portraits – were probably more accurate likenesses.

76. FH–Edith ('DD') Lyttelton [henceforth DD], 'Friday June 1898', Edith Lyttelton papers, CHAN 1/5/10/158.
77. Tim Hilton, *John Ruskin: the later years* (2000).
78. MacCarthy *The Last Pre-Raphaelite*, pp. 190–91.
79. Liddell was at Oxford with Frances's brother, Rutherford. Edith ('DD') Balfour was Frances's closest confidante. Peter Flower was passionate about hunting and the long-term lover of Margot Tennant.
80. Ellenberger, *Balfour's World*, pp. 43–52.
81. Ellenberger, *Balfour's World*, p. 71. MacCarthy hedges her bets: 'His [EBJ] fondness for the child became a lifelong passion, possibly consummated but more likely not'. MacCarthy, *The Last Pre-Raphaelite*, p. 189.
82. Mary Gladstone's Diary, 28 June 1880, Add MS 46259.
83. 'Was that really true that you heard anyone say it; about me painting always from you? Or are you teasing me? ... I hope someone did say I always painted from you, because it sounds like praise to me'. EBJ–FG, nd, vol. 1, MP, M/05/1353.
84. Originally a private gift from Morris, who was rather startled to see it promptly given to Frances by Burne-Jones.
85. Sometimes this is believed to be a twenty-first birthday present. Commissioned in 1879 and completed a year later, Frances would have been twenty-five or twenty-six. Anyway, twenty-first birthdays were not held to be of special significance in the nineteenth century.
86. MacCarthy, *The Last Pre-Raphaelite*, p. 277. Wildman, *Victorian Artist-Dreamer*, pp. 126, 275–7. Fitzgerald, *Burne-Jones*, p. 175. Garnett, 'William Graham', p. 168.
87. EBJ–FH, 13 September 1892, vol. 5 MP, M/05/1353.
88. Fitzgerald, *Burne-Jones*, p. 154.
89. 'Physical congress with one's muse is hardly possible, because her role is to penetrate the mind rather than to have her body penetrated. Dante never laid a hand on Beatrice, nor Petrarch on Laura. Gustav Klimt's "lifelong companion", Emilie Flöge, the younger sister of his sister-in-law, almost certainly died a virgin'. Germaine Greer, 'The role of the artist's muse' in *The Guardian*, 1 June 2008. Francine Prose, *The Lives of the Muses* (2002), p. 374, states that of the muses she studied, only a 'minority' had sex with their artist.

90. Margot Asquith, *Autobiography*, p. 134.
91. MacCarthy, *The Last Pre-Raphaelite*, pp. 284–7.
92. The future Edward VII.
93. Henry James, *The Painter's Eye*, pp. 144–7, cited in ODNB and MacCarthy, *The Last Pre-Raphaelite*, p. 285.
94. Fitzgerald, *Burne-Jones*, pp. 166–9.
95. Wildman, *Victorian Artist-Dreamer*, p. 212.
96. MacCarthy, *The Last Pre-Raphaelite*, pp. 294–8. Whistler sued Ruskin for denouncing Whistler's painting as 'throwing a pot of paint in the public's face'. Whistler won the case in November 1878 but was only awarded a farthing's damages. Bankrupt soon after, he left for Italy.
97. FG–Mary Gladstone [n.d., November 1879], Mary Gladstone papers, Add Ms 46251.
98. FG–Mary Gladstone, Mary Gladstone papers [November 1879] Add Ms 46251. Fitzgerald, *Burne-Jones*, pp. 174–5.
99. Fitzgerald, *Burne-Jones*, p. 146. Georgiana Burne-Jones, *Memorials of Edward Burne-Jones* (1904), I, p. 236.
100. MacCarthy, *The Last Pre-Raphaelite*, p.282. Fitzgerald, *Burne-Jones*, pp. 172–3. The Gilbert and Sullivan work was *Patience*.
101. MacCarthy, *The Last Pre-Raphaelite*, pp. 286–7. Fiona MacCarthy, 'The Golden Girls', *The Guardian*, 10 October 1998. Wildman, *Victorian Artist-Dreamer*, pp. 212–13. Phyllis Weliver, 'Liberal Dreaminess', *British Art Journal*, vol. xvii, no. 3, Spring 2017, pp. 55–63.
102. Compare the final version with an earlier sketch of Frances in this role in Alison Smith, *Edward Burne-Jones*, Tate Britain exhibition catalogue (2018), p. 76.
103. Margot Asquith, *Autobiography* (1920), p. 134.
104. Single women were supposed to be chaperoned until the age of thirty. Frances was also unusual in that when she was chaperoned, it was more often by her father and rarely by her mother. Jalland, *Women, Marriage and Politics*, pp. 24–5.
105. Jane Abdy and Charlotte Gere, *The Souls* (1984), p.131.
106. On Muses over time see Francine Prose, *The Lives of the Muses* (2002); Julia Forster, *Muses: Revealing the nature of inspiration* (2007); Zadie Smith, 'The Muse at her Easel', *New York Review of Books*, 21 November 2019.
107. See Georgie Burne-Jones's plaintive cry: 'It is pathetic to think how we women longed to keep pace with the men, and how gladly they kept us by them until their pace quick-

ened and we had to fall behind', *Memorials*, I, p. 218. Charlotte Gere, 'Model wives and Mistresses', in Jan Marsh (ed.), *Pre-Raphaelite Sisters* (2019), pp. 138–45. Many of the wellknown models of the Pre-Raphaelites were keen and talented artists in their own right, but unless they were of independent means, for the most part their work was rarely exhibited or acknowledged. The National Portrait Gallery's 2019 exhibition *Pre-Raphaelite Sisters* (curated by Jan Marsh) sought to rectify this.

108. Anderson, 'Life into Art and Art into Life', pp. 454–5.

109. Fitzgerald, *Burne-Jones*, p. 130.

110. FH, *Time Remembered*, p. 104.

PART 2 The Great Gamble (1880–1883)

1. FH, *Time Remembered*, p. 62.
2. FH, *Time Remembered*, p. 61.
3. FH, *Time Remembered*, pp. 61–4.
4. MacCarthy, *The Last Pre-Raphaelite*, pp. 366–7. Dick Swiveller is from Dickens's *The Old Curiosity Shop*. This was hardly flattering as Dick was trying to marry Little Nell to get at her grandparents' money. Presumably Burne-Jones had found out that Horner had little money and had cynically assumed that he was marrying Frances to get at her father's wealth.
5. EBJ talked of being 'dishonoured', Judith Flanders, *Circle of Sisters* (2001). On possessiveness, see his urging Laura Tennant 'never to marry but to go about being a delight to us all'. Burne-Jones attributed it to his mother dying giving birth to him, so leaving him both guilty and desperate for love. Ellenberger, *Balfour's World*, p. 52.
6. It is estimated that at this time 'two million middle-class women faced the prospect of never marrying and raising a family'. Anderson, 'Life into Art and Art into Life' p. 446.
7. All except Florence who was in an asylum and Lily who became a missionary in China. The average age for women to marry was twenty five but closer to twenty was deemed ideal. Pat Jalland, *Women, Marriage and Politics, 1860–1914*, p. 79. Interestingly in *Time Remembered*, p. 64, Frances claims she was twenty-four when she married Jack but in fact she was almost twenty-nine. In so doing she increases their age difference from twelve to seventeen years, which seems to have mattered less to her.
8. Jalland, *Women, Marriage and Politics*, pp. 257, 265.

9. Doll Liddell, *Notes*, p. 79.
10. Sheila Fletcher, *The Victorian Girls, Lord Lyttelton's daughters* (1997), p. 163.
11. In 1888 Margot Tennant claimed to Harry Cust [neither very reliable] that she had met Agnée [Clark?] who, as well as 'singing beautifully and dressing charmingly', was the heartbroken fiancée that Rutherford apparently dumped for May. Margot Tennant–Harry Cust, 7 December 1888, Margot Asquith papers, MS Eng d.3278.
12. Mary Palmer was the daughter of Sir Roundell Palmer and Lady Laura Palmer (described by Frances as a 'staunch friend'). Later Frances and Mary were neighbours when Mary married the Earl Waldegrave. FH, *Time Remembered*, p. 41.
13. Fletcher, *Victorian Girls*, p. 167.
14. FH, *Time Remembered*, pp. 41, 56. To Frances's chagrin, her parents did throw a ball for Aggie in 1881–2. Leonore Davidoff, *The Best Circles: Society, Etiquette and The Season* (1973), pp. 50, 55–61.
15. Willie Graham–FG, n.d., MP, M/04/1343.
16. FG–Alfred Lyttelton, n.d. Lyttelton papers, CHAN1/2/7/22, 24. Before taking his appointment at Cambridge, Oscar Browning had been dismissed from Eton and was rumoured to be too close to his pupils, including the future Lord Rosebery.
17. It seems as if the hostility came from the parents and especially May's mother rather than the younger generation.
18. Edith ('DD') Lyttelton declared that Alfred was 'one of her [ie Frances's] special friends even before he married Laura'. Edith Lyttelton, *Alfred Lyttelton*, p. 180. Needless to say EBJ was jealous and wrote how he wanted to be 'exactly like him all over and be always in white flannel.'
19. FH, *Time Remembered*, p. 50.
20. Lucy Masterman (ed), *Mary Gladstone: her diaries and letters* (1930), pp. 96–7.
21. FH, *Time Remembered*, p. 53.
22. W. E. Gladstone, presumably under Mary's influence, later controversially appointed him to the evangelical parish of Holy Trinity, Stroud Green, in London.
23. FH, *Time Remembered*, p. 48. Sidney Colvin– FG, 24 September [1880–2?], Autograph Letters, Mells library, vol. 2, p. 14, M/01/1260.
24. Ruskin to FG, 12 November ?, *Autograph Letters*, vol. 1, p. 9, MP, M/01/1260. Equally disconcerting was his comment 'I like to think of you sometimes sitting on the table in the hall in Grosvenor Place and looking like a piece of Dresden'. Ruskin to FG, 'New

Year', MP, *Autograph Letters* , vol. 1, p. 10, MP, M/01/1260.

25. FH, *Time Remembered*, pp. 54–7. MacCarthy, *The Last Pre-Raphaelite*, p. 276. Mary Gladstone's Diary, 26 February 1878, Add MS 46258. FG–Mary Gladstone, 28 February 1878, Add MS 46251. Masterman, p. 143 [diary,15 October 1878].

26. FH, *Time Remembered*, pp. 53–54. FG–Mary Gladstone, 'Nov 1879', Mary Gladstone papers, Add MS 46251.

27. Laura Tennant Diary, 20 March 1881, Asquith papers, MSS. Eng. d.3311, d.3198. Ellenberger, *Balfour's World*, p. 52.

28. Laura Tennant's Travel Diary 1880–1883 [20 July–10 August 1880, 15 September 1883], Bonham Carter papers, MSS Bonham Carter 705. Edith Lyttelton, 'Interwoven', CHAN/ I/6/1/B, p. 2. Ellenberger, *Balfour's World*, pp. 52–3.

29. Angela Lambert, *Unquiet Souls*, p. 23.

30. FH, *Time Remembered*, p. 62.

31. Jalland, *Women, Marriage and Politics*, pp. 100–1.

32. In *Time Remembered*, p. 59 Frances suggests that they didn't begin their 'love affair' until 1882 and the second visit.

33. Rafe Leycester–FG, 29 May 1882, 3 June 1882, 7 June 1882, MP, M/01/1261.

34. Dames at Eton ran the boys' houses although increasingly in the nineteenth century under the aegis of a 'house master'.

35. EBJ–FH, 20 July 1892, vol. 4, MP, M/05/1353. EBJ admitted that 'Gabriel' 'did wrong' and was profoundly selfish but in retrospect loved him nonetheless. In reality, they had become more detached.

36. EBJ–FH, nd [November 1886], vol. 2, MP, M/05/1353. Sir Hubert Parry, the leading English composer of the day.

37. 'Do you remember when I couldn't bear you to have any friends?... – I suppose I was dreadful but I couldn't help it – and you said that you needed many, being yourself of many facets.' EBJ–FH, 3 July 1893 vol. 7, MP, M/05/1353.

38. FH, *Time Remembered*, p. 60.

39. Jose Harris, *Private Lives, Public Spirit: a social history of Britain 1870-1914* (1993), pp. 73–9.

40. Jack held first-class degrees from Oxford in both Law and History and was called to the Bar.

41. Jack Horner [henceforth JH]–FG, 3 October 1882, MP, M/01/1263.

42. Alice's husband, Quintin Hogg, was very religious [as was she], fiercely driven, insomniac, and possibly bipolar. Amy's hus-

band 'liked to get his own way and generally got it'. FH, *Time Remembered*, pp. 43–4. Neither sister though was unhappy.

43. Jack at forty was twelve years her senior – in Victorian terms not that unusual.

44. Mary Gladstone diary, 16 September 1882, Mary Gladstone papers, Add MS 46259.

45. Sheila Goodde, *Mary Gladstone: a gentle rebel* (2003), p. 159.

46. Mary Gladstone's Diary, 16–18 September 1882, Mary Gladstone papers, Add MS 46259. Margot Asquith later confided to Frances that Mary should have seen Mells Park 'before criticising your marriage'. Margot Asquith–FH, nd [1894], Asquith Papers, MS Eng c6677, ff. 84–5.

47. FH, *Time Remembered*, p. 76.

48. *Country Life*, 10 November 1917.

49. Apart from a brief period after the Civil War when there was a flurry of Georges, Horners tended to oscillate between Thomas and John, thus causing much confusion.

50. The architect was Nathaniel Ireson.

51. *Gentleman's Magazine* (1794).

52. Dakers, *Clouds* (1993), pp. 112–13.

53. FH, *Time Remembered*, p. 179.

54. He claimed to be descended directly from James IV of Scotland.

55. There was some traditional agrarian crime, including the mutilation of Horner cattle, which at this time assumed the Chartist label.

56. Chris Roberts, *Heavy Words Lightly Thrown: The Reason Behind the Rhyme* (2005). Horners were 'longstanding Abbey tenants', cited in *The Archaeology and History of Glastonbury Abbey: Essays in honour of the 90th Birthday of C.A. Radlegh Radford* (1991), ed. Lesley Abrams and James P. Carley.

57. According to Frances's daughter Katharine, the connection between Mells and the rhyme was invented by a 'catty armchair historian' who disapproved of her mother as a popular London hostess in the 1890s. [Private information].

58. JH–FG, 11 September 1882, MP, K/02/1152.

59. JH–FG, nd, MP, M/01/1263

60. JH on Gertrude: 'I was never good enough for her and my worldly ways annoyed her.' JH–FG, 4 October 1882, MP, M/01/1263.

61. Horner Marriage Settlement, MP, K/01/1125.

62. JH–FG, 13, 14, 17 September 1882; 6, 15, 22 November 1882; 18 December 1882. MP, M/01/1263.

63. FH, *Time Remembered*, pp. 65–6.

64. FH, *Time Remembered*, pp. 66–7.

65. Mary Gladstone's diary, 15 November1882, Mary Gladstone papers, Add MS 46259.

66. JH–FG, nd, MP, M/01/1263. MacCarthy, *The Last Pre-Raphaelite*, p. 336.
67. Laura Tennant diary, 1 April 1884, Asquith papers, MSS. Eng. d.3312.
68. FH, *Time Remembered*, p. 62.
69. Masterman, *Mary Gladstone*, p. 277.
70. EBJ–FG, nd [1883], vol. 1 MP, M/05/1353. About this time he painted *The Spirit of the Downs*: 'we all', wrote Georgie, 'recognised the portrait'. To Penelope Fitzgerald this was a picture of Frances on the eve of her wedding; hence the coy reference. Christie's, when they sold the picture in 2004 found an inscription identifying the subject as Venetia Hunt who went on to marry W.A.S. Benson, the architect who worked on the Burne-Joneses' Rottingdean house. Until the sale the picture had remained with the Benson family.
71. MacCarthy, *The Last Pre-Raphaelite*, pp. 341–2.
72. MacCarthy, *The Last Pre-Raphaelite*, p. 342.
73. Graham characteristically interpreted the picture in religious terms. He suggested adding the following text from Samuel to the frame: 'He raiseth up the poor out of the dust to set them among Princes and to make them inherit the throne of glory'. Writing to Burne-Jones, he asked, 'Isn't that the real meaning and moral of it all? How the Heavenly Father's love lifts up and glorifies unworthy ones like you and me, making us worthy of the love in doing so.' Garnett, 'William Graham', p. 170.
74. EBJ–Mary Gaskell, n.d., in Josceline Dimbleby, *Profound Secret* (2004).
75. In all likelihood, over its long gestation there were numerous people who sat for this picture, including Burne-Jones's daughter, Margaret, and the model Anne Pollen. Fitzgerald, *Burne-Jones*, p. 200. Andrew Wilton and Robert Upstone (eds), *The Age of Rossetti, Burne-Jones and Watts*, Tate Gallery exhibition catalogue (1997), pp. 147–50. W. S. Taylor, 'King Cophetua and the Beggar Maid', *Apollo*, February 1973, pp. 148–55.
76. *The Times*, 1 May 1884; Wildman, *Victorian Artist-Dreamer*, pp. 253–5; Taylor, 'King Cophetua and the Beggar Maid', pp. 148–55. The cartoon that Graham bought now belongs to Birmingham Museums and Art Gallery.

PART 3 Married to Mells (1883–1886)

1. FH, *Time Remembered*, p. 77.
2. Angela Lambert, *Unquiet Souls* (1984), p. 85.
3. FH, *Time Remembered*, pp. 68–71.
4. FH, *Time Remembered*, pp. 71–80 for much of what follows.
5. See Genesis 27:46 for reference to 'daughters of Heth' who were held to be divisive and scheming. Alternatively she could be referring to the popular novel, *A Daughter of Heth* (1871) by William Black, in which the flighty Coquette wreaked havoc among a respectable Scottish household.
6. Kathleen Haldane, *Friends and Kindred: Memoirs of Louisa Kathleen Haldane* (1961), pp. 133–4.
7. FH, *Time Remembered*, pp. 72–3.
8. FH, *Time Remembered*, pp. 179–80.
9. This might refer to Wapping where Mary Elcho and Laura Tennant talked of establishing a girl's club where any daughters they had would receive the education denied their parents. Ellenberger, *Balfour's World*, p. 81.
10. Angela Lambert, *Unquiet Souls* (1984), p. 85.
11. In particular she mentions in her memoirs that on grounds of cost there was no garden party to introduce her to the local society. FH, *Time Remembered*, p. 73.
12. Laura Tennant diary, 30 November 1884, Margot Asquith papers, MS Eng. D3312. Angela Lambert, *Unquiet Souls*, p. 25.
13. Laura Tennant diary, 1 April 1884, Margot Asquith papers, MS Eng. d.3312.
14. Garnett, 'William Graham', p. 265.
15. Masterman, *Mary Gladstone*, p. 360. FH, *Time Remembered*, pp. 80–83.
16. Abdy and Gere, *The Souls*, p.133; Garnett, 'William Graham', p. 171.
17. Margot Asquith, *More Memories* (1933), pp. 96–7.
18. A.G.C. Liddell, *Notes from the life of an ordinary mortal* (1911), p. 222. Edith Lyttelton, *Alfred Lyttelton* (1917), p.180. For Clouds, see Caroline Dakers, *Clouds: The Biography of a Country House* (1993).
19. Angela Emanuel (ed.), *A Bright Remembrance: The Diaries of Julia Cartwright* (1989), p. 190 (17 August 1894).
20. Emanuel (ed.), *A Bright Remembrance*, p. 189 (17 August 1894).
21. Under Scottish law at least a third of Graham's estate of £184,321 should have gone to his wife or £61,440 (£7,300,000); and a third by law was to be distributed among the surviving offspring or £10,740 each (£1,355,681). In fact he left it all to his wife. Most of the pictures were left to his wife.

22. FH–DD, 31 January 1891, Edith Lyttelton papers, CHAN1/5/9/38–41.

23. Mortality rates at the time were 5 per 1000 but increased to 3 per 100 in women with more than five children. (Jalland, *Women, Marriage and Politics*, p. 171). Marriages in the 1880s produced 5.3 children on average. But these figures exclude death in miscarriages and still births. Precise causes were described as 'puerperal fever' which encompassed all infections; or 'accident' – often exhaustion and weakened constitution from too many births.

24. FH, *Time Remembered*, p. 84.

25. Typically George instructed her to call the child 'Elimor' after some Glastonbury ancient, conceding 'you may add Mary because her birth is within the octave of St Mary's nativity'. Another brother called for 'Nova' as in a new star. Frances ignored them both. George Horner–FH, 14 September 1885, MP, L/05/1224.

26. FH, *Time Remembered*, pp. 89–90. EBJ on hearing that 'you were calling your man-child Edward… went red and felt happy'. EBJ–FH, July 1888, vol. 3, M/05/1351.

27. FH, *Time Remembered*, p. 91.

28. FH–DD, 31 January 1891, Edith Lyttelton papers, CHAN1/5/9/38–41.

29. FH–DD, 21 January 1891, 31 January 1891, 2 May 1891, Edith Lyttelton papers, CHAN1/5/9/ 38–41, 53–5, 61–4.

30. Constance Hamlyn-Fane married John 3rd Baron Manners in 1885 and died in 1920. They lived in Avon Tyrrell – a house built from the winnings from riding his horse Seaman to victory in the 1882 Grand National.

31. FH–DD, '1891', 2 May 1891, 7 July 1891, 28 ? 1891, 19 August 1891, Edith Lyttelton papers, CHAN1/5/9/50–59, 67–9. 75–9. FH–Ettie, 30 November 1891, Desborough papers, DE/ Rv/ c1346/2.

32. FH–EBJ, 30 November 1894, vol. 9, MP, M/05/1353.

33. FH–DD, 'Thurs 1886', Edith Lyttelton papers CHAN1/5/9/1–3. FH–Violet Maxse, 5, 22 April 1894, Violet Milner papers, MS VM 43/ c368/1,3. FH–EBJ, [January 1892], 1 December 1895, vol. 7, 9, MP, M/05/1353.

34. Ellenberger, *Balfour's World*, p. 53.

35. Jeanne MacKenzie, *The Children of The Souls* (1986), p.8.

36. Abdy and Gere, *The Souls*, p. 141.

37. Mark Bonham Carter's introduction to Margot Asquith's *Autobiography*, p.xxi. 'Frances had held the first place in her heart', Edith Lyttelton (DD), *Alfred Lyttelton* (1917), p. 132.

38. DD, *Interwoven*, CHAN/I/6/1/A p.12; /B p.2 (quoting Doll's diary, 25 January 1884); /B p.29, /C 29. Jalland, *Women, Marriage and Politics*, pp. 106–8.

39. Edith Lyttelton, 'Interwoven', Edith Lyttelton papers, CHAN/I/6/1/C/29.

40. Laura Tennant's diary, 28 January 85, MS Eng. d 3312; Alfred Lyttelton–Laura Tennant, 30 January 1885, CHAN/I/C6/1. Ellenberger, *Balfour's World*, pp. 79–80.

41. 'It is the greatest blessing to me that nothing requires any interpretation. He sees you as I desire all the world to see you … as you deserve my darling.' LT–FH, [1885], MP, M/01/1275.

42. 'Goodbye dear old Darling and give yourself a hug from your very wicked far away wife who loves you with all her heart.' FH–JH 21 August 1890; 'Sept 1890', MP, M/01/1263.

43. Abdy and Gere, *The Souls*, p. 141.

44. Margot Tennant–FH, Easter Sunday 1886, 23 August 1886, 24 April 1887, nd, MP, M/01/1266. Margot Tennant's memoir of Laura's early life, MS Eng. D.3293.

45. EBJ–FH, 27 January 1887, Vol. 2 MP, M/05/1353.

46. FH, *Time Remembered*, p. 185.

47. FH, *Time Remembered*, p. 185.

48. FH, *Time Remembered*, p. 106.

49. EBJ–FH, nd, [1884] vol. 1, MP, M/05/1353.

50. Garnett, 'William Graham' p. 265. *Hidden BJ*, pp. 58, 74. This was completed in 1883. It would be sold in the 1886 sale, eventually ending up in Birmingham Museums and Art Gallery. EBJ–FH, 20 October 1884, vol. 1, MP, M/05/1353.

51. EBJ–FH, nd., [August/September 1885], vol. 1, MP, M/05/1353. MacCarthy, *The Last Pre-Raphaelite*, pp. 360–3.

52. EBJ–FH, [March 1886], vol. 1, MP, M/05/1353. BJ also anxious that the sale might go badly and ruin his reputation. But the prices were high 'especially the BJs'. JH–FH, 5 April 1886, MP, K/02/1152.

53. The original meaning of the peacock symbolism, in Persian and Phoenician art, is incorruptibility.

54. EBJ–FH, nd [August–October 1886], vol. 2, MP, M/05/1353. The result was 'soft and delicate' but perhaps missed the vivacity and impact of its subject. By contrast, the copy he made for the hall at The Grange was completely coloured in greens and blues. Another sketch was later coloured and given to Mary Elcho. MacCarthy, *The Last Pre-Raphaelite*, pp. 339–40.

55. EBJ–FH, nd [August–November 1886], vol. 2, MP, M/05/1353. Georgie recounts this commission in some detail but without any mention of Frances and referred to it being 'put up in a church'. GBJ, *Memorials*, ii, pp. 166–7.
56. 'I dare say letters will be our chief life.' EBJ–FH, 24 November 1892, vol. 6, MP, M/05/1353.
57. Caroline Dakers, 'Yours Affectionately, Angelo' in *British Art Journal* (2001), vol. 2, no. 3, p. 16. Indeed EBJ speculated on just this: 'Will Edison ever invent a thing, so that all I think up in the day might travel at night … and sound in your ear in the morning?' EBJ–FH, 21 October 1892, vol. 5, MP, M/05/1353.
58. EBJ–FH, nd, Burne-Jones papers, FM xxvii/28.
59. EBJ–FH, nd, Burne-Jones papers, FM xxvii/27. EBJ–FH, 28 October 1892, vol. 5, MP, M/05/1353.
60. EBJ–FH, nd [September 1889], vol. 3, MP, M/05/1353.
61. EBJ–FH, 27 May 1889, nd [1891], vol. 3, MP, M/05/1353. FH, *Time Remembered*, p. 117. EBJ–FH, 11 July 1892, 20 July 1892, vol. 4, MP, M/05/1353 for a discussion on Manet and the Impressionists.
62. FH–Violet Cecil, 13 September 1898, Violet Milner papers, VM 43/c368/7.
63. EBJ–FH, nd [1890?], vol. 3, MP, M/05/1353.
64. FH–DD, '1887', Edith Lyttelton papers CHAN1/5/9/17–20. Embroidery was very labour intensive. So it was quite likely that EBJ would send a design first to the Royal School who would 'pounce' the design by puckering onto the linen. They could do much of the basic stitching leaving FH to do all the challenging parts. I am grateful to Charlotte Gere for this information.
65. McCarthy, *The Last Pre-Raphaelite*, p. 410. Surviving examples of their collaboration are to be seen in the church at Mells with the 'Love' tapestry and the plaque commemorating Laura Tennant.
66. EBJ–FH, nd, [post-1882], Burne-Jones papers, FM, xxvii/11. FH, *Time Remembered*, p. 127.
67. FH, *Time Remembered*, p. 113.
68. Ibid, p. 128.
69. EBJ–FH, nd [1885 and 1888] vols 1–2, MP, M/05/1353. He also insisted that she reads 'fair and not look at the end but honourably from the beginning'.
70. FH *Time Remembered*, pp. 114–15.
71. Ibid., pp.113, 123–4. EBJ–FH, 5.3.1892, vol. 7, MP, M/05/1353.

72. EBJ–FH, 7 July 1890, 18 June 1892, Vols 3, 4, MP, M/05/1353. On this subject they had sparred before: 'About the New Testament, we will talk together; to say truth there are only two sides of Christianity for which I am fitted by the spirit which designs in me the carol part, and the Mystical part – and indeed I could not draw Paul – but we will go over this together.' FH, *Time Remembered*, p. 112.
73. EBJ–FH, nd and 15 January 1889, vol. 3, MP, M/05/1353. Clouds was destroyed on 6 January 1889, having been completed in 1885. It was restored, with the Horners arriving on 29 August 1891 as their first guests since its reincarnation. Dakers, *Clouds*, pp. 134–5. Mary Wyndham married Hugo Charteris, Lord Elcho, in 1883.
74. EBJ–FH, nd [January 1890], in FH, *Time Remembered*, p. 115.
75. EBJ–FH, 1889, in Georgiana Burne-Jones, *Memorials of Edward Burne-Jones* (1904), pp. 200–1. EBJ–FH, 9 August 1890, nd [November 1890], vol. 3, MP, M/05/1353.
76. EBJ–FH, nd [1892], vol. 4 MP, M/05/1353.
77. EBJ–FH, nd [1885], vol. 1; 31 August 1891, 6 October 1891, vol. 3; FH–EBJ, 30 November 1894, vol. 9, MP, M/05/1353.
78. EBJ–FH, nd [March 1888], vol. 2; 21 September 1888, vol. 3; 11 July 1892, vol. 4, MP, M/05/1353. GBJ, *Memorials*, p. 200. MacCarthy, *The Last Pre-Raphaelite*, pp. 377–83. EBJ– FH, 11 September 1890, Burne-Jones papers, FM xxviii/16.
79. EBJ–FH, July 1887, vol. 2, MP, M/05/1353.
80. EBJ–FH, nd [July and August, 1884], vol. 1; nd [May, June, November 1886], 1 December 1887, vol. 2; nd [1888], nd [Nov 1888], 1 July 1889, 25 November 1889, nd [1890], nd [1891], vol. 3, MP, M/05/1353.
81. EBJ–FH, nd [1890], vol. 3, MP, M/05/1353.

PART 4 Making an Entrance (1886–1892)

1. Mark Bonham Carter, 'Introduction', in Margot Asquith, *Autobiography*, pp. xxii–xxiii.
2. FH–DD, [1890s], Edith Lyttelton papers, CHAN I/5/10/94.
3. Abdy and Gere, *The Souls*, p. 141
4. EBJ–FH 2 December 1892, vol. , MP, M/05/1353.
5. 'I have seldom enjoyed anything so much as that visit to The Grange. Burne-Jones did not strike me as absurdly peculiar at all. I had imagined something objectionable and I could have listened to him with pleasure for hours… We made friends over some

Oxford windows which my Father taught me to wonder at'. George Horner–FH, 14 September 1885, MP, L/05/1224.

6. On the Souls see Nancy Ellenberger, *Balfour's World*. And her 'The Souls and London "Society" at the end of the nineteenth century', *Victorian Studies*, 25 (1982), pp. 133–60. Abdy and Gere, *The Souls*. A. Lambert, *Unquiet Souls: the Indian Summer of the British Aristocracy, 1880–1918* (1984). Jane Ridley, 'Souls', ODNB.

7. Margot Asquith to Mary Wemyss, 2 September 1932, in MacKenzie, *Children*, p. 9.

8. Ellenberger, 'Souls', pp. 140–1.

9. Abdy and Gere, *The Souls*, p. 141. FH, 'Pages from a Record of Events', MP, M/03/1309.

10. Stanway was the Elcho home in Gloucestershire; Edith ['Ettie'] Fane, society hostess, gained Taplow through her marriage to Willie Grenfell in 1887 and later in 1913 Panshanger through her grandfather, 6th Earl of Cowper. In 1905 she became Lady Desborough.

11. David Cannadine, *The Decline and Fall of the British Aristocracy* (1990), pp. 350–51. Ellenberger, 'Souls', pp. 143–4.

12. Then the royal residence of the Prince of Wales, since 1965 it has housed the Commonwealth Secretariat.

13. Lady Tweedsmuir, *The Edwardian Lady* (1966), p. 12. There were exceptions: Margot could never resist couturiers such as Worth and Ettie attended Court as a lady in waiting, enjoyed racing, and decorated Taplow extravagantly – though to much critical comment from her friends.

14. 'Nothing compares to the mad folly and deaf haste of a bicycle… I know I shall be killed if I go on', FH–DD, n.d. [1895?] Edith Lyttelton papers, CHAN1/5/10/232.

15. Frances had no Greek, although as a child she had hired a tutor in Latin, and there is no evidence that she read these translations. The consequence of an incomplete education and an ever-present source of insecurity.

16. Greywalls for the Lytteltons; Fisher's Hill for Gerald Balfour.

17. Curzon cited in Abdy and Gere, *The Souls*, p. 72.

18. FH–DD, 4 December 1890, Edith Lyttelton papers CHAN1/5/9/23–4. Ellenberger, 'The Souls', p. 134.

19. Ellenberger, *Balfour's World*, pp. 181–206. Ellenberger, 'Souls', pp. 149–52. Jane Ridley, *A Life of Edwin Lutyens: The Architect and his Wife* (2002), p. 89.

20. Ellenberger, *Balfour's World*, pp. 123–8, 155–180. Ellenberger, 'Souls', pp. 149–152. In old age Frances told Mary Elcho 'I am much too old to mind being called a "Soul"! It was a title of endearment as well as of slight acerbity'. FH–Mary Elcho, '1st September', Stanway papers, M.E.5.H.

21. MacKenzie, *Children*, pp. 6, 14.

22. Violet Bonham Carter, 'The Souls', *The Listener*, 30 October 1947. Jane Ridley, *Bertie: a Life of Edward VII* (2012), p. 434.

23. Norman and Jeanne MacKenzie (eds), *The Diary of Beatrice Webb* (1982).

24. Laura Tennant diary (20 March 1884?), Asquith papers d.3312; Ellenberger, *Balfour's World*, p. 62. Dilke's divorce case which caused such a scandal was in 1885.

25. Abdy and Gere, *Souls*, p. 127. Mark Bonham Carter's introduction to Margot's *Autobiography*, pp. xxi–xxii. Margot Tennant–Harry Cust, 8 February 1889, MS Eng d.3278. Margot Tennant–FH, 1 December 1888, MP, M/01/1266.

26. 'I am afraid we shall have to lay on the water from a well on the Mendip which will cost hundreds! It is a bore!'. FH–DD, '1891', Edith Lyttelton papers, CHAN1/5/9/50–52.

27. FH–Ettie, 20 April ?, Desborough Papers, DE/Rv/c1346/26.

28. Constantine Benckendorff, *Half a Life, Reminiscences of a Russian Gentleman* (1954), cited in Abdy and Gere, p. 132. FH, *Time Remembered*, p. 181.

29. MacKenzie, *Children*, p. 19. DD, 'Interwoven', Chandos papers, CHAN 1/6/1. Asquith, *Autobiography*, pp. 134, 189. Margot Tennant–FH, 1 December 1888, MP, M/01/1266. FH–Henry Asquith [henceforth HHA], 12 June 1892, MP, M/01/1270.

30. FH–DD, 1900, Edith Lyttelton Papers CHAN1/5/10/181. FH, *Time Remembered*, p. 161.

31. Violet Lindsay, artistic, even Bohemian, married Henry Manners in 1882, becoming Lady Granby in 1886 and Duchess of Rutland in 1906.

32. FH, *Time Remembered*, p. 162.

33. Margot Asquith, *Autobiography*, p. 122. FH–HHA, 7 June 1892, MP 405. Margot Asquith–FH, 29 ? 1901; nd, 9 May 1904, MP, M/01/1266.

34. Frances was rather in awe of the Duchesses of Rutland, Sutherland and Desborough. There would be illustrations of all three in her memoir, *Time Remembered*. Initially she was closest to the bohemian Violet Granby [Rutland] who was a genuinely accomplished artist and who 'I like very much: she is so lovely and womanly and so very gifted

too'. Jack thought her poisonous. FH–HHA, 24 November 1892, MP, M/01/1270. Abdy and Gere, *Souls*, pp. 46–52, 92. See also Catherine Bailey, *The Secret Rooms*, p. 242.

35. FH–DD, 1900, Edith Lyttelton Papers CHAN1/5/10/181.

36. FH–HHA, 7 June 1892, MP, M/01/1270.

37. Blanche Dugdale was Arthur Balfour's neice; Betty Balfour [née Lytton] was married to Arthur's brother, Gerald.

38. Claudia Renton, *The Wild Wyndhams*, p. 94.

39. FH, *Time Remembered*, p. 89. But to the outside observer Frances remained a striking figure. 'Her hair is quite white but she still has a lovely figure and her face is very graceful and animated', Angela Emanuel (ed.), *A Bright Remembrance: The Diaries of Julia Cartwright* (1989), p. 185 (8 July 1894).

40. Yet she remained a church goer, attending St Bartholomew's in Smithfield on Good Friday before going to a performance of the St John Passion ('forgotten how fine it was'). Easter Sunday would find her at Panshanger. FH– DD, 'Easter Sunday 1891' [29 March 1891], Edith Lyttelton papers CHAN1/5/9/46–9. FH, *Time Remembered*, p. 156.

41. Herbert Beerbohm Tree was a renowned actor manager of the day and half-sibling of Max Beerbohm the essayist and humourist most famous for *Zuleika Dobson*. His daughter Iris was a poet and close to Frances's children.

42. FH–Violet Cecil, 19 October 1899, Violet Milner papers, VM 43/c368/8. FH–DD, '1887', Edith Lyttelton papers CHAN1/5/9/10–12, 17–20. FH, *Time Remembered*, p. 181. FH–JH, 'Dec 1889', nd, MP, M/01/1263.

43. MP/M03/1332.

44. Charles Beresford was a British Admiral and MP.

45. Ellenberger, 'Souls', pp. 133–4. 'The New Morality', MP/ M03/1332. Frances described it as a 'skit' written by her, DD and Godfrey Webb and intended to be published anonymously in the *Westminster Gazette*. It caused 'much speculation at the time'. FH to Mary Elcho, '1 September', Stanway, ME.5.H.

46. FH is either being intellectually snobbish or mobbing up intellectual snobbery among the Souls as well as their intimidating intellect. *The Ante-Nicene Fathers* (1885) collected early Christian writings up to the Council of Nicaea in 325. It includes a reference to 'Rubilus and Zacharius the builders' [of the Church?]. Apolaustic means 'devoted to seeking enjoyment'. Thus she seeks to

emphasise the pure and the hedonistic sides of the Souls.

47. Violet Milner in Abdy and Gere, p. 126. Margot Asquith, *Autobiography*, p. 68.

48. Ellenberger, 'Souls' p. 154. Lady Walburga Paget, *Embassies of other days* (1923). Norman and Jeanne Mackenzie (ed.), *The Diaries of Beatrice Webb* (1986), vol. 2, p. 261.

49. Ellenberger, *Balfour's World*, pp. 142–7 for this and what follows.

50. Ellenberger, *Balfour's World*, p.144. FH–DD, 'Thurs 1889', Edith Lyttelton papers CHAN1/5/9/10–12.

51. Laura Tennant's diary, 28 January 1885, MSS Eng. d 3312.

52. FH–DD, '1887', Edith Lyttelton papers CHAN1/5/9/6–8. FH–DD, 'Thursday 1890', Edith Lyttelton papers CHAN1/5/9/9. Pembroke to Ettie, Desborough Papers, 1 September 1890, DE/Rv/C1293/4. Ellenberger, 'Souls', p. 151. FH travel journal, August 1890, M/02/1307–8.

53. FH, *Time Remembered*, pp. 159–160. On Pembroke see also Ellenberger, *Balfour's World*, pp. 152–3.

54. Pembroke–FH, 11 December 1891, Autograph Letters vol. 1, p. 26 MP, M/01/1260.

55. Ellenberger, *Balfour's World*, pp. 149–50, 251. Pembroke–FH, nd., 8 August 1889 Autograph Letters vol. 1, pp.22–5, MP, M/01/1260.

56. Pembroke–FH, nd., 8 August 1889, 11 December 1891, Autograph Letters vol. 1, pp. 22–6, MP, M/01/1260. FH–DD, 5 September 1887, Edith Lyttelton papers CHAN1/5/9/6–8. FH–DD, Wed 28 ? 1891, Edith Lyttelton papers, CHAN/1/5/9/67–9. Frances Horner, 'The Veil of Maya', in *Temple Bar*, 93 (1891), pp. 73–96. Charty showed it to EBJ who was full of praise but heard Frances was 'disappointed'. EBJ–FH, 28 November 1891, M/05/1353.

57. Margot Tennant–FH, nd, 16 August 18??. MP, M/01/1266. Charty Tennant-Cust, 25 September 18??, MS Eng d.3278.

58. FH–DD, 5 September 1887, Edith Lyttelton papers CHAN1/5/9/4–5.

59. Daisy White was the glamorous wife of the First Secretary at the American Legation in London and, with her husband, a fringe Soul.

60. Ellenberger, *Balfour's World*, p. 185. DD, 'Interwoven', CHAN/I/6/1/A, p. 8.

61. FH–DD, 5 September 1887, 13 August [1887], '1889', Edith Lyttelton papers CHAN1/5/9/4–5, 10–12, 17–20.

62. Was the affair with Doll seen as a betrayal of Frances? On DD and Doll, see Ellenberger,

Balfour's World, pp193–4.

63. DD, 'Interwoven', CHAN/I/6/1/A, p.12.
'Interwoven', pp. 35–6, 61. FH–DD, '1890',
Edith Lyttelton's papers CHAN1/5/9/32–33.

64. FH–DD, 30 December 1890, Edith Lyttelton's papers, CHAN I/5/9/36–7.

65. FH–DD, '1890' [??], Edith Lyttelton's papers
CHAN1/5/9/26–27. FH–DD, '1890', Edith
Lyttelton's papers, CHAN1/5/9/29–33.

66. FH–DD, [1894], Edith Lyttelton papers,
CHAN I/5/10/127–8. Lucy Graham-Smith
was Margot Asquith's older sister.

67. Claudia Renton, *Those Wild Wyndhams*
(2014), p. 237 on Balfour and Mary Wyndham.

68. Ellenberger, *Balfour's World*, pp. 181–206 for
a detailed insight on the Souls' inter-rela-
tionships

69. FH, *Time Remembered*, pp. 155, 181. FH–
Violet Cecil, 'Feb 18 [1898 at latest], BP Gate',
Violet Milner papers MS VM 43/c368/5.
Philip Zeigler, *Diana Cooper* (2011), p. 15.
Daphne Bennett, *Margot* (1984), p. 65.

70. Violet Bonham Carter, 'The Souls', *The Listener*, 30 October 1947. She was a daughter
from H.H. Asquith's first marriage.

PART 5 The Year of Living Dangerously – 1892

1. EBJ–FH, nd [*c.* 1897], vol. 10, MP,
M/05/1353.

2. FH–Margot Asquith, nd, Asquith papers,
MS Eng c 6677.

3. EBJ–FH, JANUARY 1892, VOL. 7, MP,
M/05/1353/

4. DD, 'Interwoven', Edith Lyttelton Papers,
CHAN/I/6/1/J. Lambert, *Unquiet Souls*, p.
111.

5. FH–DD [1892–5], 'April 1892', Edith Lyttelton papers, CHAN I/5/10/86, 105.

6. FH–DD, 1892, nd [1894], Edith Lyttelton
papers, CHAN I/5/10/112, 120.

7. EBJ–FH, nd, vol. 4, MP, M/05/1353. FH–DD,
1892–4? , Edith Lyttelton papers, CHAN
I/5/10/112–13, 116. HHA–FH, 17 October
1892, MP, M/01/1270.

8. EBJ–FH, 12 July 1892, vol. 4, MP, M/05/1353.
On DD's marriage: 'she is much more
oppressed and impressed with him and I
think would rather take him in sips than
in big draughts', EBJ–FH, 14 July 1892, MP,
M/05/1353.

9. EBJ–FH November 1892, vol. 5 MP,
M/05/1353. On this episode see MacCarthy,
The Last Pre-Raphaelite, pp. 405–12. On
Milford and Barbara Webb (an early patron
of Lutyens) see Jane Brown, *Lutyens and the
Edwardians*, pp. 9–24.

10. FH mocked 'middle aged ladies who knew
not what even a kiss meant'. FH–EBJ, 30
May 1892, vol. 4 MP, M/05/1353. EBJ discussing whether embracing in a cab was too
public, EBJ–FH, 23 June 1892, vol. 4, MP,
M/05/1353.

11. EBJ–FH, 22 May 1892, vol. 7, 13 May 1892,
vol. 4, MP, M/05/1353.

12. FH–HHA, 28 May 1892, MP, M/01/1270.

13. EBJ–FH, 19 June 1892, vol. 4; 13 September
1892, vol. 5, MP, M/05/1353.

14. EBJ–FH, 6 July 1892, 10–11 July 1892, vol. 4,
MP, M/05/1353.

15. EBJ–FH, 10 August 1892, vol. 4, MP,
M/05/1353. 'What nice company you are in.
But who is Ettie?'

16. Kippen House in Perthshire: 'pretentious
vulgar little house but surrounded by good
hills and lots of walking in a petticoat', FH–
HHA, nd, MP, M/01/1270.

17. FH–HHA, 25 July 1892, MP M/01/1270.
EBJ– FH, nd, vol. 4. MP, M/05/1353.

18. EBJ–FH 20, 26, 28 August 1892, vol. 5, MP,
M/05/1353.

19. EBJ–FH, 25, 26 June 1892, vol. 4, MP,
M/05/1353.

20. EBJ–FH, 13 September 1892, vol. 5, MP,
M/05/1353.

21. EBJ–FH, 13, 17, 18 August 1892, 6 October
1892, nd, vol. 5, MP, M/05/1353.

22. FH, *Time Remembered*, p.168.

23. 'I don't believe that even when one is divinely
happy it is ever quite without a sigh – at least
I never was'. EBJ–FH, 16, 18 September 1892,
vol. 5, MP, M/05/1353. FH, *Time Remembered*,
p.165. FH–DD, 10 March ?, Edith Lyttelton
Papers, CHAN1/5/10/177. FH–DD, 2 May
1891, Edith Lyttelton papers, CHAN1/5/9/53–
5. FH–HHA 12 September 1891, 22 September
1891, n.d., vol. 1, MP, M/01/1270.

24. EBJ also received a similar volume from
Frances. EBJ–FH, 18 April 1892, MP,
M/05/1353.

25. FH–DD, [April 1892], Edith Lyttelton
papers, CHAN I/5/10/92. HHA–FH, 14 May
1891, 20 November 1891, n.d., vol. 1, MP,
M/01/1270. This was not Roundell Palmer,
1st Earl of Selbourne, who had been married
for thirty years by the time they became
acquainted with the Grahams, but possibly
Mr Charles Roundell whose wife Julia wrote
an account of Cowdray in Midhurst, Kent in
1884 and lived on to 1931.

26. FH–HHA, nd; 19 May 1892, 28 May 1892;
23 December 1892, vol. 1, MP, M/01/1270.
NB the settling of accounts was an early
running gag concerning FH's attempt to pay
for her own ticket for a play they had gone

27. FH–HHA, 12 June 1892, 26 June 1892, vol. 1, MP, M/01/1270.

28. HHA–FH, 1 August 1892, vol. 1, MP, M/01/1270.

29. HHA–FH, 26 October 1891, vol. 1, MP, M/01/1270.

30. HHA–FH, 12 July 1892, 1 August 1892, 15 August 1892, 22 August 1892, vol. 1, MP, M/01/1270.

31. HHA–FH, 11 September 1892, 18 September 1892, vol. 1, MP, M/01/1270.

32. HHA–FH, 13 September 1892, 18 July 1892, 22 September 1892, 3 October 1892, vol. 1, MP, M/01/1270.

33. EBJ–FH, 19 October 1892, vol. 5, MP, M/05/1353.

34. EBJ–FH, 6 and 10 October 1892, vol. 5, M/05/1353. FH, 'Pages from a record of events', MP, M/03/1309.

35. EBJ–FH, 10, 15, 20 October 1892, vol. 5; 21 April 1896, vol. 9, MP, M/05/1353. Hopes 'that you are frightened no more, of me and for me'.

36. EBJ–FH,10, 12, 15, 20 October 1892, vol. 5, MP, M/05/1353.

37. FH–DD, 18 October 1892, Edith Lyttelton papers, CHAN I/5/10/102.

38. HHA–FH, 10 October 1892, vol. 1, MP, M/01/1270.

39. HHA–FH, 10, 11 October 1892, vol. 1 MP, M/01/1270. To meet HHA she had to stand up EBJ: EBJ–FH, 12 October 1892, vol. 5, MP, M/05/1353.

40. EBJ–FH, 12.10.1892 vol. 5, MP, M/05/1353.

41. HHA Diary 13,14, 15 October 1892, MSS Bonham Carter 571. HHA–FH, 14, 20 October 1892, vol. 1, MP, M/01/1270.

42. HHA–FH, 24 October 1892, vol. 1, MP, M/01/1270.

43. HHA–FH, 17 October 1892, vol. 1, MP, M/01/1270.

44. HHA diary 28–31 October 1892, MSS Bonham Carter 571. HHA–FH, 17, 20 October 1892, 17 December 1892, vol. 1, MP, M/01/1270.

45. HHA–FH, 24 October 1892, vol. 1, MP, M/01/1270.

46. HHA–FH, 17 October 1892 vol. 1, MP, M/01/1270.

47. HHA–FH, 24 October 1892, 8 November 1892, vol. 1, MP, M/01/1270.

48. Roy Jenkins asserts that Asquith was not in love with Frances. Colin Clifford describes a friendship that became unexpectedly intimate. Both see Frances as the first of a line of young women – dubbed by Margot his 'harem' – with whom he would 'hold hands' and exchange confidences, culminating most famously with Venetia Stanley. But these other relationships must all be seen in the context of his eventual marriage to Margot. The relationship with Frances was a decade earlier. Unlike the harem, it involved someone of similar age, independent minded, and more actively involved in his political life rather than just a confidante to whom he could let off steam. Finally it was apparently quite physically intimate. Roy Jenkins, *Asquith* (1964), p. 257. H.H. Asquith, *Letters to Venetia Stanley*, ed. M. and E. Brock (1982), p.1. Colin Clifford, *The Asquiths* (2002), pp. 49–50.

49. EBJ–FH, 9 November 1892, vol. 6, MP, M/05/1353.

50. EBJ–FH, 4–5 November 1892, vol. 6, MP, M/05/1353. She, of course. kept his in eleven leather-bound volumes.

51. EBJ–FH, 5 and 19 November 1892, vol. 6, MP, M/05/1353.

52. EBJ–FH, 24 October 1892, vol. 5, MP, M/05/1353.

53. EBJ–FH, 5 and n.d. November 1892, vol. 6, MP, M/05/1353.

54. EBJ–FH, 6–9 November 1892, vol. 6, MP, M/05/1353.

55. MacCarthy, *The Last Pre-Raphaelite*, pp. 407, 410.

56. EBJ–Helen Gaskell, nd, Ashmolean, WA2015.66. (A later hand has dated this 'Nov 1893' but it must be 1892). EBJ–FH, 20 August 1892, vol. 6, MP, M/05/1353. MacCarthy, *The Last Pre-Raphaelite*, p. 412.

57. Dimbleby, *Profound Secret*, pp. xix, 90–1. EBJ–Helen Gaskell, nd, EBJ Collection (Ashmolean), WA2015.66, 67.

58. Dimbleby, *Profound Secret*, pp. xix, 138. After reading some 'French Novels' while recuperating at a Swiss spa in 1895 she wrote to Sir Alfred Milner: 'They make me wish that the question of "sex" didn't exist… Bah! I wish they knew how little "la question du sex" interfered with most lives. I think *most*, don't you?' This was a lady to whom EBJ would send drawings of her naked in a bubble bath.

59. For much of what follows see MacCarthy, *The Last Pre-Raphaelite*, pp. 412–16. Dimbleby, *Profound Secret*, pp. 87, 101–2.

60. Thus, as he denounced Frances to May as 'of the past, dead – dead', he would admit: 'but if I give now and ask nothing back, heaven might sure let me have my dream and let me die one day, still dreaming of it. Meantime your loving heart is full of mercy to me.' EBJ–Helen Gaskell, nd, EBJ Collection

(Ashmolean), WA2015.66.
61. EBJ–Helen Gaskell, nd, EBJ Collection (Ashmolean), WA2015.66.
62. EBJ–FH 5 November 1892, vol. 6, MP, M/05/1353.
63. EBJ–FH, 5, 19, 22, 24 November 1892, vol. 6, MP, M/05/1353.
64. EBJ–FH, 13 September 1892, vol, 5; 19, 22, 25, 28 November 1892, vol. 6, MP, M/05/1353. Relations were not helped by Margot's 'impertinent' request for a drawing from him for her bazaar; or improved by her subsequent telegram: 'million thanks, you are a dear'.
65. EBJ–FH, 24 November 1892, 1 December 1892, 30 December 1892, vol. 6, MP, M/05/1353.
66. EBJ–FH, n.d., 1, 19, 25, 30 December 1892, vol. 6, MP, M/05/1353.
67. EBJ–FH, 2 December 1892, vol. 6, MP, M/05/1353.
68. EBJ–FH, nd, vol. 6, MP. HHA–FH, 23 December 1892, vol. 1, MP, M/05/1353.
69. FH–HHA, 28 May 1892; HHA–FH, 8 November 1892, vol. 1, MP, M/01/1270. See also her later rejection of Theosophy: 'a future without her present consciousness does not appeal to her'. Lutyens to Lady Emily 18 April 1911, Clayre Percy and Jane Ridley (eds.), *The Letters of Edwin Lutyens to his wife, Lady Emily* (1985), p. 216.

PART 6 Dream Endings (1893–1898)

1. EBJ–FH, nd, Vol. 5, MP, M/05/1353.
2. HHA–FH, 9 January 1910, Bonham Carter MSS 619 f. 112.
3. HHA–FH, 3 January 1893, vol. 1, MP, M/01/1270.
4. HHA Diary, 30 January 1893, 4, 10, 13, 15, 22, 24, 26 February 1893, MSS Bonham Carter 571.
5. HHA Diary, 11 March 1893, MSS Bonham Carter 571.
6. HHA Diary, 8 March 1893, MSS Bonham Carter 571–2. HHA–FH, 11 March 1893, 23 March 1893, 16 May 1893, vol. 1, MP, M/01/1270.
7. 'Pages from a Record of Events', MP, M/03/1309.
8. HHA–FH, 21, 27 July 1893, vol. 1, MP, M/01/1270.
9. Ellenberger, *Balfour's World*, pp. 246–52. Clifford, *The Asquiths*, pp. 44–6.
10. FH–DD, 21 July 1891, Edith Lyttelton papers, CHAN1/5/9/58–9.
11. Mark Bonham Carter introduction to Margot Asquith, *Autobiography*, p. xxiii.
12. HHA–FH, 2 August 1893, 19 September 1893, 26 September 1893, vol. 1, MP, M/01/1270. HHA Diary, 22–24 September 1893, 13 September 1893, MSS Bonham Carter 571.
13. Unlike the impecunious horseman, Peter Flower ('It has always been Peter'), and Evan Charteris, Hugo Elcho's brother, who adored her but whom she never quite trusted. Marrying Asquith was to enter a middle-class comfort zone. Andrew Gailey, *The Lost Imperialist, Lord Dufferin, Memory and Mythmaking in an Age of Celebrity* (2015), p. 304. Margot Asquith, *Autobiography*, p. 192.
14. See Emily Lytton's reaction after meeting Asquith in 1892 with the Horners: 'He is not quite a gentleman [and] his appearance is very much against him'; but she recognised his ability and found him 'very natural, easy and agreeable'. Emily Lytton to FH, 17 October 1892, MP, M/01/1262. Frances didn't worry about this and part of her attraction to HHA was that she gave him social support in the face of occasional snobbery.
15. Clifford, *Asquiths*, p. 52. Margot Asquith, *Autobiography*, p. 192. Jalland, *Women, Marriage and Politics*, p. 92.
16. HHA–FH, 5 December 1893, 29 December 1893, 5 January 1894, vol. 1, MP, M/01/1270. EBJ–FH, 11 December 1893, vol. 8, MP, M/05/1353.
17. It took him another five days to alert Frances. HHA–FH, 14 January 1894 vol. 1, MP, M/01/1270.
18. HHA–FH, 21 January 1894, 6 October 1894. vol. 1, MP, M/01/1270.
19. FH, *Time Remembered*, p. 169.
20. Margot Asquith, *Autobiography*, p. 189. Clifford, *Asquiths*, p. 50. 'Intensely grateful to you', wrote Margot from her honeymoon. 'You have done more than anyone to lighten the way.' Margot Asquith–FH, nd [1894], MS Eng c 6677, ff. 86–7. On the other hand, she did suspect her sister, Charty. On confidantes, for the decision to marry Asquith she seems by the end to have consulted a vast range of friends.
21. HHA–FH, 14 April 1894, vol. 1, MP, M/01/1270.
22. FH talks of HHA winning 'an unequalled position in the hearts and minds of all Liberals'. FH, *Time Remembered*, p. 168.
23. FH, *Time Remembered*, p. 167.
24. FH–HHA, 2 June 1892, 19 June 1893, vol. 1, MP, M/01/1270. Presumably those so marked would be persona non grata at Mells?

25. HHA–FH, 9 January 1910, Bonham Carter MSS 619 f.112. FH–EBJ, 20 May 1896, vol. 9. FH–DD, [1894], Edith Lyttelton papers, CHAN I/5/10/ 84.
26. EBJ–FH, nd [Nov 1893], vol. 8, MP, M/05/1353. For what follows see Claudia Renton, *Those Wild Wyndhams* (2014), pp. 144–51. Ellenberger, *Balfour's World*, pp. 253–6, 264–73.
27. FH–KH, nd, MP, M/01/1269. Violet Granby only became the Duchess of Rutland in 1906.
28. FH–DD, summer 1894, Edith Lyttelton papers, CP H3/5 and CHAN I/5/10/125.
29. Renton concludes that Cust forced Nina to have an abortion but, if so, why did he then marry her? The stress of the scandal might have been sufficient to cause a miscarriage.
30. Only on his death bed in 1917 did he relent. Her devotion to him never wavered until she died in 1955.
31. EBJ–FH, nd October 1893 vol. 8; nd [December 1894], vol. 9, MP, M/05/1353.
32. FH–DD, [1894], Edith Lyttelton papers, CHAN I/5/10/125. FH–DD, nd, Edith Lyttelton's papers CHAN1/5/9/29–33.
33. DD–Kathleen Lyttelton, 10 February 1894, CP H3/14. Ellenberger, *Balfour's World*, p. 255. HHA Diary, 14 September 1893, MSS Bonham Carter 572. Harry Cust–FH, nd [but *c.* 1893–4?], MP, M/01/1271.
34. FH–DD, [1895], Edith Lyttelton papers, CHAN I/5/10/138–9. FH–DD, [1895], Edith Lyttelton papers, CHAN I/5/10/142. Ellenberger, *Balfour's World*, pp.277–9.
35. FH–Violet Cecil, 6 October 1895, Violet Milner papers MS VM 43/c368/2.
36. FH–EBJ, 11 October 1895, vol. 9, MP, M/05/1353. Mary Crawshay was the daughter of Sir John Leslie 1st Baronet and the sister-in-law of Jennie Churchill's sister Leonie. Shane Leslie, Irish diplomat and author, was her nephew.
37. FH–JH, 7–8 October 1895, MP, M/01/1263. FH–Violet Cecil, 6 October 1895/7, Violet Milner papers MS VM 43/c368/2.
38. FH–EBJ, 11 October 1895, in *Time Remembered*, pp. 93–5.
39. FH–JH, 12 October 1895, MP, M/01/1263.
40. Violet Maxse married Lord Edward Cecil, son of the Tory Prime Minister, Lord Salisbury in 1894. After her husband's death in 1918, she would marry Viscount Milner in 1921.
41. EBJ–FH, 8 August 1894, vol. 8, MP. FH–EBJ, 20 November 1895, vol. 9, MP, M/05/1353.
42. FH–DD, [1895], Edith Lyttelton papers, CHAN I/5/10/140.

43. FH–Violet Cecil, 5 April 1894, Violet Milner Papers, MS VM 43/c368/1.
44. FH–Violet Cecil, 18 February ?, Violet Milner Papers, MS VM 43/c368/5. FH–DD, [1895], Edith Lyttelton papers, CHAN I/5/10/140, 142. I have failed to identify Lady N and have found no evidence of Jack having affairs. Indeed all who knew him emphasise that he was a man of honour.
45. EBJ–FH, May 1893, vol. 7, MP, M/05/1353.
46. EBJ–FH, 1 July 1893 and nd, vol. 7, MP, M/05/1353.
47. EBJ–FH, 25 August 1893, vol. 7, MP, M/05/1353.
48. FH–EBJ, nd [August 1893], vol. 7, MP, M/05/1353.
49. FH–DD, 1894, Edith Lyttelton papers, CHAN I/5/10/123.
50. FH–EBJ, 12 January 1894, vol. 8, MP, M/05/1353.
51. FH–DD, [1898], Edith Lyttelton papers, CHAN I/5/10/151.
52. FH–EBJ, 16 September 1894 vol. 8, MP, M/05/1353.
53. EBJ–FH, 5 September 1894, vol. 8, MP, M/05/1353.
54. EBJ–FH, nd [1894], MSS Fitz xxvii/50, 54. EBJ–FH, 17 August 93, vol. 7; 6 January 1894, vol. 8, MP, M/05/1353. FH–DD, [1895], Edith Lyttelton papers, CHAN I/5/10/130.
55. FH–EBJ 27 October 1897 and 1 November 1897, vol. 11, MP, M/05/1353. FH–DD, nd., Edith Lyttelton papers, CHAN1/5/10/244.
56. FH–EBJ, 23 April 1898, vol. 11, MP, M/05/1353.
57. FH–EBJ, 11 and 12 November 1894 vol. 9; 24 July 1897; vol. 10; 23 April 1898, vol. 11, MP, M/05/1353. Dimbleby, *Profound Secret*, p. 153. Occasionally she overplayed her hand as in 1895. When the house she was looking to rent was too expensive, she suggested 'shall we take it together and will you come and make it your town house'. It is not clear what she thought would happen to The Grange. Or where Georgie or indeed May would fit into this scheme? Anyway nothing came of it. FH–EBJ, 20 November 1895, vol. 9, MP, M/05/1353.
58. EBJ–FH, 18 November 1896; 5 June 1897, vol. 10; nd [August 1897], vol. 11, MP, M/05/1353. 'We are such ancient friends'. EBJ–FH, 14 July 1892 MP, M/05/1353.
59. EBJ–FH, nd., EBJ MSS FM xxvii/65. Miss Sara Anderson to FH, 8 May 1895, EBJ–FH, 12 May 1895 vol. 9, MP. EBJ–FH, 1897, vol. 10. FH–EBJ, nd [June 1896], vol. 9; nd [August 1897], vol. 11, MP, M/05/1353.
60. EBJ–FH, 3 September 1893. EBJ MSS FM

xxvii/38.

61. EBJ–FH, nd, vol. 8, MP, M/05/1353. EBJ–FH, 11 October 1892, EBJ MSS FM xxviii/23.

62. EBJ–FH,12 November 1894, [Jan 1895] vol. 9, MP, M/05/1353.

63. *The Yellow Book* was an art periodical [1894–7] edited by Aubrey Beardsley which attracted many notable contributors. Its yellow cover [suggestive of illicit 'French Novels'] gave it a reputation for decadence. Often associated with Oscar Wilde though he never published in it.

64. EBJ–FH, [April 1895], vol. 9, MP, M/05/1353.

65. EBJ–FH, 29 August 1895 and nd., EBJ MSS FM xxvii/56, 59. EBJ–FH, 24 June 1896, vol. 9, MP, M/05/1353.

66. FH–EBJ, 1 December 1895 vol. 9, MP, M/05/1353.

67. 1 November 1897 FH–EBJ vol. 11, MP. Frances observed Kipling 'gaining so in power and dignity …[with] a just measure of things and … contempt for the praise and blame of the crowd'. FH–DD, 1898, Edith Lyttelton papers, CHAN I/5/10/149.

68. FH, *Time Remembered*, p. 131. FH–EBJ, 27 September 1896 vol. 10, MP, M/05/1353.

69. EBJ–FH, 16 August 1894, 19 July 1894 vol. 8, MP, M/05/1353. FH–EBJ, nd [June 1896], vol. 9, MP, M/05/1353. EBJ–FH nd MSS Fitz xxvii/8-9. FH–EBJ 24 July 1897 vol. 10, MP, M/05/1353. EBJ feared he wouldn't finish Avalon 'until 1970'. EBJ–FH, 5 June 1897, vol. 10, MP, M/05/1353.

70. EBJ–FH, 12 November 1894, vol. 9; 9 July 1897, vol. 10; FH–EBJ, 19 July 1897, vol. 10, MP, M/05/1353.

71. FH–EBJ, nd [August 1897], vol. 11, MP, M/05/1353. EBJ–FH, nd [June 1897] vol. 10, MP, M/05/1353.

72. EBJ–FH, nd [1894]; 31 January 1894, vol. 8; nd [1894], vol. 9; 8 November 1897, vol. 11, MP, M/05/1353.

73. EBJ–FH, 20 Jan 1896, EBJ MSS FM xxvii/66. FH–EBJ, nd [August 1897] vol. 11, MP, M/05/1353.

74. Unfinished in part because artistically he was trying to recapture the blacks of 'the Arnolfini portrait'– then to him the greatest picture in the world but 'The magician isn't within a 100 thousand leagues of it'.

75. EBJ–FH, 17 September 1897 vol. 11, MP, M/05/1353. Caroline Dakers, 'Yours affectionately, Angelo: the Letters of Edward Burne-Jones (1833-98) and Frances Horner (1858-1940)', *British Art Journal*, vol. 2, no. 3, (Spring/Summer 2001).

76. EBJ–FH, 17 September 1897 vol. 11, MP, M/05/1353.

77. Yet that same year he would ask her 'will you come over and sit to me that I may work from you on a picture begun for you just twenty years ago' EBJ–FH, nd [1897] vol. 11, MP, M/05/1353. But at forty-three and prematurely grey, she clearly didn't model for this picture.

78. Wildman, *Victorian Artist-Dreamer*, p. 322.

79. FH–DD, 'Friday June 1898', Edith Lyttelton papers, CHAN 1/5/10/158.

80. To aid his cause, in April 1898 he rented from the St Paul's Studios, off Camden Hill, a much larger space which he could dedicate solely to *Avalon*. FH–Violet Cecil, 18 February [1898], Violet Milner papers MS VM 43/c368/5. FH–DD, 'Friday June 1898', Edith Lyttelton papers, CHAN 1/5/10/158. FH–JH, nd, MP, M/01/1263. The first reference in this paragraph is to this temporary studio, but subsequent references are to the studio at The Grange.

81. FH–JH, nd, MP, M/01/1263. FH–Violet Cecil, 19 July 1898, Violet Milner papers MS VM 43/c368/6.

82. Fitzgerald, *Burne-Jones*, p. 284; MacCarthy, *The Last Pre-Raphaelite*, pp. 504–8.

83. FH, *Time Remembered*, pp. 109–10. Henry James–FH, 25 June 1898, Autograph Letters, vol. 2, p. 21, MP, M/01/1260.

84. MacCarthy, *The Last Pre-Raphaelite*, p. 509. FH–DD, 'Friday June 1898', Edith Lyttelton papers, CHAN 1/5/10/158.

85. FH–DD, 'Friday June 1898', Edith Lyttelton papers, CHAN 1/5/10/158.

86. FH–DD, nd, Edith Lyttelton papers, CHAN I/5/10/154.

87. FH–JH, nd [1898], MP, M/01/1263. HHA–FH, 24 June 1898, vol. 2, MP, M/01/1270.

88. FH–JH, nd [1898], MP, M/01/1263. HHA–FH, 18 June 1898, vol. 2, MP, M/01/1270.

89. FH to Sydney Cockerell, 3 November 1904, Cockerell papers, Add MS 52726.

90. FH–JH, nd, MP, M/01/1263.

91. FH–Violet Cecil, Violet Milner papers, MS VM 43 /c368/14.

92. Georgiana Burne-Jones, *Memorials*, ii, pp. 166–7.

93. FH, *Time Remembered*, pp. 108–9.

94. FH–EBJ, nd [June 1896], vol. 9, MP, M/05/1353.

PART 7 Halcyon Days (1899–1914)

1. FH, *Time remembered*, p. 195.

2. FH–DD, 1895, Edith Lyttelton papers, CHAN I/5/10/131, 134-5.

3. FH–DD, 6 September ?, Edith Lyttelton papers, CHAN 1/5/10/22.

4. FH, *Time Remembered*, pp. 183–4. To her surprise, when she bemoaned her fate, EBJ recalled finding Ruskin and Cardinal Manning on their knees searching for an Ouida novel.

5. 'Everywhere I travel I hunger for more'. FH–DD, 1 October 1899, nd, Edith Lyttelton Papers CHAN1/5/10/146, 172, 189. FH–JH, nd, MP, M/01/1263. FH–Violet Cecil, 19 October 1899, Violet Milner papers, VM 43/c368/8. FH, *Time Remembered*, p.186.

6. The cause of Amy's death remains uncertain or at least unmentionable. Writing to Violet Cecil, Frances put it down to 'those arrangements which seem to me at once so intricate and so ill-conceived in regard to our sex … an anomaly unsuited to more civilised times.' FH–Violet Cecil, 29 September 1900, Violet Milner papers, VM 43/c368/17.

7. FH–DD, 1894, Edith Lyttelton papers, CHAN I/5/10/123. FH–HHA, 2 July 1892, 12 July 1892, vol. 1, MP, M/01/1270. EBJ–FH, nd [1892], EBJ MSS FM xxviii/24. FH–EBJ, 2 June 1898, nd, Vol. 11, MP, M/05/1353.

8. FH–JH, nd, MP, M/01/1263. FH–Violet Cecil, 8 January 1900, Violet Milner papers, VM 43/c368/18.

9. Crucially the position did not require Jack to resign with the fall of the government.

10. FH–DD, 1895, Edith Lyttelton papers, CHAN I/5/10/131,134–5. By contrast with her friends, Jack's brothers were less impressed: 'I wish your brothers wrote like my sisters… George's contemptuous congratulations almost as bad as Maurice's ill-natured ones'. FH–JH, nd, MP, M/01/1263.

11. In November 1913, the Archduke was a guest at Windsor Castle for a week after which he was the guest of the Duke of Portland. Was Frances exaggerating or was she housing some of his party or was this for a private part of the Archduke's visit? FH, *Time Remembered*, pp. 181, 198–204.

12. FH–Violet Cecil, 29 September 1900, Violet Milner papers MS VM 43/c368/17. Viscountess Milner, *My Picture Gallery, 1886–1901* (1951), pp. 112–17.

13. FH, *Time Remembered*, pp. 198–202. Ellen Terry to FH, nd, MP, M/01/1267.

14. FH, *Time Remembered*, p. 202. Emily Lutyens to Edwin Lutyens, January 1907, Jane Ridley, *A Life of Edwin Lutyens; the Architect and his Wife* (2002), p. 167. Frances lacked the money to commission houses from Lutyens but she took up his cause with vigour and pressed many of her rich friends to hire him. Thus, with Aggie, she secured him the commission for the 'English House' at the Paris International Exhibition in 1900. Jane Brown, *Lutyens and the Edwardians* (1996), pp. 44, 115.

15. Jane Brown, *Lutyens and the Edwardians* (1996), pp107, 114.

16. FH–DD, 19 October 1900, nd [1900], 5 September 1903 Edith Lyttelton Papers CHAN1/5/10/86, 186, 189, 209. FH, *Time Remembered*, pp. 187, 198. Yet Con Manners reported back to Frances how Norah Lindsay praised Frances's 'talent for housekeeping [and] well kept accounts'. Con Manners–FH, nd, Autograph Letters vol. 2 MP, M/01/1260. Other occupiers of Mells Park included Gilbert Thompson Bates, son of a Liverpool shipowner.

17. EBJ–FH, 21 October 1892 vol. 5; nd, [July 1896], vol. 10, MP, M/05/1353.

18. Brown, *Lutyens and the Edwardians*, p.107.

19. FH–DD, 3 January 1902, Edith Lyttelton Papers, CHAN1/5/10/204.

20. FH, *Time Remembered*. p. 195. Odd not to have asked her brother-in-law's sister, Gertrude Jekyll with whom Lutyens regularly worked.

21. FH–KH, nd, MP, M/01/1269.

22. FH–Violet Cecil, 24 April 1900, Violet Milner papers, MS VM 43/c368/16.

23. Sold at Christie's 30 June 1906. John Jolliffe, *Raymond Asquith: Life and Letters* (1980), pp. 147–50.

24. FH, *Time Remembered*, p. 182. Birrell was a Liberal cabinet minister; Herbert Paul was a radical journalist.

25. 'Do you remember you would always waylay me for fear of my speaking to anyone else on the way to a walk or on a talk… Yes…I know I haven't many woman rivals to your heart' FH–JH, nd, MP, M/01/1263.

26. FH–JH 18 January 1898, MP, M/01/1263. JH to DD, 'Tuesday' 1895, Edith Lyttelton Papers, CHAN1/5/10/145: 'I feel quite a different creature here but I wish Frances didn't fritter away so much time – it is extraordinary that she can be so happy'.

27. FH–DD, nd, Edith Lyttelton Papers, CHAN1/5/10/241. FH, *Time Remembered*, pp. 181, 190, 195.

28. FH, *Time Remembered*, pp. 145–53. EBJ–FH, nd [April 1894], vol. 8, MP, M/05/1353.

29. Raymond Asquith to Baker, 15 July 1900, Jolliffe, *Raymond*, p. 70.

30. Balfour describes Haldane reading at a party at Stanway in 1908 'the most abstruse metaphysics (Bradley!)… He looked splendid, more like a Jesuit priest than ever with his sweet sceptical smile and bland countenance … Hugo, Ed Tennant and Frances

Horner went fast asleep, while Haldane declaimed that God was a finite object or an infinite emptiness, a restless abstraction'. Balfour was one of two who understood him – indeed 'he really said some very illuminating things.' *Letters of Arthur Balfour and Lady Elcho, 1885–1917* (1992), p. 248.

31. R.B. Haldane, *Autobiography* (1929), p. 119.

32. Nicolson to Dudley Sommer, NLS, MS 20664, ff. 155–64. See also 'R.B. Haldane' by H.G.C. Matthew in ODNB.

33. Leo Amery, *My Political Life*, ii, p. 277. Jean Graham and Douglas F. Martin, *Haldane: Statesman, Lawyer, Philosopher* (1996), p. 69.

34. FH–Ettie, Lady Desborough, 21 February 1929, DE/Rv/c1346/17.

35. FH–DD, 30 December 1890, Edith Lyttelton papers, CHAN1/5/9/36–37. FH, *Time Remembered*, p. 145. FH–DD, 20 January 1891, Edith Lyttelton papers, CHAN1/5/9/61–64. Frances was only thirty-seven at the time. Yet they shared some common experiences: both brought up in Scottish, strictly Presbyterian households whose faith they would both eventually reject; both scarred by the loss of a favourite sibling when a teenager.

36. FH, *Time Remembered*, p. 146. FH–DD, 27 August 1903, Edith Lyttelton Papers, CHAN1/5/10/218.

37. FH to Ettie, 23 December 1890, DE/Rv/c1346/1. FH–DD, 18 October 1892, Edith Lyttelton papers, CHAN I/5/10/102. Stephen Koss, *Haldane, Scapegoat for Liberalism* (1969), p. 10.

38. R.B. Haldane, *Autobiography*, p. 119 Clifford, *The Asquiths*, p. 9. FH–DD, 30 December 1890, Edith Lyttelton papers, CHAN1/5/9/36– 37. Sir Frederick Maurice, *Haldane* (1937), p. 176. FH–KA, 30 December 1909, MP, M/01/1269.

39. Elizabeth 'did not care' for Haldane's English friends. In particular 'she could make nothing of Lady Horner but neither could Lady Horner make anything out of her. Mrs Haldane [R's mother] *hated* Lady Horner.' Mary Belloc Lowndes to her daughter, 30 March 1947, Susan Lowndes (ed), *Diaries and Letters of Mary Belloc Lowndes* (1971), pp. 278–9.

40. FH, *Time* Remembered, pp. 146–53. Haldane [henceforth RBH]–mother, 11 August 1904 in Maurice, *Haldane*, pp. 142–3.

41. Mary Belloc Lowndes to daughter, 30 March 1947, Susan Lowndes (ed), *Diaries and Letters of Mary Belloc Lowndes* (1971), pp. 278–9. She was the sister of Hilaire Belloc.

42. These lines from *Warum gabst du uns die tiefen Blicken* were penned to Goethe's lover, Charlotte von Stein – a passionate affair that was nevertheless unconsummated because she was a married woman. Translations by John Campbell and Gerard Evans from Wolfgang von Goethe, *Faust. Eine Tragöde*, Tübingen, 1808.

43. RBH–FH, 30 July 1909, MP, M/01/1272. FH–RBH, 13 March ?[1895], MP, M/01/1274.

44. Beatrice Webb, *Our Partnership* (1948), p. 98.

45. RBH–FH, 11, 13, 14 and 20 September 1897, MP, M/01/1272.

46. It is possible that Frances and Haldane had become closer in late 1893 but more likely that their relationship began in late spring 1894.

47. FH, *Time Remembered*, p. 147. FH–RBH, 23 September 1899, MP/ 01/1274.

48. RBH–FH, 30 October 1905; 30 July 1909, MP, M/01/1272.

49. EBJ–FH, 5 November 1892, vol. 6, MP, M/05/1353.

50. EBJ–FH, October 1896, vol. 10; 1 November 1897, vol. 11, MP, M/05/1353. FH–EBJ, 4.3.1898, vol. 11, MP, M/05/1353.

51. Laura Tennant noted how at a little over a year old Cicely would sound 'hurrahs for Gladstone and covers her face with her hands for Lord Salisbury and roars derisively at Randolph Churchill'. Angela Lambert, *Unquiet Souls*, p. 25.

52. General Gordon died in the fall of Khartoum to the forces of the Mahdi in 1885. Public opinion condemned Gladstone for delaying to send out a rescue mission.

53. Burne-Jones claimed not to have crossed Gladstone's threshold 'since he burnt down the pretty city by the sea with his filthy gunships for the sake of his filthy stock jobbery…' EBJ–FH January 1885 vol. 1, MP. Fitzgerald, *Burne-Jones*, pp163–5. Conspiracy theorists make much of the fact that at the time Gladstone was heavily invested in Egyptian bonds.

54. EBJ–FH [1884], vol. 1, MP, M/05/1353.

55. EBJ–FH, October and November 1891, vol. 3; nd, vol. 5, MP, M/01/1353. 'You didn't care for him, I know' asserted EBJ. Perhaps not for Irish Home Rule but she did care for the fate of Parnell's stepchild whom he feared he might lose in a custody battle.

56. HHA–FH, 26 October 1891, MP, M/01/1270. Even Gladstone was redeemed in his passing: 'How dull it will be… Nobody else for many a day will fill the stage as he has done – created enthusiasm and hatred as he has … he has been a mighty part of his country … the flat ones can have a fool's paradise … It's

coming … and everything will be smug and comfortable'. EBJ–FH, nd [March 1894] vol. 8, MP, M/05/1353. Frances was also struck, finding bands in the backstreets of Bath striking up the Death March on hearing the news. The impressive crowd at Gladstone's lying in state 'came for an idea as Frances Horner said'. Betty Balfour–Frances Balfour, 21 February 1898, Balfour Papers GD433/2/319.

57. EBJ–FH, 5 November 1897, vol. 11, MP, M/05/1353.

58. Jalland, *Women, Marriage and Politics*, pp, 199–200. On Parnell FH by now 'even more in favour of him – just the leader they need'. FH–DD, 18 February 1891, Edith Lyttelton papers CHAN1/5/9/4244.

59. EBH–FH, 1 July 1893, vol. 5; 1 December 1893 vol. 8, MP, M/05/1353. FH–EBJ 10 May 1898, vol. 11, MP, M/05/1353.

60. The Speaker was Arthur Peel [in post 1884–1895], the youngest son of Sir Robert Peel.

61. FH–DD, [1895], Edith Lyttelton papers, CHAN I/5/10/140.

62. FH–EBJ, 4 March 1898 vol. 11, MP, M/05/1353. Herbert Beerbohm Tree was a renowned actor of the day and half-sibling of Max Beerbohm, the essayist, caricaturist and humourist most famous for *Zuleika Dobson*.

63. EBJ–FH, 19 January1892 vol. 6, MP, M/05/1353. EBJ–FH, nd., EBJ MSS FM xxvii/49–50.

64. FH–DD, 'Easter Day 1891', Edith Lyttelton papers, CHAN1/5/9/46–9.

65. Sir William Harcourt, formerly Chancellor of the Exchequer and briefly succeeded Rosebery as leader of the Liberal Party.

66. HHA–FH, 29 April 1892, MP, M/01/1270.

67. EBJ–FH 19 January 1892, vol. 6, MP, M/05/1353.

68. FH–EBJ, nd [February 1897] vol. 10, MP, M/05/1353.

69. FH–KA, 30 December 1909, MP, M/01/1269.

70. FH, *Time Remembered*, p.188. Jalland, *Women, Marriage and Politics*, p. 197. FH–DD, 27 September 1900, Edith Lyttelton papers, CHAN1/5/9/24. FH–Violet Cecil, 22 April 1900, 17 July 1900, 27 December 1900, Violet Milner papers, MS VM 43/c368/16, 37.

71. FH–JH, nd 1895?, MP, M/01/1263. FH, *Time Remembered*, p. 149. Sir Charles Trevelyan was a Liberal (later Labour) politician.

72. FH–Ettie, 21 February 1929, DE/Rv/c1346/17. FH, *Time Remembered*, p. 146.

73. Maurice, *Haldane*, p. 73

74. FH–EBJ, 9 June 1896, vol. 9, MP, M/05/1353. FH–RBH, nd [1894], MP, M/01/1274. Apart

from Grey who was much younger, most were a little older. This was the second time that Haldane had been passed over. In 1892 he was the only one of Asquith's political friends not to get some office under Gladstone. Jenkins, *Asquith*, (1964), pp. 60–61. On Haldane's being passed over for Solicitor General, see Leo McKinstry, *Rosebery: Statesman in Turmoil* (205), p. 335.

75. FH–RBH, 13 March ?[1895], MP, M/01/1274.

76. H.W. Massingham was a Liberal editor of the *Daily Chronicle* and, after resigning over the Boer war, would later edit *The Nation*.

77. FH–EBJ 10 May 1898, vol. 11, MP, M/05/1353. FH, *Time Remembered*, pp 204–7. J.M. Morley, 15 September 1896, Autograph Letters, p. 39, MP, /01/1260.

78. Norman and Jeanne Mackenzie (ed.), *The Diaries of Beatrice Webb* (1986), vol. 2, p. 261. In retrospect Beatrice admired Frances, but in this entry she was less than generous: describing Frances as a 'kindly hostess… charming… High Priestess of the Souls in their palmy days, now somewhat elderly and faded but gracious to those she accepts as "distinguished".

79. C. Percy and J. Ridley (eds), *Letters of Edwin Lutyens to his Wife, Lady Emily* (1985), pp. 218–19.

80. FH–EBJ, 1 November 1897, vol. 11, MP, M/05/1353. Kipling: 'gaining so in power and dignity … [with] a just measure of things and … contempt for the praise and blame of the crowd'. FH–DD, 1898, Edith Lyttelton papers, CHAN I/5/10/149. EBJ–FH, nd [1896], vol. 9, MP, M/05/1353.

81. FH–DD, 11 September 1898, Edith Lyttelton papers, CHAN 1/5/10/163.

82. FH–Violet Cecil, 13 September 1898, Violet Milner papers VM 43/c368/7. FH–JH, nd [September 1899], MP, M/01/1263.

83. FH–Violet Cecil, 21 December 1899, Violet Milner papers, VM 43/c368/12; FH–DD, 29 December 1899, Edith Lyttelton Papers, CHAN1/5/10/175. Sir Alfred Lyall to FH, 3 January 1900, Autograph letters, vol. 1, pp. 50–51, MP, M/01/1260.

84. FH–Violet Cecil, 19 October 1899, 4 November 1899, 7 December 1899, Violet Milner papers, VM 43/c368/8–10.

85. FH–Violet Cecil, 7 December 1899, Violet Milner papers, VM 43/c368/10.

86. FH–Violet Cecil, 19 October 1899, Violet Milner papers, VM 43/c368/8. Julia Bush, *Edwardian Ladies and Imperial Power*, pp. 46–9.

87. FH–Violet Cecil, 7 December 1899, Violet Milner papers, VM 43/c368 /10. It is generally

accepted that Chamberlain, together with his allies in South Africa, Cecil Rhodes and Violet Cecil's lover, Alfred Milner, provoked the conflict for strategic gain.

88. FH–Violet Cecil, nd, 1 March 1900, 17 July [1900], Violet Milner papers VM 43/c368/14, 15, 37.
89. 1 Samuel 4:21–22.
90. FH–DD, nd, 27 September 1900, Edith Lyttelton Papers, CHAN1/5/9/24 & 10/166. FH–Violet Cecil, 17 July (1900?) Violet Milner papers VM 43/c368 /37. Rosebery to FH, 15 November 1896, Autograph Letter Book, MP, M/01/1260.
91. FH–JH nd, MP22/2. For this event see Leo McKinstry, *Rosebery: Statesman in Turmoil* (2005), pp. 391–8. Some years later Rosebery came to give a speech in Bath and Wells: 'He is a strange being', decided Frances. 'He has such an extraordinary pleasant smile and such a good sense of humour that I don't find him difficult to get on with – but he can also be very rude'. One bishop who Frances liked but was not clever clearly got the 'rudeness', leading FH to argue 'but I don't think Bishops ought to be clever … they should leave that to the laity'. 4 November 1899, Violet Milner papers VM 43/c368/9. H.C.G. Matthew, *Liberal Imperialists*, p. 22. Rosebery continued to be an episodic embarrassment to the Liberal Imperialists through to 1905.
92. Frances's relationship with Balfour seemed to have warmed a little. In 1901 he writes of 'very old friends like you and me'. Balfour–FH, 16 July 1901, Autograph Letter Book, pp. 56–7, MP, M/01/1260. But they would discuss Swinburne, not politics.
93. FH–Violet Cecil, 29 September 1900, Violet Milner papers, VM 43/c368 /17.
94. FH–HHA, nd [1902], MP, M/01/1270.
95. Norman and Jeanne Mackenzie (eds), *Diaries of Beatrice Webb*, 28 November 1902.
96. That Balfour should warn one of the opposition of his intentions seems an odd betrayal of party. Either it reflects their social proximity (loose talk at dinner) or more likely it was in the hope that Haldane would stir up divisions within the Liberals especially if it was forced to form a government because Balfour resigned rather than call an election.
97. For much of what follows see Haldane's Memorandum of events reproduced in Haldane, *Autobiography*, pp. 173–83; Haldane Papers NLS MS20049, ff. 92–96. See also H.G.C. Matthew, 'Haldane', ODNB; Roy Jenkins, *Asquith*, pp. 155–8; Stephen Koss,

Lord Haldane, Scapegoat for Liberalism.

98. These connections were largely through Knollys, the King's Private Secretary, but Haldane was well enough thought of to be able to brief the King personally on pressing the Prime Minister into the Lords.
99. RBH–FH, 18 October 1905, MP, M/01/1272. Frances and Haldane frequently referred to Henry Asquith by his initials 'HHA'.
100. In a tale of powerful women, Campbell-Bannerman under pressure did consider retreating to the Lords until his wife arrived from Scotland and declared her opposition! Actually he had been sorely tempted on health grounds to go to the Lords and only resisted when feeling pushed. He would die in Downing Street in 1908.
101. Graham and Martin, *Haldane*, p. 185.
102. Haldane, *Autobiography*, p. 182. A kailyard was a small cabbage patch attached to a cottage and idealized in contemporary Scottish literature. Thus to Campbell-Bannerman the War Office in 1906 was a provincial backwater where the grand philosopher would struggle to make a mark.
103. Haldane, *Autobiography*, p. 181.
104. Matthew, 'Haldane', ODNB. Haldane had wanted to be moved to the Admiralty to complete his work but was appointed Lord Chancellor instead with trouble brewing over the Parliament Act. Churchill got the Admiralty instead. 'Richard wonderful about it and won't allow a grumble', wrote Frances, not a little frustrated at his reluctance to fight his corner. FH–KA, nd [14 October ?], MP, M/01/1269. For all his modernising of the army, oddly he had little faith in the role of aircraft in war, apparently declaring in 1907 'that aeroplanes would never fly'. Koss, *Haldane*, p. 144.
105. FH, *Time Remembered*, p. 195.

PART 8 Remote Operators and Callow Youths (1890–1914)

1. FH–DD, 'Tuesday 1902', Edith Lyttelton Papers, CHAN/1/5/10/222.
2. Susan Lowndes, *Diaries and Letters of Mary Belloc Lowndes, 1911–1947* (1971), pp. 278–9. MBL–daughter [Susan], 30 March 1947.
3. Her sister Aggie by comparison in 1882 left her one-year-old child with her parents while she joined her husband as he conducted a review of the fortifications of Ceylon and Singapore.
4. FH, *Time Remembered*, pp. 84–6. FH–DD, 1 August 1890, Edith Lyttelton papers

CHAN1/5/9/21–2. FH–DD, 1895, Edith Lyttelton papers, CHAN I/5/10/131, 147. The doll was named 'Frances, DD, Lang Horner' after her mother and her godparents.

5. FH–DD, 7 August 1901, Edith Lyttelton Papers CHAN1/5/10/195. Herbert Gladstone was the youngest son of the Prime Minister. His marriage to Dorothy Paget, twenty years his junior, would not prove a happy one.

6. FH, *Time Remembered*, pp. 86–7. Frances passed Katharine's religiosity off as 'ideas to which that type of child is subject'. FH–EBJ, 9 June 1896, vol. 9; 19 July 1897, vol. 10, MP, M/05/1353. FH–JH, nd, MP, M/01/1263. FH, 'Pages from Record of Events', MP, M/01/1309.

7. They might have bonded over cricket. Jack was both passionate and talented playing first-class cricket and for the MCC. He would organise many games at the Park. Edward would captain his team but was never very keen. Mark on the other hand was very keen but not very good. Still he could happily 'talk' cricket with his father for hours. FH, 'Pages from a Record of Events', MP, M/01/1309.

8. FH, *Time Remembered*, pp. 89–90. FH–JH, nd, MP22/1. FH–DD, 21 January 1891, Edith Lyttelton papers, CHAN1/5/9/61–64. FH–DD, February 1901, Edith Lyttelton Papers, CHAN1/5/10/192.

9. FH, *Time Remembered*, pp. 91–2, 103. FH–DD, nd [1891?], Edith Lyttelton papers, CHAN/1/5/9/82. FH–Violet Cecil, 13 September 1898, Violet Milner papers, MS VM 43/c368/7. FH–EBJ, 1 May 1896, vol. 9, MP, M/05/1353.

10. FH–DD, 1 August 1890, Edith Lyttelton papers, CHAN1/5/9/21–2.

11. FH–DD, 1 October 1899, Edith Lyttelton Papers, CHAN1/5/10/172. FH–JH, nd, MP, M/01/1263. FH, *Time Remembered*, p.179

12. FH, *Time Remembered*, pp. 84–7. FH–Violet Cecil, 22 April 1900, Violet Milner papers, MS VM 43/c368/16.

13. FH–DD, '13 August [1887?]', Edith Lyttelton papers, CHAN1/5/9/15–16. FH–DD, 23 August 1903, 28 September 1904, nd, Edith Lyttelton Papers, CHAN1/5/10/207–8, 213, 236.

14. FH–EBJ, nd [June 1896], vol. 9, MP, M/05/1353. FH–Violet Cecil, 22 April 1896, Violet Milner papers, MS VM 43/c368/3.

15. Jane Ridley and Clayre Percy (eds.), *The Letters of Arthur Balfour and Lady Elcho, 1885–1917* (1992), p. 248.

16. FH–Violet Cecil, '2nd Jan', Violet Milner papers, MS VM 43/c368/4.

17. FH, *Time Remembered*, p. 88. MacKenzie, *Children of The Souls*, p. 19.

18. Georgiana BJ–FH, 5 DEcember 1899, Autograph Letters , vol. 1, p. 49, MP, M/01/1260.

19. To be fair to Frances, she was alert quite quickly to Mark's slow development. FH–Violet Cecil, 6 October1895 [but could be 1897], Violet Milner papers, MS VM 43/c368/2.

20. FH, *Time Remembered*, pp. 88–89. FH–DD, 21 January 1891, Edith Lyttelton papers, CHAN1/5/9/ 61–64.

21. MacCarthy, *The Last Pre-Raphaelite*, pp. 520–1.

22. See also EBJ's drawing of FH writing the letter in bed [*Time Remembered*, p. 102]. FH– EBJ, July 1897, vol. 10, MP, M/05/1353. 'Someday Cicely will sit for me perhaps and I will make her pretty for you.' EBJ-FH, 20 July 1892, vol 4, MP, M/05/1353.

23. EBJ–FH, January 1892, vol. 7; 19 November 1896, 9 July 1897, vol. 10. FH–EBJ, 19 July 1897, vol. 10, MP, M/05/1353. Phil Burne-Jones–FH, 22 June 1894, Autograph Letters, vol. 1, p. 28, MP, M/01/1260.

24. Canon Scott Holland–FH, 25 August ?, Autograph Letters, vol. 2, p. 16, MP, M/01/1260. EBJ–FH, nd, vol. 11, MP, M/05/1353. On Edward and his Pre-Raphaelite looks, see Wildman, *Victorian Artist-Dreamer*, p. 130.

25. EBJ–FH, 23 December 1893, vol 8, MP, M/05/1353. FH–JH, nd, MP, M/01/1263. Claudia Renton, *The Wild Wyndham Sisters* (2014), pp. xvi, 200. FH, *Time Remembered*, p. 97. Sargent was also finding it difficult to capture Cicely. In turn she never liked his portrait of her and sold it as soon as she could. Sargent to FH, nd, Autograph Letters, vol 1, M/01/1260.

26. Cynthia Asquith, *Remember and be Glad* (1952), pp. 194–7. If Mark was 'twelve or so', this portrayal is of *c*. 1904. Raymond is Raymond Asquith, son of HHA.

27. MacKenzie, *Children*, p. 22.

28. Compared to Cicely, Katharine, Frances predicted, 'will be a very different pair of shoes altogether'. FH–DD, 5 October 1892, Edith Lyttelton Papers, CHAN1/5/10/200.

29. 'Don't fancy that people don't like you as much as Cicely', FH–KH, nd, MP, M/01/1269

30. Katharine Horner–Edward Horner [henceforth EH], nd, MP?, cited in Mackenzie, *Children*, p. 20.

31. Cynthia Asquith, *Remember and be Glad* (1952), p. 88. 'Katharine was a living poem'.

32. Raymond Asquith [hereafter RA]–FH, 9 April 1904, MP, P/01/1599.

33. On Katharine's sense of 'humour … I never knew anyone who put her finger so unerringly on the weak spot'. RA–FH 10 October 1905, MP, P/01/1599.

34. Blanche Stanley to Katharine Asquith [hereafter KA], Zeigler, *Diana*, p. 46.

35. MacKenzie, *Children*, p. 19; RA to Harold Baker, 1 August 1901, Jolliffe, *Raymond*, pp. 69, 80, 112.

36. This of course was a myth. Privately Raymond worked extremely hard but Frances preferred the association with genius.

37. RA–FH, nd [November 1903], 12 January 1907, MP, P/01/1599.

38. 'Such a nice attractive boy – rather silent and studious but with quite a charm of face and manner'. FH–Violet Cecil, 17 July (1899?), MS VM 43/c368/37. FH–DD, 5 September 1903, Edith Lyttelton Papers, CHAN 1/5/10/209). RA–FH, 27 August 1905, MP, P/01/1599 and Jolliffe, *Raymond*, p. 132. RA–KH, 23 July 1904, Jolliffe, *Raymond*, pp. 113–14.

39. Clifford, *The Asquiths*, p. 111. RA–KH, 8 August 1904, 12 November 1904, Jolliffe, *Raymond*, pp. 94–5, 114, 118–19.

40. RA–KH, 6 October 1905, 26 January 1906, Jolliffe, *Raymond*, pp.137, 150–51. RA–Con Manners, 9 February 1907, Jolliffe, *Raymond*, p. 152. Clifford, *The Asquiths*, p. 129. In 1906 Raymond was twenty-eight and Katharine twenty-one.

41. MacKenzie, *Children*, pp.14–16. Clifford suggests that Katharine had Raymond's mother's looks: *The Asquiths*, p. 111.

42. RA–FH, 14 October 1903, MP, P/01/1599.

43. RA–KH, 10 October 1906, Jolliffe p.148. Conrad Russell to his mother, 'March 1907'; Conrad Russell to RA, 1 July 1907, Georgiana Blakiston (ed.) *Letters of Conrad Russell* (1987), pp. 33–5. Katharine's interest in Catholicism for the moment did not survive Raymond's mockery.

44. RA–Con Manners, 9 February 1907, Jolliffe, *Raymond*, p. 152. Clifford, *The Asquiths*, p. 130.

45. A placement error in the church saw him having to sit beside the Liberal Prime Minister, Campbell-Bannerman. Looking on, HHA commented that 'he had never known two men with a more complete antipathy to one another.' Betty Balfour to Frank Balfour, 26 July 1907, Balfour Papers (Whittinghame), GD433/2/336/1–2.

46. MacKenzie, *Children*, pp. 3–4. RA–FH, 30 July 1907, MP, P/01/1599. Jolliffe, *Raymond*, pp.154–5. Ruth Balfour to Betty Balfour, n.d., Balfour (Whittinghame) papers, GD433/2/335/78–81. As for the honeymoon, the sight of Katharine in a 'new bathing gown transcends the dreams of poets or as some would say is a little bit of all right'. RA– FH, 28 August 1907, MP, P/01/1599.

47. FH–DD, 5 October 1892, Edith Lyttelton Papers, CHAN1/5/10/200.

48. FH–JH, nd, MP, M/01/1263. The unknown suitor was Dudley Carleton, 2nd Baron Dorchester. 'On Cicely – her only serious defect is that she prefers women to men but you will agree with me it is a rather radical one'. RA–FH, 4 January 1905, MP, P/01/1599.

49. Ettie Desborough was for once the exception that proved the rule.

50. RA–FH, 31 August 1908, MP, P/01/1599. Frances resented Cicely 'springing on me what apparently most people except me knew (you amongst them I hear)'. Seemingly Cicely had been stepping out with Lambton for a year. Frances insisted that her objections were more than over money but included 'age, circumstances, profession, all what one would *not* choose'. But clearly she was hurt by the lack of trust. FH–KA, 2 August 1908, 1 September 1908, MP, M/01/1269.

51. FH, *Time Remembered*, p. 197.

52. FH–JH, nd pre-1900, MP M/01/1263. FH, *Time Remembered*, pp. 91–2.

53. FH, *Time Remembered*, p. 96. EBJ was no better. Seeing Edward and Mark at a reception of May Gaskell's, he wrote to Frances: 'such handsome things they looked and I cuddled Mark as he was too small to mind'. EBJ–FH, December 1895, vol. 9, MP, M/05/1353.

54. FH–Violet Cecil, nd, Violet Milner papers, VM 43/c368/23.

55. Much of what follows comes from FH, *Time Remembered*, pp. 208–15.

56. RA–JH, 7 March 1908, Autograph Letters vol. 2, pp. 10–11, MP, M/01/1260.

57. FH–JH, 'Sunday', MP, M/01/1263.

58. FH–JH, nd ['Wednesday', March 1908] MP, M/01/1263. RA–Violet Asquith, 10 March 1908, in Jolliffe, *Raymond*, pp. 18, 156.

59. FH–KA, 6 April 1908, MP, M/01/1269.

60. FH, *Time Remembered*, p. 197. FH–Ettie, nd, Desborough Papers, DE/Rv/C1346/35; DE/ Rv/c1347/1.

61. He also persuaded them out of making an altar tomb in the chapel for Mark who he deemed 'a small cadet of the house…people are so apt to overdo that sort of thing.' Lutyens–Lady Emily, 3 May 1908, Clayre Percy and Jane Ridley (eds.), *The Letters of Edwin Lutyens to his Wife, Lady Emily* (1985), pp.152–3.

62. FH–HHA, nd [1892], MP, M/01/1270, on Raymond Asquith winning a scholarship to Winchester.
63. This tease followed him throughout life. At Oxford he was occasionally called Jack and in the army too his roommates made the connection. MacKenzie, *Children*, p. 85. Reginald Hancock, *Memoirs of a Veterinary Surgeon* (1954), p. 83.
64. MacKenzie, *Children*, pp. 23–4.
65. MacKenzie, *Children*, p. 32.
66. FH–DD, 5 September 1903, Edith Lyttelton Papers, CHAN1/5/10/209.
67. For Edward's Eton career, see MacKenzie, *Children*, pp. 32–9. L.E. Jones, *A Victorian Boyhood* (1955).
68. FH–EH, nd., Autograph Letters, vol. 2, pp. 66–7, MP, M/01/1260.
69. EH–KA, May 1903, MP, N/01/1368. MacKenzie, *Children*, pp. 35–6.
70. MacKenzie, *Children*, p. 36.
71. MacKenzie, *Children*, pp. 54, 63.
72. MacKenzie, *Children*, p. 56. Edward's father had also been called to the Bar although he doesn't seem to have practiced much after his inheritance.
73. FH–EH, 26 October 1906, MP, M/01/1268; EH–FH 2 November 1906, MP, N/02/1361. MacKenzie, *Children*, pp. 55–7. Lister was later sent down from Oxford.
74. Clifford, *The Asquiths*, pp. 196–99. Yet privately Raymond worked very hard for his exams, as did Ronnie Knox and Patrick Shaw Stewart.
75. Eddie Marsh, *A Number of People* (1938), pp. 175–7. MacKenzie, *Children*, pp. 23, 59.
76. Edward's College bills neared £500 (*c.* £50,000 in 2019). With Jack's retirement (and loss of salary) they had considered selling Mells Park in 1906. Instead they gave up Buckingham Gate for Lower Berkeley Street [now Fitzhardinge Street]. More Marylebone than Mayfair but hardly exile.
77. MacKenzie, *Children*, pp. 78–9.
78. MacKenzie, *Children*, p. 79. L.E. Jones, *An Edwardian Youth* (1956).
79. RA–KA, 10 December 1908, Jolliffe, *Raymond*, p.159. FH–KA, 12 December 1908, MP, M/01/1269.
80. Diana Manners was the daughter of Violet Granby (from 1906 Duchess of Rutland) and Harry Cust.
81. MacKenzie, *Children*, p. 90.
82. Cynthia Asquith, *Remember and be Glad* (1952), p. 196.
83. On Ettie's determination to control her children's lives, see Richard Davenport-Hines, *Ettie* (2008), pp. 118–21.

84. MacKenzie, *Children*, pp. 92–9. See also Davenport-Hines, *Ettie*, pp. 145–7 for a row with Frances after Ettie persuaded Archie to shirk a party of Frances's and a date with Violet Asquith, in order to take her to a play. Soon Margot had joined in too in defence of her stepdaughter.
85. MacKenzie, *Children*, pp. 101–4.
86. MacKenzie, *Children*, pp. 106–7.
87. MacKenzie, *Children*, p. 107.
88. RA–FH, 3 October 1910, MP, P/01/1599, MP.
89. RA–KA, 2 August 1910, Jolliffe, *Raymond*, p. 178. RA– FH 3 August 1910, MP, P/01/1599.
90. MacKenzie, *Children*, p. 109. 'Poor Frances very upset. I am sad for her. I know she invests those rather concrete hallmarks of success with deep significance and feels them to be symbols.' Violet Bonham Carter in Mark Bonham Carter and Mark Pottle eds, *Lantern Slides: The Diaries and Letters of Violet Bonham Carter, 1904–1914*, p. 213.
91. HHA–FH, 3 January 1905, MP, M/01/1270.
92. MacKenzie, *Children*, p. 110.
93. EH–Diana Manners, nd, Diana Cooper papers, Add MS 70708.
94. Zeigler, *Diana Cooper*, p. 45. Diana Cooper, *The Rainbow comes and goes* (1958), pp. 60–1, 82.
95. Ego Charteris to mother, December 1913, in MacKenzie, *Children*, pp.132–3. Edward's losses were the equivalent of £18,000 today.
96. EH–Diana Manners, nd, Diana Cooper papers, Add MS 70708.
97. Cooper, *Rainbow*, p. 108.
98. Cooper, *Rainbow*, p. 105. MacKenzie, *Children* p. 134.
99. MacKenzie, *Children*, pp. 121–2.
100. Emerald Cunard was an heiress in her own right. Her daughter Nancy was a friend of Iris Tree and on the fringes of the Coterie; she would later become an ardent activist against fascism and racism.
101. Ziegler, *Diana Cooper*, p. 115; MacKenzie, *Children*, p.128. J.J. Norwich (ed.), *Duff Cooper Diaries 1915–51*, (15 November 1915), p. 20. This seems extraordinary. Was this Asquith's doing? Did Frances know? Is Diana a trustworthy source?
102. Claud Russell was a diplomat and the brother of Raymond's Balliol friend Conrad Russell.
103. Daughter of the leading actor manager Sir Herbert Beerbohm Tree, Iris was a poet and model for the Bloomsbury artists and led a distinctly bohemian life.
104. For much of what follows see Cooper, *Rainbow*, pp. 109–11.

105. Initially Diana claimed that Raymond had bet her £10 to do it, an allegation that Katharine would later vigorously deny. As it was, Diana in *Rainbow* was more evasive: 'who suggested bathing? I cannot tell. It may, *may* have been me.' Cooper, *Rainbow*, p. 110.
106. MacKenzie, *Children* p. 134; Clifford, *The Asquiths*, p. 225.
107. He only learnt to swim on his honeymoon, taught by Katharine.
108. HHA–Venetia Stanley, 9 July 1914, in H.H. Asquith, *Letters to Venetia Stanley*, ed. M. and E. Brock (1982), p. 98. Count Benckendorff also spoke. The prime concern of all was to deny that anyone was drunk.
109. Clifford, *The Asquiths*, p. 226.
110. More details in Cooper, *Rainbow*, pp. 109–12; Ziegler, *Diana Cooper* (1981); O. Sitwell, *Great Morning* (1948), p. 258.
111. HHA–Venetia Stanley in Asquith, *Letters to Venetia Stanley*, p. 100. Michael and Eleanor Brock, *Margot Asquith's Great War Diary, 1914–1916*, p. 278, [4 August 1916].
112. Clifford, *The Asquiths*, p. 108.
113. FH–Violet Cecil, 5 April 1894, Violet Milner papers MS VM 43/c368/1. Susan Lowndes (ed.), *Diaries of Mary Belloc Lowndes 1911–1947* (1971), pp. 33–4. 15 May 1912. She was the sister of Hilaire Belloc.
114. For this extraordinary relationship between Asquith and his children's friend and contemporary, Venetia Stanley, which on his part bordered on the obsessional and lasted from 1912 to 1915, see Michael and Eleanor Brock (eds), *H.H. Asquith: Letters to Venetia Stanley* (1982).
115. Cynthia Asquith, *Diaries*, 13 September 1915, p. 79.
116. Abdy and Gere, *The Souls*, p. 15. Nicola Beaumont, *Cynthia Asquith*.
117. Margot was heroically blind to this. 'When I look at my beautiful, delicious daughters-in-law, I wonder by what impulse they move at all! … I expect my restless energies have a dampening effect, though they worship me and I adore them'. Brocks (ed.), *War Diary*, 7 November 1914, pp. 47–8. On the Coterie's mocking of Margot, p. 296.
118. RA–KH, 19 June 1905, Jolliffe, p. 130. Diana Cooper in Clifford, *The Asquiths*, p. 201.
119. FH–DD, 'Tuesday 1902', Edith Lyttelton Papers, CHAN1/5/10/222.
120. For all her qualms over 'cant' Frances adored Raymond. Occasionally enthusiasm got the better of her ('Give Raymond a kiss from me' she wrote her daughter). She also became fast friends with Raymond's sister, Violet who in turn flattered Frances by insisting that 'you are almost the only person in the world who understands Father thoroughly'. FH–KA, nd [October 1907], MP, M/01/1269.
121. FH, *Time Remembered*, pp. 196–7.
122. Count Constantine Benckendorff, *Reminiscences of a Russian Gentleman* (1954), p. 93.
123. Cynthia Asquith, *Remember and be Glad*, p. 195. Patrick Shaw-Stewart to Diana Cooper, October 1911, in MacKenzie, *Children*, p.?
124. Abdy and Gere, *Souls*, p. 127.
125. Cynthia Asquith, *Remember and be Glad*, p. 195. FH, *Time Remembered*, p. 179.
126. Patrick Shaw Stewart to Diana Cooper, 6 November 1913, in MacKenzie, *Children*, p. 129.

PART 9 'The Shattering Years' (1914–1918)

1. Norwich, *Duff Cooper Diaries*, p. 61.
2. Diana Manners–EH, 7 August 1914, in MacKenzie, *Children*, p. 146.
3. EH–FH, 6 March 1915 MP, N/02/1361.
4. RA–Diana Manners, 'August 1914' in Jolliffe, *Raymond*, pp. 190–1. HHA–Venetia Stanley, 10 August 1914, Brocks, *Letters*, p. 163.
5. KA–Duff Cooper in John Charmley, *Duff Cooper* (1986), p. 17.
6. Diana Manners–EH, 7 August 1914, MP. Duff Cooper, *Old Men Forget* (1954). EH–Diana Manners, September 1914, Cooper papers, Add MS 70708.
7. HHA–Venetia Stanley, 10 August 1914, 11 August 1914 in Brocks, *Letters*, pp. 162–3, 165.
8. RA to Diana Manners, nd, in MacKenzie, *Children*, p.145. EH–FH, 30 October 1914, MP, N/02/1361. RBH–FH, 9 January 1915, MP, M/01/1272. FH–RBH, nd, MP, M/01/1274.
9. MacKenzie, *Children*, pp. 166–8.
10. EH–FH, 23 March 1915, MP, N/02/1361. RA–EH, 'April 1915' in Jolliffe, *Raymond*, p. 197.
11. EH–Diana Manners, 2 March 1915, Cooper papers, Add MS 70708; Diana Manners–EH, 9 March 1915, MP.
12. Catherine Bailey, *The Secret Rooms* (2012), pp. 295–310.
13. FH–RBH, nd, MP, M/01/1274. This could equally relate to her efforts to get him into the 18th Hussars. Catherine Bailey, *The Secret Rooms* (2012), p. 409.
14. EH–FH, 16 March 1915, MP, N/02/1361. MacKenzie, *Children*, pp. 186–8.
15. 'It was, I suppose, natural that this privilege – worse favouritism – was considered outrageous by the many. One cannot but sympathise with their deprecation, but which of those many would not have grasped at the

same chance?' Cooper, *The Rainbow Comes and Goes*, p. 145 and Jolliffe, *Raymond*, pp. 199.

16. Clifford, *The Asquiths*, p. 287. Brocks, *War Diary*, Sat 8 May 1915, pp. 105–6. Brocks, *Letters*, p. 592. Cooper, *The Rainbow Comes and Goes* (1958), pp. 144–5.

17. Diana Manners to Patrick Shaw Stewart, 11 June 1915, in Mackenzie, *Children*, p.187

18. HHA–Venetia Stanley, 11 May 1915, Brocks, *Letters*, p. 591. FH–Diana Manners, [1915], Cooper papers, Add MS 70711. FH–Violet Cecil, 'Tuesday', Violet Milner Papers, MS VM 43/c368/32.

19. FH–Diana Manners, nd. [1915], Add Ms 70711. FH–Ettie, nd, Desborough Papers, DE/Rv/c1346/30.

20. Margot Asquith–FH, 24 ? 1915, MP, M/01/1266.

21. Herbert ('Beb') Asquith was a son of HHA and husband of Cynthia Asquith (née Charteris).

22. *The Diaries of Lady Cynthia Asquith 1915– 1918* (1968), 17 September 1915, p. 80. Cynthia described Frances's face as a 'scene of savage grandeur.' (Cynthia Asquith, *Diaries*, 13 September 1915, p. 79). Admittedly she had heard from Bluey Frances's earlier comment that Cynthia 'only liked [people] as mirrors', though privately Cynthia acknowledged this to be true. (Cynthia Asquith, *Diaries*, 29 August 1915, p. 73).

23. Stephen Koss, *Asquith* (1976), pp. 167, 192–5. Simon Heffer, *Staring at God: Britain in the Great War* (2019), pp. 236–8.

24. Matthew, 'Haldane', ODNB.

25. FH–RBH, '1915', MP, M/01/1274.

26. RBH–FH, 26, 28 March 1915 MP, M/01/1272. 'Darling, You were wise and full of feeling this afternoon.'

27. FH–RBH, '1915', MP, M/01/1274. Margot Asquith–FH, 24 May 1915, MP, M/01/1266.

28. *Cynthia Asquith Diaries*, 14 July 1916, p. 192. FH, *Time Remembered*, pp. 204–7. Work for which she was awarded an OBE in 1919. A year earlier Aggie received a DBE for organisation of medical supplies to hospitals. Such skills were also dedicated to improving borstals for girls and maternity services in the East End of London. She later came to national renown as a regular commentator in *The Times* on the arts of domestic management. DD Lyttelton was also awarded a DBE in 1917.

29. Cynthia's husband and brother of Raymond Asquith.

30. MacKenzie, *Children*, pp. 203–4. RA–KA, 23 October 1915, Jolliffe, *Raymond*, p. 204. EH–DM, 23 November 1915, Cooper papers, Add MS 70708.

31. Ego to Mary Wemyss, 27 March 1916, Stanway papers in MacKenzie, *Children*, p. 211. Jolliffe, *Raymond*, p. 243.

32. HHA–Venetia Stanley, 23, 28, 29 March 1915, Brocks, *Letters*, pp. 503, 515, 518. Jolliffe, *Raymond*, p. 205.

33. Clifford, *The Asquiths*, p. 303. *Cynthia Asquith Diaries*, p. 92 (21 October 1915).

34. RA–FH, 19 November 1915 MP, P/01/1599 and in Jolliffe, *Raymond*, pp. 215–16. RA–Diana Manners, 19 January 1916, in Jolliffe *Raymond*, pp. 236–7.

35. RA–KA, 9 January 1916, Jolliffe, *Raymond*, p. 231. John Charmley, *Duff Cooper*, p. 18. Zeigler, *Diana*, pp. 84–5. Norwich (ed.), *Duff Cooper Diaries*, 28 August 1915, p. 15.

36. Diana Manners–KA, nd., MP, O/01/1428. Norwich, *Duff Cooper Diaries*, p. 25. On drug taking at this time, see Richard Davenport-Hines, *The Pursuit of Oblivion: A History of Narcotics* (2001); G. R. Searle, *A New England?* (2004), p. 559.

37. Zeigler, *Diana*, p. 72. Norwich, *Duff Cooper Diaries*, 11 November 1916, p. 39. FH, *Time Remembered*, p. 180.

38. Clifford, *The Asquiths*, pp. 363–9. Brocks, *War Diary*, pp. 285–6.

39. RA–Diana Manners, 19 January 1916, in Jolliffe, *Raymond*, pp. 236–7. RA–KA, 10 January 1916, 8 March 1916, 10 July 1916, 24 July 1916, Jolliffe, *Raymond*, pp. 232–3, 246, 274, 278.

40. MacKenzie, *Children*, pp. 239–40.

41. FH to Ettie, nd, [Sept 1916], Desborough papers, DE/Rv/c1346/7.

42. Jolliffe, *Raymond*, p.15. Robert Wohl, *The Generation of 1914* (1980).

43. Conrad Russell–KA, 5 July 1917, Georgiana Blakiston (ed.) *Letters of Conrad Russell* (1987), pp. 44–45. On receiving a letter from Conrad: 'sweet…but I think he likes me more than he had better'. KA, St Omer journal, 16 April 1918, Mells Papers, O/02/1501.

44. In evenings at Mesnil Warren, Newmarket with Cicely and George, Katharine wrote 'I feel like a person in a dream [as they] gossip away gently'. They have labelled her as 'a person to be sorry for without any imagination of one's feeling or why'. KA–Diana Manners, nd, Cooper papers, Add MS 70704.

45. *Cynthia Asquith Diaries*, 15–18 August 1917. KA–Diana Manners, March 1917, Cooper papers, Add MS 70704. Clifford, *The Asquiths*, p. 396.

46. EH–Diana Manners, February 1917, Cooper

papers, Add MS 70708. Norwich, *Duff Cooper Diaries*, 23 November 1917, p. 61.

47. RBH–FH, 14 February 1917, MP, M/01/1272. FH–RBH, 'September' [1917], MP, M/01/1274.

48. RA–Diana Manners, 22 August 1916, Jolliffe, *Raymond*, p. 287.

49. EH–KA, March 1917, MP, N/01/1368. MacKenzie, *Children*, p. 248.

50. Diana Manners–EH, nd., MP. EH–Patrick Shaw Stewart, 29 January 1917, 31 March 1917, MacKenzie, *Children*, p. 242. EH–Diana Manners, February 1917, Cooper papers, Add MS 70708.

51. FH to Cicely, 'Sunday' [1917]. FH–EH, nd, 1917, MP, M/01/1268. FH–Violet Cecil, nd, Violet Milner papers, VM 43/c368/31. Major house fires were not uncommon. In 1929, Hannay's rectory had burnt down.

52. KA–Diana Manners, nd., Cooper papers, Add MS 70704.

53. Patrick Shaw Stewart–Diana Manners, 16 October 1917 in MacKenzie, *Children*, pp. 255–6. EH–FH, 14 October 1917; 23 September 1917, MP, N/02/1361.

54. *Country Life*, 10 November 1917.

55. EH–FH, 17 November 1917, MP, N/02/1361.

56. FH, *Time Remembered*, pp. 223–5; MacKenzie, *Children*, p. 258.

57. *Cynthia Asquith Diaries* 3 February 1918, p. 408; MacKenzie, *Children*, p. 258. FH–Ettie, nd, Desborough Papers, DE/Rv/c1346/34. FH to RBH, nd, (*c.* November 1917), MP, M/01/1274; RBH–FH 20 [?30] December [19]17, MP, M/01/1272. Haldane's attempts at consolation were not successful as he acknowledged: 'I wish my mind did not turn to idealism, for it is shadowy to you and does not help you as it would have helped and has helped me'.

58. FH–DM, nd., 1917, Cooper papers, Add MS 70711.

59. Clifford, *The Asquiths*, p. 423. *Cynthia Asquith Diaries*, 23 November 1917, p. 370.

60. KA's Journal at St Omer Hospital 20, 27 April 1918; 6 May 1918, O/02/1501.

61. Cooper, *Rainbow*, p. 159. MacKenzie, *Children* p. 258. Marsh, *A Number of People*, pp. 175–7. Duff Cooper, *Old Men Forget*, p. 69. Viola Tree, actress and opera singer. A daughter of Beerbohm Tree, she married the critic Alan Parsons.

PART 10 Resurrection (1919–1939)

1. FH, *Time Remembered*, p. 227.

2. Between 13 and 15 August 1918 a heavily pregnant Clementine Churchill visited Mells. Mary Soames (ed.), *Speaking for Themselves: the Personal Letters of Winston and Clementine Churchill* (1998), pp. 211–12.

3. KA–Diana Cooper (née Manners), nd. [May 1918, 1919], Cooper papers, Add MS 70704. FH–DD, 6 September ?, Edith Lyttelton papers, CHAN 1/5/10/22.

4. KA–Diana Cooper, 21 December 1923, Cooper papers, Add MS 70705.

5. Katharine was now 'such a precious child to me…We have been so close for so many years…' FH–KA, nd and 4 October 1908, MP, M/01/1269.

6. *The Diaries of Lady Cynthia Asquith*, 20 July 1915, p. 56. Cynthia's prime relationship was with Basil Blackwood until his death in 1917. But in truth this was a very chaste affair. Nicola Beauman, *Cynthia Asquith* (1987).

7. FH–Violet Cecil, nd, Violet Milner papers, VM 43/c368/31.

8. Anita Leslie, *Jennie: Lady Randolph Churchill* (1969), pp. 351–3.

9. Conrad Russell–Diana Russell, 10 June 1919, Blakiston, *Letters*, p. 61. Jack was now 'so deaf' Frances rarely now entertained with him. Jack was eighty in 1923.

10. Dakers, *Clouds*, p. 205. Christie's sale 11 July 1919. RBH–FH, 6–7 August 1923. 23 April 1924, M/01/1272. KA–Diana Cooper, 23 January 1924, Add MS 70705.

11. FH, *Time Remembered*, pp. 190–1. KA–Diana Cooper, January 1924, December 1924, Add MS 70704.

12. KA–Diana Cooper, nd, Add MS 70705.

13. RA–KA, 14 May 1910, in Jolliffe, *Raymond*, p.163.

14. KA–Diana Cooper, nd [December 1923], 23 January and 16 December 1924, Add MS 70704.

15. Still for next three years he mistakenly called her Kathleen. Interestingly she never felt able to correct him.

16. A. N. Wilson, *Hilaire Belloc* (1984), pp. 231, 240–1, 334. *Duff-Cooper Diaries*, 22 June 1920. Terry Tastard, *Ronald Knox and English Catholicism* (2009), p. 174.

17. R. Speaight, *Letters from Hilaire Belloc* (1953), p. 209.

18. Joseph Pearce, *Literary Converts*. Wilson, *Belloc*, pp. 241–3. Conrad Russell admitted to Maurice Baring what he found 'strange and inexplicable…that there are a great many people about like me who would like to believe and can't.' When he 'dissects' this feeling he claims it has nothing to do with the teaching; 'so I assume it is only the historical side, the dress, the music, the Latin and a low snobbish feeling I have that Catholics are swells and have got hold of something rather good which I can't get

hold of'. But such attractions didn't stop him rejecting the Tridentine Creed: 'God can't care about rubbish like that, verbiage, bosh'. Conrad Russell to Maurice Baring, 20 July 1921; Conrad Russell to KA, 3 March 1922, Blakiston, *Letters*, pp. 66–8.

19. KA–Diana Cooper, nd. [1920s], Cooper papers, Add MS 70704, Add MS 70705.
20. KA–Diana Cooper, nd, Add MS 70705.
21. Lady Helen Asquith, 'Recollections of Canon Hannay, 1924–1934', July 1990, MP, Q/01/1737. FH–Ettie, 16 January 1929, DE/Rv/c1346/16. On religion ('Your strongest conviction') Conrad doubted if 'Raymond would have agreed to your bringing him up a Catholic… I suspect that he had anti-Catholic views which I don't much share'. Conrad Russell– KA, 17 June 1925, Blakiston, *Letters*, pp. 77–78. FH to HHA, 10 April 1926, Bonham Carter MSS 619. RBH–FH, 29 July 1922, M/01/1272. FH–KA, 9, 12, 21 April 1926, MP, M/01/1269.
22. Private information.
23. Wilson, *Belloc*, pp. 230, 246. He also satirised, in novels such as *Pongo and the Bull*, weekends at Mells Park when FH was at her height as a hostess of artists, writers and the Liberal political elite. Christopher Hollis, *Along the Road to Frome* (1958), p. 243.
24. RBH–FH, 23 April 1924, MP, M/01/1272. DD–FH, nd, MP, M/01/1290. FH–Violet Milner, nd.
25. Conrad Russell to KA, 12 February 1925, Blakiston, *Letters*, p. 75. KA–Diana Cooper, nd, Cooper papers, Add MS 70705.
26. DD–FH, nd, MP, M/01/1290. FH to Violet Milner, nd, Milner papers VM 43/c368/38. KA–Diana Cooper, nd [1925/6], Add MS 70705.
27. Conrad Russell to Diana Russell [his sister], 1 April 1927, Blakiston, *Letters*, p. 91.
28. FH–Sybil Colefax, 2 November ?, Colefax papers, MS Eng c 3163.
29. Brown, *Lutyens and the Edwardians*, p. 220.
30. FH, *Time Remembered*, p. 227.
31. Clifford, *The Asquiths*, p. 396. Jane Brown, *Lutyens and The Edwardians* (1996), pp. 172–4.
32. Abdy and Gere, *The Souls*, p. 133. FH, *Time Remembered*, pp. 192–3. Another trigger of memory. True to form the only people who objected to the memorial window for Sir John were his sisters. 'Pages from a Record of Events', MP M/03/1309. Caroline Dakers, 'Frances Horner (1854–1940) and Mells: model, muse, hostess, friend, patron, collector', forthcoming, *Collecting and Display in the British Country House*, Paul Mellon Centre for Studies in British Art.
33. FH claims that she and Edward 'so often went together' to the opera. FH–KA, 29 February 1920, MP, M/01/1269.
34. FH–Ettie, nd, Desborough Papers, DE/Rv/c1346/33. Brown, *Lutyens and the Edwardians*, pp. 172–4, 220–1. RBH–FH, 28 June 1925, MP, M/01/1272.
35. Conrad Russell–Diana Russell, 24 June 1932, Blakiston, *Letters*, pp. 118–19. KA–Diana Cooper, 31 December 1925, Cooper papers, Add MS 70705.
36. Ridley, *A life of Edwin Lutyens*, pp. 288, 328.
37. Clayre Percy and Jane Ridley (eds), *The Letters of Edwin Lutyens and his Wife, Lady Emily* (1985), p. 152. Conrad Russell–Diana Russell, 10 June 1919, Blakiston, *Letters*, p. 61. KA–Diana Cooper, 31 January 1925, Cooper papers, Add MS 70705. Christopher Hollis, *The Seven Ages* (1974), p. 194.
38. Brown, *Lutyens and The Edwardians* (1996), p. 220.
39. Herbert Paul to FH, Autograph Letter Book, Mells, 17 October 1905, p. 36, MP, M/01/1260. 'Have you seen the *Seething Pot*?' *The Seething Pot* was Hannay's breakthrough novel. On the recruitment of Hannay, see FH, 'Record of life', MP, M/01/1309.
40. Independent enough to marry divorced couples.
41. RBH–FH, 8 June 1924, MP, M/01/1272. Lady Helen Asquith, 'Recollections of Canon Hannay, 1924–1934', July 1990, MP, Q/01/1737. KA–Diana Cooper, nd [December 1925], Cooper papers, Add MS 70705. Jack too was keen to meet the author of *Spanish Gold*. MP, M/01/1309.
42. For all this see Andrew Gailey, 'An Irishman's World', *The Irish Review*, no. 13, Winter 1992–3, pp. 31–9. Hannay, *Pleasant Places* (1934), pp. 283–314. Brian Taylor, *The Life and Writings of James Owen Hannay* (1995).
43. KA–Diana Cooper, 31 December 1925, Cooper papers, Add MS 70705.
44. FH–Ettie, 25 January [1923?], Desborough papers, DE/Rv/c1346/12. Ettie must have been long recuperating to have required such a list.
45. 'I am so delighted that you are so delighted… There is nothing in life that I like so well than to be with you and dear Mells'. W. Nicholson to FH, 29 June 1936, MP, M/01/1287.
46. Frances talks of him being a 'cherished friend' and of the 'privilege of intimacy with one of the acutest minds and …finest scholars of our times'. FH, *Time Remembered*, p. 187. A close friend of Raymond's at

Winchester and later an MP, serving briefly as Financial Secretary to the War Office, he was for the most part a polished under-achiever. Nicknamed 'Bluetooth' or 'Bluey'.

47. Zeigler, *Diana Cooper*, pp. 292–4.

48. Although an elusive one: 'He is one of the good who aren't harsh to the clever and one of the clever who are never rude to the good – if one can bear with equanimity all the long voids in his friendship, it is very repaying'. (FH).

49. RBH–FH, 20 July 1924, MP, M/01/1272.

50. Eilona Derenberg (d. 1967), a professional pianist.

51. FH, *Time Remembered* p. 150. FH–KA, 16 June 1921, MP, M/01/1269. RBH–FH, 10 January 1922, MP, M/01/1272. Hannay, *Pleasant Places* (1934), pp. 304–5.

52. Katharine agreed with Conrad Russell that Barrie was 'the absolute world's crusher'. Although Barrie did give her diamonds and left her £2000 in his will. Another *bête noir* was Sibyl Colefax. KA–Diana Cooper,16 January 1925, Cooper papers Add MS 70704. FH was an 'indefatigable hostess and her week-end parties were sometimes a trial to Katharine's dejected spirits'. Blakiston, *Letters*, p. 59. FH–RBH, nd, MP, M/01/1274.

53. KA–Diana Cooper, nd, Cooper papers, Add MS 70705. KA was delighted Diana coming: 'Did mother frighten you into acquiescence. Only don't chuck her at the last moment'.

54. FH, *Time Remembered*, p. 228.

55. FH–KA, 1 May 1918, MP, M/01/1269. RBH–FH 29(?) April 1919, MP, M/01/1272.

56. RBH–FH, 16 June 1924, 26 September 1924, MP, M/01/1272. FH–RBH, nd., MP, M/01/1274.

57. FH–KA, nd, 1 March 1920, MP, M/01/1269.

58. KA–Diana Cooper, 'Jan' [1924?], Add MS 70705.

59. RBH–FH, 16 May 1924, 18 May 1924, 16 June 1924, 7 August 1924 and 19 October 1924, MP, M/01/1272. Another convert to Labour was Frances's brother-in-law, Muir Mackenzie, who was rewarded with a peerage, presumably at Haldane's suggestion. Maurice Cowling, *The Impact of Labour 1920–1924* (1971), p. 369.

60. KA–Diana Cooper, nd. [1926], Cooper papers, Add MS 70705. KA–Evelyn Waugh, 3 May 1949, Waugh papers, Add MS 81047.

61. Fiona MacCarthy, *The Last Pre-Raphaelite*, pp. 525–6.

62. FH to Violet Milner, 28 June [1933], Milner papers, MS VM 43/c368/39. Sydney Colvin–FH, MP, O/01/1410. MacCarthy, *The Last Pre-Raphaelite*, pp. 522–27.

63. FH–Sibyl Colefax, 15 August [1930s], MS Eng c3138; 21 May [?], Colefax papers, MS Eng c3163. Sibyl, Lady Colefax (1874–1950) was a socialite and interior designer who, on losing her fortune in the Wall Street Crash, set up the business that would become Colefax and Fowler. Another 'new' friend was surprisingly Belloc's sister: 'I became very fond of her and intimate with her at the end of her life'. Susan Lowndes (ed.) *Diaries and Letters of Mary Belloc Lowndes* (1971), pp. 278–9.

64. FH–Ettie, 25 January [1923?], Desborough papers, DE/Rv/c1346/12. FH–Sir Arthur Colefax, 2 December [1933?], MS Eng c 3163. Virginia Woolf to Frances Horner, 6 May 1928, MP , cited in Dakers, 'Horner', p.17.

65. Katharine would later say that she could never re-read *Time Remembered* as it would make her 'too embarrassed all over again'. [Private information].

66. Lowndes (ed) *Diaries and Letters of Mary Belloc Lowndes*, pp. 278–9.

67. FH–Violet Bonham Carter, 15 January [? 1930s], Bonham Carter MSS 181.

68. FH, *Time Remembered*, p.189.

69. *The Times*, 15 January 1931. Their complaint was over the arrival of a public telephone. This was seen as a corruption of the traditional order but only provoked a satirical response in *Punch* entitled 'The Passing of Mells', in *Mells, a Portrait* (2019).

70. FH–Ettie, 17 August [?], 27–28 September ?, Desborough papers, DE/Rv/c1346/8–10.

71. His daughter Althea disliked how her father was 'extremely attractive to women who ran after him in shoals'. Much of this he dismissed ('My father had a very dominating character and women just bowed round him.'). Althea Hannay–R.B.D. French, 24 August 1960, 30 December 1960, Hannay Papers, MS 9266. Because of her status and personality, Frances was never going to 'bow', which of course was part of her appeal. Similarly Hannay was the last in a line of strong independent men in whoe company she thrived.

72. Lady Helen Asquith, 'Recollections of Canon Hannay at Mells 1924–1934', MP Q/01/1737. Canon Hannay–KA, 5 March 1940, MP, O/01/1424.

73. Lady Helen Asquith, 'Recollections of Canon Hannay at Mells 1924–1934', MP Q/01/1737. Conrad Russell to Flora Russell, 20 October 1930, Blakiston, *Letters*, p. 114.

74. Conrad Russell to Helen Asquith, 28 January 1928, 21 March 1928, Blakiston, *Letters*, p. 95, 98. Lady Helen Asquith, 'Recollec-

tions of Canon Hannay at Mells 1924–1934',
MP, Lady Helen Asquith, 'Recollections
of Canon Hannay at Mells 1924–1934', MP
Q/01/1737. She never married.

75. Conrad Russell–Flora Russell, 8 August
1928, Blakiston, *Letters*, p. 101.

76. Conrad Russell Helen Asquith, 25 October
1930, Blakiston, *Letters*, p. 115.

77. Althea Hannay–R.B.D. French, 25 April
1960, 5 April 1961, Hannay papers, MS
9266. Lady Helen Asquith, 'Recollections
of Canon Hannay at Mells 1924–1934', MP
Q/01/1737.

78. Althea Hannay–R.B.D. French, 3 September
1957, Hannay Papers, MS 9266. Hannay,
Pleasant Places, pp. 315–16.

79. Lady Helen Asquith, 'Recollections of
Canon Hannay at Mells 1924–1934', MP
Q/01/1737. *Pleasant Places*, p. 308.

80. But not forgotten. Presumably it was
Frances who commissioned the bust of
Hannay on his leaving Mells which pres-
ently occupies a discreet corner of
the church.

81. FH–Ettie, nd, Desborough Papers, DE/Rv/
c1346/32. KA–Diana Cooper, nd, Cooper
papers, Add MS 70705.

82. Selina Hastings, *Evelyn Waugh* (1994), p.
294. H.J.A. Sire, *Father D'Arcy: Philosopher
of Christian Love* (1997), p. 67.

83. Brown, *Lutyens*, pp.222–3. Sire, *Father
D'Arcy*, p. 77.

84. Brown, *Lutyens*, p. 223.

85. Conrad Russell to Flora Russell, 16 April
1934; Conrad Russell to Diana Cooper, 25
June 1936, Blakiston, *Letters*, pp. 126–7, 140.

86. Conrad Russell–Helen Asquith, 13 June
1929, Blakiston, *Letters*, pp. 108–9.

87. KA–Diana Cooper, 16 January 1925, 24 February [1925], Cooper papers, Add MS 70705.

88. Desmond MacCarthy–FH, 7 September
38, Autograph Letters, vol. 2, pp. 61–2, MP,
M/01/1260.

89. Conrad Russell to Diana Cooper, 28 September 1938, Blakiston, *Letters*, p.158.

90. In addition to the burning of churches, 4184
priests, 2,365 monks and 300 nuns were
murdered. Joseph Pearce, *Literary Converts*
(1999), p. 204.

91. FH–Ettie, 21 September 1938, Desborough
Papers, DE/Rv/c1346/27.

92. Hollis, *The Seven Ages*, p. 145. Conrad
Russell–Flora Russell, 2 October 1938,
Blakiston, *Letters*, p. 158. Taylor, *Hannay*, p.
206.

93. Conrad Russell to Diana Cooper, 5 October
1938, Blakiston, *Letters*, p. 159. Mrs Anne
Chamberlain–FH, 24 October 1938, Auto-

graph Letters, p. 70, MP, M/01/1260.

94. FH–Sybil Colefax, '5th' [Oct? 1938], Colefax
papers, MS Eng c 3163.

95. Conrad Russell to Flora Russell, 18 October
1938, Blakiston, *Letters*, pp. 159–60.

96. Conrad Russell to Diana Cooper, 31 December 1938, Blakiston, *Letters*, pp.160–61.

97. FH–Sibyl Colefax, 29 March [39], 31 December 1939, Colefax papers, MS Eng c 3163.

98. FH, 'Journal: Brittany; Dinard.' MP,
M/02/1322. Taylor, *Hannay*, p. 207.

99. FH–KA, nd, 1 September 1939, MP,
M/01/1269.

100. Winston Churchill–KA, 4 December 1916,
in Jolliffe, *Raymond*, p. 15. FH–Ettie, 13
September 1939, Desborough papers, DE/
Rv/ c1346/19.

101. Conrad Russell–Diana Cooper, 11 February
1940, Blakiston, *Letters*, p. 179. M. Davie
(ed.), *Diaries of Evelyn Waugh* (1976), p. 443.

EPILOGUE

1. *Country Life*, February 2015.

2. Married to George V and grandmother to
HM Queen Elizabeth II. She spent the war
years nearby at Badminton with the Beauforts.
Hugo Vickers (ed.), James Pope-Hennessy,
The Quest for Queen Mary (2018), p. 299.

3. Conrad Russell to Flora Russell, 10 Sep-
tember 1939, Blakiston, *Letters*, pp. 168–9.
FH– Ettie, 13 September 1939, Desborough
Papers, DE/Rv/c1346/19.

4. Conrad Russell to Diana Cooper, 16 and 18
September 1936, Blakiston, *Letters*, pp. 142–
3. Evelyn Waugh–Mary Lygon [July 1936?],
Amory (ed.), *The Letters of Evelyn Waugh*
(1981), p. 108. Conrad Russell–Flora Russell,
25 September 1936, Blakiston, *Letters*, p. 143.

5. FH to Ettie, 21 September 38, Desborough
papers, DE/Rv/c1346/27. Brown, *Lutyens*,
p. 219. Conrad Russell–Diana Cooper, 20
October 1939, in Diana Cooper, *Trumpets
from the Steep* (1960), p. 18. May there
have been financial pressures too? In 1939,
Frances was selling in Christie's Old English
Silver sale. 1919-1949 saw half the family's
collection of Old Masters sold.

6. FH–Sibyl Colefax, 31 December 1939,
Colefax papers, MS Eng c3163. KA–Sydney
Cockerell, 1 November 1939, Cockerell
papers, Add MS 52726.

7. FH–Ettie, 'Thursday' [1939], Desborough
papers, DE/Rv/c1346/20. FH–Margot
Asquith, 8 November 1939, Asquith papers,
MS Eng c 6677. FH–Sibyl Colefax, 31
December 1939, Colefax Papers, MS Eng
c3163.

8. FH–Ettie, 20 November 1939, Desborough papers, DE/Rv/c1346/21.
9. Conrad Russell–Diana Cooper, 10 February 1940, Blakiston, *Letters*, pp. 178–9.
10. KA–Sydney Cockerell, 28 March 1940, Cockerell papers, Add MS 52726. Conrad Russell to Diana Cooper, 2–6 March 1940, Blakiston, *Letters*, pp. 179–80. Lady Helen Asquith, 'Recollections of Canon Hannay at Mells 1924–1934', MP Q/01/1737. Diana Cooper–Conrad Russell in Cooper, *Trumpets*, pp. 31–2.
11. Interestingly Frances in her will revoked the gift of Lower Berkeley Street to Cicely and, apparently with Cicely's agreement, instead arranged for it to be held in trust for Cicely's children. M/03/1335.
12. Diana Cooper–Conrad Russell, [Mar 1940], *Trumpets* p. 32. Christie's sale, 22 July 1949. Wildman, *Victorian Artist-Dreamer*, pp. 157–8. Cicely Lambton–KA, MP, N/01/1359. In which Cicely talks of selling pictures at Mells and of accepting a settlement in lieu of being 'very hard up'.
13. Conrad Russell–Diana Cooper, 20 December 1940, Blakiston, *Letters*, p. 192.
14. KA–Evelyn Waugh, 28 March 1958, Add MS 81047. Conrad Russell to Diana Cooper, 3 December 1940, Blakiston, *Letters*.
15. Max Egremont, *Siegfried Sassoon* (2005), p. 489.
16. Every graveyard tells a story. To the front are Frances and Jack, Mark and Katharine. M/03/1336. Also there is Frances's sister Amy. In close proximity are Asquith friends – Violet and Maurice Bonham Carter. Behind them are Katharine's Catholic friends including Sassoon, Knox, and Hollis, while some way off on their own are the Hannays.
17. Conrad Russell to Diana Cooper, 9 December 1939, Blakiston, *Letters*, p. 174.
18. Max Egremont, *Siegfried Sassoon* (2005), pp. 481, 489. Aristocracy and Catholic piety was a glamourous mix, which Waugh would immortalise with his novel, *Brideshead Revisited*, much to Katharine's distaste. 'Katharine loathes and hates the book because she says that in this most serious crisis in the world's history a man ought not to be writing slightly disagreeable fiction about unusually disagreeable and despicable people. I agree in a way'. Conrad Russell–Diana Cooper, 25 December 1944, Blakiston, *Letters*, p. 235.
19. Private information.
20. Conrad Russell–Diana Cooper, 26 December 1940, Blakiston, *Letters*, pp. 193–4.
21. Hannay to Katharine, 5 March 1940, MP, O/01/1424. That said, he did return to Mells to take the funeral service for McKenna in 1943. Conrad Russell–Diana Cooper, 14 December 1943, Blakiston, *Letters*, p. 217. In 1950 his ashes were buried by his wife's grave. Perhaps surprisingly, the only one of the family that stayed in touch was Cicely.
22. Conrad Russell–Diana Cooper 12 October 1940, 8 August 1941, 29 August 1941, November 1941, Blakiston, *Letters*, p.188. Diana Cooper was another who assumed that Katharine's piety would lead her to becoming a nun. The thought doesn't seem to have ever crossed her mind. The retreat into herself was a personal trait rather than specifically religious.
23. Lord Marchmain in Evelyn Waugh's *Brideshead Revisited*.
24. Conrad Russell–Diana Cooper, 28 February 1945, Blakiston, *Letters*, p. 242. Cooper, *Trumpets*, p. 243. Georgiana Blakiston's preface in Blakiston, *Letters*, pp. 11–12. Zeigler, *Diana Cooper*, pp. 292–3.
25. Evelyn Waugh, *Ronald Knox* (1959), p. 318. Hollis, *Along the Road to Frome*, p. 247. FH, *Time Remembered*, p.xv. Joseph Pierce, *Literary Converts* (1999), p. 156.
26. *Country Life*, February 2015.
27. Lutyens–Lady Emily, 22 April 1911, Percy and Ridley (eds.), *Letters of Edwin Lutyens* (1985), pp. 218–19.
28. Osbert Sitwell–KA, 7 March 1940.
29. Bongie Bonham Carter–KA, 12 March 1940, MP, M/03/1336.

Bibliography

MANUSCRIPT COLLECTIONS

Asquith, H.H., papers (Bodleian Library, Oxford)

Asquith, Margot, papers (Bodleian Library, Oxford)

Balfour, Arthur, papers (British Library and Whittingehame [National Archives of Scotland])

Bonham Carter papers (Bodleian Library, Oxford)

Burne-Jones papers (Fitzwilliam Museum, Cambridge)

Cockerell, Sydney, papers (British Library)

Colefax, Sybil, papers (Bodleian Library, Oxford)

Cooper, Diana, papers (British Library)

Desborough papers (Hertfordshire Archives and Local Studies)

Elcho, Mary, papers (Stanway House, Gloucestershire)

Gaskell, May, papers (Ashmolean Museum, Oxford)

Gladstone, Mary, papers (British Library)

Haldane, R.B., papers (National Library of Scotland)

Hannay, J.O., papers (Trinity College, Dublin)

Horner, Frances, papers (The Manor House, Mells)

Horner, John F. F., papers (The Manor House, Mells)

Horner, Katharine and Edward, papers (The Manor House, Mells)

Lyttelton papers (Churchill College Cambridge)

McKenna papers (Churchill College, Cambridge)

Milner, Alfred, Lord, papers (Bodleian Library, Oxford)

Milner, Violet, Lady, papers (Bodleian Library, Oxford)

Pembroke, George, 13th Earl, papers (Somerset Heritage Centre)

Strachey, Lytton, papers (British Library)

Waugh, Evelyn, papers (British Library)

CONTEMPORARY SOURCES

Amory, Mark (ed): *The Letters of Evelyn Waugh, 1903–1966* (2010)

Asquith, Lady Cynthia: *Diaries: 1915–18* (1968)

—— *Remember and Be Glad* (1952)

Asquith, Margot: *The Autobiography of Margot Asquith* (1920, 1922)

—— *More Memories* (1933)

Bailey, John (ed): *The Diary of Lady Frederick Cavendish* (1927)

Balfour, Arthur James, First Earl of Balfour (Mrs Edgar Dugdale ed): *Chapters of Autobiography* (1930)

Balfour, Lady Frances: *Ne Obliviscaris: Dinna Forget* (1930)

Balsan, Consuelo: *The Glitter and the Gold* (1952)

Baring, Maurice: *The Puppet Show of Memory* (1987)

Benkendorff, Count Konstantin: *Half a Life. The Reminiscences of a Russian Gentleman* (1954)

Benson, E. F.: *As We Were* (1934)

Birmingham, George A. (James O. Hannay): *Fidgets* (1926)

—— *Pleasant Places* (1934)

Blakiston, Georgiana (ed): *The Letters of Conrad Russell, 1897–1947* (1987)

Blunt, Wilfrid Scawen: *My Diaries: Being a Personal Narrative of Events, 1888–1914* (1919)

Bonham Carter, Mark and Mark Pottle (ed.): : *Lantern Slides : The Diaries of Violet Bonham Carter: 1904–14* (1996).

—— *Champion Redoubtable: The Diaries of Violet Bonham Carter: 1914–1944* (1998)

Bonham Carter, Violet: 'The Souls' in *The Listener*, 30 October 1947

Bornand, Odette (ed): *The Diary of W. M. Rossetti, 1870–1873* (1977)

Brock, Michael and Eleanor (eds): *H.H. Asquith: Letters to Venetia Stanley* (1982)

—— *Margot Asquith's Great War Diary 1914–1916* (2014)

Bryson, John (ed): *Dante Gabriel Rossetti and Jane Morris: Their Correspondence* (1976)

Burdon, Richard. *Haldane: An Autobiography* (1929)

Burne-Jones, Georgiana (GB-J): *Memorials of Edward Burne-Jones* (1904)

Churchill. Lady Randolph: *The Reminiscences of Lady Randolph Churchill* (1908)

Cooper, Artemis (ed.): *Mr Wu and Mrs Stitch: the Letters of Evelyn Waugh and Diana Cooper* (1991)

Cooper, Diana: *The Rainbow Comes and Goes* (1958)

—— *The Light of Common Day* (1959)

—— *Trumpets from the Steep* (1960)

Cooper, Duff: *Old Men Forget* (1953)

Dakers, Caroline: '"Yours affectionately Angelo": The Letters of Edward Burne-Jones and Frances Horner', *British Art Journal*, vol. 2, no. 3 (Spring/Summer 2001), pp. 16–21

Davie, Michael (ed.): *The Diaries of Evelyn Waugh* (1976)

Dugdale, Blanche E. C.: *Arthur James Balfour, First Earl of Balfour* (1936)

—— *Family Homespun* (1940)

Escott, T. H. S.: *Society in the Country House* (1907).

Fingall, Elizabeth: *Seventy Years Young. Memories of Elizabeth, Countess of Fingall* (1937)

Fitzroy, Sir Almeric: *Memoirs* (1925)

Forbes, Lady Angela: *Memories and Base Details* (1920)

Garnett, Oliver (ed.): 'The Letters and Collection of William Graham – Pre-Raphaelite Patron and Pre-Raphaelite Collector', *Journal of the Walpole Society*, vol. 62, pp. 145–393

Grey of Fallodon, Viscount: *Twenty-Five Years 1892–1916* (1925)

Hollis, Christopher: *Along the Road to Frome* (1958)

—— *The Seven Ages: Their Exits and their Entrances* (1974)

Horner, Frances: 'The Veil of Maya', *Temple Bar* (1891), 93, pp. 73–96

—— *Time Remembered* (1933)

Howard, Christopher H.D. (ed.): *The Diary of Edward Goschen 1900–1914* (1980)

Jolliffe, John (ed.): *Raymond Asquith: Life and Letters* (1980)

Liddell, A. G. C.: *Notes From the Life of an Ordinary Mortal* (1911)

Lutyens, Emily: *A Blessed Girl: Memoirs of A Victorian Childhood* (1953)

Lyttelton, Edith: *Alfred Lyttelton: an Account of his Life* (1917)

Mackail, J. W. and Guy Wyndham: *Life and Letters of George Wyndham* (1925)

MacKenzie, Norman: *Letters of Sidney and Beatrice Webb: Apprenticeships 1873–1892* (1978)

—— *Partnership 1892–1912* (2008)

MacKenzie, Norman and Jeanne: *The Diaries of Beatrice Webb* (abridged edition, 2000)

Masterman, Lucy (ed.): *Mary Gladstone (Mrs Drew): Her Diaries and Letters* (1930)

Milner, Viscountess: *My Picture Gallery 1886–1901* (1951)

Morley, John, 1st Viscount Morley of Blackburn: *Recollections* (1917)

Mosley, Charlotte (ed.): *The Letters of Nancy Mitford and Evelyn Waugh* (2010)

Nicolson, Harold: *Diaries and Letters 1930–39* (1966)

Norwich, John Julius: *The Duff Cooper Diaries 1915–1951* (2014)

Oxford and Asquith, the Earl of: *Memories and Reflections 1852–1927* (1928)

Paget, Lady Augusta: *In My Tower* (1924)

Percy, Clayre and Jane Ridley (eds): *The Letters of Edward Lutyens to his Wife, Lady Emily* (1985)

Ribblesdale, Lord: *Impressions and Memories* (1927)

Ridley, Jane and Clayre Percy (eds): *The Letters of Arthur Balfour and Lady Elcho, 1885–1917* (1992)

Speaight, Robert (ed.): *Letters from Hilaire Belloc* (1958)

Surtees, Virginia (ed.): *The Diary of Ford Madox Brown* (1981)

Watts, Mary S.: *George Frederic Watts: the Annals of an Artist's Life* (1912)

Wilson, Barbara: *Dear Youth* (1937)

SECONDARY SOURCES

Abdy, Jane and Charlotte Gere: *The Souls: An Elite in English Society 1885–1930* (1984)

Adams, R. J. Q. : *Balfour: The Last Grandee* (2007)

Anderson, Anne: 'Life into Art and Art into Life: Visualising the Aesthetic Woman or "High Art Maiden" of the Victorian "Renaissance"', *Women's History Review* (2001) 10, no. 3

Askwith, Betty: *The Lytteltons: A Family Chronicle of the 19th Century* (1975)

Bailey, Catherine: *The Secret Rooms: A True Gothic Mystery* (2012)

Beauman, Nicola: *Cynthia Asquith* (1987)

Bennett, Daphne: *Margot: A Life of the Countess of Oxford and Asquith* (1984)

Blow, Simon: *Broken Blood: The Rise and Fall of the Tennant Family* (1987)

Boym, Svetlana: *The Future of Nostalgia* (2002)

Brown, Jane: *Lutyens and the Edwardians: An English Architect and his Clients* (1996)

Bush, Julia: *Edwardian Ladies and Imperial Power* (1999)

—— 'Ladylike Lives? Upper Class Women's Autobiographies and the Politics of Later Victorian and Edwardian Women', in *Literature and History* (Autumn 2001), 10 pp. 42–61

—— *Women Against the Vote: Female Anti-Suffragism in Britain* (2007)

Byrnes, Paula: *Mad World: Evelyn Waugh and the Secrets of Brideshead* (2010)

Calloway, Stephen and Lynn Federle Orr (eds): *The Cult of Beauty: The Aesthetic Movement 1860–1900* (2011)

Campbell, Colin: *The Art of William Nicholson* (2005)

Campbell, John: *Haldane: The Forgotten Statesman who Shaped Modern Britain* (forthcoming 2020)

Cannadine, David: *The Decline and Fall of the British Aristocracy* (1990)

Carey, John: *The Intellectuals and the Masses: Pride and Prejudice among the Literary Intelligentsia 1880–1939* (1992)

Carpenter, Humphrey: *The Brideshead Generation: Evelyn Waugh and his Friends* (1989)

Cecil, Hugh and Mirabel: *Rex Whistler – Inspirations: Family, Friendships, Landscape* (2015)

Charmley, John: *Duff Cooper: The Authorised Biography* (1986)

Clifford, Colin: *The Asquiths* (2002)

Collins, Damien: *The Charmed Life: the Phenomenal World of Philip Sassoon* (2016).

Colley, Linda: *Britons: Forging the Nation* (1992)

Colls, Robert and Philip Dodd: *Englishness: Politics and Culture 1880–1920* (1986)

Cooper, Suzanne Fagence: *The Model Wife: The Passionate Lives: Effie Gray, Ruskin and Millais* (2010)

Dakers, Caroline: *Clouds: the Biography of a Country House* (1993)

Davenport-Hines, Richard: *Ettie: The Intimate Life and Dauntless Spirit of Lady Desborough* (2008)

Davidoff, Leonore: *The Best Circles: Society, Etiquette and the Season* (1973)

de Courcy, Anne: *Margot at War: Love and Betrayal in Downing Street 1912–1916* (2014)

Dimbleby, Josceline: *A Profound Secret: May Gaskell, Her Daughter Amy and Edward Burne-Jones* (2004)

Egremont, Max: *A Life of Arthur James Balfour* (1980)

—— *The Cousins: The Friendship, Opinions and Activities of Wilfrid Scawen Blunt and George Wyndham* (1977)

—— *Siegfried Sassoon: A Biography* (2005)

Ellenberger, Nancy W. : 'The Souls and London "Society" at the End of the Nineteenth Century', *Victorian Studies*, 25 (Winter 1982), pp.133–60

—— "Constructing George Wyndham: Narratives of Aristocratic Masculinity in Fin de Siècle England", *Journal of British Studies*, 39 (October 2000), pp. 487–517.

—— *Balfour's World: Aristocracy and Political Culture at the Fin de Siècle* (2015)

Fitzgerald, Penelope: *Edward Burne-Jones: A Biography* (1975)

—— *The Knox Brothers* (1977)

Flanders, Judith: *A Circle of Sisters: Alice Kipling, Georgiana Burne-Jones, Agnes Poynter and Louisa Baldwin* (2001)

Fletcher, Sheila: *Victorian Girls: Lord Lyttelton's Daughters* (1997)

Forster, Julia: *Muses: Revealing the Nature of Inspiration* (2007).

Gailey, Andrew: *The Lost Imperialist: Lord Dufferin, Memory and Myth-making in an Age of Celebrity* (2015)

Gardiner, Juliet: *The Thirties: an Intimate History* (2010)

Garnett, Henrietta: *Wives and Stunners: The Pre-Raphaelites and their Muses* (2012)

Gere, Charlotte: *Artistic Circles, Design and Decoration in the Aesthetic Movement* (2010)

Gilley, Sheridan: 'Years of Equipoise 1892–1943' in McClelland and Hodgetts (eds): *From Without the Flaminian Gate: English Catholicism 1850–2000* (1999)

Gilmour, David: *Curzon: Imperial Statesman 1859–1925* (1994)

Girouard, Mark: *The Victorian Country House* (1979)

—— *The Return to Camelot: Chivalry and the English Gentleman* (1981)

Gooddie, Sheila: *Mary Gladstone, A Gentle Rebel* (Chichester 2003)

Greensted, Mary (ed): *An Anthology of the Arts and Crafts Movement: Writings by Ashbee, Lethaby, Gimson and their Contemporaries* (2005)

Hall, Jean Graham and Douglas F. Martin: *Haldane: Statesman, Lawyer, Philosopher* (1996)

Hancock, Reginald: *Memoirs of a Veterinary Surgeon* (1954)

Harris, José: *Private Lives, Public Spirit: A Social History of Britain, 1870–1914* (1993)

Harris, Susan K. : *The Cultural Work of the Late 19th Century Hostess: Annie Adams Fields and Mary Gladstone Drew* (2002).

Hart-Davis, Duff (ed.): *End of an Era: Letters and Journals of Sir Alan Lascelles 1887–1920* (1986)

Hassall, Christopher: *Edward Marsh: Patron of the Arts, a Biography* (1959)

Hastings, Selina: *Evelyn Waugh* (1994)

Hawksley, Lucinda: *Lizzie Siddal: the Tragedy of a Pre-Raphaelite Supermodel* (2004)

Heffer, Simon: *The Age of Decadence: Britain 1880–1914* (2017)

—— *Staring at God: Britain in the Great War* (2019)

Higgin, Letitia: *The Royal School of Needlework* (1880, rev. 2010)

Hilton, Timothy: *The Pre-Raphaelites* (1970)

Horn, Pamela: *Ladies of the Manor: Wives and Daughters in Country-House Society, 1830–1918* (1991)

—— *High Society: The English Social Elite, 1880–1914* (1992)

Hoskins, W. G. : *The Age of Plunder: King Henry's England, 1500–1547* (1976)

Houghton, W. E. : *The Victorian Frame of Mind, 1830–1870* (1957)

Jalland, Patricia: *Women, Marriage and Politics, 1860–1914* (1986)

Jenkins, Roy: *Asquith* (1964)

Kaye, Richard A. : *The Flirt's Tragedy: Desire Without End in Victorian and Edwardian Fiction* (2002)

Knowles, David: *Bare Ruined Choirs: The Dissolution of the English Monasteries* (1976)

Korb, Elisa: "Models, Muses and Burne-Jones's Continuous Quest for the Ideal Female Face", in Elisa Korb and John Christian (eds): *Hidden Burne-Jones: Works on Paper* (2007)

Koss, Stephen: *Lord Haldane, Scapegoat for Liberalism* (1969)

—— *Asquith* (1976)

Lambert, Angela: *Unquiet Souls: the Indian Summer of the British Aristocracy* (1984)

Leslie, Anita: *Jennie The Life of Lady Randolph Churchill* (1969)

—— *Edwardians in Love* (1974)

Letley, Emma: *Maurice Baring: Citizen of Europe* (1991)

Longford, Elizabeth: *A Pilgrimage of Passion: The Life of Wilfrid Scawen Blunt* (1979)

Lubenow, William C. : *Liberal Intellectuals and Public Culture in Modern Britain, 1815–1914: Making Words Flesh* (2010)

MacCarthy, Fiona: *Eric Gill* (1989)

—— *William Morris: Life for our Time* (2015)

—— *The Last Pre-Raphaelite: Edward Burne-Jones and the Victorian Imagination* (2011)

MacKenzie, Jeanne: *The Children of the Souls, a Tragedy of the First World War* (1986)

McKinstry, Leo: *Rosebery: Statesman in Turmoil* (2005)

Mandler, Peter: 'Against "Englishness": English Culture and the Limits to Rural Nostalgia, 1850–1940', *TRHS*, vol. 7 (1997), pp. 155–75

Marcus, Sharon: *Between Women: Friendship, Desire and Marriage in Victorian England* (2007)

Marsh, Jan: *The Pre-Raphaelite Sisterhood* (1985)

—— *Pre-Raphaelite Women: Images of Feminity* (1987)

Masters, Brian: *Great Hostesses* (1982)

Mathew, David: 'Old Catholics and Converts 1850–1950', in G. A. Beck (ed.): *The English Catholics 1850–1950. Essays to*

Commemorate the Restoration of the Hierarchy of England and Wales (1950)

Maurice, Major General Sir Fredrick: *Haldane: The Life of the Viscount Haldane of Cloan* (1937)

Montgomery, Maureen E. : *Gilded Prostitution: Status, Money and Transatlantic Marriages, 1870–1914* (1989)

Mosley, Nicholas: *Julian Grenfell: His Life and the Times of his Death, 1888–1915* (1976)

Moyle, Franny: *Desperate Romantics: The Private Lives of the Pre-Raphaelites* (2009)

Nicholson, Andrew: *William Nicholson, Painter: Paintings, Woodcuts, Writings, Photographs* (1996)

Nicolson, Juliet: *The Great Silence: 1918–1920: Living in the Shadow of the Great War* (2009)

Norman, Edward: *Roman Catholicism in England From the Elizabethan Settlement to the Second Vatican Council* (1985)

O'Brien, Terence: *Milner: Viscount Milner of St James's and Cape Town 18454–1925* (1979)

Patey, Douglas Lane: *The Life of Evelyn Waugh: A Critical Biography* (1998)

Pearce, Joseph: *Old Thunder: A Life of Hilaire Belloc* (2002)

—— *Literary Converts: Spiritual Inspiration in an Age of Unbelief* (1999)

Postle, Martin: *The Artist's Model* (1999)

Poulson, Christine: 'Burne-Jones, Morris and God', *Journal of the William Morris Society* (1998), pp. 45–54

Prettejohn, Elizabeth: *The Cambridge Companion to the Pre-Raphaelites* (2012)

Prose Francine: *The Lives of the Muses* (2002)

Renton, Claudia: *Those Wild Wyndhams: Three Sisters at the Heart of Power* (2014)

Reynolds, K. D. : *Aristocratic Women and Political Society in Victorian Britain* (1998)

Robson, Catherine: *Men in Wonderland: the Lost Girlhood of the Victorian Gentleman* (2001)

Rose, Kenneth: *Curzon: A Most Superior Person* (1969)

Sire, H. J. A. : *Father Martin D'Arcy: Philosopher of Christian Love* (1997)

Smith, Alison (ed.): *Edward Burne-Jones*, Tate Britain exhibition catalogue (2018)

Stannard, Martin: *Evelyn Waugh: the Early Years: 1903–1939* (1986)

Sykes, Christopher: *Evelyn Waugh: a Biography* (1975)

Tastard, Terry: *Ronald Knox and English Catholicism* (2009)

Taylor, Brian: *The Life and Writings of James Owen Hannay (George A. Birmingham)* (1995)

Tinniswood, Adrian: *The Long Weekend: Life in the English Country House between the Wars* (2016)

Tombs, Robert: *The English and their History* (2014)

Walker, Kirsty Stonell: *Stunner: The Fall and Rise of Fanny Cornforth* (2006)

—— *A Curl of Copper and Pearl* (2014)

Waugh, Evelyn: *The Life of the Right Reverend Ronald Knox* (1959)

Wildman, Stephen and John Christian (ed.): *Edward Burne-Jones: Victorian, Artist, Dreamer* (1998)

Wilson, A. N. : *Hilaire Belloc* (1984)

—— *The Victorians* (2002)

Wilson, John: *CB: a Life of Sir Henry Campbell-Bannerman* (1973)

Wilton, Andrew and Robert Upstone (ed.): *Age of Rossetti, Burne-Jones and Watts: Symbolism 1860–1910* (1997)

Wohl, Robert: *The Generation of 1914* (1980)

Ziegler, Philip: *Diana Cooper* (1981)

Index

Throughout the index Frances is referred to as FG. References in italics
indicate a page on which an illustration appears

Picture Credits

The author and publishers are grateful for permission to reproduce the images in this book. Where no source is cited they are drawn from private archives and libraries.